# C# 6 FOR PROGRAMMERS
## SIXTH EDITION
### DEITEL® DEVELOPER SERIES

The publisher offers excellent discounts on this book when ordered in quantity for bulk purchases or special sales, which may include electronic versions and/or custom covers and content particular to your business, training goals, marketing focus, and branding interests.

For government sales inquiries, please contact `governmentsales@pearsoned.com`.

For questions about sales outside the U.S., please contact `intlcs@pearson.com`.

Visit us on the Web: `informit.com/ph`

Library of Congress Control Number: 2016946157



ISBN-13: 978-0-13-459632-7
ISBN-10: 0-13-459632-3

Text printed in the United States at RR Donnelley in Crawfordsville, Indiana.
2 16

# C# 6 FOR PROGRAMMERS
# SIXTH EDITION
## DEITEL® DEVELOPER SERIES



Paul Deitel
*Deitel & Associates, Inc.*

Harvey Deitel
*Deitel & Associates, Inc.*

Boston • Columbus • Indianapolis • New York • San Francisco • Amsterdam • Cape Town
Dubai • London • Madrid • Milan • Munich • Paris • Montreal • Toronto • Delhi • Mexico City
São Paulo • Sydney • Hong Kong • Seoul • Singapore • Taipei • Tokyo

# Deitel® Series Page

## Deitel® Developer Series

Android™ 6 for Programmers: An App-Driven Approach, 3/E
C for Programmers with an Introduction to C11
C++11 for Programmers
C# 6 for Programmers
iOS® 8 for Programmers: An App-Driven Approach with Swift™
Java™ for Programmers, 3/E
JavaScript for Programmers
Swift™ for Programmers

## How To Program Series

Android™ How to Program, 3/E
C++ How to Program, 10/E
C How to Program, 8/E
Java™ How to Program, Early Objects Version, 10/E
Java™ How to Program, Late Objects Version, 10/E
Internet & World Wide Web How to Program, 5/E
Visual Basic® 2012 How to Program, 6/E
Visual C#® How to Program, 6/E

## Simply Series

Simply Visual Basic® 2010: An App-Driven Approach, 4/E
Simply C++: An App-Driven Tutorial Approach

## VitalSource Web Books

`http://bit.ly/DeitelOnVitalSource`
Android™ How to Program, 2/E and 3/E
C++ How to Program, 8/E and 9/E
Java™ How to Program, 9/E and 10/E
Simply C++: An App-Driven Tutorial Approach
Simply Visual Basic® 2010: An App-Driven Approach, 4/E
Visual Basic® 2012 How to Program, 6/E
Visual C#® 2012 How to Program, 5/E
Visual C#® How to Program, 6/E

## LiveLessons Video Learning Products

`http://informit.com/deitel`
Android™ 6 App Development Fundamentals, 3/E
C++ Fundamentals
Java™ Fundamentals, 2/E
C# 6 Fundamentals
C# 2012 Fundamentals
iOS® 8 App Development Fundamentals with Swift™, 3/E
JavaScript Fundamentals
Swift™ Fundamentals

## REVEL™ Interactive Multimedia

REVEL™ for Deitel Java™

---

To receive updates on Deitel publications, Resource Centers, training courses, partner offers and more, please join the Deitel communities on

- Facebook®—`http://facebook.com/DeitelFan`
- Twitter®—`http://twitter.com/deitel` 
- LinkedIn®—`http://linkedin.com/company/deitel-&-associates`
- YouTube™—`http://youtube.com/DeitelTV`
- Google+™—`http://google.com/+DeitelFan`

and register for the free *Deitel® Buzz Online* e-mail newsletter at:

`http://www.deitel.com/newsletter/subscribe.html`

To communicate with the authors, send e-mail to:

`deitel@deitel.com`

For information on programming-languages corporate training seminars offered by Deitel & Associates, Inc. worldwide, write to `deitel@deitel.com` or visit:

`http://www.deitel.com/training/`

For continuing updates on Pearson/Deitel publications visit:

`http://www.deitel.com`
`http://www.pearsonhighered.com/deitel/`

Visit the Deitel Resource Centers, which will help you master programming languages, software development, Android™ and iOS® app development, and Internet- and web-related topics:

`http://www.deitel.com/ResourceCenters.html`

## Trademarks

*In memory of William Siebert, Professor Emeritus of Electrical Engineering and Computer Science at MIT:*

*Your use of visualization techniques in your Signals and Systems lectures inspired the way generations of engineers, computer scientists, educators and authors present their work.*

*Harvey and Paul Deitel*

# Contents

# Preface

Welcome to the world of leading-edge software development with Microsoft's® Visual C#® programming language. *C# 6 for Programmers, 6/e* is based on C# 6 and related Microsoft software technologies.[1] You'll be using the .NET platform and the Visual Studio® Integrated Development Environment on which you'll conveniently write, test and debug your applications and run them on Windows® devices. The Windows operating system runs on desktop and notebook computers, mobile phones and tablets, game systems and a great variety of devices associated with the emerging "Internet of Things." We believe that this book will give you an informative, engaging, challenging and entertaining introduction to C#.

You'll study C# in the context of four of today's most popular programming paradigms:

- object-oriented programming,
- structured programming,
- generic programming and
- functional programming (new in this edition).

If you haven't already done so, please read the back cover and check out the additional reviewer comments on the inside back cover—these capture the essence of the book concisely. In this Preface we provide more detail.

The book is loaded with "live-code" examples—most new concepts are presented in the context of complete working C# apps, followed by one or more executions showing program inputs and outputs. In the few cases where we show a code snippet, to ensure correctness first we tested it in a working program then copied the code and pasted it into the book. We include a broad range of example apps selected from business, education, computer science, personal utilities, mathematics, simulation, game playing, graphics and many other areas. We also provide abundant tables, line drawings and UML diagrams.

Read the Before You Begin section after this Preface for instructions on setting up your computer to run the 170+ code examples and to enable you to develop your own C# apps. The source code for all of the book's examples is available at

```
http://www.deitel.com/books/CSharp6FP
```

Use the source code we provide to compile and run each program as you study it—this will help you master C# and related Microsoft technologies faster and at a deeper level.

---

1. At the time of this writing, Microsoft has not yet released the official C# 6 Specification. To view an unofficial copy, visit `https://github.com/ljw1004/csharpspec/blob/gh-pages/README.md`

## Contacting the Authors

As you read the book, if you have a question, we're easy to reach at

```
deitel@deitel.com
```

We'll respond promptly.

## Join the Deitel & Associates, Inc. Social Media Communities

For book updates, visit

```
http://www.deitel.com/books/CSharp6FP
```

subscribe to the *Deitel® Buzz Online* newsletter

```
http://www.deitel.com/newsletter/subscribe.html
```

and join the conversation on

- Facebook®—`http://facebook.com/DeitelFan`
- LinkedIn®—`http://linkedin.com/company/deitel-&-associates`
- YouTube®—`http://youtube.com/DeitelTV`
- Twitter®—`http://twitter.com/Deitel`
- Instagram®—`http://instagram.com/DeitelFan`
- Google+™—`http://google.com/+DeitelFan`

## New C# 6 Features

6 We introduce key new C# 6 language features throughout the book (Fig. 1)—each defining occurrence is marked with a "6" margin icon as shown next to this paragraph.

| C# 6 new language feature | First introduced in |
|---|---|
| `string` interpolation | Section 3.5 |
| expression-bodied methods and `get` accessors | Section 7.15 |
| auto-implemented property initializers | Section 8.6.1 |
| getter-only auto-implemented properties | Section 8.6.1 |
| `nameof` operator | Section 10.5.1 |
| null-conditional operator (`?.`) | Section 13.9.1 |
| `when` clause for exception filtering | Section 13.10 |
| `using static` directive | Section 19.3.1 |
| null conditional operator (`?[]`) | Section 19.6 |
| collection initializers for any collection with an `Add` extension method | Section 19.7 |
| index initializers | Section 19.7 |

**Fig. 1** | C# 6 new language features.

## A Tour of the Book

Here's a quick walkthrough of the book's key features.

***Introduction to Visual C# and Visual Studio 2015 Community Edition***
The discussions in

- Chapter 1, Introduction
- Chapter 2, Introduction to Visual Studio and Visual Programming

introduce the C# programming language, Microsoft's .NET platform and Visual Programming. The vast majority of the book's examples will run on Windows 7, 8 and 10 using the *Visual Studio 2015 Community* edition with which we test-drive a **Painter** app in Section 1.7. Chapter 1 briefly reviews object-oriented programming terminology and concepts on which the rest of the book depends.

***Introduction to C# Fundamentals***
The discussions in

- Chapter 3, Introduction to C# App Programming
- Chapter 4, Introduction to Classes, Objects, Methods and `strings`
- Chapter 5, Control Statements: Part 1
- Chapter 6, Control Statements: Part 2
- Chapter 7, Methods: A Deeper Look
- Chapter 8, Arrays; Introduction to Exception Handling

present rich coverage of C# programming fundamentals (data types, classes, objects, operators, control statements, methods and arrays) through a series of object-oriented programming case studies. Chapter 8 briefly introduces exception handling with an example that demonstrates attempting to access an element outside an array's bounds.

***Object-Oriented Programming: A Deeper Look***
The discussions in

- Chapter 9, Introduction to LINQ and the `List` Collection
- Chapter 10, Classes and Objects: A Deeper Look
- Chapter 11, Object-Oriented Programming: Inheritance
- Chapter 12, OOP: Polymorphism and Interfaces
- Chapter 13, Exception Handling: A Deeper Look

provide a deeper look at object-oriented programming, including classes, objects, inheritance, polymorphism, interfaces and exception handling. An online two-chapter case study on designing and implementing the object-oriented software for a simple ATM is described later in this preface.

Chapter 9 introduces Microsoft's Language Integrated Query (LINQ) technology, which provides a uniform syntax for manipulating data from various data sources, such as arrays, collections and, as you'll see in later chapters, databases and XML. Chapter 9 is intentionally simple and brief to encourage readers to begin using LINQ technology early.

Section 9.4 introduces the `List` collection. Later in the book, we take a deeper look at LINQ, using LINQ to Entities (for querying databases) and LINQ to XML.

*Windows* **`Forms`** *Graphical User Interfaces (GUIs)*
The discussions in

- Chapter 14, Graphical User Interfaces with Windows Forms: Part 1
- Chapter 15, Graphical User Interfaces with Windows Forms: Part 2

present a detailed introduction to building GUIs using Windows `Forms`. We also use Windows `Forms` GUIs in several later chapters.

*Strings and Files*
The discussions in

- Chapter 16, Strings and Characters: A Deeper Look
- Chapter 17, Files and Streams

investigate `strings` in more detail, and introduce text-file processing and object-serialization for inputting and outputting entire objects.

*Generics and Generic Collections*
The discussions in

- Chapter 18, Generics
- Chapter 19, Generic Collections; Functional Programming with LINQ/PLINQ

introduce generics and generic collections. Chapter 18 introduces C# generics and demonstrates how to create type-safe generic methods and a type-safe generic class. Rather than "reinventing the wheel," most C# programmers should use .NET's built-in searching, sorting and generic collections (prepackaged data structures) capabilities, which are discussed in Chapter 19.

*Functional Programming with LINQ, PLINQ, Lambdas, Delegates and Immutability*
In addition to generic collections, Chapter 19 now introduces functional programming, showing how to use it with LINQ to Objects to write code more concisely and with fewer bugs than programs written using previous techniques. In Section 19.12, with one additional method call, we demonstrate with timing examples how PLINQ (Parallel LINQ) can improve LINQ to Objects performance substantially on multicore systems.

*Database with LINQ to Entities and SQL Server*
The discussions in

- Chapter 20, Databases and LINQ

introduce database programming with the ADO.NET Entity Framework, LINQ to Entities and Microsoft's free version of SQL Server that's installed with the Visual Studio 2015 Community edition.

*Asynchronous Programming*
The discussions in

- Chapter 21, Asynchronous Programming with `async` and `await` show how to take advantage of multicore architectures by writing applications that can process tasks asynchronously, which can improve app performance and GUI responsiveness in apps with long-running or compute-intensive tasks. The `async` modifier and `await` operator greatly simplify asynchronous programming, reduce errors and enable your apps to take advantage of the processing power in today's multicore computers, smartphones and tablets. In this edition, we added a case study that uses the Task Parallel Library (TPL), `async` and `await` in a GUI app—we keep a progress bar moving along in the GUI thread in parallel with a lengthy, compute-intensive calculation in another thread.

## Online Bonus Content

Figure 2 shows online bonus content available with the publication of the book.

| Online topics |
|---|
| XML and LINQ to XML |
| Windows Presentation Foundation (WPF) GUI and XAML |
| Windows Presentation Foundation (WPF) Graphics and Multimedia |
| ATM Case Study, Part 1: Object-Oriented Design with the UML |
| ATM Case Study, Part 2: Implementing an OO Design in C# |
| Appendix: Using the Visual Studio Debugger |

**Fig. 2** | Online topics on the *C# 6 for Programmers, 6/e* Companion Website.

### *Accessing the Bonus Content*

To access these materials—and for downloads, updates and corrections as they become available—register your copy of *C# 6 for Programmers, 6/e* at `informit.com`. To register:

1. Go to

```
http://informit.com/register
```

2. Log in or create an account.
3. Enter the product ISBN—`9780134596327`—and click **Submit.**

Once you've registered your book, you'll find any available bonus content under **Registered Products**. Here's a quick walkthrough of the initial online content.

### *XML and LINQ to XML*

The Extensible Markup Language (XML), introduced briefly in Chapter 21, is pervasive in the software-development industry, e-business and throughout the .NET platform. XML is required to understand XAML—a Microsoft XML vocabulary that's used to describe graphical user interfaces, graphics and multimedia for Windows Presentation Foundation (WPF) apps, Universal Windows Platform (UWP) apps and Windows 10 Mobile apps. We present XML in more depth, then discuss LINQ to XML, which allows you to query XML content using LINQ syntax.

### *Windows Presentation Foundation (WPF) GUI, Graphics and Multimedia*

Windows Presentation Foundation (WPF)—created after Windows `Forms` and before UWP—is another Microsoft technology for building robust GUI, graphics and multimedia desktop apps. We discuss WPF in the context of a painting app, a text editor, a color chooser, a book-cover viewer, a television video player, various animations, and speech synthesis and recognition apps.

We featured WPF in the previous edition of this book. Our plans now are to move on to UWP for creating apps that can run on desktop, mobile and other Windows devices. For this reason, the WPF chapters are provided as is from the previous edition—we'll no longer evolve this material. Many professionals are still actively using Windows `Forms` and WPF.

### *Case Study: Using the UML to Develop an Object-Oriented Design and C# Implementation of the Software for an ATM (Automated Teller Machine)*

The UML™ (Unified Modeling Language™) is a popular graphical language for visually modeling object-oriented systems. We introduce the UML in the early chapters. We then provide an online object-oriented design case study in which we use the UML to design and implement the software for a simple ATM. We analyze a typical *requirements document* that specifies the details of the system to be built, i.e., *what* the system is supposed to do. We then design the system, specifying *how* it should work—in particular, we

- determine the *classes* needed to implement that system,
- determine the *attributes* the classes need to have,
- determine the *behaviors* the classes' methods need to exhibit and
- specify how the classes must *interact* with one another to meet the system requirements.

From the design, we then produce a complete working C# implementation. Students in our professional courses often report a "light bulb moment"—the case study helps them "tie it all together" and truly understand object orientation.

## Future Online Bonus Content

Periodically, we *may* make additional bonus chapters and appendices available at

```
http://www.informit.com/title/9780134596327
```

to registered users of the book. Check this website and/or write to us at `deitel@deitel.com` for the status of this content. These *may* cover:

- Universal Windows Platform (UWP) GUI, graphics and multimedia
- ASP.NET web app development
- Web Services
- Microsoft Azure™ Cloud Computing

### *Universal Windows Platform (UWP) for Desktop and Mobile Apps*

The Universal Windows Platform (UWP) is designed to provide a common platform and user experience across all Windows devices, including personal computers, smartphones, tablets, Xbox and even Microsoft's new HoloLens virtual reality and augmented reality holographic headset—all using nearly identical code.[2]

*REST Web Services*
Web services enable you to package app functionality in a manner that turns the web into a library of *reusable* services. We used a Flickr REST-based web service in Chapter 21.

*Microsoft Azure™ Cloud Computing*
Microsoft Azure's web services enable you to develop, manage and distribute your apps in "the cloud."

## Notes About the Presentation

*C# 6 for Programmers, 6/e* contains a rich collection of examples. We concentrate on building well-engineered, high performance software and stress program clarity.

***Syntax Shading.*** For readability, we syntax shade the code, similar to the way Visual Studio colors the code. Our syntax-shading conventions are:

```
comments appear like this
keywords appear like this
constants and literal values appear like this
all other code appears in black
```

***Code Highlighting.*** We emphasize key code segments by placing them in gray rectangles.

***Using Fonts for Emphasis.*** We place the key terms and the index's page reference for each defining occurrence in **bold** text for easy reference. We show on-screen components in the **bold Helvetica** font (for example, the **File** menu) and Visual C# program text in the `Lucida` font (for example, `int count = 5;`). We use *italics* for emphasis.

***Objectives.*** The chapter objectives preview the topics covered in the chapter.

***Programming Tips.*** We include programming tips that focus on important aspects of program development. These tips and practices represent the best we've gleaned from a combined nine decades of programming, professional training and college teaching experience.

**Good Programming Practices**
*The* Good Programming Practices *call attention to techniques that will help you produce programs that are clearer, more understandable and more maintainable.*

**Common Programming Errors**
*Pointing out these* Common Programming Errors *reduces the likelihood that you'll make them.*

---

2. As of Summer 2016, Windows Forms, WPF and UWP apps all can be posted for distribution, either free or for sale, via the Windows Store. See `http://bit.ly/DesktopToUWP` for more information.

**Error-Prevention Tips**

*These tips contain suggestions for exposing and removing bugs from your programs; many of the tips describe aspects of Visual C# that prevent bugs from getting into programs.*

**Performance Tips**

*These tips highlight opportunities for making your programs run faster or minimizing the amount of memory that they occupy.*

**Software Engineering Observations**

*The* Software Engineering Observations *highlight architectural and design issues that affect the construction of software systems, especially large-scale systems.*

**Look-and-Feel Observations**

*These observations help you design attractive, user-friendly graphical user interfaces that conform to industry norms.*

***Index.*** We've included an extensive index for reference. Defining occurrences of key terms in the index are highlighted with a **bold** page number.

## Obtaining the Software Used in *C# 6 for Programmers, 6/e*

We wrote the book's code examples in *C# 6 for Programmers, 6/e* using Microsoft's free Visual Studio 2015 Community edition. See the Before You Begin section that follows this preface for download and installation instructions.

## Microsoft DreamSpark™

Microsoft provides many of its professional developer tools to students for free via a program called DreamSpark (`http://www.dreamspark.com`). If you're a student using this book in a college course, see the website for details on verifying your status so you take advantage of this program.

## Acknowledgments

We'd like to thank Barbara Deitel of Deitel & Associates, Inc. She painstakingly researched the latest versions of Visual C#, Visual Studio, .NET and other key technologies. We'd also like to acknowledge Frank McCown, Ph.D., Associate Professor of Computer Science, Harding University for his suggestion to include an example that used a `ProgressBar` with `async` and `await` in Chapter 21—so we ported to C# a similar example from our book *Java for Programmers, 3/e*.

We're fortunate to have worked with the dedicated team of publishing professionals at Pearson. We appreciate the extraordinary efforts and mentorship of our friend and professional colleague, Mark L. Taub, Editor-in-Chief of the Pearson IT Professional Group. Kristy Alaura did an extraordinary job recruiting the book's reviewers and managing the review process. Julie Nahil did a wonderful job bringing the book to publication and Chuti Prasertsith worked his magic on the cover design.

## Reviewers

The book was scrutinized by industry C# experts and academics teaching C# courses. They provided countless suggestions for improving the presentation. Any remaining flaws in the book are our own.

***Sixth Edition Reviewers:*** Lucian Wischik (Microsoft Visual C# Team), Octavio Hernandez (Microsoft Certified Solutions Developer, Principal Software Engineer at Advanced Bionics), José Antonio González Seco (Parliament of Andalusia, Spain), Bradley Sward (College of Dupage) and Qian Chen (Department of Engineering Technology: Computer Science Technology Program, Savannah State University).

***Other recent edition reviewers:*** Douglas B. Bock (MCSD.NET, Southern Illinois University Edwardsville), Dan Crevier (Microsoft), Shay Friedman (Microsoft Visual C# MVP), Amit K. Ghosh (University of Texas at El Paso), Marcelo Guerra Hahn (Microsoft), Kim Hamilton (Software Design Engineer at Microsoft and co-author of *Learning UML 2.0*), Huanhui Hu (Microsoft Corporation), Stephen Hustedde (South Mountain College), James Edward Keysor (Florida Institute of Technology), Narges Kasiri (Oklahoma State University), Helena Kotas (Microsoft), Charles Liu (University of Texas at San Antonio), Chris Lovett (Software Architect at Microsoft), Bashar Lulu (INETA Country Leader, Arabian Gulf), John McIlhinney (Spatial Intelligence; Microsoft MVP Visual Developer, Visual Basic), Ged Mead (Microsoft Visual Basic MVP, DevCity.net), Anand Mukundan (Architect, Polaris Software Lab Ltd.), Dr. Hamid R. Nemati (The University of North Carolina at Greensboro), Timothy Ng (Microsoft), Akira Onishi (Microsoft), Jeffrey P. Scott (Blackhawk Technical College), Joe Stagner (Senior Program Manager, Developer Tools & Platforms, Microsoft), Erick Thompson (Microsoft), Jesús Ubaldo Quevedo-Torrero (University of Wisconsin–Parkside, Department of Computer Science), Shawn Weisfeld (Microsoft MVP and President and Founder of UserGroup.tv) and Zijiang Yang (Western Michigan University).

As you read the book, we'd sincerely appreciate your comments, criticisms, corrections and suggestions for improvement. Please address all correspondence to:

```
deitel@deitel.com
```

We'll respond promptly. It was fun writing *C# 6 for Programmers, 6/e*—we hope you enjoy reading it!

*Paul Deitel*
*Harvey Deitel*

## About the Authors

**Paul Deitel**, CEO and Chief Technical Officer of Deitel & Associates, Inc., has over 35 years of experience in computing. He is a graduate of MIT, where he studied Information Technology. Through Deitel & Associates, Inc., he has delivered hundreds of corporate programming training courses worldwide to clients, including Cisco, IBM, Boeing, Siemens, Sun Microsystems (now Oracle), Dell, Fidelity, NASA at the Kennedy Space Center, the National Severe Storm Laboratory, NOAA (National Oceanic and Atmospheric Administration), White Sands Missile Range, Rogue Wave Software, SunGard, Nortel Networks, Puma, iRobot, Invensys and many more. He and his co-author, Dr. Harvey

Deitel, are the world's best-selling programming-language professional book/textbook/video authors.

Paul was named a Microsoft® Most Valuable Professional (MVP) for C# in 2012–2014. According to Microsoft, "the Microsoft MVP Award is an annual award that recognizes exceptional technology community leaders worldwide who actively share their high quality, real-world expertise with users and Microsoft." He also holds the Java Certified Programmer and Java Certified Developer designations and is an Oracle Java Champion.

C# MVP 2012–2014

**Dr. Harvey Deitel**, Chairman and Chief Strategy Officer of Deitel & Associates, Inc., has over 55 years of experience in the computer field. Dr. Deitel earned B.S. and M.S. degrees in Electrical Engineering from MIT and a Ph.D. in Mathematics from Boston University—he studied computing in each of these programs before they spun off Computer Science programs. He has extensive college teaching experience, including earning tenure and serving as the Chairman of the Computer Science Department at Boston College before founding Deitel & Associates, Inc., in 1991 with his son, Paul. The Deitels' publications have earned international recognition, with translations published in Japanese, German, Russian, Spanish, French, Polish, Italian, Simplified Chinese, Traditional Chinese, Korean, Portuguese, Greek, Urdu and Turkish. Dr. Deitel has delivered hundreds of programming courses to corporate, government, military and academic clients.

## About Deitel & Associates, Inc.

Deitel & Associates, Inc., founded by Paul Deitel and Harvey Deitel, is an internationally recognized authoring and corporate training organization, specializing in computer programming languages, object technology, Internet and web software technology, and Android and iOS app development. The company's clients include many of the world's largest corporations, government agencies, branches of the military and academic institutions. The company offers instructor-led training courses delivered at client sites worldwide on major programming languages and platforms, including C#®, C++, C, Java™, Android app development, iOS app development, Swift™, Visual Basic® and Internet and web programming.

Through its 40-year publishing partnership with Prentice Hall/Pearson, Deitel & Associates, Inc., creates leading-edge programming professional books, college textbooks, *LiveLessons* video products, e-books and REVEL™ interactive multimedia courses with integrated labs and assessment (`http://revel.pearson.com`). Deitel & Associates, Inc. and the authors can be reached at:

```
deitel@deitel.com
```

To learn more about Deitel's corporate training curriculum, visit

```
http://www.deitel.com/training
```

To request a proposal for worldwide on-site, instructor-led training at your organization, send an e-mail to `deitel@deitel.com`.

Individuals wishing to purchase Deitel books can do so via

```
http://bit.ly/DeitelOnAmazon
```

Individuals wishing to purchase Deitel *LiveLessons* video training can do so at:

```
http://bit.ly/DeitelOnInformit
```

Deitel books and *LiveLessons* videos are generally available electronically to Safari Books Online subscribers at:

```
http://SafariBooksOnline.com
```

You can get a free 10-day Safari Books Online trial at:

```
https://www.safaribooksonline.com/register/
```

Bulk orders by corporations, the government, the military and academic institutions should be placed directly with Pearson. For more information, visit

```
http://www.informit.com/store/sales.aspx
```

# Before You Begin

Please read this section before using the book to ensure that your computer is set up properly.

## Font and Naming Conventions

We use fonts to distinguish between features, such as menu names, menu items, and other elements that appear in the program-development environment. Our convention is

- to emphasize Visual Studio features in a **sans-serif bold font** (e.g., **Properties** window) and
- to emphasize program text in a fixed-width `sans-serif font` (e.g., `bool x = true`).

## Visual Studio 2015 Community Edition

This book uses Windows 10 and the free Microsoft Visual Studio 2015 Community edition—Visual Studio also can run on various older Windows versions. Ensure that your system meets Visual Studio 2015 Community edition's minimum hardware and software requirements listed at:

```
https://www.visualstudio.com/en-us/visual-studio-2015-system-
   requirements-vs
```

Next, download the installer from

```
https://www.visualstudio.com/products/visual-studio-express-vs
```

then execute it and follow the on-screen instructions to install Visual Studio.

Though we developed the book's examples on Windows 10, most of the examples will run on Windows 7 and higher. Most examples without graphical user interfaces (GUIs) also will run on other C# and .NET implementations—see "If You're Not Using Microsoft Visual C#..." later in this Before You Begin for more information.

## Viewing File Extensions

Several screenshots in *C# 6 for Programmers, 6/e* display file names with file-name extensions (e.g., `.txt`, `.cs`, `.png`, etc.). You may need to adjust your system's settings to display file-name extensions. If you're using Windows 7:

1. Open **Windows Explorer**.
2. Press the *Alt* key to display the menu bar, then select **Folder Options...** from the **Tools** menu.
3. In the dialog that appears, select the **View** tab.

4. In the **Advanced settings** pane, *uncheck* the box to the left of the text **Hide extensions for known file types.**
5. Click **OK** to apply the setting and close the dialog.

If you're using Windows 8 or higher:

1. Open **File Explorer**.
2. Click the **View** tab.
3. Ensure that the **File name extensions** checkbox is *checked.*

## Obtaining the Source Code

*C# 6 for Programmers, 6/e*'s source-code examples are available for download at

```
http://www.deitel.com/books/CSharp6FP
```

Click the **Examples** link to download the ZIP archive file to your computer—most browsers will save the file into your user account's `Downloads` folder. You can extract the ZIP file's contents using built-in Windows capabilities, or using a third-party archive-file tool such as WinZip (`www.winzip.com`) or 7-zip (`www.7-zip.org`).

Throughout the book, steps that require you to access our example code on your computer assume that you've extracted the examples from the ZIP file and placed them in your user account's `Documents` folder. You can extract them anywhere you like, but if you choose a different location, you'll need to update our steps accordingly. To extract the ZIP file's contents using the built-in Windows capabilities:

1. Open **Windows Explorer** (Windows 7) or **File Explorer** (Windows 8 and higher).
2. Locate the ZIP file on your system, typically in your user account's `Downloads` folder.
3. Right click the ZIP file and select **Extract All...**.
4. In the dialog that appears, navigate to the folder where you'd like to extract the contents, then click the **Extract** button.

## Configuring Visual Studio for Use with This Book

In this section, you'll use Visual Studio's **Options** dialog to configure several Visual Studio options. Setting these options is not required, but will make your Visual Studio match what we show in the book's Visual Studio screen captures.

### *Visual Studio Theme*

Visual Studio has three color themes—**Blue**, **Dark** and **Light**. We used the **Blue** theme with light colored backgrounds to make the book's screen captures easier to read. To switch themes:

1. In the Visual Studio **Tools** menu, select **Options...** to display the **Options** dialog.
2. In the left column, select **Environment**.
3. Select the **Color theme** you wish to use.

Keep the **Options** dialog open for the next step.

*Line Numbers*
Throughout the book's discussions, we refer to code in our examples by line number. Many programmers find it helpful to display line numbers in Visual Studio as well. To do so:

1. Expand the **Text Editor** node in the **Options** dialog's left pane.
2. Select **All Languages**.
3. In the right pane, check the **Line numbers** checkbox.

Keep the **Options** dialog open for the next step.

*Tab Size for Code Indents*
Microsoft recommends four-space indents in source code, which is the Visual Studio default. Due to the fixed and limited width of code lines in print, we use three-space indents—this reduces the number of code lines that wrap to a new line, making the code a bit easier to read. If you wish to use three-space indents:

1. Expand the **C#** node in the **Options** dialog's left pane and select **Tabs**.
2. Ensure that **Insert spaces** is selected.
3. Enter **3** for both the **Tab size** and **Indent size** fields.
4. Click **OK** to save your settings.

## If You're Not Using Microsoft Visual C#...

C# can be used on other platforms via two open-source projects managed by the .NET Foundation (`http://www.dotnetfoundation.org`)—the Mono Project and .NET Core.

*Mono Project*
The **Mono Project** is an open source, cross-platform C# and .NET Framework implementation that can be installed on Linux, OS X (soon to be renamed as macOS) and Windows. The code for most of the book's console (non-GUI) apps will compile and run using the Mono Project. Mono also supports Windows `Forms` GUI, which is used in Chapters 14–15 and several later examples. For more information and to download Mono, visit:

```
http://www.mono-project.com/
```

*.NET Core*
**.NET Core** is a new cross-platform .NET implementation for Windows, Linux, OS X and FreeBSD. The code for most of the book's console (non-GUI) apps will compile and run using .NET Core. At the time of this writing, a .NET Core version for Windows was available and versions were still under development for other platforms. For more information and to download .NET Core, visit:

```
https://dotnet.github.io/
```

You're now ready to get started with C# and the .NET platform using *C# 6 for Programmers, 6/e*. We hope you enjoy the book!

1

# Introduction

## Objectives

In this chapter you'll:

- Understand the history of the Visual C# programming language and the Windows operating system.
- Learn what cloud computing with Microsoft Azure is.
- Review the basics of object technology.
- Understand the parts that Windows, .NET, Visual Studio and C# play in the C# ecosystem.
- Test-drive a Visual C# drawing app.

Outline



## 1.1 Introduction

Welcome to C#[1]—a powerful computer-programming language that's used to build substantial computer applications. There are billions of personal computers in use and an even larger number of mobile devices with computers at their core. Since it was released in 2001, C# has been used primarily to build applications for personal computers and systems that support them. The explosive growth of mobile phones, tablets and other devices also is creating significant opportunities for programming mobile apps. With this new sixth edition of *C# 6 for Programmers*, you'll be able to use Microsoft's new Universal Windows Platform (UWP) with Windows 10 to build C# apps for both personal computers and Windows 10 Mobile devices. With Microsoft's purchase of Xamarin, you also can develop C# mobile apps for Android devices and for iOS devices, such as iPhones and iPads.

## 1.2 Object Technology: A Brief Review

C# is an object-oriented programming language. In this section we'll review the basics of object technology.

Building software quickly, correctly and economically remains an elusive goal at a time when demands for new and more powerful software are soaring. **Objects**, or more precisely—as we'll see in Chapter 4—the **classes** objects come from, are essentially *reusable* software components. There are date objects, time objects, audio objects, video objects, automobile objects, people objects, etc. Almost any *noun* can be reasonably represented as a software object in terms of *attributes* (e.g., name, color and size) and *behaviors* (e.g., calculating, moving and communicating). Software developers have discovered that using a modular, object-oriented design-and-implementation approach can make software-development groups much more productive than was possible with earlier techniques—object-oriented programs are often easier to understand, correct and modify.

### *The Automobile as an Object*

Let's begin with a simple analogy. Suppose you want to *drive a car and make it go faster by pressing its accelerator pedal.* What must happen before you can do this? Well, before you

1. The name C#, pronounced "C-sharp," is based on the musical # notation for "sharp" notes.

can drive a car, someone has to *design* it. A car typically begins as engineering drawings, similar to the *blueprints* that describe the design of a house. These drawings include the design for an accelerator pedal. The pedal *hides* from the driver the complex mechanisms that actually make the car go faster, just as the brake pedal hides the mechanisms that slow the car, and the steering wheel *hides* the mechanisms that turn the car. This enables people with little or no knowledge of how engines, braking and steering mechanisms work to drive a car easily.

Before you can drive a car, it must be *built* from the engineering drawings that describe it. A completed car has an *actual* accelerator pedal to make the car go faster, but even that's not enough—the car won't accelerate on its own (hopefully!), so the driver must *press* the pedal to accelerate the car.

### *Methods and Classes*

Let's use our car example to introduce some key object-oriented programming concepts. Performing a task in a program requires a **method**. The method houses the program statements that actually perform the task. It *hides* these statements from its user, just as a car's accelerator pedal hides from the driver the mechanisms of making the car go faster. In C#, we create a program unit called a class to house the set of methods that perform the class's tasks. For example, a class that represents a bank account might contain one method to *deposit* money to an account and another to *withdraw* money from an account. A class is similar in concept to a car's engineering drawings, which house the design of an accelerator pedal, steering wheel, and so on.

### *Making Objects from Classes*

Just as someone has to *build a car* from its engineering drawings before you can actually drive a car, you must *build an object* from a class before a program can perform the tasks that the class's methods define. The process of doing this is called *instantiation*. An object is then referred to as an **instance** of its class.

### *Reuse*

Just as a car's engineering drawings can be *reused* many times to build many cars, you can *reuse* a class many times to build many objects. Reuse of existing classes when building new classes and programs saves time and effort. Reuse also helps you build more reliable and effective systems, because existing classes and components often have gone through extensive *testing* (to locate problems), *debugging* (to correct those problems) and *performance tuning*. Just as the notion of *interchangeable parts* was crucial to the Industrial Revolution, reusable classes are crucial to the software revolution that's been spurred by object technology.

### *Messages and Method Calls*

When you drive a car, pressing its gas pedal sends a *message* to the car to perform a task—that is, to go faster. Similarly, you *send messages to an object*. Each message is implemented as a **method call** that tells a method of the object to perform its task. For example, a program might call a particular bank-account object's *deposit* method to increase the account's balance.

### *Attributes and Instance Variables*

A car, besides having capabilities to accomplish tasks, also has *attributes*, such as its color, its number of doors, the amount of gas in its tank, its current speed and its record of total miles driven (i.e., its odometer reading). Like its capabilities, the car's attributes are represented as part of its design in its engineering diagrams (which, for example, include an odometer and a fuel gauge). As you drive an actual car, these attributes are carried along with the car. Every car maintains its *own* attributes. For example, each car knows how much gas is in its own gas tank, but not how much is in the tanks of *other* cars.

An object, similarly, has attributes that it carries along as it's used in a program. These attributes are specified as part of the object's class. For example, a bank-account object has a *balance attribute* that represents the amount of money in the account. Each bank-account object knows the balance in the account it represents, but *not* the balances of the *other* accounts in the bank. Attributes are specified by the class's **instance variables**.

### *Properties, `get` Accessors and `set` Accessors*

Attributes are not necessarily accessible directly. The car manufacturer does not want drivers to take apart the car's engine to observe the amount of gas in its tank. Instead, the driver can check the fuel gauge on the dashboard. The bank does not want its customers to walk into the vault to count the amount of money in an account. Instead, the customers talk to a bank teller or check personalized online bank accounts. Similarly, you do not need to have access to an object's instance variables in order to use them. You should use the **properties** of an object. Properties contain **`get` accessors** for reading the values of variables, and **`set` accessors** for storing values into them.

### *Encapsulation*

Classes **encapsulate** (i.e., wrap) attributes and methods into objects created from those classes—an object's attributes and methods are intimately related. Objects may communicate with one another, but they're normally not allowed to know how other objects are implemented—implementation details are *hidden* within the objects themselves. This **information hiding**, as we'll see, is crucial to good software engineering.

### *Inheritance*

A new class of objects can be created quickly and conveniently by **inheritance**—the new class absorbs the characteristics of an existing class, possibly customizing them and adding unique characteristics of its own. In our car analogy, an object of class "convertible" certainly *is an* object of the more *general* class "automobile," but more *specifically*, the roof can be raised or lowered.

### *Object-Oriented Analysis and Design (OOAD)*

Soon you'll be writing programs in C#. How will you create the code for your programs? Perhaps, like many programmers, you'll simply turn on your computer and start typing. This approach may work for small programs (like the ones we present in the early chapters of the book), but what if you were asked to create a software system to control thousands of automated teller machines for a major bank? Or suppose you were asked to work on a team of thousands of software developers building the next generation of the U.S. air traffic control system? For projects so large and complex, you should not simply sit down and start writing programs.

To create the best solutions, you should follow a detailed **analysis** process for determining your project's **requirements** (i.e., defining *what* the system is supposed to do) and developing a **design** that satisfies them (i.e., deciding *how* the system should do it). Ideally, you'd go through this process and carefully review the design (and have your design reviewed by other software professionals) before writing any code. If this process involves analyzing and designing your system from an object-oriented point of view, it's called an **object-oriented analysis and design (OOAD) process**. Languages like C# are object oriented—programming in such a language, called **object-oriented programming (OOP)**, allows you to implement an object-oriented design as a working system.

*The UML (Unified Modeling Language)*

Although many different OOAD processes exist, a single graphical language for communicating the results of *any* OOAD process has come into wide use. This language, known as the Unified Modeling Language (UML), is now the most widely used graphical scheme for modeling object-oriented systems. We present our first UML diagrams in Chapters 4 and 5, then use them in our deeper treatment of object-oriented programming through Chapter 12. In our online ATM Software Engineering Case Study, we present a simple subset of the UML's features as we guide you through an object-oriented design and implementation experience.

## 1.3 C#

In 2000, Microsoft announced the **C#** programming language. C# has roots in the C, C++ and Java programming languages. It has similar capabilities to Java and is appropriate for the most demanding app-development tasks, especially for building today's desktop apps, large-scale enterprise apps, and web-based, mobile and cloud-based apps.

### 1.3.1 Object-Oriented Programming

C# is *object oriented*—we've discussed the basics of object technology and we present a rich treatment of object-oriented programming throughout the book. C# has access to the powerful **.NET Framework Class Library**—a vast collection of prebuilt classes that enable you to develop apps quickly (Fig. 1.1). We'll say more about .NET in Section 1.4.

| Some key capabilities in the .NET Framework Class Library | |
|---|---|
| Database | Debugging |
| Building web apps | Multithreading |
| Graphics | File processing |
| Input/output | Security |
| Computer networking | Web communication |
| Permissions | Graphical user interface |
| Mobile | Data structures |
| String processing | Universal Windows Platform GUI |

**Fig. 1.1** | Some key capabilities in the .NET Framework Class Library.

### 1.3.2 Event-Driven Programming

C# graphical user interfaces (GUIs) are **event driven**. You can write programs that respond to user-initiated **events** such as mouse clicks, keystrokes, timer expirations and *touches* and *finger swipes*—gestures that are widely used on smartphones and tablets.

### 1.3.3 Visual Programming

Visual Studio enables you to use C# as a *visual programming language*—in addition to writing program statements to build portions of your apps, you'll also use Visual Studio to drag and drop predefined GUI objects like *buttons* and *textboxes* into place on your screen, and label and resize them. Visual Studio will write much of the GUI code for you.

### 1.3.4 Generic and Functional Programming

#### *Generic Programming*

It's common to write a program that processes a collection—e.g., a collection of numbers, a collection of contacts, a collection of videos, etc. Historically, you had to program separately to handle each type of collection. With generic programming, you write code that handles a collection "in the general" and C# handles the specifics for each collection type, saving you a great deal of work. Chapters 18–19 present generics and generic collections.

#### *Functional Programming*

With *functional programming*, you specify *what* you want to accomplish in a task, but *not how* to accomplish it. For example, with Microsoft's LINQ—which we introduce in Chapter 9, then use in many later chapters—you can say, "Here's a collection of numbers, give me the sum of its elements." You do *not* need to specify the mechanics of walking through the elements and adding them into a running total one at a time—LINQ handles all that for you. Functional programming speeds application development and reduces errors. We take a deeper look at functional programming in Chapter 19.

### 1.3.5 An International Standard

C# has been standardized through ECMA International:

```
http://www.ecma-international.org
```

This enables other implementations of the language besides Microsoft's Visual C#. At the time of this writing, the C# standard document—ECMA-334—was still being updated
6 for C# 6. For information on ECMA-334, visit

```
http://www.ecma-international.org/publications/standards/Ecma-334.htm
```

Visit the Microsoft download center to find the latest version of Microsoft's C# 6 specification, other documentation and software downloads.

### 1.3.6 C# on Non-Windows Platforms

Microsoft originally developed C# for Windows development, but it can be used on other platforms via the **Mono Project** and **.NET Core**—both managed by the .NET Foundation

```
http://www.dotnetfoundation.org/
```

For more information, see the Before You Begin section after the Preface.

### 1.3.7 Internet and Web Programming

Today's apps can be written with the aim of communicating among the world's computers. As you'll see, this is the focus of Microsoft's .NET strategy. Later in the book, you'll build web-based apps with C# and Microsoft's **ASP.NET** technology.

### 1.3.8 Asynchronous Programming with async and await

In most programming today, each task in a program must finish executing before the next task can begin. This is called *synchronous programming* and is the style we use for most of this book. C# also allows *asynchronous programming* in which multiple tasks can be performed at the *same* time. Asynchronous programming can help you make your apps more responsive to user interactions, such as mouse clicks and keystrokes, among many other uses.

Asynchronous programming in early versions of Visual C# was difficult and error prone. C#'s `async` and `await` capabilities simplify asynchronous programming by enabling the compiler to hide much of the associated complexity from the developer. In Chapter 21, we provide an introduction to asynchronous programming with `async` and `await`.

## 1.4 Microsoft's .NET

In 2000, Microsoft announced its **.NET initiative** (`www.microsoft.com/net`), a broad vision for using the Internet and the web in the development, engineering, distribution and use of software. Rather than forcing you to use a single programming language, .NET permits you to create apps in *any* .NET-compatible language (such as C#, Visual Basic, Visual C++ and many others). Part of the initiative includes Microsoft's ASP.NET technology for building web-based applications.

### 1.4.1 .NET Framework

The **.NET Framework Class Library** provides many capabilities that you'll use to build substantial C# apps quickly and easily. It contains *thousands* of valuable *prebuilt* classes that have been tested and tuned to maximize performance. You'll learn how to create your own classes, but you should *re-use* the .NET Framework classes whenever possible to speed up the software-development process, while enhancing the quality and performance of the software you develop.

### 1.4.2 Common Language Runtime

The **Common Language Runtime (CLR)**, another key part of the .NET Framework, executes .NET programs and provides functionality to make them easier to develop and debug. The CLR is a **virtual machine (VM)**—software that manages the execution of programs and hides from them the underlying operating system and hardware. The source code for programs that are executed and managed by the CLR is called *managed code*. The CLR provides various services to managed code, such as

- integrating software components written in different .NET languages,
- error handling between such components,
- enhanced security,
- automatic memory management and more.

Unmanaged-code programs do not have access to the CLR's services, which makes unmanaged code more difficult to write.[2] Managed code is compiled into machine-specific instructions in the following steps:

1. First, the code is compiled into **Microsoft Intermediate Language** (MSIL). Code converted into MSIL from other languages and sources can be woven together by the CLR—this allows programmers to work in their preferred .NET programming language. The MSIL for an app's components is placed into the app's *executable file*—the file that causes the computer to perform the app's tasks.
2. When the app executes, another compiler (known as the **just-in-time compiler** or **JIT compiler**) in the CLR translates the MSIL in the executable file into machine-language code (for a particular platform).
3. The machine-language code executes on that platform.

### 1.4.3 Platform Independence

If the .NET Framework exists and is installed for a platform, that platform can run *any* .NET program. The ability of a program to run without modification across multiple platforms is known as **platform independence**. Code written once can be used on another type of computer without modification, saving time and money. In addition, software can target a wider audience. Previously, companies had to decide whether converting their programs to different platforms—a process called **porting**—was worth the cost. With .NET, porting programs is no longer an issue, at least once .NET itself has been made available on the platforms.

### 1.4.4 Language Interoperability

The .NET Framework provides a high level of **language interoperability**. Because software components written in different .NET languages (such as C# and Visual Basic) are all compiled into MSIL, the components can be combined to create a single unified program. Thus, MSIL allows the .NET Framework to be **language independent**.

The .NET Framework Class Library can be used by any .NET language. The latest release of .NET includes .NET 4.6 and .NET Core:

- NET 4.6 introduces many improvements and new features, including ASP.NET 5 for web-based applications, improved support for today's high-resolution 4K screens and more.
- .NET Core is the cross-platform subset of .NET for Windows, Linux, OS X and FreeBSD.

## 1.5 Microsoft's Windows® Operating System

Microsoft's Windows is the most widely personal-computer, desktop operating system worldwide. **Operating systems** are software systems that make using computers more convenient for users, developers and system administrators. They provide *services* that allow each app to execute safely, efficiently and *concurrently* (i.e., in parallel) with other apps.

2. `http://msdn.microsoft.com/library/8bs2ecf4.`

Other popular desktop operating systems include macOS (formerly OS X) and Linux. *Mobile operating systems* used in smartphones and tablets include Microsoft's Windows 10 Mobile, Google's Android and Apple's iOS (for iPhone, iPad and iPod Touch devices). Figure 1.2 presents the evolution of the Windows operating system.

| Version | Description |
|---|---|
| Windows in the 1990s | In the mid-1980s, Microsoft developed the **Windows operating system** based on a graphical user interface with buttons, textboxes, menus and other graphical elements. The various versions released throughout the 1990s were intended for personal computing. Microsoft entered the corporate operating systems market with the 1993 release of *Windows NT.* |
| Windows XP and Windows Vista | *Windows XP* was released in 2001 and combined Microsoft's corporate and consumer operating-system lines. At the time of this writing, it still holds more than 10% of the operating-systems market (`https://www.netmarketshare.com/operating-system-market-share.aspx`). *Windows Vista*, released in 2007, offered the attractive new Aero user interface, many powerful enhancements and new apps and enhanced security. But Vista never caught on. |
| Windows 7 | *Windows 7* is currently the world's most widely used desktop operating system with over 47% of the operating-systems market (`https://www.netmarketshare.com/operating-system-market-share.aspx`). Windows added enhancements to the Aero user interface, faster startup times, further refinement of Vista's security features, touch-screen with multitouch support, and more. |
| Windows 8 for Desktops and Tablets | Windows 8, released in 2012, provided a similar platform (the underlying system on which apps run) and *user experience* across a wide range of devices including personal computers, smartphones, tablets *and* the Xbox Live online game service. Its new look-and-feel featured a Start screen with *tiles* representing each app, similar to that of *Windows Phone* (now Windows 10 Mobile)—Microsoft's smartphone operating system. Windows 8 featured *multitouch* support for *touchpads* and *touchscreen* devices, enhanced security features and more. |
| Windows 8 UI (User Interface) | Windows 8 UI (previously called "Metro") introduced a clean look-and-feel with minimal distractions to the user. Windows 8 apps featured a *chromeless window* with no borders, title bars and menus. These elements were *hidden*, allowing apps to fill the *entire* screen—particularly helpful on smaller screens such as tablets and smartphones. The interface elements were displayed in the *app bar* when the user *swiped* the top or bottom of the screen by holding down the mouse button, moving the mouse in the swipe direction and releasing the mouse button; or using a *finger swipe* on a touchscreen device. |

**Fig. 1.2** | The evolution of the Windows operating system. (Part 1 of 2.)

| Version | Description |
|---|---|
| Windows 10 and the Universal Windows Platform | Windows 10, released in 2015, is the current version of Windows and currently holds a 15% (and growing) share of the operating-systems market (`https://www.netmarketshare.com/operating-system-market-share.aspx`). In addition to many user-interface and other updates, Windows 10 introduced the **Universal Windows Platform (UWP)**, which is designed to provide a common platform (the underlying system on which apps run) and user experience across all Windows devices including personal computers, smartphones, tablets, Xbox and even Microsoft's new HoloLens augmented reality holographic headset—all using nearly identical code. |

**Fig. 1.2** | The evolution of the Windows operating system. (Part 2 of 2.)

*Windows Store*

You can sell apps or offer them for free in the Windows Store. At the time of this writing, the fee to become a registered developer is $19 for individuals and $99 for companies. Microsoft retains 30% of the purchase price (more in some markets). See the App Developer Agreement for more information:

```
https://msdn.microsoft.com/en-us/library/windows/apps/hh694058.aspx
```

The Windows Store offers several business models for monetizing your app. You can charge full price for your app before download, with prices starting at $1.49. You also can offer a time-limited trial or feature-limited trial that allows users to try the app before purchasing the full version, sell virtual goods (such as additional app features) using in-app purchases and more. To learn more about the Windows Store and monetizing your apps, visit

```
https://msdn.microsoft.com/windows/uwp/monetize/index
```

## 1.6 Visual Studio Integrated Development Environment

C# programs can be created using Microsoft's Visual Studio—a collection of software tools called an **Integrated Development Environment** (**IDE**). The **Visual Studio Community** edition IDE enables you to *write*, *run*, *test* and *debug* C# programs quickly and conveniently. It also supports Microsoft's Visual Basic, Visual C++ and F# programming languages and many more. Most of this book's examples were built using *Visual Studio Community*, which runs on Windows 7, 8 and 10. A few of the book's examples require Windows 10.

## 1.7 Painter Test-Drive in Visual Studio Community

You'll now use *Visual Studio Community* to "test-drive" an existing app that enables you to draw on the screen using the mouse. The **Painter** app allows you to choose among several brush sizes and colors. The elements and functionality you see in this app are typical of what you'll learn to program in this text. The following steps walk you through test-driving the app. For this test drive, we assume that you placed the book's examples in your user account's `Documents` folder in a subfolder named `examples`.

### *Step 1: Checking Your Setup*

Confirm that you've set up your computer and the software properly by reading the book's Before You Begin section that follows the Preface.

### *Step 2: Locating the* **Painter** *App's Directory*

Open a **File Explorer** (Windows 8 and 10) or **Windows Explorer** (Windows 7) window and navigate to

```
C:\Users\yourUserName\Documents\examples\ch01
```

Double click the `Painter` folder to view its contents (Fig. 1.3), then double click the `Painter.sln` file to open the app's solution in Visual Studio. An app's *solution* contains all of the app's *code files*, *supporting files* (such as *images*, *videos*, *data files*, etc.) and configuration information. We'll discuss the contents of a solution in more detail in the next chapter.

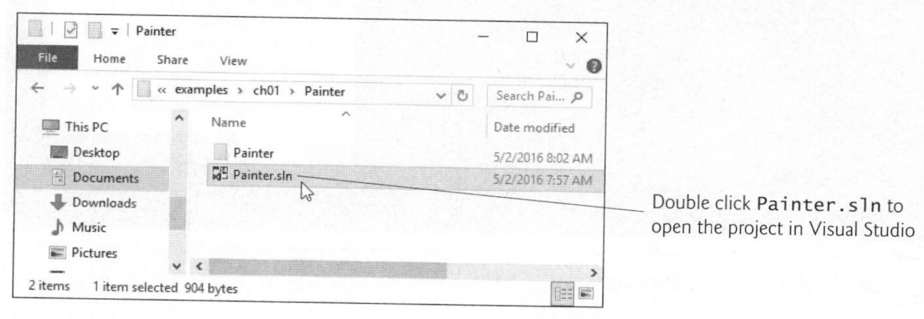


**Fig. 1.3** | Contents of `C:\examples\ch01\Painter`.

Depending on your system configuration, **File Explorer** or **Windows Explorer** might display `Painter.sln` simply as `Painter`, without the filename extension `.sln`. To display the filename extensions in Windows 8 and higher:

1. Open **File Explorer**.
2. Click the **View** tab, then ensure that the **File name extensions** checkbox is checked.

To display them in Windows 7:

1. Open **Windows Explorer**.
2. Press *Alt* to display the menu bar, then select **Folder Options...** from **Windows Explorer**'s **Tools** menu.
3. In the dialog that appears, select the **View** tab.
4. In the **Advanced settings:** pane, uncheck the box to the left of the text **Hide extensions for known file types**. [*Note*: If this item is already unchecked, no action needs to be taken.]
5. Click **OK** to apply the setting and close the dialog.

### *Step 3: Running the* Painter *App*

To see the running **Painter** app, click the **Start** button (Fig. 1.4)

or press the *F5* key.

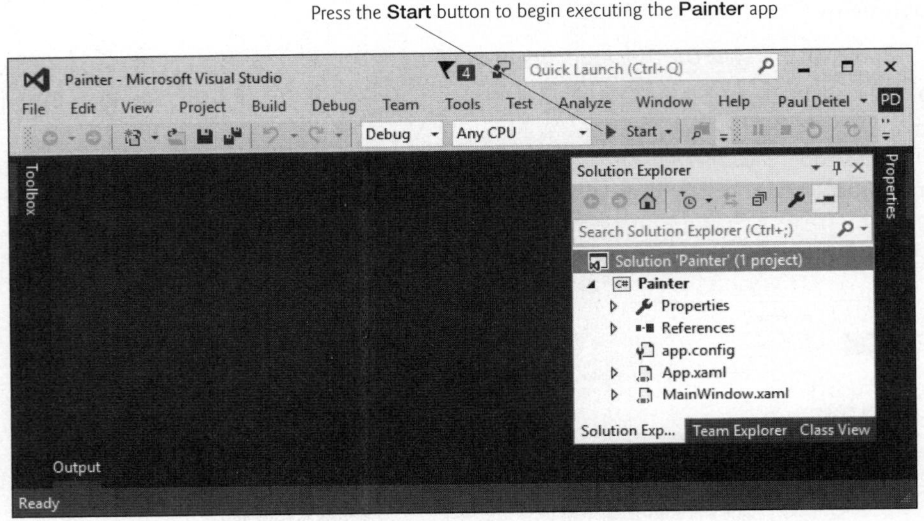


**Fig. 1.4** | Running the **Painter** app.

Figure 1.5 shows the running app and labels several of the app's graphical elements—called **controls**. These include `GroupBoxes`, `RadioButtons`, `Buttons` and a `Panel`. These controls and many others are discussed throughout the text. The app allows you to draw with a **Red, Blue, Green** or **Black** brush of **Small, Medium** or **Large** size. As you drag the mouse on the white `Panel`, the app draws circles of the specified color and size at the mouse pointer's current position. The slower you drag the mouse, the closer the circles will be. Thus, dragging slowly draws a continuous line (as in Fig. 1.6) and dragging quickly draws individual circles with space in between. You also can **Undo** your previous operation or **Clear** the drawing to start from scratch by pressing the `Buttons` below the `RadioButtons` in the GUI. By using existing *controls*—which are *objects*—you can create powerful apps much faster than if you had to write all the code yourself. This is a key benefit of *software reuse.*

The brush's properties, selected in the `RadioButtons` labeled **Black** and **Medium**, are *default settings*—the initial settings you see when you first run the app. Programmers include default settings to provide *reasonable* choices that the app will use if the user *does not* change the settings. Default settings also provide visual cues for users to choose their own settings. Now you'll choose your own settings as a user of this app.

### *Step 4: Changing the Brush Color*

Click the `RadioButton` labeled **Red** to change the brush color, then click the `RadioButton` labeled **Small** to change the brush size. Position the mouse over the white `Panel`, then drag the mouse to draw with the brush. Draw flower petals, as shown in Fig. 1.6.

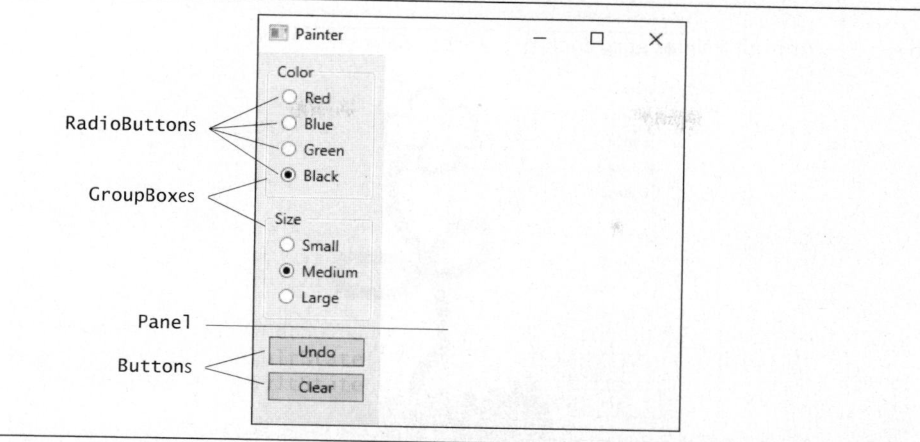


**Fig. 1.5** | **Painter** app running in Windows 10.

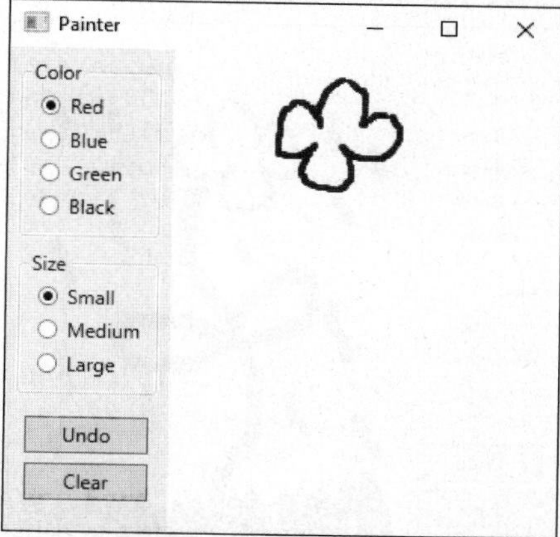


**Fig. 1.6** | Drawing flower petals with a small red brush.

### *Step 5: Changing the Brush Color and Size*

Click the **Green** `RadioButton` to change the brush color. Then, click the **Large** `RadioButton` to change the brush size. Draw grass and a flower stem, as shown in Fig. 1.7.

### *Step 6: Finishing the Drawing*

Click the **Blue** and **Medium** `RadioButtons`. Draw raindrops, as shown in Fig. 1.8, to complete the drawing.

### *Step 7: Stopping the App*

When you run an app from Visual Studio, you can terminate it by clicking the stop button

■

on the Visual Studio toolbar or by clicking the close box

**Fig. 1.7** | Drawing the flower stem and grass with a large green brush.

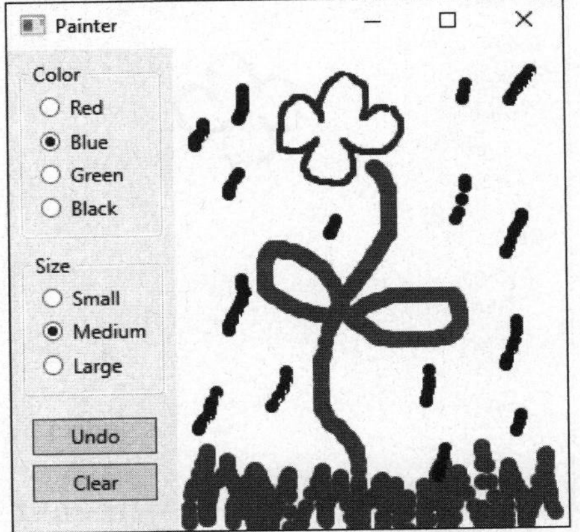


**Fig. 1.8** | Drawing rain drops with a medium blue brush.

×
on the running app's window.

Now that you've completed the test-drive, you're ready to begin developing C# apps. In Chapter 2, Introduction to Visual Studio and Visual Programming, you'll use Visual Studio to create your first C# program using *visual programming* techniques. As you'll see, Visual Studio will generate for you the code that builds the app's GUI. In Chapter 3, Introduction to C# App Programming, you'll begin writing C# programs containing conventional program code that you write.

# 2

# Introduction to Visual Studio and Visual Programming

## Objectives

In this chapter you'll:

- See an overview of the Visual Studio Community 2015 Integrated Development Environment (IDE) for writing, running and debugging your apps.
- Create a new project using Visual Studio's **Windows Forms Application** template.
- Be introduced to Windows `Forms` and the controls you'll use to build graphical user interfaces.
- Use visual app development to conveniently create, compile and execute a simple Visual C# app that displays text and an image.

**Outline**



## 2.1 Introduction

**Visual Studio** is Microsoft's Integrated Development Environment (IDE) for creating, running and debugging apps (also called applications) written in C# and various other .NET programming languages. In this chapter, we overview the Visual Studio Community 2015 IDE, then show how to create a simple Visual C# app by dragging and dropping predefined building blocks into place—a technique known as **visual app development**.

## 2.2 Overview of the Visual Studio Community 2015 IDE

There are several versions of Visual Studio. This book's examples, screen captures and discussions are based on the free **Visual Studio Community 2015** running on Windows 10. See the Before You Begin section that follows the Preface for information on installing the software. With few exceptions, this book's examples can be created and run on Windows 7, 8.x or 10—we'll point out any examples that require Windows 10.

The examples will work on full versions of Visual Studio as well—though some options, menus and instructions might differ. From this point forward, we'll refer to Visual Studio Community 2015 simply as "Visual Studio" or "the IDE."

### 2.2.1 Introduction to Visual Studio Community 2015

[*Note:* We use the > character to indicate when you should select a *menu item* from a *menu*. For example, notation **File > Save All** means that you should select the **Save All** menu item from the **File** menu.]

To begin, open Visual Studio. On Windows 10, click

then select **All Apps > Visual Studio 2015**. On Windows 7, click

then select **All Programs > Visual Studio 2015**. On Windows 8's **Start** screen, locate and click the Visual Studio 2015 tile, which will contain the following icon:

Initially, Visual Studio displays the **Start Page** (Fig. 2.1). Depending on your version of Visual Studio, your **Start Page** may look different. The **Start Page** contains a list of links to Visual Studio resources and web-based resources. At any time, you can return to the **Start Page** by selecting **View > Start Page**.

### 2.2.2 Visual Studio Themes

Visual Studio supports three themes that specify the IDE's color scheme:

- a *dark theme* (with dark window backgrounds and light text)
- a *light theme* (with light window backgrounds and dark text) and
- a *blue theme* (with light window backgrounds and dark text).

We use the blue theme throughout this book. The Before You Begin section after the Preface explains how to set this option.

### 2.2.3 Links on the Start Page

The **Start Page** links are organized into two columns. The left column's **Start** section contains options for building new apps or working on existing ones. The left column's **Recent** section contains links to projects you've recently created or modified.

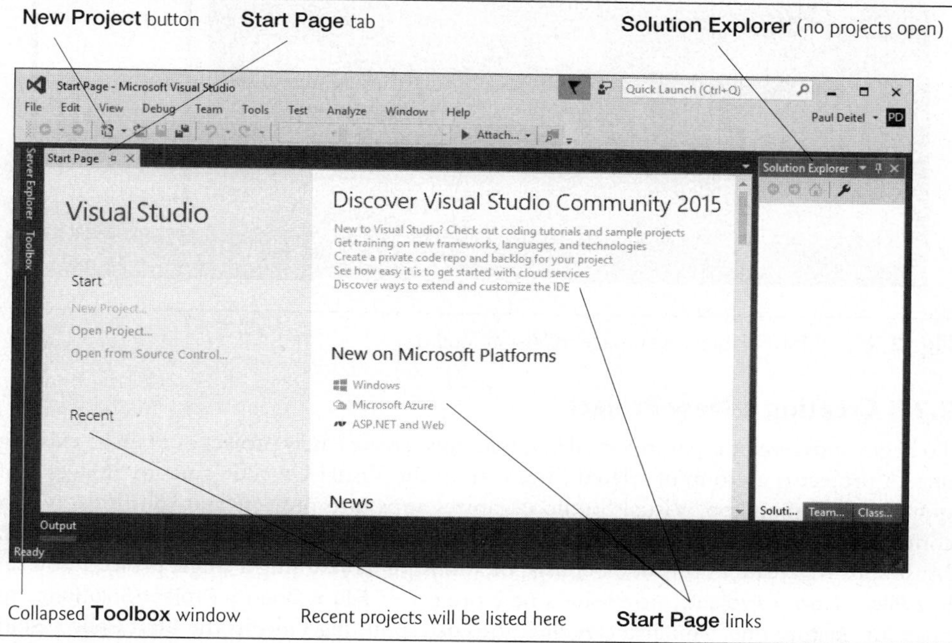


**Fig. 2.1** | **Start Page** in Visual Studio Community 2015.

The **Start Page**'s right column—with **Discover Visual Studio Community 2015** at the top—contains links to various online documentation and resources to help you get started with Visual Studio and learn about Microsoft programming technologies. An Internet connection is required for the IDE to access most of this information.

To access more extensive information on Visual Studio, you can browse the **MSDN (Microsoft Developer Network)** Library at

```
https://msdn.microsoft.com/library/dd831853
```

The MSDN site contains articles, downloads and tutorials on technologies of interest to Visual Studio developers. You also can browse the web from the IDE by selecting **View > Other Windows > Web Browser**. To request a web page, type its URL into the location bar (Fig. 2.2) and press the *Enter* key—your computer, of course, must be connected to the Internet. The web page that you wish to view appears as another tab in the IDE—Figure 2.2 shows the browser tab after entering `http://msdn.microsoft.com/library`.

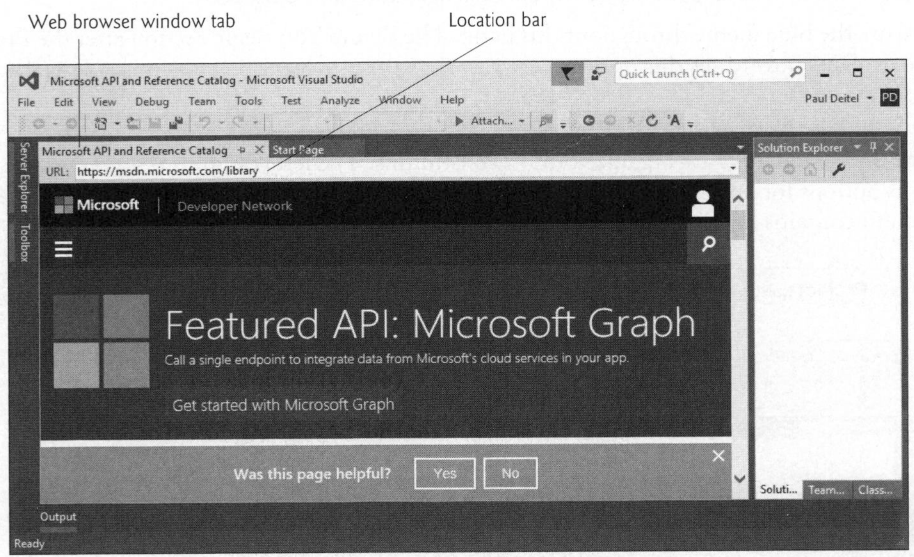


**Fig. 2.2** | MSDN Library web page in Visual Studio.

## 2.2.4 Creating a New Project

To begin app development in Visual C#, you must create a new project or open an existing one. A **project** is a group of related files, such as the Visual C# code and any images that might make up an app. Visual Studio organizes apps into projects and **solutions**, which contain one or more projects. Multiple-project solutions are used to create large-scale apps. Most apps we create in this book consist of a solution containing a single project. You select **File > New > Project...** to create a new project or **File > Open > Project/Solution...** to open an existing one. You also can click the corresponding links in the **Start Page**'s **Start** section.

### 2.2.5 New Project Dialog and Project Templates

For the discussions in the next several sections, we'll create a new project. Select **File > New > Project...** to display the **New Project dialog** (Fig. 2.3). **Dialogs** are windows that facilitate user–computer communication.

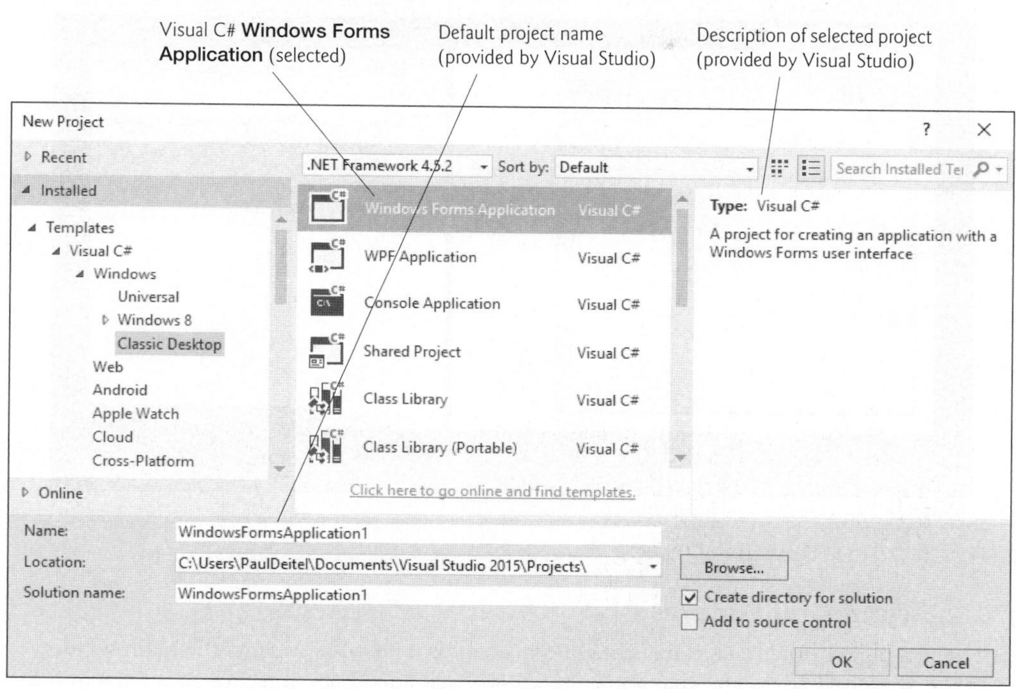


**Fig. 2.3** | **New Project** dialog.

Visual Studio provides many **templates** (left column of Fig. 2.3)—the *project types* that users can create in Visual C# and other languages. The templates include Windows Forms apps, WPF apps and others—full versions of Visual Studio provide additional templates. In this chapter, you'll build a **Windows Forms Application**—an app that executes within a Windows operating system (such as Windows 7, 8 or 10) and typically has a **graphical user interface (GUI)**. Users interact with this *visual* part of the app. GUI apps include Microsoft software products like Microsoft Word, Internet Explorer and Visual Studio, software products created by other vendors, and customized software that you and other app developers create. You'll create many Windows apps in this book.

To create a **Windows Forms Application**, under **Templates** select **Visual C# > Windows > Classic Desktop**, then in the middle column select **Windows Forms Application**. By default, Visual Studio assigns the name **WindowsFormsApplication1** to a new **Windows Forms Application** project and solution (Fig. 2.3). Click **OK** to display the IDE in **Design view** (Fig. 2.4), which contains the features that enable you to create an app's GUI.

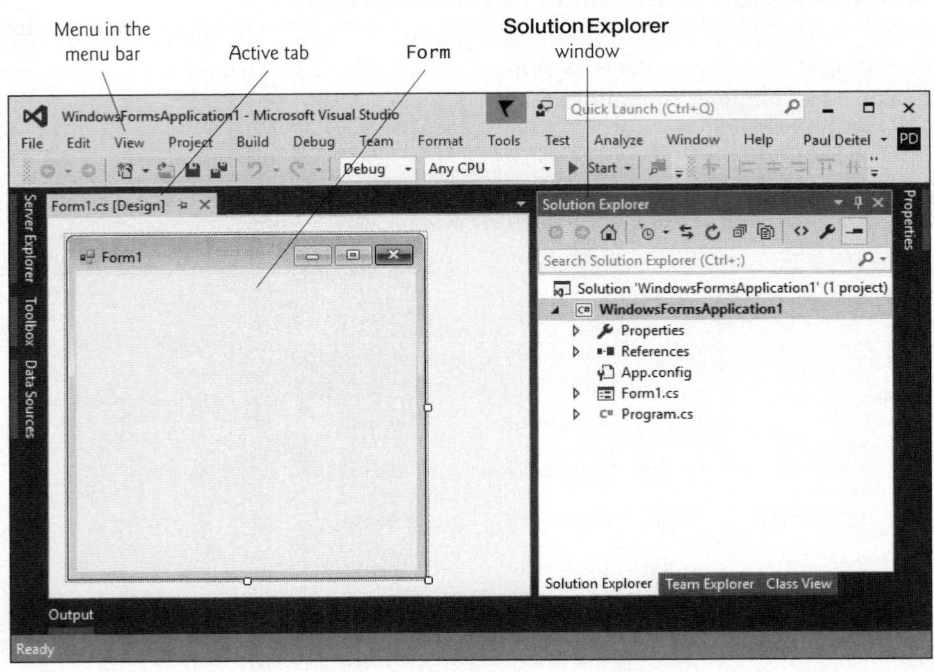


**Fig. 2.4** | **Design** view of the IDE.

### 2.2.6 Forms and Controls

The rectangle in the **Design** area titled **Form1** (called a **Form**) represents the main window of the Windows Forms app that you're creating. Each Form is an object of class Form in the .NET Framework Class Library. Apps can have multiple Forms (windows)—however, the app you'll create in Section 2.6 and most other Windows Forms apps you'll create later in this book will contain a single Form. You'll learn how to customize the Form by adding GUI **controls**—in Section 2.6, you'll add a Label and a PictureBox. A **Label** typically contains descriptive text (for example, "Welcome to Visual C#!"), and a **PictureBox** displays an image. Visual Studio has many preexisting controls and other components you can use to build and customize your apps. Many of these controls are discussed and used throughout the book. Other controls are available from third parties.

In this chapter, you'll work with preexisting controls from the .NET Framework Class Library. As you place controls on the Form, you'll be able to modify their properties (discussed in Section 2.4).

Collectively, the Form and controls make up the app's GUI. Users enter data into the app by typing at the keyboard, by clicking the mouse buttons and in a variety of other ways. Apps use the GUI to display instructions and other information for users to view. For example, the **New Project** dialog in Fig. 2.3 presents a GUI where the user clicks the mouse button to select a template type, then inputs a project name from the keyboard (the figure shows the default project name **WindowsFormsApplication1**).

Each open document's name is listed on a tab. To view a document when multiple documents are open, click its tab. The **active tab** (the tab of the currently displayed document) is highlighted (for example, **Form1.cs [Design]** in Fig. 2.4). The active tab's highlight color depends on the Visual Studio theme—the blue theme uses a yellow highlight and the light and dark themes use a blue highlight.

## 2.3 Menu Bar and Toolbar

Commands for managing the IDE and for developing, maintaining and executing apps are contained in menus, which are located on the **menu bar** of the IDE (Fig. 2.5). The set of menus displayed depends on what you're currently doing in the IDE.

File Edit View Project Build Debug Team Format Tools Test Analyze Window Help

**Fig. 2.5** | Visual Studio menu bar.

Menus contain groups of related commands called *menu items* that, when selected, cause the IDE to perform specific actions—for example, open a window, save a file, print a file and execute an app. For example, selecting **File > New > Project...** tells the IDE to display the **New Project** dialog. The menus depicted in Fig. 2.5 are summarized in Fig. 2.6.

| Menu | Contains commands for |
|---|---|
| **File** | Opening, closing, adding and saving projects, as well as printing project data and exiting Visual Studio. |
| **Edit** | Editing apps, such as cut, copy, paste, undo, redo, delete, find and select. |
| **View** | Displaying IDE windows (for example, **Solution Explorer**, **Toolbox**, **Properties** window) and for adding toolbars to the IDE. |
| **Project** | Managing projects and their files. |
| **Build** | Turning your app into an executable program. |
| **Debug** | Compiling, debugging (that is, identifying and correcting problems in apps) and running apps. |
| **Team** | Connecting to a Team Foundation Server—used by development teams that typically have multiple people working on the same app. |
| **Format** | Arranging and modifying a `Form`'s controls. The **Format** menu appears *only* when a GUI component is selected in **Design** view. |
| **Tools** | Accessing additional IDE tools and options for customizing the IDE. |
| **Test** | Performing various types of automated testing on your app. |
| **Analyze** | Locating and reporting violations of the .NET Framework Design Guidelines (`https://msdn.microsoft.com/library/ms229042`). |

**Fig. 2.6** | Summary of Visual Studio menus that are displayed when a `Form` is in **Design** view. (Part 1 of 2.)

| Menu | Contains commands for |
|---|---|
| Window | Hiding, opening, closing and displaying IDE windows. |
| Help | Accessing the IDE's help features. |

**Fig. 2.6** | Summary of Visual Studio menus that are displayed when a `Form` is in **Design** view. (Part 2 of 2.)

You can access many common menu commands from the **toolbar** (Fig. 2.7), which contains **icons** that graphically represent commands. By default, the standard toolbar is displayed when you run Visual Studio for the first time—it contains icons for the most commonly used commands, such as opening a file, saving files and running apps (Fig. 2.7). The icons that appear on the standard toolbar may vary, depending on the version of Visual Studio you're using. Some commands are initially disabled (grayed out or unavailable to use). These commands are enabled by Visual Studio only when you can use them. For example, Visual Studio enables the command for saving a file once you begin editing a file.

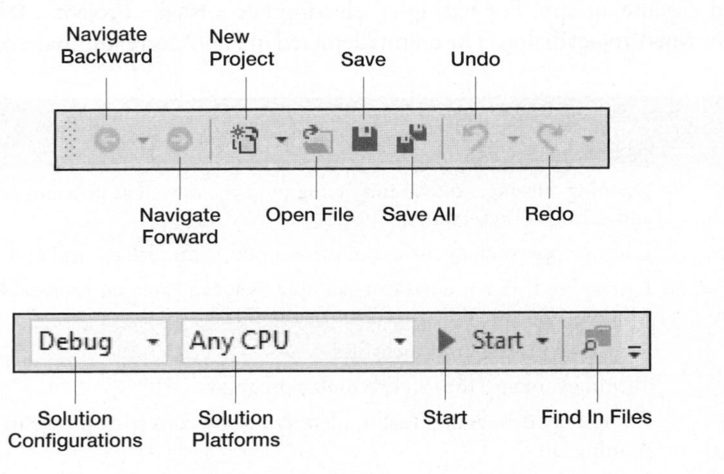


**Fig. 2.7** | Standard Visual Studio toolbar.

You can customize which toolbars are displayed by selecting **View > Toolbars** then selecting a toolbar from the list in Fig. 2.8. Each toolbar you select is displayed with the other toolbars at the top of the Visual Studio window. You move a toolbar by dragging its handle

at the left side of the toolbar. To execute a command via the toolbar, click its icon.

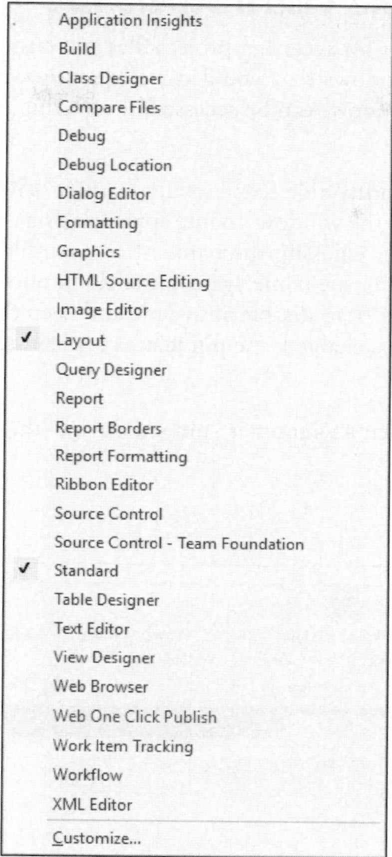


**Fig. 2.8** | List of toolbars that can be added to the top of the IDE.

It can be difficult to remember what each toolbar icon represents. *Hovering* the mouse pointer over an icon highlights it and, after a brief pause, displays a description of the icon called a **tool tip** (Fig. 2.9)—these tips help you become familiar with the IDE's features and serve as useful reminders for each toolbar icon's functionality.

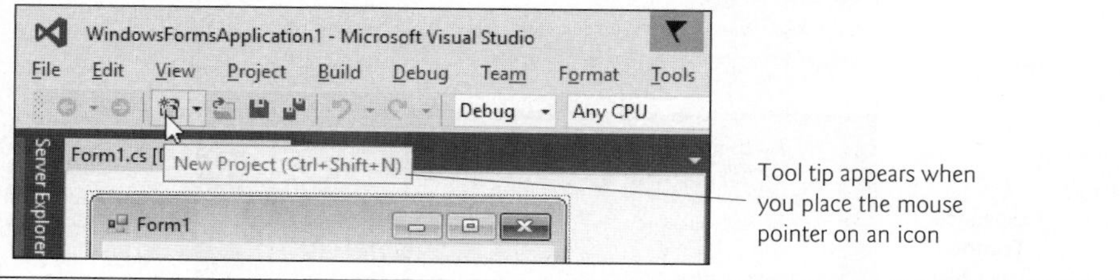


**Fig. 2.9** | Tool tip for the **New Project** button.

## 2.4 Navigating the Visual Studio IDE

The IDE provides windows for accessing project files and customizing controls. This section introduces several windows that you'll use frequently when developing Visual C# apps. Each of the IDE's windows can be accessed by selecting its name in the **View** menu.

### *Auto-Hide*

Visual Studio provides an **auto-hide** space-saving feature. When auto-hide is enabled for a window, a tab containing the window's name appears along the IDE window's left, right or bottom edge (Fig. 2.10). Clicking the name of an auto-hidden window displays that window (Fig. 2.11). Clicking the name again (or clicking outside) hides the window. To "pin down" a window (that is, to disable auto-hide and keep the window open), click the pin icon. When auto-hide is enabled, the pin icon is horizontal

as shown in Fig. 2.11. When a window is "pinned down," the pin icon is vertical

as shown in Fig. 2.12.

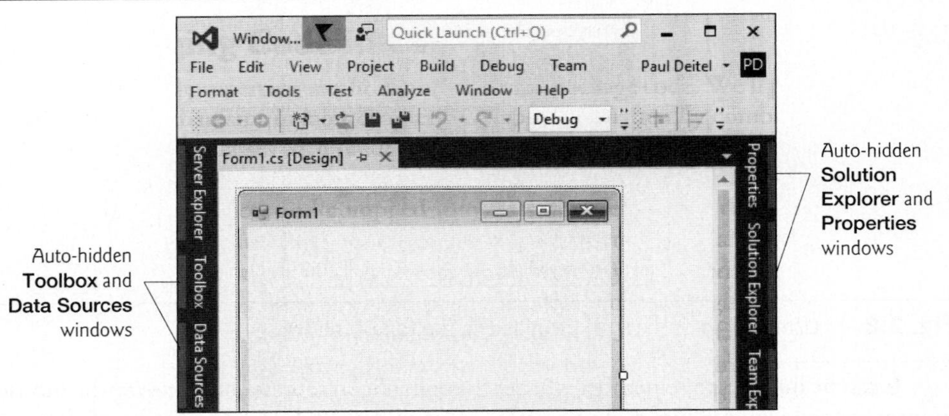


**Fig. 2.10** | Auto-hide feature demonstration.

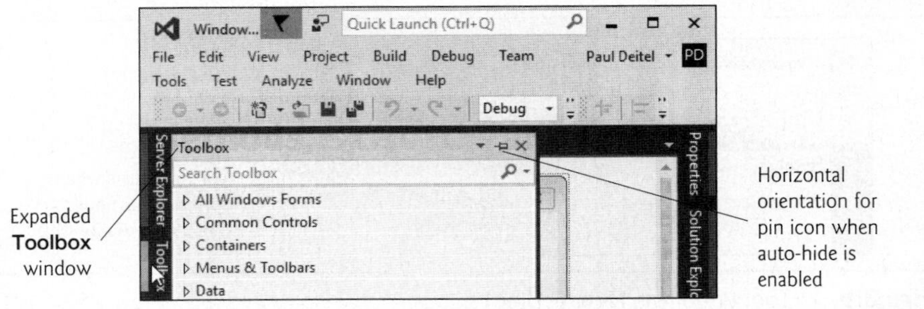


**Fig. 2.11** | Displaying the hidden **Toolbox** window when auto-hide is enabled.

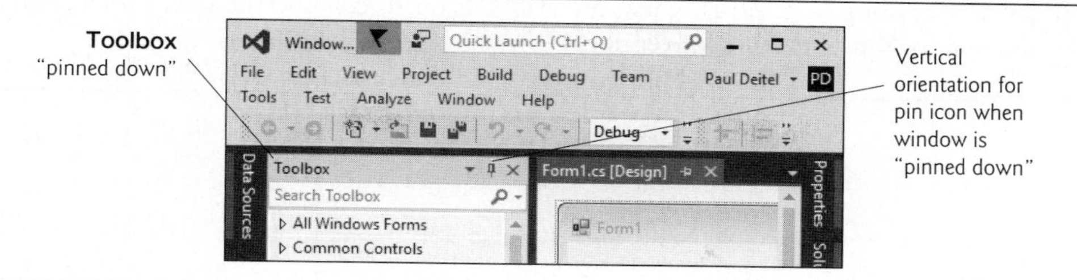


**Fig. 2.12** | Disabling auto-hide—"pinning down" a window.

The next few sections present three Visual Studio's windows that you'll use frequently—the **Solution Explorer**, the **Properties** window and the **Toolbox**. These windows display project information and include tools that help you build your apps.

### 2.4.1 Solution Explorer

The **Solution Explorer** window (Fig. 2.13) provides access to all of a solution's files. If it's not shown in the IDE, select **View > Solution Explorer**. When you open a new or existing solution, the **Solution Explorer** displays the solution's contents.

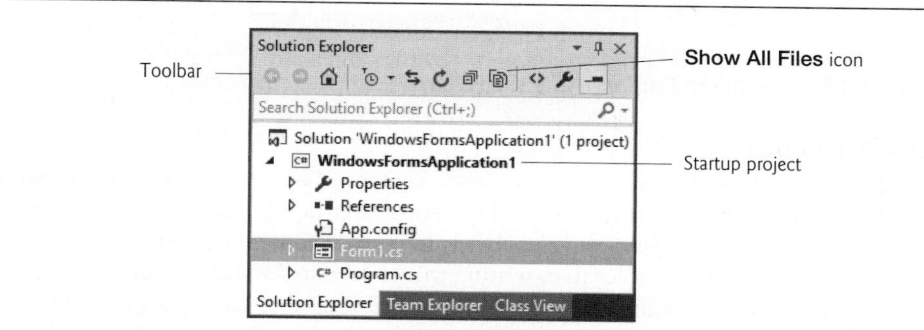


**Fig. 2.13** | **Solution Explorer** window showing the **WindowsFormsApplication1** project.

The solution's **startup project** (shown in **bold** in the **Solution Explorer**) is the one that runs when you select **Debug > Start Debugging** (or press *F5*) or select **Debug > Start Without Debugging** (or press *Ctrl* + *F5* key). For a single-project solution like the examples in this book, the startup project is the only project (in this case, **WindowsFormsApplication1**). When you create an app for the first time, the **Solution Explorer** window appears as shown in Fig. 2.13. The Visual C# file that corresponds to the `Form` shown in Fig. 2.4 is named `Form1.cs` (selected in Fig. 2.13). Visual C# files use the `.cs` file-name extension, which is short for "C#."

By default, the IDE displays only files that you may need to edit—other files that the IDE generates are hidden. The **Solution Explorer** window includes a toolbar that contains several icons. Clicking the **Show All Files icon** (Fig. 2.13) displays all the solution's files, including those generated by the IDE. Clicking the arrow to the left of a node *expands* or *collapses* that node. Click the arrow to the left of **References** to display items grouped under that heading (Fig. 2.14). Click the arrow again to collapse the tree. Other Visual Studio windows also use this convention.

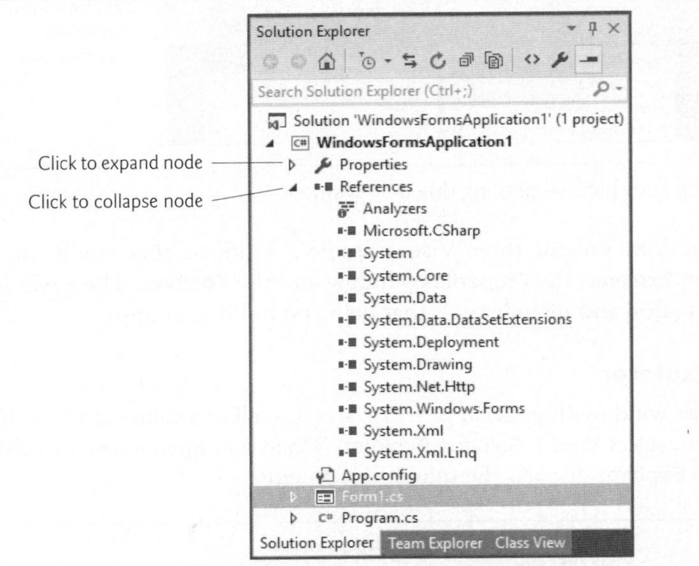


**Fig. 2.14** | **Solution Explorer** with the **References** node expanded.

### 2.4.2 Toolbox

To display the **Toolbox** window, select **View > Toolbox**. The **Toolbox** contains the controls used to customize `Forms` (Fig. 2.15). With visual app development, you can "drag and drop" controls onto the `Form` and the IDE will write the code that creates the controls for you. This is faster and simpler than writing this code yourself. Just as you do not need to know how to build an engine to drive a car, you do not need to know how to build controls to use them. *Reusing* preexisting controls saves time and money when you develop apps. You'll use the **Toolbox** when you create your first app later in the chapter.

The **Toolbox** groups the prebuilt controls into categories—**All Windows Forms**, **Common Controls**, **Containers**, **Menus & Toolbars**, **Data**, **Components**, **Printing**, **Dialogs**, **Reporting**, **WPF Interoperability** and **General** are listed in Fig. 2.15. Again, note the use of arrows for expanding or collapsing a group of controls. We discuss many of the **Toolbox**'s controls and their functionality throughout the book.

### 2.4.3 Properties Window

If the **Properties** window is not displayed below the **Solution Explorer**, select **View > Properties Window** to display it—if the window is in auto-hide mode, pin down the window by clicking its horizontal pin icon

The **Properties window** contains the properties for the currently selected `Form`, control or file in the IDE. **Properties** specify information about the `Form` or control, such as its size,

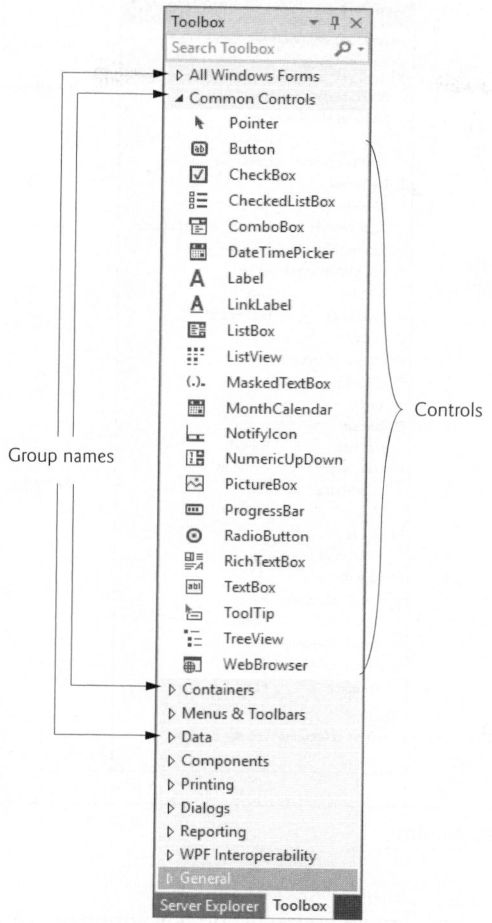


**Fig. 2.15** | **Toolbox** window displaying controls for the **Common Controls** group.

color and position. Each `Form` or control has its own set of properties. When you select a property, its description is displayed at the bottom of the **Properties** window.

Figure 2.16 shows `Form1`'s **Properties** window—you can view by clicking anywhere in the **Form1.cs [Design]** window. The left column lists the `Form`'s properties—the right column displays the current value of each property. You can sort the properties either

- *alphabetically* (by clicking the **Alphabetical** icon) or
- *categorically* (by clicking the **Categorized** icon).

Depending on the **Properties** window's size, some properties may be hidden from your view. You can scroll through the list of properties by **dragging** the **scrollbox** up or down inside the **scrollbar**, or by clicking the arrows at the top and bottom of the scrollbar. We show how to set individual properties later in this chapter.

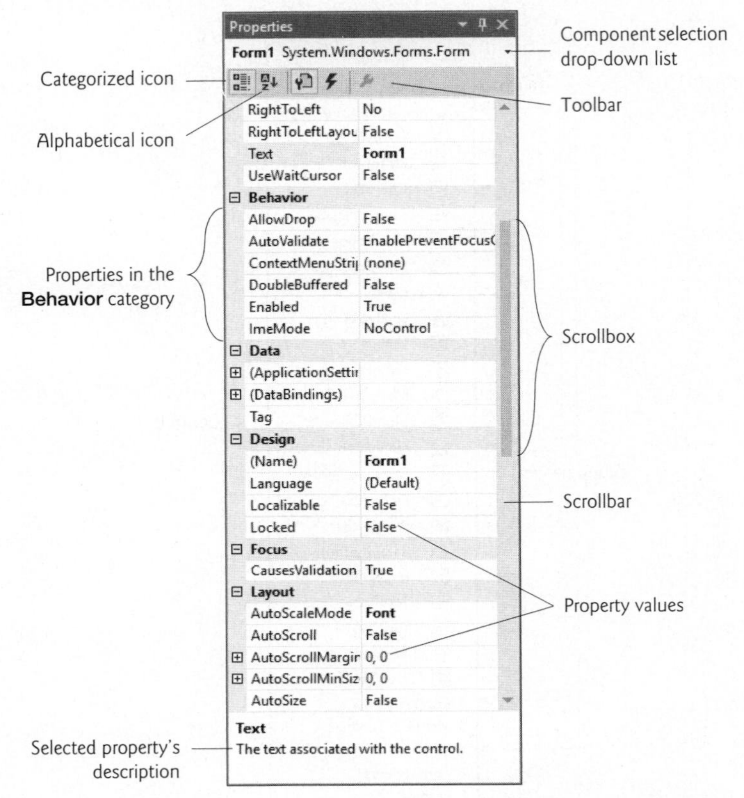


**Fig. 2.16** | **Properties** window.

The **Properties** window is crucial to visual app development—it allows you to quickly modify a control's properties and, rather than writing code yourself, lets the IDE write code for you "behind the scenes." You can see which properties are available for modification and, in many cases, can learn the range of acceptable values for a given property. The **Properties** window displays a brief description of the selected property, helping you understand its purpose.

## 2.5 Help Menu and Context-Sensitive Help

Microsoft provides extensive help documentation via the **Help menu**, which is an excellent way to get information quickly about Visual Studio, Visual C# and more. Visual Studio provides **context-sensitive help** pertaining to the "current content" (that is, the items around the location of the mouse cursor). To use context-sensitive help, click an item, then press the *F1* key. The help documentation is displayed in a web browser window. To return to the IDE, either close the browser window or select the IDE's icon in your Windows task bar.

## 2.6 Visual Programming: Creating a Simple App that Displays Text and an Image

Next, we create an app that displays the text "Welcome to C# Programming!" and an image of the Deitel & Associates bug mascot. The app consists of a Form that uses a Label and a PictureBox. Figure 2.17 shows the final app executing. The app and the bug image are available with this chapter's examples—see the Before You Begin section following the Preface for download instructions. We assume you placed the examples in your user account's Documents folder in a subfolder named examples.

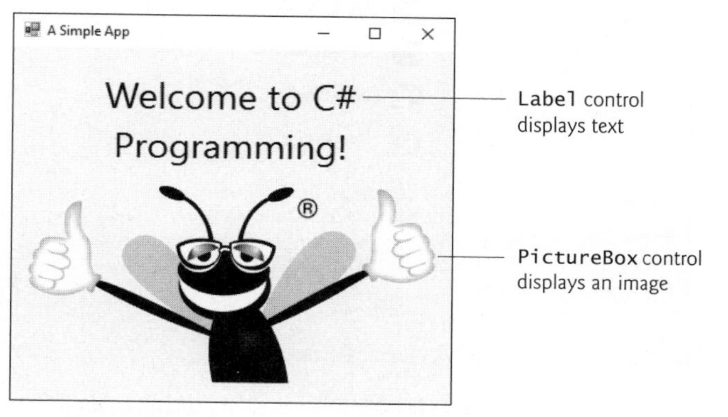


**Fig. 2.17** | Simple app executing.

In this example, you won't write any C# code—you'll use visual app-development techniques. Visual Studio processes your actions (such as mouse clicking, dragging and dropping) to generate app code. Chapter 3 begins our discussion of writing app code. Throughout the book, you'll produce increasingly substantial and powerful apps that will include code written by you and code generated by Visual Studio.

Visual app development is useful for building GUI-intensive apps that require a significant amount of user interaction. To create, save, run and terminate this first app, perform the following steps.

*Step 1: Closing the Open Project*
If the project you were working with earlier in this chapter is still open, close it by selecting **File > Close Solution**.

*Step 2: Creating the New Project*
To create a new Windows Forms app:

1. Select **File > New > Project...** to display the **New Project** dialog (Fig. 2.18).
2. Select **Windows Forms Application**. Name the project **ASimpleApp**, specify the **Location** where you want to save it and click **OK**. We stored the app in the IDE's default location—in your user account's Documents folder under the Visual Studio 2015\Projects.

As you saw earlier in this chapter, when you first create a new Windows `Forms` app, the IDE opens in **Design** view (that is, the app is being designed and is not executing). The text **Form1.cs [Design]** in the tab containing the `Form` means that we're designing the `Form` *visually* rather than *programmatically*. An asterisk (*) at the end of the text in a tab indicates that you've changed the file and the changes have not yet been saved.

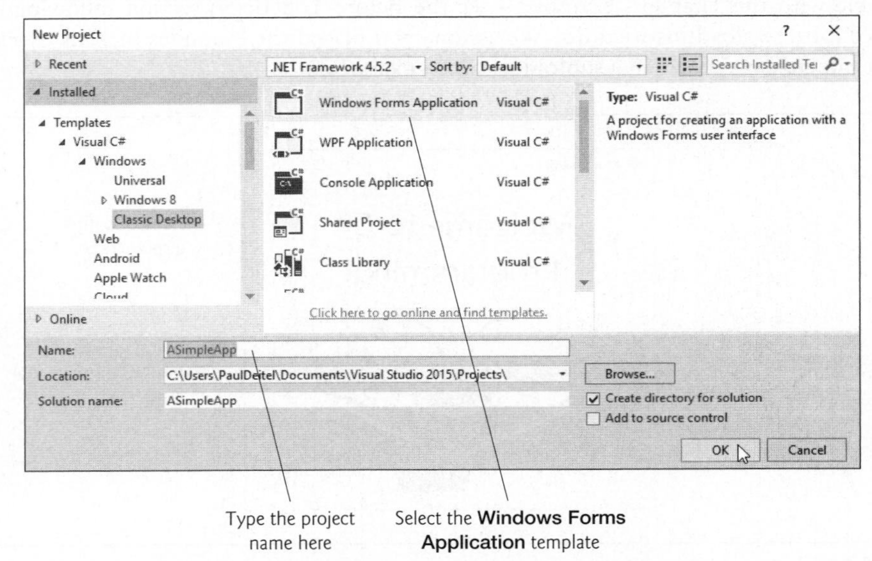


**Fig. 2.18** | **New Project** dialog.

### *Step 3: Setting the Text in the* `Form`*'s Title Bar*

The text in the `Form`'s title bar is determined by the `Form`'s **`Text` property** (Fig. 2.19). If the **Properties** window is not open, select **View > Properties Window** and pin down the window so it doesn't auto hide. Click anywhere in the `Form` to display the `Form`'s properties in the **Properties** window. In the textbox to the right of the `Text` property, type `"A Simple App"`, as in Fig. 2.19. Press the *Enter* key—the `Form`'s title bar is updated immediately (Fig. 2.20).

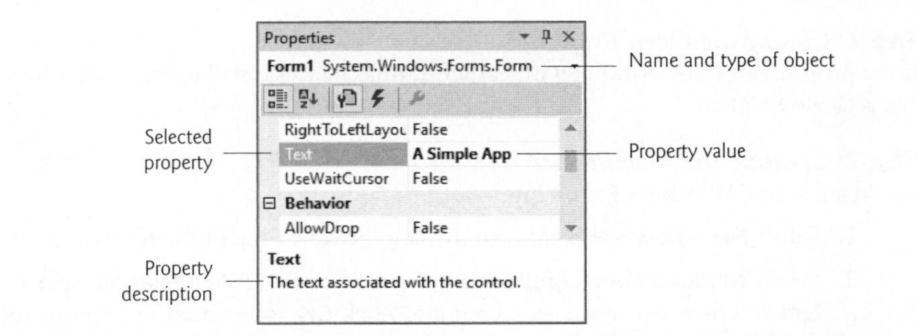


**Fig. 2.19** | Setting the `Form`'s `Text` property in the **Properties** window.

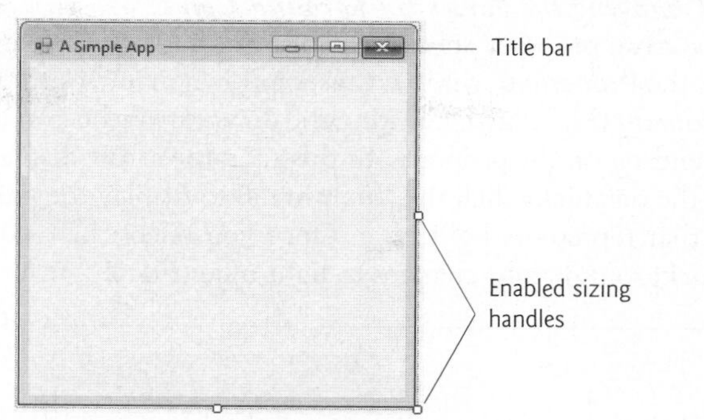


**Fig. 2.20** | `Form` with updated title-bar text and enabled sizing handles.

### *Step 4: Resizing the* `Form`

The `Form`'s size is specified in pixels (that is, dots on the screen). By default, a `Form` is 300 pixels wide and 300 pixels tall. You can resize the `Form` by dragging one of its **sizing handles** (the small white squares that appear around the `Form`, as shown in Fig. 2.20). Using the mouse, select the bottom-right sizing handle and drag it down and to the right to make the `Form` larger. As you drag the mouse (Fig. 2.21), the IDE's status bar (at the bottom of the IDE) shows the current width and height in pixels. We set the `Form` to 400 pixels wide by 360 pixels tall. You also can do this via the `Form`'s `Size` property in the **Properties** window.

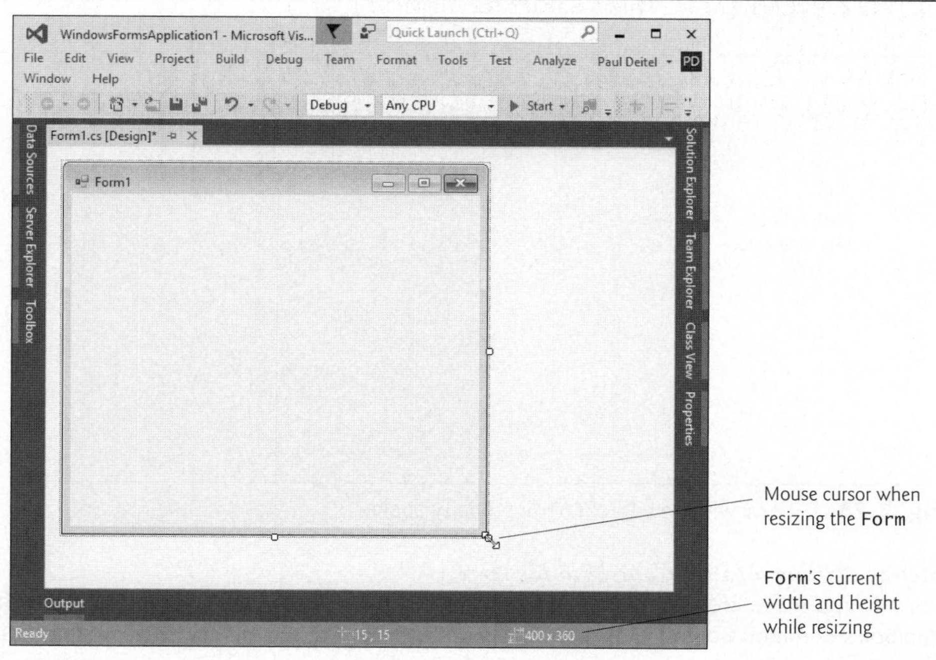


**Fig. 2.21** | Resizing the `Form`.

*Step 5: Changing the* `Form`*'s Background Color*

The **`BackColor` property** specifies a `Form`'s or control's background color. Clicking `BackColor` in the **Properties** window causes a down-arrow button to appear next to the value of the property (Fig. 2.22). Clicking the down-arrow button displays other options, which vary depending on the property. In this case, the arrow displays tabs for **Custom**, **Web** and **System** (the default). Click the **Custom tab** to display the **palette** (a grid of colors). Select the box that represents light blue. Once you select the color, the palette closes and the `Form`'s background color changes to light blue (Fig. 2.23).

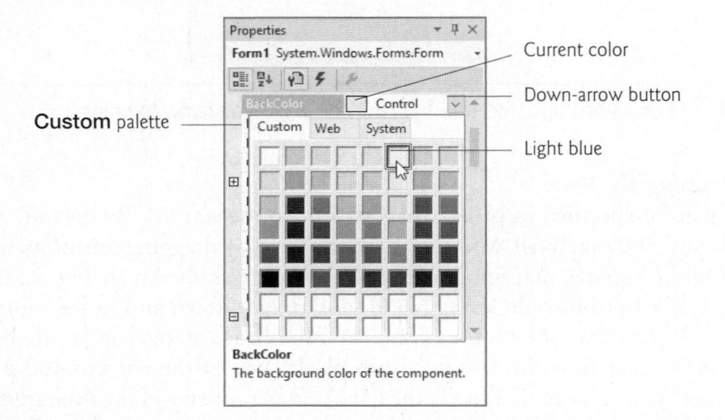


**Fig. 2.22** | Changing the `Form`'s `BackColor` property.

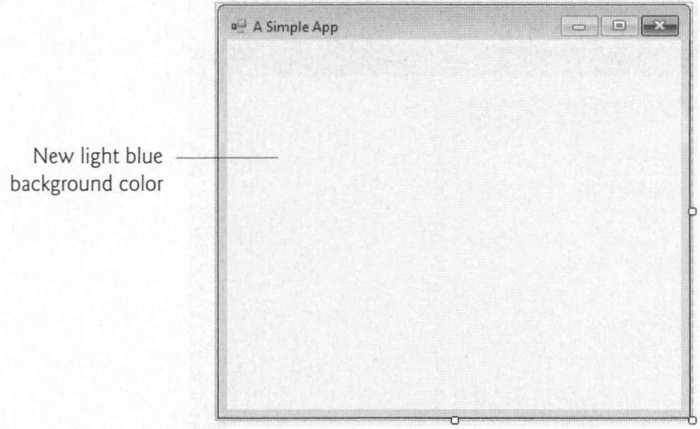


**Fig. 2.23** | `Form` with new `BackColor` property applied.

*Step 6: Adding a* `Label` *Control to the* `Form`

For the app we're creating in this chapter, the typical controls we use are located in the **Toolbox**'s **Common Controls** group, and also can be found in the **All Windows Forms** group. If the **Toolbox** is *not* already open, select **View > Toolbox** to display the set of controls you'll use for creating your apps. If either group name is collapsed, expand it by clicking the arrow to the left of the group name (the **All Windows Forms** and **Common Controls** groups are shown in Fig. 2.15). Next, double click the `Label` control in the **Toolbox** to add a `Label` in the `Form`'s upper-left corner (Fig. 2.24)—each `Label` you add to the `Form` is an object of class `Label` from the .NET Framework Class Library. [*Note:* If the `Form` is behind the **Toolbox**, you may need to hide or pin down the **Toolbox** to see the `Label`.] Although double clicking any **Toolbox** control places the control on the `Form`, you also can "drag" controls from the **Toolbox** to the `Form`—you may prefer dragging the control because you can position it wherever you want. The `Label` displays the text **label1** by default. By default, the `Label`'s `BackColor` is the same as the `Form`'s.

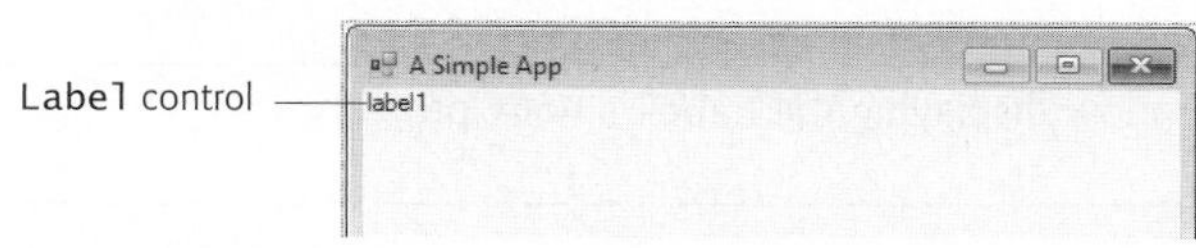


**Fig. 2.24** | Adding a `Label` to the `Form`.

### *Step 7: Customizing the `Label`'s Appearance*

Click the `Label`'s text in the `Form` to select it and display its properties in the **Properties** window. The `Label`'s `Text` property determines the text that the `Label` displays. The `Form` and `Label` each have their own `Text` property—`Form`s and controls can have the *same* property names (such as `Text`, `BackColor` etc.) without conflict. Each common properties purpose can vary by control. Perform the following steps:

1. Set the `Label`'s `Text` property to `Welcome to C# Programming!`. The `Label` resizes to fit all the typed text on one line.
2. By default, the **`AutoSize` property** of the `Label` is set to `True` so the `Label` can update its own size to fit all of its text. Set the `AutoSize` property to `False` so that you can change the `Label`'s size, then resize the `Label` (using the sizing handles) so that the text fits.
3. Move the `Label` to the top center of the `Form` by dragging it or by using the keyboard's left and right arrow keys to adjust its position (Fig. 2.25). Alternatively, when the `Label` is selected, you can center it horizontally by selecting **Format > Center In Form > Horizontally**.

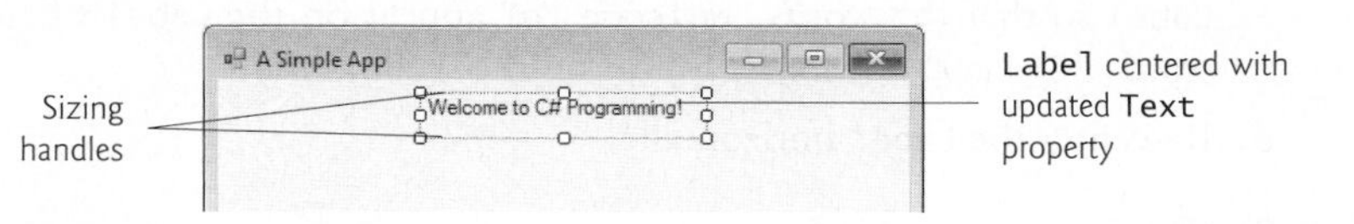


**Fig. 2.25** | GUI after the `Form` and `Label` have been customized.

### *Step 8: Setting the `Label`'s Font Size*

To change the font type and appearance of the `Label`'s text:

1. Select the value of the **`Font` property**, which causes an **ellipsis button** to appear next to the value (Fig. 2.26)—you can click this button to display a dialog of op-

tions for the property. Click the ellipsis button to display the **Font dialog** (Fig. 2.27).

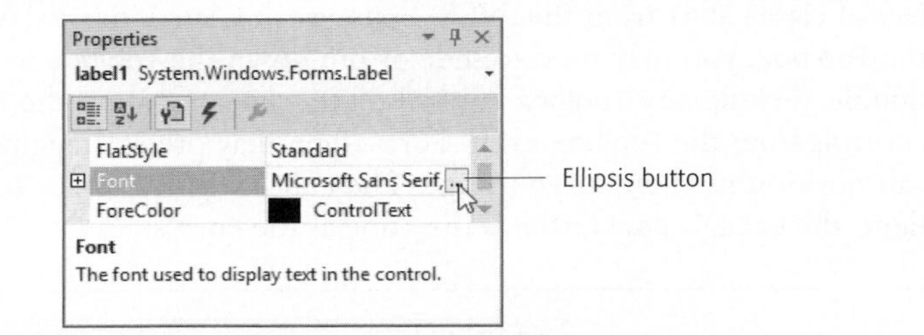


**Fig. 2.26** | **Properties** window displaying the `Label`'s `Font` property.

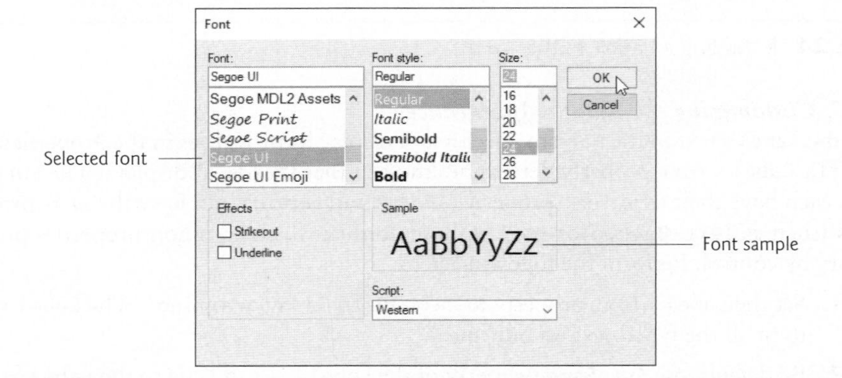


**Fig. 2.27** | **Font** dialog for selecting fonts, styles and sizes.

2. You can select the font name (the font options may be different, depending on your system), font style (**Regular**, **Italic**, **Bold**, etc.) and font size (**16**, **18**, **20**, etc.) in this dialog. The **Sample** text shows the selected font settings. Under **Font**, select **Segoe UI**, Microsoft's recommended font for user interfaces. Under **Size**, select **24** points and click **OK**.
3. If the `Label`'s text does not fit on a single line, it *wraps* to the next line. Resize the `Label` so that the words `"Welcome to"` appear on the `Label`'s first line and the words `"C# Programming!"` appear on the second line.
4. Re-center the `Label` horizontally.

### *Step 9: Aligning the `Label`'s Text*

Select the `Label`'s **`TextAlign`** property, which determines how the text is aligned within the `Label`. A three-by-three grid of buttons representing alignment choices is displayed (Fig. 2.28). The position of each button corresponds to where the text appears in the `Label`. For this app, set the `TextAlign` property to `MiddleCenter` in the three-by-three grid—this selection centers the text horizontally and vertically within the `Label`. The other `TextAlign` values, such as `TopLeft`, `TopRight`, and `BottomCenter`, can be used to position the text anywhere within a `Label`. Certain alignment values may require that you resize the `Label` to fit the text better.

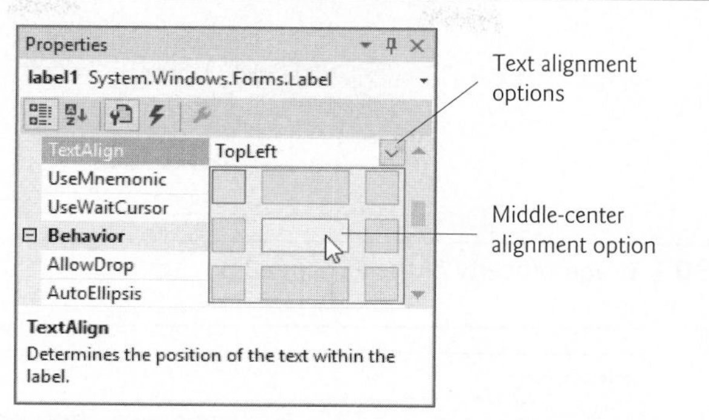


**Fig. 2.28** | Centering the `Label`'s text.

*Step 10: Adding a* **`PictureBox`** *to the* **`Form`**

The `PictureBox` control displays images. Locate the `PictureBox` in the **Toolbox** (Fig. 2.15) and double click it to add it to the `Form`—each `PictureBox` you add to the `Form` is an object of class `PictureBox` from the .NET Framework Class Library. When the `PictureBox` appears, move it underneath the `Label`, either by dragging it or by using the arrow keys (Fig. 2.29).

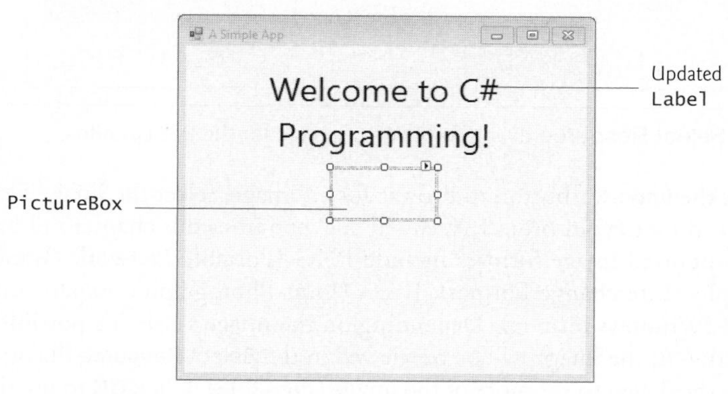


**Fig. 2.29** | Inserting and aligning a `PictureBox`.

*Step 11: Inserting an Image*

Click the `PictureBox` to display its properties in the **Properties** window (Fig. 2.30), then:

1. Locate and select the **`Image` property**, which displays a preview of the selected image or **(none)** if no image is selected.
2. Click the ellipsis button to display the **Select Resource dialog** (Fig. 2.31), which is used to import files, such as images, for use in an app.

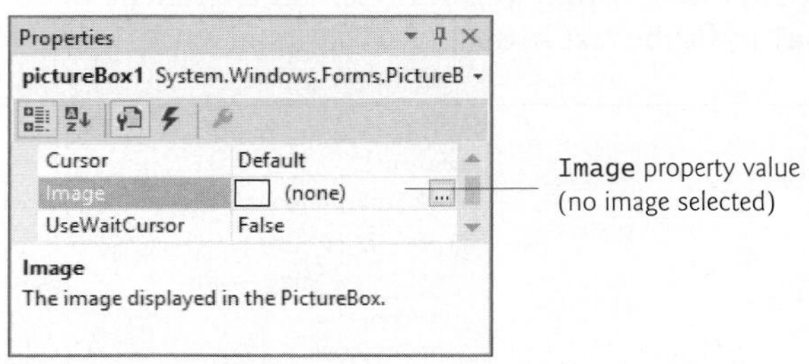


**Fig. 2.30** | `Image` property of the `PictureBox`.

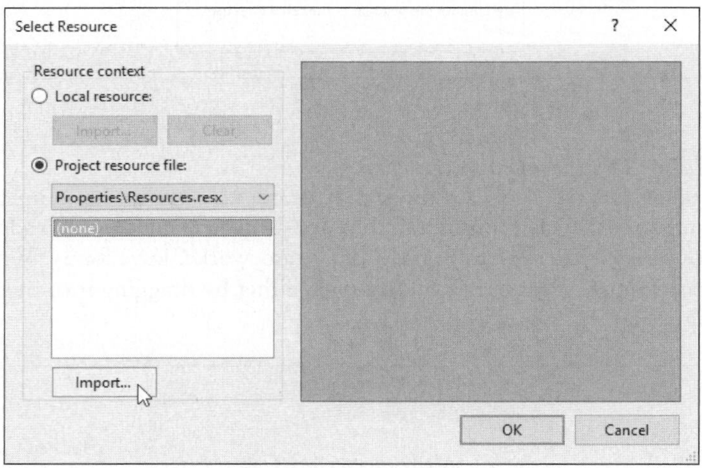


**Fig. 2.31** | **Select Resource** dialog to select an image for the `PictureBox`.

3. Click the **Import...** button to browse for an image, select the image file and click **OK** to add it to your project. We used `bug.png` from this chapter's examples folder. Supported image formats include PNG (Portable Network Graphics), GIF (Graphic Interchange Format), JPEG (Joint Photographic Experts Group) and BMP (Windows bitmap). Depending on the image's size, it's possible that only a portion of the image will be previewed in the **Select Resource** dialog—you can resize the dialog to see more of the image (Fig. 2.32). Click **OK** to use the image.
4. To scale the image to fit in the `PictureBox`, change the **`SizeMode` property** to **`StretchImage`** (Fig. 2.33). Resize the `PictureBox`, making it larger (Fig. 2.34), then re-center the `PictureBox` horizontally.

*Step 12: Saving the Project*

Select **File > Save All** to save the entire solution. The solution file (which has the filename extension `.sln`) contains the name and location of its project, and the project file (which has the filename extension `.csproj`) contains the names and locations of all the files in the project. If you want to reopen your project at a later time, simply open its `.sln` file.

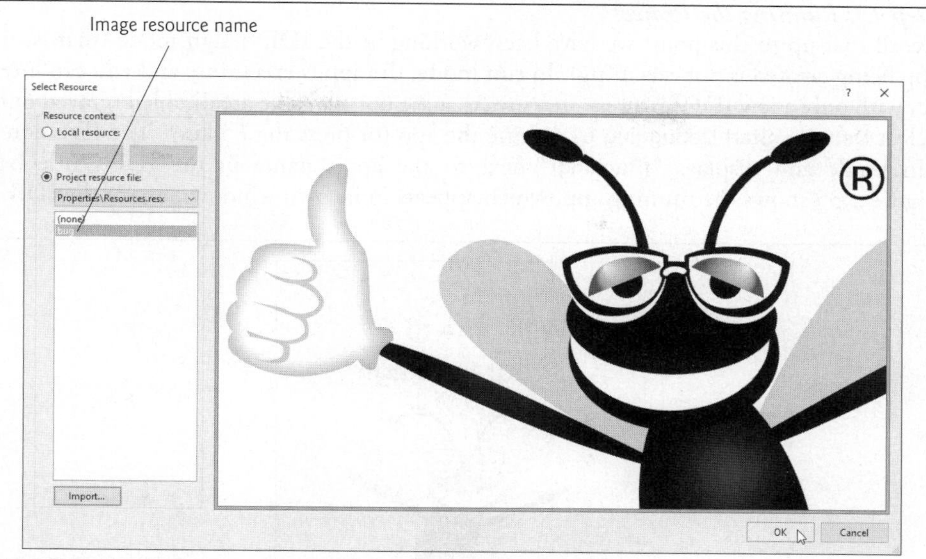


**Fig. 2.32** | **Select Resource** dialog displaying a preview of selected image.

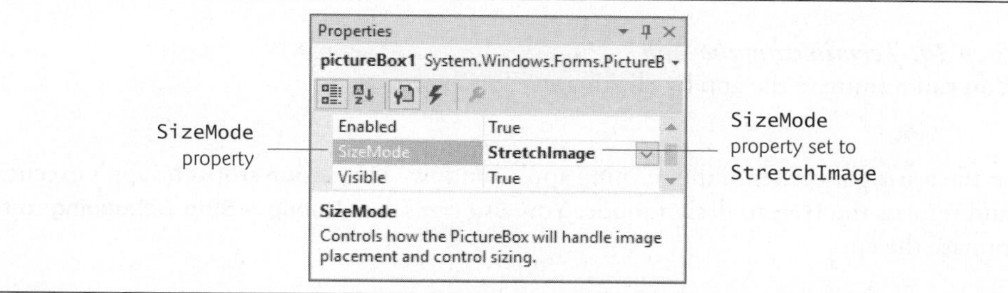


**Fig. 2.33** | Scaling an image to the size of the `PictureBox`.

**Fig. 2.34** | `PictureBox` displaying an image.

*Step 13: Running the Project*
Recall that up to this point we have been working in the IDE design mode (that is, the app being created is not executing). In **run mode**, the app is executing, and you can interact with only a few IDE features—features that are not available are disabled (grayed out). Select **Debug > Start Debugging** to execute the app (or press the *F5* key). The IDE enters run mode and displays "**(Running)**" next to the app's name in the IDE's title bar. Figure 2.35 shows the running app, which appears in its own window outside the IDE.

**Fig. 2.35** | IDE in run mode, with the running app in the foreground.

*Step 14: Terminating the App*
You can terminate the app by clicking its close box

in the top-right corner of the running app's window. This action stops the app's execution and returns the IDE to design mode. You also can select **Debug > Stop Debugging** to terminate the app.

## 2.7 Wrap-Up

In this chapter, we introduced key features of the Visual Studio IDE. You visually designed a working Visual C# app without writing any code. Visual C# app development is a mixture of the two styles—visual app development allows you to develop GUIs easily and avoid tedious GUI programming. "Conventional" programming (which we introduce in Chapter 3) allows you to specify the behavior of your apps.

You created a Visual C# Windows `Forms` app with one `Form`. You worked with the IDE's **Solution Explorer**, **Toolbox** and **Properties** windows, which are essential to developing Visual C# apps. We also demonstrated context-sensitive help, which displays help topics related to selected controls or text.

You used visual app development to design an app's GUI by adding a `Label` and a `PictureBox` control onto a `Form`. You used the **Properties** window to set a `Form`'s `Text` and `BackColor` properties. You learned that `Label` controls display text and that `PictureBoxes` display images. You displayed text in a `Label` and added an image to a `PictureBox`. You also worked with the `Label`'s `AutoSize`, `TextAlign` and `Font` properties and the `PictureBox`'s `Image` and `SizeMode` properties.

In the next chapter, we discuss "nonvisual," or "conventional," programming—you'll create your first apps with C# code that you write, instead of having Visual Studio write the code.

## 2.8 Web Resources

Please take a moment to visit each of these sites.

`https://www.visualstudio.com/`
The home page for Microsoft Visual Studio. The site includes news, documentation, downloads and other resources.

`https://social.msdn.microsoft.com/Forums/vstudio/en-US/home?forum=csharpgeneral`
This site provides access to the Microsoft Visual C# forums, which you can use to get your Visual C# language and IDE questions answered.

`https://msdn.microsoft.com/magazine/default.aspx`
This is the Microsoft Developer Network Magazine site. This site provides articles and code on many Visual C# and .NET app development topics. There is also an archive of past issues.

`http://stackoverflow.com/`
In addition to the Microsoft forums, StackOverflow is an excellent site for getting your programming questions answered for most programming languages and technologies.

# 3

# Introduction to C# App Programming

## Objectives

In this chapter you'll:

- Write simple C# apps using code rather than visual programming.
- Input data from the keyboard and output data to the screen.
- Use C# 6's `string` interpolation to create formatted `string`s by inserting values into `string` literals.
- Declare and use data of various types.
- Use arithmetic operators.
- Understand the order in which operators are applied.
- Write decision-making statements with equality and relational operators.

**Outline**



## 3.1 Introduction

We now introduce C# programming. Most of the C# apps you'll study in this book process information and display results. In this chapter, we introduce **console apps**—these input and output text in a *console window*, which in Windows is known as the **Command Prompt**.

We begin with several examples that simply display messages on the screen. We then demonstrate an app that obtains two numbers from a user, calculates their sum and displays the result. You'll perform various arithmetic calculations and save the results for later use. The last example in this chapter demonstrates decision-making fundamentals by comparing numbers and displaying messages based on the comparison results.

## 3.2 Simple App: Displaying a Line of Text

Let's consider a simple app that displays a line of text. Figure 3.1 shows the app's **source code** and its output. The app illustrates several important C# features. Each app we present in this book includes line numbers, which are *not* part of actual C# code. In the Before You Begin section following the Preface, we show how to display line numbers for your C# code in Visual Studio. We'll soon see that line 10 does the real work of the app—namely, displaying the phrase `Welcome to C# Programming!` on the screen. We now discuss each line of the app.

```
1  // Fig. 3.1: Welcome1.cs
2  // Text-displaying app.
3  using System;
4
5  class Welcome1
6  {
7     // Main method begins execution of C# app
8     static void Main()
9     {
10       Console.WriteLine("Welcome to C# Programming!");
11    } // end Main
12 } // end class Welcome1
```

```
Welcome to C# Programming!
```

**Fig. 3.1** | Text-displaying app.

### 3.2.1 Comments

Line 1 begins with //, indicating that the remainder of the line is a comment. We begin every source-code file with a comment indicating the figure number and the name of the file in which the code is stored.

A comment that begins with // is called a **single-line comment**, because it terminates at the end of the line on which it appears. A // comment also can begin in the middle of a line and continue until the end of that line (as in lines 7, 11 and 12).

**Delimited comments** such as

```
/* This is a delimited comment.
   It can be split over many lines */
```

can be split over several lines. This type of comment begins with the delimiter /* and ends with the delimiter */. All text between the delimiters is ignored by the compiler. Line 2 is a single-line comment that describes the purpose of the app.

**Common Programming Error 3.1**

*Forgetting one of the delimiters of a delimited comment is a syntax error. A programming language's* **syntax** *specifies the grammatical rules for writing code in that language. A* **syntax error** *occurs when the compiler encounters code that violates C#'s language rules. In this case, the compiler does not produce an executable file. Instead, it issues one or more error messages to help you identify and fix the incorrect code. Syntax errors are also called* **compiler errors, compile-time errors** *or* **compilation errors***, because the compiler detects them during the compilation phase. You cannot execute your app until you correct all the compilation errors in it. We'll see that some compile-time errors are not syntax errors.*

**Error-Prevention Tip 3.1**

*When the compiler reports an error, the error may not be in the line indicated by the error message. First, check the line for which the error was reported. If that line does not contain syntax errors, check several preceding lines.*

### 3.2.2 `using` Directive

Line 3

```
using System;
```

is a **`using` directive** that tells the compiler where to look for a class that's used in this app. A great strength of Visual C# is its rich set of predefined classes that you can *reuse* rather than "reinventing the wheel." These classes are organized under **namespaces**—named collections of related classes. Collectively, .NET's predefined namespaces are known as **.NET Framework Class Library**. Each `using` directive identifies a namespace containing classes that a C# app should be able to use. The `using` directive in line 3 indicates that this example intends to use classes from the `System` namespace, which contains the predefined `Console` class (discussed shortly) used in line 10, and many other useful classes.

**Error-Prevention Tip 3.2**

*Forgetting to include a `using` directive for a namespace that contains a class used in your app typically results in a compilation error, containing a message such as "`The name 'Console' does not exist in the current context.`" When this occurs, check that you provided the proper `using` directives and that the names in them are spelled correctly, including proper use of uppercase and lowercase letters. In the editor, when you hover over an error's red squiggly line, Visual Studio displays a box containing the link* "Show potential fixes." *If a `using` directive is missing, one potential fix shown is to add the `using` directive to your code—simply click that fix to have Visual Studio edit your code.*

For each new .NET class we use, we indicate the namespace in which it's located. This information is important, because it helps you locate descriptions of each class in the **.NET documentation**. A web-based version of this documentation can be found at

```
https://msdn.microsoft.com/library/w0x726c2
```

This also can be accessed via the **Help** menu. You can click the name of any .NET class or method, then press the *F1* key to get more information. Finally, you can learn about the contents of a given namespace by going to

```
https://msdn.microsoft.com/namespace
```

So

```
https://msdn.microsoft.com/System
```

takes you to namespace `System`'s documentation.

### 3.2.3 Blank Lines and Whitespace

Line 4 is simply a *blank line*. Blank lines and space characters make code easier to read, and together with tab characters are known as **whitespace**. Space characters and tabs are known specifically as **whitespace characters**. Whitespace is ignored by the compiler.

### 3.2.4 Class Declaration

Line 5

```
class Welcome1
```

begins a **class declaration** for the class named `Welcome1`. Every app consists of at least one class declaration that's defined by you. These are known as **user-defined classes.** The **`class` keyword** introduces a class declaration and is immediately followed by the **class name** (`Welcome1`). Keywords (also called **reserved words**) are reserved for use by C#.

### *Class Name Convention*

By convention, all class names begin with a capital letter and capitalize the first letter of each word they include (e.g., `SampleClassName`). This naming convention is known as **camel case**, because the uppercase letters stand out like a camel's humps. When the first letter is capitalized, it's known as **Pascal Case**. A class name is an **identifier**—a series of characters consisting of letters, digits and underscores (_) that does not begin with a digit and does not contain spaces. Some valid identifiers are `Welcome1`, `identifier`, `_value` and `m_inputField1`. The name `7button` is *not* a valid identifier because it begins with a digit, and the name `input field` is *not* a valid identifier because it contains a space. Normally, an identifier that does not begin with a capital letter is not the name of a class. C# is **case sensitive**—that is, uppercase and lowercase letters are distinct, so `a1` and `A1` are different (but both valid) identifiers. Keywords are always spelled with all lowercase letters. The complete list of C# keywords is shown in Fig. 3.2.[1]

| Keywords and contextual keywords | | | | | |
|---|---|---|---|---|---|
| `abstract` | `as` | `base` | `bool` | `break` | `byte` |
| `case` | `catch` | `char` | `checked` | `class` | `const` |
| `continue` | `decimal` | `default` | `delegate` | `do` | `double` |
| `else` | `enum` | `event` | `explicit` | `extern` | `false` |
| `finally` | `fixed` | `float` | `for` | `foreach` | `goto` |
| `if` | `implicit` | `in` | `int` | `interface` | `internal` |
| `is` | `lock` | `long` | `namespace` | `new` | `null` |
| `object` | `operator` | `out` | `override` | `params` | `private` |
| `protected` | `public` | `readonly` | `ref` | `return` | `sbyte` |
| `sealed` | `short` | `sizeof` | `stackalloc` | `static` | `string` |
| `struct` | `switch` | `this` | `throw` | `true` | `try` |
| `typeof` | `uint` | `ulong` | `unchecked` | `unsafe` | `ushort` |
| `using` | `virtual` | `void` | `volatile` | `while` | |
| ***Contextual Keywords*** | | | | | |
| `add` | `alias` | `ascending` | `async` | `await` | `by` |
| `descending` | `dynamic` | `equals` | `from` | `get` | `global` |
| `group` | `into` | `join` | `let` | `nameof` | `on` |
| `orderby` | `partial` | `remove` | `select` | `set` | `value` |
| `var` | `where` | `yield` | | | |

**Fig. 3.2** | Keywords and contextual keywords.

**Good Programming Practice 3.1**

*By convention, always begin a class name's identifier with a capital letter and start each subsequent word in the identifier with a capital letter.*

**Common Programming Error 3.2**

*C# is case sensitive. Not using the proper uppercase and lowercase letters for an identifier normally causes a compilation error.*

**Common Programming Error 3.3**

*Using a keyword as an identifier is a compilation error.*

### *Class Declaration's File Name*

A class declaration's file name is usually the class name followed by the `.cs` file-name extension, though this is not required. For our app, the file name is `Welcome1.cs`.

**Good Programming Practice 3.2**

*By convention, a file that contains a single class should have a name that's identical to the class name (plus the* `.cs` *extension) in both spelling and capitalization. This makes it easy to identify which file contains the class's declaration.*

### *Body of a Class Declaration*

A **left brace**, { (in line 6 in Fig. 3.1), begins each class declaration's **body**. A corresponding **right brace**, } (in line 12), must end each class declaration. Lines 7–11 are indented. This indentation is a *spacing convention*. We define each spacing convention and other conventions that improve program clarity as *Good Programming Practices*.

**Good Programming Practice 3.3**

*Indent the entire body of each class declaration one "level" of indentation between the left and right braces that delimit the body of the class. This format emphasizes the class declaration's structure and makes it easier to read. You can let the IDE format your code by selecting* **Edit > Advanced > Format Document**.

**Good Programming Practice 3.4**

*Set a convention for the indent size you prefer, then uniformly apply that convention. Microsoft recommends four-space indents, which is the default in Visual Studio. Due to the limited width of code lines in print books, we use three-space indents—this reduces the number of code lines that wrap to a new line, making the code a bit easier to read. We show how to set the tab size in the Before You Begin section that follows the Preface.*

**Error-Prevention Tip 3.3**

*Whenever you type an opening left brace, {, in your app, the IDE immediately inserts the closing right brace, }, then repositions the cursor between the braces so you can begin typing the body. This practice helps prevent errors due to missing braces.*

**Common Programming Error 3.4**

*It's a syntax error if braces do not occur in matching pairs.*

### 3.2.5 Main Method

Line 7 is a comment indicating the purpose of lines 8–11. Line 8

```
static void Main()
```

is where the app begins execution—this is known as the entry point. The **parentheses** after the identifier `Main` indicate that it's a **method**. Class declarations normally contain one or more methods. Method names follow the same capitalization conventions as class names. For each app, one of the methods in a class *must* be called `Main`; otherwise, the app will not execute. A method is able to perform a task and return a value when it completes its task. Keyword **`void`** (line 8) indicates that `Main` will *not* return a value after it completes its task. Later, we'll see that most methods do return values. You'll learn more about methods in Chapters 4 and 7. We discuss the contents of `Main`'s parentheses in Chapter 8. For now, simply mimic `Main`'s first line in your apps.

*Body of a Method Declaration*

The left brace in line 9 begins the **body of the method declaration**. A corresponding right brace ends the body (line 11). Line 10 in the method body is indented between the braces.

**Good Programming Practice 3.5**

*Indent each method declaration's body statements one level of indentation between the left and right braces that define the body.*

### 3.2.6 Displaying a Line of Text

Line 10

```
Console.WriteLine("Welcome to C# Programming!");
```

instructs the computer to **perform an action**—namely, to display the **string** of characters between the double quotation marks, which delimit the string. A string is sometimes called a **character string**, a **message** or a **string literal**. We refer to them simply as strings. Whitespace characters in strings are *not* ignored by the compiler.

Class **`Console`** provides **standard input/output** capabilities that enable apps to read and display text in the console window from which the app executes. The **`Console.WriteLine` method** displays a line of text in the console window. The string in the parentheses in line 10 is the **argument** to the method. Method `Console.WriteLine` performs its task by displaying its argument in the console window. When `Console.WriteLine` completes its task, it positions the **screen cursor** (the blinking symbol indicating where the next character will be displayed) at the beginning of the next line in the console window. This movement of the cursor is similar to what happens when a user presses the *Enter* key while typing in a text editor—the cursor moves to the beginning of the next line in the file.

*Statements*

The entire line 10, including `Console.WriteLine`, the parentheses, the argument `"Welcome to C# Programming!"` in the parentheses and the **semicolon** (`;`), is called a **statement**. Most statements end with a semicolon. When the statement in line 10 executes, it displays the message `Welcome to C# Programming!` in the console window. A method is typically composed of one or more statements that perform the method's task.

### 3.2.7 Matching Left ({) and Right (}) Braces

You may find it difficult when reading or writing an app to match the left and right braces ({ and }) that delimit a class's or method's body. Visual Studio can help you locate matching braces in your code. Simply place the cursor immediately in front of the left brace or immediately after the right brace, and Visual Studio will highlight both.

## 3.3 Creating a Simple App in Visual Studio

Now that we've presented our first console app (Fig. 3.1), we provide a step-by-step explanation of how to create, compile and execute it using Visual Studio Community 2015, which we'll refer to simply as Visual Studio from this point forward.

### 3.3.1 Creating the Console App

In Visual Studio, select **File > New > Project...** to display the **New Project** dialog (Fig. 3.3). At the left side, under **Installed > Templates > Visual C#** select **Windows**, then in the middle select the **Console Application** template. In the dialog's **Name** field, type `Welcome1`—your project's name—then click **OK** to create the project. The project's folder will be placed in your user account's `documents` folder under `visual studio 2015\Projects`.

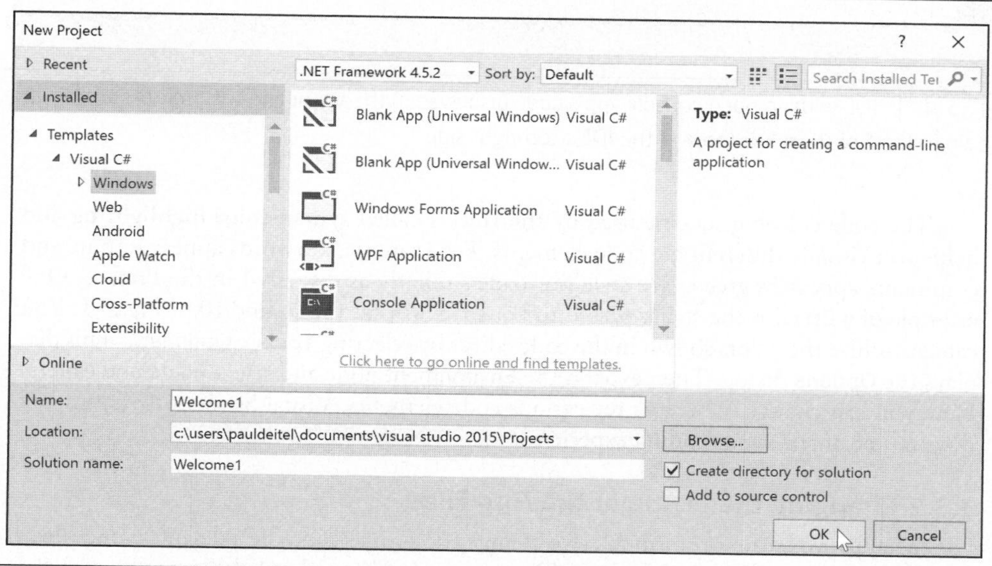


**Fig. 3.3** | Selecting **Console Application** in the **New Project** dialog.

The IDE now contains the open console app (Fig. 3.4). The editor window already contains some code provided by the IDE. Some of this code is similar to that of Fig. 3.1. Some is not and uses features that we have not yet discussed. The IDE inserts this extra code to help organize the app and to provide access to some common classes in the .NET Framework Class Library—at this point in the book, this code is neither required nor relevant to the discussion of this app; delete all of it.

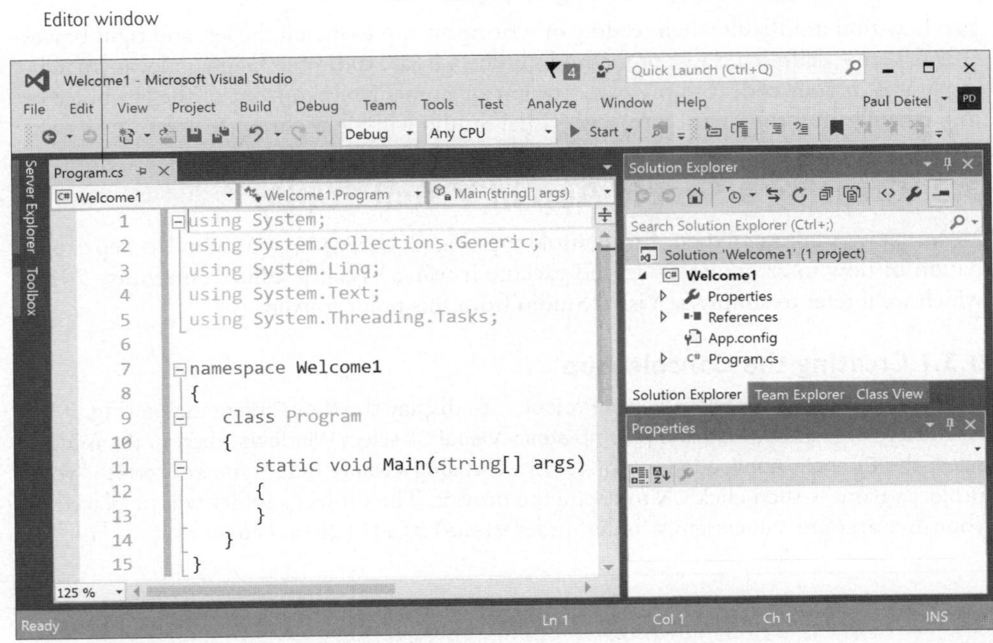


**Fig. 3.4** | IDE with an open console app's code displayed in the editor and the project's contents shown in the **Solution Explorer** at the IDE's top-right side.

The code coloring scheme used by the IDE is called **syntax-color highlighting** and helps you visually differentiate code elements. For example, keywords appear in blue and comments appear in green. We style our code similarly as discussed in the Preface. One example of a literal is the string passed to `Console.WriteLine` in line 10 of Fig. 3.1. You can customize the colors shown in the code editor by selecting **Tools > Options....** This displays the **Options** dialog. Then expand the **Environment** node and select **Fonts and Colors.** Here you can change the colors for various code elements. Visual Studio provides many ways to personalize your coding experience.

### 3.3.2 Changing the Name of the App File

For the apps we create in this book, we change the source-code file's default name (`Program.cs`) to a more descriptive name. To rename the file, right click `Program.cs` in the **Solution Explorer** and select **Rename** to make the file name editable. Windows automatically selects the file name's base part (i.e., `Program`). Type `Welcome1`, then press *Enter* to change the name to `Welcome1.cs`. Be sure to keep the `.cs` filename extension.

**Error-Prevention Tip 3.4**

*When changing a file name in a Visual Studio project, always do so in Visual Studio. Changing file names outside the IDE can break the project and prevent it from executing.*

### 3.3.3 Writing Code and Using *IntelliSense*

In the editor window (Fig. 3.4), replace the generated code with Fig. 3.1's code. As you begin typing the name `Console` (line 10), an *IntelliSense* window is displayed (Fig. 3.5).

a) *IntelliSense* window displayed as you type

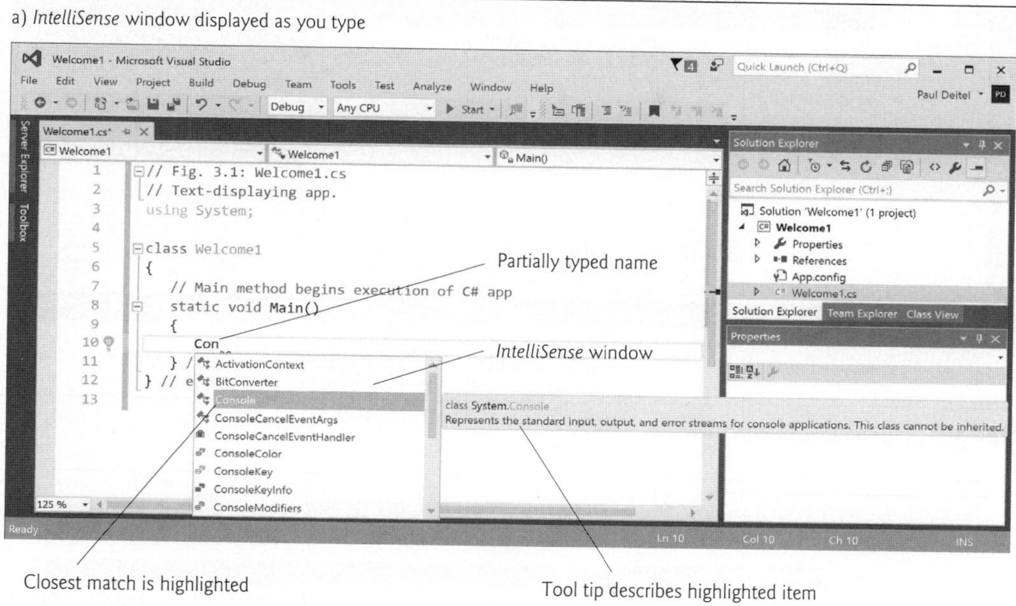


**Fig. 3.5** | *IntelliSense* window as you type "`Con`".

As you type, *IntelliSense* lists various items that start with or contain the letters you've typed so far. *IntelliSense* also displays a tool tip containing a description of the first matching item. You can either type the complete item name (e.g., `Console`), double click the item name in the member list or press the *Tab* key to complete the name. Once the complete name is provided, the *IntelliSense* window closes. While the *IntelliSense* window is displayed, pressing the *Ctrl* key makes the window transparent so you can see the code behind the window.

When you type the dot (`.`) after `Console`, the *IntelliSense* window reappears and initially shows only class `Console`'s members that can be used on the right of the dot—as you type, this list narrows to items containing what you've typed so far. Figure 3.6 shows the *IntelliSense* window narrowed down to only items that contain "`Write`". You also can type "`WL`" to find all items containing the capital letters "`W`" and "`L`" (such as `WriteLine`).

When you type the opening parenthesis character, `(`, after `Console.WriteLine`, the ***Parameter Info*** window is displayed (Fig. 3.7). This contains information about the method's parameters—the data methods require to perform their tasks. As you'll learn in Chapter 7, a method can have several versions. That is, a class can define several methods that have the *same* name, as long as they have *different* numbers and/or types of parameters—a concept known as *overloaded methods*. These methods normally all perform similar tasks.

b) *IntelliSense* window showing method names that start with `Write`

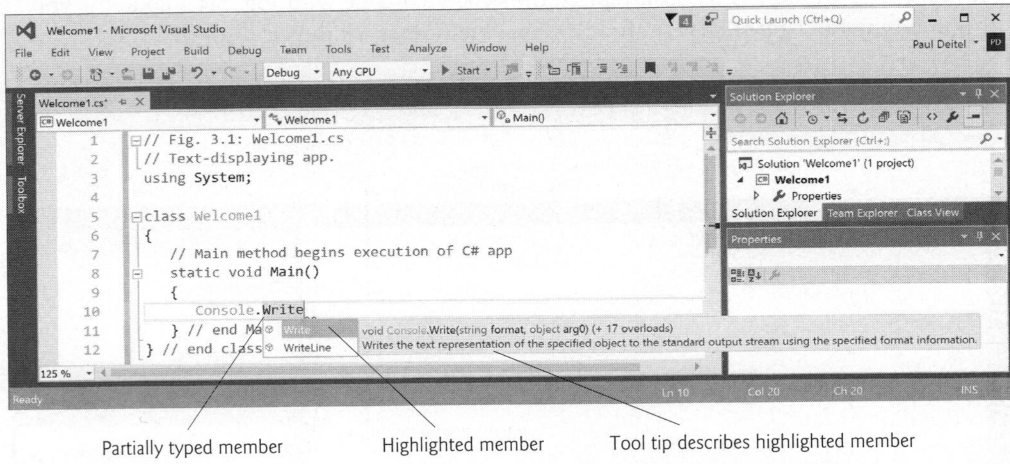


**Fig. 3.6** | *IntelliSense* window.

Parameter Info window

Down arrow

Up arrow

```
// Fig. 3.1: Welcome1.cs
// Text-displaying app.
using System;

class Welcome1
{
   // Main method begins execution of C# app
   static void Main()
   {
      Console.WriteLine()
   } // e
} // e
```

▲ 1 of 19 ▼ void Console.WriteLine()
Writes the current line terminator to the standard output stream.

**Fig. 3.7** | *Parameter Info* window.

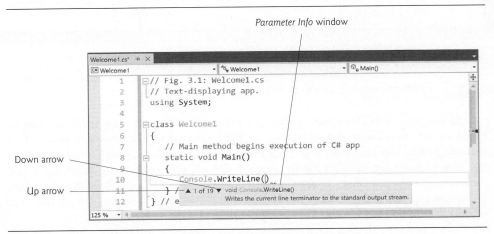

The *Parameter Info* window indicates how many versions of the selected method are available and provides up and down arrows for scrolling through the different versions. For example, there are many versions of the `WriteLine` method that enable you to display different types of data—we use the one that displays a string in our app. The *Parameter Info* window is one of many features provided by the IDE to facilitate app development. In the next several chapters, you'll learn more about the information displayed in these windows. The *Parameter Info* window is especially helpful when you want to see the different ways in which a method can be used. From the code in Fig. 3.1, we already know that we intend to display one string with `WriteLine`, so, because you know exactly which version of `WriteLine` you want to use, you can close the *Parameter Info* window by pressing the *Esc*

key, or simply keep typing and ignore it. After you type the app's code, select **File > Save All** to save the project.

### 3.3.4 Compiling and Running the App

You're now ready to compile and execute your app. Depending on the project's type, the compiler may compile the code into files with the `.exe` **(executable) extension**, the `.dll` **(dynamically linked library) extension** or one of several other extensions—you can find these files in project's subfolders on disk. Such files are called **assemblies** and are the packaging units for compiled C# code. These assemblies contain the Microsoft Intermediate Language (MSIL; Section 1.4.2) code for the app.

To compile the app, select **Build > Build Solution**. If the app contains no compile-time errors, this will compile your app and build it into an executable file (named `Welcome1.exe`, in one of the project's subdirectories). To execute it, type *Ctrl* + *F5*, which invokes the `Main` method (Fig. 3.1). If you attempt to run the app before building it, the IDE will build the app first, then run it only if there are no compilation errors. The statement in line 10 of `Main` displays `Welcome to C# Programming!`. Figure 3.8 shows the results of executing this app, displayed in a console (**Command Prompt**) window. Leave the app's project open in Visual Studio; we'll go back to it later in this section. [*Note:* The console window normally has a black background and white text. We reconfigured it to have a white background and black text for readability. If you'd like to do this, right click anywhere in the **Command Prompt** window's title bar, then select **Properties**. You can change the colors in the **Colors** tab of the dialog that appears.]

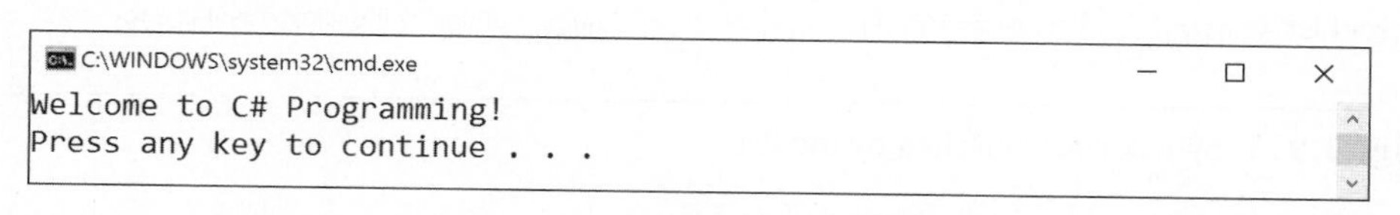


**Fig. 3.8** | Executing the app shown in Fig. 3.1.

### 3.3.5 Errors, Error Messages and the Error List Window

Go back to the app in Visual Studio. As you type code, the IDE responds either by applying syntax-color highlighting or by generating an error. When an error occurs, the IDE underlines the error's location with a red squiggly line and provides a description of it in the **Error List window** (Fig. 3.9). If the **Error List** window is not visible, select **View > Error List** to display it. In Fig. 3.9, we intentionally omitted the semicolon at the end of line 10. The error message indicates that the semicolon is missing. You can double click an error message in the **Error List** to jump to the error's location in the code.

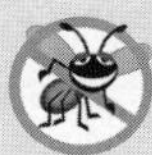

**Error-Prevention Tip 3.5**

*One compile-time error can lead to multiple entries in the* **Error List** *window. Each error you correct could eliminate several subsequent error messages when you recompile your app. So when you see an error you know how to fix, correct it—the IDE will recompile your code in the background, so fixing an error may make several other errors disappear.*

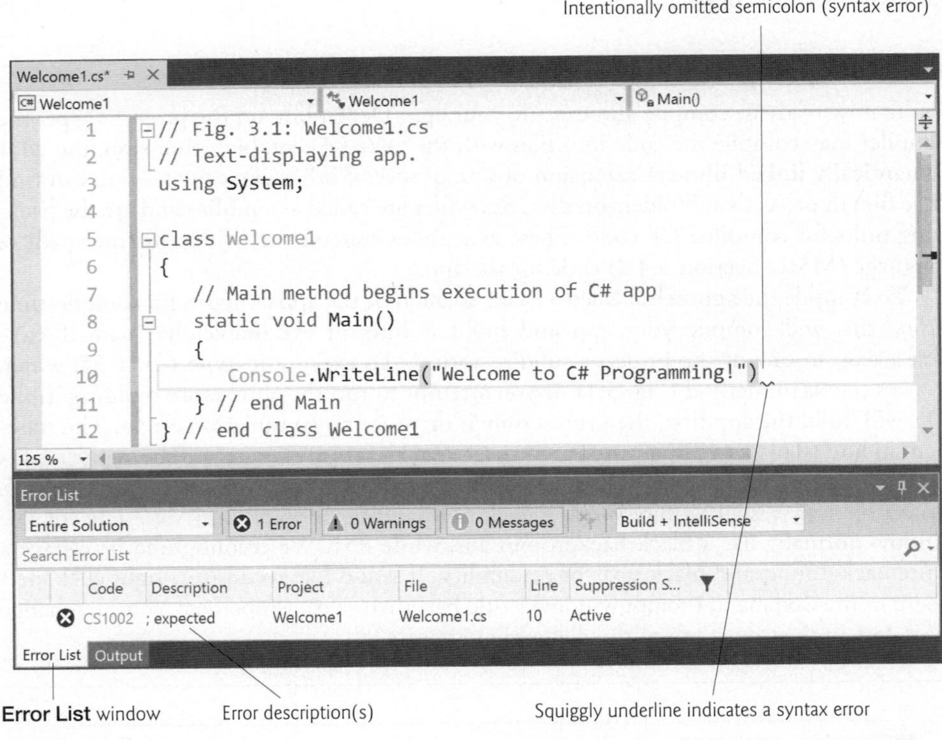


**Fig. 3.9** | Syntax error indicated by the IDE.

## 3.4 Modifying Your Simple C# App

This section continues our introduction to C# programming with two examples that modify the example of Fig. 3.1.

### 3.4.1 Displaying a Single Line of Text with Multiple Statements

Class `Welcome2`, shown in Fig. 3.10, uses two statements to produce the same output as that shown in Fig. 3.1. From this point forward, we highlight the new and key features in each code listing, as shown in lines 10–11 of Fig. 3.10.

```
1  // Fig. 3.10: Welcome2.cs
2  // Displaying one line of text with multiple statements.
3  using System;
4
5  class Welcome2
6  {
```

**Fig. 3.10** | Displaying one line of text with multiple statements. (Part 1 of 2.)

```
7       // Main method begins execution of C# app
8       static void Main()
9       {
10         Console.Write("Welcome to ");
11         Console.WriteLine("C# Programming!");
12      } // end Main
13   } // end class Welcome2
```

```
Welcome to C# Programming!
```

**Fig. 3.10** | Displaying one line of text with multiple statements. (Part 2 of 2.)

The app is almost identical to Fig. 3.1. We discuss the changes here. Line 2

```
// Displaying one line of text with multiple statements.
```

states the purpose of this app. Line 5 begins the `Welcome2` class declaration.

Lines 10–11 of method `Main`

```
Console.Write("Welcome to ");
Console.WriteLine("C# Programming!");
```

display one line of text in the console window. The first statement uses `Console`'s method **`Write`** to display a string. Unlike `WriteLine`, after displaying its argument, `Write` does *not* position the screen cursor at the beginning of the next line in the console window—the next character the app displays will appear immediately after the last character that `Write` displays. Thus, line 11 positions the first character in its argument (the letter "C") immediately *after* the last character that line 10 displays (the space character before the string's closing double-quote character). Each `Write` or `WriteLine` statement resumes displaying characters from where the last `Write` or `WriteLine` statement displayed its last character.

### 3.4.2 Displaying Multiple Lines of Text with a Single Statement

A single statement can display multiple lines by using newline characters, which indicate to `Console` methods `Write` and `WriteLine` when they should position the screen cursor to the beginning of the next line. Like space characters and tab characters, newline characters are whitespace characters. The app of Fig. 3.11 outputs four lines of text, using newline characters to indicate when to begin each new line.

```
// Fig. 3.11: Welcome3.cs
// Displaying multiple lines with a single statement.
using System;

class Welcome3
{
   // Main method begins execution of C# app
   static void Main()
   {
```

**Fig. 3.11** | Displaying multiple lines with a single statement. (Part 1 of 2.)

```
10          Console.WriteLine("Welcome\nto\nC#\nProgramming!");
11       } // end Main
12    } // end class Welcome3
```

```
Welcome
to
C#
Programming!
```

**Fig. 3.11** | Displaying multiple lines with a single statement. (Part 2 of 2.)

Most of the app is identical to the apps of Fig. 3.1 and Fig. 3.10, so we discuss only the changes here. Line 2

```
// Displaying multiple lines with a single statement.
```

states the purpose of this app. Line 5 begins the `Welcome3` class declaration.

Line 10

```
Console.WriteLine("Welcome\nto\nC#\nProgramming!");
```

displays four separate lines of text in the console window. Normally, the characters in a string are displayed exactly as they appear in the double quotes. Note, however, that the two characters `\` and `n` (repeated three times in the statement) do *not* appear on the screen. The **backslash** (\) is called an **escape character.** It indicates to C# that a "special character" is in the string. When a backslash appears in a string of characters, C# combines the next character with the backslash to form an **escape sequence.**[2]

The escape sequence `\n` represents the **newline character.** When a newline character appears in a string being output with `Console` methods, the newline character causes the screen cursor to move to the beginning of the next line in the console window. Figure 3.12 lists several common escape sequences and describes how they affect the display of characters in the console window.

| Escape sequence | Description |
|---|---|
| `\n` | Newline. Positions the screen cursor at the beginning of the next line. |
| `\t` | Horizontal tab. Moves the screen cursor to the next tab stop. |
| `\"` | Double quote. Used to place a double-quote character (") in a string—e,g., `Console.Write("\"in quotes\"");` displays `"in quotes"`. |

**Fig. 3.12** | Common escape sequences. (Part 1 of 2.)

2. There are also escape sequences that have four or eight hexadecimal characters following the \. These represent so-called Unicode characters. For more information, see the Lexical Structure section of Microsoft's C# 6 specification. For more information on the hexadecimal (base 16) number system, see our online Number Systems appendix.

| Escape sequence | Description |
|---|---|
| \r | Carriage return. Positions the screen cursor at the beginning of the current line—does not advance the cursor to the next line. Any characters output after the carriage return overwrite the characters previously output on that line. |
| \\ | Backslash. Used to place a backslash character in a string. |

**Fig. 3.12** | Common escape sequences. (Part 2 of 2.)

## 3.5 String Interpolation

Many programs format data into strings. C# 6 introduces a mechanism called **string in-** 6
**terpolation** that enables you to insert values in string literals to create formatted strings. Figure 3.13 demonstrates this capability.

```
1  // Fig. 3.13: Welcome4.cs
2  // Inserting content into a string with string interpolation.
3  using System;
4
5  class Welcome4
6  {
7     // Main method begins execution of C# app
8     static void Main()
9     {
10       string person = "Paul"; // variable that stores the string "Paul"
11       Console.WriteLine($"Welcome to C# Programming, {person}!");
12    } // end Main
13 } // end class Welcome4
```

```
Welcome to C# Programming, Paul!
```

**Fig. 3.13** | Inserting content into a `string` with `string` interpolation.

*Declaring the* **`string`** *Variable* ***person***

Line 10

```
string person = "Paul"; // variable that stores the string "Paul"
```

is a **variable declaration statement** (also called a **declaration**) that specifies the name (`person`) and type (`string`) of a variable used in this app. Variables are declared with a **name** and a **type** before they're used:

- A variable's name enables the app to access the corresponding value in memory—the name can be any valid identifier. (See Section 3.2 for identifier naming requirements.)
- A variable's type specifies what kind of information is stored at that location in memory. Variables of type **`string`** store character-based information, such as the

contents of the string literal "Paul". In fact, a string literal has type `string`. (From this point forward we'll use the type name `string` when referring to strings.)

Like other statements, declaration statements end with a semicolon (;).

### *`string` Interpolation*

Line 11

```
Console.WriteLine($"Welcome to C# Programming, {person}!");
```

uses `string` interpolation to insert the variable `person`'s value ("Paul") into the `string` that `Console.WriteLine` is about to display. An interpolated `string` must begin with a $ (dollar sign). Then, you can insert **interpolation expressions** enclosed in braces, {} (e.g., `{person}`), anywhere between the quotes (""). When C# encounters an interpolated `string`, it replaces each braced interpolation expression with the corresponding value—in this case, `{person}` is replaced with `Paul`, so line 11 displays

```
Welcome to C# Programming, Paul!
```

## 3.6 Another C# App: Adding Integers

The app in Fig. 3.14 reads (or inputs) two **integers** (whole numbers, like –22, 7, 0 and 1024) typed by a user at the keyboard, computes the sum of the values and displays the result. In the sample output, we highlight data the user enters at the keyboard in **bold**.

```
// Fig. 3.14: Addition.cs
// Displaying the sum of two numbers input from the keyboard.
using System;

class Addition
{
   // Main method begins execution of C# app
   static void Main()
   {
      int number1; // declare first number to add
      int number2; // declare second number to add
      int sum; // declare sum of number1 and number2

      Console.Write("Enter first integer: "); // prompt user
      // read first number from user
      number1 = int.Parse(Console.ReadLine());

      Console.Write("Enter second integer: "); // prompt user
      // read second number from user
      number2 = int.Parse(Console.ReadLine());

      sum = number1 + number2; // add numbers

      Console.WriteLine($"Sum is {sum}"); // display sum
   } // end Main
} // end class Addition
```

**Fig. 3.14** | Displaying the sum of two numbers input from the keyboard. (Part 1 of 2.)

```
Enter first integer: 45
Enter second integer: 72
Sum is 117
```

**Fig. 3.14** | Displaying the sum of two numbers input from the keyboard. (Part 2 of 2.)

Line 5

```
class Addition
```

begins the declaration of class `Addition`. Remember that the body of each class declaration starts with an opening left brace (line 6) and ends with a closing right brace (line 26). The app begins execution with `Main` (lines 8–25).

### 3.6.1 Declaring the `int` Variable `number1`

Line 10

```
int number1; // declare first number to add
```

is a variable declaration statement specifying that `number1` has type **`int`**—it will hold **integer** values (whole numbers such as `7`, `-11`, `0` and `31914`). The range of values for an `int` is –2,147,483,648 (`int.MinValue`) to +2,147,483,647 (`int.MaxValue`). We'll soon discuss types **`float`**, **`double`** and **`decimal`**, for specifying numbers with decimal points (as in 3.4, 0.0 and –11.19), and type **`char`**, for specifying characters. Variables of type `float` and `double` store approximations of real numbers in memory. Variables of type `decimal` store numbers with decimal points *precisely* (to 28–29 significant digits[3]), so `decimal` variables are often used with *monetary calculations*—we use type `decimal` to represent the balance in our `Account` class in Chapter 4. Variables of type `char` represent individual characters, such as an uppercase letter (e.g., `A`), a digit (e.g., `7`), a special character (e.g., `*` or `%`) or an escape sequence (e.g., the newline character, `\n`). Types such as `int`, `float`, `double`, `decimal` and `char` are called **simple types**. Simple-type names are keywords and must appear in all lowercase letters. Appendix B summarizes the characteristics of the simple types (`bool`, `byte`, `sbyte`, `char`, `short`, `ushort`, `int`, `uint`, `long`, `ulong`, `float`, `double` and `decimal`), including the amount of memory required to store a value of each type.

### 3.6.2 Declaring Variables `number2` and `sum`

The variable declaration statements at lines 11–12

```
int number2; // declare second number to add
int sum; // declare sum of number1 and number2
```

declare variables `number2` and `sum` to be of type `int`.

**Good Programming Practice 3.6**

*Declare each variable on a separate line. This format allows a comment to be easily inserted next to each declaration.*

3. See Section 4.1.7 of the *C# Language Specification*.

**Good Programming Practice 3.7**

*By convention, variable-name identifiers begin with a lowercase letter, and every word in the name after the first word begins with a capital letter (e.g.,* `firstNumber`*). This naming convention is known as camel case.*

### 3.6.3 Prompting the User for Input

Line 14

```
Console.Write("Enter first integer: "); // prompt user
```

uses `Console.Write` to prompt the user for input.

### 3.6.4 Reading a Value into Variable `number1`

Line 16

```
number1 = int.Parse(Console.ReadLine());
```

works in two steps. First, it calls the `Console`'s **`ReadLine`** method, which waits for the user to type a string of characters at the keyboard and press the *Enter* key. As we mentioned, some methods perform a task, then return the result of that task. In this case, `ReadLine` returns the text the user entered. Then the returned `string` is used as an argument to type `int`'s **`Parse`** method, which converts this sequence of characters into data of type `int`.

*Possible Erroneous User Input*

Technically, the user can type anything as the input value. `ReadLine` will accept it and pass it off to `int`'s `Parse` method. This method assumes that the `string` contains a valid integer value. In this app, if the user types a noninteger value, a runtime logic error called an *exception* will occur and the app will terminate. The `string` processing techniques you'll learn in Chapter 16 can be used to check that the input is in the correct format before attempting to convert the string to an `int`. C# also offers a technology called *exception handling* that will help you make your apps more robust by enabling them to handle exceptions and continue executing. This is also known as making your app **fault tolerant**. We introduce exception handling in Section 8.5, then use it again in Chapter 10. We take a deeper look at exception handling in Chapter 13 and throughout the book.

*Assigning a Value to a Variable*

In line 16, the result of the call to `int`'s `Parse` method (an `int` value) is placed in variable `number1` by using the **assignment operator**, `=`. The statement is read as "`number1` gets the value returned by `int.Parse`." Operator `=` is a binary operator, because it works on two pieces of information. These are known as its operands—in this case, `number1` and the result of the method call `int.Parse`. This statement is called an **assignment statement**, because it assigns a value to a variable. Everything to the right of the assignment operator, `=`, is always evaluated *before* the assignment is performed.

**Good Programming Practice 3.8**

*Place spaces on either side of a binary operator to make the code more readable.*

### 3.6.5 Prompting the User for Input and Reading a Value into number2

Line 18

```
Console.Write("Enter second integer: "); // prompt user
```

prompts the user to enter the second integer. Line 20

```
number2 = int.Parse(Console.ReadLine());
```

reads a second integer and assigns it to the variable `number2`.

### 3.6.6 Summing number1 and number2

Line 22

```
sum = number1 + number2; // add numbers
```

calculates the sum of `number1` and `number2` and assigns the result to variable `sum` by using the assignment operator, `=`. The statement is read as "`sum` *gets* the value of `number1 + number2`." When `number1 + number2` is encountered, the values stored in the variables are used in the calculation. The addition operator is a binary operator—its two operands are `number1` and `number2`. Portions of statements that contain calculations are called **expressions.** In fact, an expression is any portion of a statement that has a value associated with it. For example, the value of the expression `number1 + number2` is the sum of the numbers. Similarly, the value of the expression `Console.ReadLine()` is the string of characters typed by the user.

### 3.6.7 Displaying the sum with string Interpolation

After the calculation has been performed, line 24

```
Console.WriteLine($"Sum is {sum}"); // display sum
```

uses method `Console.WriteLine` to display the `sum`. C# replaces the interpolation expression `{sum}` with the calculated `sum` from line 22. So method `WriteLine` displays `"Sum is "`, followed by the value of `sum` and a newline.

### 3.6.8 Performing Calculations in Output Statements

Calculations also can be performed in interpolation expressions. We could have combined the statements in lines 22 and 24 into the statement

```
Console.WriteLine($"Sum is {number1 + number2}");
```

## 3.7 Arithmetic

The arithmetic operators are summarized in Fig. 3.15. The **asterisk** (`*`) indicates multiplication, and the **percent sign (`%`)** is the **remainder operator**, which we'll discuss shortly. The arithmetic operators in Fig. 3.15 are binary operators—for example, the expression `f + 7` contains the binary operator `+` and the two operands `f` and `7`.

| C# operation | Arithmetic operator | Algebraic expression | C# expression |
|---|---|---|---|
| Addition | + | $f+7$ | `f + 7` |
| Subtraction | – | $p-c$ | `p - c` |
| Multiplication | * | $b \cdot m$ | `b * m` |
| Division | / | $x / y$ or $\frac{x}{y}$ or $x \div y$ | `x / y` |
| Remainder | % | $r \bmod s$ | `r % s` |

**Fig. 3.15** | Arithmetic operators.

If both operands of the division operator (/) are integers, **integer division** is performed and the result is an integer—for example, the expression `7 / 4` evaluates to `1`, and the expression `17 / 5` evaluates to `3`. Any fractional part in integer division is simply *truncated* (i.e., discarded)—*no rounding* occurs. C# provides the remainder operator, `%`, which yields the remainder after division. The expression `x % y` yields the remainder after `x` is divided by `y`. Thus, `7 % 4` yields `3`, and `17 % 5` yields `2`. This operator is most commonly used with integer operands but also can be used with `float`s, `double`s, and `decimal`s. In later chapters, we consider several interesting applications of the remainder operator, such as determining whether one number is a multiple of another.

### 3.7.1 Arithmetic Expressions in Straight-Line Form

Arithmetic expressions must be written in **straight-line form** to facilitate entering an app's code into the computer. Thus, expressions such as "a divided by b" must be written as `a / b` in a straight line. The following algebraic notation is not acceptable to the C# compiler and cannot be typed into the Visual Studio editor:

$$\frac{a}{b}$$

### 3.7.2 Parentheses for Grouping Subexpressions

Parentheses are used to group terms in C# expressions in the same manner as in algebraic expressions. For example, to multiply `a` times the quantity `b + c`, we write

```
a * (b + c)
```

If an expression contains **nested parentheses**, such as

```
((a + b) * c)
```

the expression in the *innermost* set of parentheses (`a + b` in this case) is evaluated first.

### 3.7.3 Rules of Operator Precedence

C# applies the operators in arithmetic expressions in a precise sequence determined by the following rules of operator precedence, which are generally the same as those followed in algebra (Fig. 3.16). These rules enable C# to apply operators in the correct order.[4]

| Operators | Operations | Order of evaluation (associativity) |
|---|---|---|
| *Evaluated first* | | |
| * | Multiplication | If there are several operators of this type, |
| / | Division | they're evaluated from left to right. |
| % | Remainder | |
| *Evaluated next* | | |
| + | Addition | If there are several operators of this type, |
| - | Subtraction | they're evaluated from left to right. |

**Fig. 3.16** | Precedence of arithmetic operators.

When we say that operators are applied from left to right, we're referring to their **associativity**. You'll see that some operators associate from right to left. Figure 3.16 summarizes these rules of operator precedence. The table will be expanded as additional operators are introduced. Appendix A provides the complete precedence chart.

## 3.8 Decision Making: Equality and Relational Operators

A condition is an expression that can be either true or false. This section introduces a simple version of C#'s `if` statement that allows an app to make a **decision** based on the value of a condition. For example, the condition "grade is greater than or equal to 60" determines whether a student passed a test. If the condition in an `if` statement is true, the body of the `if` statement executes. If the condition is false, the body is skipped—it does *not* execute. We'll see an example shortly.

Conditions in `if` statements can be formed by using the **equality operators** (== and !=) and **relational operators** (>, <, >= and <=) summarized in Fig. 3.17. The two equality operators (== and !=) each have the same level of precedence, the relational operators (>, <, >= and <=) each have the same level of precedence, and the equality operators have lower precedence than the relational operators. They all associate from left to right.

**Common Programming Error 3.5**

*Confusing the equality operator, ==, with the assignment operator, =, can cause a logic error or a syntax error. The equality operator should be read as "is equal to," and the assignment operator should be read as "gets" or "gets the value of." To avoid confusion, some programmers read the equality operator as "double equals" or "equals equals."*

4. We discuss simple examples here to explain the order of evaluation. More subtle order of evaluation issues occur in the increasingly complex expressions you'll encounter later. For more details, see the following blog posts from Eric Lippert: `https://ericlippert.com/2008/05/23/` and `https://ericlippert.com/2007/08/14/`.

| Standard algebraic equality and relational operators | C# equality or relational operator | Sample C# condition | Meaning of C# condition |
|---|---|---|---|
| *Relational operators* | | | |
| > | `>` | `x > y` | x is greater than y |
| < | `<` | `x < y` | x is less than y |
| ≥ | `>=` | `x >= y` | x is greater than or equal to y |
| ≤ | `<=` | `x <= y` | x is less than or equal to y |
| *Equality operators* | | | |
| = | `==` | `x == y` | x is equal to y |
| ≠ | `!=` | `x != y` | x is not equal to y |

**Fig. 3.17** | Relational and equality operators.

### *Using the* `if` *Statement*

Figure 3.18 uses six `if` statements to compare two integers entered by the user. If the condition in any of these `if` statements is true, the statement associated with that `if` statement executes. The app uses class `Console` to prompt for and read two lines of text from the user, extracts the integers from that text with `int`'s `Parse` method, and stores them in variables `number1` and `number2`. Then the app compares the numbers and displays the results of the comparisons that are true.

```
// Fig. 3.18: Comparison.cs
// Comparing integers using if statements, equality operators
// and relational operators.
using System;

class Comparison
{
   // Main method begins execution of C# app
   static void Main()
   {
      // prompt user and read first number
      Console.Write("Enter first integer: ");
      int number1 = int.Parse(Console.ReadLine());

      // prompt user and read second number
      Console.Write("Enter second integer: ");
      int number2 = int.Parse(Console.ReadLine());

      if (number1 == number2)
      {
         Console.WriteLine($"{number1} == {number2}");
      }
```

**Fig. 3.18** | Comparing integers using `if` statements, equality operators and relational operators. (Part 1 of 2.)

```

         if (number1 != number2)
         {
            Console.WriteLine($"{number1} != {number2}");
         }

         if (number1 < number2)
         {
            Console.WriteLine($"{number1} < {number2}");
         }

         if (number1 > number2)
         {
            Console.WriteLine($"{number1} > {number2}");
         }

         if (number1 <= number2)
         {
            Console.WriteLine($"{number1} <= {number2}");
         }

         if (number1 >= number2)
         {
            Console.WriteLine($"{number1} >= {number2}");
         }
      } // end Main
   } // end class Comparison
```

```
Enter first integer: 42
Enter second integer: 42
42 == 42
42 <= 42
42 >= 42
```

```
Enter first integer: 1000
Enter second integer: 2000
1000 != 2000
1000 < 2000
1000 <= 2000
```

```
Enter first integer: 2000
Enter second integer: 1000
2000 != 1000
2000 > 1000
2000 >= 1000
```

**Fig. 3.18** | Comparing integers using `if` statements, equality operators and relational operators. (Part 2 of 2.)

### *Class* `Comparison`

The declaration of class `Comparison` begins at line 6

```
class Comparison
```

The class's `Main` method (lines 9–48) begins the execution of the app.

### *Reading the Inputs from the User*

Lines 11–13

```
// prompt user and read first number
Console.Write("Enter first integer: ");
int number1 = int.Parse(Console.ReadLine());
```

prompt for and input the first value. Line 13 also declares `number1` as an `int` variable that stores the first value entered by the user.

Lines 15–17

```
// prompt user and read second number
Console.Write("Enter second integer: ");
int number2 = int.Parse(Console.ReadLine());
```

prompt for and input the second value.

### *Comparing Numbers*

The `if` statement in lines 19–22

```
if (number1 == number2)
{
   Console.WriteLine($"{number1} == {number2}");
}
```

compares the values of variables `number1` and `number2` to test for equality. The condition `number1 == number2` is enclosed in required parentheses. If the values are equal, line 21 displays a line of text indicating that the numbers are equal. We used two interpolation expressions to insert the values of `number1` and `number2` in line 21's output. If the conditions are true in one or more of the `if` statements starting in lines 24, 29, 34, 39 and 44, the corresponding body statement displays an appropriate line of text.

Each `if` statement in Fig. 3.18 contains a single body statement that's indented. Also notice that we've enclosed each body statement in a pair of braces, `{ }`, creating what's called a **block**.

**Good Programming Practice 3.9**

*Indent the statement(s) in the body of an* `if` *statement to enhance readability.*

**Error-Prevention Tip 3.6**

*You don't need to use braces,* `{ }`*, around single-statement bodies, but you* must *include the braces around multiple-statement bodies. To avoid errors and make your code more readable, always enclose an* `if` *statement's body statement(s) in braces, even if it contains only a single statement.*

*Whitespace*

Note the use of whitespace in Fig. 3.18. Recall that whitespace characters, such as tabs, newlines and spaces, are normally ignored by the compiler. So, statements may be split over several lines and may be spaced according to your preferences without affecting the meaning of an app. It's incorrect to split identifiers, `string`s, and multicharacter operators (like >=). Ideally, statements should be kept small, but this is not always possible.

**Good Programming Practice 3.10**

*A lengthy statement can be spread over several lines. If a single statement must be split across lines, choose breaking points that make sense, such as after a comma in a comma-separated list, or after an operator in a lengthy expression. If a statement is split across two or more lines, indent all lines after the first until the end of the statement.*

*Precedence and Associativity of the Operators We've Discussed So Far*

Figure 3.19 shows the precedence of the operators introduced in this chapter. The operators are shown from top to bottom in decreasing order of precedence. All these operators, with the exception of the assignment operator, =, associate from left to right. Addition is left associative, so an expression like `x + y + z` is evaluated as if it had been written as `(x + y) + z`. The assignment operator, =, associates from right to left, so an expression like `x = y = 0` is evaluated as if it had been written as `x = (y = 0)`, which, as you'll soon see, first assigns the value `0` to variable `y`, then assigns the result of that assignment, `0`, to `x`.

**Good Programming Practice 3.11**

*Refer to the operator precedence chart (the complete chart is in Appendix A) when writing expressions containing many operators. Confirm that the operations in the expression are performed in the order you expect. If you're uncertain about the order of evaluation in a complex expression, use parentheses to force the order, as you would do in algebraic expressions. Some programmers also use parentheses to clarify the order. Observe that some operators, such as assignment, =, associate from right to left rather than left to right.*

| Operators | Associativity | Type |
|---|---|---|
| `*` `/` `%` | left to right | multiplicative |
| `+` `-` | left to right | additive |
| `<` `<=` `>` `>=` | left to right | relational |
| `==` `!=` | left to right | equality |
| `=` | right to left | assignment |

**Fig. 3.19** | Precedence and associativity of operations discussed so far.

## 3.9 Wrap-Up

We presented many important features of C# in this chapter. First you learned how to display data on the screen in a **Command Prompt** using the `Console` class's `Write` and `WriteLine` methods. Next, we showed how to use C# 6's new `string`-interpolation capabilities to insert values into `string` literals. You learned how to input data from the keyboard using the `Console` class's `ReadLine` method and how to convert `strings` to `int` values with type `int`'s `Parse` method. We discussed how to perform calculations using C#'s arithmetic operators. Finally, you made decisions using the `if` statement and the relational and equality operators. As you'll see in Chapter 4, C# apps typically contain just a few lines of code in method `Main`—these statements normally create the objects that perform the work of the app. You'll learn how to implement your own classes and use objects of those classes in apps.

# 4

# Introduction to Classes, Objects, Methods and `strings`

## Objectives

In this chapter you'll:

- Declare a class and use it to create an object.
- Implement a class's attributes as instance variables and a class's behaviors as methods.
- Call an object's methods to make them perform their tasks.
- Understand how local variables differ from instance variables of a class.
- Use validation to prevent bad data from being stored in an object.
- Understand the software engineering benefits of `private` instance variables and `public` access methods.
- Use properties to provide a friendlier notation for storing and retrieving data.
- Use a constructor to initialize an object's data when the object is created.
- Use type `decimal` for precise monetary amounts and calculations.

**Outline**



## 4.1 Introduction

[*Note:* This chapter depends on the terminology and concepts introduced in Section 1.2, Object Technology: A Brief Review.]

Section 1.2 presented a friendly introduction to object-oriented programming concepts, including classes, objects, instance variables, properties and methods. In this chapter's examples, we make those concepts real by building a simple bank-account class. The final version of the class maintains a bank account's name and balance, and provides *properties* (Name and Balance) and *methods* (Deposit and Withdraw) for behaviors including

- querying the balance (with the Balance property),
- making deposits that increase the balance (with the Deposit method) and
- making withdrawals that decrease the balance (with the Withdraw method).

We'll build the Balance property and Deposit method into the chapter's examples. As an exercise, you can add the Withdraw method.

Each *class* you create becomes a new *type* you can use to create objects, so C# is an **extensible programming language**. Major development teams in industry work on applications that contain hundreds, or even thousands, of classes.

## 4.2 Test-Driving an Account Class

A person drives a car by telling it what to do (go faster, go slower, turn left, turn right, etc.)—without having to know how the car's internal mechanisms work. Similarly, a method (such as `Main`) "drives" an `Account` object by calling its methods—without having to know how the class's internal mechanisms work. In this sense, the class containing method `Main` is referred to as a **driver class**. We show the `Main` method and its output first, so you can see an `Account` object in action.

To help you prepare for the larger programs you'll encounter later in this book and in industry, we define class `AccountTest` and its `Main` method in the file `AccountTest.cs` (Fig. 4.1). We define the `Account` class in its own file as well (file `Account.cs`, Fig. 4.2). After we present classes `AccountTest` (in this section) and `Account` (in Section 4.3), Section 4.4 discusses how to create and build a project that contains multiple `.cs` source-code files. First, let's walk through the `AccountTest` class.

```
1  // Fig. 4.1: AccountTest.cs
2  // Creating and manipulating an Account object.
3  using System;
4
5  class AccountTest
6  {
7     static void Main()
8     {
9        // create an Account object and assign it to myAccount
10       Account myAccount = new Account();
11
12       // display myAccount's initial name (there isn't one yet)
13       Console.WriteLine($"Initial name is: {myAccount.GetName()}");
14
15       // prompt for and read the name, then put the name in the object
16       Console.Write("Enter the name: "); // prompt
17       string theName = Console.ReadLine(); // read the name
18       myAccount.SetName(theName); // put theName in the myAccount object
19
20       // display the name stored in the myAccount object
21       Console.WriteLine($"myAccount's name is: {myAccount.GetName()}");
22    }
23 }
```

```
Initial name is:
Enter the name: Jane Green
myAccount's name is: Jane Green
```

**Fig. 4.1** | Creating and manipulating an `Account` object.

### 4.2.1 Instantiating an Object—Keyword new

You cannot call a method of a class until you *create an object* of that class.[1] Line 10 of Fig. 4.1

```
Account myAccount = new Account();
```

1. You'll see in Section 10.9 that `static` methods (and other `static` class members) are an exception.

uses an **object-creation expression**

```
new Account()
```

to create an `Account` object, then assigns it to the variable `myAccount`. The variable's type is `Account`—the class we'll define in Fig. 4.2. Keyword **`new`** creates a new object of the specified class—in this case, `Account`. The parentheses to the right of `Account` are required (we'll discuss these in Section 4.8).

### 4.2.2 Calling Class Account's GetName Method

The `Account` class's `GetName` method returns the account name stored in a particular `Account` object. Line 13 of Fig. 4.1

```
Console.WriteLine($"Initial name is: {myAccount.GetName()}");
```

displays `myAccount`'s initial name by calling the object's `GetName` method with the expression `myAccount.GetName()`. To call this method for a specific object, you specify

- the object's name (`myAccount`) followed by
- the **member access operator** (`.`),
- the method name (`GetName`) and
- a set of parentheses.

The *empty* parentheses indicate that `GetName` does not require any additional information to perform its task. Soon, you'll see the `SetName` method that does require additional information to perform its task.

When `Main` calls the `GetName` method:

1. The app transfers execution from the expression `myAccount.GetName()` (line 13 in `Main`) to method `GetName`'s declaration (which we'll study in Section 4.3). Because `GetName` was accessed via the object `myAccount`, `GetName` knows which object's data to manipulate.
2. Next, method `GetName` performs its task—that is, it returns the `myAccount` object's name to line 13 where the method was called.
3. `Console.WriteLine` displays the `string` returned by `GetName`—the name is inserted into the interpolated `string` in place of the call to `GetName`—then the program continues executing at line 16 in `Main`.

Because we have not yet stored a name in the `myAccount` object, line 13 does not display a name.

### 4.2.3 Inputting a Name from the User

Next, lines 16–17 prompt for and input a name. Line 17

```
string theName = Console.ReadLine(); // read a line of text
```

uses `Console` method `ReadLine` to read the name from the user and assign it to the `string` variable `theName`. The user types the name (in this case, `Jane Green`) and presses *Enter* to submit it to the app. Method `ReadLine` reads a *whole* line, including all the characters the user types until the newline that the user typed by pressing *Enter*—the newline is discarded. Pressing *Enter* also positions the output cursor to the beginning of the next line in the console window, so the program's next output begins on the line below the user's input.

### 4.2.4 Calling Class Account's SetName Method

The Account class's SetName method stores (*sets*) an account name in a particular Account object. Line 18

```
myAccount.SetName(theName); // put theName in the myAccount object
```

calls myAccounts's SetName method, passing theName's value as SetName's argument. The method stores this value in the object myAccount—we'll see exactly where it's stored in the next section.

When Main calls the SetName method:

1. The app transfers program execution from line 18 in Main to method SetName's declaration. Because method SetName was accessed via the myAccount object, SetName "knows" which object to manipulate.
2. Next, method SetName stores the argument's value in the myAccount object (we'll see exactly where in Section 4.3).
3. When SetName completes execution, program control returns to where method SetName was called (line 18 in Main), then execution continues at line 21.

*Displaying the Name That Was Entered by the User*

To demonstrate that myAccount now contains the name the user entered, line 21

```
Console.WriteLine($"myAccount's name is: {myAccount.GetName()}");
```

calls myAccounts's GetName method again. As you can see in the last line of the program's output, the name entered by the user in line 17 is displayed. When the preceding statement completes execution, the end of Main is reached, so the app terminates.

## 4.3 Account Class with an Instance Variable and *Set* and *Get* Methods

The fact that in Fig. 4.1 we could create and manipulate an Account object without knowing its implementation details is called *abstraction*. This is one of the most powerful software-engineering benefits of object-oriented programming. Now that we've seen class Account in action (Fig. 4.1), in the next several sections we'll explain its implementation in detail. Then, we present a UML diagram that summarizes class Account's *attributes* and *operations* in a concise graphical representation.

### 4.3.1 Account Class Declaration

Class Account (Fig. 4.2) contains a name *instance variable* (line 7) that stores the account holder's name—each Account object has its own copy of the name *instance variable*. In Section 4.9, we'll add a balance instance variable to keep track of the current balance in each Account. Class Account also contains method SetName that a program can call to store a name in an Account object, and method GetName that a program can call to obtain the name from an Account object.

```
1  // Fig. 4.2: Account.cs
2  // A simple Account class that contains a private instance
3  // variable name and public methods to Set and Get name's value.
4
5  class Account
6  {
7     private string name; // instance variable
8
9     // method that sets the account name in the object
10    public void SetName(string accountName)
11    {
12       name = accountName; // store the account name
13    }
14
15    // method that retrieves the account name from the object
16    public string GetName()
17    {
18       return name; // returns name's value to this method's caller
19    }
20 }
```

**Fig. 4.2** | A simple Account class that contains a private instance variable name and public methods to *Set* and *Get* name's value.

### 4.3.2 Keyword class and the Class Body

The class declaration begins in line 5 with

```
class Account
```

As we mentioned in Chapter 3, every class declaration contains the keyword class followed immediately by the class's name—in this case, Account. Also, each class declaration is typically stored in a file having the same name as the class and ending with the .cs filename extension, so we've placed class Account in the file Account.cs. The class's body is enclosed in a pair of braces (lines 6 and 20 of Fig. 4.2).

*Identifiers and Camel-Case Naming*

Class, property, method and variable names are all *identifiers* and by convention all use the naming schemes we discussed in Chapter 3:

- class, property and method names begin with an initial *uppercase* letter (i.e., Pascal case)
- variable names begin with an initial *lowercase* letter (i.e., camel case).

### 4.3.3 Instance Variable name of Type string

Recall from Section 1.2 that a class has attributes, implemented as instance variables. Objects of the class carry these instance variables with them throughout their lifetimes. Each object has its own copy of the class's instance variables. Normally, a class also contains methods and properties. These manipulate the instance variables belonging to particular objects of the class.

Instance variables are declared *inside* a class declaration but *outside* the bodies of the class's methods and properties. Line 7

```
private string name; // instance variable
```

declares instance variable `name` of type `string` *outside* the bodies of methods `SetName` and `GetName`. If there are many `Account` objects, each has its own `name`. Because `name` is an instance variable, it can be manipulated by each of the class's methods and properties. **Clients** of class `Account`—that is, any other code that calls the class's methods (such as class `AccountTest`'s `Main` method in Fig. 4.1)—cannot access the `name` instance variable because it's declared `private`. However, clients *can* access `Account`'s `public` methods `SetName` and `GetName`. These methods *can* access `private` instance variable `name`. We discuss `private` and `public` in Section 4.3.6, then discuss why this architecture of `private` instance variables and `public` *access methods* is powerful in more detail in Section 4.5.

**Good Programming Practice 4.1**

*We prefer to list a class's instance variables first in the class's body, so that you see the names and types of the variables before they're used in the class's methods and properties. You can list the class's instance variables anywhere in the class outside its method (and property) declarations, but scattering the instance variables can lead to hard-to-read code.*

### `null`—*the Default Initial Value for* `string` *Variables*

Every instance variable has a *default initial value*—a value provided by C# if you do not specify the instance variable's initial value. Thus, instance variables are not required to be explicitly initialized before they're used in a program—unless they must be initialized to values other than their default values. The default value for an instance variable of type `string` (like `name` in this example) is **`null`**, which we discuss further in Chapter 7 when we consider so-called *reference types*. When you use `Console.Write` or `Console.WriteLine` to display a `string` variable that contains the value `null`, no text is displayed on the screen—this is why line 13 in `Main` (Fig. 4.1) did not display a name the first time we called `myAccount`'s `GetName` method.

## 4.3.4 SetName Method

Let's walk through the code of method `SetName`'s declaration (Fig. 4.2, lines 10–13):

```
public void SetName(string accountName)
{
   name = accountName; // store the account name
}
```

The first line of each method declaration (line 10) is the *method header*. The method's *return type* (which appears to the left of the method's name) specifies the type of data the method returns to its *caller* after performing its task. The return type **`void`** (line 10) indicates that when `SetName` completes its task, it does not return (i.e., give back) any information to its *calling method*—in this example, line 18 of the `Main` method (Fig. 4.1). As you'll soon see, `Account` method `GetName` *does* return a value.

### SetName's *Parameter*

Our car analogy from Section 1.2 mentioned that pressing a car's gas pedal sends a message to the car to perform a task—make the car go faster. But *how fast* should the car accelerate? The farther down you press the pedal, the faster the car accelerates. So the message to the car includes both the task to perform and information that helps the car perform that task. This information is known as a *parameter*—the parameter's value helps the car determine how fast to accelerate. Similarly, a method can require one or more parameters that represent the data it needs to perform its task.

Method SetName declares the string parameter accountName—which receives the name that's passed to SetName as an argument. When line 18 in Fig. 4.1

```
myAccount.SetName(theName); // put theName in the myAccount object
```

executes, the *argument value* in the call's parentheses (i.e., the value stored in theName) is copied into the corresponding *parameter* (accountName) in the method's header (line 10 of Fig. 4.2). In Fig. 4.1's sample execution, we entered "Jane Green" for theName, so "Jane Green" was copied into the accountName parameter.

### SetName *Parameter List*

Parameters like accountName are declared in a *parameter list* located in the *required* parentheses following the method's name. Each parameter *must* specify a type (e.g., string) followed by a parameter name (e.g., accountName). When there are multiple parameters, they are placed in a *comma-separated list*, as in

```
(type1 name1, type2 name2, ...)
```

The number and order of *arguments* in a method call *must match* the number and order of *parameters* in the method declaration's parameter list.

### SetName *Method Body*

Every method body is delimited by an opening left brace (Fig. 4.2, line 11) and a closing right brace (line 13). Within the braces are one or more statements that perform the method's task(s). In this case, the method body contains a single statement (line 12)

```
name = accountName; // store the account name
```

that assigns the accountName parameter's value (a string) to the class's name instance variable, thus storing the account name in the object for which SetName was called—myAccount in this example's Main program.[2] After line 12 executes, program execution reaches the method's closing brace (line 13), so the method returns to its *caller*.

### *Parameters Are Local Variables*

In Chapter 3, we declared all of an app's variables in the Main method. Variables declared in a particular method's body (such as Main) are **local variables** which can be used *only* in that method. Each method can access only its own local variables, not those of other methods. When a method terminates, the values of its local variables are lost. A method's parameters also are local variables of the method.

---

2. We used different names for the SetName method's parameter (accountName) and the instance variable (name). It's common idiom in industry to use the same name for both. We'll show you how to do this without ambiguity in Section 10.4.

### 4.3.5 GetName Method

Method GetName (lines 16–19)

```
public string GetName()
{
   return name; // returns name's value to this method's caller
}
```

*returns* a particular Account object's name to the caller—a string, as specified by the method's return type. The method has an empty parameter list, so it does not require additional information to perform its task. When a method with a return type other than void is called and completes its task, it *must* return a result to its caller. A statement that calls method GetName on an Account object expects to receive the Account's name.

The **return** statement in line 18

```
return name; // returns name's value to this method's caller
```

passes the string value of instance variable name back to the caller, which can then use the returned value. For example, the statement in line 21 of Fig. 4.1

```
Console.WriteLine($"myAccount's name is: {myAccount.GetName()}");
```

uses the value returned by GetName to output the name stored in the myAccount object.

### 4.3.6 Access Modifiers private and public

The keyword **private** (line 7 of Fig. 4.2)

```
private string name; // instance variable
```

is an **access modifier**. Instance variable name is private to indicate that name is accessible *only* to class Account's methods (and other members, like properties, as you'll see in subsequent examples). This is known as *information hiding*—the instance variable name is hidden and can be used *only* in class Account's methods (SetName and GetName). Most instance variables are declared private.

This class also contains the **public** access modifier (line 10)

```
public void SetName(string accountName)
```

and line 16

```
public string GetName()
```

Methods (and other class members) that are declared public are "available to the public." They can be used

- by methods (and other members) of the class in which they're declared,
- by the class's clients—that is, methods (and other members) of any other classes (in this app, class AccountTest's Main method is the client of class Account).

In Chapter 11, we'll introduce the protected access modifier.

#### *Default Access for Class Members*

By default, everything in a class is private, unless you specify otherwise by providing access modifiers.

**Error-Prevention Tip 4.1**

*Making a class's instance variables* `private` *and its methods (and as you'll see, properties)* `public` *and accessing those instance variables only through the class's methods and properties facilitates debugging, because problems with data manipulations are localized to the methods (and properties).*

**Common Programming Error 4.1**

*An attempt by a method that's not a member of a particular class to access a* `private` *member of that class is a compilation error.*

### 4.3.7 `Account` UML Class Diagram

We'll often use UML class diagrams to summarize a class's *attributes* and *operations*. In industry, UML diagrams help systems designers specify systems in a concise, graphical, programming-language-independent manner, before programmers implement the systems in specific programming languages. Figure 4.3 presents a **UML class diagram** for class `Account` of Fig. 4.2.

**Account**

– name : string

+ SetName(accountName : string)
+ GetName() : string

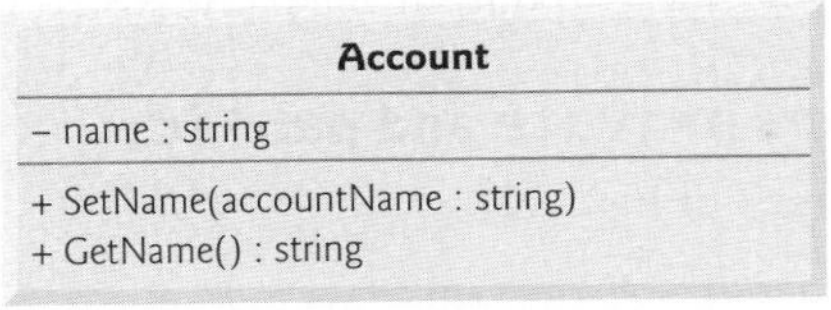

**Fig. 4.3** | UML class diagram for class `Account` of Fig. 4.2.

#### *Top Compartment*

In the UML, each class is modeled in a class diagram as a rectangle with three compartments. In this diagram the top compartment contains the *class name* `Account` centered horizontally in boldface type.

#### *Middle Compartment*

The middle compartment contains the class's attribute names, which correspond to the instance variables of the same names in C#. The single instance variable `name` in Fig. 4.2 is `private` in C#, so the UML class diagram lists a *minus sign (–) UML access modifier* before the attribute's name. Following the attribute's name are a *colon* and the *attribute type*, in this case `string`.

#### *Bottom Compartment*

The bottom compartment contains the class's **operations**, `SetName` and `GetName`, which correspond to the methods of the same names in C#. The UML models operations by listing the operation name preceded by a UML access modifier, for example, + `SetName`. This plus sign (+) indicates that `SetName` is a public operation in the UML (because it's a `public` method in C#). Operation `GetName` is also a public operation.

*Return Types*
The UML indicates an operation's return type by placing a colon and the return type *after* the parentheses following the operation name. Method `SetName` does not return a value (because it returns `void` in C#), so the UML class diagram does not specify a return type after the parentheses of this operation. Method `GetName` has a `string` return type. The UML has its own data types similar to those of C#—for simplicity, we use the C# types.

*Parameters*
The UML models a parameter by listing the parameter name, followed by a colon and the parameter type in the parentheses after the operation name. `Account` method `SetName` has a `string` parameter called `accountName`, so the class diagram lists

```
accountName : string
```

between the parentheses following the method name. Operation `GetName` does not have any parameters, so the parentheses following the operation name in the class diagram are empty, just as they are in the method's declaration in line 16 of Fig. 4.2.

## 4.4 Creating, Compiling and Running a Visual C# Project with Two Classes

When you create the project for this app, you should rename `Program.cs` to `AccountTest.cs` and add the `Account.cs` file to the project. To set up a project with two classes:

1. Create a **Console Application** as you did in Chapter 3. We named this chapter's projects `Account1`, `Account2`, `Account3` and `Account4`, respectively.
2. Rename the project's `Program.cs` file to `AccountTest.cs`. Replace the autogenerated code with class `AccountTest`'s code (Fig. 4.1).
3. Right click the project name in the **Solution Explorer** and select **Add > Class...** from the pop-up menu.
4. In the **Add New Item** dialog's **Name** field, enter the new file's name (`Account.cs`), then click **Add**. In the new `Account.cs` file, replace the auto-generated code with class `Account`'s code from Fig. 4.2.

You can open each class in the Visual Studio editor by double clicking the filename in the **Solution Explorer** window.

You must compile the classes in Figs. 4.1 and 4.2 before you can *execute* the app. This is the first time you've created an app with *multiple* classes. Class `AccountTest` has a `Main` method; class `Account` does not. The IDE automatically recognizes as the app's entry point the class that contains `Main`. When you select **Build > Build Solution** in Visual Studio, the IDE compiles all the files in the project to create the executable app. If both classes compile correctly—that is, no compilation errors are displayed—you can then run the app by typing *Ctrl* + *F5* to execute the `AccountTest` class's `Main` method. If you do not build the app before running it, typing *Ctrl* + *F5* will build the app first and run the app only if there are no compilation errors.

**Common Programming Error 4.2**

*In a given project, declaring a `Main` method in more than exactly one class results in the compilation error, "Program has more than one entry point defined."*

## 4.5 Software Engineering with *Set* and *Get* Methods

*Set* and *Get* methods can *validate* attempts to modify `private` data and control how that data is presented to the caller, respectively. These are compelling software engineering benefits. If an instance variable were `public`, any client of the class could see the data and modify it, including setting it to an *invalid* value. Also, `public` data allows client-code programmers to write code that depends on the class's data format. If the class's owner changes that format, any client code dependent on it would "break" and would need to be adjusted to the new format, making it subject to break again.

You might think that even though a client of the class cannot directly access a `private` instance variable, the client can nevertheless do whatever it wants with the variable through `public` *Set* and *Get* methods. You'd think that you could peek at the `private` data (and see exactly how it's stored in the object) any time with the `public` *Get* method and that you could modify the `private` data at will through the `public` *Set* method.

Actually, *Set* methods can be programmed to *validate* their arguments and reject any attempts to *Set* the data to bad values, such as

- a negative body temperature
- a day in March outside the range 1 through 31
- a product code not in the company's product catalog, etc.

A *Get* method can present the data in a different form, while the actual data representation remains hidden from the user. For example, a `Grade` class might store a `grade` instance variable as an `int` between 0 and 100, but a `GetGrade` method might return a letter grade as a `string`, such as `"A"` for grades between 90 and 100, `"B"` for grades between 80 and 89, …—we'll do this in Section 5.5 with a property. Tightly controlling the *access* to and *presentation* of `private` data can greatly reduce errors, while increasing the robustness, security and usability of your programs.

### *Conceptual View of an* `Account` *Object with* `private` *Data*

You can think of an `Account` object as shown in Fig. 4.4. The `private` instance variable `name` is *hidden inside* the object (represented by the inner circle containing `name`) and *guarded by an outer layer* of `public` methods (represented by the outer circle containing `GetName` and `SetName`). Any client code that needs to interact with the `Account` object can do so *only* by calling the `public` methods of the protective outer layer.

**Software Engineering Observation 4.1**

*Generally, instance variables should be `private` and methods `public`.*

**Software Engineering Observation 4.2**

*Change is the rule rather than the exception. You should anticipate that your code will be modified, and possibly often. Using `public` Set and Get methods to control access to `private` data makes programs clearer and easier to maintain.*

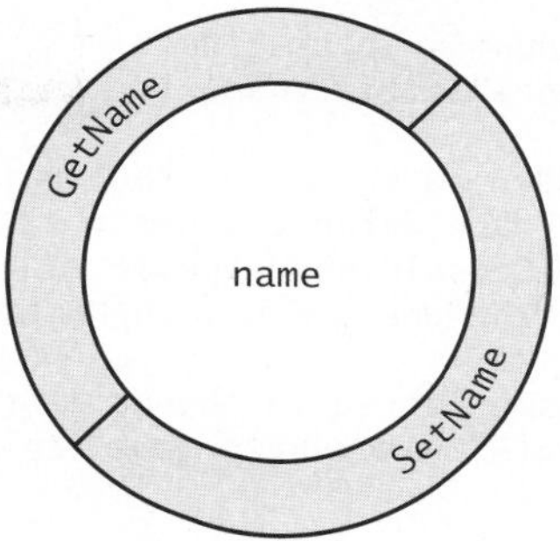


**Fig. 4.4** | Conceptual view of an Account object with its private instance variable name and guarding layer of public methods.

## 4.6 Account Class with a Property Rather Than *Set* and *Get* Methods

Our first Account class contained a private instance variable name and public methods SetName and GetName that enabled a client to assign to and retrieve from an Account's name, respectively. C# provides a more elegant solution—called **properties**—to accomplish the same tasks. A property encapsulates a **set accessor** for storing a value into a variable and a **get accessor** for getting the value of a variable.[3] In this section, we'll revisit the AccountTest class to demonstrate how to interact with an Account object containing a public Name *property*, then we'll present the updated Account class and take a detailed look at properties.

### 4.6.1 Class AccountTest Using Account's Name Property

Figure 4.5 shows the updated AccountTest class that uses class Account's Name property (declared in Fig. 4.6) to get and set an Account's name instance variable. This app produces the same output as the one in Fig. 4.1, assuming the user once again enters Jane Green when prompted to enter a name.

```
// Fig. 4.5: AccountTest.cs
// Creating and manipulating an Account object with properties.
using System;

class AccountTest
{
   static void Main()
   {
      // create an Account object and assign it to myAccount
      Account myAccount = new Account();
```

**Fig. 4.5** | Creating and manipulating an Account object with properties. (Part 1 of 2.)

3. In subsequent chapters, you'll see that properties are not required to have both a set and a get.

```
11
12           // display myAccount's initial name
13           Console.WriteLine($"Initial name is: {myAccount.Name}");
14
15           // prompt for and read the name, then put the name in the object
16           Console.Write("Please enter the name: "); // prompt
17           string theName = Console.ReadLine(); // read a line of text
18           myAccount.Name = theName; // put theName in myAccount's Name
19
20           // display the name stored in object myAccount
21           Console.WriteLine($"myAccount's name is: {myAccount.Name}");
22       }
23   }
```

```
Initial name is:
Please enter the name: Jane Green
myAccount's name is: Jane Green
```

**Fig. 4.5** | Creating and manipulating an `Account` object with properties. (Part 2 of 2.)

### *Invoking Class* `Account`*'s* `Name` *Property to Get the Name*

The `get` accessor of the `Account` class's `Name` property *gets* the account name stored in a particular `Account` object. Line 13 of Fig. 4.5

```
Console.WriteLine($"Initial name is: {myAccount.Name}");
```

displays `myAccount`'s initial name by accessing the object's `Name` property with the expression `myAccount.Name`. To access a property, you specify the object's name (`myAccount`), followed by the member-access operator (`.`) and the property's name (`Name`). When used to get the account's name, this notation *implicitly* executes the property's `get` accessor, which returns the account's name.

When `Main` accesses the `Name` property in line 13:

1. The app transfers program execution from the expression `myAccount.Name` (line 13 in `Main`) to the property `Name`'s `get` accessor).
2. Next, the `Name` property's `get` accessor performs its task—that is, it *returns* (i.e., gives back) the value of `myAccount`'s `name` instance variable to line 13 where the property was accessed.
3. `Console.WriteLine` displays the `string` returned by the `Name` property's `get` accessor—which was inserted into the interpolated `string` in place of the expression `myAccount.Name`—then the program continues executing at line 16 in `Main`.

As in Fig. 4.1, line 13 in Fig. 4.5 does not display a name, because we have not yet stored a name in the `myAccount` object.

### *Invoking Class* `Account`*'s* `Name` *Property to Set the Name*

Next, lines 16–17 prompt for and input a name. The `set` accessor `Account` class's `Name` property *sets* an account name in a particular `Account` object. Line 18

```
myAccount.Name = theName; // put theName in myAccount's Name
```

assigns to myAccounts's Name property the string entered by the user in line 17. When property Name is invoked by the expression myAccount.Name on the left of an assignment:

1. The app transfers program execution from line 18 in Main to Name's set accessor.
2. Property Name's set accessor performs its task—that is, it stores in the myAccount object's name instance variable the string value that was assigned to property Name in Main (line 18).
3. When Name's set accessor completes execution, program execution returns to where the Name property was accessed (line 18 in Main), then execution continues at line 21.

To demonstrate that myAccount now contains the name the user entered, line 21

```
Console.WriteLine($"myAccount's name is: {myAccount.Name}");
```

accesses myAccounts's Name property again, which uses the property's get accessor to obtain the name instance variable's new value. As you can see, the last line of the program's output displays the name input from the user in line 17.

### 4.6.2 Account Class with an Instance Variable and a Property

The updated Account class replaces the GetName and SetName methods from Fig. 4.2 with the property Name (lines 10–20 of Fig. 4.6). The property's get and set accessors handle the details of *getting* and *setting* data, respectively. Unlike method names, the accessor names get and set each begin with a lowercase letter.

```
1  // Fig. 4.6: Account.cs
2  // Account class that replaces public methods SetName
3  // and GetName with a public Name property.
4
5  class Account
6  {
7     private string name; // instance variable
8
9     // property to get and set the name instance variable
10    public string Name
11    {
12       get // returns the corresponding instance variable's value
13       {
14          return name; // returns the value of name to the client code
15       }
16       set // assigns a new value to the corresponding instance variable
17       {
18          name = value; // value is implicitly declared and initialized
19       }
20    }
21 }
```

**Fig. 4.6** | Account class that replaces public methods SetName and GetName with a public Name property.

### *Property* Name*'s Declaration*

Line 10

```
public string Name
```

begins the `Name` **property declaration**, which specifies that

- the property is `public` so it can be used by the class's clients,
- the property's type is `string` and
- the property's name is `Name`.

By convention, a property's identifier is the capitalized identifier of the instance variable that it manipulates—`Name` is the property that represents instance variable `name`. C# is case sensitive, so `Name` and `name` are distinct identifiers. The property's body is enclosed in the braces at lines 11 and 20.

### *Property* Name*'s* get *Accessor*

The `get` accessor (lines 12–15) performs the same task as method `GetName` in Fig. 4.2. A `get` accessor begins with the keyword **`get`**, and its body is delimited by braces. Like method `GetName`, the `get` accessor's body contains a `return` statement (line 14) that returns the value of an `Account`'s `name` instance variable. So, in line 13 of Fig. 4.5

```
Console.WriteLine($"Initial name is: {myAccount.Name}");
```

the expression `myAccount.Name` gets the value of `myAccount`'s instance variable `name`. The property notation allows the client to *think of the property as the underlying data*, but the client still *cannot* directly manipulate the `private` instance variable `name`. Keyword `get` is a *contextual keyword*, because it's a keyword only in a property's context (that is, its body)—in other contexts, `get` can be used as an identifier.

### *Property* Name*'s* set *Accessor*

The `set` accessor (lines 16–19, Fig. 4.6) begins with the identifier **`set`** followed by its body, which is delimited by braces. Method `SetName` (Fig. 4.2) declared a parameter `accountName` to receive the new name to store in an `Account` object—a `set` accessor uses the keyword **`value`** (line 18, Fig. 4.6) for the same purpose. `value` is *implicitly* declared and initialized for you with the value that the client code *assigns* to the property. So, in line 18 of Fig. 4.5

```
myAccount.Name = theName; // put theName in myAccount's Name
```

`value` is initialized with `theName` (the `string` entered by the user). Property `Name`'s `set` accessor simply assigns `value` to the instance variable `name`—we'll show a `set` accessor that performs *validation* in Fig. 4.11. Like `get`, the keywords `set` and `value` are *contextual keywords*—`set` is a keyword only in a property's context and `value` is a keyword only in a `set` accessor's context.

**Error-Prevention Tip 4.2**

*Although contextual keywords, like* `value` *in a* `set` *accessor, can be used as identifiers in some contexts, we prefer not to do so.*

The statements inside the property in lines 14 and 18 (Fig. 4.6) each access `name` even though it was declared outside the property declaration. We can use instance variable `name` in class `Account`'s property (and other properties and methods, if there are any), because `name` is an instance variable in the same class.

### 4.6.3 `Account` UML Class Diagram with a Property

Figure 4.7 presents a UML class diagram for class `Account` of Fig. 4.6. We model C# properties in the UML as attributes. The property `Name` is listed as a *public* attribute—as indicated by the plus (+) sign—followed by the word "property" in **guillemets** (« and »). Using descriptive words in guillemets (called **stereotypes** in the UML) helps distinguish properties from other attributes and operations. The UML indicates the type of the property by placing a colon and a type after the property name.

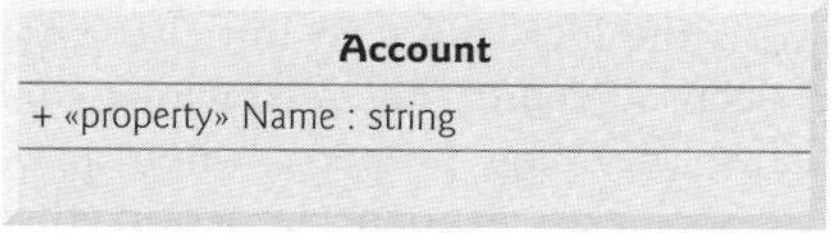

| Account |
|---|
| + «property» Name : string |
| |

**Fig. 4.7** | UML class diagram for class `Account` of Fig. 4.6.

A class diagram helps you *design* a class, so it's not required to show every *implementation* detail. Since an instance variable that's manipulated by a property is really an implementation detail of that property, our class diagram does *not* show the `name` instance variable. A programmer implementing the `Account` class based on this class diagram would create the instance variable `name` as part of the implementation process (as we did in Fig. 4.6). Similarly, a property's `get` and `set` accessors are implementation details, so they're not listed in the UML diagram.

## 4.7 Auto-Implemented Properties

In Fig. 4.6, we created an `Account` class with a `private` `name` instance variable and a `public` property `Name` to enable client code to access the `name`. When you look at the `Name` property's definition (Fig. 4.6, lines 10–20), notice that the `get` accessor simply returns `private` instance variable `name`'s value and the `set` accessor simply assigns a value to the instance variable—no other logic appears in the accessors. For such simple cases, C# provides **auto-implemented properties.**

With an auto-implemented property, the C# compiler automatically creates a *hidden* `private` instance variable, and the `get` and `set` accessors for *getting* and *setting* that hidden instance variable. This enables you to implement the property trivially, which is handy when you're first designing a class. If you later decide to include other logic in the `get` or `set` accessors, you can simply implement the property and an instance variable using the techniques shown in Fig. 4.6. To use an auto-implemented property in the `Account` class of Fig. 4.6, you'd replace the `private` instance variable at line 7 and the property at lines 10–20 with the following *single* line of code:

```
public string Name { get; set; }
```

We'll use this technique for the `Name` property in Fig. 4.8.

**Software Engineering Observation 4.3**

*In programming languages that do not have property syntax, you think of a class's attributes as instance variables. With C# property syntax, you should think of the properties themselves as the class's attributes.*

## 4.8 Account Class: Initializing Objects with Constructors

As mentioned in Section 4.6, when an object of class `Account` (Fig. 4.6) is created, its `string` instance variable `name` is initialized to `null` by *default*. But what if you want to provide an actual name when you *create* an `Account` object?

Each class you declare optionally can provide a *constructor* with parameters that can be used to initialize an object when it's created. C# *requires* a constructor call for *every* object that's created, so this is the ideal point to initialize an object's instance variables. The next example enhances class `Account` (Fig. 4.8) with a constructor that can receive a name and use it to initialize the `Name` property when an `Account` object is created (Fig. 4.9). Now that you've seen class `Account` in action, this chapter's two remaining examples present class `Account` before class `AccountTest`.

This version of class `Account` replaces the `private` `name` instance variable and the `public` `Name` property from Fig. 4.6 with a `public` *auto-implemented* `Name` property (Fig. 4.8, line 6). This property automatically creates a hidden `private` instance variable to store the property's value.

```
1  // Fig. 4.8: Account.cs
2  // Account class with a constructor that initializes an Account's name.
3
4  class Account
5  {
6     public string Name { get; set; } // auto-implemented property
7
8     // constructor sets the Name property to parameter accountName's value
9     public Account(string accountName) // constructor name is class name
10    {
11       Name = accountName;
12    }
13 }
```

**Fig. 4.8** | `Account` class with a constructor that initializes an `Account`'s name.

### 4.8.1 Declaring an Account Constructor for Custom Object Initialization

When you declare a class, you can provide your own constructor to specify *custom initialization* for objects of your class. For example, you might want to specify a name for an `Account` object when the object is created, as in line 11 of Fig. 4.9:

```
Account account1 = new Account("Jane Green");
```

In this case, the `string` argument `"Jane Green"` is passed to the `Account` object's constructor and used to initialize the `Account`'s name. A constructor's identifier *must* be the class's name. The preceding statement requires an Account constructor that can receive a string. Figure 4.8 contains a modified Account class with such a constructor.

### *Account Constructor Declaration*

Let's walk through the code of the constructor's declaration (Fig. 4.8, lines 9–12):

```
public Account(string accountName) // constructor name is class name
{
   Name = accountName;
}
```

We refer to the first line of each constructor declaration (line 9 in this case) as the *constructor header*. This constructor receives the string parameter accountName—which represents the name that's passed to the constructor as an argument. An important difference between constructors and methods is that *constructors cannot specify a return type* (not even void). Normally, constructors are declared public so they can be used by the class's client code to initialize objects of the class.

### *Constructor Body*

A constructor's *body* is delimited by a pair of *braces* containing one or more statements that perform the constructor's task(s). In this case, the body contains one statement (line 11) that assigns parameter accountName's value (a string) to the class's Name *property*, thus storing the account name in the object. After line 11 executes, the constructor has completed its task, so it returns to the line of code containing the object-creation expression that invoked the constructor. As you'll soon see, the statements in lines 11–12 of Main (Fig. 4.9) each call this constructor.

## 4.8.2 Class AccountTest: Initializing Account Objects When They're Created

The AccountTest program (Fig. 4.9) initializes two Account objects using the constructor. Line 11 creates and initializes the Account object account1. Keyword new requests memory from the system to store the Account object, then implicitly calls the class's constructor to *initialize* the object. The call is indicated by the parentheses after the class name, which contain the *argument* "Jane Green" that's used to initialize the new object's name. Line 11 then assigns the initialized object to the variable account1. Line 12 repeats this process, passing the argument "John Blue" to initialize the name for account2. Lines 15–16 use each object's Name property to obtain the names and show that they were indeed initialized when the objects were *created*. The output shows *different* names, confirming that each Account maintains its *own* name.

```
1  // Fig. 4.9: AccountTest.cs
2  // Using the Account constructor to set an Account's name
3  // when an Account object is created.
4  using System;
5
```

**Fig. 4.9** | Using the Account constructor to set an Account's name when an Account object is created. (Part 1 of 2.)

```
class AccountTest
{
   static void Main()
   {
      // create two Account objects
      Account account1 = new Account("Jane Green");
      Account account2 = new Account("John Blue");

      // display initial value of name for each Account
      Console.WriteLine($"account1 name is: {account1.Name}");
      Console.WriteLine($"account2 name is: {account2.Name}");
   }
}
```

```
account1 name is: Jane Green
account2 name is: John Blue
```

**Fig. 4.9** | Using the `Account` constructor to set an `Account`'s name when an `Account` object is created. (Part 2 of 2.)

### *Default Constructor*

Recall that line 10 of Fig. 4.5

```
Account myAccount = new Account();
```

used `new` to create an `Account` object. The *empty* parentheses in the expression

```
new Account()
```

indicate a call to the class's **default constructor**—in any class that does *not* explicitly declare a constructor, the compiler provides a `public` default constructor (which always has no parameters). When a class has only the default constructor, the class's instance variables are initialized to their *default values*:

- 0 for numeric simple types,
- `false` for simple type `bool` and
- `null` for all other types.

In Section 10.5, you'll learn that classes can have multiple constructors through a process called overloading.

### *There's No Default Constructor in a Class That Declares a Constructor*

If you declare one or more constructors for a class, the compiler will *not* create a *default constructor* for that class. In that case, you will not be able to create an `Account` object with the expression `new Account()` as we did in Fig. 4.5—unless one of the custom constructors you declare takes *no* parameters.

**Software Engineering Observation 4.4**

*Unless default initialization of your class's instance variables is acceptable, provide a custom constructor to ensure that your instance variables are properly initialized with meaningful values when each new object of your class is created.*

*Adding the Constructor to Class* **Account***'s UML Class Diagram*

The UML class diagram of Fig. 4.10 models class `Account` of Fig. 4.8, which has a constructor with a `string accountName` parameter. The UML models constructors as operations in the *third* compartment of a class diagram. To distinguish a constructor from the class's other operations, the UML requires that the word "constructor" be enclosed in guillemets (« and ») and placed before the constructor's name. It's customary to list constructors *before* other operations in the third compartment. In Fig. 4.14, you'll see a class diagram with both a constructor and an operation in the third compartment.

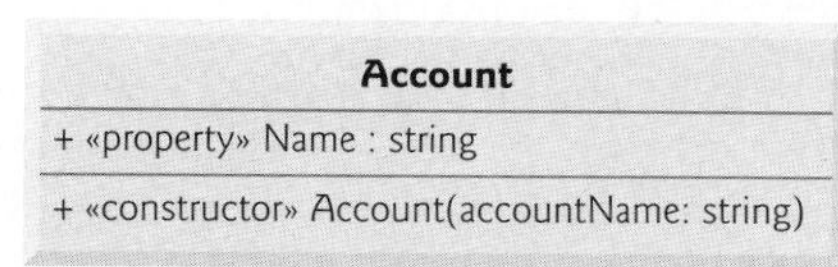


**Fig. 4.10** | UML class diagram for `Account` class of Fig. 4.8.

## 4.9 Account Class with a Balance; Processing Monetary Amounts

In this section, we'll declare an `Account` class that maintains an `Account`'s *balance* in addition to its name. Most account balances are not whole numbers (such as 0, –22 and 1024), rather they're numbers that include a decimal point, such as 99.99 or –20.15. For this reason, class `Account` represents the account balance using type **`decimal`**, which is designed to precisely represent numbers with decimal points, especially *monetary amounts*.

### 4.9.1 Account Class with a decimal balance Instance Variable

A typical bank services *many* accounts, each with its *own* balance, so our next `Account` class (Fig. 4.11) maintains a bank account's

- name—as the auto-implemented `Name` property (line 6)—and
- balance—as the `private decimal` instance variable `balance` (line 7) and a corresponding `public Balance` property (lines 17–32). We use a fully implemented `Balance` property here so we can ensure that the `set` accessor's argument is valid before assigning it to the `balance` instance variable.

A `decimal` instance variable is initialized to zero by default. Every instance (i.e., object) of class `Account` contains its *own* name and balance.

```
1  // Fig. 4.11: Account.cs
2  // Account class with a balance and a Deposit method.
3
4  class Account
5  {
```

**Fig. 4.11** | `Account` class with a `decimal` instance variable `balance` and a `Balance` property and `Deposit` method that each perform validation. (Part 1 of 2.)

```
6       public string Name { get; set; } // auto-implemented property
7       private decimal balance; // instance variable
8
9       // Account constructor that receives two parameters
10      public Account(string accountName, decimal initialBalance)
11      {
12         Name = accountName;
13         Balance = initialBalance; // Balance's set accessor validates
14      }
15
16      // Balance property with validation
17      public decimal Balance
18      {
19         get
20         {
21            return balance;
22         }
23         private set // can be used only within the class
24         {
25            // validate that the balance is greater than 0.0; if it's not,
26            // instance variable balance keeps its prior value
27            if (value > 0.0m) // m indicates that 0.0 is a decimal literal
28            {
29               balance = value;
30            }
31         }
32      }
33
34      // method that deposits (adds) only a valid amount to the balance
35      public void Deposit(decimal depositAmount)
36      {
37         if (depositAmount > 0.0m) // if the depositAmount is valid
38         {
39            Balance = Balance + depositAmount; // add it to the balance
40         }
41      }
42   }
```

**Fig. 4.11** | Account class with a decimal instance variable balance and a Balance property and Deposit method that each perform validation. (Part 2 of 2.)

#### `Account` *Class Two-Parameter Constructor*

It's common for someone opening an account to deposit money immediately, so the constructor (lines 10–14) now receives a second parameter—`initialBalance` of type `decimal` that represents the starting balance. Line 13 assigns `initialBalance` to the property `Balance`, invoking `Balance`'s `set` accessor to ensure that the `initialBalance` argument is valid before assigning a value to the instance variable `balance`.

#### `Account` *Property* `Balance`

Property `Balance` (lines 17–32) of type `decimal` provides a `get` accessor, which allows clients of the class to obtain a particular `Account` object's `balance`. The property also provides a `set` accessor.

In Fig. 4.6, class Account defined a Name property in which the set accessor simply assigned the value received in its implicit parameter value to class Account's instance variable name. The Name property did *not* ensure that name contains only *valid* data.

The Balance property's set accessor performs **validation** (also known as **validity checking**). Line 27 (Fig. 4.11) ensures that the set accessor's implicit value parameter is greater than 0.0m—the letter m (or M) indicates that 0.0 is a **decimal literal**.[4] If value is greater than 0.0m, the amount stored in value is assigned to instance variable balance (line 29). Otherwise, balance is left unchanged—we'll say more about error processing throughout the book.

Though we validated the balance in this example, we did not validate the name. Names are normally quite "free form"—there's a wide variety of acceptable name formats. Often when you fill out a form, you're asked to limit a name to a certain number of characters. In Chapter 16, Strings and Characters: A Deeper Look, you'll learn how to check a string's length, so that you can validate strings by checking that they're not too long.

### *set and get Accessors with Different Access Modifiers*

By default, a property's get and set accessors have the *same* access as the property—e.g., public property Name's accessors are public. It's possible to declare the get and set accessors with *different* access modifiers. In this case, one of the accessors must *implicitly* have the *same* access as the property and the other must be *explicitly declared* with a *more restrictive* access modifier than the property. We declared the Balance property's set accessor private—this indicates that it may be used only in class Account, not by the class's clients. This enables us to ensure that once an Account object exists, its balance can be modified *only* by method Deposit.

**Error-Prevention Tip 4.3**

*The benefits of data integrity are not automatic simply because instance variables are made private—you must provide appropriate validity checking and report the errors.*

**Error-Prevention Tip 4.4**

*set accessors that set the values of private data should verify that the intended new values are proper; if they're not, the set accessors should leave the instance variables unchanged and indicate an error. We demonstrate how to indicate errors by throwing exceptions in Chapter 10.*

### *Account Class Deposit Method*

The public method Deposit (lines 35–41 of Fig. 4.11) enables the client code to deposit money into an Account, thus increasing its balance. Line 35 indicates that

- the method does not return any information to its caller (as indicated by the return type void) and
- receives one parameter named depositAmount—a decimal value.

The depositAmount is *added* to the balance *only* if the parameter's value is *valid*—that is, it's greater than 0.0m as specified in line 37. Line 39 first adds the current Balance and

4. The m is required to indicate a decimal literal. C# treats numeric literals with decimal points as type double by default, and doubles and decimals cannot be intermixed. We introduce type double in Chapter 5.

depositAmount, forming a *temporary* sum which is *then* assigned to the Balance property. The property's set accessor then *replaces* instance variable balance's prior value (recall that addition has a *higher* precedence than the assignment operator). So line 39 uses the Balance property's get accessor on the right side of the assignment and the set accessor on the left side. It's important to understand that the calculation on the right side of the assignment operator in line 39 does *not* modify the instance variable balance—that's why the assignment is necessary.

**Software Engineering Observation 4.5**

*When implementing a method of a class, although it's possible for the method to access the class's instance variables directly, always use the class's properties for that purpose. In Chapter 10, we'll take a deeper look at this issue.*

### 4.9.2 AccountTest Class That Uses Account Objects with Balances

Class AccountTest (Fig. 4.12) creates two Account objects (lines 9–10) and initializes them with a *valid* balance of 50.00m and an *invalid* balance of -7.53m, respectively—for the purpose of our examples, we assume that balances must be greater than or equal to zero. The calls to method Console.WriteLine in lines 13–16 output the account names and initial balances, which are obtained from each Account's Name and Balance properties.

```
1  // Fig. 4.12: AccountTest.cs
2  // Reading and writing monetary amounts with Account objects.
3  using System;
4
5  class AccountTest
6  {
7     static void Main()
8     {
9        Account account1 = new Account("Jane Green", 50.00m);
10       Account account2 = new Account("John Blue", -7.53m);
11
12       // display initial balance of each object
13       Console.WriteLine(
14          $"{account1.Name}'s balance: {account1.Balance:C}");
15       Console.WriteLine(
16          $"{account2.Name}'s balance: {account2.Balance:C}");
17
18       // prompt for then read input
19       Console.Write("\nEnter deposit amount for account1: ");
20       decimal depositAmount = decimal.Parse(Console.ReadLine());
21       Console.WriteLine(
22          $"adding {depositAmount:C} to account1 balance\n");
23       account1.Deposit(depositAmount); // add to account1's balance
24
25       // display balances
26       Console.WriteLine(
27          $"{account1.Name}'s balance: {account1.Balance:C}");
28       Console.WriteLine(
29          $"{account2.Name}'s balance: {account2.Balance:C}");
```

**Fig. 4.12** | Reading and writing monetary amounts with Account objects. (Part 1 of 2.)

```
30
31          // prompt for then read input
32          Console.Write("\nEnter deposit amount for account2: ");
33          depositAmount = decimal.Parse(Console.ReadLine());
34          Console.WriteLine(
35             $"adding {depositAmount:C} to account2 balance\n");
36          account2.Deposit(depositAmount); // add to account2's balance
37
38          // display balances
39          Console.WriteLine(
40             $"{account1.Name}'s balance: {account1.Balance:C}");
41          Console.WriteLine(
42             $"{account2.Name}'s balance: {account2.Balance:C}");
43       }
44    }
```

```
Jane Green's balance: $50.00
John Blue's balance: $0.00

Enter deposit amount for account1: 25.53
adding $25.53 to account1 balance

Jane Green's balance: $75.53
John Blue's balance: $0.00

Enter deposit amount for account2: 123.45
adding $123.45 to account2 balance

Jane Green's balance: $75.53
John Blue's balance: $123.45
```

**Fig. 4.12** | Reading and writing monetary amounts with `Account` objects. (Part 2 of 2.)

### *Displaying the* `Account` *Objects' Initial Balances*

When line 14 accesses `account1`'s `Balance` property, the value of `account1`'s `balance` instance variable is returned from line 21 of Fig. 4.11 and inserted into the interpolated `string` at line 14 of Fig. 4.12 for display. Similarly, when line 16 accesses `account2`'s `Balance` property, the value of `account2`'s `balance` instance variable is returned from line 21 of Fig. 4.11 and inserted into the interpolated `string` at line 16 of Fig. 4.12 for display. The `balance` of `account2` is initially `0.00`, because the constructor rejected the attempt to start `account2` with a *negative* `balance`, so the `balance` instance variable retains its default initial value.

### `string` *Interpolation Expressions with Formatting*

This app displays each `Account`'s `balance` as a monetary amount. You can specify formatting in a C# 6 `string` interpolation expression by following the value in the braces with a colon and a **format specifier**. For example, in line 14, the interpolation expression 6

```
{account1.Balance:C}
```

uses the **format specifier** `C` to format `account1.Balance` as *currency*. The Windows culture settings on the user's machine determine the format for displaying currency amounts, such as the commas vs. periods for separating thousands, millions, etc. For example,

- 50 displays as $50.00 in the United States (U.S.), as 50,00 e (e for euros) in Germany and as ¥50 in Japan.
- 4382.51 displays as $4,382.51 in the U.S., as 4.382,51 e in Germany and as ¥4,382 in Japan.
- 1254827.40 displays as $1,254,827.40 in the U.S., as 1.254.827,40 e in Germany and as ¥1,254,827 in Japan.

Figure 4.13 lists additional format specifiers.

| Format specifier | Description |
|---|---|
| C or c | Formats the string as currency. Includes an appropriate currency symbol ($ in the U.S.) next to the number. Separates digits with an appropriate *separator character* (in the U.S. its a comma between every three digits for thousands, millions, etc.) and sets the number of decimal places to two by default. |
| D or d | Formats the string as a whole number (integer types only). |
| N or n | Formats the string with a thousands separator and a default of two decimal places. |
| E or e | Formats the number using scientific notation with a default of six decimal places. |
| F or f | Formats the string with a fixed number of decimal places (two by default). |
| G or g | Formats the number normally with decimal places or using scientific notation, depending on context. If a format item does not contain a format specifier, format G is assumed implicitly. |
| X or x | Formats the string as hexadecimal (base 16 numbers; we discuss these in the online Number Systems appendix). |

**Fig. 4.13** | string format specifiers.

### *Reading a* **decimal** *Value from the User*

Line 19 (Fig. 4.12) prompts the user to enter a deposit amount for account1. Line 20 declares *local* variable depositAmount to store each deposit amount entered by the user. Unlike *instance* variables (such as name and balance in class Account), *local* variables (like depositAmount in Main) are *not* initialized by default, so they normally must be initialized explicitly. As you'll learn momentarily, variable depositAmount's initial value will be determined by the user's input.

**Common Programming Error 4.3**

*The C# compiler will issue the compilation error* "Use of unassigned local variable 'variableName'" *if you attempt to use the value of an uninitialized local variable—in the error message,* variableName *will be the actual variable name. This helps you avoid dangerous execution-time logic errors. It's always better to get the errors out of your programs at compilation time rather than execution time.*

Line 20 obtains the input from the user by calling the Console class's ReadLine method, then passing the string entered by the user to type decimal's **Parse** method, which returns the decimal value in this string—each simple type has a Parse method. Lines 21–22 display the deposit amount in currency format.

*Making a Deposit*
Line 23 calls object `account1`'s `Deposit` method and supplies `depositAmount` as the method's argument. The method then adds the parameter's value to the `Balance` property (line 39 of Fig. 4.11). Then lines 26–29 in Fig. 4.12 output the balances of both `Accounts` again to show that *only* `account1`'s `balance` instance variable changed.

*Reading a* **`decimal`** *Value and Depositing into* **`account2`**
Line 32 prompts the user to enter a deposit amount for `account2`. Line 33 obtains the input from the user by calling method `Console.ReadLine` and passing the return value to type `decimal`'s `Parse` method. Lines 34–35 display the deposit amount. Line 36 calls object `account2`'s `Deposit` method and supplies `depositAmount` as the method's argument. Then, the method adds that value to `account2`'s `Balance` property. Finally, lines 39–42 output the `Balances` of both `Accounts` again to show that *only* `account2`'s `balance` instance variable changed.

*UML Class Diagram for Class* **`Account`**
The class diagram in Fig. 4.14 concisely models class `Account` of Fig. 4.11. The diagram models in its second compartment the `public` properties `Name` of type `string` and `Balance` of type `decimal`. Class `Account`'s constructor is modeled in the third compartment with parameters `name` of type `string` and `initialBalance` of type `decimal`. The class's `public` `Deposit` operation also is modeled in the third compartment—`Deposit` has a `depositAmount` parameter of type `decimal`. Method `Deposit` does not return a value (because it returns `void` in C#), so the UML class diagram does not specify a return type for this operation.

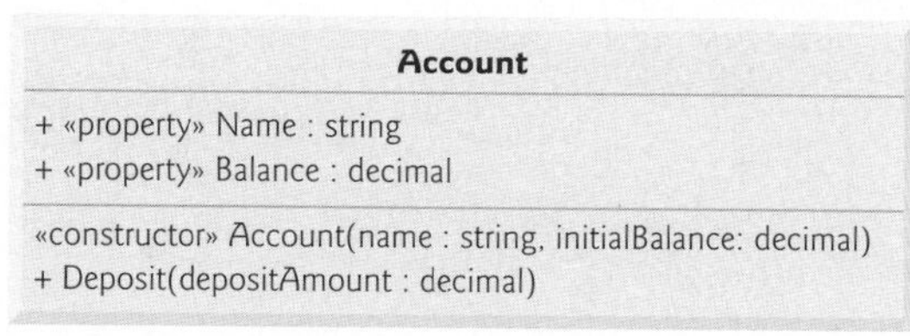


**Fig. 4.14** | UML class diagram for `Account` class of Fig. 4.11.

## 4.10 Wrap-Up

In this chapter, we discussed the object-oriented programming concepts of classes, objects, methods, instance variables, properties and constructors—these will be used in most substantial C# apps you create. You declared instance variables of a class to maintain data for each object of the class and declared *Set* and *Get* methods for operating on that data. We demonstrated how to call methods to perform their tasks and how to pass information to methods as arguments. Next, we showed C#'s elegant property syntax for setting and getting data, and we demonstrated how to access properties to execute their `set` and `get` accessors. We discussed the differences between local variables of a method and instance variables of a class and that only instance variables are initialized automatically. You learned how to create auto-implemented properties that simply `get` or `set` an instance variable without any additional logic in the accessors' declarations. You learned about type `decimal` for precise manipulation of numbers with decimal points, such as monetary amounts.

We showed how to create UML class diagrams that model the constructors, methods, properties and attributes of classes. You learned the value of declaring instance variables `private` and using `public` properties to manipulate them. For example, we demonstrated how `set` accessors in properties can be used to validate an instance variable's potential new value before modifying the variable's value.

In Chapter 5, we begin our introduction to control statements, which specify the order in which an app's actions are performed. You'll use these in your methods and properties to help specify how they should perform their tasks.

# 5

# Control Statements: Part 1

## Objectives

In this chapter you'll:

- Use the `if` and `if`...`else` selection statements to choose between actions.
- Use the `while` statement to execute statements repeatedly.
- Use counter-controlled iteration and sentinel-controlled iteration.
- Use the increment, decrement and compound assignment operators.
- Use type `decimal` for precise monetary amounts and calculations.

Outline



## 5.1 Introduction

In this chapter, we discuss C#'s `if` statement in additional detail and introduce the `if...else` and `while` statements—all of these building blocks allow you to specify the logic required for methods and properties to perform their tasks. We also introduce the compound assignment operators and the increment and decrement operators. Finally, we discuss additional details of C#'s simple types.

## 5.2 Control Structures

Normally, statements execute one after the other in the order in which they're written. This process is called **sequential execution**. Various C# statements enable you to specify that the next statement to execute is *not* necessarily the next one in sequence. This is called **transfer of control**.

During the 1960s, it became clear that the indiscriminate use of transfers of control was the root of much difficulty experienced by software development groups. The blame was pointed at the **goto statement** (used in most programming languages of the time), which allows you to specify a transfer of control to one of a wide range of destinations in a program.

The research of Bohm and Jacopini[1] had demonstrated that programs could be written *without* any `goto` statements. The challenge for programmers of the era was to shift their styles to "goto-less programming." The term **structured programming** became almost synonymous with "goto elimination." Not until the 1970s did most programmers start taking structured programming seriously. The results were impressive. Software development groups reported shorter development times, more frequent on-time delivery of systems and more frequent within-budget completion of software projects. The key to these successes was that structured programs were clearer, easier to debug and modify, and more likely to be bug free in the first place.

Bohm and Jacopini's work demonstrated that all programs could be written in terms of only three control structures—the **sequence structure**, the **selection structure** and the **iteration structure**. We'll discuss how each of these is implemented in C#.

### 5.2.1 Sequence Structure

The *sequence structure* is built into C#. Unless directed otherwise, C# statements execute one after the other in the order in which they're written—that is, in sequence. The UML **activity diagram** in Fig. 5.1 illustrates a typical sequence structure in which two calculations are performed in order. C# lets you have as many actions as you want in a sequence structure.

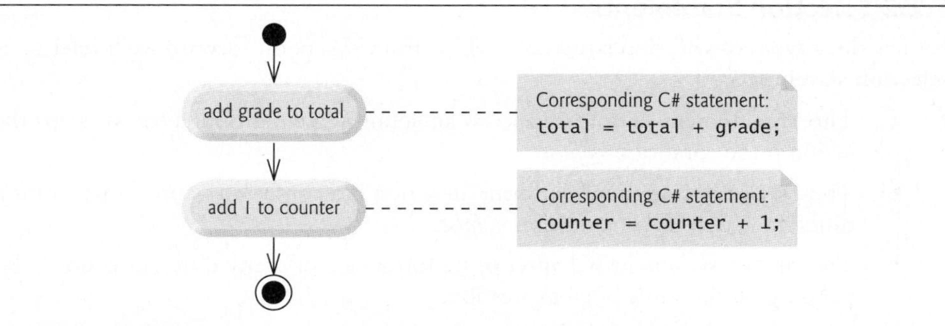


**Fig. 5.1** | Sequence structure activity diagram.

An activity diagram models the **workflow** (also called the **activity**) of a portion of a software system. Such workflows may include a portion of an algorithm, like the sequence structure in Fig. 5.1. Activity diagrams are composed of symbols, such as

- **action-state symbols** (rectangles with their left and right sides replaced with outward arcs),
- **diamonds** and
- **small circles.**

These symbols are connected by **transition arrows**, which represent the *flow of the activity*—that is, the *order* in which the actions should occur.

1. C. Bohm and G. Jacopini, "Flow Diagrams, Turing Machines, and Languages with Only Two Formation Rules," *Communications of the ACM*, Vol. 9, No. 5, May 1966, pp. 336–371.

Activity diagrams help you develop and represent algorithms. We use the UML in this chapter and the next to show the flow of control in control statements.

Consider the sequence-structure activity diagram in Fig. 5.1. It contains two **action states**, each containing an **action expression**—for example, "add grade to total" or "add 1 to counter"—that specifies a particular action to perform. The arrows in the activity diagram represent **transitions**, which indicate the *order* in which the actions represented by the action states occur. The portion of the app that implements the activities illustrated in Fig. 5.1 first adds `grade` to `total`, then adds `1` to `counter`.

The **solid circle** at the top of the activity diagram represents the **initial state**—the *beginning* of the workflow *before* the app performs the modeled actions. The **solid circle surrounded by a hollow circle** at the bottom of the diagram represents the **final state**—the *end* of the workflow *after* the app performs its actions.

Figure 5.1 also includes rectangles with the upper-right corners folded over. These are UML **notes** (like comments in C#) that describe the purpose of symbols in the diagram. Figure 5.1 uses UML notes to show the C# code associated with each action state. A **dotted line** connects each note with the element that the note describes. Activity diagrams normally do *not* show the C# code that implements the activity. We do this here to illustrate how the diagram relates to C# code.

### 5.2.2 Selection Statements

C# has three types of selection structures, which from this point forward we'll refer to as **selection statements**:

- The **`if` statement** performs (selects) an action if a condition is *true* or skips the action if the condition is *false*.
- The **`if...else` statement** performs an action if a condition is *true* or performs a different action if the condition is *false*.
- The `switch` statement (Chapter 6) performs one of many different actions, depending on the value of an expression.

The `if` statement is called a **single-selection statement** because it selects or ignores a single action (or group of actions). The `if...else` statement is called a **double-selection statement** because it selects between *two* different actions (or groups of actions). The `switch` statement is called a **multiple-selection statement** because it selects among *many* different actions (or groups of actions).

### 5.2.3 Iteration Statements

C# provides four **iteration statements** that enable programs to perform statements repeatedly as long as a condition (called the **loop-continuation condition**) remains *true*. The iteration statements are the `while`, `do...while`, `for` and `foreach` statements. (Chapter 6 presents the `do...while` and `for` statements. Chapter 8 discusses the `foreach` statement.) The `while`, `for` and `foreach` statements perform the action (or group of actions) in their bodies *zero or more times*. The `do...while` statement performs the action (or group of actions) in its body *one or more times*. The words `if`, `else`, `switch`, `while`, `do`, `for` and `foreach` are C# keywords.

### 5.2.4 Summary of Control Statements

C# has only three kinds of control statements: the *sequence*, *selection* (three types) and *iteration* (four types). Every app is formed by combining as many of these statements as is appropriate for the algorithm the app implements. We can model each control statement as an activity diagram. Like Fig. 5.1, each diagram contains an initial state and a final state that represent a control statement's entry point and exit point, respectively. **Single-entry/single-exit control statements** make it easy to build programs—we simply connect the exit point of one to the entry point of the next. We call this **control-statement stacking.** There's only one other way in which control statements may be connected—**control-statement nesting**—in which one control statement appears *inside* another. Thus, algorithms in C# apps are constructed from only three kinds of control statements, combined in only two ways. This is the essence of simplicity.

## 5.3 `if` Single-Selection Statement

We introduced the `if` single-selection statement briefly in Section 3.8. Apps use selection statements to choose among alternative courses of action. For example, suppose that the passing grade on an exam is 60. The statement

```
if (studentGrade >= 60)
{
   Console.WriteLine("Passed");
}
```

determines whether the *condition* "`studentGrade >= 60`" is *true*. If so, "`Passed`" is displayed, and the next statement in order is performed. If the condition is *false*, the `Console.Writeln` call is ignored, and the next statement in order is performed.

#### `bool` *Simple Type*

You saw in Chapter 3 that decisions can be based on conditions containing relational or equality operators. Actually, a decision can be based on *any* expression that evaluates to **`true`** or **`false`**. C# provides the simple type **`bool`** for Boolean variables that can hold only the values `true` and `false`—each of these is a C# keyword.

#### *UML Activity Diagram for an* `if` *Statement*

Figure 5.2 illustrates the single-selection `if` statement. This figure contains the most important symbol in an activity diagram—the diamond, or **decision symbol**, which indicates that a *decision* is to be made. The workflow continues along a path determined by the symbol's associated **guard conditions**, which can be *true* or *false*. Each transition arrow emerging from a decision symbol has a guard condition specified in *square brackets* next to the arrow. If a guard condition is *true*, the workflow enters the action state to which the transition arrow points. In Fig. 5.2, if the student's grade is greater than or equal to 60, the app displays "Passed" then transitions to the final state of this activity. If the grade is less than 60, the app immediately transitions to the final state without displaying a message.

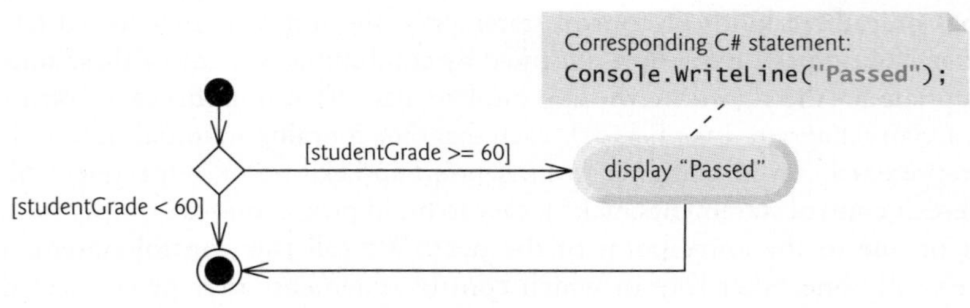


**Fig. 5.2** | `if` single-selection statement UML activity diagram.

The `if` statement is a *single-entry/single-exit* control statement. We'll see that the activity diagrams for the remaining control statements also contain initial states, transition arrows, action states that indicate actions to perform, decision symbols (with associated guard conditions) that indicate decisions to be made, and final states.

## 5.4 `if...else` Double-Selection Statement

The `if` single-selection statement performs an indicated action *only* when the condition is true; otherwise, the action is skipped. The `if...else` double-selection statement allows you to specify an action to perform when the condition is *true* and a different action when the condition is *false*. For example, the statement

```
if (grade >= 60)
{
   Console.WriteLine("Passed");
}
else
{
   Console.WriteLine("Failed");
}
```

is an `if...else` statement that displays "`Passed`" if `grade >= 60`, but displays "`Failed`" if it's less than 60. In either case, after "`Passed`" or "`Failed`" is displayed, the next statement in sequence is performed.

Note the indentation of the bodies of the `if`-part and the `else`-part for readability. Microsoft recommends four-space indentation—the default in Visual Studio. We use three-space indentation in all our print books because of line-width limitations.

### *UML Activity Diagram for an* `if...else` *Statement*

Figure 5.3 illustrates the flow of control in the preceding `if...else` statement. Once again, the symbols in the UML activity diagram (besides the initial state, transition arrows and final state) represent action states and decisions.

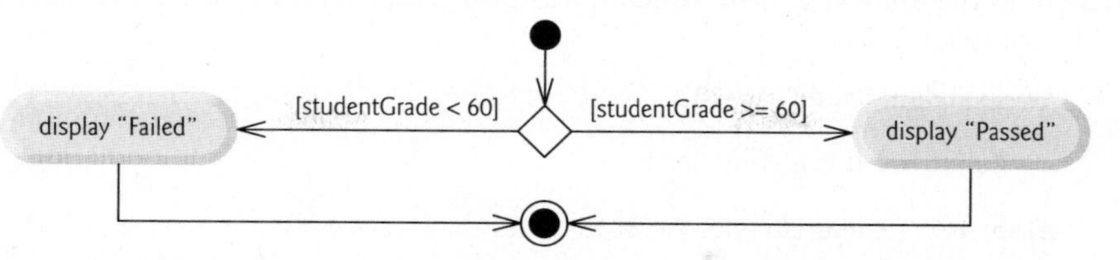


**Fig. 5.3** | `if...else` double-selection statement UML activity diagram.

### 5.4.1 Nested `if...else` Statements

An app can test multiple cases by placing `if...else` statements *inside* other `if...else` statements to create **nested `if...else` statements**. For example, the following nested `if...else` statement displays `A` for exam grades greater than or equal to 90, `B` for 80 to 89, `C` for 70 to 79, `D` for 60 to 69 and `F` for all other grades (we use shading to highlight the nesting):

```
if (studentGrade >= 90)
{
   Console.WriteLine("A")
}
else
{
   if (studentGrade >= 80)
   {
      Console.WriteLine("B")
   }
   else
   {
      if (studentGrade >= 70)
      {
         Console.WriteLine("C")
      }
      else
      {
         if (studentGrade >= 60)
         {
            Console.WriteLine("D")
         }
         else
         {
            Console.WriteLine("F")
         }
      }
   }
}
```

If variable `studentGrade` is greater than or equal to 90, the first four conditions in the nested `if...else` statement will be `true`, but only the statement in the `if` part of the first `if...else` statement will execute. After that statement executes, the `else` part of the "outermost" `if...else` statement is skipped. You can write the preceding nested `if...else` statement in the following form, which is identical except for the spacing and indentation that the compiler ignores:

```
if (studentGrade >= 90)
{
   Console.WriteLine("A");
}
else if (studentGrade >= 80)
{
   Console.WriteLine("B");
}
else if (studentGrade >= 70)
{
   Console.WriteLine("C");
}
else if (studentGrade >= 60)
{
   Console.WriteLine("D");
}
else
{
   Console.WriteLine("F");
}
```

The latter form avoids deep indentation of the code to the right. Such indentation often leaves little room on a line of code, forcing lines to wrap.

### 5.4.2 Dangling-else Problem

Throughout the text, we always enclose control statement bodies in braces. This avoids the logic error called the dangling-`else` problem in which the code indentation make it appear as though an `else` is associated with a particular `if` when, in fact, it is not.

### 5.4.3 Blocks

The `if` statement normally expects only *one* statement in its body. To include *several* statements in the body of an `if` (or the body of an `else` for an `if...else` statement), you must enclose the statements in braces. As we've done throughout the text, it's good practice to always use the braces. Statements contained in a pair of braces (such as the body of a control statement, property or method) form a **block**. A block can be placed anywhere in a control statement, property or method that a single statement can be placed.

The following example includes a block of *multiple* statements in the `else` part of an `if...else` statement:

```
if (studentGrade >= 60)
{
   Console.WriteLine("Passed");
}
else
{
   Console.WriteLine("Failed");
   Console.WriteLine("You must take this course again.");
}
```

In this case, if `studentGrade` is less than 60, the program executes *both* statements in the body of the `else` and prints

```
Failed
You must take this course again.
```

Without the braces surrounding the two statements in the `else` clause, the statement

```
Console.WriteLine("You must take this course again.");
```

would be outside the body of the `else` part of the `if...else` statement and would execute *regardless* of whether the grade was less than 60.

*Empty Statement*

Just as a block can be placed anywhere a single statement can be placed, it's also possible to have an **empty statement**, which is represented by placing a semicolon (`;`) where a statement would normally be.

### 5.4.4 Conditional Operator (?:)

C# provides the **conditional operator** (`?:`) that can be used in place of an `if...else` statement. This can make your code shorter and clearer. The conditional operator is C#'s only **ternary operator**—it takes three operands. Together, the operands and the `?:` symbols form a **conditional expression:**

- The first operand (to the left of the `?`) is a `bool` expression that evaluates to `true` or `false`.
- The second operand (between the `?` and `:`) is the value of the conditional expression if the `bool` expression is `true`.
- The third operand (to the right of the `:`) is the value of the conditional expression if the `bool` expression is `false`.

For now, the second and third operands should have the same type. In Section 7.6, we'll discuss implicit conversions that may occur if these operands do not have the same type.

For example, the statement

```
Console.WriteLine(studentGrade >= 60 ? "Passed" : "Failed");
```

displays the value of `WriteLine`'s conditional-expression argument. The conditional expression in the preceding statement evaluates to the `string` `"Passed"` if the condition

```
studentGrade >= 60
```

is `true` and to the `string` `"Failed"` if it's `false`. Thus, this statement with the conditional operator performs essentially the same task as the first `if...else` statement shown in Section 5.4. The precedence of the conditional operator is low, so the entire conditional expression is normally placed in parentheses. We'll see that conditional expressions can be used in some situations where `if...else` statements cannot.

## 5.5 Student Class: Nested if...else Statements

The example of Figs. 5.4–5.5 demonstrates a nested `if...else` statement that determines a student's letter grade based on the student's average in a course.

### *Class* Student

Class `Student` (Fig. 5.4) stores a student's name and average and provides properties for manipulating these values. The class contains:

- Auto-implemented `string` property `Name` (line 7) to store a `Student`'s name.
- Instance variable `average` of type `int` (line 8) to store a `Student`'s average in a course and a corresponding `Average` property (lines 18–36) to *get* and *set* the `Student`'s `average`. `Average`'s `set` accessor uses *nested* `if` *statements* (lines 28–34) to validate the value that's assigned to the `Average` property. These statements ensure that the value is greater than `0` *and* less than or equal to `100`; otherwise, instance variable `average`'s value is left unchanged. Each `if` statement contains a *simple condition*—i.e., one that makes only a single test. In Section 6.10, you'll see how to use *logical operators* to write *compound conditions* that conveniently combine several simple conditions. If the condition in line 28 is `true`, only then will the condition in line 30 be tested, and *only* if the conditions in both lines 28 *and* 30 are `true` will the statement in line 32 execute.
- A constructor (lines 11–15) that sets the `Name` and `Average` properties.
- Read-only property `LetterGrade` (lines 39–68), which uses *nested* `if...else` *statements* to determine the `Student`'s letter grade based on the `Student`'s average. A read-only property provides only a `get` accessor. Note that the local variable `letterGrade` is initialized to `string.Empty` (line 43), which represents the empty string (that is, a `string` containing no characters).

```
1  // Fig. 5.4: Student.cs
2  // Student class that stores a student name and average.
3  using System;
4
5  class Student
6  {
7     public string Name { get; set; } // property
8     private int average; // instance variable
9
10    // constructor initializes Name and Average properties
11    public Student(string studentName, int studentAverage)
12    {
13       Name = studentName;
14       Average = studentAverage; // sets average instance variable
15    }
16
17    // property to get and set instance variable average
18    public int Average
19    {
20       get // returns the Student's average
21       {
22          return average;
23       }
24       set  // sets the Student's average
25       {
```

**Fig. 5.4** | `Student` class that stores a student name and average. (Part 1 of 2.)

```
         // validate that value is > 0 and <= 100; otherwise,
         // keep instance variable average's current value
         if (value > 0)
         {
            if (value <= 100)
            {
               average = value; // assign to instance variable
            }
         }
      }
   }

   // returns the Student's letter grade, based on the average
   string LetterGrade
   {
      get
      {
         string letterGrade = string.Empty; // string.Empty is ""

         if (average >= 90)
         {
            letterGrade = "A";
         }
         else if (average >= 80)
         {
            letterGrade = "B";
         }
         else if (average >= 70)
         {
            letterGrade = "C";
         }
         else if (average >= 60)
         {
            letterGrade = "D";
         }
         else
         {
            letterGrade = "F";
         }

         return letterGrade;
      }
   }
}
```

**Fig. 5.4** | Student class that stores a student name and average. (Part 2 of 2.)

### *Class* StudentTest

To demonstrate the nested if statements and nested if...else statements in class Student's Average and LetterGrade properties, respectively, method Main (Fig. 5.5) creates two Student objects (lines 9–10). Next, lines 12–15 display each Student's name, average and letter grade by accessing the objects' Name, Average and LetterGrade properties, respectively.

```
// Fig. 5.5: StudentTest.cs
// Create and test Student objects.
using System;

class StudentTest
{
   static void Main()
   {
      Student student1 = new Student("Jane Green", 93);
      Student student2 = new Student("John Blue", 72);

      Console.Write($"{student1.Name}'s letter grade equivalent of ");
      Console.WriteLine($"{student1.Average} is {student1.LetterGrade}");
      Console.Write($"{student2.Name}'s letter grade equivalent of ");
      Console.WriteLine($"{student2.Average} is {student2.LetterGrade}");
   }
}
```

```
Jane Green's letter grade equivalent of 93 is A
John Blue's letter grade equivalent of 72 is C
```

**Fig. 5.5** | Create and test `Student` objects.

## 5.6 `while` Iteration Statement

An iteration statement allows you to specify that a program should repeat an action while some condition remains *true*. Consider a code segment designed to find the first power of 3 larger than 100—when the following `while` iteration statement finishes executing, `product` contains the result:

```
int product = 3;

while (product <= 100)
{
   product = 3 * product;
}
```

When this `while` statement begins execution, variable `product` contains the value `3`. Each iteration of the `while` statement multiplies `product` by 3, so `product` takes on the values 9, 27, 81 and 243 successively. When `product` becomes 243, `product <= 100` becomes `false`. This terminates the iteration, so the final value of `product` is 243. At this point, program execution continues with the next statement after the `while` statement.

**Common Programming Error 5.1**

*Not providing in the body of a `while` statement an action that eventually causes the condition in the `while` to become false results in an infinite loop.*

### `while` *Iteration Statement Activity Diagram*

The UML activity diagram in Fig. 5.6 illustrates the flow of control in the preceding `while` statement. This diagram introduces the UML's **merge symbol**. The UML represents *both* the merge symbol and the decision symbol as diamonds. The merge symbol joins multiple flows of activity into one. In this diagram, the merge symbol joins the transitions from the initial state and from the action state, so they both flow into the decision that determines whether the loop should begin (or continue) executing.

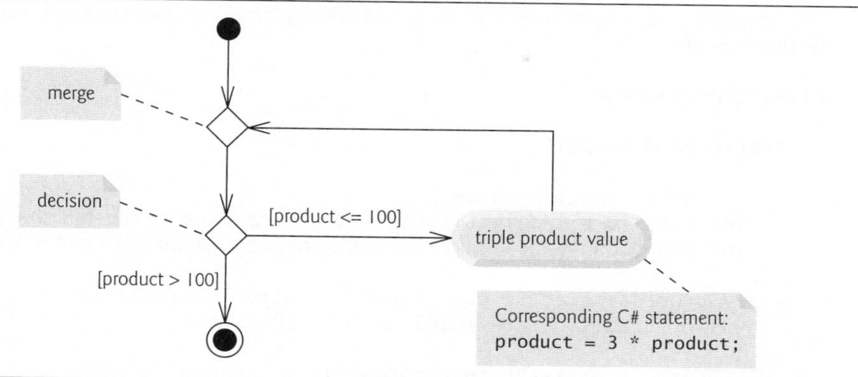


**Fig. 5.6** | `while` iteration statement UML activity diagram.

The decision and merge symbols can be distinguished by the number of "incoming" and "outgoing" transition arrows. A decision symbol has *one* transition arrow pointing *to* the diamond and *two or more* pointing out *from* it to indicate possible transitions from that point. In addition, each transition arrow pointing out of a decision symbol has a guard condition next to it. A merge symbol has two or more transition arrows pointing to the diamond and only one pointing from the diamond, to indicate multiple activity flows merging to continue the activity. None of the transition arrows associated with a merge symbol has a guard condition.

Figure 5.6 clearly shows the iteration of the `while` statement discussed earlier in this section. The transition arrow emerging from the action state points back to the merge, from which program flow transitions back to the decision that's tested at the beginning of each iteration of the loop. The loop continues executing until the guard condition `product > 100` becomes *true*. Then the `while` statement exits (reaches its final state), and control passes to the next statement in sequence in the app.

## 5.7 Counter-Controlled Iteration

Consider the following problem statement:

> *A class of 10 students took a quiz. The grades (integers in the range 0 to 100) for this quiz are available to you. Determine the class average on the quiz.*

The class average is equal to the sum of the grades divided by the number of students. The app must input each grade, keep track of the total of all grades entered, perform the averaging calculation and print the result.

We use **counter-controlled iteration** to input the grades one at a time. In this example, iteration terminates when the counter exceeds 10.

### 5.7.1 Implementing Counter-Controlled Iteration

In Fig. 5.7, method `Main` implements the class-averaging algorithm—it allows the user to enter 10 grades, then calculates and displays the average.

```
1  // Fig. 5.7: ClassAverage.cs
2  // Solving the class-average problem using counter-controlled iteration.
3  using System;
4
5  class ClassAverage
6  {
7     static void Main()
8     {
9        // initialization phase
10       int total = 0; // initialize sum of grades entered by the user
11       int gradeCounter = 1; // initialize grade # to be entered next
12
13       // processing phase uses counter-controlled iteration
14       while (gradeCounter <= 10) // loop 10 times
15       {
16          Console.Write("Enter grade: "); // prompt
17          int grade = int.Parse(Console.ReadLine()); // input grade
18          total = total + grade; // add the grade to total
19          gradeCounter = gradeCounter + 1; // increment the counter by 1
20       }
21
22       // termination phase
23       int average = total / 10; // integer division yields integer result
24
25       // display total and average of grades
26       Console.WriteLine($"\nTotal of all 10 grades is {total}");
27       Console.WriteLine($"Class average is {average}");
28    }
29 }
```

```
Enter grade: 88
Enter grade: 79
Enter grade: 95
Enter grade: 100
Enter grade: 48
Enter grade: 88
Enter grade: 92
Enter grade: 83
Enter grade: 90
Enter grade: 85

Total of all 10 grades is 848
Class average is 84
```

**Fig. 5.7** | Solving the class-average problem using counter-controlled iteration.

#### *Local Variables in `Main`*

Lines 10, 11, 17 and 23 declare local variables `total`, `gradeCounter`, `grade` and `average`, respectively. A variable declared in a method body is a local variable and can be used only from the line of its declaration to the closing right brace of the block in which the variable is declared. A local variable's declaration must appear *before* the variable is used; otherwise, a compilation error occurs. Variable `grade`—declared in the body of the `while` loop—can be used only in that block.

### *Initialization Phase: Initializing Variables* `total` *and* `gradeCounter`

C# requires local variables to be **definitely assigned**—that is, each local variable must be assigned a value before the variable's value is used. Lines 10–11 declare and initialize `total` to `0` and `gradeCounter` to `1` before their values are used, so these variables are definitely assigned (as are `grade` and `average` in lines 17 and 23, respectively).

**Common Programming Error 5.2**

*All local variables must be definitely assigned before their values are used in expressions. Using a local variable's value before it's definitely assigned results in a compilation error.*

**Error-Prevention Tip 5.1**

*Initializing local variables when they're declared helps you avoid compilation errors that might arise from attempts to use uninitialized data. While C# does not require that local-variable initializations be incorporated into declarations, it does require that local variables be initialized before their values are used in an expression.*

### *Processing Phase: Reading 10 Grades from the User*

Line 14 indicates that the `while` statement should continue **iterating** as long as `gradeCounter`'s value is less than or equal to 10. While this condition remains *true*, the `while` statement repeatedly executes the statements between the braces that delimit its body (lines 15–20).

Line 16 displays the prompt `"Enter grade: "`. Line 17 inputs the grade entered by the user and assigns it to variable `grade`. Then line 18 adds the new `grade` entered by the user to the `total` and assigns the result to `total`, replacing its previous value.

Line 19 adds `1` to `gradeCounter` to indicate that the program has processed a grade and is ready to input the next grade from the user. Incrementing `gradeCounter` eventually causes it to exceed 10. Then the loop terminates, because its condition (line 14) becomes `false`.

### *Termination Phase: Calculating and Displaying the Class Average*

When the loop terminates, line 23 performs the averaging calculation in the `average` variable's initializer. Line 26 displays the text `"Total of all 10 grades is "` followed by variable `total`'s value. Then, line 27 displays the text `"Class average is "` followed by variable `average`'s value. When execution reaches line 28, the program terminates.

Notice that this example contains only one class, with method `Main` performing all the work. In this chapter and in Chapter 4, you've seen examples consisting of two classes:

- one containing instance variables, properties and methods that perform tasks using the instance variables and properties, and
- one containing method `Main`, which creates an object of the other class and calls its methods and accesses its properties.

Occasionally, when it does not make sense to create a separate class to demonstrate a concept, we'll place the program's statements entirely within a single class's `Main` method.

### 5.7.2 Integer Division and Truncation

The averaging calculation performed in line 23 produces an integer result. The app's output indicates that the sum of the grade values in the sample execution is 848, which, when divided by 10, should yield 84.8. However, the result of the calculation `total / 10` is the integer `84`, because `total` and `10` are *both* integers. Dividing two integers results in **integer division**—any fractional part of the calculation is lost (i.e., **truncated**, not rounded). We'll see how to obtain a floating-point result from the averaging calculation in the next section.

**Common Programming Error 5.3**

*Assuming that integer division rounds (rather than truncates) can lead to incorrect results. For example, 7 ÷ 4, which yields 1.75 in conventional arithmetic, truncates to 1 in integer arithmetic, rather than rounding to 2.*

## 5.8 Sentinel-Controlled Iteration

Let us generalize Section 5.7's class-average problem. Consider the following problem:

> *Develop a class-averaging app that processes grades for an arbitrary number of students each time it's run.*

In the previous class-average example, the problem statement specified the number of students, so the number of grades (10) was known in advance. In this example, no indication is given of how many grades the user will enter during the program's execution.

One way to solve this problem is to use a special value called a **sentinel value** (also called a **signal value**, a **dummy value** or a **flag value**) to indicate "end of data entry." The user enters grades until all legitimate grades have been entered. The user then types the sentinel value to indicate that no more grades will be entered. **Sentinel-controlled iteration** is often called **indefinite iteration** because the number of iterations is *not* known before the loop begins executing. Clearly, a sentinel value must be chosen that cannot be confused with an acceptable input value. Grades on a quiz are nonnegative integers, so –1 is an acceptable sentinel value for this problem. Thus, a run of the class-averaging program might process a stream of inputs such as 95, 96, 75, 74, 89 and –1. The program would then compute and print the class average for the grades 95, 96, 75, 74 and 89; since –1 is the sentinel value, it should *not* enter into the averaging calculation.

**Error-Prevention Tip 5.2**

*When performing division by an expression whose value could be zero, explicitly test for this possibility and handle it appropriately in your app (e.g., by displaying an error message) rather than allowing the error to occur.*

### 5.8.1 Implementing Sentinel-Controlled Iteration

In Fig. 5.8, method `Main` implements the sentinel-controlled iteration solution to the class average problem. Although each grade entered by the user is an integer, the averaging calculation is likely to produce a number with a decimal point—in other words, a real number or **floating-point number** (e.g., 7.33, 0.0975 or 1000.12345). The type `int` cannot represent such a number, so this example must use another type to do so. C# provides data types **`float`** and **`double`** to store floating-point numbers in memory. The primary difference between these types is that `double` variables can typically store numbers with larger magnitude and finer detail (i.e., more digits to the right of the decimal point—also known as the number's **precision**).

```
// Fig. 5.8: ClassAverage.cs
// Solving the class-average problem using sentinel-controlled iteration.
using System;

class ClassAverage
{
   static void Main()
   {
      // initialization phase
      int total = 0; // initialize sum of grades
      int gradeCounter = 0; // initialize # of grades entered so far

      // processing phase
      // prompt for input and read grade from user
      Console.Write("Enter grade or -1 to quit: ");
      int grade = int.Parse(Console.ReadLine());

      // loop until sentinel value is read from the user
      while (grade != -1)
      {
         total = total + grade; // add grade to total
         gradeCounter = gradeCounter + 1; // increment counter

         // prompt for input and read grade from user
         Console.Write("Enter grade or -1 to quit: ");
         grade = int.Parse(Console.ReadLine());
      }

      // termination phase
      // if the user entered at least one grade...
      if (gradeCounter != 0)
      {
         // use number with decimal point to calculate average of grades
         double average = (double) total / gradeCounter;

         // display the total and average (with two digits of precision)
         Console.WriteLine(
            $"\nTotal of the {gradeCounter} grades entered is {total}");
         Console.WriteLine($"Class average is {average:F}");
      }
      else // no grades were entered, so output error message
      {
         Console.WriteLine("No grades were entered");
      }
   }
}
```

**Fig. 5.8** | Solving the class-average problem using sentinel-controlled iteration. (Part 1 of 2.)

```
Enter grade or -1 to quit: 97
Enter grade or -1 to quit: 88
Enter grade or -1 to quit: 72
Enter grade or -1 to quit: -1

Total of the 3 grades entered is 257
Class average is 85.67
```

**Fig. 5.8** | Solving the class-average problem using sentinel-controlled iteration. (Part 2 of 2.)

Recall that integer division produces an integer result. This program introduces a special operator called a **cast operator** to *force* the averaging calculation to produce a floating-point numeric result. This program also *stacks* control statements on top of one another (in sequence)—the `while` statement (lines 19–27) is followed in sequence by an `if...else` statement (lines 31–44). Much of the code in this program is identical to that in Fig. 5.7, so we concentrate on the new concepts.

### 5.8.2 Program Logic for Sentinel-Controlled Iteration

Line 11 of Fig. 5.8 initializes `gradeCounter` to `0`, because no grades have been entered yet. Remember that this program uses *sentinel-controlled iteration* to input the grades. The program increments `gradeCounter` only when the user enters a valid grade. Line 34 declares `double` variable `average`, which stores the class average as a floating-point number.

Compare the program logic for sentinel-controlled iteration in this program with that for counter-controlled iteration in Fig. 5.7. In counter-controlled iteration, each iteration of the `while` statement (lines 14–20 of Fig. 5.7) reads a value from the user, for the specified number of iterations. In sentinel-controlled iteration, the program prompts for and reads the first value (lines 15–16 of Fig. 5.8) before reaching the `while`. This value determines whether the program's flow of control should enter the body of the `while`. If the condition of the `while` is `false` (line 19), the user entered the sentinel value, so the body of the `while` does not execute (i.e., no grades were entered). If, on the other hand, the condition is `true`, the body begins execution, and the loop adds the `grade` value to the `total` and increments the `gradeCounter` (lines 21–22). Then lines 25–26 in the loop body input the next value from the user. Next, program control reaches the closing right brace of the loop body at line 27, so execution continues with the test of the `while`'s condition (line 19). The condition uses the most recent `grade` entered by the user to determine whether the loop body should execute again.

The value of variable `grade` is always input from the user immediately *before* the program tests the `while` condition. This allows the program to determine whether the value just input is the sentinel value *before* the program processes that value (i.e., adds it to the `total`). If the sentinel value is input, the loop terminates, and the program does not add –1 to the `total`.

**Good Programming Practice 5.1**

*In a sentinel-controlled loop, prompts should remind the user of the sentinel.*

After the loop terminates, the `if...else` statement at lines 31–44 executes. Line 31 determines whether any grades were input. If none were input, the `if...else` statement's `else` part executes and displays the message `"No grades were entered"`.

### 5.8.3 Braces in a `while` Statement

Notice the `while` statement's block in Fig. 5.8 (lines 20–27). Without the braces, the loop would consider its body to be *only* the first statement, which adds the `grade` to the `total`. The last three statements in the block would fall outside the loop's body, causing the computer to interpret the code incorrectly as follows:

```
while (grade != -1)
    total = total + grade; // add grade to total
gradeCounter = gradeCounter + 1; // increment counter

// prompt for input and read grade from user
Console.Write("Enter grade or -1 to quit: ");
grade = int.Parse(Console.ReadLine());
```

The preceding code would cause an *infinite loop* if the user did not enter the sentinel `-1` at line 16 (before the `while` statement).

**Error-Prevention Tip 5.3**

*Omitting the braces that delimit a block can lead to logic errors, such as infinite loops. To prevent this and other problems, always enclose the body of every control statement in braces even if the body contains only a single statement.*

### 5.8.4 Converting Between Simple Types Explicitly and Implicitly

If at least one grade was entered, line 34 of Fig. 5.8

```
double average = (double) total / gradeCounter;
```

calculates the average. Recall from Fig. 5.7 that integer division yields an integer result. Even though variable `average` is declared as a `double`, if we had written line 34 as

```
double average = total / gradeCounter;
```

it would lose the fractional part of the quotient *before* the result of the division was used to initialize `average`.

#### *Cast Operator*

To perform a floating-point calculation with integers in this example, you first create a *temporary* floating-point value using the **unary cast operator**. Line 34 uses the **`(double)`** unary cast operator—which has higher precedence than the arithmetic operators—to create a temporary `double` *copy* of its operand `total`, which appears to the right of the operator. The value stored in `total` is still an integer. Using a cast operator in this manner is called **explicit conversion**.

#### *Promotions*

After the cast operation, the calculation consists of the temporary `double` copy of `total` divided by the integer `gradeCounter`. For arithmetic, the compiler knows how to evaluate only expressions in which the operand types are *identical.* To ensure this, the compiler performs an operation called **promotion** (also called **implicit conversion**) on selected operands. In an expression containing values of types `int` and `double`, the compiler **promotes** `int` operands to `double` values. So, in line 34, the compiler creates a temporary copy of `gradeCounter`'s value of type `double`, then performs the floating-point division. Finally, `average` is initialized with the floating-point result. Section 7.6.1 discusses the allowed simple-type promotions.

*Cast Operators for Any Type*

Cast operators are available for all simple types. We'll discuss cast operators for other types in Chapter 12. The cast operator is formed by placing parentheses around the name of a type. This operator is a **unary operator**—it takes only one operand. C# also supports unary versions of the plus (+) and minus (-) operators, so you can write expressions like `+5` or `-7`. Cast operators have the second highest precedence. (See the operator precedence chart in Appendix A.)

### 5.8.5 Formatting Floating-Point Numbers

Line 39 of Fig. 5.8

```
Console.WriteLine($"Class average is {average:F}");
```

outputs the class average. In this example, we decided that we'd like to display the class average *rounded to the nearest hundredth* and output the average with exactly two digits to the right of the decimal point. The **format specifier** `F` in the interpolation expression

```
{average:F}
```

typically formats `average`'s value with two digits to the right of the decimal point—again, the Windows culture settings on the user's machine determine the actual format, including the digits to the right of the decimal point, whether commas or periods are used for separating thousands, millions, etc.

*Rounding Floating-Point Numbers*

When the `F` format specifier is used to format a floating-point value, the formatted value is **rounded** to a specific decimal position, although the value in memory remains unaltered. In many cultures a floating-point value output with `F` will be rounded to the hundredths position—for example, 123.457 will be rounded to 123.46, and 27.333 will be rounded to 27.33—though in some cultures these values are rounded to whole numbers. In this app, the three grades entered during the sample execution total 257, which yields the average 86.66666…. In the United States, the `F` format specifier rounds `average` to the hundredths position, so the average is displayed as `85.67`.

## 5.9 Nested Control Statements

We've seen that control statements can be *stacked* on top of one another (in sequence). In this case study, we examine the only other structured way control statements can be connected, namely, by **nesting** one control statement within another.

### Problem Statement

Consider the following problem statement:

> *A college offers a course that prepares students for the state licensing exam for real-estate brokers. Last year, 10 of the students who completed this course took the exam. The college wants to know how well its students did on the exam. You've been asked to write an app to summarize the results. You've been given a list of these 10 students. Next to each name is written a 1 if the student passed the exam or a 2 if the student failed.*
>
> *Your app should analyze the results of the exam as follows:*
>
> 1. *Input each test result (i.e., a 1 or a 2). Display the message "Enter result" on the screen each time the app requests a test result.*
> 2. *Count the number of test results of each type.*
> 3. *Display a summary of the test results, indicating the number of students who passed and the number who failed.*
> 4. *If more than eight students passed the exam, display the message "Bonus to instructor!"*

### Problem Statement Observations

After reading the problem statement, we make the following observations:

1. The app must process test results for 10 students. A *counter-controlled loop* can be used because the number of test results is known in advance.
2. Each test result has a numeric value—either a 1 or a 2. Each time the app reads a test result, the app must determine whether the number is a 1 or a 2. We test for a 1 in our algorithm. If the number is not a 1, we assume that it's a 2.
3. Two counters are used to keep track of the exam results—one to count the number of students who passed the exam and one to count the number of students who failed the exam.
4. After the app has processed all the results, it must determine whether more than eight students passed the exam.

The program that implements the pseudocode algorithm and two sample executions are shown in Fig. 5.9. Lines 10–12 and 19 declare the local variables that method `Main` uses to process the examination results.

```
1  // Fig. 5.9: Analysis.cs
2  // Analysis of examination results, using nested control statements.
3  using System;
4
5  class Analysis
6  {
7     static void Main()
8     {
9        // initialize variables in declarations
10       int passes = 0; // number of passes
11       int failures = 0; // number of failures
12       int studentCounter = 1; // student counter
```

**Fig. 5.9** | Analysis of examination results, using nested control statements. (Part 1 of 3.)

```
            
        // process 10 students using counter-controlled iteration
        while (studentCounter <= 10)
        {
           // prompt user for input and obtain a value from the user
           Console.Write("Enter result (1 = pass, 2 = fail): ");
           int result = int.Parse(Console.ReadLine());

           // if...else is nested in the while statement
           if (result == 1)
           {
              passes = passes + 1; // increment passes
           }
           else
           {
              failures = failures + 1; // increment failures
           }

           // increment studentCounter so loop eventually terminates
           studentCounter = studentCounter + 1;
        }

        // termination phase; prepare and display results
        Console.WriteLine($"Passed: {passes}\nFailed: {failures}");

        // determine whether more than 8 students passed
        if (passes > 8)
        {
           Console.WriteLine("Bonus to instructor!");
        }
     }
  }
```

```
Enter result (1 = pass, 2 = fail): 1
Enter result (1 = pass, 2 = fail): 2
Enter result (1 = pass, 2 = fail): 1
Enter result (1 = pass, 2 = fail): 1
Enter result (1 = pass, 2 = fail): 1
Enter result (1 = pass, 2 = fail): 1
Enter result (1 = pass, 2 = fail): 1
Enter result (1 = pass, 2 = fail): 1
Enter result (1 = pass, 2 = fail): 1
Enter result (1 = pass, 2 = fail): 1
Passed: 9
Failed: 1
Bonus to instructor!
```

```
Enter result (1 = pass, 2 = fail): 1
Enter result (1 = pass, 2 = fail): 2
Enter result (1 = pass, 2 = fail): 2
Enter result (1 = pass, 2 = fail): 2
```

**Fig. 5.9** | Analysis of examination results, using nested control statements. (Part 2 of 3.)

```
Enter result (1 = pass, 2 = fail): 1
Enter result (1 = pass, 2 = fail): 1
Enter result (1 = pass, 2 = fail): 1
Enter result (1 = pass, 2 = fail): 1
Enter result (1 = pass, 2 = fail): 2
Enter result (1 = pass, 2 = fail): 2
Passed: 5
Failed: 5
```

**Fig. 5.9** | Analysis of examination results, using nested control statements. (Part 3 of 3.)

The `while` statement (lines 15–33) loops 10 times. During each iteration, the loop inputs and processes one exam result. Notice that the `if...else` statement (lines 22–29) for processing each result is *nested* in the `while` statement. If the `result` is `1`, the `if...else` statement increments `passes`; otherwise, it *assumes* the `result` is `2` and increments `failures`. Line 32 increments `studentCounter` before the loop condition is tested again at line 15. After 10 values have been input, the loop terminates and line 36 displays the number of `passes` and the number of `failures`. Lines 39–42 determine whether more than eight students passed the exam and, if so, output the message `"Bonus to instructor!"`.

## 5.10 Compound Assignment Operators

The **compound assignment operators** abbreviate assignment expressions. Statements like

*variable* = *variable operator expression*;

where *operator* is one of the binary operators +, -, *, / or % (or others we discuss later in the text) can be written in the form

*variable operator*= *expression*;

For example, you can abbreviate the statement

```
c = c + 3;
```

with the **addition compound assignment operator**, **+=**, as

```
c += 3;
```

The += operator adds the value of the expression on its right to the value of the variable on its left and stores the result in the variable on the left of the operator. Thus, the assignment expression `c += 3` adds `3` to `c`. Figure 5.10 shows the arithmetic compound assignment operators, sample expressions using the operators and explanations of what the operators do.

| Assignment operator | Sample expression | Explanation | Assigns |
|---|---|---|---|
| *Assume:* `int c = 3, d = 5, e = 4, f = 6, g = 12;` | | | |
| `+=` | `c += 7` | `c = c + 7` | 10 to `c` |
| `-=` | `d -= 4` | `d = d - 4` | 1 to `d` |

**Fig. 5.10** | Arithmetic compound assignment operators. (Part 1 of 2.)

| Assignment operator | Sample expression | Explanation | Assigns |
|---|---|---|---|
| `*=` | `e *= 5` | `e = e * 5` | 20 to `e` |
| `/=` | `f /= 3` | `f = f / 3` | 2 to `f` |
| `%=` | `g %= 9` | `g = g % 9` | 3 to `g` |

**Fig. 5.10** | Arithmetic compound assignment operators. (Part 2 of 2.)

## 5.11 Increment and Decrement Operators

C# provides two unary operators for adding 1 to or subtracting 1 from the value of a numeric variable (summarized in Fig. 5.11). These are the unary **increment operator, ++**, and the unary **decrement operator, --**, respectively. An app can increment by `1` the value of a variable called `c` using the increment operator, `++`, rather than the expression `c = c + 1` or `c += 1`. An increment or decrement operator that's prefixed to (placed *before*) a variable is referred to as the **prefix increment operator** or **prefix decrement operator**, respectively. An increment or decrement operator that's postfixed to (placed *after*) a variable is referred to as the **postfix increment operator** or **postfix decrement operator**, respectively.

| Operator | Sample expression | Explanation |
|---|---|---|
| `++` (prefix increment) | `++a` | Increments `a` by `1` and uses the new value of `a` in the expression in which `a` resides. |
| `++` (postfix increment) | `a++` | Increments `a` by `1`, but uses the original value of `a` in the expression in which `a` resides. |
| `--` (prefix decrement) | `--b` | Decrements `b` by `1` and uses the new value of `b` in the expression in which `b` resides. |
| `--` (postfix decrement) | `b--` | Decrements `b` by `1`, but uses the original value of `b` in the expression in which `b` resides. |

**Fig. 5.11** | Increment and decrement operators.

Using the prefix increment (or decrement) operator to add 1 to (or subtract 1 from) a variable is known as **preincrementing** (or **predecrementing**). This causes the variable to be incremented (decremented) by 1; then the new value of the variable is used in the expression in which it appears.

Using the postfix increment (or decrement) operator to add 1 to (or subtract 1 from) a variable is known as **postincrementing** (or **postdecrementing**). This causes the current value of the variable to be used in the expression in which it appears; then the variable's value is incremented (decremented) by 1.

**Good Programming Practice 5.2**

*Unlike binary operators, the unary increment and decrement operators as a matter of style should be placed next to their operands, with no intervening spaces.*

### 5.11.1 Prefix Increment vs. Postfix Increment

Figure 5.12 demonstrates the difference between the prefix-increment and postfix-increment versions of the ++ increment operator. The decrement operator (--) works similarly.

```
1  // Fig. 5.12: Increment.cs
2  // Prefix-increment and postfix-increment operators.
3  using System;
4
5  class Increment
6  {
7     static void Main()
8     {
9        // demonstrate postfix increment operator
10       int c = 5; // assign 5 to c
11       Console.WriteLine($"c before postincrement: {c}"); // displays 5
12       Console.WriteLine($"    postincrementing c: {c++}"); // displays 5
13       Console.WriteLine($" c after postincrement: {c}"); // displays 6
14
15       Console.WriteLine(); // skip a line
16
17       // demonstrate prefix increment operator
18       c = 5; // assign 5 to c
19       Console.WriteLine($" c before preincrement: {c}"); // displays 5
20       Console.WriteLine($"     preincrementing c: {++c}"); // displays 6
21       Console.WriteLine($"  c after preincrement: {c}"); // displays 6
22    }
23 }
```

```
c before postincrement: 5
    postincrementing c: 5
 c after postincrement: 6

 c before preincrement: 5
     preincrementing c: 6
  c after preincrement: 6
```

**Fig. 5.12** | Prefix-increment and postfix-increment operators.

Line 10 initializes the variable c to 5, and line 11 outputs c's initial value. Line 12 outputs the value of the expression c++. This expression postincrements the variable c, so c's *original* value (5) is output, then c's value is incremented (to 6). Thus, line 12 outputs c's initial value (5) again. Line 13 outputs c's new value (6) to prove that the variable's value was indeed incremented in line 12.

Line 18 resets c's value to 5, and line 19 outputs c's value. Line 20 outputs the value of the expression ++c. This expression preincrements c, so its value is incremented; then the *new* value (6) is output. Line 21 outputs c's value again to show that the value of c is still 6 after line 20 executes.

### 5.11.2 Simplifying Increment Statements

The arithmetic compound assignment operators and the increment and decrement operators can be used to simplify statements. For example, the three assignment statements in Fig. 5.9 (lines 24, 28 and 32)

```
passes = passes + 1;
failures = failures + 1;
studentCounter = studentCounter + 1;
```

can be written more concisely with compound assignment operators as

```
passes += 1;
failures += 1;
studentCounter += 1;
```

and even more concisely with prefix-increment operators as

```
++passes;
++failures;
++studentCounter;
```

or with postfix-increment operators as

```
passes++;
failures++;
studentCounter++;
```

When incrementing or decrementing a variable in a statement by itself, the prefix increment and postfix increment forms have the *same* effect, and the prefix decrement and postfix decrement forms have the *same* effect. It's only when a variable appears in the context of a larger expression that the prefix increment and postfix increment have *different* results (and similarly for the prefix decrement and postfix decrement).

**Common Programming Error 5.4**

*Attempting to use the increment or decrement operator on an expression other than one to which a value can be assigned is a syntax error. For example, writing* ++(x + 1) *is a syntax error, because* (x + 1) *is not an expression to which a value can be assigned.*

### 5.11.3 Operator Precedence and Associativity

Figure 5.13 shows the precedence and associativity of the operators introduced to this point shown from top to bottom in decreasing order of precedence. The second column describes the associativity of the operators at each level of precedence. The conditional operator (?:); the unary operators prefix increment (++), prefix decrement (--), plus (+) and minus (-); the cast operators; and the assignment operators =, +=, -=, *=, /= and %= associate from right to left. All the other operators in the operator precedence chart in Fig. 5.13 associate from left to right. The third column names the groups of operators.

| Operators | Associativity | Type |
|---|---|---|
| `.` `new` `++`*(postfix)* `--`*(postfix)* | left to right | highest precedence |
| `++` `--` `+` `-` *(type)* | right to left | unary prefix |
| `*` `/` `%` | left to right | multiplicative |
| `+` `-` | left to right | additive |
| `<` `<=` `>` `>=` | left to right | relational |
| `==` `!=` | left to right | equality |
| `?:` | right to left | conditional |
| `=` `+=` `-=` `*=` `/=` `%=` | right to left | assignment |

**Fig. 5.13** | Precedence and associativity of the operators discussed so far.

## 5.12 Simple Types

The table in Appendix B lists C#'s **simple types**. Like its predecessor languages C and C++, C# requires *all* variables to have a type.

In C and C++, you frequently have to write separate versions of apps to support different computer platforms, because the simple types are *not* guaranteed to be identical from computer to computer. For example, an `int` value on one machine might be represented by 16 bits (2 bytes) of storage, while an `int` value on another machine might be represented by 32 bits (4 bytes) of storage. In C#, *all* C# numeric types have fixed sizes, as is shown in Appendix B. So, for example, `int` values are always 32 bits (4 bytes).

Each type in Appendix B is listed with its size in bits (there are eight bits to a byte) and its range of values. Because the designers of C# want it to be maximally portable, they use internationally recognized standards for both character formats (Unicode; `http://unicode.org`) and floating-point numbers (IEEE 754; `http://grouper.ieee.org/groups/754/`).

Recall that variables of *simple types* declared *outside* of a method as instance variables of a class are automatically assigned default values unless explicitly initialized. Instance variables of types `char`, `byte`, `sbyte`, `short`, `ushort`, `int`, `uint`, `long`, `ulong`, `float`, `double`, and `decimal` are all given the value `0` by default. Instance variables of type `bool` are given the value `false` by default. Similarly, reference-type instance variables are initialized by default to the value `null`.

## 5.13 Wrap-Up

Only three types of control statements—sequence, selection and iteration—are needed to develop any algorithm. Specifically, we demonstrated the `if` and `if...else` selection statements and the `while` iteration statement. We used control-statement stacking to compute the total and the average of a set of student grades with counter- and sentinel-controlled iteration, and we used control-statement nesting to make decisions based on a set of exam results. We introduced C#'s compound assignment, unary cast, conditional (`?:`), increment and decrement operators. Finally, we discussed the simple types. In Chapter 6, we continue our discussion of control statements, introducing the `for`, `do...while` and `switch` statements.

# 6

# Control Statements: Part 2

## Objectives

In this chapter you'll:

- Use counter-controlled iteration.
- Use the `for` and `do...while` iteration statements.
- Use the `switch` multiple-selection statement.
- Use `string`s in `switch` expressions and `string` literals in `case` labels.
- Use the `break` and `continue` program-control statements to alter the flow of control.
- Use the logical operators to form complex conditional expressions.
- Understand short-circuit evaluation of the conditional && and || operators.
- Use type `decimal` to avoid the representational errors associated with using floating-point data types to hold monetary values.

Outline



## 6.1 Introduction

In this chapter we introduce all but one of C#'s other control statements—the `foreach` statement is introduced in Chapter 8. We demonstrate C#'s `for`, `do...while` and `switch` statements. Through examples using `while` and `for`, we enumerate the essentials of counter-controlled iteration. You'll use type `decimal` to represent monetary amounts precisely, rather than incuring the representational errors that can occur with types `float` or `double`. We use a `switch` multiple-selection statement to count the number of A, B, C, D and F grade equivalents in a set of numeric grades entered by the user. We introduce the `break` and `continue` program-control statements. We discuss C#'s logical operators, which enable you to combine simple conditions in control statements.

## 6.2 Essentials of Counter-Controlled Iteration

This section uses the `while` iteration statement introduced in Chapter 5 to formalize the elements of counter-controlled iteration:

1. a **control variable** (or loop counter),
2. the control variable's **initial value**,
3. the control variable's **increment** that's applied during each iteration of the loop,
4. the **loop-continuation condition** that determines if looping should continue.

Figure 6.1 displays the numbers from 1 through 10. The elements of counter-controlled iteration are defined in lines 9, 11 and 14. Line 9 declares the control variable (`counter`) as an `int`, reserves space for it in memory and sets its initial value to `1`.

**Error-Prevention Tip 6.1**

*Floating-point values are approximate, so controlling counting loops with floating-point variables of types `float` or `double` can result in imprecise counter values and inaccurate tests for termination. Use integer values to control counting loops.*

```
// Fig. 6.1: WhileCounter.cs
// Counter-controlled iteration with the while iteration statement.
using System;

class WhileCounter
{
   static void Main()
   {
      int counter = 1; // declare and initialize control variable

      while (counter <= 10) // loop-continuation condition
      {
         Console.Write($"{counter}  ");
         ++counter; // increment control variable
      }

      Console.WriteLine();
   }
}
```

```
1  2  3  4  5  6  7  8  9  10
```

**Fig. 6.1** | Counter-controlled iteration with the `while` iteration statement.

## 6.3 for Iteration Statement

The `while` statement can be used to implement any counter-controlled loop. C# also provides the **for iteration statement**, which specifies the elements of counter-controlled iteration in a single line of code. Typically, `for` statements are used for counter-controlled iteration, and `while` statements for sentinel-controlled iteration. However, `while` and `for` can each be used for either iteration type. Figure 6.2 reimplements the app in Fig. 6.1 using the `for` statement.

```
// Fig. 6.2: ForCounter.cs
// Counter-controlled iteration with the for iteration statement.
using System;

class ForCounter
{
   static void Main()
   {
```

**Fig. 6.2** | Counter-controlled iteration with the `for` iteration statement. (Part 1 of 2.)

```
9          // for statement header includes initialization,
10         // loop-continuation condition and increment
11         for (int counter = 1; counter <= 10; ++counter)
12         {
13            Console.Write($"{counter}  ");
14         }
15
16         Console.WriteLine();
17      }
18   }
```

```
1  2  3  4  5  6  7  8  9  10
```

**Fig. 6.2** | Counter-controlled iteration with the `for` iteration statement. (Part 2 of 2.)

When the `for` statement (lines 11–14) begins executing, the control variable `counter` is *declared* and *initialized* to `1`. Next, the program checks the *loop-continuation condition*, `counter <= 10`, which is between the two required semicolons. If the condition is `true`, the body statement (line 13) displays control variable `counter`'s value (`1`). After executing the loop's body, the program increments `counter` in the expression `++counter`. Then the program performs the loop-continuation test again to determine whether to continue with the loop's next iteration. When the loop-continuation test fails, iteration terminates and the program continues executing at the first statement after the `for` (line 16).

### 6.3.1 A Closer Look at the for Statement's Header

Figure 6.3 takes a closer look at the `for` statement in Fig. 6.2. The first line—including the keyword `for` and everything in parentheses after `for` (line 11 in Fig. 6.2)—is sometimes called the **for statement header**. The `for` header "does it all"—it specifies each item needed for counter-controlled iteration with a control variable.

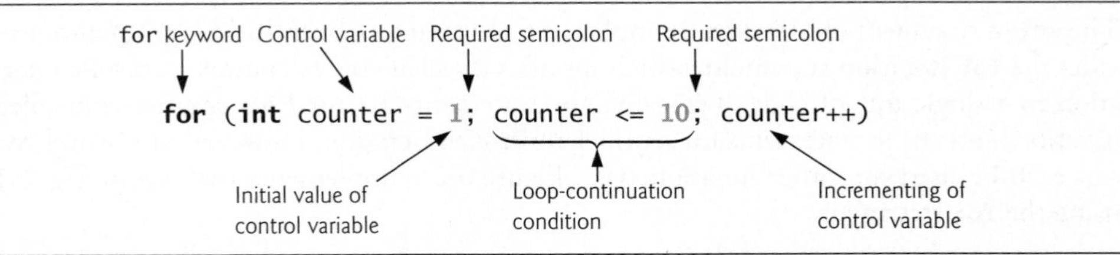


**Fig. 6.3** | `for` statement header components.

### 6.3.2 General Format of a for Statement

The general format of the `for` statement is

```
for (initialization; loopContinuationCondition; increment)
{
   statement
}
```

where the *initialization* expression names the loop's control variable and provides its initial value, the *loopContinuationCondition* determines whether looping should continue and the *increment* modifies the control variable's value (whether an increment or decrement), so that the loop-continuation condition eventually becomes `false`. The two semicolons in the `for` header are required. We don't include a semicolon after *statement*, because the semicolon is already assumed to be included in the notion of a *statement*.

### 6.3.3 Scope of a for Statement's Control Variable

If the *initialization* expression in the `for` header declares the control variable (i.e., the control variable's type is specified before the variable name, as in Fig. 6.2), the control variable can be used *only* in that `for` statement—it will not exist outside it. This restricted use of the name of the control variable is known as the variable's **scope**. The scope of a variable defines where it can be used in an app. For example, a local variable can be used only in the method that declares the variable and *only* from the point of declaration through the end of the block in which the variable has been declared. Scope is discussed in detail in Chapter 7, Methods: A Deeper Look.

**Common Programming Error 6.1**

*When a `for` statement's control variable is declared in the initialization section of a `for`'s header, using the control variable after the `for`'s body is a compilation error.*

### 6.3.4 Expressions in a for Statement's Header Are Optional

All three expressions in a `for` header are *optional*. If the *loopContinuationCondition* is omitted, C# assumes that it's *always true*, thus creating an *infinite loop*. You can omit the *initialization* expression if the app initializes the control variable *before* the loop—in this case, the scope of the control variable will *not* be limited to the loop. You can omit the *increment* expression if the app calculates the increment with statements in the loop's body or if no increment is needed. The increment expression in a `for` acts as if it were a standalone statement at the end of the `for`'s body. Therefore, the expressions

```
counter = counter + 1
counter += 1
++counter
counter++
```

are equivalent increment expressions in a `for` statement. Many programmers prefer `counter++` because it's concise and because a `for` loop evaluates its increment expression after its body executes—so the postfix increment form *seems* more natural. In this case, the variable being incremented does not appear in a larger expression, so the prefix and postfix increment operators have the *same* effect.

### 6.3.5 UML Activity Diagram for the for Statement

Figure 6.4 shows the activity diagram of the `for` statement in Fig. 6.2. The diagram makes it clear that initialization occurs only once—*before* the loop-continuation test is evaluated the first time—and that incrementing occurs *each* time through the loop *after* the body statement executes.

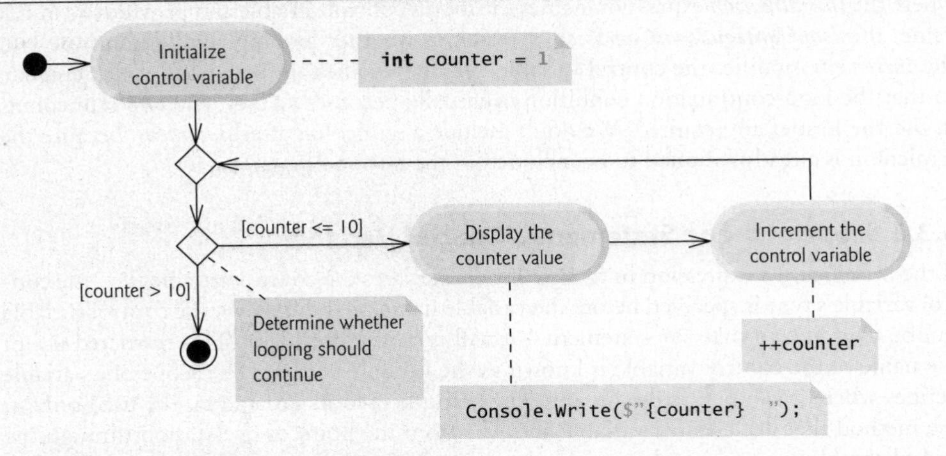


**Fig. 6.4** | UML activity diagram for the `for` statement in Fig. 6.2.

## 6.4 App: Summing Even Integers

We now consider a sample app that demonstrates a simple use of `for`. The app in Fig. 6.5 uses a `for` statement to sum the even integers from 2 to 20 and store the result in an `int` variable called `total`. Each iteration of the loop (lines 12–15) adds control variable `number`'s value to variable `total`.

```
1   // Fig. 6.5: Sum.cs
2   // Summing integers with the for statement.
3   using System;
4
5   class Sum
6   {
7      static void Main()
8      {
9         int total = 0; // initialize total
10
11        // total even integers from 2 through 20
12        for (int number = 2; number <= 20; number += 2)
13        {
14           total += number;
15        }
16
17        Console.WriteLine($"Sum is {total}"); // display results
18     }
19  }
```

```
Sum is 110
```

**Fig. 6.5** | Summing integers with the `for` statement.

The *initialization* and *increment* expressions can be comma-separated lists that enable you to use multiple initialization expressions or multiple increment expressions. For example, although this is discouraged, you could merge the `for`'s body statement (line 14) into the increment portion of the `for` header by using a comma as follows:

```
total += number, number += 2
```

## 6.5 App: Compound-Interest Calculations

The next app uses the `for` statement to compute compound interest. Consider the following problem:

> *A person invests \$1,000 in a savings account yielding 5% interest. Assuming that all the interest is left on deposit, calculate and print the amount of money in the account at the end of each year for 10 years. Use the following formula to determine the amounts:*
>
> $$a = p\,(1 + r)^n$$
>
> *where*
>
> $p$ is the original amount invested (i.e., the principal)
> $r$ is the annual interest rate (e.g., use 0.05 for 5%)
> $n$ is the number of years
> $a$ is the amount on deposit at the end of the $n$th year.

The solution to this problem (Fig. 6.6) involves a loop that performs the indicated calculation for each of the 10 years the money remains on deposit.

```
// Fig. 6.6: Interest.cs
// Compound-interest calculations with for.
using System;

class Interest
{
   static void Main()
   {
      decimal principal = 1000; // initial amount before interest
      double rate = 0.05; // interest rate

      // display headers
      Console.WriteLine("Year   Amount on deposit");

      // calculate amount on deposit for each of ten years
      for (int year = 1; year <= 10; ++year)
      {
         // calculate new amount for specified year
         decimal amount = principal *
            ((decimal) Math.Pow(1.0 + rate, year));

         // display the year and the amount
         Console.WriteLine($"{year,4}{amount,20:C}");
      }
   }
}
```

**Fig. 6.6** | Compound-interest calculations with `for`. (Part 1 of 2.)

```
Year   Amount on deposit
   1           $1,050.00
   2           $1,102.50
   3           $1,157.63
   4           $1,215.51
   5           $1,276.28
   6           $1,340.10
   7           $1,407.10
   8           $1,477.46
   9           $1,551.33
  10           $1,628.89
```

**Fig. 6.6** | Compound-interest calculations with `for`. (Part 2 of 2.)

Lines 9 and 19 declare `decimal` variables `principal` and `amount`, and line 10 declares `double` variable `rate`. Lines 9–10 also initialize `principal` to `1000` (i.e., $1,000.00) and `rate` to `0.05`. C# treats numeric literals like `0.05` as type `double`. Similarly, C# treats whole-number literals like `7` and `1000` as type `int`—unlike `double` values, `int` values *can* be assigned to `decimal` variables. When `principal` is initialized to `1000`, the `int` value `1000` is *promoted* to type `decimal` *implicitly*—no cast is required. Line 13 outputs the headers for the app's two columns of output. The first column displays the year, and the second displays the amount on deposit at the end of that year.

### 6.5.1 Performing the Interest Calculations with Math Method pow

Classes provide methods that perform common tasks on objects. Most methods must be called on a specific object. For example, to deposit money into bank accounts in Fig. 4.12, we called method `Deposit` on the `Account` objects `account1` and `account2`. Many classes also provide methods to perform common tasks that do not require specific objects—they *must* be called using a class name. Such methods are called **`static` methods**. You've used several `static` methods of class `Console`—methods `Write`, `WriteLine` and `ReadLine`. You call a `static` method by specifying the class name followed by the member-access operator (.) and the method name, as in

```
ClassName.MethodName(arguments)
```

C# does not include an exponentiation operator, so we use class `Math`'s `static` method `Pow` to perform the compound-interest calculation. The expression

```
Math.Pow(x, y)
```

calculates the value of *x* raised to the *y*th power. The method receives two `double` arguments and returns a `double` value. Lines 19–20 in Fig. 6.6 perform the calculation

$$a = p\ (1 + r)^n$$

from the problem statement, where *a* is the `amount`, *p* is the `principal`, *r* is the `rate` and *n* is the `year`. In this calculation, we need to multiply the `decimal` value `principal` by a `double` value (the value returned by the call to `Math.Pow`). C# will not *implicitly* convert `double` to a `decimal` type, or vice versa, because of the *possible loss of information* in either conversion, so line 20 contains a `(decimal)` cast operator that *explicitly* converts `Math.Pow`'s `double` return value to a `decimal`.

The `for` statement's body contains the calculation `1.0 + rate`, which appears as an argument to the `Math.Pow` method. In fact, this calculation produces the same result each time through the loop, so repeating the calculation in every iteration of the loop is wasteful.

**Performance Tip 6.1**

*In loops, avoid calculations for which the result never changes—such calculations should typically be placed before the loop. Optimizing compilers will typically do this for you.*

### 6.5.2 Formatting with Field Widths and Alignment

After each calculation, line 23

```
Console.WriteLine($"{year,4}{amount,20:C}");
```

displays the year and the amount on deposit at the end of that year. The following interpolation expression formats the `year`:

```
{year,4}
```

The integer `4` after the comma indicates that the `year` value should be displayed in a **field width** of 4—that is, `WriteLine` displays the value with at least four character positions. If the value to be output is *fewer than* four character positions wide (one or two characters in this example), the value is **right-aligned** in the field by default—in this case the value is preceded by two or three spaces, depending on the `year` value. If the value to be output were *more* than four character positions wide, the field width would be *extended to the right* to accommodate the entire value—this would push the `amount` column to the right, upsetting the neat columns of our tabular output. Similarly, the interpolation expression

```
{amount,20:C}
```

formats the `amount` as currency (`C`) right-aligned in a field of at least 20 characters. To **left align** a value, simply use a *negative* field width.

### 6.5.3 Caution: Do Not Use `float` or `double` for Monetary Amounts

Section 4.9 introduced the simple type `decimal` for precise monetary representation and calculations. You might be tempted to use the floating-point types `float` or `double` for such calculations. However, for certain values types `float` or `double` suffer from what we call **representational error**. For example, floating-point numbers often arise as a result of calculations—when we divide 10 by 3, the result is 3.3333333…, with the sequence of 3s repeating infinitely. The computer allocates only a *fixed* amount of space to hold such a value, so clearly the stored floating-point value can be only an *approximation*.

**Common Programming Error 6.2**

*Using floating-point numbers in a manner that assumes they're represented exactly (e.g., using them in comparisons for equality) can lead to incorrect results. Floating-point numbers are represented only* approximately.

**Error-Prevention Tip 6.2**

*Do not use variables of type `double` (or `float`) to perform precise monetary calculations—use type `decimal` instead. The imprecision of floating-point numbers can cause errors that will result in incorrect monetary values.*

### *Applications of Floating-Point Numbers*

Floating-point numbers have numerous applications, especially for measured values. For example, when we speak of a "normal" body temperature of 98.6 degrees Fahrenheit, we need not be precise to a large number of digits. When we read the temperature on a thermometer as 98.6, it may actually be 98.5999473210643. Calling this number simply 98.6 is fine for most applications involving body temperatures. Similarly, we used type `double` to perform class-average calculations in Chapter 5. Due to the imprecise nature of floating-point numbers, type `double` is preferred over type `float`, because `double` variables can represent floating-point numbers more precisely. For this reason, we use type `double` throughout the book, unless we're manipulating monetary amounts, in which case we use `decimal`.

## 6.6 do...while Iteration Statement

The **do...while iteration statement** is similar to the `while` statement. In the `while`, the app tests the loop-continuation condition at the beginning of the loop, *before* executing the loop's body. If the condition is false, the body *never* executes. The `do...while` statement tests the loop-continuation condition *after* executing the loop's body; therefore, the body always executes *at least once*. When a `do...while` statement terminates, execution continues with the next statement in sequence. Figure 6.7 uses a `do...while` (lines 11–15) to output the numbers 1–10.

```
1  // Fig. 6.7: DoWhileTest.cs
2  // do...while iteration statement.
3  using System;
4
5  class DoWhileTest
6  {
7     static void Main()
8     {
9        int counter = 1; // initialize counter
10
11       do
12       {
13          Console.Write($"{counter}  ");
14          ++counter;
15       } while (counter <= 10); // required semicolon
16
17       Console.WriteLine();
18    }
19 }
```

```
1  2  3  4  5  6  7  8  9  10
```

**Fig. 6.7** | do...while iteration statement.

Line 9 declares and initializes control variable `counter`. Upon entering the `do...while` statement, line 13 outputs `counter`'s value, and line 14 increments `counter`. Then the app evaluates the loop-continuation test at the *bottom* of the loop (line 15). If the condition is true, the loop continues from the first body statement (line 13). If the condition is false, the loop terminates, and the app continues with the next statement after the loop (line 17).

### *UML Activity Diagram for the* do...while *Iteration Statement*

Figure 6.8 contains the UML activity diagram for the do...while statement. This diagram makes it clear that the loop-continuation condition is not evaluated until *after* the loop performs the action state *at least once*. Compare this activity diagram with that of the while statement (Fig. 5.6).

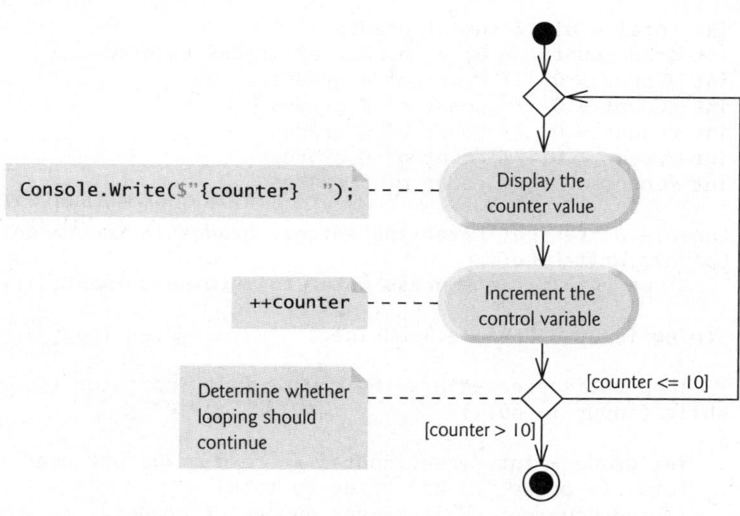


**Fig. 6.8** | do...while iteration statement UML activity diagram.

## 6.7 switch Multiple-Selection Statement

We discussed the if and if...else selection statements in Chapter 5. C# provides the **switch multiple-selection** statement to perform different actions based on the possible values of an expression, known as the **switch expression.** Each action is associated with one or more of the switch expression's possible values. These are specified as **constant integral expressions** or a **constant string expressions**:

- A constant integral expression is any expression involving character and integer constants that evaluates to an integer value—i.e., values of type sbyte, byte, short, ushort, int, uint, long, ulong and char, or a constant from an enum type (enum is discussed in Section 7.9).
- A constant string expression is any expression composed of string literals or const string variables that always results in the same string.

### 6.7.1 Using a switch Statement to Count A, B, C, D and F Grades

Figure 6.9 calculates the class average of a set of numeric grades entered by the user, and uses a switch statement to determine whether each grade is the equivalent of an A, B, C, D or F and to increment the appropriate grade counter. The program also displays a summary of the number of students who received each grade.

```
// Fig. 6.9: LetterGrades.cs
// Using a switch statement to count letter grades.
using System;

class LetterGrades
{
   static void Main()
   {
      int total = 0; // sum of grades
      int gradeCounter = 0; // number of grades entered
      int aCount = 0; // count of A grades
      int bCount = 0; // count of B grades
      int cCount = 0; // count of C grades
      int dCount = 0; // count of D grades
      int fCount = 0; // count of F grades

      Console.WriteLine("Enter the integer grades in the range 0-100.");
      Console.WriteLine(
         "Type <Ctrl> z and press Enter to terminate input:");

      string input = Console.ReadLine(); // read user input

      // loop until user enters the end-of-file indicator (<Ctrl> z)
      while (input != null)
      {
         int grade = int.Parse(input); // read grade off user input
         total += grade; // add grade to total
         ++gradeCounter; // increment number of grades

         // determine which grade was entered
         switch (grade / 10)
         {
            case 9: // grade was in the 90s
            case 10: // grade was 100
               ++aCount; // increment aCount
               break; // necessary to exit switch
            case 8: // grade was between 80 and 89
               ++bCount; // increment bCount
               break; // exit switch
            case 7: // grade was between 70 and 79
               ++cCount; // increment cCount
               break; // exit switch
            case 6: // grade was between 60 and 69
               ++dCount; // increment dCount
               break; // exit switch
            default: // grade was less than 60
               ++fCount; // increment fCount
               break; // exit switch
         }

         input = Console.ReadLine(); // read user input
      }

```

**Fig. 6.9** | Using a `switch` statement to count letter grades. (Part 1 of 2.)

```
54         Console.WriteLine("\nGrade Report:");
55
56         // if user entered at least one grade...
57         if (gradeCounter != 0)
58         {
59            // calculate average of all grades entered
60            double average = (double) total / gradeCounter;
61
62            // output summary of results
63            Console.WriteLine(
64               $"Total of the {gradeCounter} grades entered is {total}");
65            Console.WriteLine($"Class average is {average:F}");
66            Console.WriteLine("Number of students who received each grade:");
67            Console.WriteLine($"A: {aCount}"); // display number of A grades
68            Console.WriteLine($"B: {bCount}"); // display number of B grades
69            Console.WriteLine($"C: {cCount}"); // display number of C grades
70            Console.WriteLine($"D: {dCount}"); // display number of D grades
71            Console.WriteLine($"F: {fCount}"); // display number of F grades
72         }
73         else // no grades were entered, so output appropriate message
74         {
75            Console.WriteLine("No grades were entered");
76         }
77      }
78   }
```

```
Enter the integer grades in the range 0-100.
Type <Ctrl> z and press Enter to terminate input:
99
92
45
57
63
71
76
85
90
100
^Z

Grade Report:
Total of the 10 grades entered is 778
Class average is 77.80
Number of students who received each grade:
A: 4
B: 1
C: 2
D: 1
F: 2
```

**Fig. 6.9** | Using a switch statement to count letter grades. (Part 2 of 2.)

Lines 9 and 10 declare and initialize to 0 local variables total and gradeCounter to keep track of the sum of the grades entered by the user and the number of grades entered, respectively. Lines 11–15 declare and initialize to 0 counter variables for each grade category. The `Main` method has two key parts. Lines 21–52 read an arbitrary number of integer grades from the user using sentinel-controlled iteration, update variables `total` and `gradeCounter`, and increment an appropriate letter-grade counter for each grade entered. Lines 54–76 output a report containing the total of all grades entered, the average grade and the number of students who received each letter grade.

### *Reading Grades from the User*

Lines 17–19 prompt the user to enter integer grades and to type *Ctrl* + *z*, then press *Enter* to terminate the input. The notation *Ctrl* + *z* means to hold down the *Ctrl* key and tap the *z* key when typing in a **Command Prompt**. *Ctrl* + *z* is the Windows key sequence for typing the **end-of-file indicator**. This is one way to inform an app that there's no more data to input. If *Ctrl* + *z* is entered while the app is awaiting input with a `ReadLine` method, `null` is returned. (The end-of-file indicator is a system-dependent keystroke combination. On many non-Windows systems, end-of-file is entered by typing *Ctrl* + *d*.) In Chapter 17, Files and Streams, we'll see how the end-of-file indicator is used when an app reads its input from a file. Windows typically displays the characters `^Z` in a **Command Prompt** when the end-of-file indicator is typed, as shown in the program's output.

Line 21 uses `Console`'s `ReadLine` method to get the first line that the user entered and store it in variable `input`. The `while` statement (lines 24–52) processes this user input. The condition at line 24 checks whether the value of `input` is `null`—`Console`'s `ReadLine` method returns `null` only if the user typed an end-of-file indicator. As long as the end-of-file indicator has not been typed, `input` will not be `null` and the condition will pass.

Line 26 converts the `string` in `input` to an `int` type. Line 27 adds `grade` to `total`. Line 28 increments `gradeCounter`.

### *Processing the Grades*

The `switch` statement (lines 31–49) determines which counter to increment. In this example, we assume that the user enters a valid grade in the range 0–100. A grade in the range 90–100 represents A, 80–89 represents B, 70–79 represents C, 60–69 represents D and 0–59 represents F. The `switch` statement consists of a block that contains a sequence of **`case` labels** and an optional **`default` label**. These are used in this example to determine which counter to increment based on the grade.

### *The `switch` Statement*

When control reaches the `switch` statement, the app evaluates the expression `grade / 10` in the parentheses—this is the `switch` expression. The app attempts to match the value of the `switch` expression with one of the `case` labels. The `switch` expression in line 31 performs integer division, which *truncates* the fractional part of the result. Thus, when we divide any value in the range 0–100 by 10, the result is always a value from 0 to 10. We use several of these values in our `case` labels. For example, if the user enters the integer `85`, the `switch` expression evaluates to `int` value `8`. If a match occurs between the `switch` expression and a `case` (`case 8:` at line 37), the app executes the statements for that `case`. For the integer `8`, line 38 increments `bCount`, because a grade in the 80s is a B.

The **`break` statement** (line 39) causes program control to proceed with the first statement after the `switch` (line 51), which reads the next line entered by the user and assigns it to the variable `input`. Line 52 marks the end of the body of the `while` statement that inputs grades, so control flows to the while's condition (line 24) to determine whether the loop should continue executing based on the value just assigned to the variable input.

### *Consecutive* case *Labels*

The switch's cases explicitly test for the values 10, 9, 8, 7 and 6. Lines 33–34 test for the values 9 and 10 (both of which represent the grade A). Listing case labels consecutively in this manner with no statements between them enables the cases to perform the same set of statements—when the switch expression evaluates to 9 or 10, the statements in lines 35–36 execute. The switch statement does not provide a mechanism for testing ranges of values, so every value to be tested must be listed in a separate case label. Each case can have multiple statements. The switch statement differs from other control statements in that it does *not* require braces around multiple statements in each case.

### *The* default *Case*

If *no match* occurs between the switch expression's value and a case label, the statements after the default label (lines 47–48) execute. We use the default label in this example to process all switch-expression values that are less than 6—that is, all failing grades. If no match occurs and the switch does *not* contain a default label, program control simply continues with the first statement (if there's one) after the switch statement.

**Good Programming Practice 6.1**

*Although each* case *and the* default *label in a* switch *can occur in any order, place the* default *label last for clarity.*

### *No "Fall Through" in the C#* switch *Statement*

In many other programming languages containing switch, the break statement *is not* required at the end of a case. In those languages, without break statements, each time a match occurs in the switch, the statements for that case and subsequent cases execute until a break statement or the end of the switch is encountered. This is often referred to as "falling through" to the statements in subsequent cases. This leads to logic errors when you forget the break statement. C# is different from other programming languages—after the statements in a case, you're *required* to include a statement that terminates the case, such as a break, a return or a throw;[1] otherwise, a compilation error occurs.[2]

### *Displaying the Grade Report*

Lines 54–76 output a report based on the grades entered (as shown in the input/output window in Fig. 6.9). Line 57 determines whether the user entered at least one grade—this helps us avoid dividing by zero. If so, line 60 calculates the average of the grades. Lines 63–71 then output the total of all the grades, the class average and the number of students who received each letter grade. If no grades were entered, line 75 outputs an appropriate message. The output in Fig. 6.9 shows a sample grade report based on 10 grades.

---

1. We discuss the throw statement in Chapter 13, Exception Handling: A Deeper Look.
2. You can implement fall through by replacing the break statement after a case's or default's actions with a statement of the form goto case *value*; (where *value* is a literal or constant in one of the switch's cases) or goto default;.

## 6.7.2 switch Statement UML Activity Diagram

Figure 6.10 shows the UML activity diagram for the general `switch` statement. Every set of statements after a `case` label normally ends its execution with a `break` or `return` statement to terminate the `switch` statement after processing the `case`. Typically, you'll use `break` statements. Figure 6.10 emphasizes this by including `break` statements in the activity diagram. The diagram makes it clear that the `break` statement at the end of a `case` causes control to exit the `switch` statement immediately.

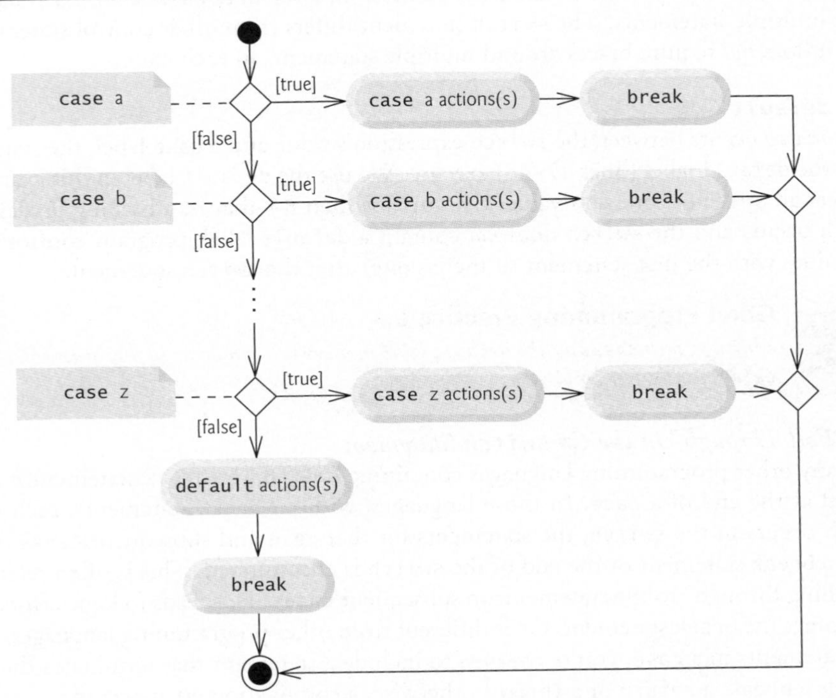


**Fig. 6.10** | `switch` multiple-selection statement UML activity diagram with `break` statements.

## 6.7.3 Notes on the Expression in Each case of a switch

In the `switch` statements cases, *constant integral expressions* can be **character constants**—specific characters in single quotes, such as `'A'`, `'7'` or `'$'`—which represent the integer values of characters. (Appendix C shows the integer values of the characters in the ASCII character set, which is a popular subset of the Unicode character set used by C#.) A *`string` constant* (or *`string` literal*) is a sequence of characters in double quotes, such as `"Welcome to C# Programming!"` or a `const string` variable. For `string`s, you also can use `null` or `string.Empty`.

The expression in each case also can be a **constant**—a value which does not change for the entire app. Constants are declared with the keyword const (discussed in Chapter 7). C# also has a feature called *enumerations*, which we also present in Chapter 7. Enumeration constants also can be used in case labels. In Chapter 12, we present a more elegant way to implement switch logic—we use a technique called *polymorphism* to create apps that are often clearer, easier to maintain and easier to extend than apps using switch logic.

## 6.8 Class AutoPolicy Case Study: strings in switch Statements

strings can be used in switch expressions, and string literals can be used in case labels. To demonstrate this, we'll implement an app that meets the following requirements:

> *You've been hired by an auto insurance company that serves these northeast states—Connecticut, Maine, Massachusetts, New Hampshire, New Jersey, New York, Pennsylvania, Rhode Island and Vermont. The company would like you to create a program that produces a report indicating for each of their auto insurance policies whether the policy is held in a state with "no-fault" auto insurance—Massachusetts, New Jersey, New York and Pennsylvania.*

The app contains two classes—AutoPolicy (Fig. 6.11) and AutoPolicyTest (Fig. 6.12).

### *Class* AutoPolicy

Class AutoPolicy (Fig. 6.11) represents an auto insurance policy. The class contains:

- auto-implemented int property AccountNumber (line 5) to store the policy's account number,
- auto-implemented string property MakeAndModel (line 6) to store the car's make and model (such as a "Toyota Camry"),
- auto-implemented string property State (line 7) to store a two-character state abbreviation representing the state in which the policy is held (e.g., "MA" for Massachusetts),
- a constructor (lines 10–15) that initializes the class's properties and
- read-only property IsNoFaultState (lines 18–37) to return a bool value indicating whether the policy is held in a no-fault auto insurance state; note the property name—a common naming convention for a bool property is to begin the name with "Is".

In property IsNoFaultState, the switch expression (line 25) is the string returned by AutoPolicy's State property. The switch statement compares the switch expression's value with the case labels (line 27) to determine whether the policy is held in Massachusetts, New Jersey, New York or Pennsylvania (the no-fault states). If there's a match, then line 28 sets local variable noFaultState to true and the switch statement terminates; otherwise, the default case sets noFaultState to false (line 31). Then IsNoFaultState's get accessor returns local variable noFaultState's value.

```
// Fig. 6.11: AutoPolicy.cs
// Class that represents an auto insurance policy.
class AutoPolicy
{
   public int AccountNumber { get; set; } // policy account number
   public string MakeAndModel { get; set; } // car that policy applies to
   public string State { get; set; } // two-letter state abbreviation

   // constructor
   public AutoPolicy(int accountNumber, string makeAndModel, string state)
   {
      AccountNumber = accountNumber;
      MakeAndModel = makeAndModel;
      State = state;
   }

   // returns whether the state has no-fault insurance
   public bool IsNoFaultState
   {
      get
      {
         bool noFaultState;

         // determine whether state has no-fault auto insurance
         switch (State) // get AutoPolicy object's state abbreviation
         {
            case "MA": case "NJ": case "NY": case "PA":
               noFaultState = true;
               break;
            default:
               noFaultState = false;
               break;
         }

         return noFaultState;
      }
   }
}
```

**Fig. 6.11** | Class that represents an auto insurance policy.

For simplicity, we do not validate an `AutoPolicy`'s properties, and we assume that state abbreviations are always two uppercase letters. In addition, a real `AutoPolicy` class would likely contain many other properties and methods for data such as the account holder's name, address, birth date, etc.

### *Class* `AutoPolicyTest`

Class `AutoPolicyTest` (Fig. 6.12) creates two `AutoPolicy` objects (lines 10–11 in `Main`). Lines 14–15 pass each object to `static` method `policyInNoFaultState` (lines 20–28), which uses `AutoPolicy` methods to determine and display whether the object it receives represents a policy in a no-fault auto insurance state.

```
// Fig. 6.12: AutoPolicyTest.cs
// Demonstrating strings in switch.
using System;

class AutoPolicyTest
{
   static void Main()
   {
      // create two AutoPolicy objects
      AutoPolicy policy1 = new AutoPolicy(11111111, "Toyota Camry", "NJ");
      AutoPolicy policy2 = new AutoPolicy(22222222, "Ford Fusion", "ME");

      // display whether each policy is in a no-fault state
      PolicyInNoFaultState(policy1);
      PolicyInNoFaultState(policy2);
   }

   // method that displays whether an AutoPolicy
   // is in a state with no-fault auto insurance
   public static void PolicyInNoFaultState(AutoPolicy policy)
   {
      Console.WriteLine("The auto policy:");
      Console.Write($"Account #: {policy.AccountNumber}; ");
      Console.WriteLine($"Car: {policy.MakeAndModel};");
      Console.Write($"State {policy.State}; ");
      Console.Write($"({policy.IsNoFaultState ? "is": "is not"})");
      Console.WriteLine(" a no-fault state\n");
   }
}
```

```
The auto policy:
Account #: 11111111; Car: Toyota Camry;
State NJ is a no-fault state

The auto policy:
Account #: 22222222; Car: Ford Fusion;
State ME is not a no-fault state
```

**Fig. 6.12** | Demonstrating strings in switch.

## 6.9 break and continue Statements

In addition to selection and iteration statements, C# provides statements break and continue to alter the flow of control. The preceding section showed how break can be used to terminate a switch statement's execution. This section discusses how to use break to terminate any iteration statement.

### 6.9.1 break Statement

The break statement, when executed in a while, for, do...while, switch, or foreach, causes immediate exit from the loop or switch. Execution continues with the first statement after the control statement. Figure 6.13 demonstrates a break statement exiting a for. When the if nested at line 13 in the for statement (lines 11–19) determines that count is 5, the break statement at line 15 executes. This terminates the for statement, and the app proceeds to line 21 (immediately after the for statement), which displays a message indicating the value of the control variable when the loop terminated. The loop fully executes its body only four times instead of 10 because of the break.

```
1  // Fig. 6.13: BreakTest.cs
2  // break statement exiting a for statement.
3  using System;
4
5  class BreakTest
6  {
7     static void Main()
8     {
9        int count; // control variable also used after loop terminates
10
11       for (count = 1; count <= 10; ++count) // loop 10 times
12       {
13          if (count == 5) // if count is 5,
14          {
15             break; // terminate loop
16          }
17
18          Console.Write($"{count} ");
19       }
20
21       Console.WriteLine($"\nBroke out of loop at count = {count}");
22    }
23 }
```

```
1 2 3 4
Broke out of loop at count = 5
```

**Fig. 6.13** | break statement exiting a for statement.

### 6.9.2 continue Statement

The **continue statement**, when executed in a while, for, do…while, or foreach, skips the remaining statements in the loop body and proceeds with the next iteration of the loop. In while and do…while statements, the app evaluates the loop-continuation test *immediately after* the continue statement executes. In a for statement, the increment expression normally executes next, then the app evaluates the loop-continuation test.

Figure 6.14 uses the continue statement in a for to skip the statement at line 16 when the nested if (line 11) determines that the value of count is 5. When the continue statement executes, program control continues with the increment of the control variable in the for statement (line 9).

**Software Engineering Observation 6.1**

*There's a tension between achieving quality software engineering and achieving the best-performing software. Often, one of these goals is achieved at the expense of the other. For all but the most performance-intensive situations, apply the following rule: First, make your code simple and correct; then make it fast, but only if necessary.*

```
// Fig. 6.14: ContinueTest.cs
// continue statement skipping an iteration of a for statement.
using System;

class ContinueTest
{
   static void Main()
   {
      for (int count = 1; count <= 10; ++count) // loop 10 times
      {
         if (count == 5) // if count is 5,
         {
            continue; // skip remaining code in loop
         }

         Console.Write($"{count} ");
      }

      Console.WriteLine("\nUsed continue to skip displaying 5");
   }
}
```

```
1 2 3 4 6 7 8 9 10
Used continue to skip displaying 5
```

**Fig. 6.14** | `continue` statement skipping an iteration of a `for` statement.

## 6.10 Logical Operators

So far, we've used only **simple conditions** expressed in terms of the relational operators >, <, >= and <=, and the equality operators == and !=, such as `number != sentinelValue`, `count <= 10` and `total > 1000`. C# provides **logical operators** to enable you to form more complex conditions by combining simple conditions. The logical operators are && (conditional AND), || (conditional OR), & (boolean logical AND), | (boolean logical inclusive OR), ^ (boolean logical exclusive OR) and ! (logical negation).

### 6.10.1 Conditional AND (&&) Operator

Suppose that we wish to ensure at some point in an app that two conditions are *both* true before we choose a certain path of execution. In this case, we can use the **&& (conditional AND)** operator, as follows:

```
if (gender == 'F' && age >= 65)
{
   ++seniorFemales;
}
```

This `if` statement contains two simple conditions—`gender == 'F'` determines whether a person is female and `age >= 65` might be evaluated to determine whether a person is a senior citizen. The `if` statement considers the combined condition

```
gender == 'F' && age >= 65
```

which is true if and only if *both* simple conditions are true. Some programmers find that the preceding combined condition is more readable with redundant parentheses, as in

```
(gender == 'F') && (age >= 65)
```

The table in Fig. 6.15 summarizes the && operator. The table shows all four possible combinations of `false` and `true` values for *expression1* and *expression2*. Such tables are called **truth tables**. C# evaluates all expressions that include relational operators, equality operators or logical operators to `bool` values—which are either `true` or `false`.

| expression1 | expression2 | expression1 && expression2 |
|---|---|---|
| false | false | false |
| false | true | false |
| true | false | false |
| true | true | true |

**Fig. 6.15** | && (conditional AND) operator truth table.

### 6.10.2 Conditional OR (||) Operator

Now suppose we wish to ensure that *either or both* of two conditions are true before we choose a certain path of execution. In this case, we use the **||** (**conditional OR**) operator, as in the following app segment:

```
if ((semesterAverage >= 90) || (finalExam >= 90))
{
   Console.WriteLine ("Student grade is A");
}
```

This statement also contains two simple conditions. The condition `semesterAverage >= 90` is evaluated to determine whether the student deserves an A in the course because of a solid performance throughout the semester. The condition `finalExam >= 90` is evaluated to determine whether the student deserves an A in the course because of an outstanding performance on the final exam. The `if` statement then considers the combined condition

```
(semesterAverage >= 90) || (finalExam >= 90)
```

and awards the student an A if either or both of the simple conditions are true. The only time the message `"Student grade is A"` is *not* displayed is when *both* of the simple conditions are *false*. Figure 6.16 is a truth table for operator conditional OR (||). Operator && has a higher precedence than operator ||. Both operators associate from left to right.

| expression1 | expression2 | expression1 \|\| expression2 |
|---|---|---|
| false | false | false |
| false | true | true |
| true | false | true |
| true | true | true |

**Fig. 6.16** | || (conditional OR) operator truth table.

### 6.10.3 Short-Circuit Evaluation of Complex Conditions

The parts of an expression containing `&&` or `||` operators are evaluated *only* until it's known whether the condition is true or false. Thus, evaluation of the expression

```
(gender == 'F') && (age >= 65)
```

stops immediately if `gender` is not equal to `'F'` (i.e., at that point, it's certain that the entire expression is `false`) and continues *only* if `gender` *is* equal to `'F'` (i.e., the entire expression could still be `true` if the condition `age >= 65` is `true`). This feature of conditional AND and conditional OR expressions is called **short-circuit evaluation.**

**Common Programming Error 6.3**

*In expressions using operator `&&`, a condition—known as the dependent condition—may require another condition to be true for the evaluation of the dependent condition to be meaningful. In this case, the dependent condition should be placed* after *the other one, or an error might occur. For example, in the expression `(i != 0) && (10 / i == 2)`, the second condition must appear after the first condition, or a divide-by-zero error might occur.*

### 6.10.4 Boolean Logical AND (&) and Boolean Logical OR (|) Operators

The **boolean logical AND** (`&`) and **boolean logical inclusive OR** (`|`) operators work identically to the `&&` (conditional AND) and `||` (conditional OR) operators, with one exception—the boolean logical operators *always* evaluate both of their operands (i.e., they do *not* perform short-circuit evaluation). Therefore, the expression

```
(gender == 'F') & (age >= 65)
```

evaluates `age >= 65` regardless of whether `gender` is equal to `'F'`. This is useful if the right operand of the `&` or `|` operator has a required **side effect**—such as a modification of a variable's value. For example, the expression

```
(birthday == true) | (++age >= 65)
```

guarantees that the condition `++age >= 65` will be evaluated. Thus, the variable `age` is incremented in the preceding expression, *regardless* of whether the overall expression is `true` or `false`.

**Error-Prevention Tip 6.3**

*For clarity, avoid expressions with side effects in conditions. The side effects may appear clever, but they can make it harder to understand code and can lead to subtle logic errors.*

### 6.10.5 Boolean Logical Exclusive OR (^)

A complex condition containing the **boolean logical exclusive OR** (`^`) operator (also called the **logical XOR operator**) is `true` *if and only if one of its operands is* `true` *and the other is* `false`. If both operands are `true` or both are `false`, the entire condition is `false`. Figure 6.17 is a truth table for the boolean logical exclusive OR operator. This operator is also guaranteed to evaluate *both* of its operands.

| expression1 | expression2 | expression1 ^ expression2 |
|---|---|---|
| false | false | false |
| false | true | true |
| true | false | true |
| true | true | false |

**Fig. 6.17** | ^ (boolean logical exclusive OR) operator truth table.

### 6.10.6 Logical Negation (!) Operator

The ! (**logical negation** or **not**) operator enables you to "reverse" the meaning of a condition. Unlike the logical operators &&, ||, &, | and ^, which are *binary* operators that combine two conditions, the logical negation operator is a *unary* operator that has only a single condition as an operand. The logical negation operator is placed before a condition to choose a path of execution if the original condition (without the logical negation operator) is `false`, as in the code segment

```
if (! (grade == sentinelValue))
{
   Console.WriteLine($"The next grade is {grade}");
}
```

which executes the `WriteLine` call *only if* `grade` is not equal to `sentinelValue`. The parentheses around the condition `grade == sentinelValue` are needed because the logical negation operator has a higher precedence than the equality operator.

In most cases, you can avoid using logical negation by expressing the condition differently with an appropriate relational or equality operator. For example, the previous statement may also be written as

```
if (grade != sentinelValue)
{
   Console.WriteLine($"The next grade is {grade}");
}
```

This flexibility can help you express a condition in a more convenient manner. Figure 6.18 is a truth table for the logical negation operator.

| expression | !expression |
|---|---|
| false | true |
| true | false |

**Fig. 6.18** | ! (logical negation) operator truth table.

### 6.10.7 Logical Operators Example

Figure 6.19 demonstrates the logical operators and boolean logical operators by producing their truth tables. The output shows the expression that was evaluated and the `bool` result of that expression. Lines 10–14 produce the truth table for `&&` (conditional AND). Lines 17–21 produce the truth table for `||` (conditional OR). Lines 24–28 produce the truth table for `&` (boolean logical AND). Lines 31–35 produce the truth table for `|` (boolean logical inclusive OR). Lines 38–42 produce the truth table for `^` (boolean logical exclusive OR). Lines 45–47 produce the truth table for `!` (logical negation).

```
1  // Fig. 6.19: LogicalOperators.cs
2  // Logical operators.
3  using System;
4
5  class LogicalOperators
6  {
7     static void Main()
8     {
9        // create truth table for && (conditional AND) operator
10       Console.WriteLine("Conditional AND (&&)");
11       Console.WriteLine($"false && false: {false && false}");
12       Console.WriteLine($"false && true: {false && true}");
13       Console.WriteLine($"true && false: {true && false}");
14       Console.WriteLine($"true && true: {true && true}\n");
15
16       // create truth table for || (conditional OR) operator
17       Console.WriteLine("Conditional OR (||)");
18       Console.WriteLine($"false || false: {false || false}");
19       Console.WriteLine($"false || true: {false || true}");
20       Console.WriteLine($"true || false: {true || false}");
21       Console.WriteLine($"true || true: {true || true}\n");
22
23       // create truth table for & (boolean logical AND) operator
24       Console.WriteLine("Boolean logical AND (&)");
25       Console.WriteLine($"false & false: {false & false}");
26       Console.WriteLine($"false & true: {false & true}");
27       Console.WriteLine($"true & false: {true & false}");
28       Console.WriteLine($"true & true: {true & true}\n");
29
30       // create truth table for | (boolean logical inclusive OR) operator
31       Console.WriteLine("Boolean logical inclusive OR (|)");
32       Console.WriteLine($"false | false: {false | false}");
33       Console.WriteLine($"false | true: {false | true}");
34       Console.WriteLine($"true | false: {true | false}");
35       Console.WriteLine($"true | true: {true | true}\n");
36
37       // create truth table for ^ (boolean logical exclusive OR) operator
38       Console.WriteLine("Boolean logical exclusive OR (^)");
39       Console.WriteLine($"false ^ false: {false ^ false}");
40       Console.WriteLine($"false ^ true: {false ^ true}");
41       Console.WriteLine($"true ^ false: {true ^ false}");
42       Console.WriteLine($"true ^ true: {true ^ true}\n");
43
```

**Fig. 6.19** | Logical operators. (Part 1 of 2.)

```
        // create truth table for ! (logical negation) operator
        Console.WriteLine("Logical negation (!)");
        Console.WriteLine($"!false: {!false}");
        Console.WriteLine($"!true: {!true}");
    }
}
```

```
Conditional AND (&&)
false && false: False
false && true: False
true && false: False
true && true: True

Conditional OR (||)
false || false: False
false || true: True
true || false: True
true || true: True

Boolean logical AND (&)
false & false: False
false & true: False
true & false: False
true & true: True

Boolean logical inclusive OR (|)
false | false: False
false | true: True
true | false: True
true | true: True

Boolean logical exclusive OR (^)
false ^ false: False
false ^ true: True
true ^ false: True
true ^ true: False

Logical negation (!)
!false: True
!true: False
```

**Fig. 6.19** | Logical operators. (Part 2 of 2.)

### *Precedence and Associativity of the Operators Presented So Far*

Figure 6.20 shows the precedence and associativity of the C# operators introduced so far. The operators are shown from top to bottom in decreasing order of precedence.

| Operators | Associativity | Type |
|---|---|---|
| `.` `new` `++`*(postfix)* `--`*(postfix)* | left to right | highest precedence |
| `++` `--` `+` `-` `!` *(type)* | right to left | unary prefix |
| `*` `/` `%` | left to right | multiplicative |

**Fig. 6.20** | Precedence/associativity of the operators discussed so far. (Part 1 of 2.)

| Operators | Associativity | Type |
|---|---|---|
| `+ -` | left to right | additive |
| `< <= > >=` | left to right | relational |
| `== !=` | left to right | equality |
| `&` | left to right | boolean logical AND |
| `^` | left to right | boolean logical exclusive OR |
| `\|` | left to right | boolean logical inclusive OR |
| `&&` | left to right | conditional AND |
| `\|\|` | left to right | conditional OR |
| `?:` | right to left | conditional |
| `= += -= *= /= %=` | right to left | assignment |

**Fig. 6.20** | Precedence/associativity of the operators discussed so far. (Part 2 of 2.)

## 6.11 Wrap-Up

Chapter 5 discussed the `if`, `if...else` and `while` control statements. In Chapter 6, we discussed the `for`, `do...while` and `switch` control statements—we'll discuss the `foreach` statement in Chapter 8. The `for` and `do...while` statements are simply more convenient ways to express certain types of iteration. The `switch` statement is in some situations a more convenient notation for multiple selection, rather than using nested `if...else` statements. You can use the `break` and `continue` statements to alter the flow of control in iteration statements. The logical operators enable you to use more complex conditional expressions in control statements. We used type `decimal` to represent monetary amounts precisely rather than incuring the representational errors associated with types `float` and `double`. In Chapter 7, we examine methods in greater depth.

# 7

# Methods: A Deeper Look

## Objectives

In this chapter you'll:

- See that `static` methods and variables are associated with classes rather than objects.
- Use common `Math` class functions.
- Learn C#'s argument promotion rules for when argument types do not match parameter types exactly.
- Get a high-level overview of various namespaces from the .NET Framework Class Library.
- Use random-number generation to implement game-playing apps.
- Understand how the visibility of identifiers is limited to specific regions of programs.
- See how the method call and return mechanism is supported by the method-call stack.
- Create overloaded methods.
- Use optional and named parameters.
- Use recursive methods.
- Understand what value types and reference types are.
- Pass method arguments by value and by reference.

Outline



## 7.1 Introduction

In this chapter, we take a deeper look at methods. We'll discuss the difference between non-static and static methods. You'll see that the Math class in the .NET Framework Class Library provides many static methods to perform mathematical calculations. We'll also discuss static variables (known as class variables) and why method Main is declared static.

You'll declare a method with multiple parameters and use operator + to perform string concatenations. We'll discuss C#'s argument promotion rules for implicitly converting simple-type values to other types and when these rules are applied by the compiler. We'll also present several commonly used Framework Class Library namespaces.

We'll take a brief, and hopefully entertaining, diversion into simulation techniques with random-number generation and develop a version of a popular casino dice game that uses most of the programming techniques you've learned so far. You'll declare named constants with the `const` keyword and with `enum` types. We'll then present C#'s scope rules, which determine where identifiers can be referenced in an app.

We'll discuss how the method-call stack enables C# to keep track of which method is currently executing, how local variables of methods are maintained in memory and how a method knows where to return after it completes execution. You'll overload methods in a class by providing methods with the same name but different numbers and/or types of parameters, and learn how to use optional and named parameters.

We'll introduce C# 6's expression-bodied methods, which provide a concise notation for methods that simply return a value to their caller. We'll also use this expression-bodied notation for a read-only property's `get` accessor.

We'll discuss how recursive methods call themselves, breaking larger problems into smaller subproblems until eventually the original problem is solved. Finally, we'll provide more insight into how value-type and reference-type arguments are passed to methods.

## 7.2 Packaging Code in C#

So far, we've used properties, methods and classes to package code. We'll present additional packaging mechanisms in later chapters. C# apps are written by combining your properties, methods and classes with predefined properties, methods and classes available in the .NET Framework Class Library and in other class libraries. Related classes are often grouped into namespaces and compiled into class libraries so that they can be reused in other apps. You'll learn how to create your own namespaces and class libraries in Chapter 15. The Framework Class Library provides many *predefined* classes that contain methods for performing common mathematical calculations, string manipulations, character manipulations, input/output operations, graphical user interfaces, graphics, multimedia, printing, file processing, database operations, networking operations, error checking, web-app development, accessibility (for people with disabilities) and more.

**Software Engineering Observation 7.1**

*Don't try to "reinvent the wheel." When possible, reuse Framework Class Library classes and methods (`https://msdn.microsoft.com/library/mt472912`). This reduces app development time and errors, contributes to good performance and often enhances security.*

## 7.3 `static` Methods, `static` Variables and Class `Math`

Although most methods are called to operate on the data of specific objects, this is not always the case. Sometimes a method performs a task that does *not* depend on the data of any object (other than the method's arguments). Such a method applies to the class in which it's declared as a whole and is known as a `static` method.

It's common for a class to contain a group of `static` methods to perform common tasks. For example, recall that we used `static` method `Pow` of class `Math` to raise a value to a power in Fig. 6.6. To declare a method as `static`, place the keyword `static` before the return type in the method's declaration. You call any `static` method by specifying the name of the class in which the method is declared, followed by the member-access operator (`.`) and the method name, as in

```
ClassName.MethodName(arguments)
```

## 7.3.1 Math Class Methods

Class `Math` (from the `System` namespace) provides a collection of `static` methods that enable you to perform common mathematical calculations. For example, you can calculate the square root of `900.0` with the `static` method call

```
double value = Math.Sqrt(900.0);
```

The expression `Math.Sqrt(900.0)` evaluates to `30.0`. Method `Sqrt` takes an argument of type `double` and returns a result of type `double`. The following statement displays in the console window the value of the preceding method call:

```
Console.WriteLine(Math.Sqrt(900.0));
```

Here, the value that `Sqrt` returns becomes the argument to `WriteLine`. We did not create a `Math` object before calling `Sqrt`, nor did we create a `Console` object before calling `WriteLine`. Also, *all* of `Math`'s methods are `static`—therefore, each is called by preceding the name of the method with the class name `Math` and the member-access operator (`.`).

Method arguments may be constants, variables or expressions. If `c = 13.0`, `d = 3.0` and `f = 4.0`, then the statement

```
Console.WriteLine(Math.Sqrt(c + d * f));
```

calculates and displays the square root of `13.0 + 3.0 * 4.0 = 25.0`—namely, `5.0`. Figure 7.1 summarizes several `Math` class methods. In the figure, *x* and *y* are of type `double`.

| Method | Description | Example |
|---|---|---|
| `Abs(`*x*`)` | absolute value of *x* | `Abs(23.7)` is `23.7`<br>`Abs(0.0)` is `0.0`<br>`Abs(-23.7)` is `23.7` |
| `Ceiling(`*x*`)` | rounds *x* to the smallest integer not less than *x* | `Ceiling(9.2)` is `10.0`<br>`Ceiling(-9.8)` is `-9.0` |
| `Floor(`*x*`)` | rounds *x* to the largest integer not greater than *x* | `Floor(9.2)` is `9.0`<br>`Floor(-9.8)` is `-10.0` |
| `Cos(`*x*`)` | trigonometric cosine of *x* (*x* in radians) | `Cos(0.0)` is `1.0` |
| `Sin(`*x*`)` | trigonometric sine of *x* (*x* in radians) | `Sin(0.0)` is `0.0` |
| `Tan(`*x*`)` | trigonometric tangent of *x* (*x* in radians) | `Tan(0.0)` is `0.0` |

**Fig. 7.1** | `Math` class methods. (Part 1 of 2.)

| Method | Description | Example |
|---|---|---|
| `Exp(x)` | exponential method $e^x$ | `Exp(1.0)` is `2.71828`<br>`Exp(2.0)` is `7.38906` |
| `Log(x)` | natural logarithm of $x$ (base $e$) | `Log(Math.E)` is `1.0`<br>`Log(Math.E * Math.E)` is `2.0` |
| `Max(x, y)` | larger value of $x$ and $y$ | `Max(2.3, 12.7)` is `12.7`<br>`Max(-2.3, -12.7)` is `-2.3` |
| `Min(x, y)` | smaller value of $x$ and $y$ | `Min(2.3, 12.7)` is `2.3`<br>`Min(-2.3, -12.7)` is `-12.7` |
| `Pow(x, y)` | $x$ raised to the power $y$ (i.e., $x^y$) | `Pow(2.0, 7.0)` is `128.0`<br>`Pow(9.0, 0.5)` is `3.0` |
| `Sqrt(x)` | square root of $x$ | `Sqrt(900.0)` is `30.0` |

**Fig. 7.1** | `Math` class methods. (Part 2 of 2.)

### 7.3.2 Math Class Constants PI and E

Each object of a class maintains its own copy of each of the class's *instance variables*. There are also variables for which each object of a class does *not* need its own separate copy (as you'll see momentarily). Such variables are declared `static` and are also known as **class variables.** When objects of a class containing `static` variables are created, all the objects of that class share *one* copy of those variables. Together a class's `static` variables and instance variables are known as its **fields**. You'll learn more about `static` fields in Section 10.9.

Class `Math` also declares two `double` constants for commonly used mathematical values:

- **`Math.PI`** (3.1415926535897931) is the ratio of a circle's circumference to its diameter, and
- **`Math.E`** (2.7182818284590451) is the base value for natural logarithms (calculated with `static` `Math` method `Log`).

These constants are declared in class `Math` with the modifiers `public` and `const`. Making them `public` allows other programmers to use these variables in their own classes. A constant is declared with the keyword **`const`**—its value cannot be changed after the constant is declared. Fields declared `const` are implicitly `static`, so you can access them via the class name `Math` and the member-access operator (`.`), as in `Math.PI` and `Math.E`.

**Common Programming Error 7.1**

*Constants declared in a class, but not inside a method or property, are implicitly `static`—it's a syntax error to declare such a constant with keyword `static` explicitly.*

### 7.3.3 Why Is Main Declared static?

Why must `Main` be declared `static`? During app *startup*, when *no objects* of the class have been created, the `Main` method must be called to begin program execution. `Main` is sometimes called the app's **entry point**. Declaring `Main` as `static` allows the execution environment to invoke `Main` without creating an instance of the class. Method `Main` is typically declared with the header:

```
static void Main()
```

but also can be declared with the header:

```
static void Main(string[] args)
```

which we'll discuss and demonstrate in Section 8.12, Shuffling and Dealing Cards. In addition, you can declare `Main` with return type `int` (instead of `void`)—this can be useful if an app is executed by another app and needs to return an indication of success or failure to that other app.

### 7.3.4 Additional Comments About `Main`

Most earlier examples have one class that contained only `Main`, and some examples had a second class that was used by `Main` to create and manipulate objects. Actually, *any* class can contain a `Main` method. In fact, each of our two-class examples could have been implemented as one class. For example, in the app in Figs. 4.11–4.12, method `Main` (lines 7–43 of Fig. 4.12) could have been moved into class `Account` (Fig. 4.11). The app results would have been identical to those of the two-class version. You can place a `Main` method in every class you declare. Some programmers take advantage of this to build a small test app into each class they declare. However, if you declare more than one `Main` method among the classes of your project, you'll need to indicate to the IDE which one you would like to be the *app's* entry point. To do so:

1. With the project open in Visual Studio, select **Project > [ProjectName] Properties...** (where **[ProjectName]** is the name of your project).
2. Select the class containing the `Main` method that should be the entry point from the **Startup object** list box.

## 7.4 Methods with Multiple Parameters

We now consider how to write a method with multiple parameters. Figure 7.2 defines `Maximum` method that determines and returns the largest of *three* `double` values. When the app begins execution, the `Main` method (lines 8–23) executes. Line 19 calls method `Maximum` (declared in lines 26–43) to determine and return the largest of its three `double` arguments. In Section 7.4.3, we'll discuss the use of the + operator in line 22. The sample outputs show that `Maximum` determines the largest value regardless of whether that value is the first, second or third argument.

```
1  // Fig. 7.2: MaximumFinder.cs
2  // Method Maximum with three parameters.
3  using System;
4
5  class MaximumFinder
6  {
7     // obtain three floating-point values and determine maximum value
8     static void Main()
9     {
```

**Fig. 7.2** | Method `Maximum` with three parameters. (Part 1 of 2.)

```
        // prompt for and input three floating-point values
        Console.Write("Enter first floating-point value: ");
        double number1 = double.Parse(Console.ReadLine());
        Console.Write("Enter second floating-point value: ");
        double number2 = double.Parse(Console.ReadLine());
        Console.Write("Enter third floating-point value: ");
        double number3 = double.Parse(Console.ReadLine());

        // determine the maximum of three values
        double result = Maximum(number1, number2, number3);

        // display maximum value
        Console.WriteLine("Maximum is: " + result);
    }

    // returns the maximum of its three double parameters
    static double Maximum(double x, double y, double z)
    {
        double maximumValue = x; // assume x is the largest to start

        // determine whether y is greater than maximumValue
        if (y > maximumValue)
        {
            maximumValue = y;
        }

        // determine whether z is greater than maximumValue
        if (z > maximumValue)
        {
            maximumValue = z;
        }

        return maximumValue;
    }
}
```

```
Enter first floating-point values: 3.33
Enter second floating-point values: 1.11
Enter third floating-point values: 2.22
Maximum is: 3.33
```

```
Enter first floating-point values: 2.22
Enter second floating-point values: 3.33
Enter third floating-point values: 1.11
Maximum is: 3.33
```

```
Enter first floating-point values: 2.22
Enter second floating-point values: 1.11
Enter third floating-point values: 3.33
Maximum is: 3.33
```

**Fig. 7.2** | Method `Maximum` with three parameters. (Part 2 of 2.)

### 7.4.1 Keyword `static`

Method `Maximum`'s declaration begins with keyword `static`, which enables the `Main` method (another `static` method) to call `Maximum` as shown in line 19 without creating an object of class `MaximumFinder` and without qualifying the method name with the class name `MaximumFinder`—`static` methods in the *same* class can call each other directly.

### 7.4.2 Method `Maximum`

Consider the declaration of method `Maximum` (lines 26–43). Line 26 indicates that the method returns a `double` value, that the method's name is `Maximum` and that the method requires *three* `double` parameters (`x`, `y` and `z`) to accomplish its task. When a method has more than one parameter, the parameters are specified as a *comma-separated list*. When `Maximum` is called in line 19, the parameter `x` is initialized with the value of the argument `number1`, the parameter `y` is initialized with the value of the argument `number2` and the parameter `z` is initialized with the value of the argument `number3`. There must be one argument in the method call for each required parameter in the method declaration. Also, each argument must be *consistent* with the type of the corresponding parameter. For example, a parameter of type `double` can receive values like `7.35` (a `double`), `22` (an `int`) or `-0.03456` (a `double`), but not `string`s like `"hello"`. Section 7.6 discusses the argument types that can be provided in a method call for each parameter of a simple type. Note the use of type `double`'s **`Parse`** method in lines 12, 14 and 16 to convert into `double` values the `string`s typed by the user.

**Common Programming Error 7.2**

*Declaring method parameters of the same type as* `double x, y` *instead of* `double x, double y` *is a syntax error—a type is required for each parameter in the parameter list.*

***Logic of Determining the Maximum Value***

To determine the maximum value, we begin with the assumption that parameter `x` contains the largest value, so line 28 declares local variable `maximumValue` and initializes it with the value of parameter `x`. Of course, it's possible that parameter `y` or `z` contains the largest value, so we must compare each of these values with `maximumValue`. The `if` statement at lines 31–34 determines whether `y` is greater than `maximumValue`. If so, line 33 assigns `y` to `maximumValue`. The `if` statement at lines 37–40 determines whether `z` is greater than `maximumValue`. If so, line 39 assigns `z` to `maximumValue`. At this point, the largest of the three values resides in `maximumValue`, so line 42 returns that value to line 19 where it's assigned to the variable `result`. When program control returns to the point in the app where `Maximum` was called, `Maximum`'s parameters `x`, `y` and `z` are no longer accessible. Methods can return *at most one* value; the returned value can be a value type that contains one or more values (implemented as a `struct`; Section 10.13) or a reference to an object that contains one or more values.

### 7.4.3 Assembling `string`s with Concatenation

C# allows `string` objects to be created by assembling smaller `string`s into larger `string`s using operator + (or the compound assignment operator +=). This is known as **`string` concatenation**. When both operands of operator + are `string` objects, the + operator creates a *new* `string` object containing copies of the characters in its left operand followed by copies of the characters in its right operand. For example, the expression `"hello " + "there"` creates the `string` `"hello there"` without disturbing the original `string`s.

In line 22, the expression `"Maximum is: " + result` uses operator `+` with operands of types `string` and `double`. Every simple-type value has a `string` representation. When one of the `+` operator's operands is a `string`, the other is implicitly converted to a `string`, then the two `string`s are *concatenated.* So, in line 22, the `double` value is converted to its `string` representation and placed at the end of `"Maximum is: "`. If there are any trailing zeros in a `double` value, these are *discarded.* Thus, the `string` representation of 9.3500 is `"9.35"`.

### *Anything Can Be Converted to a* `string`

If a `bool` is concatenated with a `string`, the `bool` is converted to the `string` `"True"` or `"False"` (each is capitalized). In addition, every object has a `ToString` method that returns a `string` representation of that object. When an object is concatenated with a `string`, the object's `ToString` method is called *implicitly* to obtain the `string` representation of the object. If the object is `null`, an *empty string* is written.

If a type does not define a `ToString` method, the default `ToString` implementation returns a `string` containing the type's **fully qualified name**—that is, the namespace in which the type is defined followed by a dot (`.`) and the type name (e.g., `System.Object` for the .NET class `Object`). Each type you create can declare a custom `ToString` method, as you'll do in Chapter 8 for a `Card` class that represents a playing card in a deck of cards.

### *Formatting* `string`*s with* `string` *Interpolation*

Line 22 of Fig. 7.2, of course, could also be written using `string` interpolation as

```
Console.WriteLine($"Maximum is: {result}");
```

As with `string` concatenation, using `string` interpolation to insert an *object* into a `string` *implicitly* calls the object's `ToString` method to obtain the object's `string` representation.

## 7.4.4 Breaking Apart Large `string` Literals

When a large `string` literal or interpolated `string` is typed into an app's source code, you can break that `string` into several smaller `string`s and place them on multiple lines for readability. The `string`s can be reassembled using `string` concatenation. We discuss the details of `string`s in Chapter 16.

**Common Programming Error 7.3**

*It's a syntax error to break a* `string` *literal or interpolated* `string` *across multiple lines of code. If a* `string` *does not fit on one line, you can split it into several smaller* `string`*s and use concatenation to form the desired* `string`*.*

**Common Programming Error 7.4**

*Confusing the string concatenation* `+` *operator with the addition* `+` *operator can lead to strange results. The* `+` *operator is left-associative. For example, if* `y` *has the* `int` *value* `5`*, the expression* `"y + 2 = " + y + 2` *results in the* `string` `"y + 2 = 52"`*, not* `"y + 2 = 7"`*, because first the value of* `y` *(*`5`*) is concatenated with the* `string` `"y + 2 = "`*, then the value* `2` *is concatenated with the new larger* `string` `"y + 2 = 5"`*. The expression* `"y + 2 = " + (y + 2)` *produces the desired result* `"y + 2 = 7"`*. Using C# 6* `string` *interpolation eliminates this problem.*

### 7.4.5 When to Declare Variables as Fields

Variable `result` is a local variable in method `Main` because it's declared in the block that represents the method's body. Variables should be declared as fields of a class (i.e., as either instance variables or `static` variables) *only* if they're required for use in more than one method of the class or if the app should save their values between calls to a given method.

### 7.4.6 Implementing Method `Maximum` by Reusing Method `Math.Max`

Recall from Fig. 7.1 that class `Math`'s `Max` method can determine the larger of two values. The entire body of our maximum method could also be implemented with nested calls to `Math.Max`, as follows:

```
return Math.Max(x, Math.Max(y, z));
```

The leftmost `Math.Max` call has the arguments `x` and `Math.Max(y, z)`. Before any method can be called, the runtime evaluates *all* the arguments to determine their values. If an argument is a method call, the call must be performed to determine its return value. So, in the preceding statement, `Math.Max(y, z)` is evaluated first to determine the larger of `y` and `z`. Then the result is passed as the second argument to the first call to `Math.Max`, which returns the larger of its two arguments. Using `Math.Max` in this manner is a good example of software reuse—we find the largest of three values by reusing `Math.Max`, which finds the larger of two values. Note how concise this code is compared to lines 28–42 of Fig. 7.2.

## 7.5 Notes on Using Methods

*Three Ways to Call a Method*

You've seen three ways to call a method:

1. Using a method name by itself to call a method of the *same* class—as in line 19 of Fig. 7.2, which calls `Maximum(number1, number2, number3)` from `Main`.
2. Using a reference to an object, followed by the member-access operator (`.`) and the method name to call a non-`static` method of the referenced object—as in line 23 of Fig. 4.12, which called `account1.Deposit(depositAmount)` from the `Main` method of class `AccountTest`.
3. Using the class name and the member-access operator (`.`) to call a `static` method of a class—as in lines 12, 14 and 16 of Fig. 7.2, which each call `Console.ReadLine()`, or as in `Math.Sqrt(900.0)` in Section 7.3.

*Three Ways to Return from a Method*

You've seen three ways to return control to the statement that calls a method:

- Reaching the method-ending right brace in a method with return type `void`.
- When the following statement executes in a method with return type `void`

```
return;
```

- When a method returns a result with a statement of the following form in which the *expression* is evaluated and its result (and control) are returned to the caller:

```
return expression;
```

**Common Programming Error 7.5**

*Declaring a method outside the body of a class declaration or inside the body of another method is a syntax error.*

**Common Programming Error 7.6**

*Redeclaring a method parameter as a local variable in the method's body is a compilation error.*

**Common Programming Error 7.7**

*Forgetting to return a value from a method that should return one is a compilation error. If a return type other than `void` is specified, the method must use a `return` statement to return a value, and that value must be consistent with the method's return type. Returning a value from a method whose return type has been declared `void` is a compilation error.*

#### `static` *Members Can Access Only the Class's Other* `static` *Members Directly*

A `static` method or property can call *only* other `static` methods or properties of the same class directly (i.e., using the method name by itself) and can manipulate *only* `static` variables in the same class directly. To access a class's non-`static` members, a `static` method or property must use a reference to an object of that class. Recall that `static` methods relate to a class as a whole, whereas non-`static` methods are associated with a specific object (instance) of the class and may manipulate the instance variables of that object (as well as the class's `static` members).

Many objects of a class, each with its own copies of the instance variables, may exist at the same time. Suppose a `static` method were to invoke a non-`static` method directly. How would the method know which object's instance variables to manipulate? What would happen if no objects of the class existed at the time the non-`static` method was invoked?

**Software Engineering Observation 7.2**

*A `static` method cannot access non-`static` members of the same class directly.*

## 7.6 Argument Promotion and Casting

Another important feature of method calls is **argument promotion**—implicitly converting an argument's value to the type that the method expects to receive (if possible) in its corresponding parameter. For example, an app can call `Math` method `Sqrt` with an integer argument even though the method expects to receive a `double` argument. The statement

```
Console.WriteLine(Math.Sqrt(4));
```

correctly evaluates `Math.Sqrt(4)` and displays the value `2.0`. `Sqrt`'s parameter list causes C# to convert the `int` value `4` to the `double` value `4.0` before passing the value to `Sqrt`. Such conversions may lead to compilation errors if C#'s **promotion rules** are not satisfied. The promotion rules specify which conversions are allowed—that is, which conversions can be performed *without losing data*. In the `Sqrt` example above, an `int` is converted to a double without changing its value. However, converting a double to an int *truncates* the fractional part of the double value—thus, part of the value is lost. Also, double variables can hold values much larger (and much smaller) than int variables, so assigning a double to an int can cause a loss of information when the double value doesn't fit in the int. Converting large integer types to small integer types (e.g., long to int) also can produce incorrect results.

### 7.6.1 Promotion Rules

The promotion rules apply to expressions containing values of two or more simple types and to simple-type values passed as arguments to methods. Each value is promoted to the appropriate type in the expression. (Actually, the expression uses a *temporary* copy of each promoted value—the types of the original values remain unchanged.) Figure 7.3 lists the simple types alphabetically and the types to which each can be promoted. Values of all simple types also can be implicitly converted to type object. We demonstrate such implicit conversions in Chapter 19.

| Type | Conversion types |
|---|---|
| bool | no possible implicit conversions to other simple types |
| byte | ushort, short, uint, int, ulong, long, decimal, float or double |
| char | ushort, int, uint, long, ulong, decimal, float or double |
| decimal | no possible implicit conversions to other simple types |
| double | no possible implicit conversions to other simple types |
| float | double |
| int | long, decimal, float or double |
| long | decimal, float or double |
| sbyte | short, int, long, decimal, float or double |
| short | int, long, decimal, float or double |
| uint | ulong, long, decimal, float or double |
| ulong | decimal, float or double |
| ushort | uint, int, ulong, long, decimal, float or double |

**Fig. 7.3** | Implicit conversions between simple types.

### 7.6.2 Sometimes Explicit Casts Are Required

By default, C# does not allow you to implicitly convert values between simple types if the target type cannot represent every value of the original type (e.g., the int value 2000000 cannot be represented as a short, and any floating-point number with nonzero digits after its decimal point cannot be represented in an integer type such as long, int or short).

To prevent a compilation error in cases where information may be lost due to an implicit conversion between simple types, the compiler requires you to use a *cast operator* to *force* the conversion. This enables you to "take control" from the compiler. You essentially say, "I know this conversion might cause loss of information, but for my purposes here, that's fine." Suppose you create a method `Square` that calculates the square of an `int` argument. To call `Square` with the whole part of a `double` argument named `doubleValue`, you'd write `Square((int) doubleValue)`. This method call explicitly casts (converts) the value of `doubleValue` to an integer for use in method `Square`. Thus, if `doubleValue`'s value is `4.5`, the method receives the value `4` and returns `16`, not `20.25`.

**Common Programming Error 7.8**

*Converting a simple-type value to a value of another simple type may change the value if the promotion is not allowed. For example, converting a floating-point value to an integral value may introduce truncation errors (loss of the fractional part) in the result.*

## 7.7 The .NET Framework Class Library

Many predefined classes are grouped into categories of related classes called *namespaces*. Together, these namespaces are referred to as the .NET Framework Class Library.

### `using` *Directives and Namespaces*

Throughout the text, `using` directives allow us to use library classes from the Framework Class Library without specifying their namespace names. For example, an app would include the declaration

```
using System;
```

in order to use the class names from the `System` namespace without fully qualifying their names. This allows you to use the *unqualified* name `Console`, rather than the *fully qualified* name `System.Console`, in your code.

**Software Engineering Observation 7.3**

*The C# compiler does not require `using` declarations in a source-code file if the fully qualified class name is specified every time a class name is used. Many programmers prefer the more concise programming style enabled by `using` declarations.*

You might have noticed in each project containing multiple classes that in each class's source-code file we did not need additional `using` directives to use the other classes in the project. There's a special relationship between classes in a project—by default, such classes are in the same namespace and can be used by other classes in the project. Thus, a `using` declaration is not required when one class in a project uses another in the same project—such as when class `AccountTest` used class `Account` in Chapter 4's examples. Also, any classes that are not *explicitly* placed in a namespace are *implicitly* placed in the so-called **global namespace**.

### *.NET Namespaces*

A strength of C# is the large number of classes in the namespaces of the .NET Framework Class Library. Some key Framework Class Library namespaces are described in Fig. 7.4, which represents only a small portion of the reusable classes in the .NET Framework Class Library.

| Namespace | Description |
|---|---|
| `System.Windows.Forms` | Contains the classes required to create and manipulate GUIs. (Various classes in this namespace are discussed in Chapter 14, Graphical User Interfaces with Windows Forms: Part 1, and Chapter 15, Graphical User Interfaces with Windows Forms: Part 2.) |
| `System.Windows.Controls`<br>`System.Windows.Input`<br>`System.Windows.Media`<br>`System.Windows.Shapes` | Contain the classes of the Windows Presentation Foundation for GUIs, 2-D and 3-D graphics, multimedia and animation. |
| `System.Linq` | Contains the classes that support Language Integrated Query (LINQ). (See Chapter 9, Introduction to LINQ and the `List` Collection, and several other chapters throughout the book.) |
| `System.Data.Entity` | Contains the classes for manipulating data in databases (i.e., organized collections of data), including support for LINQ to Entities. (See Chapter 20, Databases and LINQ.) |
| `System.IO` | Contains the classes that enable programs to input and output data. (See Chapter 17, Files and Streams.) |
| `System.Web` | Contains the classes used for creating and maintaining web apps, which are accessible over the Internet. |
| `System.Xml` | Contains the classes for creating and manipulating XML data. Data can be read from or written to XML files. |
| `System.Xml.Linq` | Contains the classes that support Language Integrated Query (LINQ) for XML documents. (See Chapter 21, Asynchronous Programming with `async` and `await`.) |
| `System.Collections`<br>`System.Collections.Generic` | Contain the classes that define data structures for maintaining collections of data. (See Chapter 19, Generic Collections; Functional Programming with LINQ/PLINQ.) |
| `System.Text` | Contains classes that enable programs to manipulate characters and `strings`. (See Chapter 16, Strings and Characters: A Deeper Look.) |

**Fig. 7.4** | .NET Framework Class Library namespaces (a subset).

### *Locating Additional Information About a .NET Class's Methods*

You can locate additional information about a .NET class's methods in the *.NET Framework Class Library* reference

```
https://msdn.microsoft.com/library/mt472912
```

When you visit this site, you'll see an alphabetical listing of all the namespaces in the Framework Class Library. Locate the namespace and click its link to see an alphabetical listing of all its classes, with a brief description of each. Click a class's link to see a more complete description of the class. Click the **Methods** link in the left-hand column to see a listing of the class's methods.

**Good Programming Practice 7.1**

*The online .NET Framework documentation is easy to search and provides many details about each class. As you learn each class in this book, you should review it in the online documentation for additional information.*

## 7.8 Case Study: Random-Number Generation

In this and the next section, we develop a nicely structured game-playing app with multiple methods. The app uses most of the control statements presented thus far in the book and introduces several new programming concepts.

There's something in the air of a casino that invigorates people—from the high rollers at the plush mahogany-and-felt craps tables to the quarter poppers at the one-armed bandits. It's the **element of chance**, the possibility that luck will convert a pocketful of money into a mountain of wealth. The element of chance can be introduced in an app via an object of class `Random` (of namespace `System`). Objects of class **`Random`** can produce random `byte`, `int` and `double` values. In the next several examples, we use objects of class `Random` to produce random numbers.

*Secure Random Numbers*

According to Microsoft's documentation for class `Random`, the random values it produces "are not completely random because a mathematical algorithm is used to select them, but they are sufficiently random for practical purposes." Such values should not be used, for example, to create randomly selected passwords. If your app requires so-called cryptographically secure random numbers, use class `RNGCryptoServiceProvider`[1] from namespace `System.Security.Cryptography`) to produce random values:

```
https://msdn.microsoft.com/library/system.security.cryptography.
   rngcryptoserviceprovider
```

### 7.8.1 Creating an Object of Type Random

A new random-number generator object can be created with class `Random` (from the `System` namespace) as follows:

```
Random randomNumbers = new Random();
```

The `Random` object can then be used to generate random `byte`, `int` and `double` values—we discuss only random `int` values here.

### 7.8.2 Generating a Random Integer

Consider the following statement:

```
int randomValue = randomNumbers.Next();
```

When called with no arguments, method **`Next`** of class `Random` generates a random `int` value in the range 0 to +2,147,483,646, inclusive. If the `Next` method truly produces values at random, then every value in that range should have an equal chance (or probability) of being chosen each time method `Next` is called. The values returned by `Next` are actually

1. Class `RNGCryptoServiceProvider` produces arrays of `bytes`. We discuss arrays in Chapter 8.

**pseudorandom numbers**—a sequence of values produced by a complex mathematical calculation. The calculation uses the current time of day (which, of course, changes constantly) to **seed** the random-number generator such that each execution of an app yields a different sequence of random values.

### 7.8.3 Scaling the Random-Number Range

The range of values produced directly by method `Next` often differs from the range of values required in a particular C# app. For example, an app that simulates coin tossing might require only 0 for "heads" and 1 for "tails." An app that simulates the rolling of a six-sided die might require random integers in the range 1–6. A video game that randomly predicts the next type of spaceship (out of four possibilities) that will fly across the horizon might require random integers in the range 1–4. For cases like these, class `Random` provides versions of method `Next` that accept arguments. One receives an `int` argument and returns a value from 0 up to, but not including, the argument's value. For example, you might use the statement

```
int randomValue = randomNumbers.Next(6); // 0, 1, 2, 3, 4 or 5
```

which returns 0, 1, 2, 3, 4 or 5. The argument `6`—called the **scaling factor**—represents the number of unique values that `Next` should produce (in this case, six—0, 1, 2, 3, 4 and 5). This manipulation is called **scaling** the range of values produced by `Random` method `Next`.

### 7.8.4 Shifting Random-Number Range

Suppose we wanted to simulate a six-sided die that has the numbers 1–6 on its faces, not 0–5. Scaling the range of values alone is not enough. So we **shift** the range of numbers produced. We could do this by adding a **shifting value**—in this case 1—to the result of method `Next`, as in

```
int face = 1 + randomNumbers.Next(6); // 1, 2, 3, 4, 5 or 6
```

The shifting value (`1`) specifies the first value in the desired set of random integers. The preceding statement assigns to `face` a random integer in the range 1–6.

### 7.8.5 Combining Shifting and Scaling

The third alternative of method `Next` provides a more intuitive way to express both shifting and scaling. This method receives two `int` arguments and returns a value from the first argument's value up to, but not including, the second argument's value. We could use this method to write a statement equivalent to our previous statement, as in

```
int face = randomNumbers.Next(1, 7); // 1, 2, 3, 4, 5 or 6
```

### 7.8.6 Rolling a Six-Sided Die

To demonstrate random numbers, let's develop an app that simulates 20 rolls of a six-sided die and displays each roll's value. Figure 7.5 shows two sample outputs, which confirm that the results of the preceding calculation are integers in the range 1–6 and that each run of the app can produce a *different* sequence of random numbers. Line 9 creates the `Random` object `randomNumbers` to produce random values. Line 15 executes 20 times in a loop to roll the die and line 16 displays the value of each roll.

```
// Fig. 7.5: RandomIntegers.cs
// Shifted and scaled random integers.
using System;

class RandomIntegers
{
   static void Main()
   {
      Random randomNumbers = new Random(); // random-number generator

      // loop 20 times
      for (int counter = 1; counter <= 20; ++counter)
      {
         // pick random integer from 1 to 6
         int face = randomNumbers.Next(1, 7);
         Console.Write($"{face}  "); // display generated value
      }

      Console.WriteLine();
   }
}
```

```
3  3  3  1  1  2  1  2  4  2  2  3  6  2  5  3  4  6  6  1
```

```
6  2  5  1  3  5  2  1  6  5  4  1  6  1  3  3  1  4  3  4
```

**Fig. 7.5** | Shifted and scaled random integers.

### *Rolling a Six-Sided Die 60,000,000 Times*

To show that the numbers produced by Next occur with approximately equal likelihood, let's simulate 60,000,000 rolls of a die (Fig. 7.6). Each integer from 1 to 6 should appear approximately 10,000,000 times.

```
// Fig. 7.6: RollDie.cs
// Roll a six-sided die 60,000,000 times.
using System;

class RollDie
{
   static void Main()
   {
      Random randomNumbers = new Random(); // random-number generator

      int frequency1 = 0; // count of 1s rolled
      int frequency2 = 0; // count of 2s rolled
      int frequency3 = 0; // count of 3s rolled
      int frequency4 = 0; // count of 4s rolled
      int frequency5 = 0; // count of 5s rolled
      int frequency6 = 0; // count of 6s rolled
```

**Fig. 7.6** | Roll a six-sided die 60,000,000 times. (Part 1 of 2.)

```

      // summarize results of 60,000,000 rolls of a die
      for (int roll = 1; roll <= 60000000; ++roll)
      {
         int face = randomNumbers.Next(1, 7); // number from 1 to 6

         // determine roll value 1-6 and increment appropriate counter
         switch (face)
         {
            case 1:
               ++frequency1; // increment the 1s counter
               break;
            case 2:
               ++frequency2; // increment the 2s counter
               break;
            case 3:
               ++frequency3; // increment the 3s counter
               break;
            case 4:
               ++frequency4; // increment the 4s counter
               break;
            case 5:
               ++frequency5; // increment the 5s counter
               break;
            case 6:
               ++frequency6; // increment the 6s counter
               break;
         }
      }

      Console.WriteLine("Face\tFrequency"); // output headers
      Console.WriteLine($"1\t{frequency1}\n2\t{frequency2}");
      Console.WriteLine($"3\t{frequency3}\n4\t{frequency4}");
      Console.WriteLine($"5\t{frequency5}\n6\t{frequency6}");
   }
}
```

```
Face    Frequency
1       10006774
2       9993289
3       9993438
4       10006520
5       9998762
6       10001217
```

```
Face    Frequency
1       10002183
2       9997815
3       9999619
4       10006012
5       9994806
6       9999565
```

**Fig. 7.6** | Roll a six-sided die 60,000,000 times. (Part 2 of 2.)

As the two sample outputs show, the values produced by method Next enable the app to realistically simulate rolling a six-sided die. The app uses nested control statements (the switch is nested inside the for) to determine the number of times each side of the die occurred. The for statement (lines 19–45) iterates 60,000,000 times. During each iteration, line 21 produces a random value from 1 to 6. This face value is then used as the switch expression (line 24). Based on the face value, the switch statement increments one of the six counter variables during each iteration of the loop. (In Section 8.4.7, we show an elegant way to replace the entire switch statement in this app with a single statement.) The switch statement has no default label because we have a case label for every possible die value that the expression in line 21 can produce. Run the app several times and observe the results. You'll see that every time you execute this apkp, it produces different results.

## 7.8.7 Scaling and Shifting Random Numbers

Previously, we demonstrated the statement

```
int face = randomNumbers.Next(1, 7);
```

which simulates the rolling of a six-sided die. This statement always assigns to variable face an integer in the range 1 ≤ face < 7. The width of this range (i.e., the number of consecutive integers in the range) is 6, and the starting number in the range is 1. Referring to the preceding statement, we see that the width of the range is determined by the difference between the two integers passed to Random method Next, and the starting number of the range is the value of the first argument. We can generalize this result as

```
int number = randomNumbers.Next(shiftingValue, shiftingValue + scalingFactor);
```

where *shiftingValue* specifies the first number in the desired range of consecutive integers and *scalingFactor* specifies how many numbers are in the range.

It's also possible to choose integers at random from sets of values *other* than ranges of consecutive integers. For this purpose, it's simpler to use the version of the Next method that takes only *one* argument. For example, to obtain a random value from the sequence 2, 5, 8, 11 and 14, you could use the statement

```
int number = 2 + 3 * randomNumbers.Next(5);
```

In this case, randomNumbers.Next(5) produces values in the range 0–4. Each value produced is multiplied by 3 to produce a number in the sequence 0, 3, 6, 9 and 12. We then add 2 to that value to *shift* the range of values and obtain a value from the sequence 2, 5, 8, 11 and 14. We can generalize this result as

```
int number = shiftingValue +
   differenceBetweenValues * randomNumbers.Next(scalingFactor);
```

where *shiftingValue* specifies the first number in the desired range of values, *differenceBetweenValues* represents the difference between consecutive numbers in the sequence and *scalingFactor* specifies how many numbers are in the range.

## 7.8.8 Repeatability for Testing and Debugging

As we mentioned earlier in this section, the methods of class Random actually generate *pseudorandom* numbers based on complex mathematical calculations. Repeatedly calling any of Random's methods produces a sequence of numbers that appears to be random. The calculation that produces the pseudorandom numbers uses the time of day as a **seed value** to change the sequence's starting point. Each new `Random` object seeds itself with a value based on the computer system's clock at the time the object is created, enabling each execution of an app to produce a *different* sequence of random numbers.

When debugging an app, it's sometimes useful to repeat the *same* sequence of pseudorandom numbers during each execution of the app. This repeatability enables you to prove that your app is working for a specific sequence of random numbers before you test the app with different sequences of random numbers. When repeatability is important, you can create a `Random` object as follows:

```
Random randomNumbers = new Random(seedValue);
```

The `seedValue` argument (an `int`) seeds the random-number calculation—using the *same* `seedValue` every time produces the *same* sequence of random numbers. Different seed values, of course, produce *different* sequences of random numbers.

## 7.9 Case Study: A Game of Chance; Introducing Enumerations

One popular game of chance is the dice game known as "craps," which is played in casinos and back alleys throughout the world. The rules of the game are straightforward:

> *You roll two dice. Each die has six faces, which contain one, two, three, four, five and six spots, respectively. After the dice have come to rest, the sum of the spots on the two upward faces is calculated. If the sum is 7 or 11 on the first throw, you win. If the sum is 2, 3 or 12 on the first throw (called "craps"), you lose (i.e., "the house" wins). If the sum is 4, 5, 6, 8, 9 or 10 on the first throw, that sum becomes your "point." To win, you must continue rolling the dice until you "make your point" (i.e., roll that same point value). You lose by rolling a 7 before making your point.*

The app in Fig. 7.7 simulates the game of craps, using methods to define the logic of the game. The `Main` method (lines 24–80) calls the `static` `RollDice` method (lines 83–94) as needed to roll the two dice and compute their sum. The four sample outputs show winning on the first roll, losing on the first roll, losing on a subsequent roll and winning on a subsequent roll, respectively. Variable `randomNumbers` (line 8) is declared `static`, so it can be created once during the program's execution and used in method `RollDice`.

```
1  // Fig. 7.7: Craps.cs
2  // Craps class simulates the dice game craps.
3  using System;
4
5  class Craps
6  {
7     // create random-number generator for use in method RollDice
8     private static Random randomNumbers = new Random();
9
10    // enumeration with constants that represent the game status
11    private enum Status {Continue, Won, Lost}
```

**Fig. 7.7** | Craps class simulates the dice game craps. (Part 1 of 4.)

```

      // enumeration with constants that represent common rolls of the dice
      private enum DiceNames
      {
         SnakeEyes = 2,
         Trey = 3,
         Seven = 7,
         YoLeven = 11,
         BoxCars = 12
      }

      // plays one game of craps
      static void Main()
      {
         // gameStatus can contain Continue, Won or Lost
         Status gameStatus = Status.Continue;
         int myPoint = 0; // point if no win or loss on first roll

         int sumOfDice = RollDice(); // first roll of the dice

         // determine game status and point based on first roll
         switch ((DiceNames) sumOfDice)
         {
            case DiceNames.Seven: // win with 7 on first roll
            case DiceNames.YoLeven: // win with 11 on first roll
               gameStatus = Status.Won;
               break;
            case DiceNames.SnakeEyes: // lose with 2 on first roll
            case DiceNames.Trey: // lose with 3 on first roll
            case DiceNames.BoxCars: // lose with 12 on first roll
               gameStatus = Status.Lost;
               break;
            default: // did not win or lose, so remember point
               gameStatus = Status.Continue; // game is not over
               myPoint = sumOfDice; // remember the point
               Console.WriteLine($"Point is {myPoint}");
               break;
         }

         // while game is not complete
         while (gameStatus == Status.Continue) // game not Won or Lost
         {
            sumOfDice = RollDice(); // roll dice again

            // determine game status
            if (sumOfDice == myPoint) // win by making point
            {
               gameStatus = Status.Won;
            }
            else
            {
```

**Fig. 7.7** | Craps class simulates the dice game craps. (Part 2 of 4.)

```
                // lose by rolling 7 before point
                if (sumOfDice == (int) DiceNames.Seven)
                {
                   gameStatus = Status.Lost;
                }
             }
          }

          // display won or lost message
          if (gameStatus == Status.Won)
          {
             Console.WriteLine("Player wins");
          }
          else
          {
             Console.WriteLine("Player loses");
          }
       }

       // roll dice, calculate sum and display results
       static int RollDice()
       {
          // pick random die values
          int die1 = randomNumbers.Next(1, 7); // first die roll
          int die2 = randomNumbers.Next(1, 7); // second die roll

          int sum = die1 + die2; // sum of die values

          // display results of this roll
          Console.WriteLine($"Player rolled {die1} + {die2} = {sum}");
          return sum; // return sum of dice
       }
    }
```

```
Player rolled 2 + 5 = 7
Player wins
```

```
Player rolled 2 + 1 = 3
Player loses
```

```
Player rolled 2 + 4 = 6
Point is 6
Player rolled 3 + 1 = 4
Player rolled 5 + 5 = 10
Player rolled 6 + 1 = 7
Player loses
```

**Fig. 7.7** | Craps class simulates the dice game craps. (Part 3 of 4.)

```
Player rolled 4 + 6 = 10
Point is 10
Player rolled 1 + 3 = 4
Player rolled 1 + 3 = 4
Player rolled 2 + 3 = 5
Player rolled 4 + 4 = 8
Player rolled 6 + 6 = 12
Player rolled 4 + 4 = 8
Player rolled 4 + 5 = 9
Player rolled 2 + 6 = 8
Player rolled 6 + 6 = 12
Player rolled 6 + 4 = 10
Player wins
```

**Fig. 7.7** | Craps class simulates the dice game craps. (Part 4 of 4.)

### 7.9.1 Method RollDice

In the rules of the game, the player must roll two dice on the first roll and must do the same on all subsequent rolls. We declare method RollDice (lines 83–94) to roll the dice and compute and display their sum. Method RollDice is declared once, but it's called from two places (lines 30 and 54) in method Main, which contains the logic for one complete game of craps. Method RollDice takes no arguments, so it has an empty parameter list. Each time it's called, RollDice returns the sum of the dice as an int. Although lines 86 and 87 look the same (except for the die names), they do not necessarily produce the same result. Each of these statements produces a random value in the range 1–6. Variable randomNumbers (used in lines 86–87) is *not* declared in the method. Rather it's declared as a private static variable of the class and initialized in line 8. This enables us to create *one* Random object that's reused in each call to RollDice.

### 7.9.2 Method Main's Local Variables

The game is reasonably involved. The player may win or lose on the first roll or may win or lose on any subsequent roll. Method Main (lines 24–80) uses local variable gameStatus (line 27) to keep track of the overall game status, local variable myPoint (line 28) to store the "point" if the player does not win or lose on the first roll and local variable sumOfDice (line 30) to maintain the sum of the dice for the most recent roll. Variable myPoint is initialized to 0 to ensure that the app will compile. If you do not initialize myPoint, the compiler issues an error, because myPoint is not assigned a value in every case of the switch statement—thus, the app could try to use myPoint before it's definitely assigned a value. By contrast, gameStatus does not require initialization because it's assigned a value in every branch of the switch statement—thus, it's guaranteed to be initialized before it's used. However, as good practice, we initialize it anyway.

### 7.9.3 enum Type Status

Local variable gameStatus (line 27) is declared to be of a new type called Status, which we declared in line 11. Status is a user-defined type called an **enumeration**, which declares a set of *constants* represented by identifiers. An enumeration is introduced by the keyword **enum** and a type name (in this case, Status). As with a class, braces ({ and }) delimit the body of an enum declaration. Inside the braces is a comma-separated list of **enumeration constants**—by default, the first constant has the value 0 and each subsequent constant's value is incremented by 1. The enum constant names must be *unique*, but the value associated with each constant need not be. Type Status is declared as a private member of class Craps, because Status is used only in that class.

Variables of type Status should be assigned only one of the three constants declared in the enumeration. When the game is won, the app sets local variable gameStatus to Status.Won (lines 37 and 59). When the game is lost, the app sets gameStatus to Status.Lost (lines 42 and 66). Otherwise, the app sets gameStatus to Status.Continue (line 45) to indicate that the dice must be rolled again.

**Good Programming Practice 7.2**

*Using enumeration constants (like* Status.Won, Status.Lost *and* Status.Continue*) rather than literal integer values (such as 0, 1 and 2) can make code easier to read and maintain.*

### 7.9.4 The First Roll

Line 30 in method Main calls RollDice, which picks two random values from 1 to 6, displays the value of the first die, the value of the second die and the sum of the dice, and returns the sum of the dice. Method Main next enters the switch statement at lines 33–49, which uses the sumOfDice value to determine whether the game has been won or lost, or whether it should continue with another roll.

### 7.9.5 enum Type DiceNames

The sums of the dice that would result in a win or loss on the first roll are declared in the DiceNames enumeration in lines 14–21. These are used in the switch statement's cases. The identifier names use casino parlance for these sums. In the DiceNames enumeration, we assign a value explicitly to each identifier name. When the enum is declared, each constant in the enum declaration is a constant value of type int. If you do not assign a value to an identifier in the enum declaration, the compiler will do so. If the first enum constant is unassigned, the compiler gives it the value 0. If any other enum constant is unassigned, the compiler gives it a value one higher than that of the preceding enum constant. For example, in the Status enumeration, the compiler implicitly assigns 0 to Status.Continue, 1 to Status.Won and 2 to Status.Lost.

### 7.9.6 Underlying Type of an enum

You could also declare an enum's underlying type to be byte, sbyte, short, ushort, int, uint, long or ulong by writing

```
private enum MyEnum : typeName {Constant1, Constant2, ...}
```

where *typeName* represents one of the integral simple types.

### 7.9.7 Comparing Integers and enum Constants

If you need to compare a simple integral type value to the underlying value of an enumeration constant, you must use a cast operator to make the two types match—there are no implicit conversions between enum and integral types. In the switch expression (line 33), we use the cast operator to convert the `int` value in `sumOfDice` to type `DiceNames` and compare it to each of the constants in `DiceNames`. Lines 35–36 determine whether the player won on the first roll with `Seven` (7) or `YoLeven` (11). Lines 39–41 determine whether the player lost on the first roll with `SnakeEyes` (2), `Trey` (3) or `BoxCars` (12). After the first roll, if the game is not over, the `default` case (lines 44–48) saves `sumOfDice` in `myPoint` (line 46) and displays the point (line 47).

### *Additional Rolls of the Dice*

If we're still trying to "make our point" (i.e., the game is continuing from a prior roll), the loop in lines 52–69 executes. Line 54 rolls the dice again. If `sumOfDice` matches `myPoint` in line 57, line 59 sets `gameStatus` to `Status.Won`, and the loop terminates because the game is complete. In line 64, we use the cast operator `(int)` to obtain the underlying value of `DiceNames.Seven` so that we can compare it to `sumOfDice`. If `sumOfDice` is equal to `Seven` (7), line 66 sets `gameStatus` to `Status.Lost`, and the loop terminates because the game is over. When the game completes, lines 72–79 display a message indicating whether the player won or lost, and the app terminates.

### *Control Statements in the* `Craps` *Example*

Note the use of the various program-control mechanisms we've discussed. The `Craps` class uses two methods—`Main` and `RollDice` (called twice from `Main`)—and the `switch`, `while`, `if...else` and nested `if` control statements. Also, notice that we use multiple `case` labels in the `switch` statement to execute the same statements for sums of `Seven` and `YoLeven` (lines 35–36) and for sums of `SnakeEyes`, `Trey` and `BoxCars` (lines 39–41).

### *Code Snippets for Auto-Implemented Properties*

Visual Studio has a feature called **code snippets** that allows you to insert *predefined code templates* into your source code. One such snippet enables you to easily create a `switch` statement with `case`s for all possible values for an `enum` type. Type `switch` in the C# code then press *Tab* twice. If you specify a variable of an `enum` type in the `switch` statement's expression and press *Enter*, a `case` for each `enum` constant will be generated automatically.

To get a list of all available code snippets, type *Ctrl* + *k*, *Ctrl* + *x*. This displays the **Insert Snippet** window in the code editor. You can navigate through the Visual C# snippet folders with the mouse to see the snippets. This feature also can be accessed by *right clicking* in the source code editor and selecting the **Insert Snippet...** menu item.

## 7.10 Scope of Declarations

You've seen declarations of C# entities, such as classes, methods, properties, variables and parameters. Declarations introduce names that can be used to refer to such C# entities. The **scope** of a declaration is the portion of the app that can refer to the declared entity by its unqualified name. Such an entity is said to be "in scope" for that portion of the app. This section introduces several important scope issues. The basic scope rules are as follows:

1. The scope of a parameter declaration is the body of the method in which the declaration appears.
2. The scope of a local-variable declaration is from the point at which the declaration appears to the end of the block containing the declaration.

3. The scope of a local-variable declaration that appears in the initialization section of a `for` statement's header is the body of the `for` statement and the other expressions in the header.
4. The scope of a method, property or field of a class is the entire body of the class. This enables non-`static` methods and properties of a class to use any of the class's fields, methods and properties, regardless of the order in which they're declared. Similarly, `static` methods and properties can use any of the `static` members of the class.

Any block may contain variable declarations. If a local variable or parameter in a method has the same name as a field, the field is hidden until the block terminates—in Chapter 10, we discuss how to access hidden fields. A compilation error occurs if a *nested block* in a method contains a variable with the same name as a local variable in an *outer block* of the method. The app in Fig. 7.8 demonstrates scoping issues with fields and local variables.

**Error-Prevention Tip 7.1**

*Use different names for fields and local variables to help prevent subtle logic errors that occur when a method is called and a local variable of the method hides a field of the same name in the class.*

```
// Fig. 7.8: Scope.cs
// Scope class demonstrates static- and local-variable scopes.
using System;

class Scope
{
   // static variable that's accessible to all methods of this class
   private static int x = 1;

   // Main creates and initializes local variable x
   // and calls methods UseLocalVariable and UseStaticVariable
   static void Main()
   {
      int x = 5; // method's local variable x hides static variable x

      Console.WriteLine($"local x in method Main is {x}");

      // UseLocalVariable has its own local x
      UseLocalVariable();

      // UseStaticVariable uses class Scope's static variable x
      UseStaticVariable();

      // UseLocalVariable reinitializes its own local x
      UseLocalVariable();

      // class Scope's static variable x retains its value
      UseStaticVariable();
```

**Fig. 7.8** | Scope class demonstrates static- and local-variable scopes. (Part 1 of 2.)

```
29
30          Console.WriteLine($"\nlocal x in method Main is {x}");
31       }
32
33       // create and initialize local variable x during each call
34       static void UseLocalVariable()
35       {
36          int x = 25; // initialized each time UseLocalVariable is called
37
38          Console.WriteLine(
39             $"\nlocal x on entering method UseLocalVariable is {x}");
40          ++x; // modifies this method's local variable x
41          Console.WriteLine(
42             $"local x before exiting method UseLocalVariable is {x}");
43       }
44
45       // modify class Scope's static variable x during each call
46       static void UseStaticVariable()
47       {
48          Console.WriteLine("\nstatic variable x on entering method " +
49             $"UseStaticVariable is {x}");
50          x *= 10; // modifies class Scope's static variable x
51          Console.WriteLine("static variable x before exiting " +
52             $"method UseStaticVariable is {x}");
53       }
54    }
```

```
local x in method Main is 5

local x on entering method UseLocalVariable is 25
local x before exiting method UseLocalVariable is 26

static variable x on entering method UseStaticVariable is 1
static variable x before exiting method UseStaticVariable is 10

local x on entering method UseLocalVariable is 25
local x before exiting method UseLocalVariable is 26

static variable x on entering method UseStaticVariable is 10
static variable x before exiting method UseStaticVariable is 100

local x in method Main is 5
```

**Fig. 7.8** | Scope class demonstrates static- and local-variable scopes. (Part 2 of 2.)

Line 8 declares and initializes the `static` variable `x` to `1`. This `static` variable is *hidden* in any block (or method) that declares a local variable named `x`. Method `Main` (lines 12–31) declares local variable `x` (line 14) and initializes it to `5`. This local variable's value is output to show that `static` variable `x` (whose value is `1`) is hidden in method `Main`. The app declares two other methods—`UseLocalVariable` (lines 34–43) and `UseStaticVariable` (lines 46–53)—that each take no arguments and do not return results. Method `Main` calls each method twice (lines 19–28). Method `UseLocalVariable` declares local variable `x` (line 36). When `UseLocalVariable` is first called (line 19), it creates local variable `x` and initializes it to `25` (line 36), outputs the value of `x` (lines 38–39), increments `x` (line 40) and outputs the value of `x` again (lines 41–42). When `UseLocalVariable` is called a second time (line 25), it re-creates local variable `x` and reinitializes it to `25`, so the output of each call to `UseLocalVariable` is identical.

Method `UseStaticVariable` does not declare any local variables. Therefore, when it refers to `x`, `static` variable `x` (line 8) of the class is used. When method `UseStaticVariable` is first called (line 22), it outputs the value (`1`) of `static` variable `x` (lines 48–49), multiplies the `static` variable `x` by `10` (line 50) and outputs the value (`10`) of `static` variable `x` again (lines 51–52) before returning. The next time method `UseStaticVariable` is called (line 28), the `static` variable has its modified value, `10`, so the method outputs `10`, then `100`. Finally, in method `Main`, the app outputs the value of local variable `x` again (line 30) to show that none of the method calls modified `Main`'s local variable `x`, because the methods all referred to variables named `x` in other scopes.

## 7.11 Method-Call Stack and Activation Records

To understand how C# performs method calls, we first need to consider a data structure (i.e., collection of related data items) known as a **stack**. Think of a stack as analogous to a pile of dishes. When a dish is placed on the pile, it's placed at the *top*—referred to as **pushing** the dish onto the stack. Similarly, when a dish is removed from the pile, it's removed from the top—referred to as **popping** the dish off the stack. Stacks are known as **last-in, first-out (LIFO) data structures**—the last item pushed (inserted) on the stack is the first item popped (removed) from the stack.

### 7.11.1 Method-Call Stack

The **method-call stack** (sometimes referred to as the **program-execution stack**) is a data structure that works behind the scenes to support the method call/return mechanism. It also supports the creation, maintenance and destruction of each called method's local variables. As we'll see in Figs. 7.10–7.12, the stack's last-in, first-out (LIFO) behavior is *exactly* what a method needs in order to return to the method that called it.

### 7.11.2 Stack Frames

As each method is called, it may, in turn, call other methods, which may, in turn, call other methods—all *before* any of the methods return. Each method eventually must return control to the method that called it. So, somehow, the system must keep track of the *return addresses* that each method needs in order to return control to the method that called it. The method-call stack is the perfect data structure for handling this information. Each time a method calls another method, an entry is *pushed* onto the stack. This entry, called a **stack frame** or an **activation record**, contains the *return address* that the called method needs in order to return to the calling method. It also contains some additional information we'll soon discuss. If the called method returns instead of calling another method before returning, the stack frame for the method call is *popped*, and control transfers to the return address in the popped stack frame. The same techniques apply when a method accesses a property or when a property calls a method.

The beauty of the call stack is that each called method *always* finds the information it needs to return to its caller at the *top* of the call stack. And, if a method makes a call to another method, a stack frame for the new method call is simply *pushed* onto the call stack. Thus, the return address required by the newly called method to return to its caller is now located at the *top* of the stack.

### 7.11.3 Local Variables and Stack Frames

The stack frames have another important responsibility. Most methods have local variables—parameters and any local variables the method declares. Local variables need to exist while a method is executing. They need to remain active if the method makes calls to other methods. But when a called method returns to its caller, the called method's local variables need to "go away." The called method's stack frame is a perfect place to reserve the memory for the called method's local variables. That stack frame exists as long as the called method is active. When that method returns—and no longer needs its local variables—its stack frame is *popped* from the stack, and those local variables no longer exist.

### 7.11.4 Stack Overflow

Of course, the amount of memory in a computer is finite, so only a certain amount of memory can be used to store activation records on the method-call stack. If more method calls occur than can have their activation records stored on the method-call stack, a fatal error known as **stack overflow** occurs[2]—typically caused by infinite recursion (Section 7.16).

### 7.11.5 Method-Call Stack in Action

Now let's consider how the call stack supports the operation of a `Square` method (lines 15–18 of Fig. 7.9) called by `Main` (lines 8–12).

```
1   // Fig. 7.9: SquareTest.cs
2   // Square method used to demonstrate the method
3   // call stack and activation records.
4   using System;
5
6   class Program
7   {
8      static void Main()
9      {
10        int x = 10; // value to square (local variable in main)
11        Console.WriteLine($"x squared: {Square(x)}");
12     }
13
14     // returns the square of an integer
15     static int Square(int y) // y is a local variable
16     {
17        return y * y; // calculate square of y and return result
18     }
19  }
```

**Fig. 7.9** | `Square` method used to demonstrate the method-call stack and activation records. (Part 1 of 2.)

2. This is how the website `stackoverflow.com` got its name. This is a popular website for getting answers to your programming questions.

```
x squared: 100
```

**Fig. 7.9** | `Square` method used to demonstrate the method-call stack and activation records. (Part 2 of 2.)

First, the operating system calls `Main`—this *pushes* an activation record onto the stack (Fig. 7.10). This tells `Main` how to return to the operating system (i.e., transfer to return address `R1`) and contains the space for `Main`'s local variable `x`, which is initialized to `10`.

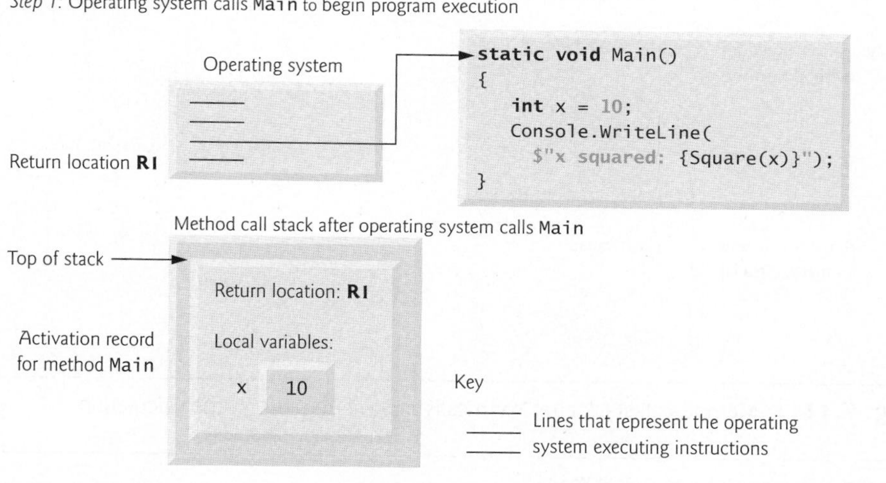


**Fig. 7.10** | Method-call stack after the operating system calls `main` to execute the program.

Method `Main`—before returning to the operating system—calls method `Square` in line 11 of Fig. 7.9. This causes a stack frame for `Square` (lines 15–18) to be pushed onto the method-call stack (Fig. 7.11). This stack frame contains the return address that `Square` needs to return to `Main` (i.e., `R2`) and the memory for `Square`'s local variable `y`.

After `Square` performs its calculation, it needs to return to `Main`—and no longer needs the memory for `y`. So `Square`'s stack frame is *popped* from the stack—giving `Square` the return location in `Main` (i.e., `R2`) and losing `Square`'s local variable (*Step 3*). Figure 7.12 shows the method-call stack *after* `Square`'s activation record has been *popped*.

Method `Main` now displays the result of calling `Square` (Fig. 7.9, line 11). Reaching the closing right brace of `Main` causes its stack frame to be *popped* from the stack, giving `Main` the address it needs to return to the operating system (i.e., `R1` in Fig. 7.10)—at this point, `Main`'s local variable `x` no longer exists.

You've now seen how valuable the stack data structure is in implementing a key mechanism that supports program execution. There's a significant omission in the sequence of illustrations in this section. See if you can spot it before reading the next sentence. The call to the method `Console.Writeln`, of course, also involves the stack, which should be reflected in this section's illustrations and discussion.

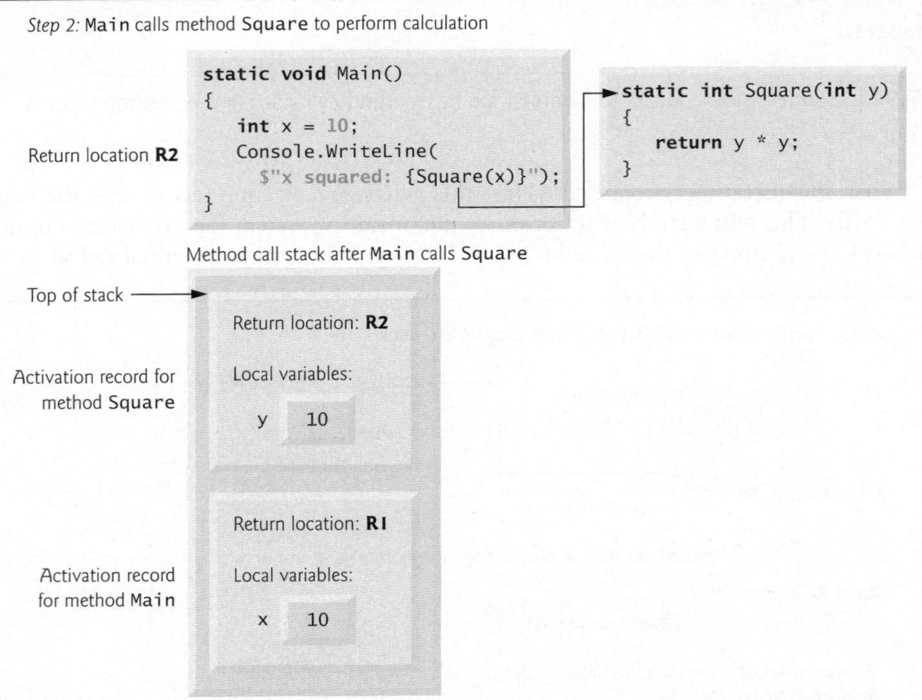


**Fig. 7.11** | Method-call stack after `Main` calls `square` to perform the calculation.

*Step 3:* `Square` returns its result to `Main`

```
static void Main()
{
   int x = 10;
   Console.WriteLine(
     $"x squared: {Square(x)}");
}
```

Return location **R2**

```
static int Square(int y)
{
   return y * y;
}
```

Method call stack after `Square` returns its result to `Main`

Top of stack

Return location: **R1**

Activation record for method `Main`

Local variables:

x 10

**Fig. 7.12** | Method-call stack after method `square` returns to `Main`.

## 7.12 Method Overloading

Methods of the same name can be declared in the same class, as long as they have different sets of parameters (determined by the number, types and order of the parameters). This is called **method overloading.** When an **overloaded method** is called, the C# compiler selects the appropriate method by examining the number, types and order of the arguments in the call. Method overloading is commonly used to create several methods with the *same name* that perform the same or similar tasks, but on *different types* or *different numbers of arguments.* For example, `Random` method `Next` (Section 7.8) has overloads that accept different numbers of arguments, and `Math` method `Max` has overloads that accept different types of arguments (`int`s vs. `double`s). These find the minimum and maximum, respectively, of two values of each of the numeric simple types. Our next example demonstrates declaring and invoking overloaded methods. You'll see examples of overloaded constructors in Chapter 10.

### 7.12.1 Declaring Overloaded Methods

In class `MethodOverload` (Fig. 7.13), we include two `Square` methods—one that calculates the square of an `int` (and returns an `int`) and one that calculates the square of a `double` (and returns a `double`). Although these methods have the same name and similar parameter lists and bodies, you can think of them simply as *different* methods. It may help to think of the method names as "`Square` of `int`" and "`Square` of `double`," respectively.

```
// Fig. 7.13: MethodOverload.cs
// Overloaded method declarations.
using System;

class MethodOverload
{
   // test overloaded square methods
   static void Main()
   {
      Console.WriteLine($"Square of integer 7 is {Square(7)}");
      Console.WriteLine($"Square of double 7.5 is {Square(7.5)}");
   }

   // square method with int argument
   static int Square(int intValue)
   {
      Console.WriteLine($"Called square with int argument: {intValue}");
      return intValue * intValue;
   }

   // square method with double argument
   static double Square(double doubleValue)
   {
      Console.WriteLine(
         $"Called square with double argument: {doubleValue}");
      return doubleValue * doubleValue;
   }
}
```

**Fig. 7.13** | Overloaded method declarations. (Part 1 of 2.)

```
Called square with int argument: 7
Square of integer 7 is 49
Called square with double argument: 7.5
Square of double 7.5 is 56.25
```

**Fig. 7.13** | Overloaded method declarations. (Part 2 of 2.)

Line 10 in `Main` invokes method `Square` with the argument `7`. Literal integer values are treated as type `int`, so the method call in line 10 invokes the version of `Square` at lines 15–19 that specifies an `int` parameter. Similarly, line 11 invokes method `Square` with the argument `7.5`. Literal real-number values are treated as type `double`, so the method call in line 11 invokes the version of `Square` at lines 22–27 that specifies a `double` parameter. Each method first outputs a line of text to prove that the proper method was called in each case.

The overloaded methods in Fig. 7.13 perform the same calculation, but with two different types. C#'s generics feature provides a mechanism for writing a single "generic method" that can perform the same tasks as an entire set of overloaded methods. We discuss generic methods in Chapter 18.

### 7.12.2 Distinguishing Between Overloaded Methods

The compiler distinguishes overloaded methods by their **signature**—a combination of the method's name and the number, types and order of its parameters. The signature also includes the way those parameters are passed, which can be modified by the `ref` and `out` keywords (discussed in Section 7.18). If the compiler looked only at method names during compilation, the code in Fig. 7.13 would be *ambiguous*—the compiler would not know how to distinguish between the `Square` methods (lines 15–19 and 22–27). Internally, the compiler uses signatures to determine whether a class's methods are unique in that class.

For example, in Fig. 7.13, the compiler will use the method signatures to distinguish between the "`Square` of `int`" method (the `Square` method that specifies an `int` parameter) and the "`Square` of `double`" method (the `Square` method that specifies a `double` parameter). As another example, if `Method1`'s declaration begins as

```
void Method1(int a, float b)
```

then that method will have a different signature than a method that begins with

```
void Method1(float a, int b)
```

The *order* of the parameter types is important—the compiler considers the preceding two `Method1` headers to be distinct.

### 7.12.3 Return Types of Overloaded Methods

In discussing the logical names of methods used by the compiler, we did not mention the methods' return types. Methods *cannot* be distinguished by return type. If in a class named `MethodOverloadError` you define overloaded methods with the following headers:

```
int Square(int x)
double Square(int x)
```

which each have the *same* signature but *different* return types, the compiler generates the following error for the second `Square` method:

```
Type 'MethodOverloadError' already defines a member called 'Square'
with the same parameter types
```

Overloaded methods can have the *same* or *different* return types if the parameter lists are *different*. Also, overloaded methods need not have the same number of parameters.

**Common Programming Error 7.9**

*Declaring overloaded methods with identical parameter lists is a compilation error regardless of whether the return types are different.*

## 7.13 Optional Parameters

Methods can have **optional parameters** that allow the calling method to *vary the number of arguments* to pass. An optional parameter specifies a **default value** that's assigned to the parameter if the optional argument is omitted. You can create methods with one or more optional parameters. *All optional parameters must be placed to the right of the method's non-optional parameters*—that is, at the end of the parameter list.

**Common Programming Error 7.10**

*Declaring a non-optional parameter to the right of an optional one is a compilation error.*

When a parameter has a default value, the caller has the *option* of passing that particular argument. For example, the method header

```
static int Power(int baseValue, int exponentValue = 2)
```

specifies an optional second parameter. Each call to `Power` must pass at least a `baseValue` argument, or a compilation error occurs. Optionally, a second argument (for the `exponentValue` parameter) can be passed to `Power`. Each optional parameter must specify a default value by using an equal (=) sign followed by the value. For example, the header for `Power` sets `2` as `exponentValue`'s default value. Consider the following calls to `Power`:

- `Power()`—This call generates a compilation error because this method requires a minimum of one argument.
- `Power(10)`—This call is valid because one argument (`10`) is being passed. The optional `exponentValue` is not specified in the method call, so the compiler uses `2` for the `exponentValue`, as specified in the method header.
- `Power(10, 3)`—This call is also valid because `10` is passed as the required argument and `3` is passed as the optional argument.

Figure 7.14 demonstrates an optional parameter. The program calculates the result of raising a base value to an exponent. Method `Power` (lines 15–25) specifies that its second parameter is optional. In `Main`, lines 10–11 call method `Power`. Line 10 calls the method without the optional second argument. In this case, the compiler provides the second argument, `2`, using the default value of the optional argument, which is not visible to you in the call.

```
// Fig. 7.14: CalculatePowers.cs
// Optional parameter demonstration with method Power.
using System;

class CalculatePowers
{
   // call Power with and without optional arguments
   static void Main()
   {
      Console.WriteLine($"Power(10) = {Power(10)}") ;
      Console.WriteLine($"Power(2, 10) = {Power(2, 10)}");
   }

   // use iteration to calculate power
   static int Power(int baseValue, int exponentValue = 2)
   {
      int result = 1;

      for (int i = 1; i <= exponentValue; ++i)
      {
         result *= baseValue;
      }

      return result;
   }
}
```

```
Power(10) = 100
Power(2, 10) = 1024
```

**Fig. 7.14** | Optional parameter demonstration with method `Power`.

## 7.14 Named Parameters

Normally, when calling a method, the argument values—in order—are assigned to the parameters from left to right in the parameter list. Consider a `Time` class that stores the time of day in 24-hour clock format as `int` values representing the hour (0–23), minute (0–59) and second (0–59). Such a class might provide a `SetTime` method with optional parameters like

```
public void SetTime(int hour = 0, int minute = 0, int second = 0)
```

In the preceding method header, all three of `SetTime`'s parameters are optional. Assuming that we have a `Time` object named `t`, consider the following calls to `SetTime`:

- `t.SetTime()`—This call specifies no arguments, so the compiler assigns the default value `0` to each parameter. The resulting time is 12:00:00 AM.
- `t.SetTime(12)`—This call specifies the argument `12` for the first parameter, `hour`, and the compiler assigns the default value `0` to the `minute` and `second` parameters. The resulting time is 12:00:00 PM.
- `t.SetTime(12, 30)`—This call specifies the arguments `12` and `30` for the parameters `hour` and `minute`, respectively, and the compiler assigns the default value `0` to the parameter `second`. The resulting time is 12:30:00 PM.

- `t.SetTime(12, 30, 22)`—This call specifies the arguments `12`, `30` and `22` for the parameters `hour`, `minute` and `second`, respectively, so the compiler does not provide any default values. The resulting time is 12:30:22 PM.

What if you wanted to specify only arguments for the `hour` and `second`? You might think that you could call the method as follows:

```
t.SetTime(12, , 22); // COMPILATION ERROR
```

C# doesn't allow you to skip an argument as shown above. C# provides a feature called **named parameters**, which enable you to call methods that receive optional parameters by providing *only* the optional arguments you wish to specify. To do so, you explicitly specify the parameter's name and value—separated by a colon (`:`)—in the argument list of the method call. For example, the preceding statement can be written as follows:

```
t.SetTime(hour: 12, second: 22); // sets the time to 12:00:22
```

In this case, the compiler assigns parameter `hour` the argument `12` and parameter `second` the argument `22`. The parameter `minute` is not specified, so the compiler assigns it the default value `0`. It's also possible to specify the arguments *out of order* when using named parameters. The arguments for the required parameters must always be supplied. The *argumentName*: *value* syntax may be used with any method's required parameters.

## 6 7.15 C# 6 Expression-Bodied Methods and Properties

C# 6 introduces a new concise syntax for:

- methods that contain only a `return` statement that returns a value
- read-only properties in which the `get` accessor contains only a `return` statement
- methods that contain single statement bodies.

Consider the following `Cube` method:

```
static int Cube(int x)
{
   return x * x * x;
}
```

In C# 6, this can be expressed with an **expression-bodied method** as

```
static int Cube(int x) => x * x * x;
```

The value of `x * x * x` is returned to `Cube`'s caller implicitly. The symbol `=>` follows the method's parameter list and introduces the method's body—no braces or `return` statement are required and this can be used with `static` and non-`static` methods alike. If the expression to the right of `=>` does not have a value (e.g., a call to a method that returns `void`), the expression-bodied method must return `void`. Similarly, a read-only property can be implemented as an **expression-bodied property**. The following reimplements the `IsNoFaultState` property in Fig. 6.11 to return the result of a logical expression:

```
public bool IsNoFaultState =>
   State == "MA" || State == "NJ" || State == "NY" || State == "PA";
```

## 7.16 Recursion

The apps we've discussed thus far are generally structured as methods that call one another in a disciplined, hierarchical manner. For some problems, however, it's useful to have a method call itself. A **recursive method** is a method that calls itself, either *directly* or *indirectly through another method.* We consider recursion conceptually first. Then we examine an app containing a recursive method.

### 7.16.1 Base Cases and Recursive Calls

Recursive problem-solving approaches have a number of elements in common. When a recursive method is called to solve a problem, it actually is capable of solving *only* the simplest case(s), or **base case(s)**. If the method is called with a base case, it returns a result. If the method is called with a more complex problem, it divides the problem into two conceptual pieces (often called *divide and conquer*): a piece that the method knows how to do and a piece that it does not know how to do. To make recursion feasible, the latter piece must resemble the original problem, but be a slightly simpler or slightly smaller version of it. Because this new problem looks like the original problem, the method calls a fresh copy (or several fresh copies) of itself to work on the smaller problem; this is referred to as a **recursive call** and is also called the **recursion step**. The recursion step normally includes a `return` statement, because its result will be combined with the portion of the problem the method knew how to solve to form a result that will be passed back to the original caller.

The recursion step executes while the original call to the method is still active (i.e., while it has not finished executing). The recursion step can result in many more recursive calls, as the method divides each new subproblem into two conceptual pieces. For the recursion to *terminate* eventually, each time the method calls itself with a slightly simpler version of the original problem, the sequence of smaller and smaller problems must converge on the base case(s). At that point, the method recognizes the base case and returns a result to the previous copy of the method. A sequence of returns ensues until the original method call returns the result to the caller. This process sounds complex compared with the conventional problem solving we've performed to this point.

### 7.16.2 Recursive Factorial Calculations

Let's write a recursive app to perform a popular mathematical calculation. The factorial of a nonnegative integer $n$, written $n!$ (and pronounced "$n$ factorial"), is the product

$$n \cdot (n-1) \cdot (n-2) \cdot \ldots \cdot 1$$

1! is equal to 1 and 0! is defined to be 1. For example, 5! is the product $5 \cdot 4 \cdot 3 \cdot 2 \cdot 1$, which is equal to 120.

The factorial of an integer, `number`, greater than or equal to 0 can be calculated iteratively (nonrecursively) using the `for` statement as follows:

```
long factorial = 1;

for (long counter = number; counter >= 1; --counter)
{
   factorial *= counter;
}
```

A recursive declaration of the factorial method is arrived at by observing the following relationship:

$$n! = n \cdot (n-1)!$$

For example, 5! is clearly equal to 5 · 4!, as is shown by the following equations:

$$5! = 5 \cdot 4 \cdot 3 \cdot 2 \cdot 1$$
$$5! = 5 \cdot (4 \cdot 3 \cdot 2 \cdot 1)$$
$$5! = 5 \cdot (4!)$$

The evaluation of 5! would proceed as shown in Fig. 7.15. Figure 7.15(a) shows how the succession of recursive calls proceeds until 1! is evaluated to be 1, which terminates the recursion. Figure 7.15(b) shows the values returned from each recursive call to its caller until the value is calculated and returned.

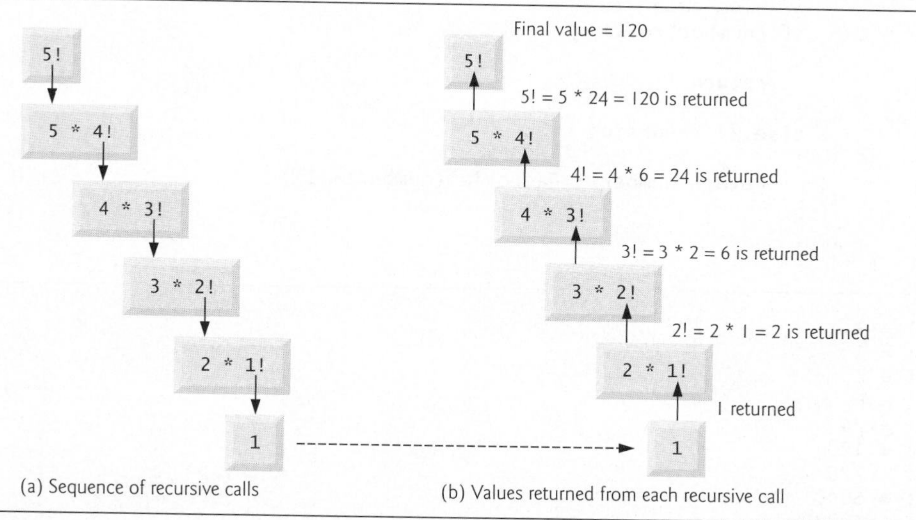


**Fig. 7.15** | Recursive evaluation of 5!.

### 7.16.3 Implementing Factorial Recursively

Figure 7.16 uses recursion to calculate and display the factorials of the integers from 0 to 10. The recursive method `Factorial` (lines 17–28) first tests to determine whether a terminating condition (line 20) is `true`. If `number` is less than or equal to `1` (the base case), `Factorial` returns `1` and no further recursion is necessary. If `number` is greater than `1`, line 26 expresses the problem as the product of `number` and a recursive call to `Factorial` evaluating the factorial of `number - 1`, which is a slightly simpler problem than the original calculation, `Factorial(number)`.

```
1  // Fig. 7.16: FactorialTest.cs
2  // Recursive Factorial method.
3  using System;
```

**Fig. 7.16** | Recursive `Factorial` method. (Part 1 of 2.)

```
4
5   class FactorialTest
6   {
7      static void Main()
8      {
9         // calculate the factorials of 0 through 10
10        for (long counter = 0; counter <= 10; ++counter)
11        {
12           Console.WriteLine($"{counter}! = {Factorial(counter)}");
13        }
14     }
15
16     // recursive declaration of method Factorial
17     static long Factorial(long number)
18     {
19        // base case
20        if (number <= 1)
21        {
22           return 1;
23        }
24        else // recursion step
25        {
26           return number * Factorial(number - 1);
27        }
28     }
29  }
```

```
0! = 1
1! = 1
2! = 2
3! = 6
4! = 24
5! = 120
6! = 720
7! = 5040
8! = 40320
9! = 362880
10! = 3628800
```

**Fig. 7.16** | Recursive `Factorial` method. (Part 2 of 2.)

Method `Factorial` (lines 17–28) receives a parameter of type `long` and returns a result of type `long`. As you can see in Fig. 7.16, factorial values become large quickly. We chose type `long` (which can represent relatively large integers) so that the app could calculate factorials greater than 20!. Unfortunately, the `Factorial` method produces large values so quickly that factorial values soon exceed even the maximum value that can be stored in a `long` variable. Due to the restrictions on the integral types, variables of type `float`, `double` or `decimal` might ultimately be needed to calculate factorials of larger numbers. This situation points to a weakness in some programming languages—the languages are *not easily extended* to handle the unique requirements of various apps. As you know, C# allows you to create new types. For example, you could create a type `HugeInteger` for arbitrarily large integers. This class would enable an app to calculate the factorials of larger numbers. In fact, the .NET Framework's `BigInteger` type (from namespace `System.Numerics`) supports arbitrarily large integers.

**Common Programming Error 7.11**

*Either omitting the base case or writing the recursion step incorrectly so that it does not converge on the base case will cause* ***infinite recursion****, eventually exhausting memory. This error is analogous to the problem of an infinite loop in an iterative (nonrecursive) solution.*

## 7.17 Value Types vs. Reference Types

Types in C# are divided into two categories—*value types* and *reference types*.

### *Value Types*

C#'s simple types (like `int`, `double` and `decimal`) are all **value types**. A variable of a value type simply contains a *value* of that type. For example, Fig. 7.17 shows an `int` variable named `count` that contains the value `7`.

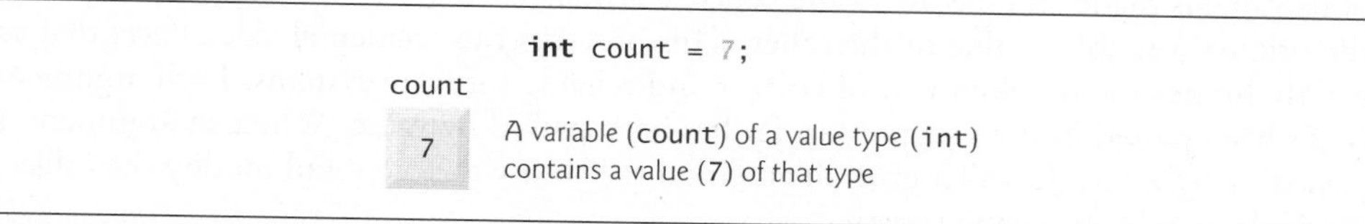


**Fig. 7.17** | Value-type variable.

### *Reference Types*

By contrast, a variable of a **reference type** (also called a **reference**) contains the *location* where the data referred to by that variable is stored. Such a variable is said to **refer to an object** in the program. For example, the statement

```
Account myAccount = new Account();
```

creates an object of our class `Account` (presented in Chapter 4), places it in memory and stores the object's reference in variable `myAccount` of type `Account`, as shown in Fig. 7.18. The `Account` object is shown with its `name` instance variable.

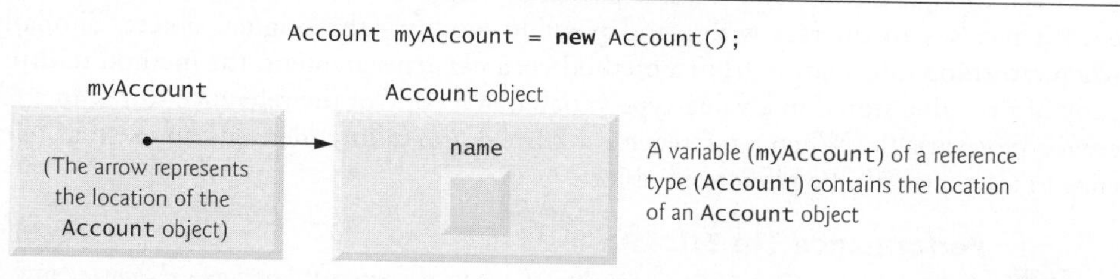


**Fig. 7.18** | Reference-type variable.

### *Reference-Type Instance Variables Are Initialized to* `null` *by Default*

Reference-type instance variables (such as `myAccount` in Fig. 7.18) are initialized by default to `null`. The type `string` is a reference type. For this reason, `string` instance variable `name` is shown in Fig. 7.18 with an empty box representing the `null`-valued variable. A `string` variable with the value `null` is *not* an empty `string`, which is represented by `""` or **`string.Empty`**. Rather, the value `null` represents a reference that does *not* refer to an object, whereas the empty `string` is a `string` object that does not contain any characters. In Section 7.18, we discuss value types and reference types in more detail.

**Software Engineering Observation 7.4**

*A variable's declared type (e.g.,* `int` *or* `Account`*) indicates whether the variable is of a value type or a reference type. If a variable's type is one of the simple types (Appendix B), an* `enum` *type or a* `struct` *type (which we introduce in Section 10.13), then it's a value type. Classes like* `Account` *are reference types.*

## 7.18 Passing Arguments By Value and By Reference

Two ways to pass arguments to methods in many programming languages are **pass-by-value** and **pass-by-reference**. When an argument is passed by *value* (the default in C#), a *copy* of its value is made and passed to the called method. Changes to the copy do *not* affect the original variable's value in the caller. This prevents the accidental side effects that so greatly hinder the development of correct and reliable software systems. Each argument that's been passed in the programs so far has been passed by value. When an argument is passed by *reference*, the caller gives the method the ability to access and modify the caller's original variable—no copy is passed.

To pass an object by reference into a method, simply provide as an argument in the method call the variable that refers to the object. Then, in the method body, reference the object using the corresponding parameter name. The parameter refers to the original object in memory, so the called method can access the original object directly.

In the previous section, we began discussing the differences between *value types* and *reference types*. A major difference is that:

- *value-type variables store values*, so specifying a value-type variable in a method call passes a *copy* of that variable's value to the method, whereas
- *reference-type variables store references to objects*, so specifying a reference-type variable as an argument passes the method a *copy of the reference* that refers to the object.

Even though the reference itself is passed by value, the method can still use the reference it receives to interact with—and possibly modify—the original object. Similarly, when returning information from a method via a `return` statement, the method returns a copy of the value stored in a value-type variable or a copy of the reference stored in a reference-type variable. When a reference is returned, the calling method can use that reference to interact with the referenced object.

**Performance Tip 7.1**

*A disadvantage of pass-by-value is that, if a large data item is being passed, copying that data can take a considerable amount of execution time and memory space.*

**Performance Tip 7.2**

*Pass-by-reference improves performance by eliminating the pass-by-value overhead of copying large objects.*

**Software Engineering Observation 7.5**

*Pass-by-reference can weaken security; the called method can corrupt the caller's data.*

### 7.18.1 `ref` and `out` Parameters

What if you would like to pass a variable by reference so the called method can modify the variable's value in the caller? To do this, C# provides keywords **`ref`** and **`out`**.

#### `ref` *Parameters*

Applying the `ref` keyword to a parameter declaration allows you to pass a variable to a method by reference—the method will be able to modify the original variable in the caller. Keyword `ref` is used for variables that already have been initialized in the calling method.

**Common Programming Error 7.12**

*When a method call contains an uninitialized variable as an argument to a* `ref` *parameter, the compiler generates an error.*

#### `out` *Parameters*

Preceding a parameter with keyword `out` creates an **output parameter**. This indicates to the compiler that the argument will be passed into the called method by reference and that the called method will assign a value to the original variable in the caller. This also prevents the compiler from generating an error message for an uninitialized variable that's passed as an argument to a method.

**Common Programming Error 7.13**

*If the method does not assign a value to the* `out` *parameter in every possible path of execution, the compiler generates an error. Also, reading an* `out` *parameter before it's assigned a value is also a compilation error.*

**Software Engineering Observation 7.6**

*A method can return only one value to its caller via a return statement, but can return many values by specifying multiple output (*`ref` *and/or* `out`*) parameters.*

#### *Passing Reference-Type Variables by Reference*

You also can pass a reference-type variable by reference, which allows you to modify it so that it refers to a new object. Passing a reference by reference is a tricky but powerful technique that we discuss in Section 8.13.

**Software Engineering Observation 7.7**

*By default, C# does not allow you to choose whether to pass each argument by value or by reference. Value types are passed by value. Objects are not passed to methods; rather, references to objects are passed—the references themselves are passed by value. When a method receives a reference to an object, the method can manipulate the object directly, but the reference value cannot be changed to refer to a new object.*

### 7.18.2 Demonstrating ref, out and Value Parameters

The app in Fig. 7.19 uses the `ref` and `out` keywords to manipulate integer values. The class contains three methods that calculate the square of an integer.

```
// Fig. 7.19: ReferenceAndOutputParameters.cs
// Reference, output and value parameters.
using System;

class ReferenceAndOutputParameters
{
   // call methods with reference, output and value parameters
   static void Main()
   {
      int y = 5; // initialize y to 5
      int z; // declares z, but does not initialize it

      // display original values of y and z
      Console.WriteLine($"Original value of y: {y}");
      Console.WriteLine("Original value of z: uninitialized\n");

      // pass y and z by reference
      SquareRef(ref y); // must use keyword ref
      SquareOut(out z); // must use keyword out

      // display values of y and z after they're modified by
      // methods SquareRef and SquareOut, respectively
      Console.WriteLine($"Value of y after SquareRef: {y}");
      Console.WriteLine($"Value of z after SquareOut: {z}\n");

      // pass y and z by value
      Square(y);
      Square(z);

      // display values of y and z after they're passed to method Square
      // to demonstrate that arguments passed by value are not modified
      Console.WriteLine($"Value of y after Square: {y}");
      Console.WriteLine($"Value of z after Square: {z}");
   }

   // uses reference parameter x to modify caller's variable
   static void SquareRef(ref int x)
   {
      x = x * x; // squares value of caller's variable
   }

   // uses output parameter x to assign a value
   // to an uninitialized variable
   static void SquareOut(out int x)
   {
      x = 6; // assigns a value to caller's variable
      x = x * x; // squares value of caller's variable
   }
```

**Fig. 7.19** | Reference, output and value parameters. (Part 1 of 2.)

```
49
50      // parameter x receives a copy of the value passed as an argument,
51      // so this method cannot modify the caller's variable
52      static void Square(int x)
53      {
54         x = x * x;
55      }
56   }
```

```
Original value of y: 5
Original value of z: uninitialized

Value of y after SquareRef: 25
Value of z after SquareOut: 36

Value of y after Square: 25
Value of z after Square: 36
```

**Fig. 7.19** | Reference, output and value parameters. (Part 2 of 2.)

Method `SquareRef` (lines 37–40) multiplies its parameter `x` by itself and assigns the new value to `x`. `SquareRef`'s parameter is declared as `ref int`, which indicates that the argument passed to this method must be an integer that's passed by reference. Because the argument is passed by reference, the assignment at line 39 modifies the original argument's value in the caller.

Method `SquareOut` (lines 44–48) assigns its parameter the value `6` (line 46), then squares that value. `SquareOut`'s parameter is declared as `out int`, which indicates that the argument passed to this method must be an integer that's passed by reference and that the argument does *not* need to be initialized in advance.

Method `Square` (lines 52–55) multiplies its parameter `x` by itself and assigns the new value to `x`. When this method is called, a *copy* of the argument is passed to the parameter `x`. Thus, even though parameter `x` is modified in the method, the original value in the caller is *not* modified.

Method `Main` (lines 8–34) invokes methods `SquareRef`, `SquareOut` and `Square`. We begin by initializing variable `y` to `5` and declaring, but *not* initializing, variable `z`. Lines 18–19 call methods `SquareRef` and `SquareOut`. Notice that when you pass a variable to a method with a reference parameter, you must precede the argument with the same keyword (`ref` or `out`) that was used to declare the reference parameter. Lines 23–24 display the values of `y` and `z` after the calls to `SquareRef` and `SquareOut`. Notice that `y` has been changed to `25` and `z` has been set to `36`.

Lines 27–28 call method `Square` with `y` and `z` as arguments. In this case, both variables are passed by *value*—only *copies* of their values are passed to `Square`. As a result, the values of `y` and `z` remain `25` and `36`, respectively. Lines 32–33 output the values of `y` and `z` to show that they were *not* modified.

**Common Programming Error 7.14**

*The `ref` and `out` arguments in a method call must match the `ref` and `out` parameters specified in the method declaration; otherwise, a compilation error occurs.*

## 7.19 Wrap-Up

In this chapter, we discussed the difference between non-`static` and `static` methods, and we showed how to call `static` methods by preceding the method name with the name of the class in which it appears and the member-access operator (`.`). You saw that the `Math` class in the .NET Framework Class Library provides many `static` methods to perform mathematical calculations. We also discussed `static` class members and why method `Main` is declared `static`.

We presented several commonly used Framework Class Library namespaces. You learned how to use operator + to perform `string` concatenations. You also learned how to declare constants with the `const` keyword and how to define sets of named constants with `enum` types. We demonstrated simulation techniques and used class `Random` to generate sets of random numbers. We discussed the scope of fields and local variables in a class. You saw how to overload methods in a class by providing methods with the same name but different signatures. You learned how to use optional and named parameters.

We showed the concise notation of C# 6's expression-bodied methods and read-only properties for implementing methods and read-only property `get` accessors that contain only a `return` statement. We discussed how recursive methods call themselves, breaking larger problems into smaller subproblems until eventually the original problem is solved. You learned the differences between value types and reference types with respect to how they're passed to methods, and how to use the `ref` and `out` keywords to pass arguments by reference.

In Chapter 8, you'll maintain lists and tables of data in arrays. You'll see a more elegant implementation of the app that rolls a die 60,000,000 times and two versions of a `GradeBook` case study. You'll also access an app's command-line arguments that are passed to method `Main` when a console app begins execution.

# 8

# Arrays; Introduction to Exception Handling

## Objectives

In this chapter you'll:

- Use arrays to store data in and retrieve data from lists and tables of values.
- Declare arrays, initialize arrays and refer to individual elements of arrays.
- Iterate through arrays with the `foreach` statement.
- Use `var` to declare implicitly typed local variables and let the compiler infer their types from their initializer values.
- Use exception handling to process runtime problems.
- Declare C# 6 getter-only auto-implemented properties.
- Initialize auto-implemented properties with C# 6 auto-property initializers.
- Pass arrays to methods.
- Declare and manipulate multidimensional arrays—both rectangular and jagged.
- Write methods that use variable-length argument lists.
- Read command-line arguments into an app.

Outline



## 8.1 Introduction

**Arrays** are data structures consisting of related data items of the *same* type. They are *fixed-length* entities—remaining the same length once they're created, although an array variable may be reassigned so that it refers to a new array of a different length.

We'll discuss how to declare, create and initialize arrays, then show several examples of common array manipulations. We'll present the `foreach` iteration statement, which provides a concise notation for accessing data in arrays (and collections, as you'll see in Section 9.4, Introduction to Collections, and in Chapter 19, Generic Collections; Functional Programming with LINQ/PLINQ).

You'll use keyword `var` to declare implicitly typed local variables—as you'll see, the compiler can determine a local variable's type, based on its initializer value. We'll introduce *exception handling* for detecting and processing problems that occur at execution time.

Many of the chapter's examples manipulate arrays of `int` simple-type values. To demonstrate that arrays also can store reference types, we'll create a card-shuffling-and-dealing simulation that manipulates an array of `Card` objects. In that example, we'll introduce C# 6's getter-only auto-implemented properties, which define properties that can be used to get, but not set, a value.

We present two versions of an instructor `GradeBook` case study that use arrays to maintain sets of student grades *in memory* and analyze them. We'll also demonstrate how to define methods that receive variable-length argument lists (which are implemented by C# as arrays) and a version of method `Main` that can receive a `string` array containing an app's so-called command-line arguments.

## 8.2 Arrays

An array is a group of variables—called **elements**—containing values of the *same type*. Arrays are reference types—an array variable is actually a reference to an array object. An array's elements can be either value types or reference types, including other arrays—e.g., every element of an `int` array is an `int` *value*, and every element of a `string` array is a *reference* to a `string` object. Array names follow the same conventions as other variable names.

### *Logical Representation of an Array; Array-Access Expressions*

Figure 8.1 shows a logical representation of an integer array called `c` that contains 12 elements. An app refers to any one of these elements with an **array-access expression** that includes the name of the reference to the array, `c`, followed by the **index** (i.e., *position number*) of the particular element in **square brackets** (`[]`). The first element in every array has **index zero** (0) and is sometimes called the **zeroth element.** Thus, the names of array `c`'s elements are `c[0]`, `c[1]`, `c[2]` and so on. The highest index in array `c` is `11`—one less than the array's number of elements, because indices begin at 0.

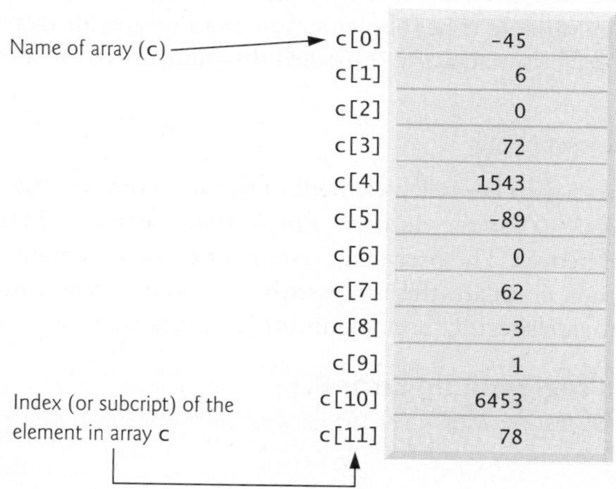


**Fig. 8.1** | A 12-element array.

### *Indices Must Be Nonnegative Integer Values*

An index must be a nonnegative integer or expression with an `int`, `uint`, `long` or `ulong` value—or a value that can be implicitly promoted to one of these types (as discussed in Section 7.6.1). If we assume that variable `a` is `5` and variable `b` is `6`, then the statement

```
c[a + b] += 2;
```

evaluates the expression `a + b` to determine the index and in this case adds `2` to element `c[11]`. Array-access expressions can be used on the left side of an assignment to place a new value into an array element.

### *Examining Array* `c` *in More Detail*

Let's examine array `c` in Fig. 8.1 more closely. The **name** of the variable that references the array is `c`. Every array instance knows its own length and provides access to this information with the **Length** property. For example, the expression `c.Length` returns array `c`'s length (that is, 12). The `Length` property of an array is *read only*, so it *cannot* be changed. The array's 12 elements are referred to as `c[0]`, `c[1]`, `c[2]`, …, `c[11]`. Referring to elements *outside* of this range, such as `c[-1]` or `c[12]`, is a runtime error (as we'll demonstrate in Fig. 8.9). The value of `c[0]` is `-45`, the value of `c[1]` is `6`, the value of `c[2]` is `0`, the value of `c[7]` is `62` and the value of `c[11]` is `78`. To calculate the sum of the values contained in the first three elements of array `c` and store the result in variable `sum`, we'd write

```
sum = c[0] + c[1] + c[2];
```

To divide the value of `c[6]` by `2` and assign the result to the variable `x`, we'd write

```
x = c[6] / 2;
```

## 8.3 Declaring and Creating Arrays

Arrays occupy space in memory. Since they're objects, they're typically created with keyword `new`.[1] To create an array object, you specify the type and the number of array elements in an **array-creation expression** that uses keyword `new` and returns a reference that can be stored in an array variable. The following statement creates an array object containing 12 `int` elements—each initialized to `0` by default—and stores the array's reference in variable `c`:

```
int[] c = new int[12];
```

When you create an array with `new`, each element of the array receives the default value for the array's element type—`0` for the numeric simple-type elements, `false` for `bool` elements and `null` for references. The preceding statement creates the memory for the array in Fig. 8.1 but does not populate the array with the values shown in that figure. In Section 8.4.2, we'll provide specific, nondefault initial values when we create an array.

**Common Programming Error 8.1**

*In an array variable declaration, specifying the number of elements in the square brackets (e.g.,* `int[12] c;`*) is a syntax error.*

Creating the array `c` also can be performed as follows:

```
int[] c; // declare the array variable
c = new int[12]; // create the array; assign to array variable
```

In the declaration, the square brackets following `int` indicate that `c` will refer to an array of `int`s (i.e., `c` will store a reference to an array object). In the assignment statement, the array variable `c` receives the reference to a new array object of 12 `int` elements. The number of elements also can be specified as an expression that's calculated at execution time.

### *Resizing an Array*

Though arrays are fixed-length entities, you can use the `static` `Array` method `Resize` to create a new array with the specified length—class `Array` defines many methods for common array manipulations. This method takes as arguments

1. Section 8.4.2 shows a case in which `new` is not required.

- the array to be resized and
- the new length

and copies the contents of the old array into the new one, then sets the variable it receives as its first argument to reference the new array. For example, in the following statements:

```
int[] newArray = new int[5];
Array.Resize(ref newArray, 10);
```

`newArray` initially refers to a five-element array. The `Resize` method then sets `newArray` to refer to a new 10-element array containing the original array's element values. If the new array is *smaller* than the old array, any content that cannot fit into the new array is *truncated without warning*. The old array's memory is reclaimed by the runtime if there are no other array variables referring to that array.[2]

## 8.4 Examples Using Arrays

This section presents several examples that demonstrate declaring arrays, creating arrays, initializing arrays and manipulating array elements.

### 8.4.1 Creating and Initializing an Array

In Fig. 8.2, line 10 of uses an array-creation expression to create a five-element `int` array with values initialized to `0` by default. The resulting array's reference initializes the variable `array` to refer to the new array object.

```
 1  // Fig. 8.2: InitArray.cs
 2  // Creating an array.
 3  using System;
 4
 5  class InitArray
 6  {
 7     static void Main()
 8     {
 9        // create the space for array and initialize to default zeros
10        int[] array = new int[5]; // array contains 5 int elements
11
12        Console.WriteLine($"{"Index"}{"Value",8}"); // headings
13
14        // output each array element's value
15        for (int counter = 0; counter < array.Length; ++counter)
16        {
17           Console.WriteLine($"{counter,5}{array[counter],8}");
18        }
19     }
20  }
```

**Fig. 8.2** | Creating an array. (Part 1 of 2.)

2. Section 10.8 discusses how the runtime reclaims the memory of objects that are no longer used.

```
Index   Value
    0       0
    1       0
    2       0
    3       0
    4       0
```

**Fig. 8.2** | Creating an array. (Part 2 of 2.)

Line 12 displays column headings for the app's output. The first column will display each array element's index (0–4 for a five-element array), and the second column contains each element's default value (0). The column head "Value" is right-aligned in a field width of 8, as specified in the string-interpolation expression

```
{"Value",8}
```

The for statement (lines 15–18) displays each array element's index (represented by counter) and value (represented by array[counter]). The loop-control variable counter is initially 0—index values start at 0, so zero-based counting allows the loop to access *every* element. The loop-continuation condition uses the property array.Length (line 15) to obtain array's length. In this example, the length is 5, so the loop continues executing as long as counter's value is less than 5. The highest index in a five-element array is 4, so using the less-than operator in the loop-continuation condition guarantees that the loop does not attempt to access an element beyond the end of the array (i.e., during the *final* iteration of the loop, counter is 4). We'll soon see what happens when an *out-of-range index* is encountered at execution time.

### 8.4.2 Using an Array Initializer

An app can create an array and initialize its elements with an **array initializer**—a comma-separated list of expressions (called an **initializer list**) enclosed in braces. The array length is determined by the number of elements in the initializer list. For example, the declaration

```
int[] n = {10, 20, 30, 40, 50};
```

creates a five-element array with index values 0, 1, 2, 3 and 4. Element n[0] is initialized to 10, n[1] is initialized to 20 and so on. This statement does *not* require new to create the array object—the compiler counts the number of initializers (5) to determine the array's size, then sets up the appropriate new operation "behind the scenes." The app in Fig. 8.3 initializes an integer array with 5 values (line 10) and displays the array in tabular format. Lines 15–18 for displaying the array's contents are identical to lines 15–18 of Fig. 8.2.

```
1  // Fig. 8.3: InitArray.cs
2  // Initializing the elements of an array with an array initializer.
3  using System;
4
5  class InitArray
6  {
```

**Fig. 8.3** | Initializing the elements of an array with an array initializer. (Part 1 of 2.)

```
    static void Main()
    {
        // initializer list specifies the value of each element
        int[] array = {32, 27, 64, 18, 95};

        Console.WriteLine($"{"Index"}{"Value",8}"); // headings

        // output each array element's value
        for (int counter = 0; counter < array.Length; ++counter)
        {
            Console.WriteLine($"{counter,5}{array[counter],8}");
        }
    }
}
```

```
Index   Value
    0      32
    1      27
    2      64
    3      18
    4      95
```

**Fig. 8.3** | Initializing the elements of an array with an array initializer. (Part 2 of 2.)

### 8.4.3 Calculating a Value to Store in Each Array Element

Figure 8.4 creates a 5-element array and assigns to its elements the even integers from 2 to 10 (2, 4, 6, 8 and 10). Then the app displays the array in tabular format. Lines 13–16 calculate an array element's value by multiplying the current value of the for loop's control variable counter by 2, then adding 2.

```
1  // Fig. 8.4: InitArray.cs
2  // Calculating values to be placed into the elements of an array.
3  using System;
4
5  class InitArray
6  {
7     static void Main()
8     {
9        const int ArrayLength = 5; // create a named constant
10       int[] array = new int[ArrayLength]; // create array
11
12       // calculate value for each array element
13       for (int counter = 0; counter < array.Length; ++counter)
14       {
15          array[counter] = 2 + 2 * counter;
16       }
17
18       Console.WriteLine($"{"Index"}{"Value",8}"); // headings
19
```

**Fig. 8.4** | Calculating values to be placed into the elements of an array. (Part 1 of 2.)

```
20          // output each array element's value
21          for (int counter = 0; counter < array.Length; ++counter)
22          {
23             Console.WriteLine($"{counter,5}{array[counter],8}");
24          }
25       }
26    }
```

```
Index    Value
    0        2
    1        4
    2        6
    3        8
    4       10
```

**Fig. 8.4** | Calculating values to be placed into the elements of an array. (Part 2 of 2.)

### *Declaring a Named Constant with* `const`

Line 9 uses the modifier `const` to declare the constant `ArrayLength`, which is initialized to 5. Constants must be initialized in their declarations and cannot be modified thereafter. Constants use the same Pascal Case naming conventions as classes, methods and properties.

**Good Programming Practice 8.1**

*Constants are also called* ***named constants****. Apps using constants often are more readable than those that use literal values (e.g.,* 5*)—a named constant such as* `ArrayLength` *clearly indicates its purpose, whereas the literal value* 5 *could have different meanings based on the context in which it's used. Another advantage to using named constants is that if the constant's value must be changed, the change is necessary only in the declaration, thus reducing code-maintenance costs.*

**Good Programming Practice 8.2**

*Defining the size of an array as a named constant instead of a literal makes code clearer. This technique eliminates so-called* ***magic numbers****. For example, repeatedly mentioning the size 5 in array-processing code for a five-element array gives the number 5 an artificial significance and can be confusing when the program includes other 5s that have nothing to do with the array size.*

**Common Programming Error 8.2**

*Assigning a value to a named constant after it's been initialized is a compilation error.*

**Common Programming Error 8.3**

*Attempting to declare a named constant without initializing it is a compilation error.*

## 8.4.4 Summing the Elements of an Array

Often, the elements of an array represent a series of values to be used in a calculation. For example, if the elements of an array represent exam grades, an instructor may wish to sum the elements then use the sum to calculate the class average. The `GradeBook` examples later in the chapter (Sections 8.8 and 8.10) use this technique. Figure 8.5 sums the values contained in a 10-element `int` array, which is declared and initialized in line 9. The `for` statement performs the calculations by adding each element's value to the `total` (line 15).[3]

```
1  // Fig. 8.5: SumArray.cs
2  // Computing the sum of the elements of an array.
3  using System;
4
5  class SumArray
6  {
7     static void Main()
8     {
9        int[] array = {87, 68, 94, 100, 83, 78, 85, 91, 76, 87};
10       int total = 0;
11
12       // add each element's value to total
13       for (int counter = 0; counter < array.Length; ++counter)
14       {
15          total += array[counter]; // add element value to total
16       }
17
18       Console.WriteLine($"Total of array elements: {total}");
19    }
20 }
```

```
Total of array elements: 849
```

**Fig. 8.5** | Computing the sum of the elements of an array.

### 8.4.5 Iterating Through Arrays with foreach

So far, we've used counter-controlled `for` statements to iterate through array elements. In this section, we introduce the **`foreach` statement**, which iterates through an entire array's elements (or the elements of a collection, as you'll see in Section 9.4). The syntax of a `foreach` statement is

```
foreach (type identifier in arrayName)
{
   statement
}
```

where *type* and *identifier* are the type and name (e.g., `int number`) of the **iteration variable**, and *arrayName* is the array through which to iterate. The iteration variable's type must be consistent with the array's element type. The iteration variable represents successive values in the array on successive iterations of the `foreach` statement.

3. The values supplied as array initializers are often read into an app, rather than specified in an initializer list. For example, an app could input the values from a user at the keyboard or from a file on disk (as discussed in Chapter 17, Files and Streams). This makes the app more reusable, because it can be used with different data sets.

Figure 8.6 uses the foreach statement (lines 13–16) to calculate the sum of array's elements. The iteration variable number's type is declared as int (line 13), because array contains int values. The foreach statement iterates through successive int values in array one by one, starting with the first element. The foreach header can be read concisely as "for each iteration, assign array's next element to int variable number, then execute the following statement." Lines 13–16 are equivalent to the counter-controlled iteration used in lines 13–16 of Fig. 8.5.

**Common Programming Error 8.4**

*Any attempt to change the iteration variable's value in the body of a* foreach *statement results in a compilation error.*

```
1  // Fig. 8.6: ForEachTest.cs
2  // Using the foreach statement to total integers in an array.
3  using System;
4
5  class ForEachTest
6  {
7     static void Main()
8     {
9        int[] array = {87, 68, 94, 100, 83, 78, 85, 91, 76, 87};
10       int total = 0;
11
12       // add each element's value to total
13       foreach (int number in array)
14       {
15          total += number;
16       }
17
18       Console.WriteLine($"Total of array elements: {total}");
19    }
20 }
```

```
Total of array elements: 849
```

**Fig. 8.6** | Using the foreach statement to total integers in an array.

### *foreach vs. for*

The foreach statement can be used in place of the for statement whenever code looping through an array does *not* require access to the current array element's *index*. For example, totaling the integers in an array requires access only to the element values—each element's index is irrelevant. If an app must use a counter for some reason other than simply to loop through an array (e.g., to calculate an element's value based on the counter's value, as in Fig. 8.4), you should use the for statement.

**Common Programming Error 8.5**

*Attempting to modify an array element's value using a* foreach *statement's iteration variable is a logic error—the iteration variable can be used only to access each array element's value, not modify it.*

### 8.4.6 Using Bar Charts to Display Array Data Graphically; Introducing Type Inference with var

Many apps present data to users in a graphical manner. For example, numeric values are often displayed as bars in a bar chart. In such a chart, longer bars represent proportionally larger numeric values. One simple way to display numeric data graphically is with a bar chart that shows each numeric value as a bar of asterisks (*).

An instructor might graph the number of grades in each of several categories to visualize the grade distribution for an exam. Suppose the grades on an exam were 87, 68, 94, 100, 83, 78, 85, 91, 76 and 87. Included were one grade of 100, two grades in the 90s, four grades in the 80s, two grades in the 70s, one grade in the 60s and no grades below 60. Our next app (Fig. 8.7) stores this grade-distribution data in an array of 11 elements, each corresponding to a category of grades. For example, `array[0]` indicates the number of grades in the range 0–9, `array[7]` the number of grades in the range 70–79 and `array[10]` the number of 100 grades. The two versions of class `GradeBook` in Sections 8.8 and 8.10 contain code that calculates these grade frequencies based on a set of grades. For now, we manually create `array` and initialize it with the number of grades in each range (Fig. 8.7, line 9). We discuss the keyword `var` (lines 14 and 27) after we present the app's logic.

```
1  // Fig. 8.7: BarChart.cs
2  // Bar chart displaying app.
3  using System;
4
5  class BarChart
6  {
7     static void Main()
8     {
9        int[] array = {0, 0, 0, 0, 0, 0, 1, 2, 4, 2, 1}; // distribution
10
11       Console.WriteLine("Grade distribution:");
12
13       // for each array element, output a bar of the chart
14       for (var counter = 0; counter < array.Length; ++counter)
15       {
16          // output bar labels ("00-09: ", ..., "90-99: ", "100: ")
17          if (counter == 10)
18          {
19             Console.Write("  100: ");
20          }
21          else
22          {
23             Console.Write($"{counter * 10:D2}-{counter * 10 + 9:D2}: ");
24          }
25
26          // display bar of asterisks
27          for (var stars = 0; stars < array[counter]; ++stars)
28          {
29             Console.Write("*");
30          }
```

**Fig. 8.7** | Bar chart displaying app. (Part 1 of 2.)

```
31
32              Console.WriteLine(); // start a new line of output
33           }
34        }
35     }
```

```
Grade distribution:
00-09:
10-19:
20-29:
30-39:
40-49:
50-59:
60-69: *
70-79: **
80-89: ****
90-99: **
  100: *
```

**Fig. 8.7** | Bar chart displaying app. (Part 2 of 2.)

The app reads the numbers from the array and graphs the information as a bar chart. Each grade range is followed by a bar of asterisks indicating the number of grades in that range. To label each bar, lines 17–24 display a grade range (e.g., "70-79: ") based on the current value of counter. When counter is 10, line 19 displays "  100: " to align the colon with the other bar labels. When counter is not 10, line 23 formats the grade range's label using the string-interpolation expressions

```
{counter * 10:D2}
```

and

```
{counter * 10 + 9:D2}
```

The format specifier D indicates that the value should be formatted as an integer, and the number after the D indicates how many digits this formatted integer must contain. The 2 indicates that values with fewer than two digits should begin with a **leading 0**.

The nested for statement (lines 27–30) displays the bars. Note the loop-continuation condition at line 27 (stars < array[counter]). Each time the app reaches the inner for, the loop counts from 0 up to one less than array[counter], thus using a value in array to determine the number of asterisks to display. In this example, array[0]–array[5] contain 0s because no students received a grade below 60. Thus, the app displays no asterisks next to the first six grade ranges.

### *Implicitly Typed Local Variables and Keyword* var

In line 14

```
for (var counter = 0; counter < array.Length; ++counter)
```

notice **var keyword** rather than a type preceding the variable counter. This declares the variable and lets the *compiler* determine the variable's type, based on the variable's *initializer*. This process is known as **type inference** and local variables declared in this manner are known as **implicitly typed local variables**. Here, the compiler *infers* that counter's type is int, because it's initialized with the literal 0, which is an int.

Similarly, consider line 11 of Fig. 4.9:

```
Account account1 = new Account("Jane Green");
```

Notice that the type `Account` appears twice—once to declare variable `account1`'s type and once to specify the type of the new object being created. From this point forward, the preferred way to write this statement is

```
var account1 = new Account("Jane Green");
```

Here, the compiler *infers* that `account1`'s type is `Account`, because the compiler can determine the type from the expression

```
new Account("Jane Green")
```

which creates an `Account` object.

The Microsoft C# Coding Conventions

```
https://msdn.microsoft.com/library/ff926074
```

recommend using type inference when a local variable's type is *obvious*, based on its initial value.[4] These coding conventions are just *guidelines*, not requirements. In industry, your employer might have its own coding requirements that differ from Microsoft's guidelines.

### *More on Implicitly Typed Local Variables*

Implicitly typed local variables also can be used to initialize an array variable via an initializer list. In the following statement, the type of `values` is inferred as `int[]`:

```
var values = new[] {32, 27, 64, 18, 95, 14, 90, 70, 60, 37};
```

`new[]` specifies that the initializer list is for an array. The array's element type, `int`, is inferred from the initializers. The following statement—in which `values` is initialized directly *without* `new[]`—generates a compilation error:

```
var values = {32, 27, 64, 18, 95, 14, 90, 70, 60, 37};
```

**Common Programming Error 8.6**

*Initializer lists can be used with both arrays and collections. If an implicitly typed local variable is initialized via an initializer list* without `new[]`*, a compilation error occurs, because the compiler cannot infer whether the variable should be an array or a collection. We use a* `List` *collection in Chapter 9 and cover collections in detail in Chapter 19.*

## 8.4.7 Using the Elements of an Array as Counters

Sometimes, apps use counter variables to summarize data, such as the results of a survey. In Fig. 7.6, we used separate counters in our die-rolling app to track the number of times each face of a six-sided die appeared as the app rolled the die 60,000,000 times. An array version of the app in Fig. 7.6 is shown in Fig. 8.8.

The app uses array `frequency` (line 10) to count the occurrences of each roll. *The single statement in line 15 replaces lines 24–44 of Fig. 7.6.* Line 15 of Fig. 8.8 uses the random value to determine which `frequency` array element to increment. The call to `Next`

4. You'll see in Chapter 9 that type inference is particularly helpful with anonymous types—that is, types that are created as the result of an expression and that do not have names.

```
1  // Fig. 8.8: RollDie.cs
2  // Roll a six-sided die 60,000,000 times.
3  using System;
4
5  class RollDie
6  {
7     static void Main()
8     {
9        var randomNumbers = new Random(); // random-number generator
10       var frequency = new int[7]; // array of frequency counters
11
12       // roll die 60,000,000 times; use die value as frequency index
13       for (var roll = 1; roll <= 60000000; ++roll)
14       {
15          ++frequency[randomNumbers.Next(1, 7)];
16       }
17
18       Console.WriteLine($"{"Face"}{"Frequency",10}");
19
20       // output each array element's value
21       for (var face = 1; face < frequency.Length; ++face)
22       {
23          Console.WriteLine($"{face,4}{frequency[face],10}");
24       }
25    }
26 }
```

```
Face Frequency
   1  10004131
   2   9998200
   3  10003734
   4   9999332
   5   9999792
   6   9994811
```

**Fig. 8.8** | Roll a six-sided die 60,000,000 times.

produces a random number from 1 to 6, so `frequency` must be large enough to store six counters. We use a seven-element array in which we ignore `frequency[0]`—it's more logical to have the face value 1 increment `frequency[1]` than `frequency[0]`. Thus, each face value is used directly as an index for array `frequency`. We also replaced lines 48–50 of Fig. 7.6 by looping through array `frequency` to output the results (Fig. 8.8, lines 21–24).

## 8.5 Using Arrays to Analyze Survey Results; Intro to Exception Handling

Our next example uses arrays to summarize data collected in a survey. Consider the following problem statement:

> *Twenty students were asked to rate on a scale of 1 to 5 the quality of the food in the student cafeteria, with 1 being "awful" and 5 being "excellent." Place the 20 responses in an integer array and determine the frequency of each rating.*

This is a typical array-processing app (Fig. 8.9). We wish to summarize the number of responses of each type (that is, 1–5). Array `responses` (lines 10–11) is a 20-element integer array containing the students' survey responses. The last value in the array is intentionally an incorrect response (`14`). When a C# program executes, the runtime checks array element indices for *validity*—all indices must be greater than or equal to 0 and less than the length of the array. Any attempt to access an element *outside* that range of indices results in a runtime error known as an `IndexOutOfRangeException`. At the end of this section, we'll discuss the invalid response, demonstrate array **bounds checking** and introduce C#'s exception-handling mechanism, which can be used to detect and handle an `IndexOutOfRangeException`.

```
1  // Fig. 8.9: StudentPoll.cs
2  // Poll analysis app.
3  using System;
4
5  class StudentPoll
6  {
7     static void Main()
8     {
9        // student response array (more typically, input at runtime)
10       int[] responses = {1, 2, 5, 4, 3, 5, 2, 1, 3, 3, 1, 4, 3, 3, 3,
11          2, 3, 3, 2, 14};
12       var frequency = new int[6]; // array of frequency counters
13
14       // for each answer, select responses element and use that value
15       // as frequency index to determine element to increment
16       for (var answer = 0; answer < responses.Length; ++answer)
17       {
18          try
19          {
20             ++frequency[responses[answer]];
21          }
22          catch (IndexOutOfRangeException ex)
23          {
24             Console.WriteLine(ex.Message);
25             Console.WriteLine(
26                $"   responses[{answer}] = {responses[answer]}\n");
27          }
28       }
29
30       Console.WriteLine($"{"Rating"}{"Frequency",10}");
31
32       // output each array element's value
33       for (var rating = 1; rating < frequency.Length; ++rating)
34       {
35          Console.WriteLine($"{rating,6}{frequency[rating],10}");
36       }
37    }
38 }
```

**Fig. 8.9** | Poll analysis app. (Part 1 of 2.)

```
Index was outside the bounds of the array.
   responses[19] = 14

Rating Frequency
     1        3
     2        4
     3        8
     4        2
     5        2
```

**Fig. 8.9** | Poll analysis app. (Part 2 of 2.)

*The* **frequency** *Array*

We use the *six-element* array `frequency` (line 12) to count the number of occurrences of each response. Each element is used as a counter for one of the possible types of survey responses—`frequency[1]` counts the number of students who rated the food as 1, `frequency[2]` counts the number of students who rated the food as 2, and so on.

## 8.5.1 Summarizing the Results

Lines 16–28 read the responses from the array `responses` one at a time and increments one of the counters `frequency[1]` to `frequency[5]`; we ignore `frequency[0]` because the survey responses are limited to the range 1–5. The key statement in the loop appears in line 20. This statement increments the appropriate `frequency` counter as determined by the value of `responses[answer]`.

Let's step through the first few iterations of the `foreach` statement:

- When the counter `answer` is `0`, `responses[answer]` is the value of `responses[0]` (that is, `1`—see line 10). In this case, `frequency[responses[answer]]` is interpreted as `frequency[1]`, and `frequency[1]` is incremented by one. To evaluate the expression, we begin with the value in the *innermost* set of brackets (`answer`, currently `0`). The value of `answer` is plugged into the expression, and the next set of brackets (`responses[answer]`) is evaluated. That value is used as the index for the `frequency` array to determine which counter to increment (in this case, `frequency[1]`).
- The next time through the loop `answer` is `1`, `responses[answer]` is the value of `responses[1]` (that is, `2`—see line 10), so `frequency[responses[answer]]` is interpreted as `frequency[2]`, causing `frequency[2]` to be incremented.
- When `answer` is `2`, `responses[answer]` is the value of `responses[2]` (that is, `5`—see line 10), so `frequency[responses[answer]]` is interpreted as `frequency[5]`, causing `frequency[5]` to be incremented, and so on.

Regardless of the number of responses processed in the survey, only a six-element array (in which we *ignore* element zero) is required to summarize the results, because all the correct response values are between 1 and 5, and the index values for a six-element array are 0–5. In the output in Fig. 8.9, the frequency column summarizes only 19 of the 20 values in the `responses` array—the last element of the array `responses` contains an *incorrect* response that was *not* counted. Lines 16–28 could be simplified, by changing line 16 to

```
foreach (var response in responses)
```

line 20 to

```
++frequency[response];
```

and modifying the error message displayed by lines 25–26.

### 8.5.2 Exception Handling: Processing the Incorrect Response

An **exception** indicates a problem that occurs while a program executes. **Exception handling** enables you to create **fault-tolerant programs** that can resolve (or handle) exceptions. In many cases, this allows a program to continue executing as if no problems were encountered. For example, the **Student Poll** app still displays results (Fig. 8.9), even though one of the responses was out of range. More severe problems might prevent a program from continuing normal execution, instead requiring the program to notify the user of the problem, then terminate. When the runtime or a method detects a problem, such as an invalid array index or an invalid method argument, it **throws** an exception—that is, an exception occurs. The exception here is thrown by the runtime. In Section 10.2, you'll see how to throw your own exceptions.

### 8.5.3 The `try` Statement

To handle an exception, place any code that might throw an exception in a **`try` statement** (Fig. 8.9, lines 18–27). The **`try` block** (lines 18–21) contains the code that might *throw* an exception, and the **`catch` block** (lines 22–27) contains the code that *handles* the exception if one occurs. You can have many `catch` blocks to handle different types of exceptions that might be thrown in the corresponding `try` block. When line 20 correctly increments an element of the `frequency` array, lines 22–27 are ignored. The braces that delimit the bodies of the `try` and `catch` blocks are required.

### 8.5.4 Executing the `catch` Block

When the program encounters the value `14` in the `responses` array, it attempts to add `1` to `frequency[14]`, which does *not* exist—the `frequency` array has only six elements. Because the runtime performs array bounds checking, it generates an exception—specifically line 20 throws an **`IndexOutOfRangeException`** to notify the program of this problem. At this point the `try` block *terminates* and the `catch` block begins executing—if you declared any variables in the `try` block, they no longer exist, so they're *not accessible* in the `catch` block.

The `catch` block declares an exception parameter's type (`IndexOutOfRangeException`) and name (`ex`). The `catch` block can handle exceptions of the specified type. Inside the `catch` block, you can use the parameter's identifier to interact with a caught exception object.

**Error-Prevention Tip 8.1**

*When writing code to access an array element, ensure that the array index remains greater than or equal to 0 and less than the length of the array. This will help prevent `IndexOutOfRangeException`s in your program.*

### 8.5.5 `Message` Property of the Exception Parameter

When lines 22–27 *catch* the exception, the program displays a message indicating the problem that occurred. Line 24 uses the exception object's built-in **`Message` property** to get the error message and display it. Once the message is displayed, the exception is considered handled and the program continues with the next statement after the `catch` block's closing brace. In this example, the end of the `foreach` statement is reached (line 28), so the program continues with the next iteration of the loop. We use exception handling again in Chapter 10, then Chapter 13 presents a deeper look at exception handling.

## 8.6 Case Study: Card Shuffling and Dealing Simulation

So far, this chapter's examples have used arrays of value-type elements. This section uses random-number generation and an *array of reference-type elements*—namely, *objects* representing playing cards—to develop a class that simulates card shuffling and dealing. This class can then be used to implement apps that play card games.

We first develop class `Card` (Fig. 8.10), which represents a playing card that has a face (e.g., `"Ace"`, `"Deuce"`, `"Three"`, …, `"Jack"`, `"Queen"`, `"King"`) and a suit (e.g., `"Hearts"`, `"Diamonds"`, `"Clubs"`, `"Spades"`). Next, we develop class `DeckOfCards` (Fig. 8.11), which creates a deck of 52 playing cards in which each element is a `Card` object. Then we build an app (Fig. 8.12) that uses class `DeckOfCards`'s card shuffling and dealing capabilities.

### 8.6.1 Class Card and Getter-Only Auto-Implemented Properties

Class `Card` (Fig. 8.10) contains two auto-implemented `string` properties—`Face` and `Suit`—that store references to the *face value* and *suit name* for a specific `Card`. Prior to C# 6, auto-implemented properties required both a `get` and a `set` accessor. `Face` and `Suit` are declared as C# 6 **getter-only auto-implemented properties**, which client code can use 6
only to *get* each property's value. Such properties are *read only*. Getter-only auto-implemented properties can be initialized *only* either in their declarations or in all of the type's constructors. Initializing an auto-implemented property in its declaration is another C# 6 6
feature known as auto-property initializers. To do so, follow the property declaration with an = and the initial value, as in

*Type PropertyName* `{ get; set; } =` *initializer*;

You can also initialize instance variables in their declarations.

```
// Fig. 8.10: Card.cs
// Card class represents a playing card.
class Card
{
   private string Face { get; } // Card's face ("Ace", "Deuce", ...)
   private string Suit { get; } // Card's suit ("Hearts", "Diamonds", ...)

   // two-parameter constructor initializes card's Face and Suit
   public Card(string face, string suit)
   {
      Face = face; // initialize face of card
      Suit = suit; // initialize suit of card
   }

```

**Fig. 8.10** | Card class represents a playing card. (Part 1 of 2.)

```
15      // return string representation of Card
16      public override string ToString() => $"{Face} of {Suit}";
17   }
```

**Fig. 8.10** | Card class represents a playing card. (Part 2 of 2.)

The constructor (lines 9–13) receives two `string`s that it uses to initialize the class's properties. Method `ToString` (line 16)—implemented here as an expression-bodied method—creates a `string` consisting of the `Face` of the card, the `string` `" of "` and the `Suit` of the card (e.g., `"Ace of Spades"`). An object's `ToString` method is called *implicitly* in many cases when the object is used where a `string` is expected, such as

- when `Write` or `WriteLine` outputs the object,
- when the object is *concatenated* to a `string` using the + operator, or
- when the object is inserted into a `string`-interpolation expression.

`ToString` also can be invoked *explicitly* to obtain a `string` representation of an object.

`ToString` must be declared with the header exactly as shown in line 16 of Fig. 8.10. We'll explain the purpose of the `override` keyword in Section 11.4.1.

### 8.6.2 Class DeckOfCards

Class `DeckOfCards` (Fig. 8.11) creates and manages an array of `Card` references. The named constant `NumberOfCards` (line 10) specifies the number of `Card`s in a deck (52). Line 11 declares an instance-variable named `deck` that refers to an array of `Card` objects with `NumberOfCards` (52) elements—the elements of the `deck` array are `null` by default. Like simple-type array-variable declarations, the declaration of a variable for an array of objects (e.g., `Card[] deck`) includes the type of the array's elements, followed by square brackets and the name of the array variable. Class `DeckOfCards` also declares `int` instance variable `currentCard` (line 12), representing the next `Card` to be dealt from the `deck` array. Note that we cannot use `var` for type inference with `NumberOfCards`, `deck` and `currentCard`, because they are not local variables of a method or property.

```
1   // Fig. 8.11: DeckOfCards.cs
2   // DeckOfCards class represents a deck of playing cards.
3   using System;
4
5   class DeckOfCards
6   {
7      // create one Random object to share among DeckOfCards objects
8      private static Random randomNumbers = new Random();
9
10     private const int NumberOfCards = 52; // number of cards in a deck
11     private Card[] deck = new Card[NumberOfCards];
12     private int currentCard = 0; // index of next Card to be dealt (0-51)
13
```

**Fig. 8.11** | DeckOfCards class represents a deck of playing cards. (Part 1 of 2.)

```
14      // constructor fills deck of Cards
15      public DeckOfCards()
16      {
17         string[] faces = {"Ace", "Deuce", "Three", "Four", "Five", "Six",
18            "Seven", "Eight", "Nine", "Ten", "Jack", "Queen", "King"};
19         string[] suits = {"Hearts", "Diamonds", "Clubs", "Spades"};
20
21         // populate deck with Card objects
22         for (var count = 0; count < deck.Length; ++count)
23         {
24            deck[count] = new Card(faces[count % 13], suits[count / 13]);
25         }
26      }
27
28      // shuffle deck of Cards with one-pass algorithm
29      public void Shuffle()
30      {
31         // after shuffling, dealing should start at deck[0] again
32         currentCard = 0; // reinitialize currentCard
33
34         // for each Card, pick another random Card and swap them
35         for (var first = 0; first < deck.Length; ++first)
36         {
37            // select a random number between 0 and 51
38            var second = randomNumbers.Next(NumberOfCards);
39
40            // swap current Card with randomly selected Card
41            Card temp = deck[first];
42            deck[first] = deck[second];
43            deck[second] = temp;
44         }
45      }
46
47      // deal one Card
48      public Card DealCard()
49      {
50         // determine whether Cards remain to be dealt
51         if (currentCard < deck.Length)
52         {
53            return deck[currentCard++]; // return current Card in array
54         }
55         else
56         {
57            return null; // indicate that all Cards were dealt
58         }
59      }
60   }
```

**Fig. 8.11** | `DeckOfCards` class represents a deck of playing cards. (Part 2 of 2.)

### *Class `DeckOfCards`: Constructor*

The constructor (lines 22–25) fills the `deck` array with `Card`s. The `for` statement initializes `count` to `0` and loops while `count` is less than `deck.Length`, causing `count` to take on each integer value from `0` to `51` (the `deck` array's indices). Each `Card` is initialized with two strings—one from the faces array at lines 17–18 (which contains "Ace" through "King") and one from the suits array at line 19 (which contains "Hearts", "Diamonds", "Clubs" and "Spades"). The calculation count % 13 (line 24) results in a value from 0 to 12—the 13 indices of array faces. Similarly, the calculation count / 13 always results in a value from 0 to 3—the four indices of array suits. When the deck array is initialized, it contains the Cards with faces "Ace" through "King" in order for each suit. Note that we cannot use a foreach loop in lines 22–25, because we need to modify each element of deck.

#### *Class* **DeckOfCards***:* **Shuffle** *Method*

Method Shuffle (lines 29–45) shuffles the Cards in the deck. The method loops through all 52 Cards and performs the following tasks:

- For each Card, a random number between 0 and 51 is picked to select another Card.
- Next, the current Card object and the randomly selected Card object are swapped. This exchange is performed by the three assignments in lines 41–43. The extra variable temp temporarily stores one of the two Card objects being swapped.

*The swap cannot be performed with only the two statements*

```
deck[first] = deck[second];
deck[second] = deck[first];
```

If deck[first] is the "Ace" of "Spades" and deck[second] is the "Queen" of "Hearts", then after the first assignment, both array elements contain the "Queen" of "Hearts", and the "Ace" of "Spades" is lost—hence, the extra variable temp is needed. After the for loop terminates, the Card objects are randomly ordered. Only 52 swaps are made in a single pass of the entire array, and the array of Card objects is shuffled.

#### *Recommendation: Use an Unbiased Shuffling Algorithm*

It's recommended that you use a so-called unbiased shuffling algorithm for real card games. Such an algorithm ensures that all possible shuffled card sequences are equally likely to occur. A popular unbiased shuffling algorithm is the Fisher-Yates algorithm

```
http://en.wikipedia.org/wiki/Fisher-Yates_shuffle
```

This webpage also uses pseudocode to shows how to implement the algorithm.

#### *Class* **DeckOfCards***:* **DealCard** *Method*

Method DealCard (lines 48–59) deals one Card. Recall that currentCard indicates the index of the Card at the top of the deck). Thus, line 51 compares currentCard to the length of the deck array. If the deck is not empty (i.e., currentCard is less than 52), line 53 returns the top Card and increments currentCard to prepare for the next call to DealCard—otherwise, line 57 returns null to indicate that the end of deck has been reached.

### 8.6.3 Shuffling and Dealing Cards

Figure 8.12 demonstrates the card shuffling and dealing capabilities of class DeckOfCards (Fig. 8.11). Line 10 of Fig. 8.12 creates a DeckOfCards object named myDeckOfCards and uses type inference to determine the variable's type. Recall that the DeckOfCards constructor creates the deck with the 52 Card objects in order by suit and face. Line 11 invokes myDeckOfCards's Shuffle method to rearrange the Card objects. The for statement in lines 14–22 deals all 52 `Cards` in the deck and displays them in four columns of 13 `Cards` each. Line 16 deals and displays a `Card` object by invoking `myDeckOfCards`'s `DealCard` method. When a `Card` object is placed in a `string`-interpolation expression, the `Card`'s `ToString` method is invoked implicitly. Because the field width is *negative*, the result is displayed *left*-aligned in a field of width 19.

```
1  // Fig. 8.12: DeckOfCardsTest.cs
2  // Card-shuffling-and-dealing app.
3  using System;
4
5  class DeckOfCardsTest
6  {
7     // execute app
8     static void Main()
9     {
10       var myDeckOfCards = new DeckOfCards();
11       myDeckOfCards.Shuffle(); // place Cards in random order
12
13       // display all 52 Cards in the order in which they are dealt
14       for (var i = 0; i < 52; ++i)
15       {
16          Console.Write($"{myDeckOfCards.DealCard(),-19}");
17
18          if ((i + 1) % 4 == 0)
19          {
20             Console.WriteLine();
21          }
22       }
23    }
24 }
```

```
Eight of Clubs     Ten of Clubs       Ten of Spades      Four of Spades
Ace of Spades      Jack of Spades     Three of Spades    Seven of Spades
Three of Diamonds  Five of Clubs      Eight of Spades    Five of Hearts
Ace of Hearts      Ten of Hearts      Deuce of Hearts    Deuce of Clubs
Jack of Hearts     Nine of Spades     Four of Hearts     Seven of Clubs
Queen of Spades    Seven of Diamonds  Five of Diamonds   Ace of Clubs
Four of Clubs      Ten of Diamonds    Jack of Clubs      Six of Diamonds
Eight of Diamonds  King of Hearts     Three of Clubs     King of Spades
King of Diamonds   Six of Spades      Deuce of Spades    Five of Spades
Queen of Clubs     King of Clubs      Queen of Hearts    Seven of Hearts
Ace of Diamonds    Deuce of Diamonds  Four of Diamonds   Nine of Clubs
Queen of Diamonds  Jack of Diamonds   Six of Hearts      Nine of Diamonds
Nine of Hearts     Three of Hearts    Six of Clubs       Eight of Hearts
```

**Fig. 8.12** | Card-shuffling-and-dealing app.

## 8.7 Passing Arrays and Array Elements to Methods

To pass an array argument to a method, specify the name of the array *without any brackets*. For example, if `hourlyTemperatures` is declared as

```
var hourlyTemperatures = new double[24];
```

then the method call

```
ModifyArray(hourlyTemperatures);
```

passes the reference of array `hourlyTemperatures` to method `ModifyArray`. Every array object "knows" its own length (and makes it available via its `Length` property). Thus, when we pass an array object's reference to a method, we need not pass the array length as an additional argument.

### *Specifying an Array Parameter*

For a method to receive an array reference through a method call, the method's parameter list must specify an array parameter. For example, the method header for method `ModifyArray` might be written as

```
void ModifyArray(double[] b)
```

indicating that `ModifyArray` receives the reference of an array of `double`s in parameter `b`. The method call passes array `hourlyTemperatures`' reference, so when the called method uses the array variable `b`, it refers to the same array object as `hourlyTemperatures` in the calling method.

### *Pass-By-Value vs. Pass-By-Reference*

When an argument is an entire array or an individual array element *of a reference type*, the called method receives a *copy of the reference*. However, when an argument to a method is an individual array element *of a value type*, the called method receives a *copy of the element's value*. To pass an individual array element to a method, use the indexed name of the array as an argument (e.g., `hourlyTemperatures[2]`). If you want to pass a value-type array element to a method by reference, you must use the `ref` keyword as shown in Section 7.18.

### *Passing an Entire Array vs. Passing a Single Array Element*

Figure 8.13 demonstrates the difference between passing an entire array and passing a value-type array element to a method. The `foreach` statement at lines 16–19 outputs the five `int` elements of `array`. Line 21 invokes method `ModifyArray`, passing `array` as an argument. Method `ModifyArray` (lines 38–44) receives a *copy* of `array`'s *reference* and uses the reference to multiply each of `array`'s elements by `2`. To prove that `array`'s elements (in `Main`) were modified, the `foreach` statement at lines 25–28 outputs the five elements of `array` again. As the output shows, method `ModifyArray` doubled the value of each element.

```
1  // Fig. 8.13: PassArray.cs
2  // Passing arrays and individual array elements to methods.
3  using System;
4
5  class PassArray
6  {
7     // Main creates array and calls ModifyArray and ModifyElement
8     static void Main()
9     {
10       int[] array = {1, 2, 3, 4, 5};
```

**Fig. 8.13** | Passing arrays and individual array elements to methods. (Part 1 of 2.)

```
      Console.WriteLine("Effects of passing reference to entire array:");
      Console.WriteLine("The values of the original array are:");

      // output original array elements
      foreach (var value in array)
      {
         Console.Write($"   {value}");
      }

      ModifyArray(array); // pass array reference
      Console.WriteLine("\n\nThe values of the modified array are:");

      // output modified array elements
      foreach (var value in array)
      {
         Console.Write($"   {value}");
      }

      Console.WriteLine("\n\nEffects of passing array element value:\n" +
         $"array[3] before ModifyElement: {array[3]}");

      ModifyElement(array[3]); // attempt to modify array[3]
      Console.WriteLine($"array[3] after ModifyElement: {array[3]}");
   }

   // multiply each element of an array by 2
   static void ModifyArray(int[] array2)
   {
      for (var counter = 0; counter < array2.Length; ++counter)
      {
         array2[counter] *= 2;
      }
   }

   // multiply argument by 2
   static void ModifyElement(int element)
   {
      element *= 2;
      Console.WriteLine($"Value of element in ModifyElement: {element}");
   }
}
```

```
Effects of passing reference to entire array:
The values of the original array are:
   1   2   3   4   5

The values of the modified array are:
   2   4   6   8   10

Effects of passing array element value:
array[3] before ModifyElement: 8
Value of element in ModifyElement: 16
array[3] after ModifyElement: 8
```

**Fig. 8.13** | Passing arrays and individual array elements to methods. (Part 2 of 2.)

Figure 8.13 next demonstrates that when a copy of an individual value-type array element is passed to a method, modifying the copy in the called method does *not* affect the original value of that element in the calling method's array. To show the value of `array[3]` before invoking method `ModifyElement`, lines 30–31 display the value of `array[3]`, which is `8`. Line 33 calls method `ModifyElement` (lines 47–51) and passes `array[3]` as an argument. Remember that `array[3]` is actually one `int` value (`8`) in `array`. Therefore, the app passes a copy of the value of `array[3]`. Method `ModifyElement` multiplies the value received as an argument by 2, stores the result in its parameter `element`, then outputs the value of `element` (`16`). Since method parameters, like local variables, cease to exist when the method in which they're declared completes execution, the method parameter `element` is destroyed when method `ModifyElement` terminates. When the app returns control to `Main`, line 34 displays the unmodified value of `array[3]` (i.e., `8`).

## 8.8 Case Study: GradeBook Using an Array to Store Grades

We now present the first version of a `GradeBook` class that instructors can use to maintain students' grades on an exam and display a grade report that includes the grades, class average, lowest grade, highest grade and a grade distribution bar chart. The version of class `GradeBook` presented in this section stores the grades for one exam in a one-dimensional array. In Section 8.10, we present a second version of class `GradeBook` that uses a two-dimensional array to store students' grades for *several* exams.

### *Storing Student Grades in an* **array** *in Class* **GradeBook**

Figure 8.14 shows the output that summarizes the 10 grades we store in an object of class `GradeBook` (Fig. 8.15), which uses an `array` of integers to store the grades of 10 students for a single exam. The array `grades` is declared as an instance variable in line 7 of Fig. 8.15—therefore, each `GradeBook` object maintains its own set of grades.

```
Welcome to the grade book for
CS101 Introduction to C# Programming!

The grades are:

Student  1:  87
Student  2:  68
Student  3:  94
Student  4: 100
Student  5:  83
Student  6:  78
Student  7:  85
Student  8:  91
Student  9:  76
Student 10:  87

Class average is 84.90
Lowest grade is 68
Highest grade is 100
```

**Fig. 8.14** | Output of the `GradeBook` example that stores one exam's grades in an array. (Part 1 of 2.)

```
Grade distribution:
00-09:
10-19:
20-29:
30-39:
40-49:
50-59:
60-69: *
70-79: **
80-89: ****
90-99: **
  100: *
```

**Fig. 8.14** | Output of the GradeBook example that stores one exam's grades in an array. (Part 2 of 2.)

```
// Fig. 8.15: GradeBook.cs
// Grade book using an array to store test grades.
using System;

class GradeBook
{
   private int[] grades; // array of student grades

   // getter-only auto-implemented property CourseName
   public string CourseName { get; }

   // two-parameter constructor initializes
   // auto-implemented property CourseName and grades array
   public GradeBook(string name, int[] gradesArray)
   {
      CourseName = name; // set CourseName to name
      grades = gradesArray; // initialize grades array
   }

   // display a welcome message to the GradeBook user
   public void DisplayMessage()
   {
      // auto-implemented property CourseName gets the name of course
      Console.WriteLine(
         $"Welcome to the grade book for\n{CourseName}!\n");
   }

   // perform various operations on the data
   public void ProcessGrades()
   {
      // output grades array
      OutputGrades();

      // call method GetAverage to calculate the average grade
      Console.WriteLine($"\nClass average is {GetAverage():F}");
```

**Fig. 8.15** | Grade book using an array to store test grades. (Part 1 of 4.)

```

      // call methods GetMinimum and GetMaximum
      Console.WriteLine($"Lowest grade is {GetMinimum()}");
      Console.WriteLine($"Highest grade is {GetMaximum()}\n");

      // call OutputBarChart to display grade distribution chart
      OutputBarChart();
   }

   // find minimum grade
   public int GetMinimum()
   {
      var lowGrade = grades[0]; // assume grades[0] is smallest

      // loop through grades array
      foreach (var grade in grades)
      {
         // if grade lower than lowGrade, assign it to lowGrade
         if (grade < lowGrade)
         {
            lowGrade = grade; // new lowest grade
         }
      }

      return lowGrade; // return lowest grade
   }

   // find maximum grade
   public int GetMaximum()
   {
      var highGrade = grades[0]; // assume grades[0] is largest

      // loop through grades array
      foreach (var grade in grades)
      {
         // if grade greater than highGrade, assign it to highGrade
         if (grade > highGrade)
         {
            highGrade = grade; // new highest grade
         }
      }

      return highGrade; // return highest grade
   }

   // determine average grade for test
   public double GetAverage()
   {
      var total = 0.0; // initialize total as a double

```

**Fig. 8.15** | Grade book using an array to store test grades. (Part 2 of 4.)

```
      // sum students' grades
      foreach (var grade in grades)
      {
         total += grade;
      }

      // return average of grades
      return total / grades.Length;
   }

   // output bar chart displaying grade distribution
   public void OutputBarChart()
   {
      Console.WriteLine("Grade distribution:");

      // stores frequency of grades in each range of 10 grades
      var frequency = new int[11];

      // for each grade, increment the appropriate frequency
      foreach (var grade in grades)
      {
         ++frequency[grade / 10];
      }

      // for each grade frequency, display bar in chart
      for (var count = 0; count < frequency.Length; ++count)
      {
         // output bar label ("00-09: ", ..., "90-99: ", "100: ")
         if (count == 10)
         {
            Console.Write("  100: ");
         }
         else
         {
            Console.Write($"{count * 10:D2}-{count * 10 + 9:D2}: ");
         }

         // display bar of asterisks
         for (var stars = 0; stars < frequency[count]; ++stars)
         {
            Console.Write("*");
         }

         Console.WriteLine(); // start a new line of output
      }
   }

   // output the contents of the grades array
   public void OutputGrades()
   {
      Console.WriteLine("The grades are:\n");
```

**Fig. 8.15** | Grade book using an array to store test grades. (Part 3 of 4.)

```
137
138          // output each student's grade
139          for (var student = 0; student < grades.Length; ++student)
140          {
141             Console.WriteLine(
142                $"Student {student + 1, 2}: {grades[student],3}");
143          }
144       }
145    }
```

**Fig. 8.15** | Grade book using an array to store test grades. (Part 4 of 4.)

The constructor (lines 14–18) receives the name of the course and an array of grades. When an app (e.g., class `GradeBookTest` in Fig. 8.16) creates a `GradeBook` object, the app passes an existing `int` array to the constructor, which assigns the array's reference to instance variable `grades` (Fig. 8.15, line 17). The size of `grades` is determined by the class that passes the array to the constructor. Thus, a `GradeBook` can process a variable number of grades—as many as are in the array in the caller. The grade values in the passed array could have been input from a user at the keyboard or read from a file on disk (as discussed in Chapter 17). In our test app, we simply initialize an array with a set of grade values (Fig. 8.16, line 9). Once the grades are stored in instance variable `grades` of class `GradeBook`, all the class's methods can access the elements of `grades` as needed to perform various calculations.

### *Methods* `ProcessGrades` *and* `OutputGrades`

Method `ProcessGrades` (Fig. 8.15, lines 29–43) contains a series of method calls that result in the output of a report summarizing the grades. Line 32 calls method `OutputGrades` to display the contents of array `grades`. Lines 139–143 in method `OutputGrades` use a `for` statement to output the student grades. We use a `for` statement, rather than a `foreach`, because lines 141–142 use counter variable `student`'s value to output each grade next to a particular student number (see Fig. 8.14). Although array indices start at 0, an instructor would typically number students starting at 1. Thus, lines 141–142 (Fig. 8.15) output `student + 1` as the student number to produce grade labels `"Student 1: "`, `"Student 2: "` and so on.

### *Method* `GetAverage`

Method `ProcessGrades` next calls method `GetAverage` (line 35) to obtain the average of the grades in the array. Method `GetAverage` (lines 82–94) uses a `foreach` statement to total the values in array `grades` before calculating the average. The iteration variable in the `foreach`'s header indicates that for each iteration, `grade` takes on a value in array `grades`. The average calculation in line 93 uses `grades.Length` to determine the number of grades being averaged. Note that we initialized total as a `double` (`0.0`), so no cast is necessary.

### *Methods* `GetMinimum` *and* `GetMaximum`

Lines 38–39 in method `ProcessGrades` call methods `GetMinimum` and `GetMaximum` to determine the lowest and highest grades of any student on the exam, respectively. Each of these methods uses a `foreach` statement to loop through array `grades`. Lines 51–58 in method `GetMinimum` loop through the array, and lines 54–57 compare each grade to `lowGrade`. If a grade is less than `lowGrade`, `lowGrade` is set to that grade. When line 60 executes, lowGrade contains the lowest grade in the array. Method GetMaximum (lines 64–79) works the same way as method GetMinimum.

### *Method* OutputBarChart

Finally, line 42 in method ProcessGrades calls method OutputBarChart to display a distribution chart of the grade data, using a technique similar to that in Fig. 8.7. In that example, we manually calculated the number of grades in each category (i.e., 0–9, 10–19, …, 90–99 and 100) by simply looking at a set of grades. In this example, lines 102–108 (Fig. 8.15) use a technique similar to that in Figs. 8.8 and 8.9 to calculate the frequency of grades in each category. Line 102 declares variable frequency and initializes it with an array of 11 ints to store the frequency of grades in each grade category. For each grade in array grades, lines 105–108 increment the appropriate element of the frequency array. To determine which element to increment, line 107 divides the current grade by 10, using integer division. For example, if grade is 85, line 107 increments frequency[8] to update the count of grades in the range 80–89. Lines 111–130 next display the bar chart (see Fig. 8.7) based on the values in array frequency. Like lines 27–30 of Fig. 8.7, lines 124–127 of Fig. 8.15 use a value in array frequency to determine the number of asterisks to display in each bar.

### *Class* GradeBookTest *That Demonstrates Class* GradeBook

Lines 11–12 of Fig. 8.16 create an object of class GradeBook (Fig. 8.15) using int array gradesArray (declared and initialized in line 9 of Fig. 8.16). Line 13 displays a welcome message, and line 14 invokes the GradeBook object's ProcessGrades method. The output reveals the summary of the 10 grades in myGradeBook.

**Software Engineering Observation 8.1**

*A **test harness** (or test app) creates an object of the class to test and provides it with data, which could be placed directly into an array with an array initializer, come from the user at the keyboard or come from a file (as you'll see in Chapter 17). After initializing an object, the test harness uses the object's members to manipulate the data. Gathering data in the test harness like this allows the class to manipulate data from several sources.*

```
1  // Fig. 8.16: GradeBookTest.cs
2  // Create a GradeBook object using an array of grades.
3  class GradeBookTest
4  {
5     // Main method begins app execution
6     static void Main()
7     {
8        // one-dimensional array of student grades
9        int[] gradesArray = {87, 68, 94, 100, 83, 78, 85, 91, 76, 87};
10
11       var myGradeBook = new GradeBook(
12          "CS101 Introduction to C# Programming", gradesArray);
13       myGradeBook.DisplayMessage();
14       myGradeBook.ProcessGrades();
15    }
16 }
```

**Fig. 8.16** | Create a GradeBook object using an array of grades.

## 8.9 Multidimensional Arrays

**Two-dimensional arrays** are often used to represent **tables of values** consisting of information arranged in **rows** and **columns**. To identify a particular table element, we must specify *two* indices. By convention, the first identifies the element's row and the second its column. (**Multidimensional arrays** can have more than two dimensions, but such arrays are beyond the scope of this book.) C# supports two types of two-dimensional arrays—**rectangular arrays** and **jagged arrays**.

### 8.9.1 Rectangular Arrays

Rectangular arrays are used to represent tables of information in the form of rows and columns, where each row has the same number of columns. Figure 8.17 illustrates a rectangular array named a containing three rows and four columns—a three-by-four array. In general, an array with *m* rows and *n* columns is called an ***m*-by-*n* array**.

| | Column 0 | Column 1 | Column 2 | Column 3 |
|---|---|---|---|---|
| Row 0 | `a[0, 0]` | `a[0, 1]` | `a[0, 2]` | `a[0, 3]` |
| Row 1 | `a[1, 0]` | `a[1, 1]` | `a[1, 2]` | `a[1, 3]` |
| Row 2 | `a[2, 0]` | `a[2, 1]` | `a[2, 2]` | `a[2, 3]` |

Column index
Row index
Array name

**Fig. 8.17** | Rectangular array with three rows and four columns.

#### *Array-Access Expression for a Two-Dimensional Rectangular Array*

Every element in array a is identified in by an array-access expression of the form a[*row*, *column*]; a is the name of the array, and *row* and *column* are the indices that uniquely identify each element in array a by row and column number. The element names in row 0 all have a first index of 0, and the element names in column 3 all have a second index of 3.

#### *Array Initializer for a Two-Dimensional Rectangular Array*

Like one-dimensional arrays, multidimensional arrays can be initialized with array initializers in declarations. A rectangular array b with two rows and two columns could be declared and initialized with **nested array initializers** as follows:

```
int[,] b = {{1, 2}, {3, 4}};
```

The initializer values are grouped by row in braces. So, 1 and 2 initialize b[0, 0] and b[0, 1], respectively, and 3 and 4 initialize b[1, 0] and b[1, 1], respectively. The compiler counts the number of nested array initializers (represented by sets of two inner braces within the outer braces) in the initializer list to determine the number of rows in array b. The compiler counts the initializer values in the nested array initializer for a row to determine the number of columns (two) in that row. The compiler will generate an error if the number of initializers in each row is not the same, because every row of a rectangular array must have the *same* length (i.e., the same number of columns.

### 8.9.2 Jagged Arrays

A jagged array is a one-dimensional array in which each element refers to a one-dimensional array. This makes them quite flexible, because the lengths of the rows in the array need *not* be the same. For example, jagged arrays could be used to store a single student's exam grades across multiple courses, where the number of exams may vary from course to course.

#### *Array Initializer for a Two-Dimensional Jagged Array*

We can access the elements in a jagged array by an array-access expression of the form *arrayName*[*row*][*column*]—similar to the array-access expression for rectangular arrays, but with a separate set of square brackets for each dimension. A jagged array with three rows of different lengths could be declared and initialized as follows:

```
int[][] jagged = {new int[] {1, 2},
                  new int[] {3},
                  new int[] {4, 5, 6}};
```

where 1 and 2 initialize jagged[0][0] and jagged[0][1], respectively; 3 initializes jagged[1][0]; and 4, 5 and 6 initialize jagged[2][0], jagged[2][1] and jagged[2][2], respectively. So array jagged is actually composed of four separate one-dimensional arrays—one for the rows, one per row. Thus, array jagged itself is an array of three elements, each a reference to a one-dimensional array of int values.

#### *Diagram of a Two-Dimensional Jagged Array in Memory*

Observe the differences between the array-creation expressions for rectangular arrays and for jagged arrays. Two sets of square brackets follow the type of jagged, indicating that this is an array of int arrays. Furthermore, in the array initializer, C# requires the keyword new to create an array object for each row. Figure 8.18 illustrates the array reference jagged after it's been declared and initialized.

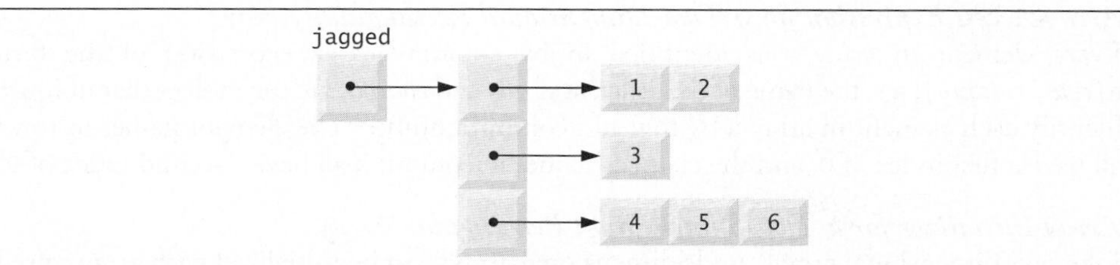


**Fig. 8.18** | Jagged array with three rows of different lengths.

#### *Creating Two-Dimensional Arrays with Array-Creation Expressions*

A rectangular array can be created with an array-creation expression. For example, the following lines declare variable b and assign it a reference to a three-by-four rectangular array:

```
int[,] b;
b = new int[3, 4];
```

In this case, we use the literal values 3 and 4 to specify the number of rows and number of columns, respectively, but this is *not* required—apps also can use variables and expressions to specify array dimensions. As with one-dimensional arrays, the elements of a rectangular array are initialized when the array object is created.

A jagged array cannot be completely created with a single array-creation expression. The following statement is a syntax error:

```
int[][] c = new int[2][5]; // error
```

Instead, each one-dimensional array in the jagged array must be initialized separately. A jagged array can be created as follows:

```
int[][] c;
c = new int[2][]; // create 2 rows
c[0] = new int[5]; // create 5 columns for row 0
c[1] = new int[3]; // create 3 columns for row 1
```

The preceding statements create a jagged array with two rows. Row `0` has five columns, and row `1` has three columns.

### 8.9.3 Two-Dimensional Array Example: Displaying Element Values

Figure 8.19 demonstrates initializing rectangular and jagged arrays with array initializers and using nested `for` loops to **traverse** the arrays (i.e., visit every element of each array). Class `InitArray`'s `Main` method creates two arrays. Line 12 uses nested array initializers to initialize variable `rectangular` with an array in which row 0 has the values `1`, `2` and `3`, and row 1 has the values `4`, `5` and `6`. Lines 17–19 use nested initializers of different lengths to initialize variable `jagged`. In this case, the initializer uses the keyword `new` to create a one-dimensional array for each row. Row 0 is initialized to have two elements with values `1` and `2`, respectively. Row 1 is initialized to have one element with value `3`. Row 2 is initialized to have three elements with the values `4`, `5` and `6`, respectively.

```
1  // Fig. 8.19: InitArray.cs
2  // Initializing rectangular and jagged arrays.
3  using System;
4
5  class InitArray
6  {
7     // create and output rectangular and jagged arrays
8     static void Main()
9     {
10       // with rectangular arrays,
11       // every row must be the same length.
12       int[,] rectangular = {{1, 2, 3}, {4, 5, 6}};
13
14       // with jagged arrays,
15       // we need to use "new int[]" for every row,
16       // but every row does not need to be the same length.
17       int[][] jagged = {new int[] {1, 2},
18                         new int[] {3},
19                         new int[] {4, 5, 6}};
20
21       OutputArray(rectangular); // displays array rectangular by row
22       Console.WriteLine(); // output a blank line
23       OutputArray(jagged); // displays array jagged by row
24    }
```

**Fig. 8.19** | Initializing jagged and rectangular arrays. (Part 1 of 2.)

```
25
26      // output rows and columns of a rectangular array
27      static void OutputArray(int[,] array )
28      {
29         Console.WriteLine("Values in the rectangular array by row are");
30
31         // loop through array's rows
32         for (var row = 0; row < array.GetLength(0); ++row)
33         {
34            // loop through columns of current row
35            for (var column = 0; column < array.GetLength(1); ++column)
36            {
37               Console.Write($"{array[row, column]}  ");
38            }
39
40            Console.WriteLine(); // start new line of output
41         }
42      }
43
44      // output rows and columns of a jagged array
45      static void OutputArray(int[][] array)
46      {
47         Console.WriteLine("Values in the jagged array by row are");
48
49         // loop through each row
50         foreach (var row in array)
51         {
52            // loop through each element in current row
53            foreach (var element in row)
54            {
55               Console.Write($"{element}  ");
56            }
57
58            Console.WriteLine(); // start new line of output
59         }
60      }
61   }
```

```
Values in the rectangular array by row are
1  2  3
4  5  6

Values in the jagged array by row are
1  2
3
4  5  6
```

**Fig. 8.19** | Initializing jagged and rectangular arrays. (Part 2 of 2.)

### *Overloaded Method* `OutputArray`

Method `OutputArray` is overloaded. The first version (lines 27–42) specifies the array parameter as `int[,] array` to indicate that it takes a rectangular array. The second version (lines 45–60) takes a jagged array, because its array parameter is listed as `int[][] array`.

### *Method* **OutputArray** *for Rectangular Arrays*

Line 21 invokes method `OutputArray` with argument `rectangular`, so the version of `OutputArray` at lines 27–42 is called. The nested `for` statement (lines 32–41) outputs the rows of a rectangular array. The loop-continuation condition of each `for` statement (lines 32 and 35) uses the rectangular array's `GetLength` method to obtain the length of each dimension. Dimensions are numbered starting from 0, so the method call `GetLength(0)` on `array` returns the size of the first dimension of the array (the number of rows), and the call `GetLength(1)` returns the size of the second dimension (the number of columns). A `foreach` statement also can iterate through all the elements in a rectangular array. In this case, `foreach` iterates through all the rows and columns starting from row `0`, as if the elements were in a one-dimensional array.

### *Method* **OutputArray** *for Jagged Arrays*

Line 23 invokes method `OutputArray` with argument `jagged`, so `OutputArray` at lines 45–60 is called. The nested `foreach` statement (lines 50–59) outputs the rows of a jagged array. The inner `foreach` statement (lines 53–56) iterates through each element in the current row. This allows the loop to determine the exact number of columns in each row. Since the jagged array is created as an array of arrays, we can use nested `foreach` statements to output the elements in the console window. The outer loop iterates through the elements of `array`, which are references to one-dimensional arrays of `int` values that represent each row. The inner loop iterates through the elements of the current row.

### *Common Multidimensional-Array Manipulations Performed with* **for** *Statements*

Many common array manipulations use `for` statements. As an example, the following `for` statement sets all the elements in row 2 of rectangular array a in Fig. 8.17 to `0`:

```
for (int column = 0; column < a.GetLength(1); ++column)
{
   a[2, column] = 0;
}
```

We specified row `2`; therefore, we know that the first index is always `2` (`0` is the first row, and `1` is the second row). This `for` loop varies only the second index (i.e., the **column index**). The preceding `for` statement is equivalent to the assignment statements

```
a[2, 0] = 0;
a[2, 1] = 0;
a[2, 2] = 0;
a[2, 3] = 0;
```

The following nested `for` statement totals the values of all the elements in array `a` one row at a time:

```
int total = 0;

for (int row = 0; row < a.GetLength(0); ++row)
{
   for (int column = 0; column < a.GetLength(1); ++column)
   {
      total += a[row, column];
   }
}
```

The outer loop begins by setting the row index to 0 so that row 0's elements can be totaled by the inner loop. The outer loop then increments row to 1 so that row 1's elements can be totaled, then increments row to 2 so that row 2's elements can be totaled. The total can be displayed when the outer for statement terminates. The next example shows how to process a rectangular array in a more concise manner using foreach statements.

## 8.10 Case Study: GradeBook Using a Rectangular Array

In Section 8.8, we presented class GradeBook (Fig. 8.15), which used a one-dimensional array to store student grades on a single exam. In most courses, students take several exams. Instructors are likely to want to analyze grades across the entire course, both for a single student and for the class as a whole.

### *Storing Student Grades in a Rectangular Array in Class* **GradeBook**

Figure 8.20 shows the output that summarizes 10 students' grades on three exams. Figure 8.21 contains a version of class GradeBook that uses a rectangular array grades to store the grades of a number of students on multiple exams. Each row of the array represents a single student's grades for the entire course, and each column represents the grades for the whole class on one of the exams the students took during the course. An app such as GradeBookTest (Fig. 8.22) passes the array as an argument to the GradeBook constructor. In this example, we use a 10-by-3 array containing 10 students' grades on three exams.

```
Welcome to the grade book for
CS101 Introduction to C# Programming!

The grades are:

            Test 1  Test 2  Test 3  Average
Student  1      87      96      70    84.33
Student  2      68      87      90    81.67
Student  3      94     100      90    94.67
Student  4     100      81      82    87.67
Student  5      83      65      85    77.67
Student  6      78      87      65    76.67
Student  7      85      75      83    81.00
Student  8      91      94     100    95.00
Student  9      76      72      84    77.33
Student 10      87      93      73    84.33

Lowest grade in the grade book is 65
Highest grade in the grade book is 100

Overall grade distribution:
00-09:
10-19:
20-29:
30-39:
40-49:
50-59:
```

**Fig. 8.20** | Output of GradeBook that uses two-dimensional arrays. (Part 1 of 2.)

```
60-69: ***
70-79: ******
80-89: ***********
90-99: *******
  100: ***
```

**Fig. 8.20** | Output of GradeBook that uses two-dimensional arrays. (Part 2 of 2.)

```
// Fig. 8.21: GradeBook.cs
// Grade book using a rectangular array to store grades.
using System;

class GradeBook
{
   private int[,] grades; // rectangular array of student grades

   // auto-implemented property CourseName
   public string CourseName { get; }

   // two-parameter constructor initializes
   // auto-implemented property CourseName and grades array
   public GradeBook(string name, int[,] gradesArray)
   {
      CourseName = name; // set CourseName to name
      grades = gradesArray; // initialize grades array
   }

   // display a welcome message to the GradeBook user
   public void DisplayMessage()
   {
      // auto-implemented property CourseName gets the name of course
      Console.WriteLine(
         $"Welcome to the grade book for\n{CourseName}!\n");
   }

   // perform various operations on the data
   public void ProcessGrades()
   {
      // output grades array
      OutputGrades();

      // call methods GetMinimum and GetMaximum
      Console.WriteLine(
         $"\nLowest grade in the grade book is {GetMinimum()}" +
         $"\nHighest grade in the grade book is {GetMaximum()}\n");

      // output grade distribution chart of all grades on all tests
      OutputBarChart();
   }

```

**Fig. 8.21** | Grade book using a rectangular array to store grades. (Part 1 of 4.)

```
    // find minimum grade
    public int GetMinimum()
    {
       // assume first element of grades array is smallest
       var lowGrade = grades[0, 0];

       // loop through elements of rectangular grades array
       foreach (var grade in grades)
       {
          // if grade less than lowGrade, assign it to lowGrade
          if (grade < lowGrade)
          {
             lowGrade = grade;
          }
       }

       return lowGrade; // return lowest grade
    }

    // find maximum grade
    public int GetMaximum()
    {
       // assume first element of grades array is largest
       var highGrade = grades[0, 0];

       // loop through elements of rectangular grades array
       foreach (var grade in grades)
       {
          // if grade greater than highGrade, assign it to highGrade
          if (grade > highGrade)
          {
             highGrade = grade;
          }
       }

       return highGrade; // return highest grade
    }

    // determine average grade for particular student
    public double GetAverage(int student)
    {
       // get the number of grades per student
       var gradeCount = grades.GetLength(1);
       var total = 0.0; // initialize total

       // sum grades for one student
       for (var exam = 0; exam < gradeCount; ++exam)
       {
          total += grades[student, exam];
       }

```

**Fig. 8.21** | Grade book using a rectangular array to store grades. (Part 2 of 4.)

```
      // return average of grades
      return total / gradeCount;
   }

   // output bar chart displaying overall grade distribution
   public void OutputBarChart()
   {
      Console.WriteLine("Overall grade distribution:");

      // stores frequency of grades in each range of 10 grades
      var frequency = new int[11];

      // for each grade in GradeBook, increment the appropriate frequency
      foreach (var grade in grades)
      {
         ++frequency[grade / 10];
      }

      // for each grade frequency, display bar in chart
      for (var count = 0; count < frequency.Length; ++count)
      {
         // output bar label ("00-09: ", ..., "90-99: ", "100: ")
         if (count == 10)
         {
            Console.Write("  100: ");
         }
         else
         {
            Console.Write($"{count * 10:D2}-{count * 10 + 9:D2}: ");
         }

         // display bar of asterisks
         for (var stars = 0; stars < frequency[count]; ++stars)
         {
            Console.Write("*");
         }

         Console.WriteLine(); // start a new line of output
      }
   }

   // output the contents of the grades array
   public void OutputGrades()
   {
      Console.WriteLine("The grades are:\n");
      Console.Write("           "); // align column heads

      // create a column heading for each of the tests
      for (var test = 0; test < grades.GetLength(1); ++test)
      {
         Console.Write($"Test {test + 1}  ");
      }
```

**Fig. 8.21** | Grade book using a rectangular array to store grades. (Part 3 of 4.)

```
146
147         Console.WriteLine("Average"); // student average column heading
148
149         // create rows/columns of text representing array grades
150         for (var student = 0; student < grades.GetLength(0); ++student)
151         {
152            Console.Write($"Student {student + 1,2}");
153
154            // output student's grades
155            for (var grade = 0; grade < grades.GetLength(1); ++grade)
156            {
157               Console.Write($"{grades[student, grade],8}");
158            }
159
160            // call method GetAverage to calculate student's average grade;
161            // pass row number as the argument to GetAverage
162            Console.WriteLine($"{GetAverage(student),9:F}");
163         }
164      }
165   }
```

**Fig. 8.21** | Grade book using a rectangular array to store grades. (Part 4 of 4.)

Five methods perform array manipulations to process the grades. Each is similar to its counterpart in Fig. 8.15. Method `GetMinimum` (lines 44–60 in Fig. 8.21) determines the lowest grade of any student. Method `GetMaximum` (lines 63–79) determines the highest grade of any student. Method `GetAverage` (lines 82–96) determines a particular student's semester average. Method `OutputBarChart` (lines 99–133) outputs a bar chart of the distribution of all student grades for the semester. Method `OutputGrades` (lines 136–164) outputs the two-dimensional array in tabular format, along with each student's semester average.

### *Processing a Two-Dimensional Array with a* **foreach** *Statement*

Methods `GetMinimum`, `GetMaximum` and `OutputBarChart` each loop through array `grades` using `foreach`—e.g., lines 50–57 in method `GetMinimum`. To find the lowest overall grade, this `foreach` statement iterates through rectangular array `grades` and compares each element to variable `lowGrade`. If a grade is less than `lowGrade`, `lowGrade` is set to that grade.

When the `foreach` statement traverses the elements of array `grades`, it looks at each element of the first row in order by index, then each element of the second row in order by index and so on. The `foreach` statement (lines 50–57) traverses the elements of `grades` in the same order as the following equivalent code, expressed with nested `for` statements:

```
for (var row = 0; row < grades.GetLength(0); ++row)
{
   for (var column = 0; column < grades.GetLength(1); ++column)
   {
      if (grades[row, column] < lowGrade)
      {
         lowGrade = grades[row, column];
      }
   }
}
```

When the foreach statement completes, lowGrade contains the lowest grade in the rectangular array. Method GetMaximum works similarly to method GetMinimum. Note the simplicity of using foreach vs. the preceding nested for statement.

**Software Engineering Observation 8.2**

*"Keep it simple" is good advice for most of the code you'll write.*

### *Method* OutputBarChart

Method OutputBarChart (lines 99–133) displays the grade distribution as a bar chart. The syntax of the foreach statement (lines 107–110) is identical for one-dimensional and two-dimensional arrays.

### *Method* OutputGrades

Method OutputGrades (lines 136–164) uses nested for statements to output grades' values, in addition to each student's semester average. The output in Fig. 8.20 shows the result, which resembles the tabular format of an instructor's physical grade book. Lines 142–145 (in Fig. 8.21) display the column headings for each test. We use the for statement rather than the foreach statement here so that we can identify each test with a number. Similarly, the for statement in lines 150–163 first outputs a row label using a counter variable to identify each student (line 152). Although array indices start at 0, lines 144 and 152 output test + 1 and student + 1, respectively, to produce test and student numbers starting at 1 (see Fig. 8.20). The inner for statement in lines 155–158 of Fig. 8.21 uses the outer for statement's counter variable student to loop through a specific row of array grades and output each student's test grade. Finally, line 162 obtains each student's semester average by passing the row index of grades (i.e., student) to method GetAverage.

### *Method* GetAverage

Method GetAverage (lines 82–96) takes one argument—the row index for a particular student. When line 162 calls GetAverage, the argument is int value student, which specifies the particular row of rectangular array grades. Method GetAverage calculates the sum of the array elements on this row, divides the total by the number of test results and returns the floating-point result as a double value (line 95).

### *Class* GradeBookTest *That Demonstrates Class* GradeBook

Figure 8.22 creates an object of class GradeBook (Fig. 8.21) using the two-dimensional array of ints that gradesArray references (Fig. 8.22, lines 9–18). Lines 20–21 pass a course name and gradesArray to the GradeBook constructor. Lines 22–23 then invoke myGradeBook's DisplayMessage and ProcessGrades methods to display a welcome message and obtain a report summarizing the students' grades for the semester, respectively.

```
1  // Fig. 8.22: GradeBookTest.cs
2  // Create a GradeBook object using a rectangular array of grades.
3  class GradeBookTest
4  {
```

**Fig. 8.22** | Create a GradeBook object using a rectangular array of grades. (Part 1 of 2.)

```
   // Main method begins app execution
   static void Main()
   {
      // rectangular array of student grades
      int[,] gradesArray = {{87, 96, 70},
                            {68, 87, 90},
                            {94, 100, 90},
                            {100, 81, 82},
                            {83, 65, 85},
                            {78, 87, 65},
                            {85, 75, 83},
                            {91, 94, 100},
                            {76, 72, 84},
                            {87, 93, 73}};

      GradeBook myGradeBook = new GradeBook(
         "CS101 Introduction to C# Programming", gradesArray);
      myGradeBook.DisplayMessage();
      myGradeBook.ProcessGrades();
   }
}
```

**Fig. 8.22** | Create a `GradeBook` object using a rectangular array of grades. (Part 2 of 2.)

## 8.11 Variable-Length Argument Lists

**Variable-length argument lists** allow you to create methods that receive an arbitrary number of arguments. A one-dimensional array-type argument preceded by the keyword **`params`** in a method's parameter list indicates that the method receives a variable number of arguments with the type of the array's elements. This use of a `params` modifier can occur only in the parameter list's last parameter. While you can use method overloading and array passing to accomplish much of what is accomplished with variable-length argument lists, using the `params` modifier is more concise.

Figure 8.23 demonstrates method `Average` (lines 8–19), which receives a variable-length sequence of `double`s (line 8). C# treats the variable-length argument list as a one-dimensional array whose elements are all of the same type. Hence, the method body can manipulate the parameter `numbers` as an array of `double`s. Lines 13–16 use the `foreach` loop to walk through the array and calculate the total of the `double`s in the array. Line 18 accesses `numbers.Length` to obtain the size of the `numbers` array for use in the averaging calculation. Lines 30, 32 and 34 in `Main` call method `Average` with two, three and four arguments, respectively. Method `Average` has a variable-length argument list, so it can average as many `double` arguments as the caller passes. The output reveals that each call to method `Average` returns the correct value.

**Common Programming Error 8.7**

*The* `params` *modifier may be used only with the last parameter of the parameter list.*

```
// Fig. 8.23: ParamArrayTest.cs
// Using variable-length argument lists.
using System;

class ParamArrayTest
{
   // calculate average
   static double Average(params double[] numbers)
   {
      var total = 0.0; // initialize total

      // calculate total using the foreach statement
      foreach (var d in numbers)
      {
         total += d;
      }

      return numbers.Length != 0 ? total / numbers.Length : 0.0;
   }

   static void Main()
   {
      var d1 = 10.0;
      var d2 = 20.0;
      var d3 = 30.0;
      var d4 = 40.0;

      Console.WriteLine(
         $"d1 = {d1:F1}\nd2 = {d2:F1}\nd3 = {d3:F1}\nd4 = {d4:F1}\n");
      Console.WriteLine($"Average of d1 and d2 is {Average(d1, d2):F1}");
      Console.WriteLine(
         $"Average of d1, d2 and d3 is {Average(d1, d2, d3):F1}");
      Console.WriteLine(
         $"Average of d1, d2, d3 and d4 is {Average(d1, d2, d3, d4):F1}");
   }
}
```

```
d1 = 10.0
d2 = 20.0
d3 = 30.0
d4 = 40.0

Average of d1 and d2 is 15.0
Average of d1, d2 and d3 is 20.0
Average of d1, d2, d3 and d4 is 25.0
```

**Fig. 8.23** | Using variable-length argument lists.

## 8.12 Using Command-Line Arguments

On many systems, it's possible to pass arguments from the command line (these are known as **command-line arguments**) to an app by including a parameter of type `string[]` (i.e., an array of `string`s) in the parameter list of `Main`. By convention, this parameter is named `args` (Fig. 8.24, line 7). You can execute an app directly from the **Command Prompt** by changing to the directory containing the app's `.exe` file, typing the file's name (possibly followed by command-line arguments) and pressing *Enter*. When you do this, the execution environment passes any command-line arguments that appear after the app name to the app's `Main` method as `string`s in the one-dimensional array `args`. The number of arguments passed from the command line is obtained by accessing the array's `Length` property. For example, the command "`MyApp a b`" passes two command-line arguments to app `MyApp`. You must enter command-line arguments separated by whitespace, not commas. When the preceding command executes, the `Main` method entry point receives the two-element array `args` (i.e., `args.Length` is 2) in which `args[0]` contains the `string` `"a"` and `args[1]` contains the `string` `"b"`. Common uses of command-line arguments include passing options and filenames to apps.

```
1  // Fig. 8.24: InitArray.cs
2  // Using command-line arguments to initialize an array.
3  using System;
4
5  class InitArray
6  {
7     static void Main(string[] args)
8     {
9        // check number of command-line arguments
10       if (args.Length != 3)
11       {
12          Console.WriteLine(
13             "Error: Please re-enter the entire command, including\n" +
14             "an array size, initial value and increment.");
15       }
16       else
17       {
18          // get array size from first command-line argument
19          var arrayLength = int.Parse(args[0]);
20          var array = new int[arrayLength]; // create array
21
22          // get initial value and increment from command-line argument
23          var initialValue = int.Parse(args[1]);
24          var increment = int.Parse(args[2]);
25
26          // calculate value for each array element
27          for (var counter = 0; counter < array.Length; ++counter)
28          {
29             array[counter] = initialValue + increment * counter;
30          }
31
32          Console.WriteLine($"{"Index"}{"Value",8}");
33
34          // display array index and value
35          for (int counter = 0; counter < array.Length; ++counter)
36          {
```

**Fig. 8.24** | Using command-line arguments to initialize an array. (Part 1 of 2.)

```
37                  Console.WriteLine($"{counter,5}{array[counter],8}");
38              }
39          }
40      }
41  }
```

```
C:\Users\PaulDeitel\Documents\examples\ch08\fig08_24>InitArray.exe
Error: Please re-enter the entire command, including
an array size, initial value and increment.
```

```
C:\Users\PaulDeitel\Documents\examples\ch08\fig08_24>InitArray.exe 5 0 4
Index   Value
    0       0
    1       4
    2       8
    3      12
    4      16
```

```
C:\Users\PaulDeitel\Documents\examples\ch08\fig08_24>InitArray.exe 10 1 2
Index   Value
    0       1
    1       3
    2       5
    3       7
    4       9
    5      11
    6      13
    7      15
    8      17
    9      19
```

**Fig. 8.24** | Using command-line arguments to initialize an array. (Part 2 of 2.)

Figure 8.24 uses three command-line arguments to initialize an array. When the app executes, if `args.Length` is not 3, the app displays an error message and terminates (lines 10–15). Otherwise, lines 16–39 initialize and display the array based on the values of the command-line arguments.

The command-line arguments become available to `Main` as `strings` in `args`. Line 19 gets `args[0]`—a `string` that specifies the array size—and converts it to an `int` value, which the app uses to create the array in line 20.

Lines 23–24 convert the `args[1]` and `args[2]` command-line arguments to `int` values and store them in `initialValue` and `increment`, respectively—as always, these lines could result in exceptions if the user does not enter valid integers. Line 29 calculates the value for each array element.

The first sample execution indicates that the app received an insufficient number of command-line arguments. The second sample execution uses command-line arguments `5`, `0` and `4` to specify the size of the array (`5`), the value of the first element (`0`) and the increment of each value in the array (`4`), respectively. The corresponding output indicates that these values create an array containing the integers `0`, `4`, `8`, `12` and `16`. The output from the third sample execution illustrates that the command-line arguments `10`, `1` and `2` produce an array whose 10 elements are the nonnegative odd integers from `1` to `19`.

***Specifying Command-Line Arguments in Visual Studio***
We ran this example from a **Command Prompt** window. You also can supply command-line arguments in the IDE. To do so, right click the project's **Properties** node in the **Solution Explorer**, then select **Open**. Select the **Debug** tab, then enter the arguments in the text box labeled **Command line arguments**. When you run the app, the IDE will pass the command-line arguments to the app.

## 8.13 (Optional) Passing Arrays by Value and by Reference

In C#, a variable that "stores" an object, such as an array, does not actually store the object itself. Instead, such a variable stores a *reference* to the object. The distinction between reference-type variables and value-type variables raises some subtle issues that you must understand to create secure, stable programs.

As you know, when an app passes an argument to a method, the called method receives a *copy* of that argument's value. Changes to the *local copy* in the called method do *not* affect the original variable in the caller. If the argument is a *reference* type, the method makes a *copy* of the *reference*, *not* a *copy* of the actual object that's referenced. The local copy of the reference also refers to the original object, which means that changes to the object in the called method affect the original object.

**Performance Tip 8.1**

*Passing references to arrays and other objects makes sense for performance reasons. If arrays were passed by value, a copy of each element would be passed. For large, frequently passed arrays, this would waste time and consume considerable storage for the copies of the arrays.*

Section 7.18 showed that C# allows variables to be passed by reference with keyword `ref`. You also can use keyword `ref` to pass a *reference-type variable* by reference, which allows the called method to modify the original variable in the caller and make that variable refer to a different object. This is a capability, which, if misused, can lead to subtle problems. For instance, when a reference-type object like an array is passed with `ref`, the called method actually gains control over the *reference itself*, allowing the called method to replace the original reference in the caller with a reference to a different object, or even with `null`. Such behavior can lead to *unpredictable effects*, which can be disastrous in mission-critical apps.

Figure 8.25 demonstrates the subtle difference between passing a reference by value and passing a reference by reference with keyword `ref`. Lines 11 and 14 declare two integer array variables, `firstArray` and `firstArrayCopy`. Line 11 initializes `firstArray` with the values `1`, `2` and `3`. The assignment statement at line 14 copies the reference stored in `firstArray` to variable `firstArrayCopy`, causing these variables to reference the same array object. We make the copy of the reference so that we can determine later whether reference `firstArray` gets overwritten. The `foreach` statement at lines 21–24 displays the contents of `firstArray` before it's passed to method `FirstDouble` (line 27) so that we can verify that the called method indeed changes the array's contents.

```
// Fig. 8.25: ArrayReferenceTest.cs
// Testing the effects of passing array references
// by value and by reference.
using System;

class ArrayReferenceTest
{
   static void Main(string[] args)
   {
      // create and initialize firstArray
      int[] firstArray = {1, 2, 3};

      // copy the reference in variable firstArray
      int[] firstArrayCopy = firstArray;

      Console.WriteLine("Test passing firstArray reference by value");
      Console.Write(
         "Contents of firstArray before calling FirstDouble:\n\t");

      // display contents of firstArray
      foreach (var element in firstArray)
      {
         Console.Write($"{element} ");
      }

      // pass variable firstArray by value to FirstDouble
      FirstDouble(firstArray);

      Console.Write(
         "\nContents of firstArray after calling FirstDouble\n\t");

      // display contents of firstArray
      foreach (var element in firstArray)
      {
         Console.Write($"{element} ");
      }

      // test whether reference was changed by FirstDouble
      if (firstArray == firstArrayCopy)
      {
         Console.WriteLine("\n\nThe references refer to the same array");
      }
      else
      {
         Console.WriteLine(
            "\n\nThe references refer to different arrays");
      }

      // create and initialize secondArray
      int[] secondArray = {1, 2, 3};

      // copy the reference in variable secondArray
      int[] secondArrayCopy = secondArray;
```

**Fig. 8.25** | Testing the effects of passing an array reference by value and by reference. (Part 1 of 3.)

```

         Console.WriteLine(
            "\nTest passing secondArray reference by reference");
         Console.Write(
            "Contents of secondArray before calling SecondDouble:\n\t");

         // display contents of secondArray before method call
         foreach (var element in secondArray)
         {
            Console.Write($"{element} ");
         }

         // pass variable secondArray by reference to SecondDouble
         SecondDouble(ref secondArray);

         Console.Write(
            "\nContents of secondArray after calling SecondDouble:\n\t");

         // display contents of secondArray after method call
         foreach (var element in secondArray)
         {
            Console.Write($"{element} ");
         }

         // test whether reference was changed by SecondDouble
         if (secondArray == secondArrayCopy)
         {
            Console.WriteLine("\n\nThe references refer to the same array");
         }
         else
         {
            Console.WriteLine(
               "\n\nThe references refer to different arrays");
         }
      }

      // modify elements of array and attempt to modify reference
      static void FirstDouble(int[] array)
      {
         // double each element's value
         for (var i = 0; i < array.Length; ++i)
         {
            array[i] *= 2;
         }

         // create new object and assign its reference to array
         array = new int[] {11, 12, 13};
      }

      // modify elements of array and change reference array
      // to refer to a new array
      static void SecondDouble(ref int[] array)
      {
```

**Fig. 8.25** | Testing the effects of passing an array reference by value and by reference. (Part 2 of 3.)

```
107         // double each element's value
108         for (var i = 0; i < array.Length; ++i)
109         {
110            array[i] *= 2;
111         }
112
113         // create new object and assign its reference to array
114         array = new int[] {11, 12, 13};
115      }
116   }
```

```
Test passing firstArray reference by value
Contents of firstArray before calling FirstDouble:
        1 2 3
Contents of firstArray after calling FirstDouble
        2 4 6

The references refer to the same array

Test passing secondArray reference by reference
Contents of secondArray before calling SecondDouble:
        1 2 3
Contents of secondArray after calling SecondDouble:
        11 12 13

The references refer to different arrays
```

**Fig. 8.25** | Testing the effects of passing an array reference by value and by reference. (Part 3 of 3.)

### *Method* `FirstDouble`

Lines 94–97 in `FirstDouble` multiply the values of the array's elements by `2`. Line 100 creates a new array containing the values `11`, `12` and `13`, and assigns the array's reference to parameter `array` in an attempt to overwrite reference `firstArray` in the caller—this, of course, does not happen, because the reference was passed by value. After method `FirstDouble` executes, the `foreach` statement at lines 33–36 displays `firstArray`'s contents, demonstrating that the values of the elements have been changed by the method. The `if...else` statement at lines 39–47 uses the == operator to compare references `firstArray` (which we just attempted to overwrite) and `firstArrayCopy`. The expression in line 39 evaluates to `true` if the operands of operator == reference the same object. In this case, the object represented by `firstArray` is the array created in line 11—not the array created in method `FirstDouble` (line 100)—so the original reference stored in `firstArray` was not modified.

### *Method* `SecondDouble`

Lines 50–87 perform similar tests, using array variables `secondArray` and `secondArrayCopy`, and method `SecondDouble` (lines 105–115). Method `SecondDouble` performs the same operations as `FirstDouble`, but receives its array argument using keyword `ref`. In this case, the reference stored in `secondArray` after the method call is a reference to the array created in line 114 of `SecondDouble`, demonstrating that a variable passed with keyword `ref` can be modified by the called method so that the variable in the caller actually points to a *different* object—in this case, an array created in `SecondDouble`. The `if...else` statement in lines 79–87 confirms that `secondArray` and `secondArrayCopy` no longer refer to the same array.

**Software Engineering Observation 8.3**

*When a method receives a reference-type parameter by value, a copy of the object's reference is passed. This prevents a method from overwriting references passed to that method. In the vast majority of cases, protecting the caller's reference from modification is the desired behavior. If you encounter a situation where you truly want the called procedure to modify the caller's reference, pass the reference-type parameter using keyword* `ref`*—but, again, such situations are rare.*

**Software Engineering Observation 8.4**

*In C#, references to objects (including arrays) are passed to called methods. A called method—receiving a reference to an object in a caller—can interact with, and possibly change, the caller's object.*

## 8.14 Wrap-Up

This chapter began our discussion of C# data structures, using arrays to store data in and retrieve data from lists and tables of values. You declared, created and initialized arrays. We presented examples demonstrating common array manipulations. We introduced C#'s last control statement—the `foreach` iteration statement—which provides a concise and less error-prone notation for accessing data in arrays and other data structures.

We demonstrated implicitly typed local variables (with keyword `var`) for which the compiler determines variable types, based on their initializer values. We introduced the exception-handling mechanism and used it to allow a program to continue executing when it attempted to access an array element outside the array's bounds.

We used arrays to simulate shuffling and dealing playing cards. In that example, we introduced C# 6's getter-only auto-implemented properties, which define properties that can be used to get, but not set, a value. We also discussed auto-property initialization for auto-implemented properties.

We presented two versions of an instructor `GradeBook` case study that used arrays to maintain sets of student grades in memory and analyze student grades. Finally, we demonstrate how to define methods that receive variable-length argument lists and how to process command-line arguments passed to `Main` as a `string` array.

We continue our coverage of data structures in Chapter 9, where we discuss `List`, which is a dynamically resizable array-based collection. Chapter 18 presents generics, which provide the means to create general models of methods and classes that can be declared once, but used with many different data types. Chapter 19 introduces the data-structure classes provided by the .NET Framework, which use generics to allow you to specify the exact types of objects that a particular data structure will store. You should almost always use these predefined data structures instead of building your own. The .NET Framework also provides class `Array`, which contains utility methods for array manipulation, such as the `Resize` method introduced in this chapter.

In Chapter 9, we introduce Language Integrated Query (LINQ), which enables you to write expressions that can retrieve information from a wide variety of data sources, such as arrays. You'll see how to search, sort and filter data using LINQ.

# 9

# Introduction to LINQ and the `List` Collection

## Objectives

In this chapter you'll:

- Learn basic LINQ concepts.
- Query an array using a range variable and the `from`, `where` and `select` clauses.
- Iterate over LINQ query results.
- Sort a LINQ query's results with the `orderby` clause.
- Learn basic interface concepts and how the `IEnumerable<T>` interface enables a `foreach` to iterate over an array or collection's elements.
- Learn basic .NET collections concepts.
- Become familiar with commonly used methods of generic class `List`.
- Create and use a generic `List` collection.
- Query a generic `List` collection using LINQ.
- Declare multiple range variables in a LINQ query with the `let` clause.
- Understand how deferred execution helps make LINQ queries reusable.

Outline



## 9.1 Introduction

Chapter 8 introduced arrays—simple data structures used to store items of a specific type. Although commonly used, arrays have limited capabilities. For instance, you must specify an array's size when you create it. If, at execution time, you wish to modify that size, you must do so manually by creating a new array and copying elements into it or by using class Array's Resize method, which performs those tasks for you.

In this chapter, we introduce the .NET Framework's List *collection* class—which offers greater capabilities than traditional arrays. A List is similar to an array but provides additional functionality, such as **dynamic resizing**—a List can increase its size when items are added to it. We use the List collection to implement several data manipulations similar to those in the preceding chapter. List and the .NET Framework's other collections are reusable, reliable, powerful and efficient and have been carefully designed and tested to ensure correctness and good performance.

Large amounts of data that need to persist beyond an app's execution are typically stored in a *database*—an organized collection of data (discussed in Chapter 20). A *database management system (DBMS)* provides mechanisms for storing, organizing, retrieving and modifying data in a database. A language called SQL (Structured Query Language)—pronounced "sequel"—is the international standard used to perform **queries** (i.e., to request information that satisfies given criteria) and to manipulate data in *relational databases*. These organize data in tables that maintain relationships between pieces of data stored in each table—a key goal is to eliminate duplicate data. For years, programs accessing a relational database passed SQL queries to the database management system, then processed the returned results. This chapter introduces C#'s **LINQ** (**Language Integrated Query**) capabilities. LINQ allows you to write **query expressions**, similar to SQL queries, that retrieve information from a *variety* of data sources, not just databases. In this chapter, we use **LINQ to Objects** to manipulate objects in memory, such as arrays and Lists.

### *LINQ Providers*

The syntax of LINQ is built into C#, but LINQ queries may be used in many contexts via libraries known as *providers*. A **LINQ provider** is a set of classes that implement LINQ operations and enable programs to interact with *data sources* to perform tasks such as *sorting*, *grouping* and *filtering* elements. Many LINQ providers are more specialized, allowing you to interact with a specific website or data format. Figure 9.1 shows where and how we use LINQ throughout the book.

| Chapter | Used to |
|---|---|
| Chapter 9, Introduction to LINQ and the `List` Collection | Query arrays and `List`s. |
| Chapter 16, Strings and Characters: A Deeper Look | Select GUI controls in a Windows Forms app (located in the online Regular Expressions section of the chapter on this book's webpage at `www.deitel.com/books/CSharp6FP`). |
| Chapter 17, Files and Streams | Search a directory and manipulate text files. |
| Chapter 19, Generic Collections; Functional Programming with LINQ/PLINQ | Show LINQ method-call syntax with delegates and lambdas. Introduces functional-programming concepts, using LINQ to Objects to write code more concisely and with fewer bugs than programs written with previous techniques. Shows how PLINQ (Parallel LINQ) can improve LINQ to Objects performance substantially with multicore systems. |
| Chapter 20, Databases and LINQ | Query information from a database using *LINQ to Entities*. Like LINQ to Objects, LINQ to Entities is built into C# and the .NET Framework. |
| Chapter 21, Asynchronous Programming with `async` and `await` | Query an XML response from a web service using *LINQ to XML*. Like LINQ to Objects, LINQ to XML is built into C# and the .NET Framework. |

**Fig. 9.1** | LINQ usage throughout the book.

### *LINQ Query Syntax vs. Method-Call Syntax*

There are two LINQ approaches—one uses a SQL-like syntax and the other uses method-call syntax. This chapter shows the simpler SQL-like syntax. In Chapter 19, we'll show the method-call syntax, introducing the notions of delegates and lambdas—mechanisms that enable you to pass methods to other methods to help them perform their tasks.

## 9.2 Querying an Array of `int` Values Using LINQ

Figure 9.2 shows how to use *LINQ to Objects* to query an array of integers, selecting elements that satisfy a set of conditions—a process called **filtering**. Iteration statements that *filter* arrays focus on the process of getting the results—iterating through the elements and checking whether they satisfy the desired criteria. LINQ specifies the conditions that selected elements must satisfy. This is known as **declarative programming**—as opposed to **imperative programming** (which we've been doing so far) in which you specify the actual actions to perform a task. The query in lines 22–24 specifies that the results should consist of all the ints in the values array that are greater than 4. It *does not* specify *how* those results are obtained—the C# compiler generates all the necessary code, which is one of the great strengths of LINQ. Using LINQ to Objects requires the System.Linq namespace (line 4).

```
1  // Fig. 9.2: LINQWithSimpleTypeArray.cs
2  // LINQ to Objects using an int array.
3  using System;
4  using System.Linq;
5
6  class LINQWithSimpleTypeArray
7  {
8     static void Main()
9     {
10       // create an integer array
11       var values = new[] {2, 9, 5, 0, 3, 7, 1, 4, 8, 5};
12
13       // display original values
14       Console.Write("Original array:");
15       foreach (var element in values)
16       {
17          Console.Write($" {element}");
18       }
19
20       // LINQ query that obtains values greater than 4 from the array
21       var filtered =
22          from value in values // data source is values
23          where value > 4
24          select value;
25
26       // display filtered results
27       Console.Write("\nArray values greater than 4:");
28       foreach (var element in filtered)
29       {
30          Console.Write($" {element}");
31       }
32
33       // use orderby clause to sort original values in ascending order
34       var sorted =
35          from value in values // data source is values
36          orderby value
37          select value;
38
39       // display sorted results
40       Console.Write("\nOriginal array, sorted:");
41       foreach (var element in sorted)
42       {
43          Console.Write($" {element}");
44       }
45
```

**Fig. 9.2** | LINQ to Objects using an int array. (Part 1 of 2.)

```
46          // sort the filtered results into descending order
47          var sortFilteredResults =
48             from value in filtered  // data source is LINQ query filtered
49             orderby value descending
50             select value;
51
52          // display the sorted results
53          Console.Write(
54             "\nValues greater than 4, descending order (two queries):");
55          foreach (var element in sortFilteredResults)
56          {
57             Console.Write($" {element}");
58          }
59
60          // filter original array and sort results in descending order
61          var sortAndFilter =
62             from value in values      // data source is values
63             where value > 4
64             orderby value descending
65             select value;
66
67          // display the filtered and sorted results
68          Console.Write(
69             "\nValues greater than 4, descending order (one query):");
70          foreach (var element in sortAndFilter)
71          {
72             Console.Write($" {element}");
73          }
74
75          Console.WriteLine();
76       }
77    }
```

```
Original array: 2 9 5 0 3 7 1 4 8 5
Array values greater than 4: 9 5 7 8 5
Original array, sorted: 0 1 2 3 4 5 5 7 8 9
Values greater than 4, descending order (two queries): 9 8 7 5 5
Values greater than 4, descending order (one query): 9 8 7 5 5
```

**Fig. 9.2** | LINQ to Objects using an `int` array. (Part 2 of 2.)

### 9.2.1 The `from` Clause

A LINQ query begins with a **`from` clause** (line 22), which specifies a **range variable** (`value`) and the data source to query (`values`). The range variable represents each item in the data source (one at a time), much like the control variable in a `foreach` statement. Since `value` is assigned one element at a time from the array `values`—an `int` array—the compiler *infers* that `value` should be of type `int`. You also may declare the range variable's type explicitly between the `from` keyword and the range-variable's name.

Introducing the range variable in the `from` clause allows the IDE to provide *IntelliSense* as you type the rest of the query. When you enter the range variable's name followed by a dot (`.`) in the code editor, the IDE displays the range variable's methods and properties, making it easier for you to construct queries.

*Implicitly Typed Local Variables*

Typically, implicitly typed local variables (declared with `var`) are used for the collections of data returned by LINQ queries, as we do in lines 21, 34, 47 and 61. We also use this feature to declare the control variable in the `foreach` statements.

## 9.2.2 The where Clause

If the condition in the **`where` clause** (line 23) evaluates to `true`, the element is *selected*—i.e., it's included in the results. Here, the `int`s in the array are included in the result only if they're greater than `4`. An expression that takes a value and returns `true` or `false` by testing a condition on that value is known as a **predicate**.

## 9.2.3 The `select` Clause

For each item in the data source, the **`select` clause** (line 24) determines what value appears in the results. In this case, it's the `int` that the range variable currently represents, but you'll soon see that the `select` clause may contain an expression that transforms a value before including it in the results. Most LINQ queries end with a `select` clause.

## 9.2.4 Iterating Through the Results of the LINQ Query

Lines 28–31 use a `foreach` statement to display the query results. As you know, a `foreach` statement can iterate through the contents of an array, allowing you to process each element in the array. Actually, the `foreach` statement can iterate through the contents of arrays, collections and the results of LINQ queries. The `foreach` statement in lines 28–31 iterates over the query result `filtered`, displaying each of its `int` items.

*LINQ vs. Iteration Statements*

It would be simple to display the integers greater than `4` using a iteration statement that tests each value before displaying it. However, this would intertwine the code that selects elements and the code that displays them. With LINQ, these are kept separate:

- the LINQ query specifies how to locate the values and
- a loop accesses the results

making the code easier to understand and maintain.

## 9.2.5 The orderby Clause

The **`orderby` clause** (line 36) sorts the query results in *ascending* order. Lines 49 and 64 use the **`descending`** modifier in the `orderby` clause to sort the results in *descending* order. An **`ascending`** modifier also exists but isn't normally used, because it's the default. Any value that can be compared with other values of the same type may be used with the `orderby` clause. A value of a *simple type* (e.g., `int`) can always be compared to another value of the *same* type; we'll discuss how to compare values of *reference types* in Chapter 12.

The queries in lines 48–50 and 62–65 generate the same results, but in different ways. Lines 48–50 uses LINQ to sort the results of the query `filtered` from lines 22–24. The second query uses both the `where` and `orderby` clauses. Because queries can operate on the results of other queries, it's possible to build a query one step at a time, passing the results of queries between methods for further processing.

### 9.2.6 Interface IEnumerable<T>

As we mentioned, the foreach statement can iterate through the contents of *arrays*, *collections* and *LINQ query results*. Actually, foreach iterates over any so-called IEnumerable<T> object, which just happens to be what most LINQ queries return.

IEnumerable<T> is an **interface**. Interfaces define and standardize the ways in which people and systems can interact with one another. For example, the controls on a radio serve as an *interface* between radio users and the radio's internal components. The controls allow users to perform a limited set of *operations* (e.g., changing the station, adjusting the volume, and choosing between AM and FM), and different radios may implement the controls in different ways (e.g., using push buttons, dials or voice commands). The interface specifies *what* operations a radio permits users to perform but does not specify *how* the operations are implemented. Similarly, the interface between a driver and a car with a manual transmission includes the steering wheel, the gear shift, the clutch, the gas pedal and the brake pedal. This same interface is found in nearly all manual-transmission cars, enabling someone who knows how to drive one manual-transmission car to drive another.

Software objects also communicate via interfaces. A C# interface describes a set of methods and properties that can be called on an object—to tell the object, for example, to perform some task or return some piece of information. The IEnumerable<T> interface describes the functionality of any object that can be iterated over and thus offers methods and properties to access each element. A class that *implements* an interface must declare all the methods and properties described by that interface.

Most LINQ queries return an IEnumerable<T> object—some queries return a single value (e.g., the sum of an int array's elements). For queries that return an IEnumerable<T> object, you can use a foreach statement to iterate over the query results. The notation <T> indicates that the interface is a *generic* interface that can be used with any type of data (for example, ints, strings or Employees). You'll learn more about the <T> notation in Section 9.4. In Section 12.7, we'll discuss interfaces and show how to define your own interfaces. In Chapter 18, we'll cover generics in detail.

## 9.3 Querying an Array of Employee Objects Using LINQ

LINQ is not limited to querying arrays of simple types such as ints. It can be used with arrays of any data type, including strings and user-defined classes. It cannot be used when a query does not have a defined meaning—for example, you cannot use orderby on values that are not *comparable*. Comparable types in .NET are those that implement the IComparable interface, which is discussed in Section 18.4. All built-in types, such as string, int and double implement IComparable. Figure 9.3 presents an Employee class. Figure 9.4 uses LINQ to query an array of Employee objects.

```
// Fig. 9.3: Employee.cs
// Employee class with FirstName, LastName and MonthlySalary properties.
class Employee
{
```

**Fig. 9.3** | Employee class with FirstName, LastName and MonthlySalary properties. (Part 1 of 2.)

```
   public string FirstName { get; } // read-only auto-implemented property
   public string LastName { get; } // read-only auto-implemented property
   private decimal monthlySalary; // monthly salary of employee

   // constructor initializes first name, last name and monthly salary
   public Employee(string firstName, string lastName,
      decimal monthlySalary)
   {
      FirstName = firstName;kll
      LastName = lastName;
      MonthlySalary = monthlySalary;
   }

   // property that gets and sets the employee's monthly salary
   public decimal MonthlySalary
   {
      get
      {
         return monthlySalary;
      }
      set
      {
         if (value >= 0M) // validate that salary is nonnegative
         {
            monthlySalary = value;
         }
      }
   }

   // return a string containing the employee's information
   public override string ToString() =>
      $"{FirstName,-10} {LastName,-10} {MonthlySalary,10:C}";
}
```

**Fig. 9.3** | Employee class with FirstName, LastName and MonthlySalary properties. (Part 2 of 2.)

```
// Fig. 9.4: LINQWithArrayOfObjects.cs
// LINQ to Objects querying an array of Employee objects.
using System;
using System.Linq;

class LINQWithArrayOfObjects
{
   static void Main()
   {
      // initialize array of employees
      var employees = new[] {
         new Employee("Jason", "Red", 5000M),
         new Employee("Ashley", "Green", 7600M),
         new Employee("Matthew", "Indigo", 3587.5M),
         new Employee("James", "Indigo", 4700.77M),
```

**Fig. 9.4** | LINQ to Objects querying an array of Employee objects. (Part 1 of 3.)

```
         new Employee("Luke", "Indigo", 6200M),
         new Employee("Jason", "Blue", 3200M),
         new Employee("Wendy", "Brown", 4236.4M)};

      // display all employees
      Console.WriteLine("Original array:");
      foreach (var element in employees)
      {
         Console.WriteLine(element);
      }

      // filter a range of salaries using && in a LINQ query
      var between4K6K =
         from e in employees
         where (e.MonthlySalary >= 4000M) && (e.MonthlySalary <= 6000M)
         select e;

      // display employees making between 4000 and 6000 per month
      Console.WriteLine("\nEmployees earning in the range" +
         $"{4000:C}-{6000:C} per month:");
      foreach (var element in between4K6K)
      {
         Console.WriteLine(element);
      }

      // order the employees by last name, then first name with LINQ
      var nameSorted =
         from e in employees
         orderby e.LastName, e.FirstName
         select e;

      // header
      Console.WriteLine("\nFirst employee when sorted by name:");

      // attempt to display the first result of the above LINQ query
      if (nameSorted.Any())
      {
         Console.WriteLine(nameSorted.First());
      }
      else
      {
         Console.WriteLine("not found");
      }

      // use LINQ to select employee last names
      var lastNames =
         from e in employees
         select e.LastName;

      // use method Distinct to select unique last names
      Console.WriteLine("\nUnique employee last names:");
```

**Fig. 9.4** | LINQ to Objects querying an array of Employee objects. (Part 2 of 3.)

```
        foreach (var element in lastNames.Distinct())
        {
           Console.WriteLine(element);
        }

        // use LINQ to select first and last names
        var names =
           from e in employees
           select new {e.FirstName, e.LastName};

        // display full names
        Console.WriteLine("\nNames only:");
        foreach (var element in names)
        {
           Console.WriteLine(element);
        }

        Console.WriteLine();
     }
  }
```

```
Original array:
Jason      Red         $5,000.00
Ashley     Green       $7,600.00
Matthew    Indigo      $3,587.50
James      Indigo      $4,700.77
Luke       Indigo      $6,200.00
Jason      Blue        $3,200.00
Wendy      Brown       $4,236.40

Employees earning in the range $4,000.00-$6,000.00 per month:
Jason      Red         $5,000.00
James      Indigo      $4,700.77
Wendy      Brown       $4,236.40

First employee when sorted by name:
Jason      Blue        $3,200.00

Unique employee last names:
Red
Green
Indigo
Blue
Brown

Names only:
{ FirstName = Jason, LastName = Red }
{ FirstName = Ashley, LastName = Green }
{ FirstName = Matthew, LastName = Indigo }
{ FirstName = James, LastName = Indigo }
{ FirstName = Luke, LastName = Indigo }
{ FirstName = Jason, LastName = Blue }
{ FirstName = Wendy, LastName = Brown }
```

**Fig. 9.4** | LINQ to Objects querying an array of Employee objects. (Part 3 of 3.)

### 9.3.1 Accessing the Properties of a LINQ Query's Range Variable

The `where` clause in line 30 (Fig. 9.4) accesses the range variable's properties. The compiler infers that the range variable is of type `Employee`, because `employees` was defined as an array of `Employee` objects (lines 11–18). Any `bool` expression can be used in a `where` clause. Line 30 uses the `&&` (conditional AND) operator to combine conditions. Here, only employees that have a salary between $4,000 and $6,000 per month, inclusive, are included in the query result, which is displayed in lines 36–39.

### 9.3.2 Sorting a LINQ Query's Results by Multiple Properties

Line 44 uses `orderby` to sort the results according to *multiple* properties—specified in a comma-separated list. Here, the employees are sorted alphabetically by last name. `Employees` that have the same last name are sorted by first name.

### 9.3.3 Any, `First` and `Count` Extension Methods

Line 51 introduces the **`Any`** method, which returns `true` if the query to which it's applied has at least one element. The query result's **`First`** method (line 53) returns the first element in the result. You should check that the query result is not empty (line 51) *before* calling `First`, which throws an `InvalidOperationException` if the collection is empty.

We've not specified the class that defines methods `First` and `Any`. Your intuition probably tells you they're methods of interface `IEnumerable<T>`, but they aren't. They're actually **extension methods** that enhance a class's capabilities without modifying the class's definition. The LINQ extension methods can be used as if they were methods of `IEnumerable<T>`. Section 10.14 shows how to create extension methods.

LINQ defines many more extension methods, such as **`Count`**, which returns the number of elements in the results. Rather than using `Any`, we could have checked that `Count` was nonzero, but it's more efficient to determine whether there's at least one element than to count all the elements. The LINQ query syntax is actually transformed by the compiler into extension method calls, with the results of one method call used in the next. It's this design that allows queries to be run on the results of previous queries, as it simply involves passing the result of a method call to another method. For a complete list of `IEnumerable<T>` extension methods, visit

```
https://msdn.microsoft.com/library/9eekhta0
```

### 9.3.4 Selecting a Property of an Object

Line 63 uses the `select` clause to select the range variable's `LastName` property rather than the range variable itself. This causes the results of the query to consist of only the last names (as `strings`), instead of complete `Employee` objects. Lines 67–70 display the unique last names. The **`Distinct` extension method** (line 67) removes duplicate elements, causing all elements in the resulting collection to be unique.

### 9.3.5 Creating New Types in the `select` Clause of a LINQ Query

The last LINQ query in the example (lines 74–75) selects the properties `FirstName` and `LastName`. The syntax

```
new {e.FirstName, e.LastName}
```

creates a new object of an **anonymous type** (a type with no name), which the compiler generates for you, based on the properties listed in the curly braces ({}). In this case, each new object of the anonymous type is initialized with the FirstName and LastName values from the corresponding Employee object. These selected properties can then be accessed when iterating over the results. Implicitly typed local variables allow you to use *anonymous types* because you do not have to explicitly state the type when declaring such variables.

When the compiler creates an anonymous type, it automatically generates a ToString method that returns a string representation of the object. You can see this in the program's output—it consists of the property names and their values, enclosed in braces. Anonymous types are discussed more in Chapter 20.

#### *Projections*

The query in lines 74–75 is an example of a **projection**, which transforms an object into a new form. In this case, the transformation creates new objects containing only the FirstName and LastName properties, but projections also can manipulate the data. For example, a projection that includes the MonthlySalary could give all employees a 10% raise by multiplying their MonthlySalary properties by 1.1 with the expression

```
e.MonthlySalary * 1.1M
```

#### *Changing the Names of Properties in Anonymous Types*

You can specify a new name for a selected property in an anonymous type. For example, if line 75 is written as

```
new {First = e.FirstName, Last = e.LastName}
```

the anonymous type would have properties named First and Last, rather than FirstName and LastName. If you don't specify a new name, the property's original name is used.

## 9.4 Introduction to Collections

The .NET Framework Class Library provides several classes, called *collections*, used to store groups of related objects. These classes provide efficient methods that organize, store and retrieve your data *without* requiring knowledge of how the data is being stored. This reduces app development time.

You've used arrays to store sequences of objects. Arrays do not automatically change their size at execution time to accommodate additional elements—you must do so manually by creating a new array or by using the Array class's Resize method.

### 9.4.1 List<T> Collection

The generic collection class **List<T>** (from namespace System.Collections.Generic) provides a convenient solution to this problem. The T is a placeholder—when declaring a new List, replace it with the type of elements that you want the List to hold. This is similar to specifying the type when declaring an array. For example,

```
List<int> intList;
```

declares intList as a List collection that can store only int values, and

```
List<string> stringList;
```

declares `stringList` as a `List` of references to `string`s. Classes with this kind of placeholder enabling them to be used with any type are called **generic classes.** Generic classes are discussed in Chapter 18. Additional generic collection classes are discussed in Chapter 19. Figure 19.2 provides a table of collection classes. Figure 9.5 shows some common methods and properties of class `List<T>`.

| Method or property | Description |
|---|---|
| `Add` | Adds an element to the end of the `List`. |
| `AddRange` | Adds the elements of its collection argument to the end of the `List`. |
| `Capacity` | Property that *gets* or *sets* the number of elements a `List` can store without resizing. |
| `Clear` | Removes all the elements from the `List`. |
| `Contains` | Returns `true` if the `List` contains the specified element and `false` otherwise. |
| `Count` | Property that returns the number of elements stored in the `List`. |
| `IndexOf` | Returns the index of the first occurrence of the specified value in the `List`. |
| `Insert` | Inserts an element at the specified index. |
| `Remove` | Removes the first occurrence of the specified value. |
| `RemoveAt` | Removes the element at the specified index. |
| `RemoveRange` | Removes a specified number of elements starting at a specified index. |
| `Sort` | Sorts the `List`. |
| `TrimExcess` | Sets the `Capacity` of the `List` to the number of elements the `List` currently contains (`Count`). |

**Fig. 9.5** | Some methods and properties of class `List<T>`.

### 9.4.2 Dynamically Resizing a `List<T>` Collection

Figure 9.6 demonstrates dynamically resizing a `List` object. Line 11 creates a `List` of `string`s, then lines 14–15 display the `List`'s initial `Count` and `Capacity`, respectively:

- The **`Count`** property returns the number of elements currently in the `List`.
- The **`Capacity`** property indicates how many items the `List` can hold without having to grow.

When the `List` is created, both are initially `0`—though the `Capacity` is implementation dependent.

```
1  // Fig. 9.6: ListCollection.cs
2  // Generic List<T> collection demonstration.
3  using System;
4  using System.Collections.Generic;
5
6  class ListCollection
7  {
```

**Fig. 9.6** | Generic `List<T>` collection demonstration. (Part 1 of 3.)

```
      static void Main()
      {
         // create a new List of strings
         var items = new List<string>();

         // display List's Count and Capacity before adding elements
         Console.WriteLine("Before adding to items: " +
            $"Count = {items.Count}; Capacity = {items.Capacity}");

         items.Add("red"); // append an item to the List
         items.Insert(0, "yellow"); // insert the value at index 0

         // display List's Count and Capacity after adding two elements
         Console.WriteLine("After adding two elements to items: " +
            $"Count = {items.Count}; Capacity = {items.Capacity}");

         // display the colors in the list
         Console.Write(
            "\nDisplay list contents with counter-controlled loop:");
         for (var i = 0; i < items.Count; i++)
         {
            Console.Write($" {items[i]}");
         }

         // display colors using foreach
         Console.Write("\nDisplay list contents with foreach statement:");
         foreach (var item in items)
         {
            Console.Write($" {item}");
         }

         items.Add("green"); // add "green" to the end of the List
         items.Add("yellow"); // add "yellow" to the end of the List

         // display List's Count and Capacity after adding two more elements
         Console.WriteLine("\n\nAfter adding two more elements to items: " +
            $"Count = {items.Count}; Capacity = {items.Capacity}");

         // display the List
         Console.Write("\nList with two new elements:");
         foreach (var item in items)
         {
            Console.Write($" {item}");
         }

         items.Remove("yellow"); // remove the first "yellow"

         // display the List
         Console.Write("\n\nRemove first instance of yellow:");
         foreach (var item in items)
         {
            Console.Write($" {item}");
         }
```

**Fig. 9.6** | Generic `List<T>` collection demonstration. (Part 2 of 3.)

```

         items.RemoveAt(1); // remove item at index 1

         // display the List
         Console.Write("\nRemove second list element (green):");
         foreach (var item in items)
         {
            Console.Write($" {item}");
         }

         // display List's Count and Capacity after removing two elements
         Console.WriteLine("\nAfter removing two elements from items: " +
            $"Count = {items.Count}; Capacity = {items.Capacity}");

         // check if a value is in the List
         Console.WriteLine("\n\"red\" is " +
            $"{(items.Contains("red") ? string.Empty : "not ")}in the list");

         items.Add("orange"); // add "orange" to the end of the List
         items.Add("violet"); // add "violet" to the end of the List
         items.Add("blue"); // add "blue" to the end of the List

         // display List's Count and Capacity after adding three elements
         Console.WriteLine("\nAfter adding three more elements to items: " +
            $"Count = {items.Count}; Capacity = {items.Capacity}");

         // display the List
         Console.Write("List with three new elements:");
         foreach (var item in items)
         {
            Console.Write($" {item}");
         }
         Console.WriteLine();
      }
   }
```

```
Before adding to items: Count = 0; Capacity = 0
After adding two elements to items: Count = 2; Capacity = 4

Display list contents with counter-controlled loop: yellow red
Display list contents with foreach statement: yellow red

After adding two more elements to items: Count = 4; Capacity = 4
List with two new elements: yellow red green yellow

Remove first instance of yellow: red green yellow
Remove second list element (green): red yellow
After removing two elements from items: Count = 2; Capacity = 4

"red" is in the list

After adding three more elements to items: Count = 5; Capacity = 8
List with three new elements: red yellow orange violet blue
```

**Fig. 9.6** | Generic `List<T>` collection demonstration. (Part 3 of 3.)

### *Adding and Inserting Elements*

The Add and Insert methods add elements to the List (lines 17–18):

- The **Add** method *appends* its argument to the end of the List.
- The **Insert** method inserts a new element at the specified position.

Insert's first argument is an index—as with arrays, collection indices start at zero. The second argument is the value to insert at the specified index. To make room for the new element, the indices of the elements at the specified index and above each *increase* by one—in this case, "red" initially was at index 0, but now is at index 1, so that "yellow" can be inserted at index 0.

### *Count and Capacity*

Lines 21–22 display the List's Count (2) and Capacity (4) after the Add and Insert operations. When line 17 executes, the List grows, increasing its Capacity to 4 so that the List can accommodate *four* elements. One of these elements is immediately occupied by "red". At this point, the List's Count is 1. When line 18 executes, there's still room for three more elements, so "yellow" is inserted and the Count becomes 2.

### *Iterating Through a **List's** Contents*

Lines 27–30 display the items in the List. Like array elements, List elements can be accessed by placing the index in square brackets after the List variable's name. The indexed List expression can be used to modify the element at the index. Lines 34–37 display the List using the preferred foreach statement.

### *Adding More Elements and Growing the **List***

Lines 39–51 add more elements to the List, then display its Count, Capacity and contents once again.

### *Removing Elements*

The **Remove** method deletes the *first* element with a specific value (line 53), returning true if successful and false otherwise. Lines 57–60 show the List's contents after line 53 executes. A similar method, **RemoveAt**, removes the element at the specified index (line 62). When an element is removed through either of these methods, the indices of all elements above that index *decrease* by one—the opposite of the Insert method. Lines 66–69 show the List's contents after line 62 executes. Lines 72–73 display the List's Count (2) and Capacity (4) after the remove operations. At this point, there's room in the List for two more elements.

### *Determining Whether an Element Is in the **List***

Line 77 uses the **Contains** method to check whether an item is in the List. The Contains method returns true if the element is found in the List and false otherwise. The method compares its argument to each element of the List in order until the item is found, so using Contains on a large List is inefficient.

### *Adding More Elements and Growing the **List***

Lines 79–81 add three more elements to the List. Before lines 79–80 execute, Count is 2 and Capacity is 4, so there's room in the List for the two new elements added by those statements. When Line 81 executes, however, Count and Capacity are both 4, so the List doubles its Capacity to 8 and the Count becomes 5, leaving room for three more elements.

### *Doubling the Capacity*

When a List grows, it must (behind the scenes) create a larger internal array and copy each element to the new array. This is a time-consuming operation. It would be inefficient for the List to grow each time an element is added. To minimize the number of memory reallocations, a List *doubles* its capacity when more memory is required.[1]

**Performance Tip 9.1**

*Doubling a* List*'s* Capacity *is an efficient way for a* List *to grow quickly to be "about the right size." This operation is much more efficient than growing a* List *by only as much space as it takes to hold the element(s) being added. A disadvantage is that the* List *might occupy more space than it requires. This is a classic example of the space/time trade-off.*

**Performance Tip 9.2**

*It can be wasteful to double a* List*'s size when more space is needed. For example, a full* List *of 1,000,000 elements resizes to accommodate 2,000,000 elements when one new element is added. This leaves 999,999 unused elements. You can use* TrimExcess *(as in* yourListObject.TrimExcess()*) to reduce a* List*'s* Capacity *to its current* Count*. You also can set the* Capacity *directly to control space usage better—for example, if you know a* List *will never grow beyond 100 elements, you can preallocate that space by assigning 100 to the* List*'s* Capacity *or using the* List *constructor that receives an initial capacity.*

## 9.5 Querying the Generic List Collection Using LINQ

As with arrays, you can use LINQ to Objects to query Lists. In Fig. 9.7, a List of strings is converted to uppercase and searched for those that begin with "R".

```
// Fig. 9.7: LINQWithListCollection.cs
// LINQ to Objects using a List<string>.
using System;
using System.Linq;
using System.Collections.Generic;

class LINQWithListCollection
{
   static void Main()
   {
      // populate a List of strings
      var items = new List<string>();
      items.Add("aQua"); // add "aQua" to the end of the List
      items.Add("RusT"); // add "RusT" to the end of the List
      items.Add("yElLow"); // add "yElLow" to the end of the List
      items.Add("rEd"); // add "rEd" to the end of the List

```

**Fig. 9.7** | LINQ to Objects using a List<string>. (Part 1 of 2.)

1. This is not required and could be implementation dependent.

```
      // display initial List
      Console.Write("items contains:");
      foreach (var item in items)
      {
         Console.Write($" {item}");
      }

      Console.WriteLine(); // output end of line

      // convert to uppercase, select those starting with "R" and sort
      var startsWithR =
         from item in items
         let uppercaseString = item.ToUpper()
         where uppercaseString.StartsWith("R")
         orderby uppercaseString
         select uppercaseString;

      // display query results
      Console.Write("results of query startsWithR:");
      foreach (var item in startsWithR)
      {
         Console.Write($" {item}");
      }

      Console.WriteLine(); // output end of line

      items.Add("rUbY"); // add "rUbY" to the end of the List
      items.Add("SaFfRon"); // add "SaFfRon" to the end of the List

      // display initial List
      Console.Write("items contains:");
      foreach (var item in items)
      {
         Console.Write($" {item}");
      }

      Console.WriteLine(); // output end of line

      // display updated query results
      Console.Write("results of query startsWithR:");
      foreach (var item in startsWithR)
      {
         Console.Write($" {item}");
      }

      Console.WriteLine(); // output end of line
   }
}
```

```
items contains: aQua RusT yElLow rEd
results of query startsWithR: RED RUST
items contains: aQua RusT yElLow rEd rUbY SaFfRon
results of query startsWithR: RED RUBY RUST
```

**Fig. 9.7** | LINQ to Objects using a `List<string>`. (Part 2 of 2.)

### 9.5.1 The let Clause

Line 30 uses LINQ's **let clause** to create a new range variable. This is useful if you need to store a temporary result for use later in the LINQ query. Typically, let declares a new range variable to which you assign the result of an expression that operates on the query's original range variable. In this case, we use string method **ToUpper** to convert each item to uppercase, then store the result in the new range variable uppercaseString. We then use uppercaseString in the where, orderby and select clauses. The where clause (line 31) uses string method **StartsWith** to determine whether uppercaseString starts with the character "R". Method StartsWith performs a case-sensitive comparison to determine whether a string starts with the string received as an argument. If uppercaseString starts with "R", method StartsWith returns true, and the element is included in the query results. More powerful string matching can be done using the *regular-expression* capabilities introduced in the online part of Chapter 16, Strings and Characters: A Deeper Look (http://www.deitel.com/books/CSharp6FP).

### 9.5.2 Deferred Execution

We create the query only once (lines 29–33), yet iterating over the results (lines 37–40 and 58–61) gives two *different* lists of colors. This demonstrates LINQ's **deferred execution.** A LINQ query executes *only* when you access the results—such as iterating over them or using the Count method—*not* when you define the query. This allows you to create a query once and execute it many times. Any changes to the data source are reflected in the results each time the query executes.

**Performance Tip 9.3**

*Deferred execution can improve performance when a query's results are not immediately needed.*

### 9.5.3 Extension Methods ToArray and ToList

There may be times when you want to retrieve a collection of the results immediately. LINQ provides extension methods ToArray and ToList for this purpose. These methods execute the query on which they're called and give you the results as an array or List<T>, respectively. We use ToArray in Section 19.12.

**Performance Tip 9.4**

*Methods ToArray and ToList also can improve efficiency if you'll be iterating over the same results multiple times, as you execute the query only once.*

### 9.5.4 Collection Initializers

**Collection initializers** provide a convenient syntax (similar to *array initializers*) for initializing a collection. For example, lines 12–16 of Fig. 9.7 could be replaced with the following statement:

```
var items = new List<string> {"aQua", "RusT", "yElLow", "rEd"};
```

In the preceding declaration, we explicitly created the `List<string>` with `new`, so the compiler knows that the initializer list contains elements for a `List<string>`. The following declaration would generate a compilation error, because the compiler cannot determine whether you wish to create an array or a collection

```
var items = {"aQua", "RusT", "yElLow", "rEd"};
```

## 9.6 Wrap-Up

This chapter introduced LINQ (Language Integrated Query), a powerful feature for querying data. We showed how to filter an array or collection using LINQ's `where` clause, and how to sort the query results using the `orderby` clause. We used the `select` clause to select specific properties of an object, and the `let` clause to introduce a new range variable to make writing queries more convenient. The `StartsWith` method of class `string` was used to filter `strings` starting with a specified character or series of characters. We used several LINQ extension methods to perform operations not provided by the query syntax—the `Distinct` method to remove duplicates from the results, the `Any` method to determine if the results contain any items, and the `First` method to retrieve the first element in the results.

We introduced the `List<T>` generic collection, which provides all the functionality of arrays, along with other useful capabilities such as dynamic resizing. We used method `Add` to append new items to the end of the `List`, method `Insert` to insert new items into specified locations in the `List`, method `Remove` to remove the first occurrence of a specified item, method `RemoveAt` to remove an item at a specified index and method `Contains` to determine if an item was in the `List`. We used property `Count` to get the number of items in the `List`, and property `Capacity` to determine the number of elements the `List` can hold without growing. We use more advanced features of LINQ in later chapters.

In Chapter 10 we take a deeper look at class concepts. We'll discuss the `this` reference, additional constructor concepts, how the runtime manages memory with garbage collection, `static` class members, read-only class members, object initializers and operator overloading.

## 9.7 Deitel LINQ Resource Center

Our LINQ Resource Center (`http://www.deitel.com/LINQ/`) contains many links to additional information, including blogs by Microsoft LINQ team members, books, sample chapters, FAQs, tutorials, videos, webcasts and more.

10

# Classes and Objects: A Deeper Look

## Objectives

In this chapter you'll:

- Use composition to allow a class to have references to objects of other classes as members.
- Throw an exception to indicate that an argument is out of range.
- Enable an object to refer to itself with the keyword `this`.
- Use `static` variables and methods.
- Use `readonly` fields.
- Take advantage of C#'s memory-management features.
- Use the IDE's **Class View** and **Object Browser** windows.
- Use object initializers to create an object and initialize it in the same statement.
- Overload built-in operators to work with objects of your own types.
- Define your own value type with `struct`.
- Use extension methods to enhance an existing class's capabilities.

Outline



## 10.1 Introduction

In this chapter, we take a deeper look at building classes, controlling access to members of a class and creating constructors. We discuss *composition*—a capability that allows a class to have references to objects of other classes as members. The chapter also discusses `static` class members and `readonly` instance variables and properties.

We also introduce operator overloading. In previous chapters, we declared our own classes and used methods to perform tasks on objects of those classes. Operator overloading allows us to define the behavior of the built-in operators, such as + and -, when used on objects of our own classes. This can provide a more convenient notation than calling methods for performing certain tasks (such as arithmetic) using objects.

We show how to create your own value types using `struct`, discuss key differences between `struct`s and classes, and discuss when `struct` types should be used. Finally, we demonstrate how to create your own extension methods to add functionality to an existing type that you did not define.

## 10.2 `Time` Class Case Study; Throwing Exceptions

Our first example consists of classes `Time1` (Fig. 10.1) and `Time1Test` (Fig. 10.2). Class `Time1` represents the time of day.[1] Class `Time1Test`'s `Main` method creates an object of class `Time1` and invokes its methods. The output of this app appears in Fig. 10.2.

1. C# has the types like `DateTime` and `DateTimeOffset` for date and time manipulations. Our time examples are for demonstration purposes—you do not need to create your own types for dates and times. We use `DateTime` in Section 15.4.

### 10.2.1 Time1 Class Declaration

Class `Time1` contains three `public` properties of type `int`—`Hour`, `Minute` and `Second` (Fig. 10.1, lines 7–9). These represent the time in universal-time format (24-hour clock format, in which hours are in the range 0–23). Class `Time1` contains `public` methods `SetTime` (lines 13–25), `ToUniversalString` (lines 28–29) and `ToString` (lines 32–34). These are the **`public` services** or the **`public` interface** that this class provides to its clients. In this example, class `Time1` does not declare a constructor, so the compiler defines a default constructor. Each property receives the default value `0` for an `int`. Instance variables and auto-implemented properties also can be assigned values in their declarations.

```
1  // Fig. 10.1: Time1.cs
2  // Time1 class declaration maintains the time in 24-hour format.
3  using System; // namespace containing ArgumentOutOfRangeException
4
5  public class Time1
6  {
7     public int Hour { get; set; } // 0 - 23
8     public int Minute { get; set; } // 0 - 59
9     public int Second { get; set; } // 0 - 59
10
11    // set a new time value using universal time; throw an
12    // exception if the hour, minute or second is invalid
13    public void SetTime(int hour, int minute, int second)
14    {
15       // validate hour, minute and second
16       if ((hour < 0 || hour > 23) || (minute < 0 || minute > 59) ||
17          (second < 0 || second > 59))
18       {
19          throw new ArgumentOutOfRangeException();
20       }
21
22       Hour = hour;
23       Minute = minute;
24       Second = second;
25    }
26
27    // convert to string in universal-time format (HH:MM:SS)
28    public string ToUniversalString() =>
29       $"{Hour:D2}:{Minute:D2}:{Second:D2}";
30
31    // convert to string in standard-time format (H:MM:SS AM or PM)
32    public override string ToString() =>
33       $"{((Hour == 0 || Hour == 12) ? 12 : Hour % 12)}:" +
34       $"{Minute:D2}:{Second:D2} {(Hour < 12 ? "AM" : "PM")}";
35 }
```

**Fig. 10.1** | `Time1` class declaration maintains the time in 24-hour format.

***`public` Class***

In Fig. 10.1, we declared class `Time1` as a **`public`** class, meaning that it potentially can be reused in other projects. Although we use class `Time1` only in this project, from this point forward, we'll declare as `public` any class that could potentially be reused in another project.

### *Method* SetTime *and Throwing Exceptions*

Method SetTime (lines 13–25) is a public method that declares three int parameters and uses them to set the time. Lines 16–17 test each argument to determine whether the value is out of range. If all the values are in range, lines 22–24 assign the values to the Hour, Minute and Second properties. The hour (line 13) must be in the range 0 to 23, because universal-time format represents hours as integers from 0 to 23 (e.g., 1 PM is hour 13 and 11 PM is hour 23; midnight is hour 0 and noon is hour 12). Similarly, both minute and second values must be in the range 0 to 59. For values outside these ranges, line 19 **throws an exception** of type **ArgumentOutOfRangeException** (namespace System), which notifies the client code that an invalid argument was passed to the method. As you learned in Chapter 8, you can use try...catch to catch exceptions and attempt to recover from them, which we'll do in Fig. 10.2. The **throw statement** (line 19) creates a new object of type ArgumentOutOfRangeException. The parentheses following the class name indicate a call to the ArgumentOutOfRangeException constructor. After the exception object is created, the throw statement immediately terminates method SetTime and the exception is returned to the code that attempted to set the time, where it can be *caught* and dealt with.

### *Method* ToUniversalString

Method ToUniversalString (lines 28–29) is an expression-bodied method—recall this is a shorthand notation for a method that contains only a return statement. The method takes no arguments and returns a string in universal-time format, consisting of six digits—two for the hour, two for the minute and two for the second. For example, if the time were 1:30:07 PM, method ToUniversalString would return 13:30:07. The method implicitly returns the value of the string-interpolation expression in line 29. The D2 format specifier formats an integer with two digits and, where needed, a leading 0 if the integer has fewer than two digits.

### *Method* ToString

Method ToString (lines 32–34) is an expression-bodied method that takes no arguments and returns a string in which the Hour, Minute and Second values are separated by colons and followed by an AM or PM indicator (e.g., 1:27:06 PM). Like method ToUniversalString, method ToString implicitly returns the value of a string-interpolation expression. In this case, we do not format the Hour, but we format the Minute and Second as two-digit values with leading 0s, if necessary. Line 33 uses a conditional operator (?:) to determine the value for Hour in the string—if the hour is 0 or 12 (AM or PM), it appears as 12—otherwise, it appears as a value from 1 to 11. The conditional operator in line 34 determines whether AM or PM will be inserted in the string.

## 10.2.2 Using Class Time1

The Time1Test app class (Fig. 10.2) uses class Time1. Line 10 creates a Time1 object and assigns it to local variable time. Operator new invokes class Time1's *default constructor*, since Time1 does not declare any constructors. Lines 13–17 output the time, first in universal-time format (by invoking time's ToUniversalString method in line 14), then in standard-time format (by explicitly invoking time's ToString method in line 16) to confirm that the Time1 object was initialized properly. Line 20 invokes method SetTime of the time object to change the time. Then lines 21–24 output the time again in both formats to confirm that the time was set correctly.

```
// Fig. 10.2: Time1Test.cs
// Time1 object used in an app.
using System;

class Time1Test
{
   static void Main()
   {
      // create and initialize a Time1 object
      var time = new Time1(); // invokes Time1 constructor

      // output string representations of the time
      Console.WriteLine(
         $"The initial universal time is: {time.ToUniversalString()}");
      Console.WriteLine(
         $"The initial standard time is: {time.ToString()}");
      Console.WriteLine(); // output a blank line

      // change time and output updated time
      time.SetTime(13, 27, 6);
      Console.WriteLine(
         $"Universal time after SetTime is: {time.ToUniversalString()}");
      Console.WriteLine(
         $"Standard time after SetTime is: {time.ToString()}");
      Console.WriteLine(); // output a blank line

      // attempt to set time with invalid values
      try
      {
         time.SetTime(99, 99, 99);
      }
      catch (ArgumentOutOfRangeException ex)
      {
         Console.WriteLine(ex.Message + "\n");
      }

      // display time after attempt to set invalid values
      Console.WriteLine("After attempting invalid settings:");
      Console.WriteLine($"Universal time: {time.ToUniversalString()}");
      Console.WriteLine($"Standard time: {time.ToString()}");
   }
}
```

```
The initial universal time is: 00:00:00
The initial standard time is: 12:00:00 AM

Universal time after SetTime is: 13:27:06
Standard time after SetTime is: 1:27:06 PM

Specified argument was out of the range of valid values.

After attempting invalid settings:
Universal time: 13:27:06
Standard time: 1:27:06 PM
```

**Fig. 10.2** | Time1 object used in an app.

#### *Calling `Time` Method `SetTime` with Invalid Values*

To illustrate that method `SetTime` validates its arguments, line 30 calls method `SetTime` with invalid arguments of `99` for the `hour`, `minute` and `second`. This statement is placed in a `try` block (lines 28–31) in case `SetTime` throws an `ArgumentOutOfRangeException`, which it will do since the arguments are all invalid. When this occurs, the exception is caught at lines 32–35 and the exception's `Message` property is displayed. Lines 38–40 output the time again in both formats to confirm that `SetTime` did *not* change the time when invalid arguments were supplied.

#### *Notes on the `Time1` Class Declaration*

Consider several class-design issues with respect to class `Time1`. The time is represented as three integers for the hour, minute and second. However, the actual data representation used within the class is of no concern to the class's clients. For example, it would be perfectly reasonable for `Time1` to represent the time internally as the number of seconds since midnight or the number of minutes and seconds since midnight. Clients could use the same `public` methods and properties to get the same results without being aware of this—of course, the `Hour`, `Minute` and `Second` properties would need to be reimplemented to work with the new data representation. As an exercise, you can change the time representation to the number of seconds since midnight, then use the updated class with the existing client code.

**Software Engineering Observation 10.1**

*Classes simplify programming because the client can use only the `public` members exposed by the class. Such members are usually client oriented rather than implementation oriented. Clients are neither aware of, nor involved in, a class's implementation. Clients generally care about* what *the class does but not* how *the class does it. Clients do, of course, care that the class operates correctly and efficiently.*

**Software Engineering Observation 10.2**

*Interfaces change less frequently than implementations. When an implementation changes, implementation-dependent code must change accordingly. Hiding the implementation reduces the possibility that other parts of the app become dependent on class-implementation details.*

**Software Engineering Observation 10.3**

*Date and time manipulations are more complex than the simplified classes we use in this book. For applications that require date and time processing, check out .NET's `DateTimeOffest`, `DateTime`, `TimeSpan` and `TimeZoneInfo` value types in namespace `System`.*

## 10.3 Controlling Access to Members

The access modifiers `public` and `private` control access to a class's variables, methods and properties. (In Chapter 11, we'll introduce the additional access modifier `protected`.) As we stated in Section 10.2, the primary purpose of `public` methods and properties is to present to the class's clients a view of the services the class provides (that is, the class's *public interface*). Clients of the class need not be concerned with how the class accomplishes its tasks. For this reason, a class's `private` variables, properties and methods (i.e., the class's implementation details) are not directly accessible to the class's clients.

Figure 10.3 demonstrates that `private` class members are not directly accessible outside the class. In this app, we use a modified version of class `Time1` that declares `private` instance variables `hour`, `minute` and `second`, rather than `public` properties `Hour`, `Minute` and `Second`. Lines 9–11 attempt to directly access `private` instance variables `hour`, `minute` and `second` of `Time1` object `time`. When this app is compiled, the compiler generates error messages stating that these `private` members are not accessible.

```
1  // Fig. 10.3: MemberAccessTest.cs
2  // Private members of class Time1 are not accessible outside the class.
3  class MemberAccessTest
4  {
5     static void Main()
6     {
7        var time = new Time1(); // create and initialize Time1 object
8
9        time.hour = 7; // error: hour has private access in Time1
10       time.minute = 15; // error: minute has private access in Time1
11       time.second = 30; // error: second has private access in Time1
12    }
13 }
```

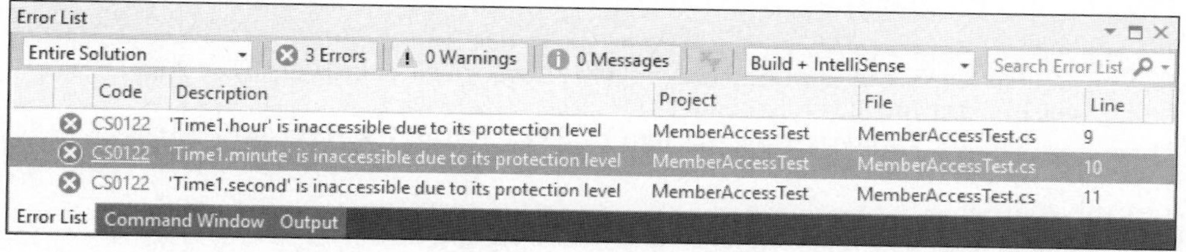


**Fig. 10.3** | Private members of class `Time1` are not accessible outside the class.

## 10.4 Referring to the Current Object's Members with the `this` Reference

Every object can access a *reference to itself* with keyword **`this`** (also called the **`this` reference**). When a non-`static` method (or property) is called for a particular object, the method's body *implicitly* uses keyword `this` to refer to the object's instance variables and other non-static class members. As you'll see in Fig. 10.4, you also can use keyword `this` *explicitly* in a non-`static` method's body. Section 10.5 shows a more interesting use of keyword `this`. Section 10.9 explains why keyword `this` cannot be used in a `static` method.

```
// Fig. 10.4: ThisTest.cs
// this used implicitly and explicitly to refer to members of an object.
using System;

class ThisTest
{
```

**Fig. 10.4** | `this` used implicitly and explicitly to refer to members of an object. (Part 1 of 2.)

```
7      static void Main()
8      {
9         var time = new SimpleTime(15, 30, 19);
10        Console.WriteLine(time.BuildString());
11     }
12  }
13
14  // class SimpleTime demonstrates the "this" reference
15  public class SimpleTime
16  {
17     private int hour; // 0-23
18     private int minute; // 0-59
19     private int second; // 0-59
20
21     // if the constructor uses parameter names identical to
22     // instance-variable names, the "this" reference is
23     // required to distinguish between the names
24     public SimpleTime(int hour, int minute, int second)
25     {
26        this.hour = hour; // set "this" object's hour instance variable
27        this.minute = minute; // set "this" object's minute
28        this.second = second; // set "this" object's second
29     }
30
31     // use explicit and implicit "this" to call ToUniversalString
32     public string BuildString() =>
33        $"{"this.ToUniversalString()",24}: {this.ToUniversalString()}" +
34        $"\n{"ToUniversalString()",24}: {ToUniversalString()}";
35
36     // convert to string in universal-time format (HH:MM:SS);
37     // "this" is not required here to access instance variables,
38     // because the method does not have local variables with the same
39     // names as the instance variables
40     public string ToUniversalString() =>
41        $"{this.hour:D2}:{this.minute:D2}:{this.second:D2}";
42  }
```

```
this.ToUniversalString(): 15:30:19
     ToUniversalString(): 15:30:19
```

**Fig. 10.4** | `this` used implicitly and explicitly to refer to members of an object. (Part 2 of 2.)

Figure 10.4 demonstrates implicit and explicit use of the `this` reference to enable class `ThisTest`'s `Main` method to display the `private` data of a `SimpleTime` object. For the sake of brevity, we declare two classes in one file—class `ThisTest` is declared in lines 5–12, and class `SimpleTime` is declared in lines 15–42.

Class `SimpleTime` declares three `private` instance variables—`hour`, `minute` and `second` (lines 17–19). The constructor (lines 24–29) receives three `int` arguments to initialize a `SimpleTime` object (without validation for simplicity). Here, we used parameter names that are *identical* to the class's instance-variable names (lines 17–19). We did this intentionally to *hide* the corresponding instance variables so that we could illustrate explicit use of the `this` reference. If a method contains a local variable with the *same* name as an instance variable, the local variable is said to *shadow* (or hide) the instance variable in the method's body. However, you can use `this` to access the hidden instance variable explicitly, as shown in lines 26–28 for `SimpleTime`'s hidden instance variables.

**Software Engineering Observation 10.4**

*Using properties throughout a class to access the class's instance variables normally eliminates shadowing because property names use Pascal Case naming (capital first letter) and parameter names use Camel Case (lowercase first letter).*

Method `BuildString` (lines 32–34) returns a `string` created by a statement that uses the `this` reference explicitly and implicitly. Line 33 uses the `this` reference *explicitly* to call method `ToUniversalString`. Line 34 uses the `this` reference *implicitly* to call the same method. Programmers typically do not use the `this` reference explicitly to reference other methods in the current object. Also, line 41 in method `ToUniversalString` explicitly uses the `this` reference to access each instance variable. This is not necessary here, because the method does *not* have any local variables that hide the instance variables of the class.

Class `ThisTest` (lines 5–12) demonstrates class `SimpleTime`. Line 9 creates an instance of class `SimpleTime` and invokes its constructor. Line 10 invokes the object's `BuildString` method, then displays the results.

## 10.5 Time Class Case Study: Overloaded Constructors

Next, we demonstrate a class with several **overloaded constructors** that enable objects of that class to be conveniently initialized in different ways. To overload constructors, simply provide multiple constructor declarations with different signatures.

### 10.5.1 Class Time2 with Overloaded Constructors

By default, the properties `Hour`, `Minute` and `Second` of class `Time1` (Fig. 10.1) are initialized to their default values of `0`—midnight in universal time. Class `Time1` doesn't enable the class's clients to initialize the time with specific nonzero values, because it does not define such a constructor. Class `Time2` (Fig. 10.5) contains overloaded constructors. In this app, one constructor invokes the other, which in turn calls `SetTime` to set the `private` instance variables `hour`, `minute` and `second` via the class's `Hour`, `Minute` and `Second` properties, which perform validation. The compiler invokes the appropriate `Time2` constructor by matching the number and types of the arguments specified in the constructor call with the number and types of the parameters specified in each constructor declaration.

```
// Fig. 10.5: Time2.cs
// Time2 class declaration with overloaded constructors.
using System; // for class ArgumentOutOfRangeException

public class Time2
{
   private int hour; // 0 - 23
   private int minute; // 0 - 59
   private int second; // 0 - 59
```

**Fig. 10.5** | Time2 class declaration with overloaded constructors. (Part 1 of 3.)

```

   // constructor can be called with zero, one, two or three arguments
   public Time2(int hour = 0, int minute = 0, int second = 0)
   {
      SetTime(hour, minute, second); // invoke SetTime to validate time
   }

   // Time2 constructor: another Time2 object supplied as an argument
   public Time2(Time2 time)
      : this(time.Hour, time.Minute, time.Second) { }

   // set a new time value using universal time; invalid values
   // cause the properties' set accessors to throw exceptions
   public void SetTime(int hour, int minute, int second)
   {
      Hour = hour; // set the Hour property
      Minute = minute; // set the Minute property
      Second = second; // set the Second property
   }

   // property that gets and sets the hour
   public int Hour
   {
      get
      {
         return hour;
      }
      set
      {
         if (value < 0 || value > 23)
         {
            throw new ArgumentOutOfRangeException(nameof(value),
               value, $"{nameof(Hour)} must be 0-23");
         }

         hour = value;
      }
   }

   // property that gets and sets the minute
   public int Minute
   {
      get
      {
         return minute;
      }
      set
      {
         if (value < 0 || value > 59)
         {
            throw new ArgumentOutOfRangeException(nameof(value),
               value, $"{nameof(Minute)} must be 0-59");
         }
```

**Fig. 10.5** | Time2 class declaration with overloaded constructors. (Part 2 of 3.)

```
63
64             minute = value;
65          }
66       }
67
68       // property that gets and sets the second
69       public int Second
70       {
71          get
72          {
73             return second;
74          }
75          set
76          {
77             if (value < 0 || value > 59)
78             {
79                throw new ArgumentOutOfRangeException(nameof(value),
80                   value, $"{nameof(Second)} must be 0-59");
81             }
82
83             second = value;
84          }
85       }
86
87       // convert to string in universal-time format (HH:MM:SS)
88       public string ToUniversalString() =>
89          $"{Hour:D2}:{Minute:D2}:{Second:D2}";
90
91       // convert to string in standard-time format (H:MM:SS AM or PM)
92       public override string ToString() =>
93          $"{((Hour == 0 || Hour == 12) ? 12 : Hour % 12)}:" +
94          $"{Minute:D2}:{Second:D2} {(Hour < 12 ? "AM" : "PM")}";
95    }
```

**Fig. 10.5** | Time2 class declaration with overloaded constructors. (Part 3 of 3.)

### *Class `Time2`'s Three-Argument Constructor*

Lines 12–15 declare a constructor with three *default parameters*. We did not define a constructor with an empty parameter list, so for class `Time2` the constructor at lines 12–15 is also considered to be the class's **parameterless constructor**—you can call the constructor without arguments and the compiler will provide the default values. This constructor also can be called with one argument for the hour, two for the hour and minute, or three for the hour, minute and second. This constructor calls `SetTime` to set the time.

**Common Programming Error 10.1**

*A constructor can call methods of its class. Be aware that the instance variables might not yet be initialized, because the constructor is in the process of initializing the object. Using instance variables before they have been initialized properly is a logic error.*

### *Constructor Initializers*

Lines 18–19 declare another `Time2` constructor that receives a reference to a `Time2` object. In this case, the values from the `Time2` argument are passed to the three-parameter constructor at lines 12–15 to initialize the `hour`, `minute` and `second`. In this constructor, we use `this` in a manner that's allowed *only* in the constructor's header. In line 19,

```
    : this(time.Hour, time.Minute, time.Second) { }
```

`: this` followed by parentheses containing arguments indicates a call to one of the class's other constructors—in this case, the `Time2` constructor that takes three `int` arguments (lines 12–15). Line 19 passes the values of the `time` argument's `Hour`, `Minute` and `Second` properties to initialize the `Time2` object being constructed. Any initialization code in the body of the constructor at lines 18–19 would execute *after* the other constructor is called.

Using `this` as in line 19 is called a **constructor initializer**. It enables a class to reuse initialization code provided by a constructor, rather than defining similar code in another constructor. If we needed to change how objects of class `Time2` are initialized, only the constructor at lines 12–15 would need to be modified. Even that constructor might not need modification—it simply calls the `SetTime` method to perform the actual initialization, so it's possible that the changes the class might require would be localized to `SetTime`.

**Software Engineering Observation 10.5**

*Constructor initializers make classes easier to maintain, modify and debug, because the common initialization code can be defined in one constructor and called by others.*

Line 19 could have directly accessed instance variables `hour`, `minute` and `second` of the constructor's `time` argument with the expressions `time.hour`, `time.minute` and `time.second`—even though they're declared as `private` variables of class `Time2`.

**Software Engineering Observation 10.6**

*When executing a method of a class, if that method has a reference to another object of the same class (typically received via a parameter), the method can access* all *of that other object's data and methods (including those that are* `private`*).*

### `SetTime` *Method and the* `Hour`, `Minute` *and* `Second` *Properties*

Method `SetTime` (lines 23–28) invokes the `set` accessors of the properties `Hour` (lines 31–47), `Minute` (lines 50–66) and `Second` (lines 69–85), which ensure that the hour is in the range 0 to 23 and that the values for the minute and second are each in the range 0 to 59. If a value is out of range, each `set` accessor throws an `ArgumentOutOfRangeException` (lines 41–42, 60–61 and 79–80). In this example, we use the exception class's overloaded constructor that receives three arguments:

- the `string` name of the item that was out of range
- the value that was supplied for that item and
- a `string` error message.

It's common to include in an exception's error message a variable's or property's identifier. This information can help a client-code programmer understand the context in which the exception occurred. Prior to C# 6, you had to hard code these identifiers into your error-message `string`s. As of C# 6, you can instead use the **`nameof`** operator (lines 41–42, 60–61 and 79–80), which returns a `string` representation of the identifier enclosed in parentheses. For example, the expression

```
    nameof(value)
```

in line 41 returns the `string` `"value"` and the expression

```
nameof(Hour)
```

in line 42 returns the `string` `"Hour"`.

**Good Programming Practice 10.1**

*When you need to include an identifier in a* `string` *literal, use the* `nameof` *operator rather than hard coding the identifier's name in the* `string`*. If you right click an identifier in Visual Studio then use the* **Rename...** *option to change the identifier's name throughout your code, the* `string` *that* `nameof` *returns will be updated automatically with the identifier's new name.*

### *Notes Regarding Class `Time2`'s Methods, Properties and Constructors*

`Time2`'s properties are accessed throughout the class's body—`SetTime` assigns values to `Hour`, `Minute` and `Second` in lines 25–27, and `ToUniversalString` and `ToString` use properties `Hour`, `Minute` and `Second` in line 89 and lines 93–94, respectively. These methods could access the class's `private` data directly. However, consider changing the time's representation from three `int` values (requiring 12 bytes of memory) to one `int` value representing the total number of elapsed seconds since midnight (requiring only four bytes of memory). If we make this change, only code that accesses the `private` data *directly* would need to change—for class `Time2`, the bodies of properties `Hour`, `Minute` and `Second`. There would be no need to modify `SetTime`, `ToUniversalString` or `ToString`, because they access the `private` data *indirectly* through `Hour`, `Minute` and `Second`. Designing a class in this manner reduces the likelihood of programming errors when altering the class's implementation.

Similarly, each constructor could include a copy of the appropriate statements from method `SetTime`. Doing so may be slightly more efficient, because the extra constructor call and the call to `SetTime` are eliminated. However, duplicating statements in multiple methods or constructors makes changing the class's internal data representation more difficult and error-prone. Having one constructor call the other or even call `SetTime` directly allows any changes to `SetTime`'s implementation to be made only once.

**Software Engineering Observation 10.7**

*When implementing a method of a class, using the class's properties to access the class's* `private` *data simplifies code maintenance and reduces the likelihood of errors.*

## 10.5.2 Using Class `Time2`'s Overloaded Constructors

Class `Time2Test` (Fig. 10.6) creates six `Time2` objects (lines 9–13 and 41) to invoke the overloaded `Time2` constructors.

```
1  // Fig. 10.6: Time2Test.cs
2  // Overloaded constructors used to initialize Time2 objects.
3  using System;
4
5  public class Time2Test
6  {
```

**Fig. 10.6** | Overloaded constructors used to initialize `Time2` objects. (Part 1 of 3.)

```
    static void Main()
    {
        var t1 = new Time2(); // 00:00:00
        var t2 = new Time2(2); // 02:00:00
        var t3 = new Time2(21, 34); // 21:34:00
        var t4 = new Time2(12, 25, 42); // 12:25:42
        var t5 = new Time2(t4); // 12:25:42

        Console.WriteLine("Constructed with:\n");
        Console.WriteLine("t1: all arguments defaulted");
        Console.WriteLine($"   {t1.ToUniversalString()}"); // 00:00:00
        Console.WriteLine($"   {t1.ToString()}\n"); // 12:00:00 AM

        Console.WriteLine(
            "t2: hour specified; minute and second defaulted");
        Console.WriteLine($"   {t2.ToUniversalString()}"); // 02:00:00
        Console.WriteLine($"   {t2.ToString()}\n"); // 2:00:00 AM

        Console.WriteLine(
            "t3: hour and minute specified; second defaulted");
        Console.WriteLine($"   {t3.ToUniversalString()}"); // 21:34:00
        Console.WriteLine($"   {t3.ToString()}\n"); // 9:34:00 PM

        Console.WriteLine("t4: hour, minute and second specified");
        Console.WriteLine($"   {t4.ToUniversalString()}"); // 12:25:42
        Console.WriteLine($"   {t4.ToString()}\n"); // 12:25:42 PM

        Console.WriteLine("t5: Time2 object t4 specified");
        Console.WriteLine($"   {t5.ToUniversalString()}"); // 12:25:42
        Console.WriteLine($"   {t5.ToString()}"); // 12:25:42 PM

        // attempt to initialize t6 with invalid values
        try
        {
            var t6 = new Time2(27, 74, 99); // invalid values
        }
        catch (ArgumentOutOfRangeException ex)
        {
            Console.WriteLine("\nException while initializing t6:");
            Console.WriteLine(ex.Message);
        }
    }
}
```

```
Constructed with:

t1: all arguments defaulted
   00:00:00
   12:00:00 AM

t2: hour specified; minute and second defaulted
   02:00:00
   2:00:00 AM
```

**Fig. 10.6** | Overloaded constructors used to initialize `Time2` objects. (Part 2 of 3.)

```
t3: hour and minute specified; second defaulted
   21:34:00
   9:34:00 PM

t4: hour, minute and second specified
   12:25:42
   12:25:42 PM

t5: Time2 object t4 specified
   12:25:42
   12:25:42 PM

Exception while initializing t6:
Hour must be 0-23
Parameter name: value
Actual value was 27.
```

**Fig. 10.6** | Overloaded constructors used to initialize `Time2` objects. (Part 3 of 3.)

Lines 9–13 demonstrate passing arguments to the `Time2` constructors. C# invokes the appropriate overloaded constructor by matching the number and types of the arguments in the constructor call with the number and types of the parameters in each constructor declaration. Lines 9–12 each invoke the constructor at lines 12–15 of Fig. 10.5:

- Line 9 of Fig. 10.6 invokes the constructor with no arguments—the compiler supplies the default value `0` for each of the three parameters.
- Line 10 invokes the constructor with one argument that represents the hour—the compiler supplies the default value `0` for the minute and second.
- Line 11 invokes the constructor with two arguments that represent the hour and minute—the compiler supplies the default value `0` for the second.
- Line 12 invoke the constructor with values for the hour, minute and second.

Line 13 invokes the constructor at lines 18–19 of Fig. 10.5. Lines 15–36 (Fig. 10.6) display the `string` representation of each initialized `Time2` object to confirm that each was initialized properly.

Line 41 attempts to initialize `t6` by creating a new `Time2` object and passing three invalid values to the constructor. When the constructor attempts to use the invalid hour value to initialize the `Hour` property, an `ArgumentOutOfRangeException` occurs. We catch this exception at line 43 and display its `Message` property, which results in the last three lines of the output in Fig. 10.6. Because we used the three-argument `ArgumentOutOfRangeException` constructor when the exception object was created, the exception's `Message` property also includes the *information about the out-of-range value.*

## 10.6 Default and Parameterless Constructors

Every class *must* have at least one constructor—if you do not provide any constructors in a class's declaration, the compiler creates a *default constructor* that takes no arguments when it's invoked. In Section 11.4.1, you'll learn that the default constructor implicitly performs a special task.

The compiler will *not* create a default constructor for a class that *explicitly* declares at least one constructor. In this case, if you want to be able to invoke the constructor with no arguments, you must declare a *parameterless constructor*—that is, one that's declared with no parameters *or* one in which all the parameters have default values (e.g., line 12 of Fig. 10.5). Like a default constructor, a parameterless constructor is invoked with *empty parentheses*. If you call class `Time2`'s three-argument constructor with no arguments, the compiler explicitly passes `0` to each parameter. If we omit from class `Time2` a constructor that can be called with no arguments, clients of this class would not be able to create a `Time2` object with the expression `new Time2()`. If a class provides both a parameterless constructor *and* a constructor with a default arguments for all of its parameters, the compiler will use the parameterless constructor when you pass no arguments to the constructor.

## 10.7 Composition

A class can have objects of values types or references to objects of other classes as members. This is called **composition** and is sometimes referred to as a ***has-a* relationship**. For example, an object of class `AlarmClock` needs to know the current time *and* the time when it's supposed to sound its alarm, so it's reasonable to include *two* references to `Time` objects in an `AlarmClock` object.

**Software Engineering Observation 10.8**

*One form of software reuse is composition, in which a class contains references to other objects. Recall that classes are reference types. A class can have a property of its own type—for example, a `Person` class could have `Mother` and `Father` properties of type `Person` that reference other `Person` objects.*

### 10.7.1 Class Date

Our example of composition contains three classes—`Date` (Fig. 10.7), `Employee` (Fig. 10.8) and `EmployeeTest` (Fig. 10.9). Class `Date` (Fig. 10.7) declares `int` instance variables `month` and `day` (lines 7–8) and *auto-implemented property* `Year` (line 9) to represent a date.

```
1  // Fig. 10.7: Date.cs
2  // Date class declaration.
3  using System;
4
5  public class Date
6  {
7     private int month; // 1-12
8     private int day; // 1-31 based on month
9     public int Year { get; private set; } // auto-implemented property Year
10
11    // constructor: use property Month to confirm proper value for month;
12    // use property Day to confirm proper value for day
13    public Date(int month, int day, int year)
14    {
15       Month = month; // validates month
```

**Fig. 10.7** | `Date` class declaration. (Part 1 of 3.)

```
      Year = year; // could validate year
      Day = day; // validates day
      Console.WriteLine($"Date object constructor for date {this}");
   }

   // property that gets and sets the month
   public int Month
   {
      get
      {
         return month;
      }
      private set // make writing inaccessible outside the class
      {
         if (value <= 0 || value > 12) // validate month
         {
            throw new ArgumentOutOfRangeException(
               nameof(value), value, $"{nameof(Month)} must be 1-12");
         }

         month = value;
      }
   }

   // property that gets and sets the day
   public int Day
   {
      get
      {
         return day;
      }
      private set // make writing inaccessible outside the class
      {
         int[] daysPerMonth =
            {0, 31, 29, 31, 30, 31, 30, 31, 31, 30, 31, 30, 31};

         // check if day in range for month
         if (value <= 0 || value > daysPerMonth[Month])
         {
            throw new ArgumentOutOfRangeException(nameof(value), value,
               $"{nameof(Day)} out of range for current month/year");
         }
         // check for leap year
         if (Month == 2 && value == 29 &&
            !(Year % 400 == 0 || (Year % 4 == 0 && Year % 100 != 0)))
         {
            throw new ArgumentOutOfRangeException(nameof(value), value,
               $"{nameof(Day)} out of range for current month/year");
         }

         day = value;
      }
   }
```

**Fig. 10.7** | Date class declaration. (Part 2 of 3.)

```
69
70      // return a string of the form month/day/year
71      public override string ToString() => $"{Month}/{Day}/{Year}";
72   }
```

**Fig. 10.7** | Date class declaration. (Part 3 of 3.)

*Constructor*

The constructor (lines 13–19) receives three `int`s. Line 15 invokes property `Month`'s `set` accessor (lines 28–37) to validate the month—if the value is out-of-range the accessor throws an exception. Line 16 uses property `Year` to set the year. Since `Year` is an auto-implemented property, it provides no validation—we're assuming in this example that `Year`'s value is correct. Line 17 uses property `Day`'s `set` accessor (lines 47–67) to validate and assign the value for `day` based on the current `Month` and `Year` (by using properties `Month` and `Year` in turn to obtain the values of `month` and `Year`).

The *order of initialization is important*, because property `Day`'s `set` accessor performs its validation assuming that `Month` and `Year` are correct. Line 53 determines whether the day is out of range, based on the number of days in the `Month` and, if so, throw an exception. Lines 59–60 determine whether the `Month` is February, the day is `29` and the `Year` is *not* a leap year (in which case, `29` is out of range) and, if so, throw an exception. If no exceptions are thrown, the value for `day` is correct and assigned to the instance variable at line 66. Line 18 in the constructor formats the `this` reference as a `string`. Since `this` is a reference to the current `Date` object, the object's `ToString` method (line 71) is called *implicitly* to obtain the `Date`'s `string` representation.

***private set** Accessors*

Class `Date` uses access modifiers to ensure that *clients* of the class must use the appropriate methods and properties to access `private` data. In particular, the properties `Year`, `Month` and `Day` declare `private set` accessors (lines 9, 28 and 47, respectively)—these `set` accessors can be used only within the class. We declare these `private` for the same reasons that we declare instance variables `private`—to simplify code maintenance and control access to the class's data. Although the constructor, method and properties in class `Date` still have all the advantages of using the `set` accessors to perform validation, clients of the class must use the class's constructor to initialize the data in a `Date` object. The `get` accessors of `Year`, `Month` and `Day` are *implicitly* `public`—when there's no access modifier before a `get` or `set` accessor, the property's access modifier is used.

## 10.7.2 Class Employee

Class `Employee` (Fig. 10.8) has `public` auto-implemented, getter-only properties `FirstName`, `LastName`, `BirthDate` and `HireDate`. `BirthDate` and `HireDate` (lines 7–8) refer to `Date` objects, demonstrating that *a class can have references to objects of other classes as members*. This, of course, also is true of `FirstName` and `LastName`, which refer to `String` objects. The `Employee` constructor (lines 11–18) uses its four parameters to initialize the class's properties. When class `Employee`'s `ToString` method is called, it returns a `string` containing the `string` representations of the two `Date` objects. Each of these `string`s is obtained with an *implicit* call to the `Date` class's `ToString` method.

```
// Fig. 10.8: Employee.cs
// Employee class with references to other objects.
public class Employee
{
   public string FirstName { get; }
   public string LastName { get; }
   public Date BirthDate { get; }
   public Date HireDate { get; }

   // constructor to initialize name, birth date and hire date
   public Employee(string firstName, string lastName,
      Date birthDate, Date hireDate)
   {
      FirstName = firstName;
      LastName = lastName;
      BirthDate = birthDate;
      HireDate = hireDate;
   }

   // convert Employee to string format
   public override string ToString() => $"{LastName}, {FirstName} " +
      $"Hired: {HireDate}  Birthday: {BirthDate}";
}
```

**Fig. 10.8** | Employee class with references to other objects.

### 10.7.3 Class EmployeeTest

Class EmployeeTest (Fig. 10.9) creates two Date objects (lines 9–10) to represent an Employee's birthday and hire date, respectively. Line 11 creates an Employee and initializes its instance variables by passing to the constructor two strings (representing the Employee's first and last names) and two Date objects (representing the birthday and hire date). Line 13 *implicitly* invokes the Employee's ToString method to display the Employee's string representation and demonstrate that the object was initialized properly.

```
1  // Fig. 10.9: EmployeeTest.cs
2  // Composition demonstration.
3  using System;
4
5  class EmployeeTest
6  {
7     static void Main()
8     {
9        var birthday = new Date(7, 24, 1949);
10       var hireDate = new Date(3, 12, 1988);
11       var employee = new Employee("Bob", "Blue", birthday, hireDate);
12
13       Console.WriteLine(employee);
14    }
15 }
```

**Fig. 10.9** | Composition demonstration. (Part 1 of 2.)

```
Date object constructor for date 7/24/1949
Date object constructor for date 3/12/1988
Blue, Bob  Hired: 3/12/1988  Birthday: 7/24/1949
```

**Fig. 10.9** | Composition demonstration. (Part 2 of 2.)

## 10.8 Garbage Collection and Destructors

Every object you create uses various system resources, such as memory. In many programming languages, these system resources are reserved for the object's use until they're explicitly released by the programmer. If all the references to the object that manages a resource are lost before the resource is explicitly released, the app can no longer access the resource to release it. This is known as a **resource leak**.

To avoid resource leaks, we need a disciplined way to give resources back to the system when they're no longer needed. The Common Language Runtime (CLR) performs automatic memory management by using a **garbage collector** that *reclaims* the memory occupied by objects no longer in use, so the memory can be used for other objects. When there are no more references to an object, the object becomes **eligible for destruction**. Every object has a special member, called a **destructor**, that's invoked by the garbage collector to perform **termination housekeeping** on an object before the garbage collector reclaims the object's memory. A destructor is declared like a parameterless constructor, except that its name is the class name, preceded by a tilde (~), and it has no access modifier in its header. After the garbage collector calls the object's destructor, the object becomes **eligible for garbage collection**. The memory for such an object can be reclaimed by the garbage collector.

**Memory leaks**, which are common in other languages such as C and C++ (because memory is *not* automatically reclaimed in those languages), are less likely in C#, but some can still happen in subtle ways. Other types of resource leaks can occur. For example, an app could open a file on disk to modify its contents. If the app does not close the file, no other app can modify (or possibly even use) the file until the app that opened it terminates.

A problem with the garbage collector is it doesn't guarantee that it will perform its tasks at a specified time. Therefore, the garbage collector may call the destructor any time after the object becomes eligible for destruction, and may reclaim the memory any time after the destructor executes. In fact, it's possible that neither will happen before the app terminates. Thus, it's unclear whether, or when, the destructor will be called. For this reason, destructors are rarely used.

**Software Engineering Observation 10.9**

*A class that uses resources, such as files on disk, should provide a method to eventually release the resources. Many Framework Class Library classes provide* `Close` *or* `Dispose` *methods for this purpose. Section 13.6 introduces the* `Dispose` *method, which is then used in many later examples.* `Close` *methods are typically used with objects that are associated with files (Chapter 17) and other types of so-called streams of data.*

## 10.9 `static` Class Members

Every object has its *own* copy of its class's instance variables. In certain cases, only one copy of a particular variable should be *shared* by all objects of a class. A **`static` variable** (or property) is used in such cases. A `static` variable or property represents **classwide information**—all objects of the class share the same piece of data. The declaration of a `static` variable or property begins with the keyword `static`.

Let's motivate `static` data with an example. Suppose that we have a video game with `Martian`s and other space creatures. Each `Martian` tends to be brave and willing to attack other space creatures when it's aware that there are at least four other `Martian`s present. If fewer than five `Martian`s are present, each `Martian` becomes cowardly. Thus each `Martian` needs to know the `martianCount`. We could endow class `Martian` with `martianCount` as an instance variable (or as a property, but we'll use an instance variable for discussion purposes here). If we do this, every `Martian` will have a separate copy of the instance variable, and every time we create a new `Martian`, we'll have to update the instance variable `martianCount` in every `Martian`. This wastes space on redundant copies, wastes time updating the separate copies and is error prone. Instead, we declare `martianCount` to be `static`, making `martianCount` classwide data. Every `Martian` can access the `martianCount`, but only one copy of the `static` `martianCount` is maintained. This saves space. We save time by having the `Martian` constructor increment the `static` `martianCount`—there's *only one copy*, so we do not have to increment separate copies of `martianCount` for each `Martian` object.

**Software Engineering Observation 10.10**

*Use a `static` variable when all objects of a class must share the same copy of the variable.*

### `static` *Variable Scope*

The scope of a `static` variable is the body of its class. A class's `public static` members can be accessed by qualifying the member name with the class name and the member access (`.`) operator, as in `Math.PI`. A class's `private static` class members can be accessed *only* through the class's methods and properties. To access a `private static` member from outside its class, a `public static` method or property can be provided.

**Common Programming Error 10.2**

*It's a compilation error to access or invoke a `static` member by referencing it through an instance of the class, like a non-`static` member.*

**Software Engineering Observation 10.11**

*`static` variables, methods and properties exist, and can be used, even if no objects of that class have been instantiated. `static` members are available as soon as the class is loaded into memory at execution time.*

### `static` *Methods and Non-*`static` *Class Members*

A `static` method (or property) cannot access non-`static` class members directly, because a `static` method (or property) can be called even when *no* objects of the class exist. For the same reason, `this` cannot be used in a `static` method—the `this` reference always refers to a *specific object* of the class. When a `static` method is called, it does not know which object to manipulate and there might *not* be *any* objects of its class in memory.

### *Class* `Employee`

Our next app contains classes `Employee` (Fig. 10.10) and `EmployeeTest` (Fig. 10.11). Class `Employee` declares `private static` auto-implemented property `Count` to maintain a count of the number of `Employee` objects that have been created. We declare `Count`'s `set` accessor `private`, because only class `Employee` should be able to modify `Count`'s value. `Count` is a `static` auto-implemented property, so the compiler creates a corresponding `private` `static` variable that `Count` manages. When you declare a `static` variable and do not initialize it, the compiler initializes it to the type's default value (in this case, `0`).

When `Employee` objects exist, `Count` can be used in any method or property of class `Employee`—this example increments `Count` in the constructor (line 19). Client code can access the `Count` with the expression `Employee.Count`, which evaluates to the number of `Employee` objects that have been created.

```
1  // Fig. 10.10: Employee.cs
2  // static property used to maintain a count of the number of
3  // Employee objects that have been created.
4  using System;
5
6  public class Employee
7  {
8     public static int Count { get; private set; } // objects in memory
9
10    public string FirstName { get; }
11    public string LastName { get; }
12
13    // initialize employee, add 1 to static Count and
14    // output string indicating that constructor was called
15    public Employee(string firstName, string lastName)
16    {
17       FirstName = firstName;
18       LastName = lastName;
19       ++Count; // increment static count of employees
20       Console.WriteLine("Employee constructor: " +
21          $"{FirstName} {LastName}; Count = {Count}");
22    }
23 }
```

**Fig. 10.10** | `static` property used to maintain a count of the number of `Employee` objects that have been created.

### *Class* `EmployeeTest`

`EmployeeTest` method `Main` (Fig. 10.11) instantiates two `Employee` objects (lines 14–15). When each object's constructor is invoked, lines 17–18 of Fig. 10.10 assign the `Employee`'s first name and last name to properties `FirstName` and `LastName`. These two statements do *not* make copies of the original `string` arguments.

**Software Engineering Observation 10.12**

*Actually,* `string` *objects in C# are* ***immutable****—they cannot be modified after they're created. Therefore, it's safe to have many references to one* `string`*. This is not normally the case for objects of most other classes. If* `string` *objects are immutable, you might wonder why we're able to use operators + and += to concatenate* `strings`*. String-concatenation operations actually result in a* new `string` *object containing the concatenated values. The original string objects are not modified.*

```
1  // Fig. 10.11: EmployeeTest.cs
2  // static member demonstration.
3  using System;
4
5  class EmployeeTest
6  {
7     static void Main()
8     {
9        // show that Count is 0 before creating Employees
10       Console.WriteLine(
11          $"Employees before instantiation: {Employee.Count}");
12
13       // create two Employees; Count should become 2
14       var e1 = new Employee("Susan", "Baker");
15       var e2 = new Employee("Bob", "Blue");
16
17       // show that Count is 2 after creating two Employees
18       Console.WriteLine(
19          $"\nEmployees after instantiation: {Employee.Count}");
20
21       // get names of Employees
22       Console.WriteLine($"\nEmployee 1: {e1.FirstName} {e1.LastName}");
23       Console.WriteLine($"Employee 2: {e2.FirstName} {e2.LastName}");
24
25       // in this example, there is only one reference to each Employee,
26       // so the following statements cause the CLR to mark each
27       // Employee object as being eligible for garbage collection
28       e1 = null; // mark object referenced by e1 as no longer needed
29       e2 = null; // mark object referenced by e2 as no longer needed
30    }
31 }
```

```
Employees before instantiation: 0
Employee constructor: Susan Baker; Count = 1
Employee constructor: Bob Blue; Count = 2

Employees after instantiation: 2

Employee 1: Susan Baker
Employee 2: Bob Blue
```

**Fig. 10.11** | static member demonstration.

Lines 18–19 of Fig. 10.11 display the updated Count. When Main has finished using the two Employee objects, references e1 and e2 are set to null at lines 28–29, so they no longer refer to the objects that were instantiated in lines 14–15. The objects become *eligible for destruction* because there are *no more references to them*. After the objects' destructors are called, the objects become *eligible* for garbage collection. (Note that we did not need to set e1 and e2 are set to null here as they're local variables—when a local variable of a reference type goes out of scope, the object's reference count is decremented automatically.)

Eventually, the garbage collector might reclaim the memory for these objects (or the operating system will reclaim it when the app terminates). C# does not guarantee when, or even whether, the garbage collector will execute. When the garbage collector does run, it's possible that no objects or only a subset of the eligible objects will be collected.

## 10.10 readonly Instance Variables

The **principle of least privilege** is fundamental to good software engineering. In the context of an app, the principle states that *code should be granted the amount of privilege and access needed to accomplish its designated task, but no more.* Let's see how this principle applies to instance variables.

Some instance variables need to be modifiable, and some do not. In Section 8.4, we used keyword `const` to declare a constant, which must be initialized in its declaration—all objects of the class have the same value for that constant. Suppose, however, we want a constant that can have a *different* value for each object of a class. For this purpose, C# provides keyword **`readonly`** to specify that an instance variable of an object is *not* modifiable and that any attempt to modify it *after* the object is constructed is an error. For example,

```
private readonly int Increment;
```

declares `readonly` instance variable `Increment` of type `int`. Like a constant, a `readonly` variable's identifier uses Pascal Case by convention. Although `readonly` instance variables can be initialized when they're declared, this isn't required. A `readonly` variable should be initialized *by each* of the class's constructors or in the variable's declaration. Each constructor can assign values to a `readonly` instance variable multiple times—the variable doesn't become unmodifiable until *after* the constructor completes execution. If a constructor does not initialize the `readonly` variable, the variable uses the same default value as any other instance variable (`0` for numeric simple types, `false` for `bool` type and `null` for reference types)—these values actually are set before a constructor executes and can be overwritten by the called constructor.

**Software Engineering Observation 10.13**

*Declaring an instance variable as `readonly` helps enforce the principle of least privilege. If an instance variable should not be modified after the object is constructed, declare it to be `readonly` to prevent modification.*

`const` members must be assigned values at compile time. Therefore, `const` members can be initialized *only* with other constant values, such as integers, `string` literals, characters and other `const` members. Constant members with values that cannot be determined at compile time—such as constants that are initialized with the result of a method call—must be declared with keyword `readonly`, so they can be initialized at *execution time*. Variables that are `readonly` can be initialized with more complex expressions, such as an array initializer or a method call that returns a value or a reference to an object.

**Common Programming Error 10.3**

*Attempting to modify a `readonly` instance variable anywhere but in its declaration or the object's constructors is a compilation error.*

**Error-Prevention Tip 10.1**

*Attempts to modify a `readonly` instance variable are caught at compilation time rather than causing execution-time errors. It's always preferable to get bugs out at compile time, if possible, rather than allowing them to slip through to execution time (where studies have found that repairing bugs is often much more costly).*

**Software Engineering Observation 10.14**

*If a* `readonly` *instance variable is initialized to a constant only in its declaration, it's not necessary to have a separate copy of the instance variable for every object of the class. The variable should be declared* `const` *instead. Constants declared with* `const` *are implicitly* `static`*, so there will only be one copy for the entire class.*

6 *C# 6 Getter-Only Auto-Implemented Properties and* **`readonly`**

Section 8.6.1 introduced C# 6's getter-only auto-implemented properties. When an auto-implemented property has only a `get` accessor, the property can be used only to read the value, so the compiler implicitly declares the corresponding `private` instance variable as `readonly`. Getter-only auto-implemented properties can be initialized in their declarations or in constructors.

## 10.11 Class View and Object Browser

Now that we have introduced key concepts of object-oriented programming, we present two Visual Studio features that facilitate the design of object-oriented apps—the **Class View** and the **Object Browser**.

### 10.11.1 Using the Class View Window

The **Class View** displays the fields, methods and properties for all classes in a project. Select **View > Class View** to display the **Class View** as a tab in the same position within the IDE as the **Solution Explorer**. Figure 10.12 shows the **Class View** for the `Time1` project of Fig. 10.1 (class `Time1`) and Fig. 10.2 (class `Time1Test`).

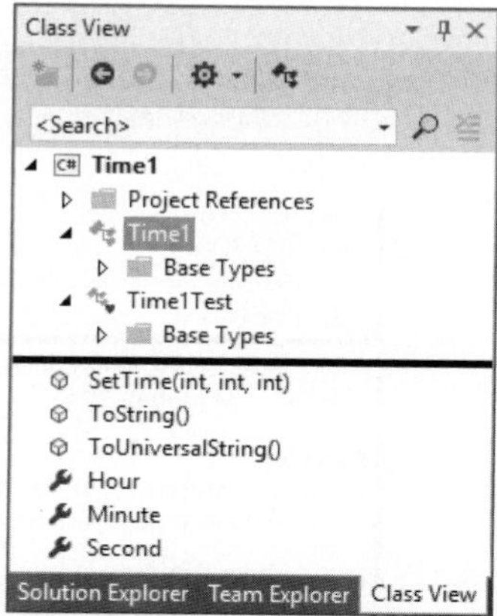


**Fig. 10.12** | **Class View** of class `Time1` (Fig. 10.1) and class `Time1Test` (Fig. 10.2).

The view follows a hierarchical structure, positioning the project name (`Time1`) as the *root* and including a series of nodes that represent the classes, variables, methods and properties in the project. If a

▷

appears to the left of a node, that node can be *expanded* to show other nodes. If a

appears to the left of a node, that node can be *collapsed*. According to the **Class View**, project `Time1` contains class `Time1` and class `Time1Test` as children. When class `Time1` is selected, the class's members appear in the lower half of the window. Class `Time1` contains methods `SetTime`, `ToString` and `ToUniversalString`, indicated by purple boxes

and `public` properties `Hour`, `Minute` and `Second`, indicated by wrench icons

If a class has any `private` members, those members' icons contain small padlocks. Both class `Time1` and class `Time1Test` contain the **Base Types** node. If you expand this node, you'll see class `Object` in each case, because each class *inherits* from class `System.Object`—we discuss this concept in Chapter 11.

### 10.11.2 Using the Object Browser

Visual Studio's **Object Browser** lists all classes in the .NET library. You can use the **Object Browser** to learn about the functionality provided by a specific class. To open the **Object Browser**, select **View > Object Browser**. Figure 10.13 depicts the **Object Browser** when the user navigates to the `Math` class in namespace `System`. To do this, we expanded the node for `mscorlib` (Microsoft Core Library) in the upper-left pane of the **Object Browser**, then expanded its subnode for `System`. The most common classes from the `System` namespace, such as `System.Math`, are in `mscorlib`.

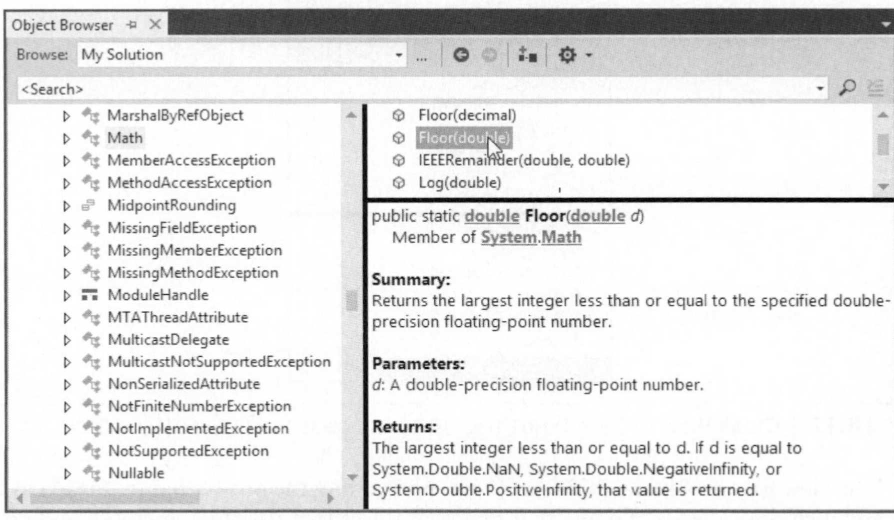


**Fig. 10.13** | **Object Browser** for class `Math`.

The **Object Browser** lists all methods provided by class `Math` in the upper-right pane—this offers you "instant access" to information regarding the functionality of various objects. Clicking the name of a member in the upper-right pane displays a description of that member in the lower-right pane. The **Object Browser** can be used to quickly learn about a class or one of its methods. You also can view the complete description of a class or a method in the online documentation by selecting the type or member in the **Object Browser** and pressing *F1*.

## 10.12 Object Initializers

**Object initializers** allow you to create an object and initialize its `public` properties (and `public` instance variables, if any) in the same statement. This can be useful when a class does not provide an appropriate constructor to meet your needs, but does provide a constructor that can be called with no arguments and properties that you can use to set the class's data. The following statements demonstrate object initializers using the class `Time2` from Fig. 10.5.

```
// create a Time2 object and initialize its properties
var aTime = new Time2 {Hour = 14, Minute = 30, Second = 12};

// create a Time2 object and initialize only its Minute property
var anotherTime = new Time2 {Minute = 45};
```

The first statement creates a `Time2` object (`aTime`), initializes it with class `Time2`'s constructor that can be called with no arguments, then uses an object initializer to set its `Hour`, `Minute` and `Second` properties. Notice that `new Time2` is immediately followed by an **object-initializer list**—a comma-separated list in curly braces (`{ }`) of properties and their values. Each property name can appear only *once* in the object-initializer list. The object initializer executes the property initializers in the order in which they appear.

The second statement creates a new `Time2` object (`anotherTime`), initializes it with class `Time2`'s constructor that can be called with no arguments, then sets only its `Minute` property using an object initializer. When the `Time2` constructor is called with no arguments, it initializes the time to midnight. The object initializer then sets each specified property to the supplied value. In this case, the `Minute` property is set to `45`. The `Hour` and `Second` properties retain their default values, because no values are specified for them in the object initializer.

## 10.13 Operator Overloading; Introducing `struct`

Method-call notation can be cumbersome for certain kinds of operations, such as arithmetic. In these cases, it would be convenient to use C#'s rich set of built-in operators instead. This section shows how to create operators that work with objects of your own types—via a process called **operator overloading**.

You can overload most operators. Some are overloaded more frequently than others, especially the arithmetic operators, such as `+` and `-`, where operator notation is more natural than calling methods. For a list of overloadable operators, see

```
https://msdn.microsoft.com/library/8edha89s
```

### 10.13.1 Creating Value Types with `struct`

To demonstrate operator overloading, we'll define type `ComplexNumber` (Section 10.13.2). Complex numbers have the form

```
realPart + imaginaryPart * i
```

where `i` is $\sqrt{-1}$. Like integers and floating-point numbers, complex numbers are arithmetic types that are commonly used in calculations. As you know, C#'s simple numeric types are *value types*. To mimic the simple numeric types, we'll define `ComplexNumber` as a value type by using a **`struct`** (short for "structure") rather than a `class`. C#'s simple types like `int` and `double` are actually aliases for `struct` types—an `int` is defined by the `struct System.Int32`, a `long` by `System.Int64`, a `double` by `System.Double` and so on. The operator overloading techniques shown in Section 10.13.2 also can be applied to classes.

#### *When to Declare a `struct` Type*

Microsoft recommends using classes for most new types, but recommends a `struct` if:

- the type represents a single value—a complex number represents one number that happens to have a real part and an imaginary part.
- the size of an object is 16 bytes or smaller—we'll represent a complex number's real and imaginary parts using two `double`s (a total of 16 bytes).

For the complete list of `struct` recommendations, see

```
https://msdn.microsoft.com/library/ms229017
```

### 10.13.2 Value Type `ComplexNumber`

Value type `ComplexNumber` (Fig. 10.14) overloads the plus (+), minus (-) and multiplication (*) operators to enable programs to add, subtract and multiply instances of class `ComplexNumber` using common mathematical notation. Lines 9–10 define getter-only auto-implemented properties for the `ComplexNumber`'s `Real` and `Imaginary` components.

```
1  // Fig. 10.14: ComplexNumber.cs
2  // Value type that overloads operators for adding, subtracting
3  // and multiplying complex numbers.
4  using System;
5
6  public struct ComplexNumber
7  {
8     // read-only properties that get the real and imaginary components
9     public double Real { get; }
10    public double Imaginary { get; }
11
12    // constructor
13    public ComplexNumber(double real, double imaginary)
14    {
```

**Fig. 10.14** | Value type that overloads operators for adding, subtracting and multiplying complex numbers. (Part 1 of 2.)

```
15          Real = real;
16          Imaginary = imaginary;
17       }
18
19       // return string representation of ComplexNumber
20       public override string ToString() =>
21          $"({Real} {(Imaginary < 0 ? "-" : "+")} {Math.Abs(Imaginary)}i)";
22
23       // overload the addition operator
24       public static ComplexNumber operator+(ComplexNumber x, ComplexNumber y)
25       {
26          return new ComplexNumber(x.Real + y.Real,
27             x.Imaginary + y.Imaginary);
28       }
29
30       // overload the subtraction operator
31       public static ComplexNumber operator-(ComplexNumber x, ComplexNumber y)
32       {
33          return new ComplexNumber(x.Real - y.Real,
34             x.Imaginary - y.Imaginary );
35       }
36
37       // overload the multiplication operator
38       public static ComplexNumber operator*(ComplexNumber x, ComplexNumber y)
39       {
40          return new ComplexNumber(
41             x.Real * y.Real - x.Imaginary * y.Imaginary,
42             x.Real * y.Imaginary + y.Real * x.Imaginary);
43       }
44    }
```

**Fig. 10.14** | Value type that overloads operators for adding, subtracting and multiplying complex numbers. (Part 2 of 2.)

### *Constructor*

Lines 13–17 define a `ComplexNumber` constructor that receives parameters to initialize the `Real` and `Imaginary` properties. Unlike a `class`, you cannot define a parameterless constructor for a `struct`—the compiler always provides a default constructor that initializes the `struct`'s instance variables to their default values. Also, `struct`s cannot specify initial values in instance variable or property declarations.

### *Overloaded Operators*

Lines 24–28 overload the plus operator (+) to add `ComplexNumber`s. Keyword **`operator`**, followed by an operator symbol (such as +), indicates that a method overloads the specified operator. Overloaded operator methods are *required* to be `public` and `static`.

Methods that overload binary operators must take two arguments—the *first* is the *left* operand and the *second* is the *right* operand. Class `ComplexNumber`'s overloaded + operator takes two `ComplexNumber`s as arguments and returns a `ComplexNumber` that represents the sum of the arguments. The method's body adds the `ComplexNumber`s and returns the result as a new `ComplexNumber`.

We do *not* modify the contents of either of the original operands passed as arguments x and y. This matches our intuitive sense of how this operator should behave—adding two numbers does not modify either of the original values. Lines 31–43 declare similar overloaded operators to subtract and multiply ComplexNumbers.

**Software Engineering Observation 10.15**

*Overload operators to perform the same function or similar functions on objects as the operators perform on objects of simple types. Avoid nonintuitive use of operators.*

**Software Engineering Observation 10.16**

*At least one parameter of an overloaded operator method must be of the type in which the operator is overloaded. This prevents you from changing how operators work on simple types.*

**Software Engineering Observation 10.17**

*Though you cannot overload the arithmetic assignment operators (e.g., += and -=), C# allows you to use them with any type that declares the corresponding arithmetic operator (e.g., + and -).*

### 10.13.3 Class ComplexTest

Class ComplexTest (Fig. 10.15) demonstrates the overloaded ComplexNumber operators +, - and *. Lines 10–21 prompt the user to enter the real and imaginary parts of two complex numbers, then use this input to create two ComplexNumber objects for use in calculations.

```
1  // Fig. 10.15: ComplexTest.cs
2  // Overloading operators for complex numbers.
3  using System;
4
5  class ComplexTest
6  {
7     static void Main()
8     {
9        // prompt the user to enter the first complex number
10       Console.Write("Enter the real part of complex number x: ");
11       double realPart = double.Parse(Console.ReadLine());
12       Console.Write("Enter the imaginary part of complex number x: ");
13       double imaginaryPart = double.Parse(Console.ReadLine());
14       var x = new ComplexNumber(realPart, imaginaryPart);
15
16       // prompt the user to enter the second complex number
17       Console.Write("\nEnter the real part of complex number y: ");
18       realPart = double.Parse(Console.ReadLine());
19       Console.Write("Enter the imaginary part of complex number y: ");
20       imaginaryPart = double.Parse(Console.ReadLine());
21       var y = new ComplexNumber(realPart, imaginaryPart);
22
23       // display the results of calculations with x and y
24       Console.WriteLine();
```

**Fig. 10.15** | Overloading operators for complex numbers. (Part 1 of 2.)

```
25         Console.WriteLine($"{x} + {y} = {x + y}");
26         Console.WriteLine($"{x} - {y} = {x - y}");
27         Console.WriteLine($"{x} * {y} = {x * y}");
28     }
29 }
```

```
Enter the real part of complex number x: 2
Enter the imaginary part of complex number x: 4

Enter the real part of complex number y: 4
Enter the imaginary part of complex number y: -2

(2 + 4i) + (4 - 2i) = (6 + 2i)
(2 + 4i) - (4 - 2i) = (-2 + 6i)
(2 + 4i) * (4 - 2i) = (16 + 12i)
```

**Fig. 10.15** | Overloading operators for complex numbers. (Part 2 of 2.)

Lines 25–27 add, subtract and multiply `x` and `y` with the overloaded operators (in `string`-interpolation expressions), then output the results. In line 25, we use the `+` operator with `ComplexNumber` operands `x` and `y`. Without operator overloading, the expression `x + y` wouldn't make sense—the compiler wouldn't know how to add two `ComplexNumber` objects. This expression makes sense here because we've defined the `+` operator for two `ComplexNumbers` in lines 24–28 of Fig. 10.14. When the two `ComplexNumbers` are "added" in line 25 of Fig. 10.15, this invokes the `operator+` declaration, passing the left operand as the first argument and the right operand as the second argument. When we use the subtraction and multiplication operators in lines 26–27, their respective overloaded operator declarations are invoked similarly.

Each calculation's result is the new `ComplexNumber` object returned by the corresponding overloaded operator method. When this new object is placed in a `string`-interpolation expression, its `ToString` method (Fig. 10.14, lines 20–21) is implicitly invoked. The expression `x + y` in line 25 of Fig. 10.15 could be rewritten to explicitly invoke the `ToString` method of the resulting `ComplexNumber` object, as in:

```
(x + y).ToString()
```

## 10.14 Time Class Case Study: Extension Methods

You can use **extension methods** to add functionality to an existing type without modifying the type's source code. You saw in Section 9.3.3 that LINQ's capabilities are implemented as extension methods. Figure 10.16 uses extension methods to add two new methods to class `Time2` (Section 10.5)—`DisplayTime` and `AddHours`.

```
// Fig. 10.16: TimeExtensionsTest.cs
// Demonstrating extension methods.
using System;

class TimeExtensionsTest
{
```

**Fig. 10.16** | Demonstrating extension methods. (Part 1 of 2.)

```
   static void Main()
   {
      var myTime = new Time2(); // call Time2 constructor
      myTime.SetTime(11, 34, 15); // set the time to 11:34:15

      // test the DisplayTime extension method
      Console.Write("Use the DisplayTime extension method: ");
      myTime.DisplayTime();

      // test the AddHours extension method
      Console.Write("Add 5 hours with the AddHours extension method: ");
      var timeAdded = myTime.AddHours(5); // add five hours
      timeAdded.DisplayTime(); // display the new Time2 object

      // add hours and display the time in one statement
      Console.Write("Add 15 with the AddHours extension method: ");
      myTime.AddHours(15).DisplayTime(); // add hours and display time

      // use fully qualified extension-method name to display the time
      Console.Write("Use fully qualified extension-method name: ");
      TimeExtensions.DisplayTime(myTime);
   }
}

// extension-methods class
static class TimeExtensions
{
   // display the Time2 object in console
   public static void DisplayTime(this Time2 aTime)
   {
      Console.WriteLine(aTime.ToString());
   }

   // add the specified number of hours to the time
   // and return a new Time2 object
   public static Time2 AddHours(this Time2 aTime, int hours)
   {
      // create a new Time2 object
      var newTime = new Time2() {
         Minute = aTime.Minute, Second = aTime.Second};

      // add the specified number of hours to the given time
      newTime.Hour = (aTime.Hour + hours) % 24;

      return newTime; // return the new Time2 object
   }
}
```

```
Use the DisplayTime extension method: 11:34:15 AM
Add 5 hours with the AddHours extension method: 4:34:15 PM
Add 15 hours with the AddHours extension method: 2:34:15 AM
Use fully qualified extension-method name: 11:34:15 AM
```

**Fig. 10.16** | Demonstrating extension methods. (Part 2 of 2.)

### *Extension Method* `DisplayTime`

Extension method `DisplayTime` (lines 35–38) displays the `string` representation of the time. The key new feature of method `DisplayTime` is the `this` keyword that precedes the `Time2` parameter in the method header (line 35)—this notifies the compiler that `DisplayTime` is an extension method for an existing class (`Time2`). The type of an extension method's first parameter specifies the type of object on which you can call the method—for this reason, each extension method *must* define at least one parameter. Also, extension methods must be defined as `static` methods in a `static` class such as `TimeExtensions` (lines 32–53). A `static` class can contain only `static` members and cannot be instantiated.

### *Calling Extension Method* `DisplayTime`

Line 14 uses `Time2` object `myTime` to call the `DisplayTime` extension method. Note that we do not provide an argument to the method call. The compiler implicitly passes the object that calls the method (`myTime`) as the extension method's first argument. This allows you to call `DisplayTime` as if it were a `Time2` instance method. In fact, *IntelliSense* displays extension methods with the class's instance methods and identifies them with a distinct icon

The down-arrow in the icon denotes an extension method. Also, when you select an extension method in the *IntelliSense* window, the tool tip that describes the method includes the text **(extension)** for each extension method.

### *Extension Method* `AddHours`

Lines 42–52 of Fig. 10.16 declare the `AddHours` extension method. Again, the `this` keyword in the first parameter's declaration indicates that `AddHours` can be called on a `Time2` object. The second parameter is an `int` value specifying the number of hours to add to the time. The `AddHours` method returns a new `Time2` object with the specified number of hours added.

Lines 45–46 create the new `Time2` object and use an object initializer to set its `Minute` and `Second` properties to the corresponding values in the parameter `aTime`—these are not modified when we add hours to the time. Line 49 adds the second argument's number of hours to the original `Time2` object's `Hour` property, then uses the `%` operator to ensure the value remains in the range 0–23. The result is assigned to the new `Time2` object's `Hour` property. Line 51 returns the new `Time2` object to the caller.

### *Calling Extension Method* `AddHours`

Line 18 calls the `AddHours` extension method to add five hours to the `myTime` object's hour value. Note that the method call specifies only one argument—the number of hours to add. Again, the compiler implicitly passes the object that's used to call the method (`myTime`) as the extension method's first argument. The `Time2` object returned by `AddHours` is assigned to a local variable (`timeAdded`) and displayed in the console using the `DisplayTime` extension method (line 19).

### *Calling Both Extension Methods in a Single Statement*

Line 23 uses both extension methods (`DisplayTime` and `AddHours`) in a single statement to add 15 hours to the original `myTime` and display the result in the console. Multiple method calls in the same statement are known as **cascaded method calls**. When a method returns an object, you can follow the method call with a member access operator (`.`) then call a method on the object that was returned. The methods are called from left to right. In line 23, the `DisplayTime` method is called on the `Time2` object returned by method `AddHours`. This eliminates the need to assign the object returned by `AddHours` to a variable, then call `DisplayTime` in a separate statement.

### *Calling an Extension Method With Its Fully Qualified Name*

Line 27 calls extension method `DisplayTime` using its fully qualified name—the name of the class in which the extension method is defined (`TimeExtensions`), followed by the member access operator (`.`), the method name (`DisplayTime`) and its argument list. Note in line 27 that the call to `DisplayTime` passes a `Time2` object as an argument to the method. When using the fully qualified method name, you must specify an argument for extension method's first parameter. This use of the extension method uses the syntax of a `static` method call.

### *Extension Method Cautions*

If a type for which you declare an extension method already defines an instance method with the same name and a compatible signature, the instance method will shadow (i.e., hide) the extension method. Also, if a predefined type is later updated to include an instance method that shadows an extension method, the compiler does not report any errors and the extension method does not appear in *IntelliSense*.

## 10.15 Wrap-Up

In this chapter, we discussed additional class concepts. The time examples concluded with a complete class declaration consisting of `private` data, overloaded `public` constructors for initialization flexibility, properties for manipulating the class's data and methods that returned `string` representations of a time in two different formats.

We mentioned that the `this` reference is used implicitly in a class's non-`static` methods and properties to access the current object's instance variables and other non-`static` members. You saw explicit uses of the `this` reference to access the class's members (including shadowed instance variables) and how to use keyword `this` in a constructor to call another constructor of the same class.

You saw that composition enables a class to have references to objects of other classes as members. We discussed garbage collection and how it reclaims the memory of objects that are no longer used. We motivated the notion of `static` class variables and demonstrated how to declare and use `static` variables and methods in your own classes. You saw how to declare and initialize `readonly` variables and we discussed that the compiler automatically marks as `readonly` the instance variable for a getter-only auto-implemented variable.

We also showed how to use Visual Studio's **Class View** and **Object Browser** windows to navigate the classes of the Framework Class Library and your own apps to discover information about those classes. You initialized an object's properties as you created it with an object initializer. We showed how to define the behavior of the built-in operators on objects of your own classes with operator overloading, and demonstrated how to create your own value types with `struct`. Finally, we showed how to use extension methods to add capabilities to existing types without modifying their source code.

In the next chapter, you'll learn about inheritance. You'll see that all classes in C# are related directly or indirectly to the `object` root class and begin to understand how inheritance enables you to build related classes faster.

# 11

# Object-Oriented Programming: Inheritance

## Objectives

In this chapter you'll:

- Understand how inheritance promotes software reusability.
- Create a derived class that inherits attributes and behaviors from a base class.
- Override base-class methods in derived classes.
- Use access modifier `protected` to give derived-class methods access to base-class members.
- Access base-class members with `base`.
- Understand how constructors are used in inheritance hierarchies.
- See an overview of the methods of class `object`, the direct or indirect base class of all classes.

Outline



## 11.1 Introduction

This chapter continues our discussion of object-oriented programming (OOP) by introducing one of its primary features—**inheritance**, a form of *software reuse* in which a new class is created by absorbing an existing class's members and enhancing them with new or modified capabilities. Inheritance lets you save time during app development by reusing proven, high-performance and debugged high-quality software. This also increases the likelihood that a system will be implemented effectively.

The existing class from which a new class inherits members is called the **base class**, and the new class is the **derived class.** Each derived class can become the base class for future derived classes. A derived class normally adds its own fields, properties and methods. Therefore, it's more *specific* than its base class and represents a more *specialized* group of objects. Typically, the derived class exhibits the behaviors of its base class and additional ones that are specific to itself.

The **direct base class** is the base class from which a derived class explicitly inherits. An **indirect base class** is any class above the direct base class in the **class hierarchy**, which defines the inheritance relationships among classes. The class hierarchy begins with class **`object`**—a C# keyword that's an alias for `System.Object` in the Framework Class Library. Every class directly or indirectly **extends** (or "inherits from") `object`. Section 11.7 lists class `object`'s methods, which every other class inherits. In **single inheritance**, a class is derived from *one* direct base class. C# supports only single inheritance. In Chapter 12, OOP: Polymorphism and Interfaces, we explain how you can use interfaces to realize many of the benefits of multiple inheritance (i.e., inheriting from multiple direct base classes) while avoiding the associated problems that occur in some programming languages.

Experience in building software systems indicates that significant amounts of code deal with closely related special cases. When you're preoccupied with special cases, the details can obscure the big picture. With object-oriented programming, you can, when appropriate, focus on the *commonalities* among objects in the system rather than the special cases.

We distinguish between the ***is-a*** **relationship** and the ***has-a*** **relationship**. *Is-a* represents inheritance. In an *is-a* relationship, an object of a derived class also can be treated as an object of its base class. For example, a car *is a* vehicle, and a truck *is a* vehicle. By contrast, *has-a* represents composition (see Chapter 10). In a *has-a* relationship, an object contains as members references to other objects. For example, a car *has a* steering wheel, and a car object *has a* reference to a steering-wheel object.

New classes can inherit from classes in **class libraries**. Organizations develop their own class libraries and can take advantage of others available worldwide. Some day, most new software likely will be constructed from **standardized reusable components**, just as automobiles and most computer hardware are constructed today. This will facilitate the development of more powerful, abundant and economical software.

## 11.2 Base Classes and Derived Classes

Often, an object of one class *is an* object of another class as well. For example, in geometry, a rectangle *is a* quadrilateral (as are squares, parallelograms and trapezoids). Thus, class `Rectangle` can be said to inherit from class `Quadrilateral`. In this context, class `Quadrilateral` is a *base class* and class `Rectangle` is a *derived class*. A rectangle *is a* specific type of quadrilateral, but it's incorrect to claim that every quadrilateral *is a* rectangle—the quadrilateral could be a parallelogram or some other shape. Figure 11.1 lists several simple examples of base classes and derived classes—base classes tend to be more *general*, and derived classes tend to be more *specific*.

| Base class | Derived classes |
|---|---|
| `Student` | `GraduateStudent, UndergraduateStudent` |
| `Shape` | `Circle, Triangle, Rectangle` |
| `Loan` | `CarLoan, HomeImprovementLoan, MortgageLoan` |
| `Employee` | `Faculty, Staff, HourlyWorker, CommissionWorker` |
| `SpaceObject` | `Star, Moon, Planet, FlyingSaucer` |
| `BankAccount` | `CheckingAccount, SavingsAccount` |

**Fig. 11.1** | Inheritance examples.

Because every derived-class object *is an* object of its base class, and one base class can have *many* derived classes, the set of objects represented by a base class is typically larger than the set of objects represented by any of its derived classes. For example, the base class `Vehicle` represents *all* vehicles—cars, trucks, boats, bicycles and so on. By contrast, derived class `Car` represents a smaller, more specific subset of vehicles.

Inheritance relationships form treelike hierarchical structures (Figs. 11.2 and 11.3). A base class exists in a hierarchical relationship with its derived classes. When classes participate in inheritance relationships, they become "affiliated" with other classes. A class becomes either a base class, supplying members to other classes, or a derived class, inheriting its members from another class. Sometimes, a class is *both* a base and a derived class.

Let us develop a sample class hierarchy, also called an **inheritance hierarchy** (Fig. 11.2). The UML class diagram of Fig. 11.2 shows a university community that has many types of members, including employees, students and alumni. Employees are either faculty members or staff members. Faculty members are either administrators (such as deans and department chairpersons) or teachers. The hierarchy could contain many other classes. For example, students can be graduate or undergraduate students. Undergraduate students can be freshmen, sophomores, juniors or seniors.

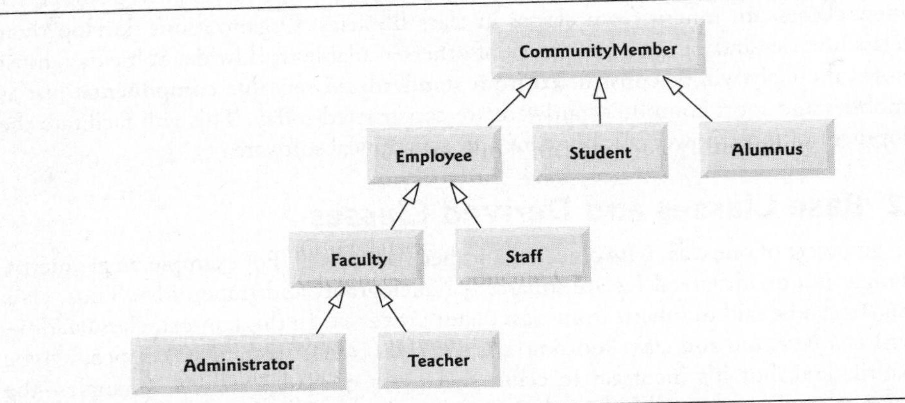


**Fig. 11.2** | Inheritance hierarchy UML class diagram for university `CommunityMember`s.

Each arrow with a *hollow triangular arrowhead* in the hierarchy diagram represents an *is-a* relationship. As we follow the arrows, we can state, for instance, that "an `Employee` *is a* `CommunityMember`" and "a `Teacher` *is a* `Faculty` member." `CommunityMember` is the *direct* base class of `Employee`, `Student` and `Alumnus` and is an *indirect* base class of all the other classes in the diagram. Starting from the bottom, you can follow the arrows and apply the *is-a* relationship up to the topmost base class. For example, an `Administrator` *is a* `Faculty` member, *is an* `Employee` and *is a* `CommunityMember`.

Now consider the `Shape` hierarchy in Fig. 11.3, which begins with base class `Shape`. This class is extended by derived classes `TwoDimensionalShape` and `ThreeDimensionalShape`—a `Shape` is either a `TwoDimensionalShape` or a `ThreeDimensionalShape`. The third level of this hierarchy contains *specific* `TwoDimensionalShapes` and `ThreeDimensionalShapes`. We can follow the arrows from the bottom to the topmost base class in this hierarchy to identify the *is-a* relationships. For instance, a `Triangle` *is a* `TwoDimensionalShape` and *is a* `Shape`, while a `Sphere` *is a* `ThreeDimensionalShape` and *is a* `Shape`. This hierarchy could contain many other classes. For example, ellipses and trapezoids also are `TwoDimensionalShapes`.

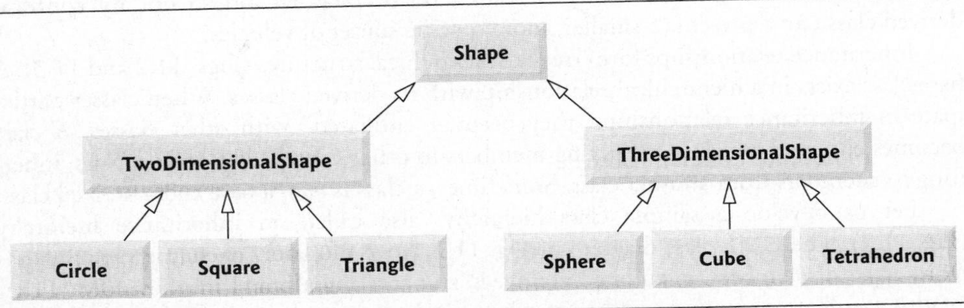


**Fig. 11.3** | UML class diagram showing an inheritance hierarchy for `Shapes`.

Not every class relationship is an inheritance relationship. In Chapter 10 we discussed the *has-a* relationship, in which classes have members that are references to objects of other classes. Such relationships create classes by *composition* of existing classes. For example, given the classes `Employee`, `BirthDate` and `TelephoneNumber`, it's improper to say that an `Employee` *is a* `BirthDate` or that an `Employee` *is a* `TelephoneNumber`. However, an `Employee` *has a* `BirthDate`, and an `Employee` *has a* `TelephoneNumber`.

It's possible to treat base-class objects and derived-class objects similarly—their commonalities are expressed in the base class's members. Objects of all classes that extend a common base class can be treated as objects of that base class—such objects have an *is-a* relationship with the base class. However, *base-class objects cannot be treated as objects of their derived classes*. For example, all cars are vehicles, but not all vehicles are cars (other vehicles could be trucks, planes, bicycles, etc.). This chapter and Chapter 12 consider many examples of *is-a* relationships.

A derived class can customize methods it inherits from its base class. In such cases, the derived class can **override** (redefine) the base-class method with an appropriate implementation, as we'll see often in the chapter's code examples.

## 11.3 protected Members

Chapter 10 discussed access modifiers `public` and `private`. A class's `public` members are accessible wherever the app has a reference to an object of that class or one of its derived classes. A class's `private` members are accessible *only* within the class itself. A base class's `private` members *are* inherited by its derived classes, but are *not* directly accessible by derived-class methods and properties. In this section, we introduce access modifier `protected`. Using `protected` access offers an intermediate level of access between `public` and `private`. A base class's `protected` members can be accessed by members of that base class *and* by members of its derived classes, but not by clients of the class.

All non-`private` base-class members retain their original access modifier when they become members of the derived class—`public` members of the base class become `public` members of the derived class, and `protected` members of the base class become `protected` members of the derived class.

Derived-class methods can refer to `public` and `protected` members inherited from the base class simply by using the member names. When a derived-class method overrides a base-class method, the base-class version can be accessed from the derived class by preceding the base-class method name with the keyword `base` and the member access (`.`) operator. We discuss accessing overridden members of the base class in Section 11.4.

**Software Engineering Observation 11.1**

*Properties and methods of a derived class cannot directly access* `private` *members of the base class. A derived class can change the state of* `private` *base-class fields only through non-*`private` *methods and properties provided in the base class.*

**Software Engineering Observation 11.2**

*Declaring* `private` *fields in a base class helps you test, debug and correctly modify systems. If a derived class could access its base class's* `private` *fields, classes that inherit from that derived class could access the fields as well. This would propagate access to what should be* `private` *fields, and the benefits of information hiding would be lost.*

## 11.4 Relationship between Base Classes and Derived Classes

In this section, we use an inheritance hierarchy containing types of employees in a company's payroll app to discuss the relationship between a base class and a derived class. In this company:

- *commission employees*—who will be represented as objects of a base class—are paid a percentage of their sales, while
- *base-salaried commission employees*—who will be represented as objects of a derived class—receive a base salary *plus* a percentage of their sales.

We divide our discussion of the relationship between these employee types into an evolutionary set of five examples that was carefully designed to teach key capabilities for good software engineering with inheritance:

1. The first example creates class `CommissionEmployee`, which directly inherits from class `object`. The class declares `public` auto-implemented properties for the first name, last name and social security number, and `private` instance variables for the commission rate and gross (i.e., total) sales amount.
2. The second example declares class `BasePlusCommissionEmployee`, which also directly inherits from `object`. The class declares `public` auto-implemented properties for the first name, last name and social security number, and `private` instance variables for the commission rate, gross sales amount *and* base salary. We create the class by writing *every* line of code the class requires—we'll soon see that it's more efficient to create this class by inheriting from `CommissionEmployee`.
3. The third example declares a separate `BasePlusCommissionEmployee` class that extends class `CommissionEmployee`—that is, a `BasePlusCommissionEmployee` *is a* `CommissionEmployee` who also has a base salary. `BasePlusCommissionEmployee` attempts to access class `CommissionEmployee`'s `private` members, but this results in compilation errors because a derived class *cannot* access its base class's `private` instance variables.
4. The fourth example shows that if base class `CommissionEmployee`'s instance variables are declared as `protected`, a `BasePlusCommissionEmployee` class that inherits from `CommissionEmployee` can access that data directly.
5. The fifth and final example demonstrates *best practice* by setting the `CommissionEmployee` instance variables back to `private` in class `CommissionEmployee` to enforce good software engineering. Then we show how a separate `BasePlusCommissionEmployee` class that inherits from class `CommissionEmployee` can use `CommissionEmployee`'s `public` methods and properties to manipulate `CommissionEmployee`'s `private` instance variables in a controlled manner.

In the first four examples, we'll directly access instance variables in several cases where properties should be used. In the fifth example, we'll apply effective software engineering techniques that we've presented up to this point in the book to create classes that are easy to maintain, modify and debug.

### 11.4.1 Creating and Using a CommissionEmployee Class

We begin with class `CommissionEmployee` (Fig. 11.4). The colon (`:`) followed by class name `object` in line 5 indicates that class `CommissionEmployee` *extends* (i.e., *inherits from*) class `object` (an alias for class `Object` in namespace `System`). You use inheritance to create classes from existing classes. *Every* class (except `object`) extends an existing class. Because class `CommissionEmployee` extends `object`, class `CommissionEmployee` inherits `object`'s methods—`object` has no fields. (Section 11.7 summarizes `object`'s methods.) Every C# class directly or indirectly inherits `object`'s methods. If a class does not specify that it inherits from another class, the new class *implicitly* inherits from `object`. For this reason, you typically do *not* include "`: object`" in your code—we do so in this example, then not again in the book.

```
1  // Fig. 11.4: CommissionEmployee.cs
2  // CommissionEmployee class represents a commission employee.
3  using System;
4
5  public class CommissionEmployee : object
6  {
7     public string FirstName { get; }
8     public string LastName { get; }
9     public string SocialSecurityNumber { get; }
10    private decimal grossSales; // gross weekly sales
11    private decimal commissionRate; // commission percentage
12
13    // five-parameter constructor
14    public CommissionEmployee(string firstName, string lastName,
15       string socialSecurityNumber, decimal grossSales,
16       decimal commissionRate)
17    {
18       // implicit call to object constructor occurs here
19       FirstName = firstName;
20       LastName = lastName;
21       SocialSecurityNumber = socialSecurityNumber;
22       GrossSales = grossSales; // validates gross sales
23       CommissionRate = commissionRate; // validates commission rate
24    }
25
26    // property that gets and sets commission employee's gross sales
27    public decimal GrossSales
28    {
29       get
30       {
31          return grossSales;
32       }
33       set
34       {
35          if (value < 0) // validation
36          {
37             throw new ArgumentOutOfRangeException(nameof(value),
38                value, $"{nameof(GrossSales)} must be >= 0");
39          }
```

**Fig. 11.4** | `CommissionEmployee` class represents a commission employee. (Part 1 of 2.)

```
40
41          grossSales = value;
42       }
43    }
44
45    // property that gets and sets commission employee's commission rate
46    public decimal CommissionRate
47    {
48       get
49       {
50          return commissionRate;
51       }
52       set
53       {
54          if (value <= 0 || value >= 1) // validation
55          {
56             throw new ArgumentOutOfRangeException(nameof(value),
57                value, $"{nameof(CommissionRate)} must be > 0 and < 1");
58          }
59
60          commissionRate = value;
61       }
62    }
63
64    // calculate commission employee's pay
65    public decimal Earnings() => commissionRate * grossSales;
66
67    // return string representation of CommissionEmployee object
68    public override string ToString() =>
69       $"commission employee: {FirstName} {LastName}\n" +
70       $"social security number: {SocialSecurityNumber}\n" +
71       $"gross sales: {grossSales:C}\n" +
72       $"commission rate: {commissionRate:F2}";
73 }
```

**Fig. 11.4** | `CommissionEmployee` class represents a commission employee. (Part 2 of 2.)

### *`CommissionEmployee` Class Overview*

`CommissionEmployee`'s attributes include `public`, getter-only, auto-implemented properties `FirstName`, `LastName` and `SocialSecurityNumber`, and `private` instance variables `grossSales` and `commissionRate`. The class provides

- a constructor (lines 14–24)
- `public` properties (lines 27–62) to *set* and *get* `grossSales` and `commissionRate`, and
- expression-bodied methods `Earnings` (line 65) and `ToString` (lines 68–72).

Because instance variables `grossSales` and `commissionRate` are `private`, other classes cannot directly access these variables. Declaring instance variables as `private` and providing `public` properties to manipulate and validate them helps enforce good software engineering. The `set` accessors of properties `GrossSales` and `CommissionRate` *validate* their arguments before assigning the values to instance variables `grossSales` and `commissionRate`, respectively.

### `CommissionEmployee` *Constructor*

Constructors are *not* inherited, so class `CommissionEmployee` does not inherit class `object`'s constructor. However, class `CommissionEmployee`'s constructor calls `object`'s constructor *implicitly*. In fact, before executing the code in its own body, every derived class's constructor calls a constructor in its direct base class, either explicitly or implicitly (if no constructor call is specified), to ensure that the instance variables inherited from the base class are initialized properly.

Calling a base-class constructor *explicitly* is discussed in Section 11.4.3. If the code does not *explicitly* call the base-class constructor, the compiler generates an *implicit* call to the base class's *default* or *parameterless* constructor, or a constructor with all default arguments. The comment in line 18 indicates where the implicit call to the base class `object`'s constructor is made (you do not write the code for this call). Even if a class does not have constructors, the default constructor that the compiler implicitly declares for the class will call the base class's default or parameterless constructor. Class `object` is the *only* class that does not have a base class.

After the implicit call to `object`'s constructor occurs, lines 19–23 in the constructor assign values to the class's properties. We do *not* validate the values of arguments `firstName`, `lastName` and `socialSecurityNumber`. We certainly could validate the first and last names—perhaps by ensuring that they're of a reasonable length. Similarly, a social security number could be validated to ensure that it contains nine digits, with or without dashes (e.g., `123-45-6789` or `123456789`).

### `CommissionEmployee` *Method* `Earnings`

Method `Earnings` (line 65) calculates a `CommissionEmployee`'s earnings by multiplying the `commissionRate` and the `grossSales`, then returns the result. As a best practice, we should use the properties `CommissionRate` and `GrossSales` to access the instance variables in line 65. We access them directly here and in the next few examples to help motivate then demonstrate the `protected` access modifier. In this chapter's final example, we'll follow best practice.

### `CommissionEmployee` *Method* `ToString`

Method `ToString` (lines 68–72) is special—it's one of the methods that *every* class inherits directly or indirectly from class `object`. Method `ToString` returns a `string` representing an object. It can be called explicitly, but it's called *implicitly* by an app whenever an object must be converted to a `string` representation, such as when displaying an object with `Console`'s `Write` or `WriteLine` methods or inserting an object in a `string`-interpolation expression. By default, class `object`'s `ToString` method returns the object's fully qualified class name. For `object`, `ToString` returns

```
System.Object
```

because `object` is an alias for class `Object` in the `System` namespace. `ToString` is primarily a placeholder that can be (and typically should be) *overridden* by a derived class to specify an appropriate `string` representation of the data in a derived class object.

Method `ToString` of class `CommissionEmployee` overrides (redefines) class `object`'s `ToString` method. When invoked, `CommissionEmployee`'s `ToString` method returns a `string` containing information about the `CommissionEmployee`. Line 71 uses the format specifier `C` (in `"{grossSales:C}"`) to format `grossSales` as currency and line 72 uses the format specifier `F2` (in `"{commissionRate:F2}"`) to format the `commissionRate` with two digits to the right of the decimal point.

To override a base-class method, a derived class must declare a method with keyword **`override`** and with the *same signature* (method name, number of parameters and parameter types) *and* return type as the base-class method—`object`'s `ToString` method takes *no* parameters and returns type `string`, so `CommissionEmployee` declares `ToString` with the same parameter list and return type. As you'll soon see, the base-class method also must be declared `virtual`, which is the case for `object` method `ToString`.

**Common Programming Error 11.1**

*It's a compilation error to override a method with one that has a* different *access modifier. Overriding a method with a* more restrictive *access modifier would break the* is-a *relationship. If a* `public` *method could be overridden as a* `protected` *or* `private` *method, the derived-class objects would not be able to respond to the same method calls as base-class objects. In particular, once a method is declared in a base class, the method* must *have the* same *access modifier for all that class's direct and indirect derived classes.*

### *Class* `CommissionEmployeeTest`

Figure 11.5 tests class `CommissionEmployee`. Lines 10–11 create a `CommissionEmployee` object and invoke its constructor (lines 14–24 of Fig. 11.4) to initialize it. Again, we append the `M` suffix to the gross sales amount and the commission rate to indicate these are `decimal` literals. Lines 16–22 in Fig. 11.5 use `CommissionEmployee`'s properties to retrieve the object's instance-variable values for output. Line 23 outputs the amount calculated by the `Earnings` method. Lines 25–26 invoke the `set` accessors of the object's `GrossSales` and `CommissionRate` properties to change the values of instance variables `grossSales` and `commissionRate`. Line 30 outputs the `string` representation of the updated `CommissionEmployee`. When an object is output by `Console`'s `WriteLine` method, which displays the object's `string` representation, the `ToString` method is invoked *implicitly*. Line 31 outputs the updated earnings.

```
1  // Fig. 11.5: CommissionEmployeeTest.cs
2  // Testing class CommissionEmployee.
3  using System;
4
5  class CommissionEmployeeTest
6  {
7     static void Main()
8     {
9        // instantiate CommissionEmployee object
10       var employee = new CommissionEmployee("Sue", "Jones",
11          "222-22-2222", 10000.00M, .06M);
12
13       // display CommissionEmployee data
14       Console.WriteLine(
15          "Employee information obtained by properties and methods: \n");
16       Console.WriteLine($"First name is {employee.FirstName}");
```

**Fig. 11.5** | Testing class `CommissionEmployee`. (Part 1 of 2.)

```
         Console.WriteLine($"Last name is {employee.LastName}");
         Console.WriteLine(
            $"Social security number is {employee.SocialSecurityNumber}");
         Console.WriteLine($"Gross sales are {employee.GrossSales:C}");
         Console.WriteLine(
            $"Commission rate is {employee.CommissionRate:F2}");
         Console.WriteLine($"Earnings are {employee.Earnings():C}");

         employee.GrossSales = 5000.00M; // set gross sales
         employee.CommissionRate = .1M; // set commission rate

         Console.WriteLine(
            "\nUpdated employee information obtained by ToString:\n");
         Console.WriteLine(employee);
         Console.WriteLine($"earnings: {employee.Earnings():C}");
      }
   }
```

```
Employee information obtained by properties and methods:

First name is Sue
Last name is Jones
Social security number is 222-22-2222
Gross sales are $10,000.00
Commission rate is 0.06
Earnings are $600.00

Updated employee information obtained by ToString:

commission employee: Sue Jones
social security number: 222-22-2222
gross sales: $5,000.00
commission rate: 0.10
earnings: $500.00
```

**Fig. 11.5** | Testing class `CommissionEmployee`. (Part 2 of 2.)

### 11.4.2 Creating a `BasePlusCommissionEmployee` Class without Using Inheritance

We now discuss the second part of our introduction to inheritance by declaring and testing the completely new and independent class `BasePlusCommissionEmployee` (Fig. 11.6), which contains a first name, last name, social security number, gross sales amount, commission rate *and* base salary—"`Base`" in the class name stands for "base salary" not base class.

```
// Fig. 11.6: BasePlusCommissionEmployee.cs
// BasePlusCommissionEmployee class represents an employee that receives
// a base salary in addition to a commission.
using System;

```

**Fig. 11.6** | `BasePlusCommissionEmployee` class represents an employee that receives a base salary in addition to a commission. (Part 1 of 3.)

```
public class BasePlusCommissionEmployee
{
   public string FirstName { get; }
   public string LastName { get; }
   public string SocialSecurityNumber { get; }
   private decimal grossSales; // gross weekly sales
   private decimal commissionRate; // commission percentage
   private decimal baseSalary; // base salary per week

   // six-parameter constructor
   public BasePlusCommissionEmployee(string firstName, string lastName,
      string socialSecurityNumber, decimal grossSales,
      decimal commissionRate, decimal baseSalary)
   {
      // implicit call to object constructor occurs here
      FirstName = firstName;
      LastName = lastName;
      SocialSecurityNumber = socialSecurityNumber;
      GrossSales = grossSales; // validates gross sales
      CommissionRate = commissionRate; // validates commission rate
      BaseSalary = baseSalary; // validates base salary
   }

   // property that gets and sets gross sales
   public decimal GrossSales
   {
      get
      {
         return grossSales;
      }
      set
      {
         if (value < 0) // validation
         {
            throw new ArgumentOutOfRangeException(nameof(value),
               value, $"{nameof(GrossSales)} must be >= 0");
         }

         grossSales = value;
      }
   }

   // property that gets and sets commission rate
   public decimal CommissionRate
   {
      get
      {
         return commissionRate;
      }
      set
      {
```

**Fig. 11.6** | BasePlusCommissionEmployee class represents an employee that receives a base salary in addition to a commission. (Part 2 of 3.)

```
57             if (value <= 0 || value >= 1) // validation
58             {
59                throw new ArgumentOutOfRangeException(nameof(value),
60                   value, $"{nameof(CommissionRate)} must be > 0 and < 1");
61             }
62 
63             commissionRate = value;
64          }
65       }
66 
67       // property that gets and sets BasePlusCommissionEmployee's base salary
68       public decimal BaseSalary
69       {
70          get
71          {
72             return baseSalary;
73          }
74          set
75          {
76             if (value < 0) // validation
77             {
78                throw new ArgumentOutOfRangeException(nameof(value),
79                   value, $"{nameof(BaseSalary)} must be >= 0");
80             }
81 
82             baseSalary = value;
83          }
84       }
85 
86       // calculate earnings
87       public decimal Earnings() =>
88          baseSalary + (commissionRate * grossSales);
89 
90       // return string representation of BasePlusCommissionEmployee
91       public override string ToString() =>
92          $"base-salaried commission employee: {FirstName} {LastName}\n" +
93          $"social security number: {SocialSecurityNumber}\n" +
94          $"gross sales: {grossSales:C}\n" +
95          $"commission rate: {commissionRate:F2}\n" +
96          $"base salary: {baseSalary:C}";
97    }
```

**Fig. 11.6** | `BasePlusCommissionEmployee` class represents an employee that receives a base salary in addition to a commission. (Part 3 of 3.)

`BasePlusCommissionEmployee`'s attributes include `public`, getter-only, auto-implemented properties for the `FirstName`, `LastName` and `SocialSecurityNumber`, and `private` instance variables for the `grossSales`, `commissionRate` *and* `baseSalary`. The class provides

- a constructor (lines 16–27)
- `public` properties (lines 30–84) for manipulating the `grossSales`, `commissionRate` and `baseSalary`, and
- expression-bodied methods `Earnings` (lines 87–88) and `ToString` (lines 91–96).

Instance variables `grossSales`, `commissionRate` and `baseSalary` are `private`, so objects of other classes cannot directly access these variables. The `set` accessors of properties `GrossSales`, `CommissionRate` and `BaseSalary` *validate* their arguments before assigning the values to instance variables `grossSales`, `commissionRate` and `baseSalary`, respectively.

`BasePlusCommissionEmployee`'s variables, properties and methods *encapsulate* all the necessary features of a base-salaried commission employee. Note the similarity between this class and class `CommissionEmployee` (Fig. 11.4)—in this example, *we do not yet exploit that similarity*.

Class `BasePlusCommissionEmployee` does *not* specify that it extends `object` with the syntax "`: object`" in line 6, so the class *implicitly* extends `object`. Also, like class `CommissionEmployee`'s constructor (lines 14–24 of Fig. 11.4), class `BasePlusCommissionEmployee`'s constructor invokes class `object`'s default constructor *implicitly*, as noted in the comment in line 20 of Fig. 11.6.

Class `BasePlusCommissionEmployee`'s `Earnings` method (lines 87–88) computes the earnings of a base-salaried commission employee. Line 88 adds the employee's base salary to the product of the commission rate and the gross sales, and returns the result.

Class `BasePlusCommissionEmployee` overrides `object` method `ToString` (lines 91–96) to return a `string` containing the `BasePlusCommissionEmployee`'s information. Once again, we use format specifier `C` to format the gross sales and base salary as currency and format specifier `F2` to format the commission rate with two digits of precision to the right of the decimal point.

### *Class* ***BasePlusCommissionEmployeeTest***

Figure 11.7 tests class `BasePlusCommissionEmployee`. Lines 10–11 instantiate a `BasePlusCommissionEmployee` object and pass `"Bob"`, `"Lewis"`, `"333-33-3333"`, `5000.00M`, `.04M` and `300.00M` to the constructor as the first name, last name, social security number, gross sales, commission rate and base salary, respectively. Lines 16–24 use `BasePlusCommissionEmployee`'s properties and methods to retrieve the values of the object's instance variables and calculate the earnings for output. Line 26 invokes the object's `BaseSalary` property to *change* the base salary. Property `BaseSalary`'s `set` accessor (Fig. 11.6, lines 68–84) ensures that instance variable `baseSalary` is not assigned a negative value, because an employee's base salary cannot be negative. Lines 30–31 of Fig. 11.7 invoke the object's `ToString` method *implicitly* and invoke the object's `Earnings` method.

```
1  // Fig. 11.7: BasePlusCommissionEmployeeTest.cs
2  // Testing class BasePlusCommissionEmployee.
3  using System;
4
5  class BasePlusCommissionEmployeeTest
6  {
7     static void Main()
8     {
9        // instantiate BasePlusCommissionEmployee object
10       var employee = new BasePlusCommissionEmployee("Bob", "Lewis",
11          "333-33-3333", 5000.00M, .04M, 300.00M);
12
```

**Fig. 11.7** | Testing class `BasePlusCommissionEmployee`. (Part 1 of 2.)

```
        // display BasePlusCommissionEmployee's data
        Console.WriteLine(
           "Employee information obtained by properties and methods: \n");
        Console.WriteLine($"First name is {employee.FirstName}");
        Console.WriteLine($"Last name is {employee.LastName}");
        Console.WriteLine(
           $"Social security number is {employee.SocialSecurityNumber}");
        Console.WriteLine($"Gross sales are {employee.GrossSales:C}");
        Console.WriteLine(
           $"Commission rate is {employee.CommissionRate:F2}");
        Console.WriteLine($"Earnings are {employee.Earnings():C}");
        Console.WriteLine($"Base salary is {employee.BaseSalary:C}");

        employee.BaseSalary = 1000.00M; // set base salary

        Console.WriteLine(
           "\nUpdated employee information obtained by ToString:\n");
        Console.WriteLine(employee);
        Console.WriteLine($"earnings: {employee.Earnings():C}");
    }
}
```

```
Employee information obtained by properties and methods:

First name is Bob
Last name is Lewis
Social security number is 333-33-3333
Gross sales are $5,000.00
Commission rate is 0.04
Earnings are $500.00
Base salary is $300.00

Updated employee information obtained by ToString:

base-salaried commission employee: Bob Lewis
social security number: 333-33-3333
gross sales: $5,000.00
commission rate: 0.04
base salary: $1,000.00
earnings: $1,200.00
```

**Fig. 11.7** | Testing class `BasePlusCommissionEmployee`. (Part 2 of 2.)

### *Code Duplication*

*Much of the code for class `BasePlusCommissionEmployee` (Fig. 11.6) is similar, or identical, to that of class `CommissionEmployee` (Fig. 11.4).* For example, in class `BasePlusCommissionEmployee`, properties `FirstName`, `LastName` and `SocialSecurityNumber` are identical to those of class `CommissionEmployee`. Classes `CommissionEmployee` and `BasePlusCommissionEmployee` also both contain `private` instance variables `commissionRate` and `grossSales`, as well as identical properties to manipulate these variables. In addition, the `BasePlusCommissionEmployee` constructor is almost identical to that of class `CommissionEmployee`, except that `BasePlusCommissionEmployee`'s constructor also sets the `BaseSalary`.

The other additions to class `BasePlusCommissionEmployee` are `private` instance variable `baseSalary` and `public` property `BaseSalary`. Class `BasePlusCommissionEmployee`'s `Earnings` method is nearly identical to that of class `CommissionEmployee`, except that `BasePlusCommissionEmployee`'s `Earnings` also adds the `baseSalary`. Similarly, class `BasePlusCommissionEmployee`'s `ToString` method is nearly identical to that of class `CommissionEmployee`, except that `BasePlusCommissionEmployee`'s `ToString` also formats the value of instance variable `baseSalary` as currency.

We literally *copied* the code from class `CommissionEmployee` and *pasted* it into class `BasePlusCommissionEmployee`, then modified class `BasePlusCommissionEmployee` to include a base salary and methods and properties that manipulate the base salary. This "copy-and-paste" approach is error prone and time consuming. Worse yet, it can spread many physical copies of the same code throughout a system, creating a code-maintenance nightmare. Is there a way to "absorb" the members of one class in a way that makes them part of other classes without copying code? In the next several examples we answer this question, using a more elegant approach to building classes—namely, *inheritance.*

**Error-Prevention Tip 11.1**

*Copying and pasting code from one class to another can spread errors across multiple source-code files. To avoid duplicating code (and possibly errors) in situations where you want one class to "absorb" the members of another class, use inheritance rather than the "copy-and-paste" approach.*

**Software Engineering Observation 11.3**

*With inheritance, the common members of all the classes in the hierarchy are declared in a base class. When changes are required for these common features, you need to make the changes* only *in the base class—derived classes then inherit the changes. Without inheritance, changes would need to be made to all the source-code files that contain a copy of the code in question.*

### 11.4.3 Creating a `CommissionEmployee`–`BasePlusCommissionEmployee` Inheritance Hierarchy

Now we declare class `BasePlusCommissionEmployee` (Fig. 11.8), which extends (inherits from) class `CommissionEmployee` (Fig. 11.4).[1] A `BasePlusCommissionEmployee` object *is a* `CommissionEmployee` (because inheritance passes on the capabilities of class `CommissionEmployee`), but class `BasePlusCommissionEmployee` also has instance variable `baseSalary` (Fig. 11.8, line 7). The colon (`:`) in line 5 of the class declaration indicates inheritance. As a derived class, `BasePlusCommissionEmployee` inherits `CommissionEmployee`'s members and can access only those that are non-`private`. `CommissionEmployee`'s constructor is *not* inherited. Thus, the `public` services of `BasePlusCommissionEmployee` include its constructor (lines 11–18), `public` methods and properties inherited from class `CommissionEmployee`, property `BaseSalary` (lines 22–38), method `Earnings` (lines 41–42) and method `ToString` (lines 45–51). We'll explain the errors in Fig. 11.8 momentarily.

1. For this purpose, we created a project containing a copy of `CommissionEmployee.cs` from Fig. 11.4.

```
// Fig. 11.8: BasePlusCommissionEmployee.cs
// BasePlusCommissionEmployee inherits from CommissionEmployee.
using System;

public class BasePlusCommissionEmployee : CommissionEmployee
{
   private decimal baseSalary; // base salary per week

   // six-parameter derived-class constructor
   // with call to base class CommissionEmployee constructor
   public BasePlusCommissionEmployee(string firstName, string lastName,
      string socialSecurityNumber, decimal grossSales,
      decimal commissionRate, decimal baseSalary)
      : base(firstName, lastName, socialSecurityNumber,
         grossSales, commissionRate)
   {
      BaseSalary = baseSalary; // validates base salary
   }

   // property that gets and sets
   // BasePlusCommissionEmployee's base salary
   public decimal BaseSalary
   {
      get
      {
         return baseSalary;
      }
      set
      {
         if (value < 0) // validation
         {
            throw new ArgumentOutOfRangeException(nameof(value),
               value, $"{nameof(BaseSalary)} must be >= 0");
         }

         baseSalary = value;
      }
   }

   // calculate earnings
   public override decimal Earnings() =>
      baseSalary + (commissionRate * grossSales);

   // return string representation of BasePlusCommissionEmployee
   public override string ToString() =>
      // not allowed: attempts to access private base-class members
      $"base-salaried commission employee: {FirstName} {LastName}\n" +
      $"social security number: {SocialSecurityNumber}\n" +
      $"gross sales: {grossSales:C}\n" +
      $"commission rate: {commissionRate:F2}\n" +
      $"base salary: {baseSalary}";
}
```

**Fig. 11.8** | BasePlusCommissionEmployee inherits from CommissionEmployee. (Part 1 of 2.)

Error List

Entire Solution | 6 Errors | 0 Warnings | 0 Messages | Build + IntelliSense | Search Error List

| Code | Description | File | Line |
|---|---|---|---|
| CS0506 | 'BasePlusCommissionEmployee.Earnings()': cannot override inherited member 'CommissionEmployee.Earnings()' because it is not marked virtual, abstract, or override | BasePlusCommissionEmployee.cs | 41 |
| CS0122 | 'CommissionEmployee.commissionRate' is inaccessible due to its protection level | BasePlusCommissionEmployee.cs | 42 |
| CS0122 | 'CommissionEmployee.commissionRate' is inaccessible due to its protection level | BasePlusCommissionEmployee.cs | 50 |
| CS0122 | 'CommissionEmployee.grossSales' is inaccessible due to its protection level | BasePlusCommissionEmployee.cs | 42 |
| CS0122 | 'CommissionEmployee.grossSales' is inaccessible due to its protection level | BasePlusCommissionEmployee.cs | 49 |
| CS1022 | Type or namespace definition, or end-of-file expected | BasePlusCommissionEmployee.cs | 53 |

**Fig. 11.8** | `BasePlusCommissionEmployee` inherits from `CommissionEmployee`. (Part 2 of 2.)

### *A Derived Class's Constructor Must Call Its Base Class's Constructor*

Each derived-class constructor *must* implicitly or explicitly call its base-class constructor to ensure that the instance variables inherited from the base class are initialized properly. `BasePlusCommissionEmployee`'s six-parameter constructor explicitly calls class `CommissionEmployee`'s five-parameter constructor to initialize the `CommissionEmployee` portion of a `BasePlusCommissionEmployee` object—that is, the `FirstName`, `LastName`, `SocialSecurityNumber`, `GrossSales` and `CommissionRate`.

Lines 14–15 in `BasePlusCommissionEmployee`'s constructor invoke `CommissionEmployee`'s constructor (declared at lines 14–24 of Fig. 11.4) via a *constructor initializer*. In Section 10.5, we used a constructor initializer with keyword `this` to call an overloaded constructor in the *same* class. Line 14 of Fig. 11.8 uses a constructor initializer with keyword **`base`** to invoke the *base-class constructor*, passing arguments to initialize the base class's corresponding properties that were inherited into the derived-class object. If `BasePlusCommissionEmployee`'s constructor did not invoke `CommissionEmployee`'s constructor explicitly, C# would attempt to invoke class `CommissionEmployee`'s parameterless or default constructor *implicitly*. `CommissionEmployee` does *not* have such a constructor, so the compiler would issue an error.

**Common Programming Error 11.2**

*A compilation error occurs if a derived-class constructor calls one of its base-class constructors with arguments that do not match the number and types of parameters specified in one of the base-class constructor declarations.*

### *`BasePlusCommissionEmployee` Method `Earnings`*

Lines 41–42 of Fig. 11.8 declare method `Earnings` using keyword `override` to override the `CommissionEmployee`'s `Earnings` method, as we did with method `ToString` in previous examples. Line 41 causes the first compilation error shown in Fig. 11.8, indicating that we cannot override the base class's `Earnings` method because it was not explicitly "marked virtual, abstract, or override." The **`virtual`** and `abstract` keywords indicate that a base-class method can be overridden in derived classes.[2] The `override` modifier declares

2. As you'll learn in Section 12.4, `abstract` methods are *implicitly* `virtual`.

that a derived-class method overrides a `virtual` or `abstract` base-class method. This modifier also *implicitly* declares the derived-class method `virtual` and allows it to be overridden in derived classes further down the inheritance hierarchy. Adding the keyword `virtual` to method `Earnings`' declaration in Fig. 11.4, as in

```
public virtual decimal Earnings()
```

eliminates the first compilation error in Fig. 11.8.

The compiler generates additional errors for line 42 of Fig. 11.8, because base class `CommissionEmployee`'s instance variables `commissionRate` and `grossSales` are `private`—derived class `BasePlusCommissionEmployee`'s methods are not allowed to access the base class's `private` members. The compiler also issues errors at lines 49–50 in method `ToString` for the same reason. The errors in `BasePlusCommissionEmployee` could have been prevented by using the `public` properties inherited from class `CommissionEmployee`. For example, lines 42, 49 and 50 could have invoked the `get` accessors of properties `CommissionRate` and `GrossSales` to access `CommissionEmployee`'s `private` instance variables `commissionRate` and `grossSales`, respectively.

### 11.4.4 CommissionEmployee–BasePlusCommissionEmployee Inheritance Hierarchy Using protected Instance Variables

To enable class `BasePlusCommissionEmployee` to directly access base-class instance variables `grossSales` and `commissionRate`, we can declare those members as `protected` in the base class. As we discussed in Section 11.3, a base class's `protected` members *are* accessible to all derived classes of that base class. Class `CommissionEmployee` in this example is a modification of the version from Fig. 11.4 that declares its instance variables `grossSales` and `commissionRate` as

```
protected decimal grossSales; // gross weekly sales
protected decimal commissionRate; // commission percentage
```

rather than `private`. We also declare the `Earnings` method `virtual` so that `BasePlusCommissionEmployee` can override the method. The rest of class `CommissionEmployee` in this example is identical to Fig. 11.4. The complete source code for class `CommissionEmployee` is included in this example's project.

#### *Class* BasePlusCommissionEmployee

Class `BasePlusCommissionEmployee` (Fig. 11.9) in this example extends the version of class `CommissionEmployee` with `protected` instance variables `grossSales` and `commissionRate`. Each `BasePlusCommissionEmployee` object contains these `CommissionEmployee` instance variables, which are inherited into `BasePlusCommissionEmployee` as `protected` members. As a result, directly accessing instance variables `grossSales` and `commissionRate` no longer generates compilation errors in methods `Earnings` and `ToString`. If another class extends `BasePlusCommissionEmployee`, the new derived class also inherits `grossSales` and `commissionRate` as `protected` members.

Class `BasePlusCommissionEmployee` does *not* inherit class `CommissionEmployee`'s constructor. However, class `BasePlusCommissionEmployee`'s constructor (lines 12–19) calls class `CommissionEmployee`'s constructor with a constructor initializer. Again, `BasePlusCommissionEmployee`'s constructor must *explicitly* call `CommissionEmployee`'s constructor, because CommissionEmployee does *not* provide a parameterless constructor that could be invoked implicitly.

```
// Fig. 11.9: BasePlusCommissionEmployee.cs
// BasePlusCommissionEmployee inherits from CommissionEmployee and has
// access to CommissionEmployee's protected members.
using System;

public class BasePlusCommissionEmployee : CommissionEmployee
{
   private decimal baseSalary; // base salary per week

   // six-parameter derived-class constructor
   // with call to base class CommissionEmployee constructor
   public BasePlusCommissionEmployee(string firstName, string lastName,
      string socialSecurityNumber, decimal grossSales,
      decimal commissionRate, decimal baseSalary)
      : base(firstName, lastName, socialSecurityNumber,
         grossSales, commissionRate)
   {
      BaseSalary = baseSalary; // validates base salary
   }

   // property that gets and sets
   // BasePlusCommissionEmployee's base salary
   public decimal BaseSalary
   {
      get
      {
         return baseSalary;
      }
      set
      {
         if (value < 0) // validation
         {
            throw new ArgumentOutOfRangeException(nameof(value),
               value, $"{nameof(BaseSalary)} must be >= 0");
         }

         baseSalary = value;
      }
   }

   // calculate earnings
   public override decimal Earnings() =>
      baseSalary + (commissionRate * grossSales);

   // return string representation of BasePlusCommissionEmployee
   public override string ToString() =>
      $"base-salaried commission employee: {FirstName} {LastName}\n" +
      $"social security number: {SocialSecurityNumber}\n" +
```

**Fig. 11.9** | BasePlusCommissionEmployee inherits from CommissionEmployee and has access to CommissionEmployee's protected members. (Part 1 of 2.)

```
        $"gross sales: {grossSales:C}\n" +
        $"commission rate: {commissionRate:F2}\n" +
        $"base salary: {baseSalary}";
}
```

**Fig. 11.9** | `BasePlusCommissionEmployee` inherits from `CommissionEmployee` and has access to `CommissionEmployee`'s `protected` members. (Part 2 of 2.)

### *Testing Class* `BasePlusCommissionEmployee`

The `BasePlusCommissionEmployeeTest` class in this example's project is identical to that of Fig. 11.7 and produces the same output, so we do not show the code here. Although the version of class `BasePlusCommissionEmployee` in Fig. 11.6 does not use inheritance and the version in Fig. 11.9 does, both classes provide the *same* functionality. The source code in Fig. 11.9 (52 lines) is considerably shorter than that in Fig. 11.6 (97 lines), because a large portion of the class's functionality is now inherited from `CommissionEmployee`—there's now only one copy of the `CommissionEmployee` functionality. This makes the code easier to maintain, modify and debug, because the code related to a `CommissionEmployee` exists *only* in that class.

### `public` *vs.* `protected` *Data*

We could have declared base class `CommissionEmployee`'s instance variables `grossSales` and `commissionRate` as `public` to enable derived class `BasePlusCommissionEmployee` to access the base-class instance variables. However, declaring `public` instance variables is poor software engineering, because it allows unrestricted access to the instance variables by *any* of the class's clients, greatly increasing the chance of errors and inconsistencies. With `protected` instance variables, the derived class gets access to the instance variables, but classes that are not derived from the base class cannot access its variables directly.

### *Problems with* `protected` *Instance Variables*

In this example, we declared base-class instance variables as `protected` so that derived classes could access them. Inheriting `protected` instance variables enables you to directly access the variables in the derived class *without* invoking the `set` or `get` accessors of the corresponding property, thus violating encapsulation. In most cases, it's better to use `private` instance variables and access them via properties to encourage proper software engineering. Your code will be easier to maintain, modify and debug.

Using `protected` instance variables creates several potential problems. First, since the derived-class object can set an inherited variable's value directly *without* using a property's `set` accessor, a derived-class object can assign an *invalid* value to the variable. For example, if we were to declare `CommissionEmployee`'s instance variable `grossSales` as `protected`, a derived-class object (e.g., `BasePlusCommissionEmployee`) could then directly assign a *negative* value to `grossSales`, making it invalid.

The second problem with `protected` instance variables is that derived-class methods are more likely to be written to *depend* on the base class's data implementation. In practice, derived classes should depend only on the base-class *services* (i.e., non-`private` methods and properties) and *not* on the base-class data implementation. With `protected` instance variables in the base class, we may need to modify all the derived classes of the base class if the base-class implementation changes. For example, if for some reason we were to change the names of instance variables `grossSales` and `commissionRate`, then we'd have to do so for all occurrences in which a derived class directly references base-class instance variables `grossSales` and `commissionRate`. In such a case, the software is said to be **fragile** or **brittle**, because a small change in the base class can "break" derived-class implementation. You should be able to *change* the base-class *implementation* while still providing the *same services* to the derived classes. Of course, if the base-class services change, we must reimplement our derived classes.

**Software Engineering Observation 11.4**

*Declaring base-class instance variables* `private` *(as opposed to* `protected`*) enables the base-class implementation of these instance variables to change without affecting derived-class implementations.*

## 11.4.5 CommissionEmployee–BasePlusCommissionEmployee Inheritance Hierarchy Using private Instance Variables

We now reexamine our hierarchy, this time using the best software engineering practices.

### *Base Class* CommissionEmployee

Class `CommissionEmployee` (Fig. 11.10) once again declares instance variables `grossSales` and `commissionRate` as `private` (lines 10–11). Methods `Earnings` (line 65) and `ToString` (lines 68–72) no longer directly access these instance variables—rather they use properties `GrossSales` and `CommissionRate` to access the data. If we decide to change the instance-variable names, the `Earnings` and `ToString` declarations will *not* require modification—only the bodies of the properties `GrossSales` and `CommissionRate` that directly manipulate the instance variables will need to change. These changes occur solely within the base class—no changes to the derived class are needed. Localizing the effects of changes like this is a good software engineering practice. Derived class `BasePlusCommissionEmployee` (Fig. 11.11) inherits from `CommissionEmployee`'s and can access the `private` base-class members via the inherited `public` properties.

```
1  // Fig. 11.10: CommissionEmployee.cs
2  // CommissionEmployee class represents a commission employee.
3  using System;
4
5  public class CommissionEmployee
6  {
7     public string FirstName { get; }
8     public string LastName { get; }
9     public string SocialSecurityNumber { get; }
10    private decimal grossSales; // gross weekly sales
11    private decimal commissionRate; // commission percentage
12
13    // five-parameter constructor
14    public CommissionEmployee(string firstName, string lastName,
15       string socialSecurityNumber, decimal grossSales,
16       decimal commissionRate)
17    {
```

**Fig. 11.10** | `CommissionEmployee` class represents a commission employee. (Part 1 of 3.)

```
      // implicit call to object constructor occurs here
      FirstName = firstName;
      LastName = lastName;
      SocialSecurityNumber = socialSecurityNumber;
      GrossSales = grossSales; // validates gross sales
      CommissionRate = commissionRate; // validates commission rate
   }

   // property that gets and sets commission employee's gross sales
   public decimal GrossSales
   {
      get
      {
         return grossSales;
      }
      set
      {
         if (value < 0) // validation
         {
            throw new ArgumentOutOfRangeException(nameof(value),
               value, $"{nameof(GrossSales)} must be >= 0");
         }

         grossSales = value;
      }
   }

   // property that gets and sets commission employee's commission rate
   public decimal CommissionRate
   {
      get
      {
         return commissionRate;
      }
      set
      {
         if (value <= 0 || value >= 1) // validation
         {
            throw new ArgumentOutOfRangeException(nameof(value),
               value, $"{nameof(CommissionRate)} must be > 0 and < 1");
         }

         commissionRate = value;
      }
   }

   // calculate commission employee's pay
   public virtual decimal Earnings() => CommissionRate * GrossSales;

   // return string representation of CommissionEmployee object
   public override string ToString() =>
      $"commission employee: {FirstName} {LastName}\n" +
      $"social security number: {SocialSecurityNumber}\n" +
```

**Fig. 11.10** | CommissionEmployee class represents a commission employee. (Part 2 of 3.)

```
        $"gross sales: {GrossSales:C}\n" +
        $"commission rate: {CommissionRate:F2}";
}
```

**Fig. 11.10** | CommissionEmployee class represents a commission employee. (Part 3 of 3.)

### *Derived Class* BasePlusCommissionEmployee

Class BasePlusCommissionEmployee (Fig. 11.11) has several changes to its method implementations that distinguish it from the version in Fig. 11.9. Methods Earnings (Fig. 11.11, line 43) and ToString (lines 46–47) each invoke property BaseSalary's get accessor to obtain the base-salary value, rather than accessing baseSalary directly. If we decide to rename instance variable baseSalary, only the body of property BaseSalary will need to change.

```
1  // Fig. 11.11: BasePlusCommissionEmployee.cs
2  // BasePlusCommissionEmployee inherits from CommissionEmployee and has
3  // controlled access to CommissionEmployee's private data via
4  // its public properties.
5  using System;
6
7  public class BasePlusCommissionEmployee : CommissionEmployee
8  {
9     private decimal baseSalary; // base salary per week
10
11    // six-parameter derived-class constructor
12    // with call to base class CommissionEmployee constructor
13    public BasePlusCommissionEmployee(string firstName, string lastName,
14       string socialSecurityNumber, decimal grossSales,
15       decimal commissionRate, decimal baseSalary)
16       : base(firstName, lastName, socialSecurityNumber,
17            grossSales, commissionRate)
18    {
19       BaseSalary = baseSalary; // validates base salary
20    }
21
22    // property that gets and sets
23    // BasePlusCommissionEmployee's base salary
24    public decimal BaseSalary
25    {
26       get
27       {
28          return baseSalary;
29       }
30       set
31       {
32          if (value < 0) // validation
33          {
```

**Fig. 11.11** | BasePlusCommissionEmployee inherits from CommissionEmployee and has access to CommissionEmployee's private data via its public properties. (Part 1 of 2.)

```
34                 throw new ArgumentOutOfRangeException(nameof(value),
35                    value, $"{nameof(BaseSalary)} must be >= 0");
36              }
37
38              baseSalary = value;
39           }
40        }
41
42        // calculate earnings
43        public override decimal Earnings() => BaseSalary + base.Earnings();
44
45        // return string representation of BasePlusCommissionEmployee
46        public override string ToString() =>
47           $"base-salaried {base.ToString()}\nbase salary: {BaseSalary:C}";
48     }
```

**Fig. 11.11** | `BasePlusCommissionEmployee` inherits from `CommissionEmployee` and has access to `CommissionEmployee`'s `private` data via its `public` properties. (Part 2 of 2.)

### `BasePlusCommissionEmployee` *Method* `Earnings`

Class `BasePlusCommissionEmployee`'s `Earnings` method (Fig. 11.11, line 43) overrides class `CommissionEmployee`'s `Earnings` method (Fig. 11.10, line 65) to calculate the earnings of a `BasePlusCommissionEmployee`. The new version obtains the portion of the employee's earnings based on commission alone by calling `CommissionEmployee`'s `Earnings` method with the expression `base.Earnings()` (Fig. 11.11, line 43), then adds the base salary to this value to calculate the total earnings of the employee. Note the syntax used to invoke an overridden base-class method from a derived class—place the keyword `base` and the member access operator (`.`) before the base-class method name. This method invocation is a good software engineering practice—by having `BasePlusCommissionEmployee`'s `Earnings` method invoke `CommissionEmployee`'s `Earnings` method to calculate part of a `BasePlusCommissionEmployee` object's earnings, we avoid duplicating the code and reduce code-maintenance problems.

**Common Programming Error 11.3**

*When a base-class method is overridden in a derived class, the derived-class version often calls the base-class version to do a portion of the work. Failure to prefix the base-class method name with the keyword* `base` *and the member access (*`.`*) operator when referencing the base class's method from the derived-class version causes the derived-class method to call itself, creating infinite recursion.*

### `BasePlusCommissionEmployee` *Method* `ToString`

Similarly, `BasePlusCommissionEmployee`'s `ToString` method (Fig. 11.11, lines 46–47) overrides `CommissionEmployee`'s (Fig. 11.10, lines 68–72) to return a `string` representation that's appropriate for a base-salaried commission employee. The new version creates part of `BasePlusCommissionEmployee` `string` representation (i.e., the `string` `"commission employee"` and the values of `CommissionEmployee`'s data) by calling `CommissionEmployee`'s `ToString` method with the expression `base.ToString()` (Fig. 11.11, line 47) and incorporating the result into the `string` returned by the derived class's `ToString` method, which includes the base salary.

### *Testing Class* `BasePlusCommissionEmployee`

Class `BasePlusCommissionEmployeeTest` performs the same manipulations on a `BasePlusCommissionEmployee` object as in Fig. 11.7 and produces the same output, so we do not show it here. Although each `BasePlusCommissionEmployee` class you've seen behaves identically, the version in Fig. 11.11 is the best engineered. *By using inheritance and by using properties that hide the data and ensure consistency, we have efficiently and effectively constructed a well-engineered class.*

## 11.5 Constructors in Derived Classes

As we explained in the preceding section, instantiating a derived-class object begins a chain of constructor calls. The derived-class constructor, before performing its own tasks, invokes its direct base class's constructor either explicitly (via a constructor initializer with the `base` reference) or implicitly (calling the base class's default constructor or parameterless constructor). Similarly, if the base class is derived from another class, the base-class constructor invokes the constructor of the next class up in the hierarchy, and so on. The *last* constructor called in the chain is always the constructor for class `object`. The original derived-class constructor's body finishes executing last. Each base class's constructor manipulates the base-class data that the derived-class object inherits.

For example, consider again the `CommissionEmployee`–`BasePlusCommissionEmployee` hierarchy from Figs. 11.10 and 11.11. When an app creates a `BasePlusCommissionEmployee` object, the `BasePlusCommissionEmployee` constructor is called. That constructor *immediately* calls `CommissionEmployee`'s constructor, which in turn *immediately* calls `object`'s constructor implicitly. Class `object`'s constructor performs its task, then immediately returns control to `CommissionEmployee`'s constructor, which then initializes the `CommissionEmployee` data that's part of the `BasePlusCommissionEmployee` object. When `CommissionEmployee`'s constructor completes execution, it returns control to `BasePlusCommissionEmployee`'s constructor, which then initializes the `BasePlusCommissionEmployee` object's `BaseSalary`.

## 11.6 Software Engineering with Inheritance

This section discusses customizing existing software with inheritance. When a new class extends an existing class, the new class inherits the members of the existing class. We can customize the new class to meet our needs by including additional members and by overriding base-class members. C# simply requires access to the compiled base-class code, so it can compile and execute any app that uses or extends the base class. This powerful capability is attractive to independent software vendors (ISVs), who can develop proprietary classes for sale or license and make them available to users in class libraries. Users then can derive new classes from these library classes rapidly, without accessing the ISVs' proprietary source code.

**Software Engineering Observation 11.5**

*Although inheriting from a class does not require access to the class's source code, developers often insist on seeing the source code to understand how the class is implemented. They may, for example, want to ensure that they're extending a class that performs well and is implemented securely.*

People experienced with the scope of the problems faced by designers who work on large-scale software projects say that effective software reuse improves the software-development process. Object-oriented programming facilitates software reuse, potentially shortening development times. The availability of substantial and useful class libraries helps deliver the maximum benefits of software reuse through inheritance.

**Software Engineering Observation 11.6**

*At the design stage in an object-oriented system, the designer often finds that certain classes are closely related. The designer should "factor out" common members and place them in a base class. Then the designer should use inheritance to develop derived classes, specializing them with capabilities beyond those inherited from the base class.*

**Software Engineering Observation 11.7**

*Declaring a derived class does not affect its base class's source code. Inheritance preserves the integrity of the base class.*

Reading derived-class declarations can be confusing, because inherited members are not declared explicitly in the derived classes, but are nevertheless present in them. A similar problem exists in documenting derived-class members.

## 11.7 Class object

As we discussed earlier in this chapter, all classes inherit directly or indirectly from class `object`—an alias for `System.Object` in the Framework Class Library—so its non-`static` methods are inherited by *all* classes. Figure 11.12 summarizes `object`'s methods. You can learn more about `object`'s methods at:

```
http://msdn.microsoft.com/library/system.object
```

| Method | Description |
|---|---|
| `Equals` | This method compares the current object to another object for equality and returns `true` if they're equal and `false` otherwise. It takes any object as an argument. When objects of a particular class must be compared for equality, the class should override method `Equals` to compare the *contents* of the two objects. The website `http://bit.ly/OverridingEqualsCSharp` explains the requirements for a properly overridden `Equals` method. |
| `Finalize` | This method cannot be explicitly declared or called. When a class contains a destructor, the compiler implicitly renames it to override the `protected` method `Finalize`, which is called *only* by the garbage collector before it reclaims an object's memory. The garbage collector is not guaranteed to reclaim an object, thus it's *not* guaranteed that an object's `Finalize` method will execute. When a derived class's `Finalize` method executes, it performs its task, then invokes the base class's `Finalize` method. In general, you should avoid using `Finalize`. |

**Fig. 11.12** | `object` methods that are inherited directly or indirectly by all classes. (Part 1 of 2.)

| Method | Description |
|---|---|
| `GetHashCode` | A hashtable data structure relates objects, called *keys*, to corresponding objects, called *values*. When a value is initially inserted in a hashtable, the key's `GetHashCode` method is called. The value returned is used by the hashtable to determine the location at which to insert the corresponding value. The key's hashcode is also used by the hashtable to locate the key's corresponding value. |
| `GetType` | Every object knows its own type at execution time. Method `GetType` (used in Section 12.5) returns an object of class `Type` (namespace `System`) that contains information about the object's type, such as its class name (obtained from `Type` property `FullName`). |
| `MemberwiseClone` | This `protected` method, which takes no arguments and returns an `object` reference, makes a copy of the object on which it's called. The implementation of this method performs a **shallow copy**—instance-variable values in one object are copied into another object of the same type. For reference types, only the references are copied. |
| `ReferenceEquals` | This `static` method receives two `object` references and returns `true` if they're the same instance or if they're `null` references. Otherwise, it returns `false`. |
| `ToString` | This method (introduced in Section 7.4) returns a `string` representation of the current object. The default implementation of this method returns the namespace followed by a dot and the class name of the object's class. |

**Fig. 11.12** | `object` methods that are inherited directly or indirectly by all classes. (Part 2 of 2.)

## 11.8 Wrap-Up

This chapter introduced inheritance—the ability to create classes by absorbing an existing class's members and enhancing them with new capabilities. You learned the notions of base classes and derived classes and created a derived class that inherits members from a base class and overrides inherited `virtual` methods. We introduced access modifier `protected`; derived-class members can access `protected` base-class members. You learned how to access base-class members with `base`. You also saw how constructors are used in inheritance hierarchies. Finally, you learned about the methods of class `object`, the direct or indirect base class of *all* classes.

In Chapter 12, we build on our discussion of inheritance by introducing polymorphism—an object-oriented concept that enables us to write apps that handle, in a more general manner, objects of a wide variety of classes related by inheritance. After studying Chapter 12, you'll be familiar with classes, objects, encapsulation, inheritance and polymorphism—the most essential aspects of object-oriented programming.

12

# OOP: Polymorphism and Interfaces

## Objectives

In this chapter you'll:

- Understand how polymorphism enables you to "program in the general" and make systems extensible.
- Use overridden methods to effect polymorphism.
- Create abstract classes and methods.
- Determine an object's type at execution time with operator `is`, then use downcasting to perform type-specific processing.
- Create `sealed` methods and classes.
- Declare and implement interfaces.
- Be introduced to interfaces `IComparable`, `IComponent`, `IDisposable` and `IEnumerator` of the .NET Framework Class Library.

Outline



## 12.1 Introduction

We now continue our study of object-oriented programming by explaining and demonstrating **polymorphism** with inheritance hierarchies. Polymorphism enables us to *program in the general* rather than *program in the specific*. In particular, polymorphism enables us to write apps that process objects that share the *same* base class in a class hierarchy as if they were all objects of the base class.

Let's consider a polymorphism example. Suppose we create an app that simulates moving several types of animals for a biological study. Classes `Fish`, `Frog` and `Bird` represent the types of animals under investigation. Imagine that each class extends base class `Animal`, which contains a method `Move` and maintains an animal's current location as *x–y–z* coordinates. Each derived class implements method `Move` differently. Our app maintains a collection of references to objects of the various `Animal`-derived classes. To simulate an animal's movements, the app sends each object the *same* message once per second—namely, `Move`. Each specific type of `Animal` responds to a `Move` message in a unique way—a `Fish` might swim three feet, a `Frog` might jump five feet and a `Bird` might fly 10 feet. The app issues the `Move` message to each animal object *generically*, but each object modifies its *x–y–z* coordinates appropriately for its *specific* type of movement. Relying on each object to "do the right thing" in response to the *same* method call is the key concept of polymorphism. The *same* message (in this case, `Move`) sent to a *variety* of objects has *many forms* of results—hence the term polymorphism.

### *Systems Are Easy to Extend*

With polymorphism, we can design and implement systems that are easily *extensible*—new classes can be added with little or no modification to the polymorphic portions of the app, as long as the new classes are part of the inheritance hierarchy that the app processes generically. The only parts of an app that must be altered to accommodate new classes are those that require direct knowledge of the new classes that you add to the hierarchy. For example, if we extend class `Animal` to create class `Tortoise` (which might respond to a `Move` message by crawling one inch), we need to write only the `Tortoise` class and the part of the simulation that instantiates a `Tortoise` object. The portions of the simulation that process each `Animal` generically can remain the *same*.

This chapter has several parts. First, we discuss common examples of polymorphism. We then provide an example demonstrating polymorphic behavior. As you'll soon see, you'll use base-class references to manipulate both base-class objects *and* derived-class objects polymorphically.

### *Polymorphic* `Employee` *Inheritance Hierarchy*

We then present a case study that revisits the `Employee` hierarchy of Section 11.4.5. We develop a simple payroll app that polymorphically calculates the weekly pay of several different types of employees using each employee's `Earnings` method. Though the earnings of each type of employee are calculated in a *specific* way, polymorphism allows us to process the employees "in the *general*." In the case study, we enlarge the hierarchy to include two new classes—`SalariedEmployee` (for people paid a fixed weekly salary) and `HourlyEmployee` (for people paid an hourly salary and "time-and-a-half" for overtime). We declare a *common set of functionality* for all the classes in the updated hierarchy in a base class `Employee` (Section 12.5.1) from which classes `SalariedEmployee`, `HourlyEmployee` and `CommissionEmployee` *inherit directly* and class `BasePlusCommissionEmployee` *inherits indirectly*. As you'll soon see, when we invoke each employee's `Earnings` method via a base-class `Employee` reference, the correct earnings calculation is performed due to C#'s polymorphic capabilities.

### *Determining the Type of an Object at Execution Time*

Occasionally, when performing polymorphic processing, we need to program "in the *specific*." Our `Employee` case study demonstrates that an app can determine the type of an object at *execution* time and act on that object accordingly. In the case study, we use these capabilities to determine whether a particular employee object *is a* `BasePlusCommissionEmployee`. If so, we increase that employee's base salary by 10%.

### *Interfaces*

The chapter continues with an introduction to C# interfaces. An interface describes a set of methods and properties that can be called on an object, but does *not* provide *concrete* implementations for them. You can declare classes that **implement** (i.e., provide *concrete* implementations for the methods and properties of) one or more interfaces. Each interface member must be defined for *all* the classes that implement the interface. Once a class implements an interface, all objects of that class have an *is-a* relationship with the interface type, and all objects of the class are *guaranteed* to provide the functionality described by the interface. This is true of all *derived* classes of that class as well.

Interfaces are particularly useful for assigning common functionality to possibly *unrelated* classes. This allows objects of unrelated classes to be processed polymorphically—objects of classes that implement the *same* interface can respond to the *same* method calls. To demonstrate creating and using interfaces, we modify our payroll app to create a general accounts-payable app that can calculate payments due for the earnings of company employees and for invoice amounts to be billed for purchased goods. As you'll see, interfaces enable polymorphic capabilities similar to those enabled by inheritance.

## 12.2 Polymorphism Examples

Let's consider several additional examples of polymorphism.

### Quadrilateral *Inheritance Hierarchy*

If class `Rectangle` is derived from class `Quadrilateral` (a four-sided shape), then a `Rectangle` *is a* more specific version of a `Quadrilateral`. Any operation (e.g., calculating the perimeter or the area) that can be performed on a `Quadrilateral` object also can be performed on a `Rectangle` object. These operations also can be performed on other `Quadrilaterals`, such as `Squares`, `Parallelograms` and `Trapezoids`. The polymorphism occurs when an app invokes a method through a base-class variable—at execution time, the correct derived-class version of the method is called, based on the type of the referenced object. You'll see a simple code example that illustrates this process in Section 12.3.

### *Video Game* `SpaceObject` *Inheritance Hierarchy*

As another example, suppose we design a video game that manipulates objects of many different types, including objects of classes `Martian`, `Venusian`, `Plutonian`, `SpaceShip` and `LaserBeam`. Imagine that each class inherits from the common base class `SpaceObject`, which contains method `Draw`. Each derived class implements this method. A screen-manager app maintains a collection (e.g., a `SpaceObject` array) of references to objects of the various classes. To refresh the screen, the screen manager periodically sends each object the *same message*—namely, `Draw`. However, each object responds in a unique way. For example, a `Martian` object might *draw itself* in red with the appropriate number of antennae. A `SpaceShip` object might *draw itself* as a bright silver flying saucer. A `LaserBeam` object might *draw itself* as a bright red beam across the screen. Again, the *same message* (in this case, `Draw`) sent to a variety of objects has *many forms* of results.

A screen manager might use polymorphism to facilitate adding new classes to a system with minimal modifications to the system's code. Suppose we want to add `Mercurian` objects to our video game. To do so, we must build a `Mercurian` class that extends `SpaceObject` and provides its own `Draw` method implementation. When objects of class `Mercurian` appear in the `SpaceObject` collection, the screen-manager code invokes method `Draw`, exactly as it does for every other object in the collection, *regardless of its type*, so the new `Mercurian` objects simply "plug right in" without any modification of the screen-manager code by the programmer. Thus, without modifying the system (other than to build new classes and modify the code that creates new objects), you can use polymorphism to include additional types that might not have been envisioned when the system was created.

**Software Engineering Observation 12.1**

*Polymorphism promotes extensibility: Software that invokes polymorphic behavior is independent of the object types to which messages are sent. New object types that can respond to existing method calls can be incorporated into a system without requiring modification of the polymorphic system logic. Only client code that instantiates new objects must be modified to accommodate new types.*

## 12.3 Demonstrating Polymorphic Behavior

Section 11.4 created a commission-employee class hierarchy, in which class `BasePlusCommissionEmployee` inherited from class `CommissionEmployee`. The examples in that section manipulated `CommissionEmployee` and `BasePlusCommissionEmployee` objects by using references to them to invoke their methods. We aimed base-class references at base-class objects and derived-class references at derived-class objects. These assignments are natural and straightforward—base-class references are intended to refer to base-class objects, and derived-class references are intended to refer to derived-class objects. However, other assignments are possible.

The next example aims a base-class reference at a derived-class object, then shows how invoking a method on a derived-class object via a base-class reference invokes the derived-class functionality—*the type of the actual referenced object, not the type of the reference, determines which method is called.* This demonstrates the key concept that a derived-class object can be treated as an object of its base class, which enables various interesting manipulations. An app can create a collection of base-class references that refer to objects of many derived-class types, because each derived-class object *is an* object of its base class. For instance, we can assign the reference of a `BasePlusCommissionEmployee` object to a base-class `CommissionEmployee` variable because a `BasePlusCommissionEmployee` *is a* `CommissionEmployee`—so we can treat a `BasePlusCommissionEmployee` as a `CommissionEmployee`.

*A base-class object is not an object of any of its derived classes.* For example, we cannot directly assign the reference of a `CommissionEmployee` object to a derived-class `BasePlusCommissionEmployee` variable, because a `CommissionEmployee` *is not* a `BasePlusCommissionEmployee`—a `CommissionEmployee` does not, for example, have a `baseSalary` instance variable and does not have a `BaseSalary` property. The compiler allows the assignment of a base-class reference to a derived-class variable *if* we explicitly cast the base-class reference to the derived-class type—a technique we discuss in greater detail in Section 12.5.6.

**Software Engineering Observation 12.2**

*The* is-a *relationship applies from a derived class to its direct and indirect base classes, but not vice versa.*

Figure 12.1 demonstrates three ways to use base-class and derived-class variables to store references to base-class and derived-class objects. The first two are straightforward—as in Section 11.4, we assign a base-class reference to a base-class variable, and we assign a derived-class reference to a derived-class variable. Then we demonstrate the relationship between derived classes and base classes (i.e., the *is-a* relationship) by assigning a derived-class reference to a base-class variable. [*Note:* This app uses classes `CommissionEmployee` and `BasePlusCommissionEmployee` from Fig. 11.10 and Fig. 11.11, respectively.]

```
// Fig. 12.1: PolymorphismTest.cs
// Assigning base-class and derived-class references to base-class and
// derived-class variables.
using System;

```

**Fig. 12.1** | Assigning base-class and derived-class references to base-class and derived-class variables. (Part 1 of 3.)

```
class PolymorphismTest
{
   static void Main()
   {
      // assign base-class reference to base-class variable
      var commissionEmployee = new CommissionEmployee(
         "Sue", "Jones", "222-22-2222", 10000.00M, .06M);

      // assign derived-class reference to derived-class variable
      var basePlusCommissionEmployee = new BasePlusCommissionEmployee(
         "Bob", "Lewis", "333-33-3333", 5000.00M, .04M, 300.00M);

      // invoke ToString and Earnings on base-class object
      // using base-class variable
      Console.WriteLine(
         "Call CommissionEmployee's ToString and Earnings methods " +
         "with base-class reference to base class object\n");
      Console.WriteLine(commissionEmployee.ToString());
      Console.WriteLine($"earnings: {commissionEmployee.Earnings()}\n");

      // invoke ToString and Earnings on derived-class object
      // using derived-class variable
      Console.WriteLine("Call BasePlusCommissionEmployee's ToString and" +
         " Earnings methods with derived class reference to" +
         " derived-class object\n");
      Console.WriteLine(basePlusCommissionEmployee.ToString());
      Console.WriteLine(
         $"earnings: {basePlusCommissionEmployee.Earnings()}\n");

      // invoke ToString and Earnings on derived-class object
      // using base-class variable
      CommissionEmployee commissionEmployee2 = basePlusCommissionEmployee;
      Console.WriteLine(
         "Call BasePlusCommissionEmployee's ToString and Earnings " +
         "methods with base class reference to derived-class object");
      Console.WriteLine(commissionEmployee2.ToString());
      Console.WriteLine(
         $"earnings: {basePlusCommissionEmployee.Earnings()}\n");
   }
}
```

```
Call CommissionEmployee's ToString and Earnings methods with base class
reference to base class object:

commission employee: Sue Jones
social security number: 222-22-2222
gross sales: $10,000.00
commission rate: 0.06
earnings: $600.00
```

**Fig. 12.1** | Assigning base-class and derived-class references to base-class and derived-class variables. (Part 2 of 3.)

```
Call BasePlusCommissionEmployee's ToString and Earnings methods with derived
class reference to derived class object:

base-salaried commission employee: Bob Lewis
social security number: 333-33-3333
gross sales: $5,000.00
commission rate: 0.04
base salary: $300.00
earnings: $500.00

Call BasePlusCommissionEmployee's ToString and Earnings methods with base
class reference to derived class object:

base-salaried commission employee: Bob Lewis
social security number: 333-33-3333
gross sales: $5,000.00
commission rate: 0.04
base salary: $300.00
earnings: $500.00
```

**Fig. 12.1** | Assigning base-class and derived-class references to base-class and derived-class variables. (Part 3 of 3.)

In Fig. 12.1, lines 11–12 create a new `CommissionEmployee` object and assign its reference to a `CommissionEmployee` variable and lines 15–16 create a new `BasePlusCommissionEmployee` object and assign its reference to a `BasePlusCommissionEmployee` variable. These assignments are *natural*—a `CommissionEmployee` variable's primary purpose is to hold a reference to a `CommissionEmployee` object. Lines 23–24 use the reference `commissionEmployee` to invoke methods `ToString` and `Earnings`. Because `commissionEmployee` refers to a `CommissionEmployee` object, *base class* `CommissionEmployee`'s version of the methods are called. Similarly, lines 31–33 use the reference `basePlusCommissionEmployee` to invoke the methods `ToString` and `Earnings` on the `BasePlusCommissionEmployee` object. This invokes *derived class* `BasePlusCommissionEmployee`'s version of the methods.

Line 37 then assigns the reference to derived-class object `basePlusCommissionEmployee` to a *base-class* `CommissionEmployee` variable, which lines 41–43 use to invoke methods `ToString` and `Earnings`. Note that the call `commissionEmployee2.ToString()` in line 41 actually calls *derived* class `BasePlusCommissionEmployee`'s `ToString` method. The compiler allows this "crossover" because an object of a derived class *is an* object of its base class (but not vice versa). When the compiler encounters a `virtual` method call made through a variable, the compiler checks the *variable's* class type to determine if the method can be called. If that class contains the proper method declaration (or inherits one), the call compiles. At execution time, *the type of the object to which the variable refers* determines the actual method to use.

**Software Engineering Observation 12.3**

*A base-class variable that contains a reference to a derived-class object and is used to call a `virtual` method actually calls the overriding derived-class version of the method.*

## 12.4 Abstract Classes and Methods

When we think of a class type, we assume that apps will create objects of that type. In some cases, however, it's useful to declare *classes for which you never intend to instantiate objects*. Such classes are called **abstract classes**. Because they're used only as base classes in inheritance hierarchies, we refer to them as **abstract base classes**. These classes *cannot* be used to instantiate objects, because, as you'll soon see, abstract classes are *incomplete*—derived classes must define the "missing pieces." Section 12.5.1 demonstrates abstract classes.

### *Purpose of an Abstract Class*

The purpose of an abstract class is primarily to provide an appropriate base class from which other classes can inherit, and thus *share a common design*. In the `Shape` hierarchy of Fig. 11.3, for example, derived classes inherit the notion of what it means to be a `Shape`—common attributes such as `Location`, `Color` and `BorderThickness`, and behaviors such as `Draw`, `Move`, `Resize` and `ChangeColor`. Classes that can be used to instantiate objects are called **concrete classes**. Such classes provide implementations of *every* method they declare (some of the implementations can be inherited). For example, we could derive concrete classes `Circle`, `Square` and `Triangle` from abstract base class `TwoDimensionalShape`. Similarly, we could derive concrete classes `Sphere`, `Cube` and `Tetrahedron` from abstract base class `ThreeDimensionalShape`. Abstract classes are too *general* to create real objects—they specify only what is common among derived classes. We need to be more *specific* before we can create objects. For example, if you send the `Draw` message to abstract class `TwoDimensionalShape`, the class knows that two-dimensional shapes should be drawable, but it does *not* know what *specific* shape to draw, so it cannot implement a real `Draw` method. *Concrete* classes provide the *specifics* needed to instantiate objects.

### *Client Code That Uses Only Abstract Base-Class Types*

Not all inheritance hierarchies contain abstract classes. However, you'll often write client code that uses only abstract base-class types to reduce client code's dependencies on a range of specific derived-class types. For example, you can write a method with a parameter of an abstract base-class type. When called, such a method can be passed an object of any concrete class that directly or indirectly extends the abstract base class specified as the parameter's type.

### *Multiple Levels of Abstract Base-Class Types in a Hierarchy*

Abstract classes sometimes constitute several levels of the hierarchy. For example, the `Shape` hierarchy of Fig. 11.3 begins with *abstract* class `Shape`. On the next level of the hierarchy are two more *abstract* classes, `TwoDimensionalShape` and `ThreeDimensionalShape`. The next level of the hierarchy declares *concrete* classes for `TwoDimensionalShapes` (`Circle`, `Square` and `Triangle`) and for `ThreeDimensionalShapes` (`Sphere`, `Cube` and `Tetrahedron`).

### *Creating an Abstract Class*

You make a class abstract by declaring it with the keyword **`abstract`**. An abstract class normally contains one or more **abstract methods**. An abstract method is one with keyword `abstract` in its declaration, as in

```
public abstract void Draw(); // abstract method
```

*Abstract methods are implicitly virtual and do not provide implementations.* A class that contains abstract methods must be declared as an abstract class *even if* it contains some concrete (non-`abstract`) methods. Each *concrete* derived class of an abstract base class also must provide concrete implementations of the base class's abstract methods. We show an example of an abstract class with an abstract method in Fig. 12.4.

### *Abstract Properties*

Properties also can be declared `abstract` or `virtual`, then overridden in derived classes with the `override` keyword, just like methods. This allows an abstract base class to specify common properties of its derived classes. Abstract property declarations have the form:

```
public abstract PropertyType MyProperty { get; set; }
```

The semicolons after the `get` and `set` keywords indicate that we provide *no implementation* for these accessors. An abstract property omits implementations for the `get` accessor and/or the `set` accessor. Concrete derived classes *must* provide implementations for *every* accessor declared in the abstract property. When both `get` and `set` accessors are specified, every concrete derived class must implement both. If one accessor is omitted, the derived class is *not* allowed to implement that accessor. Doing so causes a compilation error.

### *Constructors and `static` Methods Cannot be `abstract` or `virtual`*

Constructors and `static` methods *cannot* be declared `abstract` or `virtual`. Constructors are not inherited, so such a constructor could never be implemented. Similarly, derived classes cannot override `static` methods, so such as `static` method could never be implemented.

**Software Engineering Observation 12.4**

*An abstract class declares common attributes and behaviors of the various classes that inherit from it, either directly or indirectly, in a class hierarchy. An abstract class typically contains one or more abstract methods or properties that concrete derived classes must override. The instance variables, concrete methods and concrete properties of an abstract class are subject to the normal rules of inheritance.*

**Common Programming Error 12.1**

*Attempting to instantiate an object of an abstract class is a compilation error.*

**Common Programming Error 12.2**

*Failure to implement a base class's abstract methods and properties in a derived class is a compilation error unless the derived class is also declared* `abstract`.

### *Declaring Variables of Abstract Base-Class Types*

Although we cannot instantiate objects of abstract base classes, you'll soon see that we *can* use abstract base classes to declare variables that can hold references to objects of *any* concrete classes *derived* from those abstract classes. Apps typically use such variables to manipulate derived-class objects polymorphically. Also, you can use abstract base-class names to invoke `static` methods declared in those abstract base classes.

### *Polymorphism and Device Drivers*

Polymorphism is particularly effective for implementing so-called *layered software systems*. In operating systems, for example, each different type of physical device could operate quite differently from the others. Even so, common commands can read or write data from and to the devices. For each device, the operating system uses a piece of software called a *device driver* to control all communication between the system and the device. The write message sent to a device-driver object needs to be interpreted *specifically* in the context of that driver and how it manipulates a specific device. However, the write call itself really is no different from the write to any other device in the system: Place some number of bytes from memory onto that device. An object-oriented operating system might use an abstract base class to provide an "interface" appropriate for all device drivers. Then, through inheritance from that abstract base class, derived classes are formed that all behave similarly. The device-driver methods are declared as abstract methods in the abstract base class. The implementations of these abstract methods are provided in the derived classes that correspond to the specific types of device drivers. New devices are always being developed, often long after the operating system has been released. When you buy a new device, it comes with a device driver provided by the device vendor. The device is immediately operational after you connect it to your computer and install the device driver. This is another elegant example of how polymorphism makes systems *extensible*.

## 12.5 Case Study: Payroll System Using Polymorphism

This section reexamines the `CommissionEmployee-BasePlusCommissionEmployee` hierarchy that we explored in Section 11.4. Now we use an abstract method and polymorphism to perform payroll calculations based on the type of employee. We create an enhanced employee hierarchy to solve the following problem:

> *A company pays its employees on a weekly basis. The employees are of four types:*
>
> 1. *Salaried employees are paid a fixed weekly salary regardless of the number of hours worked.*
> 2. *Hourly employees are paid by the hour and receive "time-and-a-half" overtime pay for all hours worked in excess of 40 hours*
> 3. *Commission employees are paid a percentage of their sales.*
> 4. *Salaried-commission employees receive a base salary plus a percentage of their sales.*
>
> *For the current pay period, the company has decided to reward salaried-commission employees by adding 10% to their base salaries. The company wants to implement an app that performs its payroll calculations polymorphically.*

We use `abstract` class `Employee` to represent the general concept of an employee. The classes that extend `Employee` are `SalariedEmployee`, `CommissionEmployee` and `HourlyEmployee`. Class `BasePlusCommissionEmployee`—which extends `CommissionEmployee`—represents the last employee type. The UML class diagram in Fig. 12.2 shows the inheritance hierarchy for our polymorphic employee payroll app. Abstract class `Employee` is *italicized*, as per the convention of the UML.

Abstract base class `Employee` declares the "interface" to the hierarchy—that is, the set of members that an app can invoke on all `Employee` objects. We use the term "interface" here in a general sense to refer to the various ways apps can communicate with objects of any `Employee` derived class. Be careful not to confuse the general notion of an "interface" with the formal notion of a C# interface, the subject of Section 12.7. Each employee, regardless of the way his or her earnings are calculated, has a first name, a last name and a social security number, so those pieces of data appear in abstract base class `Employee`.

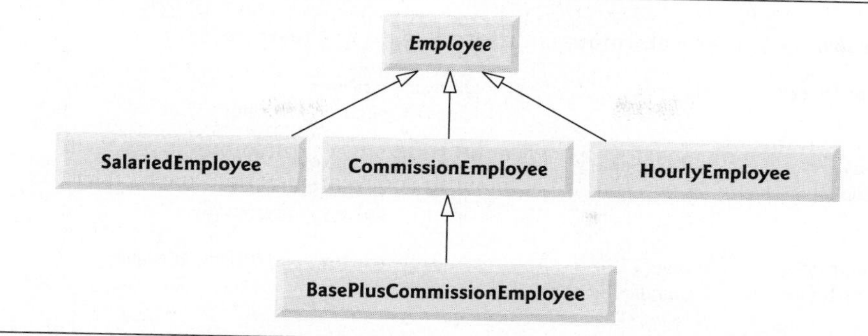


**Fig. 12.2** | `Employee` hierarchy UML class diagram.

The following subsections implement the `Employee` class hierarchy. Section 12.5.1 implements `abstract` base class `Employee`. Sections 12.5.2–12.5.5 each implement one of the concrete classes. Section 12.5.6 implements a test app that builds objects of all these classes and processes those objects polymorphically.

### 12.5.1 Creating Abstract Base Class `Employee`

Class `Employee` (Fig. 12.4) provides methods `Earnings` and `ToString`, in addition to the auto-implemented properties that manipulate `Employee`'s data. An `Earnings` method certainly applies generically to all employees. But each earnings calculation depends on the employee's class. So we declare `Earnings` as `abstract` in base class `Employee`, because a default implementation does not make sense for that method—there's not enough information to determine what amount `Earnings` should return. Each derived class overrides `Earnings` with a specific implementation. To calculate an employee's earnings, the app assigns a reference to the employee's object to a base class `Employee` variable, then invokes the `Earnings` method on that variable. We maintain a `List` of `Employee` variables, each of which holds a reference to an `Employee` object (of course, there *cannot* be `Employee` objects because `Employee` is an *abstract* class—because of inheritance, however, all objects of all derived classes of `Employee` may nevertheless be thought of as `Employee` objects). The app iterates through the `List` and calls method `Earnings` for each `Employee` object. These method calls are processed polymorphically. Including `Earnings` as an abstract method in `Employee` *forces* every directly derived *concrete* class of `Employee` to override `Earnings` with a method that performs an appropriate pay calculation.

Method `ToString` in class `Employee` returns a `string` containing the employee's first name, last name and social security number. Each derived class of `Employee` overrides method `ToString` to create a `string` representation of an object of that class containing the employee's type (e.g., `"salaried employee:"`), followed by the rest of the employee's information.

The diagram in Fig. 12.3 shows each of the five classes in the hierarchy down the left side and methods `Earnings` and `ToString` across the top. For each class, the diagram shows the desired results of each method. [*Note:* We do not list base class `Employee`'s properties because they're not overridden in any of the derived classes—each of these properties is inherited and used "as is" by each of the derived classes.]

| | Earnings | ToString |
|---|---|---|
| Employee | abstract | *firstName lastName*<br>social security number: *SSN* |
| Salaried-<br>Employee | weeklySalary | salaried employee: *firstName lastName*<br>social security number: *SSN*<br>weekly salary: *weeklysalary* |
| Hourly-<br>Employee | *If hours <= 40*<br>wage * hours<br>*If hours > 40*<br>40 * wage +<br>(hours - 40) *<br>wage * 1.5 | hourly employee: *firstName lastName*<br>social security number: *SSN*<br>hourly wage: *wage*<br>hours worked: *hours* |
| Commission-<br>Employee | commissionRate *<br>grossSales | commission employee: *firstName lastName*<br>social security number: *SSN*<br>gross sales: *grossSales*<br>commission rate: *commissionRate* |
| BasePlus-<br>Commission-<br>Employee | baseSalary +<br>(commissionRate *<br>grossSales) | base salaried commission employee:<br>*firstName lastName*<br>social security number: *SSN*<br>gross sales: *grossSales*<br>commission rate: *commissionRate*<br>base salary: *baseSalary* |

**Fig. 12.3** | Polymorphic interface for the Employee hierarchy classes.

### *Class* Employee

Let's consider class Employee's declaration (Fig. 12.4). The class includes auto-implemented, getter-only properties for the first name, last name and social security number (lines 5–7); a constructor that initializes the first name, last name and social security number (lines 10–16); expression-bodied method ToString (lines 19–20), which uses properties to return an Employee's string representation; and abstract method Earnings (line 23), which *must* be implemented by *concrete* derived classes. The Employee constructor does not validate the social security number in this example. Normally, such validation should be provided.

```
1  // Fig. 12.4: Employee.cs
2  // Employee abstract base class.
3  public abstract class Employee
4  {
5     public string FirstName { get; }
6     public string LastName { get; }
7     public string SocialSecurityNumber { get; }
```

**Fig. 12.4** | Employee abstract base class. (Part 1 of 2.)

```

   // three-parameter constructor
   public Employee(string firstName, string lastName,
      string socialSecurityNumber)
   {
      FirstName = firstName;
      LastName = lastName;
      SocialSecurityNumber = socialSecurityNumber;
   }

   // return string representation of Employee object, using properties
   public override string ToString() => $"{FirstName} {LastName}\n" +
      $"social security number: {SocialSecurityNumber}";

   // abstract method overridden by derived classes
   public abstract decimal Earnings(); // no implementation here
}
```

**Fig. 12.4** | `Employee` abstract base class. (Part 2 of 2.)

Why did we declare `Earnings` as an `abstract` method? As explained earlier, it simply does not make sense to provide an implementation of this method in class `Employee`. We cannot calculate the earnings for a *general* `Employee`—we first must know the *specific* `Employee` type to determine the appropriate earnings calculation. By declaring this method `abstract`, we indicate that each *concrete* derived class *must* provide an appropriate `Earnings` implementation and that an app will be able to use base-class `Employee` variables to invoke method `Earnings` polymorphically for *any* type of `Employee`.

### 12.5.2 Creating Concrete Derived Class `SalariedEmployee`

Class `SalariedEmployee` (Fig. 12.5) extends class `Employee` (line 5) and overrides `Earnings` (line 37), which makes `SalariedEmployee` a concrete class. The class includes a constructor (lines 10–15) that takes a first name, a last name, a social security number and a weekly salary as arguments; property `WeeklySalary` (lines 18–34) to manipulate instance variable `weeklySalary`, including a `set` accessor that ensures we assign only nonnegative values to `weeklySalary`; method `Earnings` (line 37) to calculate a `SalariedEmployee`'s earnings; and method `ToString` (lines 40–42), which returns a `string` including the employee's type, namely, `"salaried employee: "`, followed by employee-specific information produced by base class `Employee`'s `ToString` method and `SalariedEmployee`'s `WeeklySalary` property. Class `SalariedEmployee`'s constructor passes the first name, last name and social security number to the `Employee` constructor (line 12) via a constructor initializer to initialize the base class's data. Method `Earnings` overrides `Employee`'s `abstract` method `Earnings` to provide a concrete implementation that returns the `SalariedEmployee`'s weekly salary. If we do not implement `Earnings`, class `SalariedEmployee` must be declared `abstract`—otherwise, a compilation error occurs (and, of course, we want `SalariedEmployee` to be a concrete class).

```
1  // Fig. 12.5: SalariedEmployee.cs
2  // SalariedEmployee class that extends Employee.
3  using System;
4
5  public class SalariedEmployee : Employee
6  {
7     private decimal weeklySalary;
8
9     // four-parameter constructor
10    public SalariedEmployee(string firstName, string lastName,
11       string socialSecurityNumber, decimal weeklySalary)
12       : base(firstName, lastName, socialSecurityNumber)
13    {
14       WeeklySalary = weeklySalary; // validate salary
15    }
16
17    // property that gets and sets salaried employee's salary
18    public decimal WeeklySalary
19    {
20       get
21       {
22          return weeklySalary;
23       }
24       set
25       {
26          if (value < 0) // validation
27          {
28             throw new ArgumentOutOfRangeException(nameof(value),
29                value, $"{nameof(WeeklySalary)} must be >= 0");
30          }
31
32          weeklySalary = value;
33       }
34    }
35
36    // calculate earnings; override abstract method Earnings in Employee
37    public override decimal Earnings() => WeeklySalary;
38
39    // return string representation of SalariedEmployee object
40    public override string ToString() =>
41       $"salaried employee: {base.ToString()}\n" +
42       $"weekly salary: {WeeklySalary:C}";
43 }
```

**Fig. 12.5** | `SalariedEmployee` class that extends `Employee`.

`SalariedEmployee` method `ToString` (lines 40–42) overrides `Employee`'s version. If class `SalariedEmployee` did *not* override `ToString`, `SalariedEmployee` would have inherited the `Employee` version. In that case, `SalariedEmployee`'s `ToString` method would simply return the employee's full name and social security number, which does not adequately represent a `SalariedEmployee`.

To produce a complete `SalariedEmployee` `string` representation, the derived class's `ToString` method returns `"salaried employee: "`, followed by the base-class `Employee`-

specific information (i.e., first name, last name and social security number) obtained by invoking the base class's `ToString` via keyword `base` (line 41)—this is a nice example of code reuse. The `string` representation also contains the employee's weekly salary, obtained via property `WeeklySalary`.

### 12.5.3 Creating Concrete Derived Class `HourlyEmployee`

Class `HourlyEmployee` (Fig. 12.6) also extends class `Employee` (line 5). The class includes a constructor (lines 11–18) that takes as arguments a first name, a last name, a social security number, an hourly wage and the number of hours worked. Lines 21–37 and 40–56 declare properties `Wage` and `Hours` for instance variables `wage` and `hours` (lines 7–8), respectively. `Wage`'s `set` accessor ensures that `wage` is nonnegative, and `Hours`' `set` accessor ensures that `hours` is in the range `0–168` (the total number of hours in a week) inclusive. The class overrides method `Earnings` (lines 59–69) to calculate an `HourlyEmployee`'s earnings and method `ToString` (lines 72–74) to return an `HourlyEmployee`'s `string` representation. The `HourlyEmployee` constructor passes the first name, last name and social security number to the base-class `Employee` constructor (line 14) to initialize the base class's data. Also, method `ToString` calls base-class method `ToString` (line 73) to get the `string` representation of the `Employee`-specific information (i.e., first name, last name and social security number).

```
1  // Fig. 12.6: HourlyEmployee.cs
2  // HourlyEmployee class that extends Employee.
3  using System;
4
5  public class HourlyEmployee : Employee
6  {
7     private decimal wage; // wage per hour
8     private decimal hours; // hours worked for the week
9
10    // five-parameter constructor
11    public HourlyEmployee(string firstName, string lastName,
12       string socialSecurityNumber, decimal hourlyWage,
13       decimal hoursWorked)
14       : base(firstName, lastName, socialSecurityNumber)
15    {
16       Wage = hourlyWage; // validate hourly wage
17       Hours = hoursWorked; // validate hours worked
18    }
19
20    // property that gets and sets hourly employee's wage
21    public decimal Wage
22    {
23       get
24       {
25          return wage;
26       }
27       set
28       {
```

**Fig. 12.6** | `HourlyEmployee` class that extends `Employee`. (Part 1 of 2.)

```
         if (value < 0) // validation
         {
            throw new ArgumentOutOfRangeException(nameof(value),
               value, $"{nameof(Wage)} must be >= 0");
         }

         wage = value;
      }
   }

   // property that gets and sets hourly employee's hours
   public decimal Hours
   {
      get
      {
         return hours;
      }
      set
      {
         if (value < 0 || value > 168) // validation
         {
            throw new ArgumentOutOfRangeException(nameof(value),
               value, $"{nameof(Hours)} must be >= 0 and <= 168");
         }

         hours = value;
      }
   }

   // calculate earnings; override Employee's abstract method Earnings
   public override decimal Earnings()
   {
      if (Hours <= 40) // no overtime
      {
         return Wage * Hours;
      }
      else
      {
         return (40 * Wage) + ((Hours - 40) * Wage * 1.5M);
      }
   }

   // return string representation of HourlyEmployee object
   public override string ToString() =>
      $"hourly employee: {base.ToString()}\n" +
      $"hourly wage: {Wage:C}\nhours worked: {Hours:F2}";
}
```

**Fig. 12.6** | HourlyEmployee class that extends Employee. (Part 2 of 2.)

## 12.5.4 Creating Concrete Derived Class CommissionEmployee

Class CommissionEmployee (Fig. 12.7) extends class Employee (line 5). The class includes a constructor (lines 11–18) that takes a first name, a last name, a social security number, a sales amount and a commission rate; properties `GrossSales` and `CommissionRate` (lines 21–37 and 40–56) to manipulate instance variables `grossSales` and `commissionRate`, respectively; overridden method `Earnings` (line 59) to calculate a `CommissionEmployee`'s earnings; and overridden method `ToString` (lines 62–65), which returns a `CommissionEmployee`'s `string` representation. The constructor also passes the first name, last name and social security number to the `Employee` constructor (line 14) to initialize `Employee`'s data. Method `ToString` calls base-class method `ToString` (line 63) to get the `string` representation of the `Employee`-specific information (i.e., first name, last name and social security number).

```
1  // Fig. 12.7: CommissionEmployee.cs
2  // CommissionEmployee class that extends Employee.
3  using System;
4
5  public class CommissionEmployee : Employee
6  {
7     private decimal grossSales; // gross weekly sales
8     private decimal commissionRate; // commission percentage
9
10    // five-parameter constructor
11    public CommissionEmployee(string firstName, string lastName,
12       string socialSecurityNumber, decimal grossSales,
13       decimal commissionRate)
14       : base(firstName, lastName, socialSecurityNumber)
15    {
16       GrossSales = grossSales; // validates gross sales
17       CommissionRate = commissionRate; // validates commission rate
18    }
19
20    // property that gets and sets commission employee's gross sales
21    public decimal GrossSales
22    {
23       get
24       {
25          return grossSales;
26       }
27       set
28       {
29          if (value < 0) // validation
30          {
31             throw new ArgumentOutOfRangeException(nameof(value),
32                value, $"{nameof(GrossSales)} must be >= 0");
33          }
34
35          grossSales = value;
36       }
37    }
38
39    // property that gets and sets commission employee's commission rate
40    public decimal CommissionRate
41    {
```

**Fig. 12.7** | `CommissionEmployee` class that extends `Employee`. (Part 1 of 2.)

```
      get
      {
         return commissionRate;
      }
      set
      {
         if (value <= 0 || value >= 1) // validation
         {
            throw new ArgumentOutOfRangeException(nameof(value),
               value, $"{nameof(CommissionRate)} must be > 0 and < 1");
         }

         commissionRate = value;
      }
   }

   // calculate earnings; override abstract method Earnings in Employee
   public override decimal Earnings() => CommissionRate * GrossSales;

   // return string representation of CommissionEmployee object
   public override string ToString() =>
      $"commission employee: {base.ToString()}\n" +
      $"gross sales: {GrossSales:C}\n" +
      $"commission rate: {CommissionRate:F2}";
}
```

**Fig. 12.7** | CommissionEmployee class that extends Employee. (Part 2 of 2.)

### 12.5.5 Creating Indirect Concrete Derived Class BasePlusCommissionEmployee

Class BasePlusCommissionEmployee (Fig. 12.8) extends class CommissionEmployee (line 5) and therefore is an *indirect* derived class of class Employee. BasePlusCommissionEmployee has a constructor (lines 10–17) that takes as arguments a first name, a last name, a social security number, a sales amount, a commission rate and a base salary. It then passes the first name, last name, social security number, sales amount and commission rate to the CommissionEmployee constructor (lines 13–14) to initialize the base class's data. BasePlusCommissionEmployee also contains property BaseSalary (lines 21–37) to manipulate instance variable baseSalary. Overridden method Earnings (line 40) calculates a BasePlusCommissionEmployee's earnings, calling base class CommissionEmployee's Earnings to calculate the commission-based portion of the BasePlusCommissionEmployee's earnings. Again, this shows the benefits of code reuse. The overridden ToString method (lines 43–44) creates a string representation of a BasePlusCommissionEmployee that contains "base-salaried", followed by the string returned by base class CommissionEmployee's ToString method (another example of code reuse), then the base salary. The result is a string beginning with "base-salaried commission employee", followed by the rest of the BasePlusCommissionEmployee's information. Recall that CommissionEmployee's ToString method obtains the employee's first name, last name and social security number by invoking the ToString method of *its* base class (i.e., Employee)—a further demonstration of code reuse. BasePlusCommissionEmployee's ToString initiates a *chain of method calls* that spans all three levels of the Employee hierarchy.

```
// Fig. 12.8: BasePlusCommissionEmployee.cs
// BasePlusCommissionEmployee class that extends CommissionEmployee.
using System;

public class BasePlusCommissionEmployee : CommissionEmployee
{
   private decimal baseSalary; // base salary per week

   // six-parameter constructor
   public BasePlusCommissionEmployee(string firstName, string lastName,
      string socialSecurityNumber, decimal grossSales,
      decimal commissionRate, decimal baseSalary)
      : base(firstName, lastName, socialSecurityNumber,
          grossSales, commissionRate)
   {
      BaseSalary = baseSalary; // validates base salary
   }

   // property that gets and sets
   // BasePlusCommissionEmployee's base salary
   public decimal BaseSalary
   {
      get
      {
         return baseSalary;
      }
      set
      {
         if (value < 0) // validation
         {
            throw new ArgumentOutOfRangeException(nameof(value),
               value, $"{nameof(BaseSalary)} must be >= 0");
         }

         baseSalary = value;
      }
   }

   // calculate earnings
   public override decimal Earnings() => BaseSalary + base.Earnings();

   // return string representation of BasePlusCommissionEmployee
   public override string ToString() =>
      $"base-salaried {base.ToString()}\nbase salary: {BaseSalary:C}";
}
```

**Fig. 12.8** | `BasePlusCommissionEmployee` class that extends `CommissionEmployee`.

### 12.5.6 Polymorphic Processing, Operator `is` and Downcasting

To test our `Employee` hierarchy, the app in Fig. 12.9 creates an object of each of the four concrete classes `SalariedEmployee`, `HourlyEmployee`, `CommissionEmployee` and `BasePlusCommissionEmployee` (lines 11–19). The app manipulates these objects, first via variables of each object's own type (lines 23–30), then polymorphically, using a `List` of

`Employee` variables (lines 33–56)—each object's `ToString` method is called *implicitly* by `WriteLine` when the object is output as a `string`. While processing the objects polymorphically, the app increases the base salary of each `BasePlusCommissionEmployee` by 10% (this, of course, requires determining the object's type at *execution* time). Finally, lines 59–63 polymorphically determine and output the type of each object in the `Employee List`.

```
1  // Fig. 12.9: PayrollSystemTest.cs
2  // Employee hierarchy test app.
3  using System;
4  using System.Collections.Generic;
5
6  class PayrollSystemTest
7  {
8     static void Main()
9     {
10       // create derived-class objects
11       var salariedEmployee = new SalariedEmployee("John", "Smith",
12           "111-11-1111", 800.00M);
13       var hourlyEmployee = new HourlyEmployee("Karen", "Price",
14          "222-22-2222", 16.75M, 40.0M);
15       var commissionEmployee = new CommissionEmployee("Sue", "Jones",
16          "333-33-3333", 10000.00M, .06M);
17       var basePlusCommissionEmployee =
18          new BasePlusCommissionEmployee("Bob", "Lewis",
19          "444-44-4444", 5000.00M, .04M, 300.00M);
20
21       Console.WriteLine("Employees processed individually:\n");
22
23       Console.WriteLine($"{salariedEmployee}\nearned: " +
24           $"{salariedEmployee.Earnings():C}\n");
25       Console.WriteLine(
26          $"{hourlyEmployee}\nearned: {hourlyEmployee.Earnings():C}\n");
27       Console.WriteLine($"{commissionEmployee}\nearned: " +
28           $"{commissionEmployee.Earnings():C}\n");
29       Console.WriteLine($"{basePlusCommissionEmployee}\nearned: " +
30           $"{basePlusCommissionEmployee.Earnings():C}\n");
31
32       // create List<Employee> and initialize with employee objects
33       var employees = new List<Employee>() {salariedEmployee,
34          hourlyEmployee, commissionEmployee, basePlusCommissionEmployee};
35
36       Console.WriteLine("Employees processed polymorphically:\n");
37
38       // generically process each element in employees
39       foreach (var currentEmployee in employees)
40       {
41          Console.WriteLine(currentEmployee); // invokes ToString
42
43          // determine whether element is a BasePlusCommissionEmployee
44          if (currentEmployee is BasePlusCommissionEmployee)
45          {
```

**Fig. 12.9** | `Employee` hierarchy test app. (Part 1 of 3.)

```
            // downcast Employee reference to
            // BasePlusCommissionEmployee reference
            var employee = (BasePlusCommissionEmployee) currentEmployee;

            employee.BaseSalary *= 1.10M;
            Console.WriteLine("new base salary with 10% increase is: " +
               $"{employee.BaseSalary:C}");
         }

         Console.WriteLine($"earned: {currentEmployee.Earnings():C}\n");
      }

      // get type name of each object in employees
      for (int j = 0; j < employees.Count; j++)
      {
         Console.WriteLine(
            $"Employee {j} is a {employees[j].GetType()}");
      }
   }
}
```

```
Employees processed individually:

salaried employee: John Smith
social security number: 111-11-1111
weekly salary: $800.00
earned: $800.00

hourly employee: Karen Price
social security number: 222-22-2222
hourly wage: $16.75
hours worked: 40.00
earned: $670.00

commission employee: Sue Jones
social security number: 333-33-3333
gross sales: $10,000.00
commission rate: 0.06
earned: $600.00

base-salaried commission employee: Bob Lewis
social security number: 444-44-4444
gross sales: $5,000.00
commission rate: 0.04
base salary: $300.00
earned: $500.00


Employees processed polymorphically:

salaried employee: John Smith
social security number: 111-11-1111
weekly salary: $800.00
earned: $800.00
```

**Fig. 12.9** | Employee hierarchy test app. (Part 2 of 3.)

```
hourly employee: Karen Price
social security number: 222-22-2222
hourly wage: $16.75
hours worked: 40.00
earned: $670.00

commission employee: Sue Jones
social security number: 333-33-3333
gross sales: $10,000.00
commission rate: 0.06
earned: $600.00

base-salaried commission employee: Bob Lewis
social security number: 444-44-4444
gross sales: $5,000.00
commission rate: 0.04
base salary: $300.00
new base salary with 10% increase is: $330.00
earned: $530.00

Employee 0 is a SalariedEmployee
Employee 1 is a HourlyEmployee
Employee 2 is a CommissionEmployee
Employee 3 is a BasePlusCommissionEmployee
```

**Fig. 12.9** | `Employee` hierarchy test app. (Part 3 of 3.)

### *Assigning Derived-Class Objects to Base-Class References*

Lines 33–34 create the `List<Employee>` named `employees` and initialize it with the `SalariedEmployee`, `HourlyEmployee`, `CommissionEmployee` and `BasePlusCommissionEmployee` created in lines 11–19. Each element of the `List` is an `Employee` variable. The derived-class objects can each be assigned to an element of `employees`, because a `SalariedEmployee` *is an* `Employee`, an `HourlyEmployee` *is an* `Employee`, a `CommissionEmployee` *is an* `Employee` and a `BasePlusCommissionEmployee` *is an* `Employee`. This is allowed even though `Employee` is an *abstract* class.

### *Polymorphic Processing of* `Employee`*s*

Lines 39–56 iterate through `employees` and invoke methods `ToString` and `Earnings` with `Employee` variable `currentEmployee`, which is assigned the reference of a different `Employee` during each iteration. The output illustrates that the appropriate methods for each class are indeed invoked. All calls to `virtual` methods `ToString` and `Earnings` are resolved at *execution* time, based on the type of the object to which `currentEmployee` refers. This process is known as **dynamic binding** or **late binding**. For example, line 41 *implicitly* invokes method `ToString` of the object to which `currentEmployee` refers. Only the methods of class `Employee` can be called via an `Employee` variable—and `Employee` includes class `object`'s methods, such as `ToString`. (Section 11.7 discussed the methods that all classes inherit from class `object`.) A base-class reference can be used to invoke only methods that were originally declared in the base class or higher in the class hierarchy.

### *Giving* `BasePlusCommissionEmployee`*s 10% Raises*

We perform special processing on `BasePlusCommissionEmployee` objects—as we encounter them, we increase their base salary by 10%. When processing objects polymorphically, we typically do not need to worry about the *specifics*, but to adjust the base salary, we do have to determine the specific type of each `Employee` object at execution time. Line 44 uses the `is` operator to determine whether a particular `Employee` object's type is `BasePlusCommissionEmployee`. The condition in line 44 is true only if the object referenced by `currentEmployee` *is a* `BasePlusCommissionEmployee`. This would also be true for any object of a `BasePlusCommissionEmployee` derived class (if there were any), because an object of any `BasePlusCommissionEmployee` derived class *is a* `BasePlusCommissionEmployee`.

Line 48 casts `currentEmployee` from type `Employee` to type `BasePlusCommissionEmployee` and assigns the result to `BasePlusCommissionEmployee` variable `employee`. This is known as a **downcast**, because the cast is to a type lower down in the class hierarchy. This downcast is allowed only if the object to which `currentEmployee` refers has an *is-a* relationship with `BasePlusCommissionEmployee`—the condition at line 44 ensures this is the case. Why would we ever want to perform such a downcast? *A base-class reference can be used to invoke only the methods declared in the base class*—attempting to invoke a derived-class-only method through a base-class reference results in a compilation error. If an app needs to perform a derived-class-specific operation on a derived-class object referenced by a base-class variable, the app must first cast the base-class reference to a derived-class reference. So, this cast is *required* in this program for us to use derived class `BasePlusCommissionEmployee`'s `BaseSalary` property on the `currentEmployee`.

**Common Programming Error 12.3**

*Assigning a base-class variable to a derived-class variable (without an explicit downcast) is a compilation error.*

**Software Engineering Observation 12.5**

*If at execution time the reference to a derived-class object has been assigned to a variable of one of its direct or indirect base classes, it's acceptable to cast the reference stored in that base-class variable back to a reference of the derived-class type. Before performing such a cast, use the `is` operator to ensure that the object is indeed an object of an appropriate derived-class type.*

When *downcasting* an object, an `InvalidCastException` (of namespace `System`) occurs if at execution time the object does not have an *is a* relationship with the type specified in the cast operator. An object can be cast only to its own type or to the type of one of its base classes. You can avoid a potential `InvalidCastException` by using the **`as`** operator to perform a downcast rather than a cast operator. For example, in the statement

```
var employee = currentEmployee as BasePlusCommissionEmployee;
```

`employee` is assigned a reference to an object that *is a* `BasePlusCommissionEmployee`, or the value `null` if `currentEmployee` is not a `BasePlusCommissionEmployee`. You can then compare `employee` with `null` to determine whether the cast succeeded.

If the `is` expression in line 44 is `true`, the `if` statement (lines 44–53) performs the special processing required for the `BasePlusCommissionEmployee` object. Using `BasePlusCommissionEmployee` variable `employee`, line 50 accesses the derived-class-only property `BaseSalary` to retrieve and update the employee's base salary with the 10% raise.

Line 55 invokes method `Earnings` on `currentEmployee`, which calls the appropriate derived-class object's `Earnings` method polymorphically. Obtaining the earnings of the `Sal-`

SalariedEmployee, HourlyEmployee and CommissionEmployee polymorphically in line 55 produces the same result as obtaining these employees' earnings individually in lines 24, 26 and 28. However, the earnings amount obtained for the BasePlusCommissionEmployee in lines 55 is higher than that obtained in line 30, due to the 10% increase in its base salary.

### *Every Object Knows Its Own Type*

Lines 59–63 display each employee's *type* as a string. Every object knows its own type and can access this information through method **GetType**, which all classes inherit from class object. This method returns an object of class Type (of namespace System), which contains information about the object's type, including its class name, the names of its methods and the name of its base class. Line 62 invokes method GetType on the object to get its **runtime class** (i.e., a Type object that represents the object's type). Then method ToString is *implicitly* invoked on the object returned by GetType. The Type class's ToString method returns the class name.

### *Avoiding Compilation Errors with Downcasting*

In the previous example, we avoid compilation errors by *downcasting* an Employee variable to a BasePlusCommissionEmployee variable in line 48—the type BasePlusCommissionEmployee is inferred from the cast operation. If we remove the cast operator and attempt to assign Employee variable currentEmployee directly to a BasePlusCommissionEmployee variable named employee (with its type explicitly declared, rather than using var), we'd receive a "Cannot implicitly convert type" compilation error. This error indicates that the attempt to assign the reference of base-class object currentEmployee to derived-class variable employee is *not* allowed without an appropriate cast operator. The compiler prevents this assignment, because a CommissionEmployee is *not* a BasePlusCommissionEmployee—again, the *is-a* relationship applies only between the derived class and its base classes, not vice versa.

Similarly, if lines 50 and 52 use base-class variable currentEmployee, rather than derived-class variable employee, when accessing derived-class-only property BaseSalary, we receive an "'Employee' does not contain a definition for 'BaseSalary'" compilation error on each of these lines. *Attempting to invoke derived-class-only methods or properties on a base-class reference is not allowed.* While lines 50 and 52 execute only if is in line 44 returns true to indicate that currentEmployee refers to a BasePlusCommissionEmployee object, we *cannot* attempt to use derived-class BasePlusCommissionEmployee property BaseSalary with base-class Employee reference currentEmployee. The compiler would generate errors in lines 50 and 52, because BaseSalary is not a base-class member and cannot be used with a base-class variable. Although the actual method that's called depends on the object's type at execution time, *a variable can be used to invoke only those methods that are members of that variable's type*, which the compiler verifies. Using a base-class Employee variable, we can invoke only methods and properties found in class Employee—methods Earnings and ToString, and properties FirstName, LastName and SocialSecurityNumber—and methods inherited from class object.

## 12.5.7 Summary of the Allowed Assignments Between Base-Class and Derived-Class Variables

Now that you've seen a complete app that processes diverse derived-class objects polymorphically, we summarize what you can and cannot do with base-class and derived-class objects and variables. Although a derived-class object also *is a* base-class object, the two are nevertheless different. As discussed previously, derived-class objects can be treated as if they were base-class objects. However, the derived class can have additional derived-class-only members. For this reason, assigning a base-class reference to a derived-class variable is *not* allowed without an *explicit* cast—such an assignment would leave the derived-class members *undefined* for a base-class object.

We've discussed four ways to assign base-class and derived-class references to variables of base-class and derived-class types:

1. *Assigning a base-class reference to a base-class variable* is straightforward.
2. *Assigning a derived-class reference to a derived-class variable* is straightforward.
3. *Assigning a derived-class reference to a base-class variable* is safe, because the derived-class object *is an* object of its base class. However, this reference can be used to refer *only* to base-class members. If this code refers to derived-class-only members through the base-class variable, the compiler reports errors.
4. *Attempting to assign a base-class reference to a derived-class variable* is a compilation error. To avoid this error, the base-class reference must be cast to a derived-class type explicitly or must be converted using the `as` operator. At execution time, if the object to which the reference refers is *not* a derived-class object, an exception will occur (unless you use the `as` operator, in which case you'll have to check the expression's result for `null`). The `is` operator can be used to ensure that such a cast is performed *only* if the object is a derived-class object.

## 12.6 `sealed` Methods and Classes

Only methods declared `virtual`, `override` or `abstract` can be *overridden* in derived classes. A method declared **`sealed`** in a base class *cannot* be overridden in a derived class. Methods that are declared `private` are implicitly `sealed`, because it's impossible to override them in a derived class (though the derived class can declare a new method with the same signature as the `private` method in the base class). Methods that are declared `static` also are implicitly `sealed`, because `static` methods cannot be overridden either. A derived-class method declared both `override` and `sealed` can override a base-class method, but cannot be overridden in derived classes further down the inheritance hierarchy.

A `sealed` method's declaration can never change, so all derived classes use the same method implementation, and calls to `sealed` methods (and non-`virtual` methods) are resolved at *compile time*—this is known as **static binding**. Since the compiler knows that `sealed` methods cannot be overridden, it can often *optimize* code by removing calls to `sealed` methods and replacing them with the expanded code of their declarations at each method-call location—a technique known as **inlining the code**.

**Performance Tip 12.1**

*The compiler can decide to inline a* `sealed` *method call and will do so for small, simple* `sealed` *methods. Inlining does not violate encapsulation or information hiding, but does improve performance, because it eliminates the overhead of making a method call.*

A class that's declared `sealed` *cannot* be a base class (i.e., a class cannot extend a `sealed` class). All methods in a `sealed` class are implicitly `sealed`. Class `string` is a `sealed` class. This class cannot be extended, so apps that use `strings` can rely on the functionality of `string` objects as specified in the Framework Class Library.

**Common Programming Error 12.4**

*Attempting to declare a derived class of a* `sealed` *class is a compilation error.*

## 12.7 Case Study: Creating and Using Interfaces

Our next example (Figs. 12.11–12.14) reexamines the payroll system of Section 12.5. Suppose that the company involved wishes to perform several accounting operations in a single accounts-payable app—in addition to calculating the payroll earnings that must be paid to each employee, the company must also calculate the payment due on each of several invoices (i.e., bills for goods purchased). Though applied to unrelated things (i.e., employees and invoices), both operations have to do with calculating some kind of payment amount. For an employee, the payment refers to the employee's earnings. For an invoice, the payment refers to the total cost of the goods listed on the invoice. Can we calculate such different things as the payments due for employees and invoices polymorphically in a single app? Is there a capability that can require *unrelated* classes to implement a set of common methods (e.g., a method that calculates a payment amount)? *Interfaces* offer exactly this capability.

### *Standardized Interactions*

Interfaces define and standardize the ways in which people and systems can interact with one another. For example, the controls on a radio serve as an interface between a radio's users and its internal components. The controls allow users to perform a limited set of operations (e.g., changing the station, adjusting the volume, choosing between AM and FM), and different radios may implement the controls in different ways (e.g., using push buttons, dials, voice commands). The interface specifies *what* operations a radio must permit users to perform but does not specify *how* they're performed. Similarly, the interface between a driver and a car with a manual transmission includes the steering wheel, the gear shift, the clutch pedal, the gas pedal and the brake pedal. This same interface is found in nearly all manual-transmission cars, enabling someone who knows how to drive one particular manual-transmission car to drive just about any other. The components of each car may look a bit different, but the *general* purpose is the same—to allow people to drive the car.

### *Interfaces in Software*

Software objects also communicate via interfaces. A C# interface describes a set of methods and properties that can be called on an object—to tell it, for example, to perform some task or return some piece of information. The next example introduces an interface named `IPayable` that describes the functionality of any object that must be capable of being paid and thus must offer a method to determine the proper payment amount due. An **interface declaration** begins with the keyword **`interface`** and can contain only

- abstract methods,
- abstract properties,
- abstract indexers (not covered in this book) and
- abstract events (events are discussed in Chapter 14, Graphical User Interfaces with Windows Forms: Part 1).

All interface members are *implicitly* declared both `public` and `abstract`. In addition, each interface can extend one or more other interfaces to create a more elaborate interface that other classes can implement.

**Common Programming Error 12.5**

*It's a compilation error to explicitly declare an interface member* `public` *or* `abstract`*, because they're redundant in interface-member declarations. It's also a compilation error to specify in an interface any implementation details, such as concrete method declarations.*

### *Implementing an Interface*

A class must specify that it **implements** the interface by listing the interface name after the colon (`:`) in the class declaration. This is the *same* syntax used to indicate inheritance from a base class. A concrete class implementing the interface must declare each member of the interface with the signature specified in the interface declaration. A class that implements an interface but does *not* implement all its members is an abstract class—it must be declared `abstract` and must contain an `abstract` declaration for each unimplemented member of the interface. Implementing an interface is like signing a contract with the compiler that states, "I will provide an implementation for all the members specified by the interface, or I will declare them `abstract`."

**Common Programming Error 12.6**

*Failing to define or declare any member of an interface in a class that implements the interface results in a compilation error.*

### *Common Methods for Unrelated Classes*

An interface is typically used when *unrelated* classes need to *share* common methods. This allows objects of unrelated classes to be processed polymorphically—objects of classes that implement the same interface can respond to the *same* method calls. You can create an interface that describes the desired functionality, then implement this interface in any classes requiring that functionality. For example, in the accounts-payable app developed in this section, we implement interface `IPayable` in each class (e.g., `Employee`, `Invoice`) that must be able to calculate a payment amount.

### *Interfaces vs. Abstract Classes*

An interface often is used in place of an `abstract` class when there's no default implementation to inherit—that is, no fields and no default method implementations. Like `abstract` classes, interfaces are typically `public` types, so they're normally declared in files by themselves with the same name as the interface and the `.cs` filename extension.

## 12.7.1 Developing an `IPayable` Hierarchy

To build an app that can determine payments for employees and invoices alike, we first create an interface named `IPayable`. Interface `IPayable` contains method `GetPaymentAmount` that returns a `decimal` amount to be paid for an object of any class that implements the interface. Method `GetPaymentAmount` is a general-purpose version of method `Earnings` of the `Employee` hierarchy—method `Earnings` calculates a payment amount specifically for an `Employee`, while `GetPaymentAmount` can be applied to a broad range of *unrelated* objects. After declaring interface `IPayable`, we introduce class `Invoice`, which implements interface IPayable. We then modify class Employee such that it also implements interface IPayable.

Classes Invoice and Employee both represent things for which the company must be able to calculate a payment amount. Both classes implement IPayable, so an app can invoke method GetPaymentAmount on Invoice objects and Employee objects alike. This enables the polymorphic processing of Invoices and Employees required for our company's accounts-payable app.

**Good Programming Practice 12.1**

*By convention, the name of an interface begins with* I *(e.g.,* IPayable*). This helps distinguish interfaces from classes, improving code readability.*

**Good Programming Practice 12.2**

*When declaring a method in an interface, choose a name that describes the method's purpose in a general manner, because the method may be implemented by a broad range of unrelated classes.*

### *UML Diagram Containing an Interface*

The UML class diagram in Fig. 12.10 shows the interface and class hierarchy used in our accounts-payable app. The hierarchy begins with interface IPayable. The UML distinguishes an interface from a class by placing the word "interface" in guillemets (« and ») above the interface name. The UML expresses the relationship between a class and an interface through a **realization**. A class is said to "realize," or implement, an interface. A class diagram models a realization as a dashed arrow with a *hollow arrowhead* pointing from the implementing class to the interface. The diagram in Fig. 12.10 indicates that classes Invoice and Employee each realize (i.e., implement) interface IPayable. As in the class diagram of Fig. 12.2, class Employee appears in italics, indicating that it's an abstract class. Concrete class SalariedEmployee extends Employee and inherits its base class's realization relationship with interface IPayable. Figure 12.10 could include Section 12.5's entire Employee class hierarchy—to keep the forthcoming example small, we did not include classes HourlyEmployee, CommissionEmployee and BasePlusCommissionEmployee.

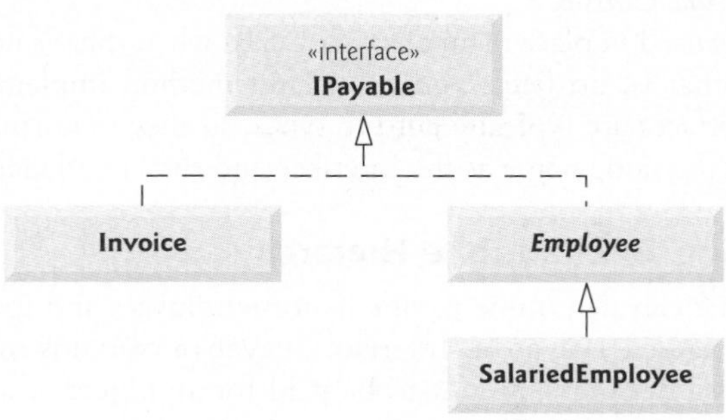


**Fig. 12.10** | IPayable interface and class hierarchy UML class diagram.

### 12.7.2 Declaring Interface IPayable

The declaration of interface `IPayable` begins in Fig. 12.11 at line 3. Interface `IPayable` contains `public abstract` method `GetPaymentAmount` (line 5). The method cannot be *explicitly* declared `public` or `abstract`. Interfaces can have *any* number of members and interface methods can have parameters.

```
1  // Fig. 12.11: IPayable.cs
2  // IPayable interface declaration.
3  public interface IPayable
4  {
5     decimal GetPaymentAmount(); // calculate payment; no implementation
6  }
```

**Fig. 12.11** | `IPayable` interface declaration.

### 12.7.3 Creating Class Invoice

We now create class `Invoice` (Fig. 12.12) to represent a simple invoice that contains billing information for one kind of part. The class contains properties `PartNumber` (line 7), `PartDescription` (line 8), `Quantity` (lines 23–39) and `PricePerItem` (lines 42–58) that indicate the part number, the description of the part, the quantity of the part ordered and the price per item. Class `Invoice` also contains a constructor (lines 13–20) and a `ToString` method (lines 61–63) that returns a string representation of an `Invoice` object. The `set` accessors of properties `Quantity` and `PricePerItem` ensure that `quantity` and `pricePerItem` are assigned only nonnegative values.

```
1  // Fig. 12.12: Invoice.cs
2  // Invoice class implements IPayable.
3  using System;
4
5  public class Invoice : IPayable
6  {
7     public string PartNumber { get; }
8     public string PartDescription { get; }
9     private int quantity;
10    private decimal pricePerItem;
11
12    // four-parameter constructor
13    public Invoice(string partNumber, string partDescription, int quantity,
14       decimal pricePerItem)
15    {
16       PartNumber = partNumber;
17       PartDescription = partDescription;
18       Quantity = quantity; // validate quantity
19       PricePerItem = pricePerItem; // validate price per item
20    }
21
```

**Fig. 12.12** | `Invoice` class implements `IPayable`. (Part 1 of 2.)

```
22     // property that gets and sets the quantity on the invoice
23     public int Quantity
24     {
25        get
26        {
27           return quantity;
28        }
29        set
30        {
31           if (value < 0) // validation
32           {
33              throw new ArgumentOutOfRangeException(nameof(value),
34                 value, $"{nameof(Quantity)} must be >= 0");
35           }
36
37           quantity = value;
38        }
39     }
40
41     // property that gets and sets the price per item
42     public decimal PricePerItem
43     {
44        get
45        {
46           return pricePerItem;
47        }
48        set
49        {
50           if (value < 0) // validation
51           {
52              throw new ArgumentOutOfRangeException(nameof(value),
53                 value, $"{nameof(PricePerItem)} must be >= 0");
54           }
55
56           pricePerItem = value;
57        }
58     }
59
60     // return string representation of Invoice object
61     public override string ToString() =>
62        $"invoice:\npart number: {PartNumber} ({PartDescription})\n" +
63        $"quantity: {Quantity}\nprice per item: {PricePerItem:C}";
64
65     // method required to carry out contract with interface IPayable
66     public decimal GetPaymentAmount() => Quantity * PricePerItem;
67  }
```

**Fig. 12.12** | `Invoice` class implements `IPayable`. (Part 2 of 2.)

Line 5 indicates that class `Invoice` implements interface `IPayable`. Like all classes, class `Invoice` also implicitly inherits from class `object`. All objects of a class can implement multiple interfaces, in which case they have the *is-a* relationship with each implemented interface type.

To implement more than one interface, use a comma-separated list of interface names after the colon (:) in the class declaration, as in

```
public class ClassName : BaseClassName, FirstInterface, SecondInterface, …
```

When a class inherits from a base class and implements one or more interfaces, the class declaration *must* list the base-class name *before* any interface names.

**Software Engineering Observation 12.6**

*C# does not allow derived classes to inherit from more than one base class, but it does allow a class to inherit from a base class and implement any number of interfaces.*

Class `Invoice` implements the one method in interface `IPayable`—method `GetPaymentAmount` is declared in line 66. The method calculates the amount required to pay the invoice. The method multiplies the values of `quantity` and `pricePerItem` (obtained through the appropriate properties) and returns the result. This method satisfies the implementation requirement for the method in interface `IPayable`—we've *fulfilled the interface contract* with the compiler.

### 12.7.4 Modifying Class `Employee` to Implement Interface `IPayable`

We now modify class `Employee` to implement interface `IPayable` (Fig. 12.13). This class declaration is identical to that of Fig. 12.4 with two exceptions:

- Line 3 of Fig. 12.13 indicates that class `Employee` now implements interface `IPayable`.
- Line 27 implements interface `IPayable`'s `GetPaymentAmount` method.

Notice that `GetPaymentAmount` simply calls `Employee`'s `abstract` method `Earnings`. At execution time, when `GetPaymentAmount` is called on an object of an `Employee` derived class, `GetPaymentAmount` calls that class's concrete `Earnings` method, which knows how to calculate earnings for objects of that derived-class type.

```
1  // Fig. 12.13: Employee.cs
2  // Employee abstract base class that implements interface IPayable.
3  public abstract class Employee : IPayable
4  {
5     public string FirstName { get; }
6     public string LastName { get; }
7     public string SocialSecurityNumber { get; }
8
9     // three-parameter constructor
10    public Employee(string firstName, string lastName,
11       string socialSecurityNumber)
12    {
13       FirstName = firstName;
14       LastName = lastName;
15       SocialSecurityNumber = socialSecurityNumber;
16    }
17
```

**Fig. 12.13** | `Employee` abstract base class that implements interface `IPayable`. (Part 1 of 2.)

```
   // return string representation of Employee object, using properties
   public override string ToString() => $"{FirstName} {LastName}\n" +
      $"social security number: {SocialSecurityNumber}";

   // abstract method overridden by derived classes
   public abstract decimal Earnings(); // no implementation here

   // implementing GetPaymentAmount here enables the entire Employee
   // class hierarchy to be used in an app that processes IPayables
   public decimal GetPaymentAmount() => Earnings();
}
```

**Fig. 12.13** | `Employee` abstract base class that implements interface `IPayable`. (Part 2 of 2.)

### *Derived Classes of* `Employee` *and Interface* `IPayable`

When a class implements an interface, the same *is-a* relationship as inheritance applies. Class `Employee` implements `IPayable`, so we can say that an `Employee` *is an* `IPayable`, and thus any object of an `Employee` derived class also *is an* `IPayable`. So, if we update the class hierarchy in Section 12.5 with the new `Employee` class in Fig. 12.13, then `SalariedEmployees`, `HourlyEmployees`, `CommissionEmployees` and `BasePlusCommissionEmployees` are all `IPayable` objects. Just as we can assign the reference of a `SalariedEmployee` derived-class object to a base-class `Employee` variable, we can assign the reference of a `SalariedEmployee` object (or any other `Employee` derived-class object) to an `IPayable` variable. `Invoice` implements `IPayable`, so an `Invoice` object also *is an* `IPayable` object, and we can assign the reference of an `Invoice` object to an `IPayable` variable.

**Software Engineering Observation 12.7**

*Inheritance and interfaces are similar in their implementation of the* is-a *relationship. An object of a class that implements an interface may be thought of as an object of that interface type. An object of any derived classes of a class that implements an interface also can be thought of as an object of the interface type.*

**Software Engineering Observation 12.8**

*The* is-a *relationship that exists between base classes and derived classes, and between interfaces and the classes that implement them, holds when passing an object to a method. When a method parameter receives an argument of a base class or interface type, the method polymorphically processes the object received as an argument.*

## 12.7.5 Using Interface `IPayable` to Process `Invoices` and `Employees` Polymorphically

`PayableInterfaceTest` (Fig. 12.14) illustrates that interface `IPayable` can be used to process a set of `Invoices` and `Employees` polymorphically in a single app. Lines 12–16 create a `List<IPayable>` named `payableObjects` and initialize it with four new objects—two `Invoice` objects (lines 13–14) and two `SalariedEmployee` objects (lines 15–16). These assignments are allowed because an `Invoice` *is an* `IPayable`, a `SalariedEmployee` *is an* `Employee` and an `Employee` *is an* `IPayable`. Lines 22–28 use a `foreach` statement to process each `IPayable` object in `payableObjects` polymorphically, displaying the object as a `string`, along with the payment due. Line 25 implicitly invokes method `ToString` using the IPayable interface reference payable, even though ToString is not declared in interface IPayable—all references (including those of interface types) refer to objects of classes that extend object and therefore have a ToString method. Line 27 invokes IPayable method GetPaymentAmount to obtain the payment amount for each object in payableObjects, regardless of the actual type of the object. The output reveals that the method calls in lines 25 and 27 invoke the appropriate class's implementation of methods ToString and GetPaymentAmount.

**Software Engineering Observation 12.9**

*All methods of class* object *can be called by using a reference of an interface type—the reference refers to an object, and all objects inherit the methods of class* object.

```
1  // Fig. 12.14: PayableInterfaceTest.cs
2  // Tests interface IPayable with disparate classes.
3  using System;
4  using System.Collections.Generic;
5
6  class PayableInterfaceTest
7  {
8     static void Main()
9     {
10       // create a List<IPayable> and initialize it with four
11       // objects of classes that implement interface IPayable
12       var payableObjects = new List<IPayable>() {
13          new Invoice("01234", "seat", 2, 375.00M),
14          new Invoice("56789", "tire", 4, 79.95M),
15          new SalariedEmployee("John", "Smith", "111-11-1111", 800.00M),
16          new SalariedEmployee("Lisa", "Barnes", "888-88-8888", 1200.00M)};
17
18       Console.WriteLine(
19          "Invoices and Employees processed polymorphically:\n");
20
21       // generically process each element in payableObjects
22       foreach (var payable in payableObjects)
23       {
24          // output payable and its appropriate payment amount
25          Console.WriteLine($"{payable}");
26          Console.WriteLine(
27             $"payment due: {payable.GetPaymentAmount():C}\n");
28       }
29    }
30 }
```

```
Invoices and Employees processed polymorphically:

invoice:
part number: 01234 (seat)
quantity: 2
price per item: $375.00
payment due: $750.00
```

**Fig. 12.14** | Tests interface IPayable with disparate classes. (Part 1 of 2.)

```
invoice:
part number: 56789 (tire)
quantity: 4
price per item: $79.95
payment due: $319.80

salaried employee: John Smith
social security number: 111-11-1111
weekly salary: $800.00
payment due: $800.00

salaried employee: Lisa Barnes
social security number: 888-88-8888
weekly salary: $1,200.00
payment due: $1,200.00
```

**Fig. 12.14** | Tests interface `IPayable` with disparate classes. (Part 2 of 2.)

### 12.7.6 Common Interfaces of the .NET Framework Class Library

In this section, we overview several common interfaces defined in the .NET Framework Class Library. These interfaces are implemented and used in the same manner as those you create (e.g., interface `IPayable` in Section 12.7.2). Implementing these interfaces enables you to incorporate objects of your own types into many important aspects of the Framework Class Library. Figure 12.15 overviews several commonly used Framework Class Library interfaces and why you might implement them in your own types.

| Interface | Description |
|---|---|
| `IComparable` | C# contains several comparison operators (e.g., <, <=, >, >=, ==, !=) that allow you to compare simple-type values. Section 10.13 showed that you can overload these operators for your own types. Interface `IComparable` can be used to allow objects of a class that implements the interface to be compared to one another. The interface contains one method, `CompareTo`, which compares the object that calls the method to the object passed as an argument. Classes must implement `CompareTo` to return a value indicating whether the object on which it's invoked is less than (negative integer return value), equal to (`0` return value) or greater than (positive integer return value) the object passed as an argument, using any criteria you specify. For example, if class `Employee` implements `IComparable`, its `CompareTo` method could compare `Employee` objects by their earnings amounts. Interface `IComparable` is commonly used for ordering objects in a collection such as an array. We use `IComparable` in Chapter 18, Generics, and Chapter 19, Generic Collections; Functional Programming with LINQ/PLINQ. |
| `IComponent` | Implemented by any class that represents a component, including Graphical User Interface (GUI) controls (such as buttons or labels). Interface `IComponent` defines the behaviors that components must implement. We discuss `IComponent` and many GUI controls that implement this interface in Chapter 14, Graphical User Interfaces with Windows Forms: Part 1, and Chapter 15, Graphical User Interfaces with Windows Forms: Part 2. |

**Fig. 12.15** | Common interfaces of the .NET Framework Class Library. (Part 1 of 2.)

| Interface | Description |
|---|---|
| `IDisposable` | Implemented by classes that must provide an explicit mechanism for *releasing* resources. Some resources can be used by only one program at a time. In addition, some resources, such as files on disk, are unmanaged resources that, unlike memory, cannot be released by the garbage collector. Classes that implement interface `IDisposable` provide a `Dispose` method that can be called to explicitly release resources that are explicitly associated with an object. We discuss `IDisposable` briefly in Chapter 13, Exception Handling: A Deeper Look. You can learn more about this interface at `http://msdn.microsoft.com/library/system.idisposable`. The MSDN article *Implementing a Dispose Method* at `http://msdn.microsoft.com/library/fs2xkftw` discusses the proper implementation of this interface in your classes. |
| `IEnumerator` | Used for iterating through the elements of a *collection* (such as an array or a `List`) one element at a time—the `foreach` statement uses an `IEnumerator` object to iterate through elements. Interface `IEnumerator` contains method `MoveNext` to move to the next element in a collection, method `Reset` to move to the position before the first element and property `Current` to return the object at the current location. We use `IEnumerator` in Chapter 19. All `IEnumberable` objects (Chapter 9) provide a `GetEnumerator` method that returns an `IEnumerator` object. |

**Fig. 12.15** | Common interfaces of the .NET Framework Class Library. (Part 2 of 2.)

## 12.8 Wrap-Up

This chapter introduced polymorphism—the ability to process objects that share the same base class in a class hierarchy as if they were all objects of the base class. The chapter discussed how polymorphism makes systems extensible and maintainable, then demonstrated how to use overridden methods to effect polymorphic behavior. We introduced the notion of an abstract class, which allows you to provide an appropriate base class from which other classes can inherit. You learned that an abstract class can declare abstract methods that each derived class must implement to become a concrete class. We also discussed that an app can use variables of an abstract class to invoke concrete derived-class implementations of `abstract` methods polymorphically. You also learned how to determine an object's type at execution time. We showed how to create `sealed` methods and classes. Finally, the chapter discussed declaring and implementing an interface as another way to achieve polymorphic behavior, often among objects of different, unrelated classes.

You should now be familiar with classes, objects, encapsulation, inheritance, interfaces and polymorphism—the most essential aspects of object-oriented programming. Next, we take a deeper look at using exception handling to deal with runtime errors.

# 13

# Exception Handling: A Deeper Look

## Objectives

In this chapter you'll:

- Learn when to use exception handling.
- Use `try` blocks to delimit code that may throw exceptions.
- Use `throw` to indicate a problem at runtime.
- Use `catch` blocks to specify exception handlers.
- Understand what happens to uncaught exceptions.
- Understand the mechanics of exception handling.
- Use the `finally` block to release resources.
- See how a `using` statement can auto-release resources.
- Understand .NET exception class hierarchy.
- Use `Exception` properties.
- Create new exception types.
- Use C# 6's null-conditional operator (`?.`) to determine whether a reference is null before using it to call a method or access a property.
- Use nullable value types to specify that a variable may contain a value or `null`.
- Use C# 6 exception filters to specify a condition for catching an exception.

**Outline**



## 13.1 Introduction

In this chapter, we take a deeper look at **exception handling**. As you know from Section 8.5, an **exception** indicates that a problem occurred during a program's execution. The name "exception" comes from the fact that, although the problem can occur, it occurs infrequently. As we showed in Section 8.5 and in Chapter 10, exception handling enables you to create apps that can *handle* exceptions—in many cases allowing a program to continue executing as if no problems had been encountered. More severe problems may prevent a program from continuing normal execution, instead requiring it to notify the user of the problem, then terminate in a controlled manner. The features presented in this chapter enable you to write clear, **robust** and more **fault-tolerant programs** (i.e., programs that are able to deal with problems that may arise and continue executing). "Best practices" for exception handling in Visual C# are specified in the Visual Studio documentation.[1]

After reviewing exception-handling concepts and basic exception-handling techniques, we overview .NET's exception-handling class hierarchy. Programs typically *request* and *release* resources (such as files on disk) during program execution. Often, the supply of these resources is limited, or the resources can be used by only one program at a time. We demonstrate a part of the exception-handling mechanism that enables a program to use a resource, then *guarantee* that it will be released for use by other programs, even if an

1. "Best Practices for Handling Exceptions [C#]," *.NET Framework Developer's Guide*, Visual Studio .NET Online Help. Available at `https://msdn.microsoft.com/library/seyhszts`.

exception occurs. We show several properties of class `System.Exception` (the base class of all exception classes) and discuss how you can create and use your own exception classes.

You'll see various C# features for working with values that can be null, including:

- C# 6's null-conditional operator (`?.`), which determines whether a reference is `null` before using it to call a method or access a property.
- The null-coalescing operator (`??`), which returns its left operand's value if it's not `null` and returns its right operand's value, otherwise.
- Nullable types, which specify that a value-type variable may contain a value or `null`.

Finally, we'll present C# 6's exception filters that specify a condition for catching an exception.

## 13.2 Example: Divide by Zero without Exception Handling

Let's revisit what happens when errors arise in a console app that does not use exception handling. Figure 13.1 inputs two integers from the user, then divides the first integer by the second, using integer division to obtain an `int` result. In this example, an exception is **thrown** (i.e., an exception occurs) when a method detects a problem and is unable to handle it.

```
// Fig. 13.1: DivideByZeroNoExceptionHandling.cs
// Integer division without exception handling.
using System;

class DivideByZeroNoExceptionHandling
{
   static void Main()
   {
      // get numerator
      Console.Write("Please enter an integer numerator: ");
      var numerator = int.Parse(Console.ReadLine());

      // get denominator
      Console.Write("Please enter an integer denominator: ");
      var denominator = int.Parse(Console.ReadLine());

      // divide the two integers, then display the result
      var result = numerator / denominator;
      Console.WriteLine(
         $"\nResult: {numerator} / {denominator} = {result}");
   }
}
```

```
Please enter an integer numerator: 100
Please enter an integer denominator: 7

Result: 100 / 7 = 14
```

**Fig. 13.1** | Integer division without exception handling. (Part 1 of 2.)

```
Please enter an integer numerator: 100
Please enter an integer denominator: 0

Unhandled Exception: System.DivideByZeroException:
  Attempted to divide by zero.
  at DivideByZeroNoExceptionHandling.Main()
     in C:\Users\PaulDeitel\Documents\examples\ch13\Fig13_01\
     DivideByZeroNoExceptionHandling\DivideByZeroNoExceptionHandling\
     DivideByZeroNoExceptionHandling.cs:line 18
```

```
Please enter an integer numerator: 100
Please enter an integer denominator: hello

Unhandled Exception: System.FormatException:
  Input string was not in a correct format.
  at System.Number.StringToNumber(String str, NumberStyles options,
     NumberBuffer& number, NumberFormatInfo info, Boolean parseDecimal)
  at System.Number.ParseInt32(String s, NumberStyles style,
     NumberFormatInfo info)
  at System.Int32.Parse(String s)
  at DivideByZeroNoExceptionHandling.Main()
     in C:\Users\PaulDeitel\Documents\examples\ch13\Fig13_01\
     DivideByZeroNoExceptionHandling\DivideByZeroNoExceptionHandling\
     DivideByZeroNoExceptionHandling.cs:line 15
```

**Fig. 13.1** | Integer division without exception handling. (Part 2 of 2.)

*Running the App*

In most of our examples, an app appears to run the same regardless of whether you run it by choosing **Start Debugging** or **Start Without Debugging** from the **Debug** menu. As we'll discuss shortly, the example in Fig. 13.1 might cause exceptions, depending on the user's input. For this example, we do not wish to debug the app; we simply want to see what happens when errors arise. For this reason, we executed this app with **Debug > Start Without Debugging**. If an exception occurs during execution, a dialog appears indicating that the app "has stopped working." You can simply click **Cancel** or **Close Program** to terminate the app. An error message describing the exception that occurred is displayed in the program's output. We formatted the error messages in Fig. 13.1 for readability. In the first sample execution, the program performs a successful division and runs to completion with no exceptions.

### 13.2.1 Dividing By Zero

In the second sample execution, the user enters `0` as the denominator. Several lines of information are displayed in response to the invalid input. This information—known as a **stack trace**—includes the exception class's name (`System.DivideByZeroException`) in a message indicating the problem that occurred and the path of execution that led to the exception, method by method. Stack traces help you debug a program. The first line of the error message specifies that a `DivideByZeroException` occurred. When a program divides an integer by 0, the CLR throws a **`DivideByZeroException`** (namespace `System`). The text after the exception name, "`Attempted to divide by zero`," is an error message that indicates why this exception occurred. Division by zero is not allowed in integer arithmetic.[2]

Each "at" line in a stack trace indicates a line of code in a particular method that was executing when the exception occurred. The "at" line contains the namespace, class and method in which the exception occurred

```
DivideByZeroNoExceptionHandling.Main
```

the location and name of the file containing the code

```
C:\Users\PaulDeitel\Documents\examples\ch13\Fig13_01\
   DivideByZeroNoExceptionHandling\
   DivideByZeroNoExceptionHandling\
   DivideByZeroNoExceptionHandling.cs
```

and the line number

```
:line 18
```

where the exception occurred. (Class `DivideByZeroNoExceptionHandling` is not declared in a namespace, so no namespace is displayed before the class name in the stack traces.)

In this case, the stack trace indicates that the `DivideByZeroException` occurred when the program was executing line 18 of method `Main`. The first "at" line in the stack trace indicates the exception's **throw point**—the initial point at which the exception occurred (i.e., line 18 in `Main`). This information makes it easy for you to see which method call caused the exception. Subsequent "at" lines in the stack trace specify what method calls were made to get to the throw point in the program.

### 13.2.2 Enter a Non-Numeric Denominator

In the third sample execution, the user enters `"hello"` as the denominator. This causes a `FormatException`, and another stack trace is displayed. Our earlier examples that read numeric values from the user assumed that the user would input an integer value, but a noninteger value could be entered. A **`FormatException`** (namespace `System`) occurs, for example, when `int.Parse` receives a `string` that does not represent a valid integer. Starting from the last "at" line in the stack trace, we see that the exception was detected in line 15 of method `Main`. The stack trace also shows the other methods that led to the exception being thrown:

- `Main` called `Int32.Parse`—recall that `int` is just an alias for `Int32`,
- `Int32.Parse` called method `Number.ParseInt32`, and
- `Number.ParseInt32` called `Number.StringToNumber`.

The throw point occurred in `Number.StringToNumber`, as indicated by the first "at" line in the stack trace. Note that the stack trace's actual text depends on your locale.

### 13.2.3 Unhandled Exceptions Terminate the App

In the sample executions in Fig. 13.1, the program terminates when an *unhandled* exception occurs and a stack trace is displayed. This does not always happen—sometimes a pro-

2. Division by zero with floating-point values *is* allowed and results in the value infinity—represented by either constant **`Double.PositiveInfinity`** or constant **`Double.NegativeInfinity`**, depending on whether the numerator is positive or negative. These values are displayed as `Infinity` or `-Infinity`. If *both* the numerator and denominator are *zero*, the result of the calculation is the constant **`Double.NaN`** ("not a number"), which is returned when a calculation's result is *undefined*.

gram may continue executing even though an exception has occurred and a stack trace has been displayed. In such cases, the app may produce incorrect results. The next section demonstrates how to handle exceptions to enable the program to run to completion.

## 13.3 Example: Handling DivideByZeroExceptions and FormatExceptions

Now, let's consider a simple example of exception handling. The app in Fig. 13.2 uses exception handling to process any `DivideByZeroException`s and `FormatException`s that might arise. The app reads two integers from the user (lines 18–21). Assuming that the user provides integers as input and does not specify `0` as the denominator for the division, line 25 performs the division and lines 28–29 display the result. However, if the user inputs a noninteger value or supplies `0` as the denominator, an exception occurs. This program demonstrates how to **catch** and **handle** such exceptions—in this case, displaying an error message and allowing the user to enter another set of values.

```
1  // Fig. 13.2: DivideByZeroExceptionHandling.cs
2  // FormatException and DivideByZeroException handlers.
3  using System;
4
5  class DivideByZeroExceptionHandling
6  {
7     static void Main(string[] args)
8     {
9        var continueLoop = true; // determines whether to keep looping
10
11       do
12       {
13          // retrieve user input and calculate quotient
14          try
15          {
16             // int.Parse generates FormatException
17             // if argument cannot be converted to an integer
18             Console.Write("Enter an integer numerator: ");
19             var numerator = int.Parse(Console.ReadLine());
20             Console.Write("Enter an integer denominator: ");
21             var denominator = int.Parse(Console.ReadLine());
22
23             // division generates DivideByZeroException
24             // if denominator is 0
25             var result = numerator / denominator;
26
27             // display result
28             Console.WriteLine(
29                $"\nResult: {numerator} / {denominator} = {result}");
30             continueLoop = false;
31          }
32          catch (FormatException formatException)
33          {
34             Console.WriteLine($"\n{formatException.Message}");
```

**Fig. 13.2** | `FormatException` and `DivideByZeroException` handlers. (Part 1 of 2.)

```
                Console.WriteLine(
                   "You must enter two integers. Please try again.\n");
             }
             catch (DivideByZeroException divideByZeroException)
             {
                Console.WriteLine($"\n{divideByZeroException.Message}");
                Console.WriteLine(
                   "Zero is an invalid denominator. Please try again.\n");
             }
          } while (continueLoop);
       }
    }
```

```
Please enter an integer numerator: 100
Please enter an integer denominator: 7

Result: 100 / 7 = 14
```

```
Enter an integer numerator: 100
Enter an integer denominator: 0

Attempted to divide by zero.
Zero is an invalid denominator. Please try again.

Enter an integer numerator: 100
Enter an integer denominator: 7

Result: 100 / 7 = 14
```

```
Enter an integer numerator: 100
Enter an integer denominator: hello

Input string was not in a correct format.
You must enter two integers. Please try again.

Enter an integer numerator: 100
Enter an integer denominator: 7

Result: 100 / 7 = 14
```

**Fig. 13.2** | `FormatException` and `DivideByZeroException` handlers. (Part 2 of 2.)

### *Sample Outputs*

Before we discuss the details of the program, let's consider the sample outputs in Fig. 13.2. The first sample output shows a successful calculation in which the user enters the numerator `100` and the denominator `7`. The result (`14`) is an `int`, because integer division always yields an `int` result. The second sample output demonstrates the result of an attempt to divide by zero. In integer arithmetic, the CLR tests for division by zero and generates a `DivideByZeroException` if the denominator is zero. The program detects the exception and displays an error message indicating the attempt to divide by zero. The last sample output depicts the result of inputting a non-int value—in this case, the user enters the string "hello" as the denominator. The program attempts to convert the input strings to ints using method int.Parse (lines 19 and 21). If an argument cannot be converted to an int, the method throws a FormatException. The program catches the exception and displays an error message indicating that the user must enter two ints.

### *Another Way to Convert Strings to Integers*

Another way to validate the input is to use the **int.TryParse** method, which converts a string to an int value *if possible*. Like int.Parse, each of the numeric simple types has a TryParse method. TryParse requires two arguments—one is the string to parse and the other is the variable in which the converted value is to be stored. The method returns a bool value that's true only if the string was converted successfully to an int. If not, TryParse assigns the value 0 to the second argument—that argument is passed by reference so TryParse can modify its value.

**Error-Prevention Tip 13.1**

*Method TryParse can be used to validate input in code rather than allowing the code to throw an exception—this technique is generally preferred.*

## 13.3.1 Enclosing Code in a try Block

Now we consider the user interactions and flow of control that yield the results shown in the sample output windows. Lines 14–31 define a **try block** enclosing the code that might throw exceptions, as well as some code that will be skipped when an exception occurs. For example, the program should not display a new result (lines 28–29) unless the calculation in line 25 completes successfully.

The user inputs values that represent the numerator and denominator. The two statements that read the ints (lines 19 and 21) call method int.Parse to convert strings to int values. This method throws a FormatException if it cannot convert its string argument to an int. If lines 19 and 21 convert the values properly (i.e., no exceptions occur), then line 25 divides the numerator by the denominator and assigns the result to variable result. If denominator is 0, line 25 causes the CLR to throw a DivideByZeroException. If line 25 does not cause an exception to be thrown, then lines 28–29 display the result of the division.

## 13.3.2 Catching Exceptions

Exception-handling code appears in a **catch block**. In general, when an exception occurs in a try block, a corresponding catch block *catches* the exception and *handles* it. The try block in this example is followed by two catch blocks—one that handles a FormatException (lines 32–37) and one that handles a DivideByZeroException (lines 38–43). A catch block specifies an exception parameter representing the exception that the catch block can handle. The catch block can use the parameter's identifier (which you choose) to interact with a caught exception object. If there's no need to use the exception object in the catch block, the exception parameter's identifier can be omitted. The type of the catch's parameter is the type of the exception that the catch block handles. Optionally, you can include a `catch` block that does *not* specify an exception type—such a `catch` block (known as a **general `catch` clause**) catches all exception types. At least one `catch` block and/or a **`finally` block** (discussed in Section 13.5) must immediately follow a `try` block.

In Fig. 13.2, the first `catch` block catches `FormatException`s (thrown by method `int.Parse`), and the second `catch` block catches `DivideByZeroException`s (thrown by the CLR). If an exception occurs, the program executes only the first matching `catch` block. Both exception handlers in this example display an error-message dialog. After either `catch` block terminates, program control continues with the first statement after the last `catch` block (the end of the method, in this example). We'll soon take a deeper look at how this flow of control works in exception handling.

### 13.3.3 Uncaught Exceptions

An **uncaught exception** (or **unhandled exception**) is one for which there's no matching `catch` block. You saw the results of uncaught exceptions in the second and third outputs of Fig. 13.1. Recall that when exceptions occur in that example, the app terminates early (after displaying the exception's stack trace). The result of an uncaught exception depends on how you execute the program—Fig. 13.1 demonstrated the results of an uncaught exception when an app is executed using **Debug > Start Without Debugging**. If you run the app by using **Debug > Start Debugging** and the runtime environment detects an uncaught exception, the app pauses, and the **Exception Assistant** window (Fig. 13.3) appears.

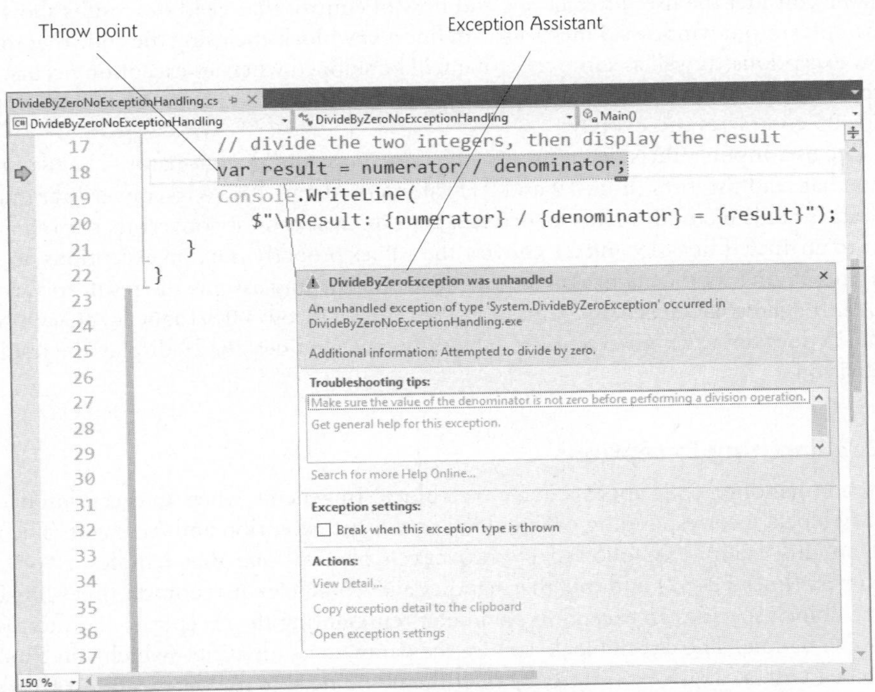


**Fig. 13.3** | Exception Assistant.

The Exception Assistant window contains

- a line pointing from the Exception Assistant to the line of code that caused the exception,
- the type of the exception,
- **Troubleshooting tips** with links to helpful information on what might have caused the exception and how to handle it, and
- links to view or copy the complete exception details

Figure 13.3 shows the Exception Assistant that's displayed if the user attempts to divide by zero in the app of Fig. 13.1.

### 13.3.4 Termination Model of Exception Handling

Recall that the point in the program at which an exception occurs is called the *throw point*—this is an important location for debugging purposes (as we demonstrate in Section 13.7). If an exception occurs in a `try` block (such as a `FormatException` being thrown as a result of the code in lines 19 and 21 in Fig. 13.2), the `try` block terminates immediately, and program control transfers to the first of the following `catch` blocks in which the exception parameter's type matches that of the thrown exception. After the exception is handled, program control does *not* return to the throw point because the `try` block has *exited* (which also causes any of its local variables to go out of scope). Rather, control resumes after the last `catch` block. This is known as the **termination model of exception handling**. [*Note:* Some languages use the **resumption model of exception handling**, in which, after an exception is handled, control resumes just after the throw point.]

If no exceptions occur in the `try` block, the program successfully completes the `try` block (setting `continueLoop` to `false`) and ignores the `catch` blocks in lines 32–37 and 38–43. Then the program executes the first statement following the `try` and `catch` blocks. In this example, the program reaches the end of the `do...while` loop (line 44) in which the condition is now `false`, so the program terminates because the end of `Main` is reached.

The `try` block and its corresponding `catch` and `finally` blocks together form a **`try` statement**. It's important not to confuse the terms "`try` block" and "`try` statement"—the term "`try` block" refers to the block of code following the keyword `try` (but before any `catch` or `finally` blocks), while the term "`try` statement" includes all the code from the opening `try` keyword to the end of the last `catch` or `finally` block. This includes the `try` block, as well as any associated `catch` blocks and `finally` block.

When a `try` block terminates, its local variables go out of scope. If a `try` block terminates due to an exception, the CLR searches for the first `catch` block that can process the type of exception that occurred—in an outer block in the same method or in a previous method in the method-call stack. The CLR locates the matching `catch` by comparing the type of the thrown exception to each `catch`'s parameter type. A match occurs if the types are identical or if the thrown exception's type is a derived class of the `catch`'s parameter type. Once an exception is matched to a `catch` block, the code in that block executes and the other `catch` blocks in the `try` statement are ignored.

### 13.3.5 Flow of Control When Exceptions Occur

In the third sample output of Fig. 13.2, the user inputs `hello` as the denominator. When line 21 executes, `int.Parse` cannot convert this `string` to an `int`, so the method throws a FormatException object to indicate that the method was unable to convert the string to an int. When the exception occurs, the try block exits (terminates). Next, the CLR attempts to locate a matching catch block. A match occurs with the catch block in line 32, so the exception handler displays the exception's Message property (to retrieve the error message associated with the exception) and the program ignores all other exception handlers following the try block. Program control continues with line 44 once the catch block completes execution.

**Common Programming Error 13.1**

*Specifying a comma-separated list of parameters in a* catch *block is a syntax error. A* catch *block can have at most one parameter. Section 13.10 shows how you can use exception filters to specify additional conditions for which an exception can be caught.*

In the second sample output of Fig. 13.2, the user inputs 0 as the denominator. When the division in line 25 executes, a DivideByZeroException occurs. Once again, the try block terminates, and the program attempts to locate a matching catch block. In this case, the first catch block does not match—the exception type in the catch-handler declaration is not the same as the type of the thrown exception, and FormatException is not a base class of DivideByZeroException. Therefore the program continues to search for a matching catch block, which it finds in line 38. Line 40 displays the exception's Message property. Again, program control continues with line 44 once the catch block completes execution.

## 13.4 .NET Exception Hierarchy

In C#, the exception-handling mechanism allows only objects of class **Exception** (namespace System) and its derived classes to be thrown and caught. Note, however, that C# programs may interact with software components written in other .NET languages (such as C++) that do not restrict exception types. The general catch clause can be used to catch such exceptions.

This section overviews several of the .NET Framework's exception classes and focuses exclusively on exceptions that derive from class Exception. In addition, we discuss how to determine whether a particular method throws exceptions.

### 13.4.1 Class SystemException

Class Exception (namespace System) is the base class of .NET's exception class hierarchy. An important derived class is **SystemException**. The CLR generates SystemExceptions. Many of these can be avoided if apps are coded properly. For example, if a program attempts to access an **out-of-range array index**, the CLR throws an exception of type **IndexOutOfRangeException** (a derived class of SystemException). Similarly, an exception occurs when a program uses a reference-type variable to call a method when the reference has a value of null. This causes a **NullReferenceException** (another derived class of SystemException). You saw earlier in this chapter that a DivideByZeroException occurs in integer division when a program attempts to divide by zero.

Other exceptions thrown by the CLR include **OutOfMemoryException**, **StackOverflowException** and **ExecutionEngineException**, which are thrown when something goes wrong that causes the CLR to become unstable. Sometimes such exceptions cannot even be caught. It's best to simply log such exceptions (using a tool such as Apache's *log4net*—`http://logging.apache.org/log4net/`), then terminate your app.

A benefit of the exception class hierarchy is that a `catch` block can catch exceptions of a particular type or—because of the *is-a* relationship of inheritance—can use a base-class type to catch exceptions in a hierarchy of related exception types. For example, Section 13.3.2 discussed the `catch` block with no parameter, which catches exceptions of all types (including those that are not derived from `Exception`). A `catch` block that specifies a parameter of type `Exception` can catch all exceptions that derive from `Exception`, because `Exception` is the base class of all exception classes in the .NET Framework. The advantage of this approach is that the exception handler can access the caught exception's information via the parameter in the `catch`. We'll say more about accessing exception information in Section 13.7.

Using inheritance with exceptions enables a `catch` block to catch related exceptions using a concise notation. A set of exception handlers could catch each derived-class exception type individually, but catching the base-class exception type is more concise. However, this technique makes sense *only* if the handling behavior is the same for a base class and all derived classes. Otherwise, catch each derived-class exception individually.

**Common Programming Error 13.2**

*The compiler issues an error if a `catch` block that catches a base-class exception is placed* before *a `catch` block for any of that class's derived-class types. In this case, the base-class `catch` block would catch all base-class and derived-class exceptions, so the derived-class exception handler would never execute.*

### 13.4.2 Which Exceptions Might a Method Throw?

How do we determine that an exception might occur in a program? For methods contained in the .NET Framework classes, read the detailed descriptions of the methods in the online documentation. If a method may throw an exception, its description contains a section called **Exceptions** that specifies the types of exceptions the method may throw and briefly describes what causes them. For an example, search for "`int.Parse` method" in the Visual Studio online documentation. The **Exceptions** section of this method's web page indicates that method `int.Parse` throws three exception types:

- `ArgumentNullException`,
- `FormatException`, and
- `OverflowException`

and describes the reasons for each. [*Note:* You also can find this information in the **Object Browser** described in Section 10.11.]

**Software Engineering Observation 13.1**

*If a method may throw exceptions, statements that invoke the method directly or indirectly should be placed in `try` blocks, and those exceptions should be caught and handled.*

It's more difficult to determine when the CLR may throw exceptions. Such information appears in the *C# Language Specification*, which specifies cases in which exceptions are thrown. At time of writing, the C# specification has not yet been officially released by Microsoft. You can view an unofficial copy at:

```
https://github.com/ljw1004/csharpspec/blob/gh-pages/README.md
```

## 13.5 `finally` Block

Programs frequently request and release resources dynamically (i.e., at execution time). For example, a program that reads a file from disk first makes a file-open request (as we'll see in Chapter 17, Files and Streams). If that request succeeds, the program reads the contents of the file. Operating systems typically prevent more than one program from manipulating a file at once. Therefore, when a program finishes processing a file, the program should close the file (i.e., release the resource) so other programs can use it. If the file is not closed, a **resource leak** occurs. In such a case, the file resource is not available to other programs.

In programming languages such as C and C++, in which the programmer is responsible for dynamic memory management, the most common type of resource leak is a **memory leak**. A memory leak occurs when a program allocates memory (as C# programmers do via keyword `new`), but does not deallocate the memory when it's no longer needed. Normally, this is *not* an issue in C#, because the CLR performs *garbage collection* of memory that's no longer needed by an executing program (Section 10.8). However, other kinds of resource leaks (such as unclosed files) can occur.

**Error-Prevention Tip 13.2**

*The CLR does not completely eliminate memory leaks. It will not garbage-collect an object until the program contains no more references to that object, and even then there may be a delay until the memory is required. Thus, memory leaks can occur if you inadvertently keep references to unwanted objects.*

### 13.5.1 Moving Resource-Release Code to a `finally` Block

Exceptions often occur when an app uses resources that require explicit release. For example, a program that processes a file might receive `IOException`s during the processing. For this reason, file-processing code normally appears in a `try` block. Regardless of whether a program experiences exceptions while processing a file, the program should close the file when it's no longer needed. Suppose a program places all resource-request and resource-release code in a `try` block. If no exceptions occur, the `try` block executes normally and releases the resources after using them. However, if an exception occurs, the `try` block may exit *before* the resource-release code can execute. We could duplicate all the resource-release code in each of the `catch` blocks, but this would make the code more difficult to modify and maintain. We could also place the resource-release code after the `try` statement; however, if the `try` block terminated due to a `return` statement or an exception occurred, code following the `try` statement would never execute.

To address these problems, C#'s exception-handling mechanism provides the `finally` block, which is *guaranteed* to execute regardless of whether the `try` block executes successfully or an exception occurs. This makes the `finally` block an ideal location in which to place resource-release code for resources that are acquired and manipulated in the corresponding `try` block:

- If the `try` block executes successfully, the `finally` block executes immediately after the `try` block terminates—either by reaching the block's closing brace or if a `return` statement executes in the block.
- If an exception occurs in the `try` block, the `finally` block executes immediately after a `catch` block completes—either by reaching the block's closing brace or if a `return` statement executes in the block.
- If there is no `catch` block, if the exception is not caught by a `catch` block associated with the `try` block, or if a `catch` block associated with the `try` block throws an exception itself, the `finally` block executes before the exception is processed by the next enclosing `try` block, which could be in the calling method.

By placing the resource-release code in a `finally` block, we ensure that even if the program terminates due to an uncaught exception, the resource will be deallocated. Local variables in a `try` block cannot be accessed in the corresponding `finally` block. For this reason, variables that must be accessed in both a `try` block and its corresponding `finally` block should be declared before the `try` block.

**Error-Prevention Tip 13.3**

*A `finally` block typically contains code to release resources acquired in the corresponding `try` block, which makes the `finally` block an effective mechanism for eliminating resource leaks.*

**Performance Tip 13.1**

*As a rule, resources should be released as soon as they're no longer needed in a program. This makes them available for reuse promptly.*

If one or more `catch` blocks follow a `try` block, the `finally` block is optional. However, if no `catch` blocks follow a `try` block, a `finally` block must appear immediately after the `try` block. If any `catch` blocks follow a `try` block, the `finally` block (if there is one) appears *after* the last `catch` block. Only whitespace and comments can separate the blocks in a `try` statement.

### 13.5.2 Demonstrating the `finally` Block

The app in Fig. 13.4 demonstrates that the `finally` block *always* executes, regardless of whether an exception occurs in the corresponding `try` block. The app consists of method `Main` (lines 8–47) and four other methods that `Main` invokes to demonstrate `finally`. These methods are `DoesNotThrowException` (lines 50–67), `ThrowExceptionWithCatch` (lines 70–89), `ThrowExceptionWithoutCatch` (lines 92–108) and `ThrowException-CatchRethrow` (lines 111–136).

```
1  // Fig. 13.4: UsingExceptions.cs
2  // finally blocks always execute, even when no exception occurs.
3
4  using System;
5
```

**Fig. 13.4** | `finally` blocks always execute, even when no exception occurs. (Part 1 of 4.)

```
class UsingExceptions
{
   static void Main()
   {
      // Case 1: No exceptions occur in called method
      Console.WriteLine("Calling DoesNotThrowException");
      DoesNotThrowException();

      // Case 2: Exception occurs and is caught in called method
      Console.WriteLine("\nCalling ThrowExceptionWithCatch");
      ThrowExceptionWithCatch();

      // Case 3: Exception occurs, but is not caught in called method
      // because there is no catch block.
      Console.WriteLine("\nCalling ThrowExceptionWithoutCatch");

      // call ThrowExceptionWithoutCatch
      try
      {
         ThrowExceptionWithoutCatch();
      }
      catch
      {
         Console.WriteLine(
            "Caught exception from ThrowExceptionWithoutCatch in Main");
      }

      // Case 4: Exception occurs and is caught in called method,
      // then rethrown to caller.
      Console.WriteLine("\nCalling ThrowExceptionCatchRethrow");

      // call ThrowExceptionCatchRethrow
      try
      {
         ThrowExceptionCatchRethrow();
      }
      catch
      {
         Console.WriteLine(
            "Caught exception from ThrowExceptionCatchRethrow in Main");
      }
   }

   // no exceptions thrown
   static void DoesNotThrowException()
   {
      // try block does not throw any exceptions
      try
      {
         Console.WriteLine("In DoesNotThrowException");
      }
      catch
      {
```

**Fig. 13.4** | `finally` blocks always execute, even when no exception occurs. (Part 2 of 4.)

```
         Console.WriteLine("This catch never executes");
      }
      finally
      {
         Console.WriteLine("finally executed in DoesNotThrowException");
      }

      Console.WriteLine("End of DoesNotThrowException");
   }

   // throws exception and catches it locally
   static void ThrowExceptionWithCatch()
   {
      // try block throws exception
      try
      {
         Console.WriteLine("In ThrowExceptionWithCatch");
         throw new Exception("Exception in ThrowExceptionWithCatch");
      }
      catch (Exception exceptionParameter)
      {
         Console.WriteLine($"Message: {exceptionParameter.Message}");
      }
      finally
      {
         Console.WriteLine(
            "finally executed in ThrowExceptionWithCatch");
      }

      Console.WriteLine("End of ThrowExceptionWithCatch");
   }

   // throws exception and does not catch it locally
   static void ThrowExceptionWithoutCatch()
   {
      // throw exception, but do not catch it
      try
      {
         Console.WriteLine("In ThrowExceptionWithoutCatch");
         throw new Exception("Exception in ThrowExceptionWithoutCatch");
      }
      finally
      {
         Console.WriteLine(
            "finally executed in ThrowExceptionWithoutCatch");
      }

      // unreachable code; logic error
      Console.WriteLine("End of ThrowExceptionWithoutCatch");
   }

```

**Fig. 13.4** | finally blocks always execute, even when no exception occurs. (Part 3 of 4.)

```
110     // throws exception, catches it and rethrows it
111     static void ThrowExceptionCatchRethrow()
112     {
113        // try block throws exception
114        try
115        {
116           Console.WriteLine("In ThrowExceptionCatchRethrow");
117           throw new Exception("Exception in ThrowExceptionCatchRethrow");
118        }
119        catch (Exception exceptionParameter)
120        {
121           Console.WriteLine("Message: " + exceptionParameter.Message);
122
123           // rethrow exception for further processing
124           throw;
125
126           // unreachable code; logic error
127        }
128        finally
129        {
130           Console.WriteLine(
131              "finally executed in ThrowExceptionCatchRethrow");
132        }
133
134        // any code placed here is never reached
135        Console.WriteLine("End of ThrowExceptionCatchRethrow");
136     }
137  }
```

```
Calling DoesNotThrowException
In DoesNotThrowException
finally executed in DoesNotThrowException
End of DoesNotThrowException

Calling ThrowExceptionWithCatch
In ThrowExceptionWithCatch
Message: Exception in ThrowExceptionWithCatch
finally executed in ThrowExceptionWithCatch
End of ThrowExceptionWithCatch

Calling ThrowExceptionWithoutCatch
In ThrowExceptionWithoutCatch
finally executed in ThrowExceptionWithoutCatch
Caught exception from ThrowExceptionWithoutCatch in Main

Calling ThrowExceptionCatchRethrow
In ThrowExceptionCatchRethrow
Message: Exception in ThrowExceptionCatchRethrow
finally executed in ThrowExceptionCatchRethrow
Caught exception from ThrowExceptionCatchRethrow in Main
```

**Fig. 13.4** | `finally` blocks always execute, even when no exception occurs. (Part 4 of 4.)

Line 12 of `Main` invokes method `DoesNotThrowException`. This method's `try` block outputs a message (line 55). Because the `try` block does *not* throw any exceptions, program control ignores the catch block (lines 57–60) and executes the finally block (lines 61–64), which outputs a message. At this point, program control continues with the first statement after the close of the finally block (line 66), which outputs a message indicating that the end of the method has been reached. Then program control returns to Main.

### 13.5.3 Throwing Exceptions Using the throw Statement

Line 16 of Main invokes method ThrowExceptionWithCatch (lines 70–89), which begins in its try block (lines 73–77) by outputting a message. Next, the try block creates an Exception object and uses a **throw statement** to throw it (line 76). Executing the throw statement indicates that a problem has occurred in the code. As you've seen in earlier chapters, you can throw exceptions by using the throw statement. Just as with exceptions thrown by the Framework Class Library's methods and the CLR, this indicates to client apps that an error has occurred. A throw statement specifies an object to be thrown. The operand of a throw statement can be of type Exception or of any type derived from it.

The string passed to the constructor becomes the exception object's error message. When a throw statement in a try block executes, the try block *exits immediately*, and program control continues with the first matching catch block (lines 78–81) following the try block. In this example, the type thrown (Exception) matches the type specified in the catch, so line 80 outputs a message indicating the exception that occurred. Then, the finally block (lines 82–86) executes and outputs a message. At this point, program control continues with the first statement after the close of the finally block (line 88), which outputs a message indicating that the end of the method has been reached. Program control then returns to Main. In line 80, we use the exception object's Message property to retrieve the error message associated with the exception (i.e., the message passed to the Exception constructor). Section 13.7 discusses several properties of class Exception.

Lines 23–31 of Main define a try statement in which Main invokes method ThrowExceptionWithoutCatch (lines 92–108). The try block enables Main to catch any exceptions thrown by ThrowExceptionWithoutCatch. The try block in lines 95–99 of ThrowExceptionWithoutCatch begins by outputting a message. Next, the try block throws an Exception (line 98) and exits immediately.

Normally, program control would continue at the first catch following this try block. However, this try block does not have any catch blocks. Therefore, the exception is not caught in method ThrowExceptionWithoutCatch. Program control proceeds to the finally block (lines 100–104), which outputs a message. At this point, program control returns to Main in search of an appropriate catch block—any statements appearing after the finally block (e.g., line 107) do not execute. (In fact, the compiler issues a warning about this.) In this example, such statements could cause logic errors, because the exception thrown in line 98 is not caught. In Main, the catch block in lines 27–31 catches the exception and displays a message indicating that the exception was caught in Main.

### 13.5.4 Rethrowing Exceptions

Lines 38–46 of Main define a try statement in which Main invokes method ThrowExceptionCatchRethrow (lines 111–136). The try statement enables Main to catch any exceptions thrown by ThrowExceptionCatchRethrow. The try statement in lines 114–132 of ThrowExceptionCatchRethrow begins by outputting a message. Next, the try block throws an Exception (line 117). The try block *exits immediately*, and program control continues at the first `catch` (lines 119–127) following the `try` block. In this example, the type thrown (`Exception`) matches the type specified in the `catch`, so line 121 outputs a message indicating where the exception occurred. Line 124 uses the `throw` statement to **rethrow** the exception. This indicates that the `catch` block performed partial processing of the exception and now is throwing the exception again (in this case, back to the method `Main`) for further processing.

You also can rethrow an exception with a version of the `throw` statement which takes an operand that's the reference to the exception that was caught. It's important to note, however, that this form of `throw` statement *resets the throw point*, so the original throw point's stack-trace information is *lost*. Section 13.7 demonstrates using a `throw` statement with an operand from a `catch` block. In that section, you'll see that after an exception is caught, you can create and throw a different type of exception object from the `catch` block and you can include the original exception as part of the new exception object. Class library designers often do this to *customize* the exception types thrown from methods in their class libraries or to provide additional debugging information.

**Software Engineering Observation 13.2**

*In general, it's considered better practice to throw a new exception and pass the original one to the new exception's constructor, rather than rethrowing the original exception. This maintains all of the stack-trace information from the original exception. We demonstrate passing an existing exception to a new exception's constructor in Section 13.7.3.*

The exception handling in method `ThrowExceptionCatchRethrow` does not complete, because the `throw` statement in line 124 immediately terminates the `catch` block—if there were any code between line 124 and the end of the block, it would not execute. When line 124 executes, method `ThrowExceptionCatchRethrow` terminates and returns control to `Main` in search of an appropriate `catch`. Once again, the `finally` block (lines 128–132) executes and outputs a message before control returns to `Main`. When control returns to `Main`, the `catch` block in lines 42–46 catches the exception and displays a message indicating that the exception was caught. Then the program terminates.

### 13.5.5 Returning After a `finally` Block

The next statement to execute after a `finally` block terminates depends on the exception-handling state. If the `try` block successfully completes, or if a `catch` block catches and handles an exception, the program continues its execution with the next statement after the `finally` block. However, if an exception is not caught, or if a `catch` block rethrows an exception, program control continues in the next enclosing `try` block. The enclosing `try` could be in the calling method or in one of its callers. It also is possible to nest a `try` statement in a `try` block; in such a case, the outer `try` statement's `catch` blocks would process any exceptions that were not caught in the inner `try` statement. If a `try` block executes and has a corresponding `finally` block, the `finally` block executes even if the `try` block terminates due to a `return` statement. The `return` occurs after the execution of the `finally` block.

**Common Programming Error 13.3**

*If an uncaught exception is awaiting processing when the `finally` block executes, and the `finally` block throws a new exception that's not caught in the `finally` block, the first exception is lost, and the new exception is passed to the next enclosing `try` block.*

**Error-Prevention Tip 13.4**

*When placing code that can throw an exception in a `finally` block, always enclose the code in a `try` statement that catches the appropriate exception types. This prevents the loss of any uncaught and rethrown exceptions that occur before the `finally` block executes.*

**Software Engineering Observation 13.3**

*Do not place `try` blocks around every statement that might throw an exception—this can make programs difficult to read. Instead, place one `try` block around a significant portion of code, and follow this `try` block with `catch` blocks that handle each possible exception. Then follow the `catch` blocks with a single `finally` block. Use separate `try` blocks to distinguish between multiple statements that can throw the same exception type.*

## 13.6 The using Statement

Typically resource-release code should be placed in a `finally` block to ensure that a resource is released, *regardless* of whether there were exceptions when the resource was used in the corresponding `try` block. An alternative notation—the **`using`** statement (not to be confused with the `using` directive for using namespaces)—simplifies writing code in which you obtain a resource, use the resource in a `try` block and release the resource in a corresponding `finally` block. For example, a file-processing app (Chapter 17) could process a file with a `using` statement to ensure that the file is closed properly when it's no longer needed. The resource must be an object that implements the `IDisposable` interface and therefore has a `Dispose` method. The general form of a `using` statement is

```
using (var exampleObject = new ExampleClass())
{
   exampleObject.SomeMethod(); // do something with exampleObject
}
```

where `ExampleClass` is a class that implements the `IDisposable` interface. This code creates an object of type `ExampleClass` and uses it in a statement, then calls its `Dispose` method to release any resources used by the object. The `using` statement implicitly places the code in its body in a `try` block with a corresponding `finally` block that calls the object's `Dispose` method. For instance, the preceding brief code segment is equivalent to

```
{
   var exampleObject = new ExampleClass();
   try
   {
      exampleObject.SomeMethod();
   }
   finally
   {
      if (exampleObject != null)
      {
         exampleObject.Dispose();
      }
   }
}
```

The `if` statement in the `finally` block ensures that `exampleObject` is not null—that is, it references an object—otherwise, a `NullReferenceException` would occur when attempting to call `Dispose`. Section 13.9 introduces C# 6's new `?.` operator, which can be used to express the above `if` statement more elegantly as a single line of code.

## 13.7 Exception Properties

As we discussed in Section 13.4, exception types derive from class `Exception`, which has several properties. These frequently are used to formulate error messages indicating a caught exception. Two important properties are `Message` and **`StackTrace`**. Property `Message` stores the `string` error message associated with an `Exception` object. This message can be a default message defined in the exception type or a customized message passed to an `Exception` object's constructor when the `Exception` object is thrown. Property `StackTrace` contains a `string` that represents the method-call stack. Recall that the runtime environment at all times keeps a list of open method calls that have been made but have not yet returned. The `StackTrace` represents the series of methods that have not finished processing at the time the exception occurs. If the debugging information that's generated by the compiler for the method is accessible to the IDE (e.g., the code is part of your project, rather than some third party library), the stack trace also includes line numbers; the first line number indicates the *throw point*, and subsequent line numbers indicate the locations from which the methods in the stack trace were called.

### 13.7.1 Property InnerException

Another frequently used property is **`InnerException`**. When an exception occurs in a class library, it's common for the library to catch that exception, then `throw` a new one containing information that helps the client code programmer determine the exception's cause. Class library programmers typically "wrap" the original exception object in the new exception object—this gives the client code programmer complete details of what led to the exception.

For example, a programmer implementing libraries used in an accounting system might have account-number processing code in which account numbers are input as `string`s but represented as `int`s in the code. Recall that a program can convert `string`s to `int` values with `int.Parse`, which throws a `FormatException` if it encounters an invalid number format. When this happens, the library programmer might wish to employ a different error message than the default message supplied by `FormatException` or might wish to indicate a new exception type, such as `InvalidAccountNumberException`.

In such cases, the library programmer would provide code to catch the `FormatException`, then create an `InvalidAccountNumberException` object in the `catch` block, passing the original exception as a constructor argument. The original exception object becomes the `InvalidAccountNumberException` object's `InnerException`. Section 13.8 shows how to create a custom exception class.

When an `InvalidAccountNumberException` occurs in code that uses the accounting-system library, the `catch` handler can reference the original exception via property `InnerException`. So the `InvalidAccountNumberException` can indicate *both* that the user specified an invalid account number and that the number format was invalid. If the `InnerException` property is `null`, this indicates that the exception was not caused by another exception.

### 13.7.2 Other Exception Properties

Class `Exception` provides other properties, including **`HelpLink`**, **`Source`** and **`TargetSite`**:

- Property `HelpLink` specifies a link to the help file that describes the problem that occurred. This property is `null` if no such file exists.
- Property `Source` specifies the name of the assembly (i.e., app or library) that caused the exception.
- Property `TargetSite` specifies the method where the exception originated.

### 13.7.3 Demonstrating Exception Properties and Stack Unwinding

Our next example (Fig. 13.5) demonstrates properties `Message`, `StackTrace` and `InnerException` of class `Exception`. In addition, the example formally introduces **stack unwinding**—when an exception is thrown but not caught in a particular scope, the method-call stack is "unwound," and an attempt is made to catch the exception in the next outer `try` block. We keep track of the methods on the call stack as we discuss property `StackTrace` and the stack-unwinding mechanism. To see the proper stack trace, you should execute this program using steps similar to those presented in Section 13.2.

```
// Fig. 13.5: Properties.cs
// Stack unwinding and Exception class properties.
// Demonstrates using properties Message, StackTrace and InnerException.
using System;

class Properties
{
   static void Main()
   {
      // call Method1; any Exception generated is caught
      // in the catch block that follows
      try
      {
         Method1();
      }
      catch (Exception exceptionParameter)
      {
         // output the string representation of the Exception, then output
         // properties Message, StackTrace and InnerException
         Console.WriteLine("exceptionParameter.ToString: \n" +
            exceptionParameter);
         Console.WriteLine("\nexceptionParameter.Message: \n" +
            exceptionParameter.Message);
         Console.WriteLine("\nexceptionParameter.StackTrace: \n" +
            exceptionParameter.StackTrace);
         Console.WriteLine("\nexceptionParameter.InnerException: \n" +
            exceptionParameter.InnerException);
      }
   }

```

**Fig. 13.5** | Stack unwinding and `Exception` class properties. (Part 1 of 3.)

```
   // calls Method2
   static void Method1()
   {
      Method2();
   }

   // calls Method3
   static void Method2()
   {
      Method3();
   }

   // throws an Exception containing an InnerException
   static void Method3()
   {
      // attempt to convert string to int
      try
      {
         int.Parse("Not an integer");
      }
      catch (FormatException formatExceptionParameter)
      {
         // wrap FormatException in new Exception
         throw new Exception("Exception occurred in Method3",
            formatExceptionParameter);
      }
   }
}
```

```
exceptionParameter.ToString:
System.Exception: Exception occurred in Method3 --->
   System.FormatException: Input string was not in a correct format.
   at System.Number.StringToNumber(String str, NumberStyles options,
      NumberBuffer& number, NumberFormatInfo info, Boolean parseDecimal)
   at System.Number.ParseInt32(String s, NumberStyles style,
      NumberFormatInfo info)
   at System.Int32.Parse(String s)
   at Properties.Method3() in C:\Users\PaulDeitel\Documents\examples\
      ch13\Fig13_05\Properties\Properties\Properties.cs:line 49
   --- End of inner exception stack trace ---
   at Properties.Method3() in C:\Users\PaulDeitel\Documents\examples\
      ch13\Fig13_05\Properties\Properties\Properties.cs:line 54
   at Properties.Method2() in C:\Users\PaulDeitel\Documents\examples\
      ch13\Fig13_05\Properties\Properties\Properties.cs:line 40
   at Properties.Method1() in C:\Users\PaulDeitel\Documents\examples\
      ch13\Fig13_05\Properties\Properties\Properties.cs:line 34
   at Properties.Main() in C:\Users\PaulDeitel\Documents\examples\
      ch13\Fig13_05\Properties\Properties\Properties.cs:line 14

exceptionParameter.Message:
Exception occurred in Method3
```

**Fig. 13.5** | Stack unwinding and `Exception` class properties. (Part 2 of 3.)

```
exceptionParameter.StackTrace:
   at Properties.Method3() in C:\Users\PaulDeitel\Documents\examples\
      ch13\Fig13_05\Properties\Properties\Properties.cs:line 54
   at Properties.Method2() in C:\Users\PaulDeitel\Documents\examples\
      ch13\Fig13_05\Properties\Properties\Properties.cs:line 40
   at Properties.Method1() in C:\Users\PaulDeitel\Documents\examples\
      ch13\Fig13_05\Properties\Properties\Properties.cs:line 34
   at Properties.Main() in C:\Users\PaulDeitel\Documents\examples\
      ch13\Fig13_05\Properties\Properties\Properties.cs:line 14

exceptionParameter.InnerException:
System.FormatException: Input string was not in a correct format.
   at System.Number.StringToNumber(String str, NumberStyles options,
      NumberBuffer& number, NumberFormatInfo info, Boolean parseDecimal)
   at System.Number.ParseInt32(String s, NumberStyles style,
      NumberFormatInfo info)
   at System.Int32.Parse(String s)
   at Properties.Method3() in C:\Users\PaulDeitel\Documents\examples\
      ch13\Fig13_05\Properties\Properties\Properties.cs:line 49
```

**Fig. 13.5** | Stack unwinding and `Exception` class properties. (Part 3 of 3.)

Program execution begins with `Main`, which becomes the first method on the method-call stack. Line 14 (Fig. 13.5) of the `try` block in `Main` invokes `Method1` (declared in lines 32–35), which becomes the second method on the stack. If `Method1` throws an exception, the `catch` block in lines 16–28 handles the exception and outputs information about the exception that occurred. Line 34 of `Method1` invokes `Method2` (lines 38–41), which becomes the third method on the stack. Then line 40 of `Method2` invokes `Method3` (lines 44–57), which becomes the fourth method on the stack.

At this point, the method-call stack (from top to bottom) for the program is

```
Method3
Method2
Method1
Main
```

The method called *most recently* (`Method3`) appears at the *top* of the stack; the *first* method called (`Main`) appears at the *bottom*. The `try` statement (lines 47–56) in `Method3` invokes method `int.Parse` (line 49), which attempts to convert a `string` to an `int`. At this point, `int.Parse` becomes the fifth and final method on the call stack.

### 13.7.4 Throwing an Exception with an InnerException

Because the argument to `int.Parse` is not in `int` format, line 49 throws a `FormatException` that's caught in line 51 of `Method3`. The exception terminates the call to `int.Parse`, so the method is *unwound* (i.e., removed) from the method-call stack. The `catch` block in `Method3` then creates and throws an `Exception` object. The first argument to the `Exception` constructor is the custom error message for our example, "`Exception occurred in Method3.`" The second argument is the `InnerException`—the `FormatException` that was caught. The `StackTrace` for this new exception object reflects the point at which the exception was thrown (lines 54–55). Now `Method3` terminates, because the exception thrown in the `catch` block is not caught in the method body. Thus, control returns to the statement that invoked `Method3` in the prior method in the call stack (`Method2`). This *unwinds* `Method3` from the method-call stack.

When control returns to line 40 in `Method2`, the CLR determines that line 40 is not in a `try` block. Therefore the exception cannot be caught in `Method2`, and `Method2` terminates. This *unwinds* `Method2` from the call stack and returns control to line 34 in `Method1`.

Here again, line 34 is not in a `try` block, so `Method1` cannot catch the exception. The method terminates and is *unwound* from the call stack, returning control to line 14 in `Main`, which *is* located in a `try` block. The `try` block in `Main` exits and the `catch` block (lines 16–28) catches the exception. The `catch` block uses properties `Message`, `StackTrace` and `InnerException` to create the output. Stack unwinding continues until a `catch` block catches the exception or the program terminates.

### 13.7.5 Displaying Information About the Exception

The first block of output (which we reformatted for readability) in Fig. 13.5 contains the exception's `string` representation, which is returned from an *implicit* call to method `ToString`. The `string` begins with the name of the exception class followed by the `Message` property value. The next four items present the stack trace of the `InnerException` object. The remainder of the block of output shows the `StackTrace` for the exception thrown in lines 54–55 of `Method3`. The `StackTrace` represents the state of the method-call stack at the throw point of the exception, rather than at the point where the exception eventually is caught. Each `StackTrace` line that begins with "`at`" represents a method on the call stack. These lines indicate the method in which the exception occurred, the file in which the method resides and the line number of the throw point in the file. The inner-exception information includes the *inner-exception stack trace.*

**Error-Prevention Tip 13.5**

*When catching and rethrowing an exception, provide additional debugging information in the rethrown exception. To do so, create an object of an* `Exception` *subclass containing more specific debugging information, then pass the original caught exception to the new exception object's constructor to initialize the* `InnerException` *property.*

The next block of output (two lines) simply displays the `Message` property's value (`Exception occurred in Method3`) of the exception thrown in `Method3`.

The third block of output displays the `StackTrace` property of the exception thrown in `Method3`. This `StackTrace` property contains the stack trace starting from line 54 in `Method3`, because that's the point at which the `Exception` object was created and thrown. The stack trace *always* begins from the exception's throw point.

Finally, the last block of output displays the `string` representation of the `InnerException` property, which includes the namespace and class name of the exception object, as well as its `Message` and `StackTrace` properties.

## 13.8 User-Defined Exception Classes

In many cases, you can use existing exception classes from the .NET Framework Class Library to indicate exceptions that occur in your programs. In some cases, however, you might wish to create new exception classes specific to the problems that occur in your programs. **User-defined exception classes** should derive directly or indirectly from class `Ex-`

ception of namespace System. When you create code that throws exceptions, they should be well documented, so that other developers who use your code will know how to handle them.

**Good Programming Practice 13.1**

*Associating each type of malfunction with an appropriately named exception class improves program clarity.*

**Software Engineering Observation 13.4**

*Before creating a user-defined exception class, investigate the existing exceptions in the .NET Framework Class Library to determine whether an appropriate exception type already exists.*

### *Class* `NegativeNumberException`

Figures 13.6–13.7 demonstrate a user-defined exception class. NegativeNumberException (Fig. 13.6) represents exceptions that occur when a program performs an illegal operation on a negative number, such as attempting to calculate its square root. According to Microsoft's "Best Practices for Handling Exceptions" (bit.ly/Exceptions-BestPractices), user-defined exceptions should typically extend class Exception, have a class name that ends with Exception and define three constructors:

- a *parameterless constructor,*
- a *constructor that receives a* string *argument* (the error message), and
- a *constructor that receives a* string *argument and an* Exception *argument* (the error message and the inner-exception object).

Defining these three constructors makes your exception class more flexible, allowing other programmers to easily use and extend it.

```
// Fig. 13.6: NegativeNumberException.cs
// NegativeNumberException represents exceptions caused by
// illegal operations performed on negative numbers.
using System;

public class NegativeNumberException : Exception
{
   // default constructor
   public NegativeNumberException()
      : base("Illegal operation for a negative number")
   {
      // empty body
   }

   // constructor for customizing error message
   public NegativeNumberException(string messageValue)
      : base(messageValue)
   {
```

**Fig. 13.6** | NegativeNumberException represents exceptions caused by illegal operations performed on negative numbers. (Part 1 of 2.)

```
        // empty body
    }

    // constructor for customizing the exception's error
    // message and specifying the InnerException object
    public NegativeNumberException(string messageValue, Exception inner)
        : base(messageValue, inner)
    {
        // empty body
    }
}
```

**Fig. 13.6** | `NegativeNumberException` represents exceptions caused by illegal operations performed on negative numbers. (Part 2 of 2.)

`NegativeNumberException`s most frequently occur during arithmetic operations, so it seems logical to derive class `NegativeNumberException` from class `ArithmeticException`. However, class `ArithmeticException` derives from class `SystemException`—the category of exceptions thrown by the CLR. Per Microsoft's best practices for exception handling, *user-defined exception classes should inherit from* `Exception` rather than `SystemException`. In this case, we could have used the built-in `ArgumentOutOfRangeException` class (introduced in Chapter 10), which is recommended in the best practices for invalid argument values. We create our own exception type here simply for demonstration purposes.

### *Using Class* `NegativeNumberException`

Class `SquareRootTest` (Fig. 13.7) demonstrates our user-defined exception class. The app enables the user to input a numeric value, then invokes method `SquareRoot` (lines 40–52) to calculate the square root of that value. To perform this calculation, `SquareRoot` invokes class `Math`'s `Sqrt` method, which receives a `double` value as its argument. Normally, if the argument is *negative*, method `Sqrt` returns `NaN`. In this program, we'd like to *prevent* the user from calculating the square root of a negative number. If the numeric value that the user enters is negative, method `SquareRoot` throws a `NegativeNumberException` (lines 45–46). Otherwise, `SquareRoot` invokes class `Math`'s method `Sqrt` to compute the square root (line 50).

```
1  // Fig. 13.7: SquareRootTest.cs
2  // Demonstrating a user-defined exception class.
3  using System;
4
5  class SquareRootTest
6  {
7     static void Main(string[] args)
8     {
9        var continueLoop = true;
10
11       do
12       {
```

**Fig. 13.7** | Demonstrating a user-defined exception class. (Part 1 of 3.)

```
         // catch any NegativeNumberException thrown
         try
         {
            Console.Write(
               "Enter a value to calculate the square root of: ");
            double inputValue = double.Parse(Console.ReadLine());
            double result = SquareRoot(inputValue);

            Console.WriteLine(
               $"The square root of {inputValue} is {result:F6}\n");
            continueLoop = false;
         }
         catch (FormatException formatException)
         {
            Console.WriteLine("\n" + formatException.Message);
            Console.WriteLine("Please enter a double value.\n");
         }
         catch (NegativeNumberException negativeNumberException)
         {
            Console.WriteLine("\n" + negativeNumberException.Message);
            Console.WriteLine("Please enter a non-negative value.\n");
         }
      } while (continueLoop);
   }

   // computes square root of parameter; throws
   // NegativeNumberException if parameter is negative
   public static double SquareRoot(double value)
   {
      // if negative operand, throw NegativeNumberException
      if (value < 0)
      {
         throw new NegativeNumberException(
            "Square root of negative number not permitted");
      }
      else
      {
         return Math.Sqrt(value); // compute square root
      }
   }
}
```

```
Enter a value to calculate the square root of: 30
The square root of 30 is 5.477226
```

```
Enter a value to calculate the square root of: hello

Input string was not in a correct format.
Please enter a double value.

Enter a value to calculate the square root of: 25
The square root of 25 is 5.000000
```

**Fig. 13.7** | Demonstrating a user-defined exception class. (Part 2 of 3.)

```
Enter a value to calculate the square root of: -2

Square root of negative number not permitted
Please enter a non-negative value.

Enter a value to calculate the square root of: 2
The square root of 2 is 1.414214
```

**Fig. 13.7** | Demonstrating a user-defined exception class. (Part 3 of 3.)

When the user inputs a value, the `try` statement (lines 14–34) attempts to invoke `SquareRoot` using the value input by the user. If the user input is not a number, a `FormatException` occurs, and the `catch` block in lines 25–29 processes the exception. If the user inputs a negative number, method `SquareRoot` throws a `NegativeNumberException` (lines 45–46); the `catch` block in lines 30–34 catches and handles this type of exception.

## 13.9 Checking for `null` References; Introducing C# 6's `?.` Operator

In Section 13.6, we showed the following code snippet:

```
{
   var exampleObject = new ExampleClass();
   try
   {
      exampleObject.SomeMethod();
   }
   finally
   {
      if (exampleObject != null)
      {
         exampleObject.Dispose();
      }
   }
}
```

The `if` statement in the preceding `finally` block ensures that if `exampleObject` is `null`, the call to `Dispose` is skipped, thus preventing a `NullReferenceException`.

**Error-Prevention Tip 13.6**

*Always ensure that a reference is not* `null` *before using it to call a method or access a property of an object.*

### 13.9.1 Null-Conditional Operator (`?.`)

6 C# 6's new **null-conditional operator** (`?.`) provides a more elegant way to check for `null`. The following statement replaces the four-line `if` statement above:

```
exampleObject?.Dispose();
```

In this statement, `Dispose` is called *only* if `exampleObject` is not `null`—exactly as in the preceding `if` statement.

### 13.9.2 Revisiting Operators is and as

In Section 12.5.6, we introduced downcasting with the is operator and mentioned that downcasting can cause InvalidCastExceptions. We then mentioned that you can avoid the InvalidCastException by using the as operator as follows:

```
var employee = currentEmployee as BasePlusCommissionEmployee;
```

If currentEmployee *is a* BasePlusCommissionEmployee, employee is assigned the BasePlusCommissionEmployee; otherwise, it's assigned null. Since employee could be null, you must ensure that it's not null before using it. For example, to give the BasePlusCommissionEmployee a 10% raise, we could use the statement

```
employee?.BaseSalary *= 1.10M;
```

which accesses and modifies the BaseSalary property *only* if employee is not null.

### 13.9.3 Nullable Types

Suppose you'd like to capture the value of the expression employee?.BaseSalary, as in

```
decimal salary = employee?.BaseSalary;
```

This statement actually results in a compilation error indicating that you cannot implicitly convert type decimal? to type decimal.

Normally a value-type variable cannot be assigned null. Because the employee reference might be null, the expression

```
employee?.BaseSalary
```

returns a **nullable type**—a value type that also can be null. You specify a nullable type by following a value type's name with a question mark (?)—so decimal? represents a nullable decimal. The statement

```
decimal? salary = employee?.BaseSalary;
```

indicates that salary either will be null or the employee's BaseSalary.

Nullable types have the following capabilities for accessing their underlying values:

- The **GetValueOrDefault** method checks whether a nullable-type variable contains a value. If so, the method returns that value; otherwise, it returns the value type's default value. An overload of this method receives one argument that enables you to specify a custom default value.
- The **HasValue** property returns true if a nullable-type variable contains a value; otherwise, it returns false.
- The **Value** property returns the nullable-type variable's underlying value or throws an InvalidOperationException if the underlying value is null.

Variables of nullable types also may be used as the left operand of the null-conditional operator (?.) or the null coalescing operator (??—discussed in the next section).

**Error-Prevention Tip 13.7**

*Before using a nullable-type variable's* Value *property, use the* HasValue *property to check whether the variable has a value. If the nullable-type variable is* null*, accessing* Value *results in an* InvalidOperationException.

### 13.9.4 Null Coalescing Operator (??)

C# also offers the **null coalescing operator** (??) for working with values that can be `null`. The operator has two operands. If the left operand is not `null`, the entire ?? expression evaluates to the left operand's value; otherwise, it evaluates to the right operand's value. For example, in the statement

```
decimal salary = employee?.BaseSalary ?? 0M;
```

if `employee` is not `null`, `salary` is assigned the `employee`'s `BaseSalary`; otherwise, `salary` is assigned `0M`. The preceding statement is equivalent to

```
decimal salary = (employee?.BaseSalary).GetValueOrDefault();
```

As you can see, the preceding statements are more elegant and more compact than writing the following equivalent code, which must explicitly test for `null`:

```
decimal salary = 0M;

if (employee != null)
{
   salary = employee.BaseSalary
}
```

## 13.10 Exception Filters and the C# 6 when Clause

6

Prior to C# 6, you could catch an exception based only on its type. C# 6 introduces **exception filters** that enable you to catch an exception based on a `catch`'s exception type and a condition that's specified with a **`when` clause**, as in

**`catch`**(*ExceptionType name*) **`when`**(*condition*)

You also can specify an exception filter for a general `catch` clause that does not provide an exception type. This allows you to catch an exception based only on a condition, as in

**`catch when`**(*condition*)

In each case, the exception is caught only if the `when` clause's condition is `true`; otherwise, the exception is not caught and the search for an appropriate `catch` continues.

A typical use of an exception filter is to determine whether a property of an exception object has a specific value. Consider an app that connects to a web server to download videos. Such an app would call methods that may throw `HttpException`s—for example, the web server might not be found, you might not have permission to access the web server, etc. Class `HttpException` has an `ErrorCode` property that contains a numeric code, which apps can use to determine what went wrong and handle the exception accordingly. The following `catch` handler catches an `HttpException` *only* if the exception object's `ErrorCode` property contains `401`, indicating your app does not have permission to access the web server:

```
catch (HttpException ex) when (exception.ErrorCode == 401)
```

You might provide several similar `catch` handlers with exception filters that test for various other `ErrorCode`s.

**Common Programming Error 13.4**

*Following a `try` block with multiple `catch` clauses for the same type results in a compilation error, unless they provide different `when` clauses. If there are multiple such `catches` and one does not have a `when` clause, it must appear last; otherwise, a compilation error occurs.*

## 13.11 Wrap-Up

In this chapter, you learned how to use exception handling to deal with errors in an app. You saw exception handling in the context of a divide-by-zero example. You learned how to use `try` blocks to enclose code that may throw an exception, and how to use `catch` blocks to deal with exceptions that may arise. We explained the termination model of exception handling, in which, after an exception is handled, program control does not return to the throw point.

We discussed several important classes of the .NET `Exception` hierarchy, including `Exception` (from which user-defined exception classes are derived) and `SystemException`. Next you learned how to use the `finally` block to release resources whether or not an exception occurs, and how to throw and rethrow exceptions with the `throw` statement. We showed how the `using` statement can be used to automate the process of releasing a resource. You then saw how to obtain information about an exception using `Exception` properties `Message`, `StackTrace` and `InnerException`, and method `ToString`. We demonstrated how to create your own exception classes.

We introduced C# 6's new `?.` null-conditional operator for testing whether a reference is `null` before accessing the referenced object. We also introduced nullable value types and the `??` null coalescing operator. Finally, we showed how to use C# 6's new `when` clause for adding exception filters to `catch` clauses.

In the next two chapters, we present an in-depth treatment of graphical user interfaces. In these chapters and throughout the rest of the book, we use exception handling to make our examples more robust, while demonstrating new features of the language.

# 14

# Graphical User Interfaces with Windows Forms: Part 1

## Objectives

In this chapter you'll:

- Design principles of graphical user interfaces (GUIs).
- Create graphical user interfaces.
- Process events in response to user interactions with GUI controls.
- Understand the namespaces that contain the classes for GUI controls and event handling.
- Create and manipulate various controls.
- Add descriptive `ToolTip`s to GUI controls.
- Process mouse and keyboard events.

Outline



## 14.1 Introduction

A graphical user interface (GUI) allows a user to interact *visually* with a program. A GUI gives a program a distinctive "look" and "feel." As an example of a GUI, consider Fig. 14.1, which shows a Visual Studio window containing various GUI controls.

**Look-and-Feel Observation 14.1**

*Consistent user interfaces enable a user to learn new apps more quickly because the apps have the same "look" and "feel."*

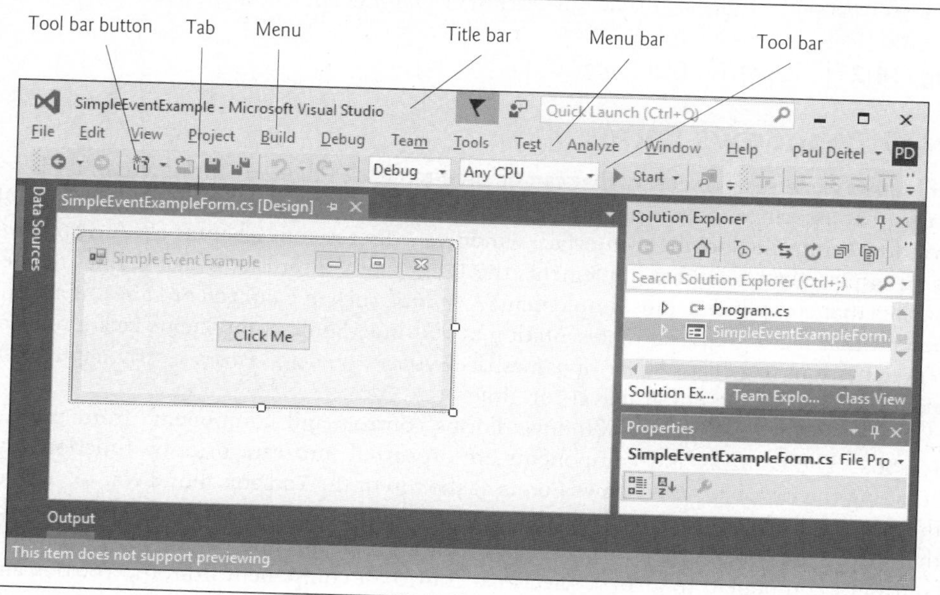


**Fig. 14.1** | GUI controls in Visual Studio.

Near the top, there's a *menu bar* containing the menus **File**, **Edit**, **View**, etc. Below that is a *tool bar* of buttons, each with a defined task, such as creating a new project or opening a file. Below that is a *tab* representing a currently open file—this *tabbed view* allows users to switch between the open files. These controls form a user-friendly interface through which you have been interacting with the IDE.

GUIs are built from *GUI controls* (which are sometimes called **components** or **widgets**—short for **window gadgets**). GUI controls are *objects* that can display information on the screen or enable users to interact with an app via the mouse, keyboard or some other form of input (such as voice commands). Several common GUI controls are listed in Fig. 14.2—in the sections that follow and in Chapter 15, we discuss each of these in detail. Chapter 15 explores the features and properties of additional GUI controls.

| Control | Description |
|---|---|
| `Label` | Displays *images* or *uneditable text*. |
| `TextBox` | Enables the user to *enter data via the keyboard*. It also can be used to *display editable or uneditable text*. |
| `Button` | Triggers an *event* when clicked with the mouse. |
| `CheckBox` | Specifies an option that can be *selected* (checked) or *unselected* (not checked). |
| `ComboBox` | Provides a *drop-down list* of items from which the user can make a *selection* either by clicking an item in the list or by typing in a box. |
| `ListBox` | Provides a *list* of items from which the user can make a *selection* by clicking one or more items. |
| `Panel` | A *container* in which controls can be placed and organized. |
| `NumericUpDown` | Enables the user to select from a *range* of numeric input values. |

**Fig. 14.2** | Some basic GUI controls.

## 14.2 Windows Forms

**Windows Forms** is one library that can be used to create GUIs. A `Form` is a graphical element that appears on your computer's desktop; it can be a dialog, a window or an **MDI window (multiple document interface window)**—discussed in Chapter 15. A *component* is an instance of a class that implements the **`IComponent` interface**, which defines the behaviors that components must implement. A *control*, such as a `Button` or `Label`, is a component that has a graphical representation at runtime. Some components lack graphical representations (e.g., class `Timer` of namespace `System.Windows.Forms`—see Chapter 15). Such components are not visible at run time.

Figure 14.3 displays the Windows Forms controls and components from the C# **Toolbox**. The controls and components are organized into categories by functionality. Selecting the category **All Windows Forms** at the top of the **Toolbox** allows you to view all the controls and components from the other tabs in one list (as shown in Fig. 14.3). In this chapter and the next, we discuss many of these controls and components. To add a control or component to a `Form`, select that control or component from the **Toolbox** and drag it onto the `Form`. To *deselect* a control or component, select the **Pointer** item in the **Toolbox** (the icon at the top of the list).

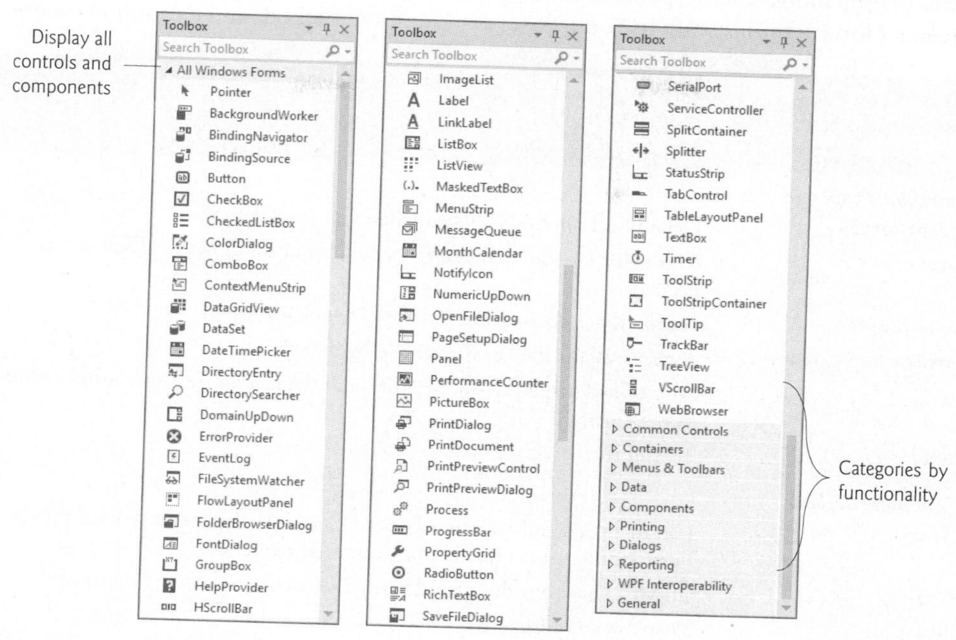


**Fig. 14.3** | Components and controls for Windows Forms.

### *Active Window and Focus*

When there are several windows on the screen, the **active window** is the *frontmost* and has a *highlighted title bar*. A window becomes the active window when the user clicks somewhere inside it. The active window is said to "have the **focus**." For example, in Visual Studio the active window is the **Toolbox** when you're selecting an item from it, or the **Properties** window when you're editing a control's properties.

### *Auto-Generated Code Stored in Separate File*

A `Form` is a **container** for controls and components. When you drag an item from the **Toolbox** onto the `Form`, Visual Studio generates code that creates the object and sets its basic properties. This code is updated when the control or component's properties are modified in the IDE. Removing a control or component from the `Form` *deletes* the corresponding generated code. The IDE maintains the generated code in a separate file using **`partial` classes**—classes that are split among multiple files and assembled into a single class by the compiler. You could write this code yourself, but it's much easier to allow Visual Studio to handle the details. We introduced visual programming concepts in Section 2.6. In this chapter and the next, we use visual programming to build more substantial GUIs.

### *Common `Form` Properties, Methods and an Event*

Each control or component we present in this chapter is located in namespace `System.Windows.Forms`. To create a Windows Forms app, you generally create a Windows `Form`, set its properties, add controls to the `Form`, set their properties and implement *event handlers* (methods) that respond to *events* generated when a user interacts with the controls. Figure 14.4 lists common Form properties, common methods and a common event.

| Form properties, methods and an event | Description |
|---|---|
| *Common Properties* | |
| AcceptButton | Default Button that's clicked when you press *Enter*. |
| AutoScroll | bool value (false by default) that allows or disallows *scrollbars* when needed. |
| CancelButton | Button that's clicked when the *Escape* key is pressed. |
| FormBorderStyle | *Border style* for the Form (Sizable by default). |
| Font | Font of text displayed on the Form, and the *default font* for controls added to the Form. |
| Text | Text in the Form's title bar. |
| *Common Methods* | |
| Close | Closes a Form and *releases all resources*, such as the memory used for the Form's contents. A closed Form cannot be reopened. |
| Hide | Hides a Form, but does *not* destroy the Form or release its resources. |
| Show | Displays a *hidden* Form. |
| *Common Event* | |
| Load | Occurs before a Form is displayed to the user. You'll learn about events and event-handling in the next section. |

**Fig. 14.4** | Common Form properties, methods and an event.

## 14.3 Event Handling

Normally, a user interacts with an app's GUI to indicate the tasks that the app should perform. For example, when you write an e-mail in an e-mail app, clicking the **Send** button tells the app to send the e-mail to the specified e-mail addresses. GUIs are **event driven**. When the user interacts with a GUI component, the interaction—known as an **event**—drives the program to perform a task. Before GUIs, the program told the user what to do next. With GUIs, the user tells the program what to do. Common events (user interactions) that might cause an app to perform a task include

- *clicking* a Button,
- *typing* in a TextBox,
- *selecting* an item from a menu,
- *closing* a window and
- *moving* the mouse.

All GUI controls have events associated with them. Objects of other types also can have associated events as well. A method that performs a task in response to an event is called an **event handler**, and the overall process of responding to events is known as **event handling**.

### 14.3.1 A Simple Event-Driven GUI

The `Form` in the app of Fig. 14.5 contains a `Button` that a user can click to display a `MessageBox`. In line 6, notice the `namespace` declaration, which is inserted for every class you create—we've been removing these from earlier simple examples. Namespaces organize groups of related classes. Recall from Section 7.4.3 that each class's name is actually a combination of its namespace name, a dot (`.`) and the class name—again, this is known as the class's fully qualified name. We'll use namespaces like this in Chapter 15. If another namespace also contains a class with the same name, the fully qualified class names must be used to distinguish between the classes in the app and prevent a **name conflict** (also called a **name collision**).

```
1  // Fig. 14.5: SimpleEventExampleForm.cs
2  // Simple event handling example.
3  using System;
4  using System.Windows.Forms;
5
6  namespace SimpleEventExample
7  {
8     // Form that shows a simple event handler
9     public partial class SimpleEventExampleForm : Form
10    {
11       // default constructor
12       public SimpleEventExampleForm()
13       {
14          InitializeComponent();
15       }
16
17       // handles click event of Button clickButton
18       private void clickButton_Click(object sender, EventArgs e)
19       {
20          MessageBox.Show("Button was clicked.");
21       }
22    }
23 }
```

Simple Event Example

Click Me

Button was clicked.

OK

**Fig. 14.5** | Simple event-handling example.

#### *Renaming the* `Form1.cs` *File*

Using the techniques presented in Section 2.6, create a `Form` containing a `Button`. First, create a new Windows Forms app names `SimpleEventExample`. Then:

1. Rename the `Form1.cs` file to `SimpleEventExampleForm.cs` in the **Solution Explorer**.

2. Click the `Form` in the designer, then use the **Properties** window to set the `Form`'s `Text` property to `"Simple Event Example"`.
3. Set the `Form`'s `Font` property to Segoe UI, 9pt. To do so, select the `Font` property in the **Properties** window, then click the *ellipsis (...) button* in the property's value field to display a font dialog.

#### *Adding a* `Button` *to the* `Form`

Drag a `Button` from the **Toolbox** onto the `Form`. In the **Properties** window, set the `(Name)` property (which specifies the `Button`'s variable name) to `clickButton` and the `Text` property to `Click Me`. By convention, a control's variable name ends with the control's type. For example, in the variable name `clickButton`, "`Button`" is the control's type.

#### *Adding an Event Handler for the* `Button`*'s* `Click` *Event*

When the user clicks the `Button` in this example, we want the app to respond by displaying a `MessageBox`. To do this, you must create an *event handler* for the `Button`'s `Click` *event*, which you can do by *double clicking* the `Button` on the `Form`. This opens the file containing the following *empty* event handler in the program code:

```
private void clickButton_Click(object sender, EventArgs e)
{
}
```

By convention, the IDE names the event-handler method as *objectName_eventName* (e.g., `clickButton_Click`). The `clickButton_Click` event handler *executes* when the user *clicks* the `clickButton` control.

#### *Event Handler Parameters*

Each event handler receives two parameters when it's called. The first—an `object` reference named `sender` by default—is a reference to the *object that the user interacted with to generate the event.* The second is a reference to an `EventArgs` object (or an object of an `EventArgs` derived class), which is typically named `e`. This object contains additional information about the event that occurred. `EventArgs` is the *base class* of all classes that represent event information.

#### *Displaying a* `MessageBox`

To display a `MessageBox` in response to the event, insert the statement

```
MessageBox.Show("Button was clicked.");
```

in the event handler's body. The resulting event handler appears in lines 18–21 of Fig. 14.5. When you execute the app and click the `Button`, a `MessageBox` appears displaying the text `"Button was clicked."`.

### 14.3.2 Auto-Generated GUI Code

Visual Studio places the *auto-generated* GUI code in the `Form` class's `Designer.cs` file—in this example, the file `SimpleEventExampleForm.Designer.cs`. You can open this file by expanding the `Form` class's node in the **Solution Explorer** window and double clicking the file name that ends with `Designer.cs`. Figs. 14.6 and 14.7 show this file's contents. The IDE collapses the code in lines 23–57 of Fig. 14.7 by default—you can click the

icon next to line 23 to *expand* the code, then click the

icon next to that line to *collapse* it.

SimpleEventExampleForm.Designer.cs

SimpleEventExample | SimpleEventExample.SimpleEventExampleForm | components

```
1   namespace SimpleEventExample
2   {
3      partial class SimpleEventExampleForm
4      {
5         /// <summary>
6         /// Required designer variable.
7         /// </summary>
8         private System.ComponentModel.IContainer components = null;
9
10        /// <summary>
11        /// Clean up any resources being used.
12        /// </summary>
13        /// <param name="disposing">true if managed resources should be disposed; oth
14        protected override void Dispose(bool disposing)
15        {
16           if (disposing && (components != null))
17           {
18              components.Dispose();
19           }
20           base.Dispose(disposing);
21        }
22
```

123 %

**Fig. 14.6** | First half of the Visual Studio generated code file.

Now that you have studied classes and objects in detail, this code will be easier to understand. Since this code is created and maintained by Visual Studio, you generally do not need to look at it. In fact, you do not need to understand most of the code shown here to build GUI apps. However, we now take a closer look to help you understand how GUI apps work.

The auto-generated code that defines the GUI is actually part of the `Form`'s *class*—in this case, `SimpleEventExampleForm`. Line 3 of Fig. 14.6 (and line 9 of Fig. 14.5) uses the `partial` modifier, which allows this class to be split among multiple files, including the files that contain auto-generated code and those in which you write your own code. Line 59 of Fig. 14.7 declares the `clickButton` that we created in **Design** mode. It's declared as an instance variable of class `SimpleEventExampleForm`. By default, all variable declarations for controls created through C#'s *design window* have a `private` access modifier. The code also includes the ***`Dispose`*** ***method*** for *releasing resources* (Fig. 14.6, lines 14–21) and method `InitializeComponent` (Fig. 14.7, lines 29–55), which contains the code that creates the `Button`, then sets some of the `Button`'s and the `Form`'s properties. The property values correspond to the values set in the **Properties** window for each control. Visual Studio adds comments to the code that it generates, as in lines 33–35. Line 42 was generated when we created the event handler for the `Button`'s `Click` event.

SimpleEventExampleForm.Designer.cs

SimpleEventExample | SimpleEventExample.SimpleEventExampleForm | components

```
    #region Windows Form Designer generated code

    /// <summary>
    /// Required method for Designer support - do not modify
    /// the contents of this method with the code editor.
    /// </summary>
    private void InitializeComponent()
    {
       this.clickButton = new System.Windows.Forms.Button();
       this.SuspendLayout();
       //
       // clickButton
       //
       this.clickButton.Location = new System.Drawing.Point(120, 37);
       this.clickButton.Name = "clickButton";
       this.clickButton.Size = new System.Drawing.Size(75, 23);
       this.clickButton.TabIndex = 0;
       this.clickButton.Text = "Click Me";
       this.clickButton.UseVisualStyleBackColor = true;
       this.clickButton.Click += new System.EventHandler(this.clickButton_Click);
       //
       // SimpleEventExampleForm
       //
       this.AutoScaleDimensions = new System.Drawing.SizeF(7F, 15F);
       this.AutoScaleMode = System.Windows.Forms.AutoScaleMode.Font;
       this.ClientSize = new System.Drawing.Size(314, 97);
       this.Controls.Add(this.clickButton);
       this.Font = new System.Drawing.Font("Segoe UI", 9F, System.Drawing.FontSty
       this.Name = "SimpleEventExampleForm";
       this.Text = "Simple Event Example";
       this.ResumeLayout(false);

    }

    #endregion

    private System.Windows.Forms.Button clickButton;
  }
}
```

123 %

**Fig. 14.7** | Second half of the Visual Studio generated code file.

Method `InitializeComponent` is called when the `Form` is created, and establishes such properties as the `Form` title, the `Form` size, control sizes and text. Visual Studio also uses the code in this method to create the GUI you see in design view. Changing the code in `InitializeComponent` may prevent Visual Studio from displaying the GUI properly.

### Error-Prevention Tip 14.1

*The code in the* `Designer.cs` *file that's generated by building a GUI in* **Design** *mode is not meant to be modified directly, which is why this code is placed in a separate file. Modifying this code can prevent the GUI from being displayed correctly in* **Design** *mode and might cause an app to function incorrectly. In* **Design** *mode, it's recommended that you modify control properties only in the* **Properties** *window, not in the* `Designer.cs` *file.*

### 14.3.3 Delegates and the Event-Handling Mechanism

The control that generates an event is known as the **event sender**. An event-handling method—known as the *event handler*—responds to a particular event that a control generates. When the event occurs, the event sender calls its event handler to perform a task (i.e., to "handle the event").

The .NET event-handling mechanism allows you to choose your own names for event-handling methods. However, each event-handling method must declare the proper parameters to receive information about the event that it handles. Since you can choose your own method names, an event sender such as a `Button` cannot know in advance which method will respond to its events. So, we need a mechanism to indicate which method is the event handler for an event.

*Delegates*

Event handlers are connected to a control's events via special objects called **delegates**. A delegate type declaration specifies the return type and signature of a method—in event handling, the delegate specifies the return type and arguments for an event handler. GUI controls have predefined delegates that correspond to every event they can generate. For example, the delegate for a `Button`'s `Click` event is of type `EventHandler` (namespace `System`). The online help documentation declares this type as follows:

```
public delegate void EventHandler(object sender, EventArgs e);
```

This uses the **`delegate`** keyword to declare a delegate type named `EventHandler`, which can hold references to methods that return `void` and receive two parameters—one of type `object` (the *event sender*) and one of type `EventArgs`. If you compare the delegate declaration with `clickButton_Click`'s first line (Fig. 14.5, line 18), you'll see that this event handler returns the same type and receives the same parameters specified by the `EventHandler` delegate—the parameters' names need not match. The preceding declaration actually creates an entire class for you. The details of this special class's declaration are handled by the compiler.

*Indicating the Method that a Delegate Should Call*

Since each event handler is declared as a delegate, the *event sender* can simply call the appropriate delegate when an event occurs—a `Button` calls the `EventHandler` delegate that corresponds to its `Click` event in response to a click. The delegate's job is to invoke the appropriate method. To enable the `clickButton_Click` method to be called, Visual Studio assigns `clickButton_Click` to the click `Button`'s `Click` `EventHandler` delegate, as shown in line 42 of Fig. 14.7. This code is added by Visual Studio when you double click the `Button` control in **Design** mode. The expression

```
new System.EventHandler(this.clickButton_Click);
```

creates an `EventHandler` delegate object and initializes it with the `clickButton_Click` method. Line 42 uses the += operator to *add* the delegate to the `Button`'s `Click` `EventHandler` delegate. This enables `clickButton_Click` to respond when a user clicks the `Button`. The += operator is overloaded by the delegate class that's created by the compiler.

*(Optional) Multicast Delegates*

You can actually specify that several methods should be invoked in response to one event by adding other delegates to the `Button`'s `Click` event with statements similar to line 42 of Fig. 14.7. Event delegates are **multicast**—they represent a *set of delegate objects* that all have the *same signature.* When an event occurs, the event sender calls *every* method referenced by the multicast delegate. This is known as **event multicasting.** Event delegates derive from class **`MulticastDelegate`**, which derives from class **`Delegate`** (both from namespace `System`). For most cases, you'll specify only one event handler for a particular event on a control.

### 14.3.4 Another Way to Create Event Handlers

For the GUI app in Fig. 14.5, you double clicked the `Button` control on the `Form` to create its event handler. This technique creates an event handler for a control's **default event**—the event that's most frequently used with that control. Controls can generate many different events, and each one can have its own event handler. For instance, your app also can provide an event handler for a `Button`'s `MouseHover` event, which occurs when the mouse pointer remains positioned over the `Button` for a short period of time. We now discuss how to create an event handler for an event that's not a control's default event.

#### *Using the* Properties *Window to Create Event Handlers*

You can create event handlers through the **Properties** window. If you select a control on the `Form`, then click the **Events** icon (the lightning bolt icon in Fig. 14.8) in the **Properties** window, that control's events are listed in the window. You can double click an event's name to display in the editor an existing event handler for that event, or to create the event handler if it does not yet exist in your code. You also can select an event, then use the drop-down list to its right to choose an existing method that should be used as the event handler for that event. The methods that appear in this drop-down list are the `Form` class's methods that have the proper signature to be an event handler for the selected event. You can return to viewing the properties of a control by selecting the **Properties** icon (Fig. 14.8).

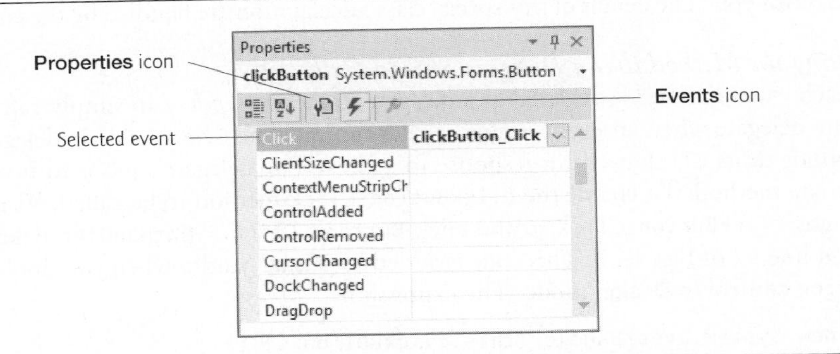


**Fig. 14.8** | Viewing events for a `Button` control in the **Properties** window.

A single method can handle events from multiple controls. For example, consider an app that displays `CheckBox`es that represent bold and italic fonts. The user could select bold, italic or both. In this case, the font's style depends on both `CheckBox`es, so their events could be handled by the same method, which would determine each `CheckBox`'s state to determine the user's selected font style.

You can specify an event handler for multiple events by selecting multiple controls (drag over them, hold *Shift* and click each or hold *Ctrl* and click each) and selecting a single method in the **Properties** window's **Events** tab. If you create a new event handler this way, you should rename it appropriately so that it does not contain one control's name. You could also select each control individually and specify the same method for each one's event.

### 14.3.5 Locating Event Information

Read the Visual Studio documentation to learn about the different events raised by each control. To do this, select a control in the IDE (either in your `Form`'s design or in the **Toolbox** and press the *F1* key to display that control's online help (Fig. 14.9).

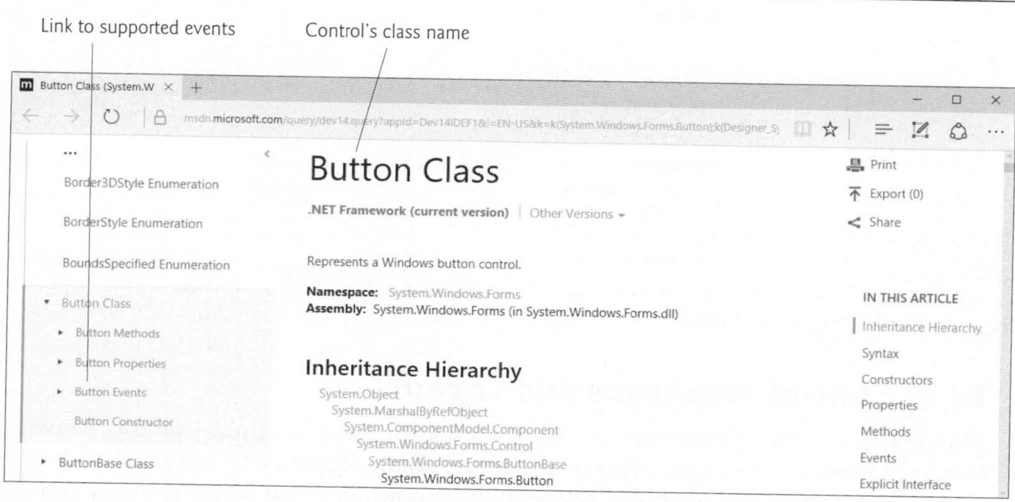


**Fig. 14.9** | Link to list of `Button` events.

The web page that's displayed contains basic information about the control's class. In the left column of the page are several links to more information about the class—**Button Methods, Button Properties, Button Events** and **Button Constructor.** Each link displays a subset of the class's members. Click the link to the list of events for that control (**Button Events** in this case) to display the supported events for that control.

Next, click the name of an event to view its description and examples of its use. We selected the `Click` event to display the information in Fig. 14.10. The `Click` event is a member of class `Control`, an indirect base class of class `Button`. The **Remarks** section of the page discusses the details of the selected event. Alternatively, you could use the **Object Browser** to look up this information in the `System.Windows.Forms` namespace. The **Object Browser** shows only the members *originally* defined in a given class. The `Click` event is originally defined in class `Control` and inherited into `Button`. For this reason, you must look at class `Control` in the **Object Browser** to see the documentation for the `Click` event. See Section 10.11 for more information regarding the **Object Browser**.

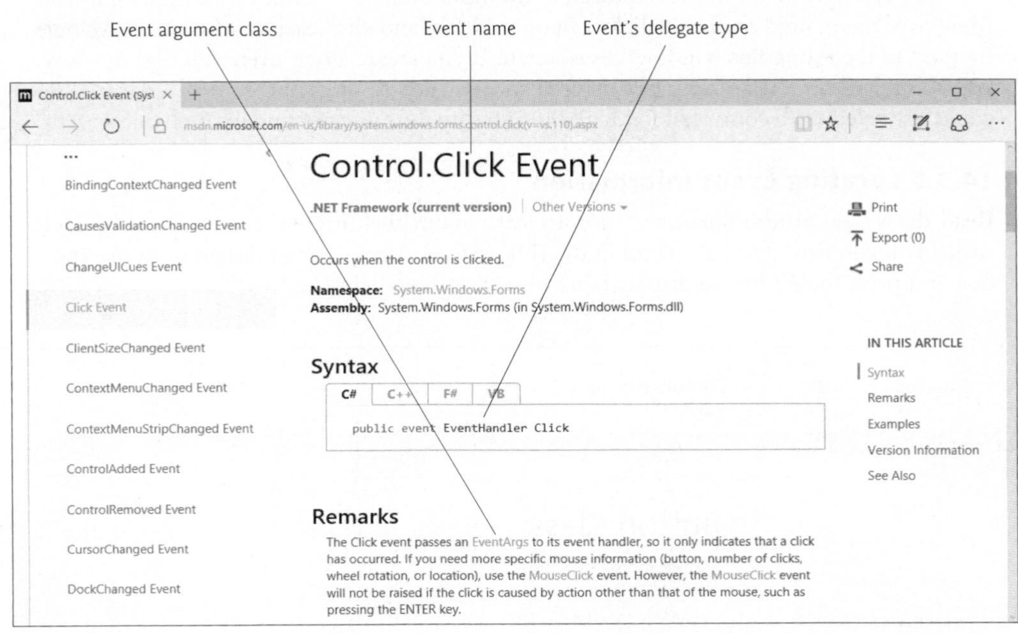


**Fig. 14.10** | `Click` event details.

## 14.4 Control Properties and Layout

This section overviews properties that are common to many controls. Controls derive from class **`Control`** (namespace `System.Windows.Forms`). Figure 14.11 lists some of class `Control`'s properties and methods. The properties shown here can be set for many controls. For example, the `Text` property specifies the text that appears on a control. The location of this text varies depending on the control. In a `Form`, the text appears in the title bar, but the text of a `Button` appears on its face.

| Class `Control` properties and methods | Description |
|---|---|
| *Common Properties* | |
| `BackColor` | The control's background color. |
| `BackgroundImage` | The control's background image. |
| `Enabled` | Specifies whether the control is *enabled* (i.e., if the user can interact with it). Typically, portions of a *disabled* control appear "grayed out" as a visual indication to the user that the control is disabled. |
| `Focused` | Indicates whether the control *has the focus* (only available at run-time). |

**Fig. 14.11** | Class `Control` properties and methods. (Part 1 of 2.)

| Class `Control` properties and methods | Description |
|---|---|
| `Font` | The `Font` used to display the control's text. |
| `ForeColor` | The control's foreground color. This usually determines the color of the text in the `Text` property. |
| `TabIndex` | The *tab order* of the control. When the *Tab* key is pressed, the focus transfers between controls based on the tab order. You can set this order. |
| `TabStop` | If `true`, then a user can give focus to this control via the *Tab* key. |
| `Text` | The text associated with the control. The location and appearance of the text vary depending on the type of control. |
| `Visible` | Indicates whether the control is visible. |
| ***Common Methods*** | |
| `Hide` | Hides the control (sets the `Visible` property to `false`). |
| `Select` | *Acquires the focus.* |
| `Show` | Shows the control (sets the `Visible` property to `true`). |

**Fig. 14.11** | Class `Control` properties and methods. (Part 2 of 2.)

Method **`Select`** transfers the focus to a control and makes it the **active control**. When you press the *Tab* key in an executing Windows `Forms` app, controls *receive the focus* in the order specified by their **`TabIndex`** property. This property is set by Visual Studio based on the order in which controls are added to a `Form`, but you can change the *tabbing order* using **View > Tab Order**. `TabIndex` is helpful for users who enter information in many controls, such as a set of `TextBox`es that represent a user's name, address and telephone number. The user can enter information, then quickly select the next control by pressing the *Tab* key.

Property **`Enabled`** indicates whether the user can interact with a control to generate an event. Often, if a control is *disabled*, it's because an option is unavailable to the user at that time. For example, text editor apps often disable the "paste" command until the user cuts or copies some text. In most cases, a disabled control's text appears in gray (rather than in black). You also can hide a control from the user without disabling the control by setting the `Visible` property to `false` or by calling method `Hide`. In each case, the control still exists but is not visible on the `Form`.

### 14.4.1 Anchoring and Docking

You can use anchoring and docking to specify the layout of controls inside a **container**—such as a `Form` or, within a `Form`, a control that groups other controls (such as a `Panel`, discussed in Section 14.6). **Anchoring** places controls a fixed distance from the sides of the container. Anchoring enhances the user experience. For example, if the user expects a control to appear in a particular corner of the app, anchoring ensures that the control will always be in that corner—even if the user *resizes* the `Form`. **Docking** attaches a control to a container such that the control stretches across an entire side or fills an entire area. For example, a control such as a status bar typically should remain at the bottom of the `Form` and stretch across the entire bottom of that `Form`, regardless of the `Form`'s width. When the parent control is resized, the docked control resizes as well.

### *Anchoring Demonstration*

When a window (or other type of *container* like a `Panel`) is resized, anchored controls are moved (and possibly resized) so that the distance from the sides to which they're anchored does not vary. By default, most controls are anchored to the top-left corner of the `Form`. To see the effects of anchoring a control, create a simple Windows `Forms` app that contains two `Buttons`. Anchor one control to the right and bottom sides by setting the **Anchor** property as shown in Fig. 14.12. Leave the other control with its default anchoring (top, left). Execute the app and enlarge the `Form`. The `Button` anchored to the bottom-right corner is always the same distance from the bottom right (Fig. 14.13). The other control stays its original distance from the top left.

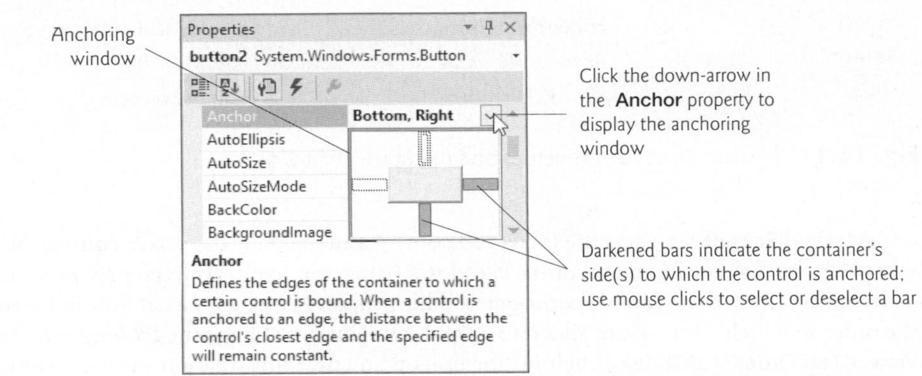


**Fig. 14.12** | Manipulating the **Anchor** property of a control.

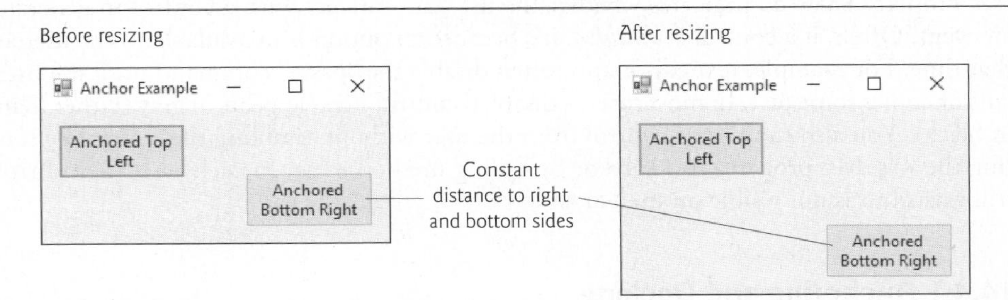


**Fig. 14.13** | Anchoring demonstration.

In Fig. 14.14, a `Button` is docked at the top of the `Form` (spanning the top portion). When the `Form` is resized, the `Button` is resized to the `Form`'s new width. `Forms` have a **`Padding`** property that specifies the distance between the docked controls and the `Form` edges. This property specifies four values (one for each side), and each value is set to `0` by default. Some common control layout properties are summarized in Fig. 14.15.

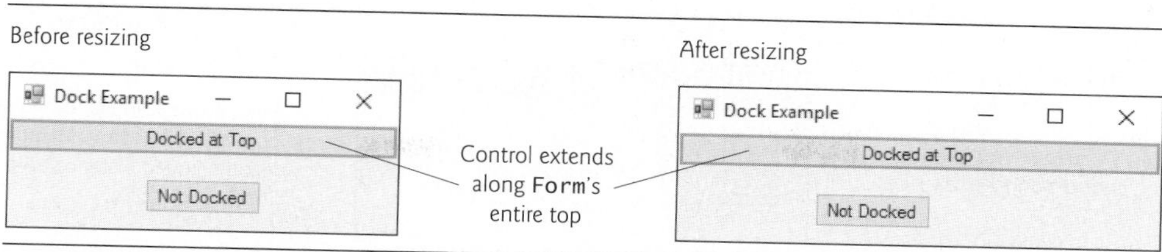


**Fig. 14.14** | Docking a `Button` to the top of a `Form`.

| `Control` layout properties | Description |
|---|---|
| `Anchor` | Causes a control to remain at a fixed distance from the side(s) of the container even when the container is resized. |
| `Dock` | Allows a control to span one side of its container or to fill the remaining space in the container. |
| `Padding` | Sets the space between a container's edges and docked controls. The default is `0`, causing the control to appear flush with the container's sides. |
| `Location` | Specifies the location (as a set of coordinates) of the upper-left corner of the control, in relation to its container's upper-left corner. |
| `Size` | Specifies the size of the control in pixels as a `Size` object, which has properties `Width` and `Height`. |
| `MinimumSize`, `MaximumSize` | Indicates the minimum and maximum size of a `Control`, respectively. |

**Fig. 14.15** | `Control` layout properties.

A `Control`'s `Anchor` and `Dock` properties are set with respect to the container in which the `Control` resides—known as the **parent container**—which could be a `Form` or another container (such as a `Panel`). The minimum and maximum `Form` (or other `Control`) sizes can be set via properties **`MinimumSize`** and **`MaximumSize`**, respectively. Both are of type **`Size`**, which has properties **`Width`** and **`Height`**. Properties `MinimumSize` and `MaximumSize` allow you to design the GUI layout for a given size range. The user cannot make a `Form` smaller than the size specified by property `MinimumSize` and cannot make a `Form` larger than the size specified by property `MaximumSize`. To set a `Form` to a *fixed* size (where the `Form` cannot be resized by the user), set its minimum and maximum size to the same value.

### 14.4.2 Using Visual Studio To Edit a GUI's Layout

Visual Studio helps you with GUI layout. When you drag a control across a `Form`, blue **snap lines** appear to help you position the control with respect to others (Fig. 14.16) and the `Form`'s edges. This feature makes the control you're dragging appear to "snap into place" alongside other controls. Visual Studio also provides the **Format** menu, which contains options for modifying your GUI's layout. The **Format** menu does not appear in the IDE unless you select one or more controls in design view. When you select multiple controls, you can align them with the **Format** menu's **Align** submenu. The **Format** menu also enables you to modify the space between controls or to center a control on the `Form`.

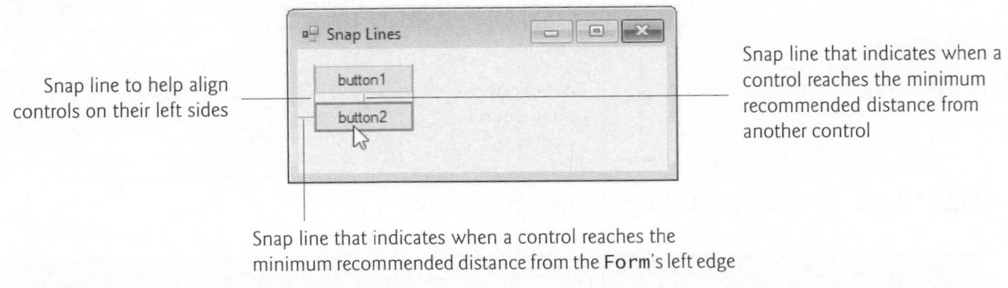


**Fig. 14.16** | Snap lines for aligning controls.

## 14.5 Labels, TextBoxes and Buttons

Labels provide text information (as well as optional images) and are defined with class Label (a derived class of Control). A Label displays text that the *user cannot directly modify*. A Label's text can be changed programmatically by modifying the Label's Text property. Figure 14.17 lists common Label properties.

| Common Label properties | Description |
|---|---|
| Font | The font of the text on the Label. |
| Text | The text on the Label. |
| TextAlign | The alignment of the Label's text on the control—horizontally (left, center or right) and vertically (top, middle or bottom). The default is top, left. |

**Fig. 14.17** | Common Label properties.

A **textbox** (class TextBox) is an area in which either text can be displayed by a program or the user can type text via the keyboard. A **password TextBox** is a TextBox that hides the information entered by the user. As the user types characters, the password TextBox masks the user input by displaying a password character. If you set the property **UseSystemPasswordChar** to true, the TextBox becomes a password TextBox. Users often encounter both types of TextBoxes, when logging into a computer or website—the username TextBox allows users to input their usernames; the password TextBox allows users to enter their passwords. Figure 14.18 lists the common properties and a common event of TextBoxes.

A button is a control that the user clicks to trigger a specific action or to select an option in a program. As you'll see, a program can use several types of buttons, such as **checkboxes** and **radio buttons**. All the button classes derive from class **ButtonBase** (namespace System.Windows.Forms), which defines common button features. In this section, we discuss class Button, which typically enables a user to issue a command to an app. Figure 14.19 lists common properties and a common event of class Button.

| TextBox properties and an event | Description |
|---|---|
| ***Common Properties*** | |
| AcceptsReturn | If true in a multiline TextBox, pressing *Enter* in the TextBox creates a new line. If false (the default), pressing *Enter* is the same as pressing the default Button on the Form. The default Button is the one assigned to a Form's AcceptButton property. |
| Multiline | If true, the TextBox can span multiple lines. The default value is false. |
| ReadOnly | If true, the TextBox has a gray background, and its text cannot be edited. The default value is false. |
| ScrollBars | For multiline textboxes, this property indicates which scrollbars appear (None—the default, Horizontal, Vertical or Both). |
| Text | The TextBox's text content. |
| UseSystemPasswordChar | When true, the TextBox becomes a password TextBox, and the system-specified character masks each character the user types. |
| ***Common Event*** | |
| TextChanged | Generated when the text changes in a TextBox (i.e., when the user adds or deletes characters). When you double click the TextBox control in **Design** mode, an empty event handler for this event is generated. |

**Fig. 14.18** | TextBox properties and an event.

| Button properties and an event | Description |
|---|---|
| ***Common Properties*** | |
| Text | Specifies the text displayed on the Button face. |
| FlatStyle | Modifies a Button's appearance—Flat (for the Button to display without a three-dimensional appearance), Popup (for the Button to appear flat until the user moves the mouse pointer over the Button), Standard (three-dimensional) and System, where the Button's appearance is controlled by the operating system. The default value is Standard. |
| ***Common Event*** | |
| Click | Generated when the user clicks the Button. When you double click a Button in design view, an empty event handler for this event is created. |

**Fig. 14.19** | Button properties and an event.

Figure 14.20 uses a TextBox, a Button and a Label. The user enters text into a password box and clicks the Button, causing the text input to be displayed in the Label. Normally, we would not display this text—the purpose of password TextBoxes is to hide the text being entered by the user. When the user clicks the **Show Me** Button, this app retrieves the text that the user typed in the password TextBox and displays it in a Label.

```
// Fig. 14.20: LabelTextBoxButtonTestForm.cs
// Using a TextBox, Label and Button to display
// the hidden text in a password TextBox.
using System;
using System.Windows.Forms;

namespace LabelTextBoxButtonTest
{
   // Form that creates a password TextBox and
   // a Label to display TextBox contents
   public partial class LabelTextBoxButtonTestForm : Form
   {
      // default constructor
      public LabelTextBoxButtonTestForm()
      {
         InitializeComponent();
      }

      // display user input in Label
      private void displayPasswordButton_Click(object sender, EventArgs e)
      {
         // display the text that the user typed
         displayPasswordLabel.Text = inputPasswordTextBox.Text;
      }
   }
}
```

**Fig. 14.20** | Program to display hidden text in a password box.

First, create the GUI by dragging the controls (a `TextBox`, a `Button` and a `Label`) onto the `Form`. Once the controls are positioned, change their names in the **Properties** window from the default values—`textBox1`, `button1` and `label1`—to the more descriptive `displayPasswordLabel`, `displayPasswordButton` and `inputPasswordTextBox`. The `(Name)` property in the **Properties** window enables us to change the variable name for a control. Visual Studio creates the necessary code and places it in method `InitializeComponent` of the partial class in the file `LabelTextBoxButtonTestForm.Designer.cs`.

We set `displayPasswordButton`'s `Text` property to "`Show Me`" and clear the `Text` of `displayPasswordLabel` so that it's blank when the program begins executing. The `BorderStyle` property of `displayPasswordLabel` is set to `Fixed3D`, giving our `Label` a three-dimensional appearance. We also changed its `TextAlign` property to `MiddleLeft` so that the `Label`'s text is displayed centered between its top and bottom. The password character for `inputPasswordTextBox` is determined by the user's system settings when you set `UseSystemPasswordChar` to `true`.

We create an event handler for `displayPasswordButton` by double clicking this control in **Design** mode. We added line 23 to the event handler's body. When the user clicks the **Show Me** `Button` in the executing app, line 23 obtains the text entered by the user in `inputPasswordTextBox` and displays the text in `displayPasswordLabel`.

## 14.6 GroupBoxes and Panels

**GroupBoxes** and **Panels** arrange controls on a GUI. `GroupBoxes` and `Panels` are typically used to group several controls of similar functionality or several controls that are related in a GUI. All of the controls in a `GroupBox` or `Panel` move together when the `GroupBox` or `Panel` is moved. Furthermore, a `GroupBoxes` and `Panels` also can be used to show or hide a set of controls at once. When you modify a container's `Visible` property, it toggles the visibility of all the controls within it.

The primary difference between these two controls is that `GroupBoxes` can display a caption (i.e., text) and do *not* include scrollbars, whereas `Panels` can include scrollbars and do not include a caption. `GroupBoxes` have thin borders by default; `Panels` can be set so that they also have borders by changing their `BorderStyle` property. Figures 14.21–14.22 list the common properties of `GroupBoxes` and `Panels`, respectively.

**Look-and-Feel Observation 14.2**

*`Panels` and `GroupBoxes` can contain other `Panels` and `GroupBoxes` for more complex layouts.*

**Look-and-Feel Observation 14.3**

*You can organize a GUI by anchoring and docking controls inside a `GroupBox` or `Panel`. The `GroupBox` or `Panel` then can be anchored or docked inside a `Form`. This divides controls into functional "groups" that can be arranged easily.*

| GroupBox properties | Description |
|---|---|
| `Controls` | The set of controls that the `GroupBox` contains. |
| `Text` | Specifies the caption text displayed at the top of the `GroupBox`. |

**Fig. 14.21** | `GroupBox` properties.

| Panel properties | Description |
|---|---|
| `AutoScroll` | Indicates whether scrollbars appear when the `Panel` is too small to display all of its controls. The default value is `false`. |
| `BorderStyle` | Sets the border of the `Panel`. The default value is `None`; other options are `Fixed3D` and `FixedSingle`. |
| `Controls` | The set of controls that the `Panel` contains. |

**Fig. 14.22** | `Panel` properties.

To create a GroupBox, drag its icon from the **Toolbox** onto a Form. Then, drag new controls from the **Toolbox** into the GroupBox. These controls are added to the GroupBox's **Controls** property and become part of the GroupBox. The GroupBox's Text property specifies the caption at the top of the GroupBox.

To create a Panel, drag its icon from the **Toolbox** onto the Form. You can then add controls directly to the Panel by dragging them from the **Toolbox** onto the Panel. To enable the scrollbars, set the Panel's AutoScroll property to true. If the Panel is resized and cannot display all of its controls, scrollbars appear (Fig. 14.23). The scrollbars can be used to view *all* the controls in the Panel—at design time *and* at execution time. In Fig. 14.23, we set the Panel's BorderStyle property to FixedSingle so that you can see the Panel in the Form.

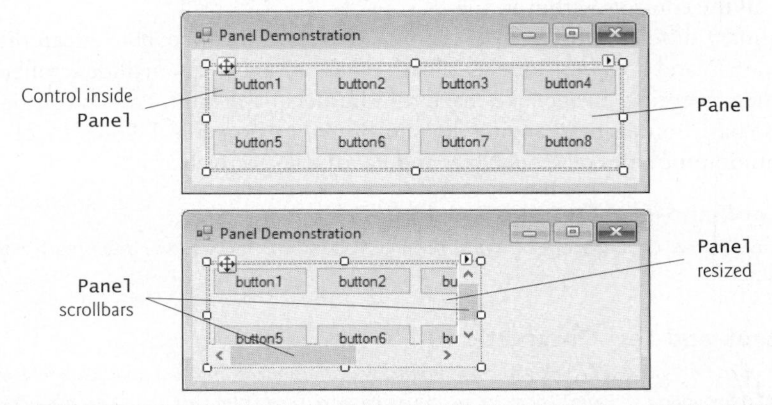


**Fig. 14.23** | Creating a Panel with scrollbars.

The program in Fig. 14.24 uses a GroupBox and a Panel to arrange Buttons. When these Buttons are clicked, their event handlers change the text on a Label.

```
// Fig. 14.24: GroupBoxPanelExampleForm.cs
// Using GroupBoxes and Panels to arrange Buttons.
using System;
using System.Windows.Forms;

namespace GroupBoxPanelExample
{
   // Form that displays a GroupBox and a Panel
   public partial class GroupBoxPanelExampleForm : Form
   {
      // default constructor
      public GroupBoxPanelExampleForm()
      {
         InitializeComponent();
      }
```

**Fig. 14.24** | Using GroupBoxes and Panels to arrange Buttons. (Part 1 of 2.)

```
16
17          // event handler for Hi Button
18          private void hiButton_Click(object sender, EventArgs e)
19          {
20             messageLabel.Text = "Hi pressed"; // change text in Label
21          }
22
23          // event handler for Bye Button
24          private void byeButton_Click(object sender, EventArgs e)
25          {
26             messageLabel.Text = "Bye pressed"; // change text in Label
27          }
28
29          // event handler for Far Left Button
30          private void leftButton_Click(object sender, EventArgs e)
31          {
32             messageLabel.Text = "Far Left pressed"; // change text in Label
33          }
34
35          // event handler for Far Right Button
36          private void rightButton_Click(object sender, EventArgs e)
37          {
38             messageLabel.Text = "Far Right pressed"; // change text in Label
39          }
40       }
41    }
```

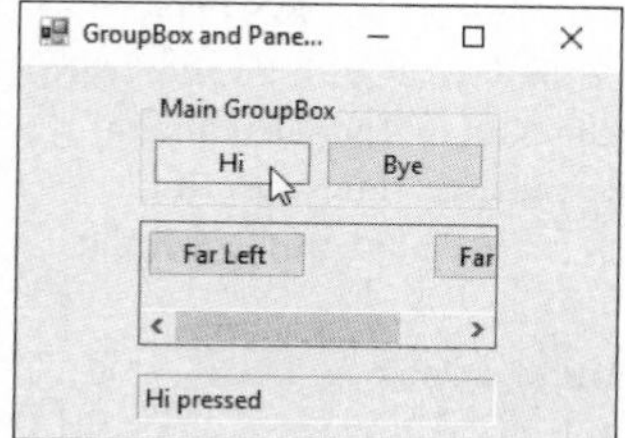


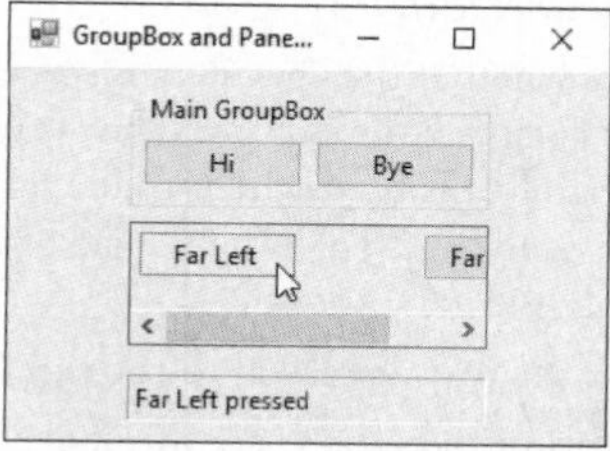


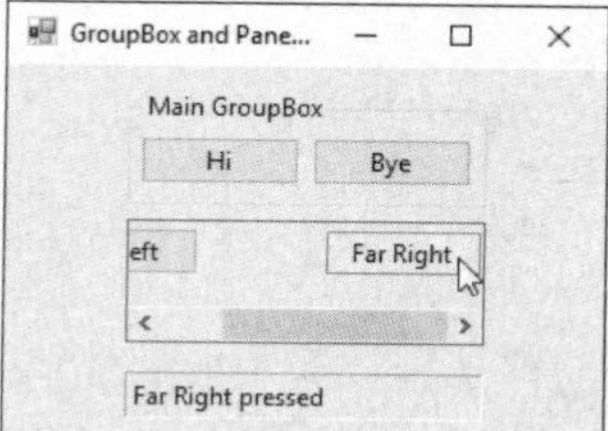


**Fig. 14.24** | Using GroupBoxes and Panels to arrange Buttons. (Part 2 of 2.)

The mainGroupBox has two Buttons—hiButton (which displays the text **Hi**) and byeButton (which displays the text **Bye**). The Panel (named mainPanel) also has two Buttons, leftButton (which displays the text **Far Left**) and rightButton (which displays the text **Far Right**). The mainPanel has its AutoScroll property set to true, allowing scrollbars to appear when the contents of the Panel require more space than the Panel's visible area. The Label (named messageLabel) is initially blank. To add controls to mainGroupBox or mainPanel, Visual Studio calls method Add of each container's Controls property. This code is placed in the partial class located in the file GroupBoxPanelExampleForm.Designer.cs.

The event handlers for the four Buttons are located in lines 18–39. Lines 20, 26, 32 and 38 change the text of messageLabel to indicate which Button the user pressed.

## 14.7 CheckBoxes and RadioButtons

C# has two types of **state buttons** that can be in the on/off or true/false states—**CheckBoxes** and **RadioButtons**. Like class Button, classes CheckBox and RadioButton are derived from class ButtonBase.

### 14.7.1 CheckBoxes

A CheckBox is a small square that either is blank or contains a check mark. When the user clicks a CheckBox to select it, a check mark appears in the box. If the user clicks the CheckBox again to deselect it, the check mark is removed. You also can configure a CheckBox to toggle between three states (*checked*, *unchecked* and *indeterminate*) by setting its **ThreeState** property to true. Any number of CheckBoxes can be selected at a time. A list of common CheckBox properties and a common event appears in Fig. 14.25.

| CheckBox properties and an event | Description |
|---|---|
| *Common Properties* | |
| Appearance | By default, this property is set to Normal, and the CheckBox displays as a traditional checkbox. If it's set to Button, the CheckBox displays as a Button that looks pressed when the CheckBox is checked. |
| Checked | Indicates whether the CheckBox is *checked* (contains a check mark) or unchecked (blank). This property returns a bool value. The default is false (*unchecked*). |
| CheckState | Indicates whether the CheckBox is *checked* or *unchecked* with a value from the CheckState enumeration (Checked, Unchecked or Indeterminate). Indeterminate is used when it's unclear whether the state should be Checked or Unchecked. When CheckState is set to Indeterminate, the CheckBox is usually shaded. |
| Text | Specifies the text displayed to the right of the CheckBox. |
| ThreeState | When this property is true, the CheckBox has three states—*checked*, *unchecked* and *indeterminate*. By default, this property is false and the CheckBox has only two states—*checked* and *unchecked*. When true, Checked returns true for both the *checked* and *indeterminate* states. |
| *Common Event* | |
| CheckedChanged | Generated *any* time the Checked or CheckState property changes. This is a CheckBox's default event. When a user double clicks the CheckBox control in design view, an empty event handler for this event is generated. |

**Fig. 14.25** | CheckBox properties and an event.

The program in Fig. 14.26 allows the user to select CheckBoxes to change a Label's font style. The event handler for one CheckBox applies bold and the event handler for the other applies italic. If both CheckBoxes are selected, the font style is set to bold and italic. Initially, neither CheckBox is checked.

```
// Fig. 14.26: CheckBoxTestForm.cs
// Using CheckBoxes to toggle italic and bold styles.
using System;
using System.Drawing;
using System.Windows.Forms;

namespace CheckBoxTest
{
   // Form contains CheckBoxes to allow the user to modify sample text
   public partial class CheckBoxTestForm : Form
   {
      // default constructor
      public CheckBoxTestForm()
      {
         InitializeComponent();
      }

      // toggle the font style between bold and
      // not bold based on the current setting
      private void boldCheckBox_CheckedChanged(object sender, EventArgs e)
      {
         outputLabel.Font = new Font(outputLabel.Font,
            outputLabel.Font.Style ^ FontStyle.Bold);
      }

      // toggle the font style between italic and
      // not italic based on the current setting
      private void italicCheckBox_CheckedChanged(
         object sender, EventArgs e)
      {
         outputLabel.Font = new Font(outputLabel.Font,
            outputLabel.Font.Style ^ FontStyle.Italic);
      }
   }
}
```

**Fig. 14.26** | Using CheckBoxes to toggle italic and bold styles.

The boldCheckBox has its Text property set to Bold. The italicCheckBox has its Text property set to Italic. The Text property of outputLabel is set to Watch the font style change. After creating the controls, we define their event handlers. Double clicking the CheckBoxes at design time creates empty CheckedChanged event handlers.

To change a `Label`'s font style, set its `Font` property to a new **`Font` object** (lines 22–23 and 31–32). Class `Font` is in the `System.Drawing` namespace. The `Font` constructor used here takes a `Font` and new style as arguments. The argument `outputLabel.Font` uses `outputLabel`'s original font name and size. The style is specified with a member of the **`FontStyle` enumeration**, which contains `Regular`, `Bold`, `Italic`, `Strikeout` and `Underline`. (The `Strikeout` style displays text with a line through it.) A `Font` object's **`Style`** property is read-only, so it can be set only when the `Font` object is created.

## 14.7.2 Combining Font Styles with Bitwise Operators

Styles can be combined via **bitwise operators**—operators that perform manipulation on bits of information. All data is represented in the computer as combinations of 0s and 1s. Each 0 or 1 represents a bit. The `FontStyle` (namespace `System.Drawing`) is represented as a set of bits that are selected in a way that allows us to combine different `FontStyle` elements to create compound styles, using bitwise operators. These styles are *not mutually exclusive*, so we can combine different styles and remove them without affecting the combination of previous `FontStyle` elements.

We can combine the various font styles, using either the *logical OR (|) operator* or the *logical exclusive OR (^) operator* (also called XOR). When the *logical OR operator* is applied to two bits, if at least one bit of the two has the value 1, then the result is 1. Combining styles using the *logical OR operator* works as follows. Assume that `FontStyle.Bold` is represented by bits `01` and that `FontStyle.Italic` is represented by bits `10`. When we use the *logical OR (|)* to combine the styles, we obtain the bits `11`.

```
01   =   Bold
10   =   Italic
--
11   =   Bold and Italic
```

The *logical OR operator* helps create style combinations. However, what happens if we want to *undo* a style combination, as we did in Fig. 14.26?

The *logical exclusive OR operator* enables us to combine styles and to *undo* existing style settings. When *logical exclusive OR* is applied to two bits, if both bits have the same value, then the result is 0. If both bits are different, then the result is 1.

Combining styles using *logical exclusive OR* works as follows. Assume, again, that `FontStyle.Bold` is represented by bits `01` and that `FontStyle.Italic` is represented by bits `10`. When we use *logical exclusive OR (^)* on both styles, we obtain the bits `11`.

```
01   =   Bold
10   =   Italic
--
11   =   Bold and Italic
```

Now, suppose that we'd like to *remove* the `FontStyle.Bold` style from the previous combination of `FontStyle.Bold` and `FontStyle.Italic`. The easiest way to do so is to reapply the *logical exclusive OR (^) operator* to the compound style and `FontStyle.Bold`.

```
11   =   Bold and Italic
01   =   Bold
--
10   =   Italic
```

This is a simple example. The advantages of using bitwise operators to combine FontStyle values become more evident when we consider that there are five FontStyle values (Bold, Italic, Regular, Strikeout and Underline), resulting in 16 FontStyle combinations. Using bitwise operators to combine font styles greatly reduces the amount of code required to check all possible font combinations.

In Fig. 14.26, we need to set the FontStyle so that the text appears in bold if it was not bold originally, and vice versa. Line 23 uses the *bitwise logical exclusive OR operator* to do this. If outputLabel.Font.Style is bold, then the resulting style is not bold. If the text is originally italic, the resulting style is bold and italic, rather than just bold. The same applies for FontStyle.Italic in line 32.

If we didn't use bitwise operators to compound FontStyle elements, we'd have to test for the current style and change it accordingly. In boldCheckBox_CheckedChanged, we could test for the regular style and make it bold, test for the bold style and make it regular, test for the italic style and make it bold italic and test for the italic bold style and make it italic. This is cumbersome because, for every new style we add, we double the number of combinations. Adding a CheckBox for underline would require testing eight additional styles. Adding a CheckBox for strikeout would require testing 16 additional styles.

### 14.7.3 RadioButtons

Radio buttons (defined with class RadioButton) are similar to CheckBoxes in that they also have two states—**selected** and **not selected** (also called **deselected**). However, RadioButtons normally appear as a **group**, in which only one RadioButton can be selected at a time. Selecting one RadioButton in the group forces all the others to be deselected. Therefore, RadioButtons are used to represent a set of **mutually exclusive** options (i.e., a set in which multiple options *cannot* be selected at the same time).

**Look-and-Feel Observation 14.4**

*Use RadioButtons when the user should choose only one option in a group. Use CheckBoxes when the user should be able to choose multiple options in a group.*

All RadioButtons added in a container are in the same group. To divide RadioButtons into several groups, they must be added to *separate* containers, such as GroupBoxes or Panels. RadioButton's common properties and a common event are listed in Fig. 14.27.

| RadioButton properties and an event | Description |
|---|---|
| *Common Properties* | |
| Checked | Indicates whether the RadioButton is checked. |
| Text | Specifies the RadioButton's text. |
| *Common Event* | |
| CheckedChanged | Generated every time the RadioButton is checked or unchecked. When you double click a RadioButton control in design view, an empty event handler for this event is generated. |

**Fig. 14.27** | RadioButton properties and an event.

**Software Engineering Observation 14.1**

*Forms, GroupBoxes, and Panels can act as logical groups for RadioButtons. The RadioButtons within each group are mutually exclusive to each other, but not to RadioButtons in different logical groups.*

The program in Fig. 14.28 uses RadioButtons to enable users to select options for a MessageBox. After selecting the desired attributes, the user presses the **Display** Button to display the MessageBox. A Label in the lower-left corner shows the result of the MessageBox (i.e., which Button the user clicked—**Yes**, **No**, **Cancel**, etc.).

```
// Fig. 14.28: RadioButtonsTestForm.cs
// Using RadioButtons to set message window options.
using System;
using System.Windows.Forms;

namespace RadioButtonsTest
{
   // Form contains several RadioButtons--user chooses one
   // from each group to create a custom MessageBox
   public partial class RadioButtonsTestForm : Form
   {
      // create variables that store the user's choice of options
      private MessageBoxIcon IconType { get; set; }
      private MessageBoxButtons ButtonType { get; set; }

      // default constructor
      public RadioButtonsTestForm()
      {
         InitializeComponent();
      }

      // change Buttons based on option chosen by sender
      private void buttonType_CheckedChanged(object sender, EventArgs e)
      {
         if (sender == okRadioButton) // display OK Button
         {
            ButtonType = MessageBoxButtons.OK;
         }
         // display OK and Cancel Buttons
         else if (sender == okCancelRadioButton)
         {
            ButtonType = MessageBoxButtons.OKCancel;
         }
         // display Abort, Retry and Ignore Buttons
         else if (sender == abortRetryIgnoreRadioButton)
         {
            ButtonType = MessageBoxButtons.AbortRetryIgnore;
         }
```

**Fig. 14.28** | Using RadioButtons to set message-window options. (Part 1 of 4.)

```
         // display Yes, No and Cancel Buttons
         else if (sender == yesNoCancelRadioButton)
         {
            ButtonType = MessageBoxButtons.YesNoCancel;
         }
         // display Yes and No Buttons
         else if (sender == yesNoRadioButton)
         {
            ButtonType = MessageBoxButtons.YesNo;
         }
         // only one option left--display Retry and Cancel Buttons
         else
         {
            ButtonType = MessageBoxButtons.RetryCancel;
         }
      }

      // change Icon based on option chosen by sender
      private void iconType_CheckedChanged(object sender, EventArgs e)
      {
         if (sender == asteriskRadioButton) // display asterisk Icon
         {
            IconType = MessageBoxIcon.Asterisk;
         }
         // display error Icon
         else if (sender == errorRadioButton)
         {
            IconType = MessageBoxIcon.Error;
         }
         // display exclamation point Icon
         else if (sender == exclamationRadioButton)
         {
            IconType = MessageBoxIcon.Exclamation;
         }
         // display hand Icon
         else if (sender == handRadioButton)
         {
            IconType = MessageBoxIcon.Hand;
         }
         // display information Icon
         else if (sender == informationRadioButton)
         {
            IconType = MessageBoxIcon.Information;
         }
         // display question mark Icon
         else if (sender == questionRadioButton)
         {
            IconType = MessageBoxIcon.Question;
         }
```

**Fig. 14.28** | Using RadioButtons to set message-window options. (Part 2 of 4.)

```
         // display stop Icon
         else if (sender == stopRadioButton)
         {
            IconType = MessageBoxIcon.Stop;
         }
         // only one option left--display warning Icon
         else
         {
            IconType = MessageBoxIcon.Warning;
         }
      }

      // display MessageBox and Button user pressed
      private void displayButton_Click(object sender, EventArgs e)
      {
         // display MessageBox and store
         // the value of the Button that was pressed
         DialogResult result = MessageBox.Show(
            "This is your Custom MessageBox.", "Custon MessageBox",
            ButtonType, IconType);

         // check to see which Button was pressed in the MessageBox
         // change text displayed accordingly
         switch (result)
         {
            case DialogResult.OK:
               displayLabel.Text = "OK was pressed.";
               break;
            case DialogResult.Cancel:
               displayLabel.Text = "Cancel was pressed.";
               break;
            case DialogResult.Abort:
               displayLabel.Text = "Abort was pressed.";
               break;
            case DialogResult.Retry:
               displayLabel.Text = "Retry was pressed.";
               break;
            case DialogResult.Ignore:
               displayLabel.Text = "Ignore was pressed.";
               break;
            case DialogResult.Yes:
               displayLabel.Text = "Yes was pressed.";
               break;
            case DialogResult.No:
               displayLabel.Text = "No was pressed.";
               break;
         }
      }
   }
}
```

**Fig. 14.28** | Using RadioButtons to set message-window options. (Part 3 of 4.)

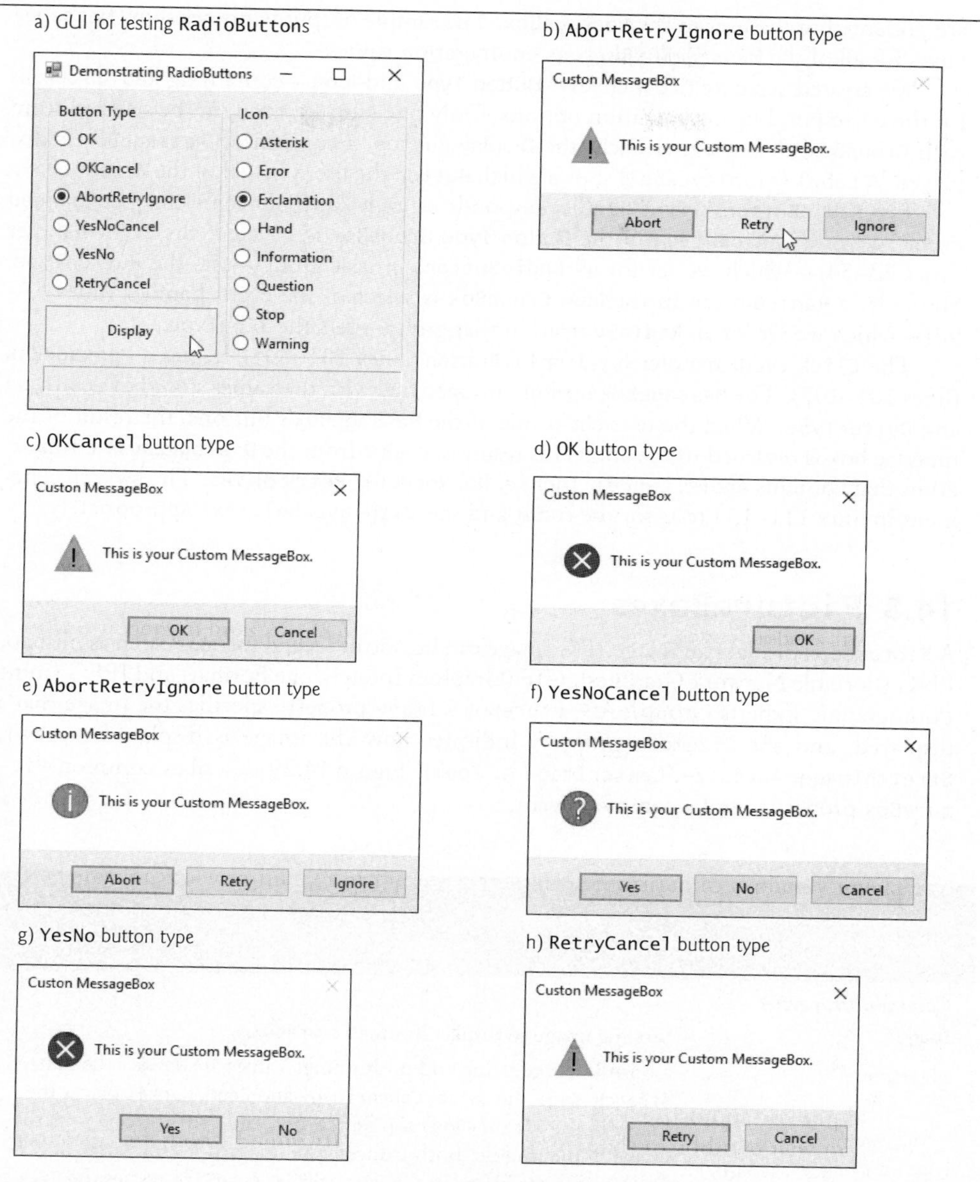


**Fig. 14.28** | Using `RadioButtons` to set message-window options. (Part 4 of 4.)

We store the user's choices in properties `IconType` and `ButtonType` (declared in lines 13–14). `IconType` is of type `MessageBoxIcon`, and can have values `Asterisk`, `Error`, `Exclamation`, `Hand`, `Information`, `None`, `Question`, `Stop` and `Warning`. The sample output shows only `Error`, `Exclamation`, `Information` and `Question` icons.

`ButtonType` is of type `MessageBoxButtons`, and can have values `AbortRetryIgnore`, `OK`, `OKCancel`, `RetryCancel`, `YesNo` and `YesNoCancel`. The name indicates the options that are presented to the user in the `MessageBox`. The sample output windows show `MessageBox`es for all of the `MessageBoxButtons` enumeration values.

We created separate `GroupBox`es—**Button Type** and **Icon**—containing `RadioButtons` for the corresponding enumeration options. Only one `RadioButton` can be selected from each `GroupBox`. When a user clicks the **Display** `Button`, a customized `MessageBox` is displayed. A `Label` (`displayLabel`) shows which `Button` the user pressed in the `MessageBox`.

The `RadioButtons`' event handler responds to each `RadioButton`'s `CheckedChanged` event. When a `RadioButton` in the **Button Type** `GroupBox` is selected, the event handler (lines 23–54)—which we set for all `RadioButtons` in that group—sets the `ButtonType`. Similarly, a `RadioButton` in the **Icon** `GroupBox` is selected, the event handler (lines 57–98)—which we set for all `RadioButtons` in that group—sets the `IconType`.

The `Click` event handler for `displayButton` (lines 101–135) creates a `MessageBox` (lines 105–107). The `MessageBox` options are specified with the values stored in `IconType` and `ButtonType`. When the user clicks one of the `MessageBox`'s buttons, the result of the message box is returned to the app. This result is a value from the **`DialogResult` enumeration** that contains `Abort`, `Cancel`, `Ignore`, `No`, `None`, `OK`, `Retry` or `Yes`. The `switch` statement in lines 111–134 tests for the result and sets `displayLabel.Text` appropriately.

## 14.8 PictureBoxes

A `PictureBox` displays an image. The image can be one of several formats, such as bitmap, PNG (Portable Network Graphics), GIF (Graphics Interchange Format) and JPEG (Joint Photographic Experts Group). A `PictureBox`'s `Image` property specifies the image that's displayed, and the `SizeMode` property indicates how the image is displayed (`Normal`, `StretchImage`, `Autosize`, `CenterImage` or `Zoom`). Figure 14.29 describes common `PictureBox` properties and a common event.

| `PictureBox` properties and an event | Description |
|---|---|
| *Common Properties* | |
| `Image` | Sets the image to display in the `PictureBox`. |
| `SizeMode` | Controls image sizing and positioning. Values are `Normal` (default), `StretchImage`, `AutoSize`, `CenterImage` and `Zoom`. `Normal` places the image in the `PictureBox`'s top-left corner, and `CenterImage` puts the image in the middle. Both truncate the image if it's too large. `StretchImage` fits the image in the `PictureBox`. `AutoSize` resizes the `PictureBox` to fit the image. `Zoom` resizes the image to to fit the `PictureBox` but maintains the original aspect ratio. |
| *Common Event* | |
| `Click` | Occurs when the user clicks a control. When you double click this control in the designer, an event handler is generated for this event. |

**Fig. 14.29** | `PictureBox` properties and an event.

Figure 14.30 uses a `PictureBox` named `imagePictureBox` to display one of three bitmap images—`image0.bmp`, `image1.bmp` or `image2.bmp`. These images are provided in the `Images` subdirectory of this chapter's examples directory. Whenever a user clicks the **Next Image** `Button`, the image changes to the next image in sequence. When the last image is displayed and the user clicks the **Next Image** `Button`, the first image is displayed again.

```
// Fig. 14.30: PictureBoxTestForm.cs
// Using a PictureBox to display images.
using System;
using System.Drawing;
using System.Windows.Forms;

namespace PictureBoxTest
{
   // Form to display different images when Button is clicked
   public partial class PictureBoxTestForm : Form
   {
      private int ImageNumber { get; set; } = -1; // image to display

      // default constructor
      public PictureBoxTestForm()
      {
         InitializeComponent();
      }

      // change image whenever Next Button is clicked
      private void nextButton_Click(object sender, EventArgs e)
      {
         ImageNumber = (ImageNumber + 1) % 3; // cycles from 0 to 2

         // retrieve image from resources and load into PictureBox
         imagePictureBox.Image =
            (Image) (Properties.Resources.ResourceManager.GetObject(
            $"image{ImageNumber}"));
      }
   }
}
```

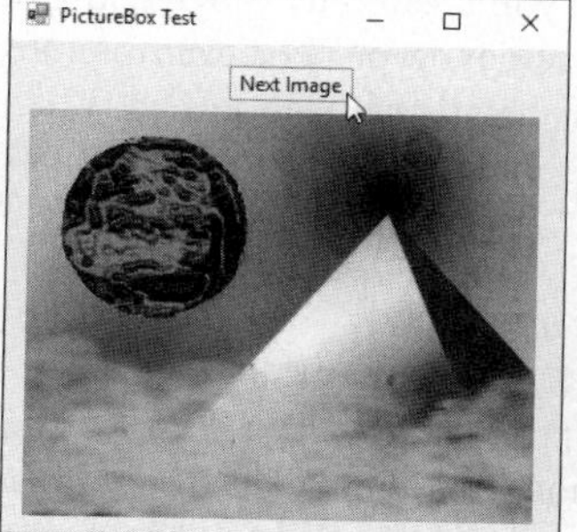

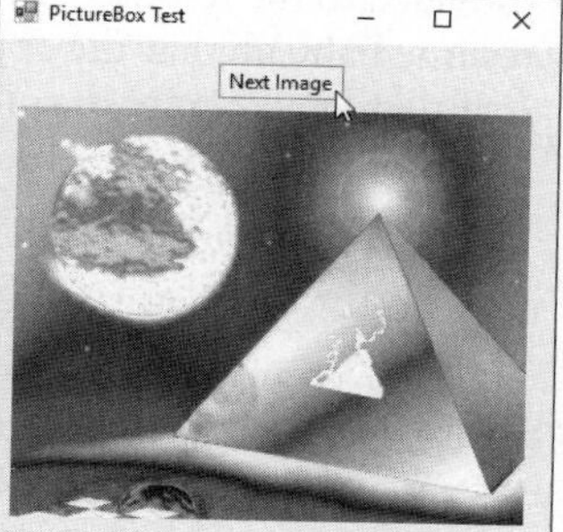


**Fig. 14.30** | Using a `PictureBox` to display images.

*Using Resources Programmatically*

In this example, we added the images to the project as **resources**. This causes the IDE to to copy the images into the app's executable file and enables the app to access the images through the project's `Properties` namespace. When you do this, you don't need to worry about wrapping the images with the app when you move it to another location or computer.

If you're creating a new project, use the following steps to add images to the project as resources:

1. After creating your project, right click the project's **Properties** node in the **Solution Explorer** and select **Open** to display the project's properties.
2. From the tabs on the left, click the **Resources** tab.
3. At the top of the **Resources** tab, click the down arrow next to **Add Resource** and select **Add Existing File...** to display the **Add existing file to resources** dialog.
4. Locate the image files you wish to add as resources and click the **Open** button. We provided three sample images in the `Images` folder with this chapter's examples.
5. Save your project.

The files now appear in a folder named **Resources** in the **Solution Explorer**. We'll use this technique in most examples that use images going forward.

A project's resources are accessible to the app via its **`Resources`** class (of the project's `Properties` namespace). The `Resources` class contains a **`ResourceManager`** object for interacting with the resources programmatically. To access an image, you can use the method **`GetObject`**, which takes as an argument the resource name as it appears in the **Resources** tab (e.g., `"image0"`) and returns the resource as an `Object`. Lines 27–28 invoke `GetObject` with the result of the `string`-interpolation expression

```
$"image{ImageNumber}"
```

which builds the name of the resource by placing the index of the next picture (`ImageNumber`, which was obtained earlier in line 23) at the end of the word `"image"`. You must convert this `Object` to type `Image` (namespace `System.Drawing`) to assign it to the `PictureBox`'s `Image` property (lines 26–28).

The `Resources` class also provides direct access to the resources you define with expressions of the form `Resources.`*resourceName*, where *resourceName* is the name you provided to the resource when you created it. When using such an expression, the resource returned already has the appropriate type. For example, `Properties.Resources.image0` is an `Image` object representing the first image.

## 14.9 ToolTips

In Chapter 2, we demonstrated *tool tips*—the helpful text that appears when the mouse hovers over an item in a GUI. Recall that the tool tips in Visual Studio (and most apps with GUIs) help you become familiar with the IDE's features and serve as useful reminders for each toolbar icon's functionality. This section demonstrates how to use the **`ToolTip` component** to add tool tips to your apps. Figure 14.31 describes common properties and a common event of class `ToolTip`.

| ToolTip properties and an event | Description |
|---|---|
| *Common Properties* | |
| AutoPopDelay | The amount of time (in milliseconds) that the tool tip appears while the mouse is over a control. |
| InitialDelay | The amount of time (in milliseconds) that a mouse must hover over a control before a tool tip appears. |
| ReshowDelay | The amount of time (in milliseconds) between which two different tool tips appear (when the mouse is moved from one control to another). |
| *Common Event* | |
| Draw | Raised when the tool tip is about to be displayed. This event allows programmers to modify the appearance of the tool tip. |

**Fig. 14.31** | ToolTip properties and an event.

When you add a ToolTip component from the **Toolbox**, it appears in the **component tray**—at the bottom of the window when the Form is in **Design** mode. Once a ToolTip is added to a Form, a new property appears in the **Properties** window for the Form's other controls. This property appears in the **Properties** window as **ToolTip on**, followed by the name of the ToolTip component. For instance, if our Form's ToolTip were named helpfulToolTip, you would set a control's **ToolTip on helpfulToolTip** property value to specify the control's tool tip text. Figure 14.32 demonstrates the ToolTip component. For this example, we create a GUI containing two Labels, so we can demonstrate different tool tip text for each Label. Since there's no event-handling code in this example, we do not show you the code for the Form class.

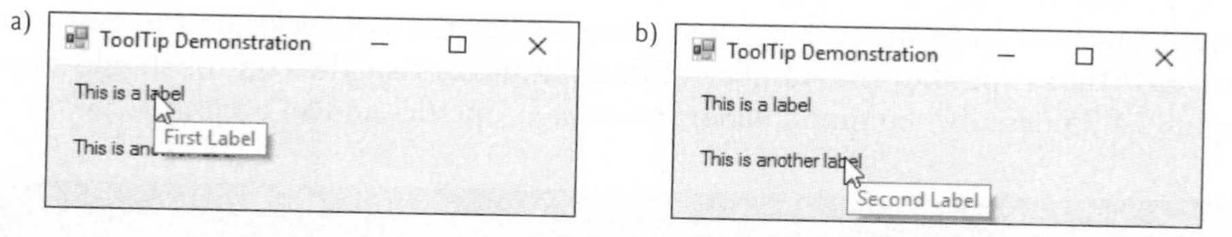


**Fig. 14.32** | Demonstrating the ToolTip component.

In this example, the IDE named the ToolTip component toolTip1. Figure 14.33 shows the ToolTip in the component tray. We set the tool tip text for the first Label to "First Label" and the tool tip text for the second Label to "Second Label". Figure 14.34 demonstrates setting the tool tip text for the first Label.

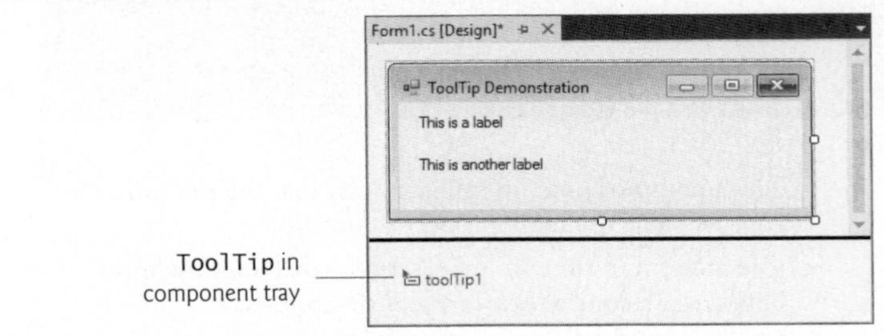


**Fig. 14.33** | Demonstrating the component tray.

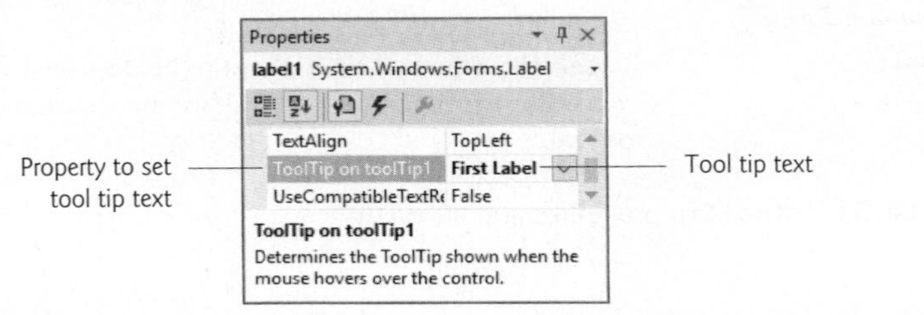


**Fig. 14.34** | Setting a control's tool tip text.

## 14.10 NumericUpDown Control

At times, you'll want to restrict a user's input choices to a specific *range of numeric values*. This is the purpose of the **NumericUpDown control**. This control appears as a `TextBox`, with two small `Buttons` on the right side—one with an up arrow and one with a down arrow. By default, a user can type numeric values into this control as if it were a `TextBox` or click the up and down arrows to increase or decrease the value in the control, respectively. The largest and smallest values in the range are specified with the **`Maximum`** and **`Minimum`** properties, respectively (both of type `decimal`). The **`Increment`** property (also of type `decimal`) specifies by how much the current value changes when the user clicks the arrows. Property **`DecimalPlaces`** specifies the number of decimal places that the control should display. Figure 14.35 describes common `NumericUpDown` properties and an event.

| `NumericUpDown` properties and an event | Description |
|---|---|
| *Common Properties* | |
| `DecimalPlaces` | Specifies how many decimal places to display in the control. |
| `Increment` | Specifies by how much the current number in the control changes when the user clicks the control's up and down arrows. |

**Fig. 14.35** | `NumericUpDown` properties and an event. (Part 1 of 2.)

| NumericUpDown properties and an event | Description |
|---|---|
| Maximum | Largest value in the control's range. |
| Minimum | Smallest value in the control's range. |
| UpDownAlign | Modifies the alignment of the up and down Buttons on the NumericUpDown control. This property can be used to display these Buttons either to the left or to the right of the control. |
| Value | The numeric value currently displayed in the control. |
| *Common Event* | |
| ValueChanged | This event is raised when the value in the control is changed. This is the default event for the NumericUpDown control. |

**Fig. 14.35** | NumericUpDown properties and an event. (Part 2 of 2.)

Figure 14.36 demonstrates a NumericUpDown control in a GUI that calculates interest rate. The calculations performed in this app are similar to those in Fig. 6.6. TextBoxes are used to input the principal and interest rate amounts, and a NumericUpDown control is used to input the number of years for which we want to calculate interest.

```
// Fig. 14.36: InterestCalculatorForm.cs
// Demonstrating the NumericUpDown control.
using System;
using System.Windows.Forms;

namespace NumericUpDownTest
{
   public partial class InterestCalculatorForm : Form
   {
      // default constructor
      public InterestCalculatorForm()
      {
         InitializeComponent();
      }

      private void calculateButton_Click(object sender, EventArgs e)
      {
         // retrieve user input
         decimal principal = decimal.Parse(principalTextBox.Text);
         double rate = double.Parse(interestTextBox.Text);
         int year = (int) yearUpDown.Value;

         // set output header
         string output = "Year\tAmount on Deposit\r\n";

```

**Fig. 14.36** | Demonstrating the NumericUpDown control. (Part 1 of 2.)

```
26            // calculate amount after each year and append to output
27            for (int yearCounter = 1; yearCounter <= year; ++yearCounter)
28            {
29               decimal amount = principal *
30                  ((decimal) Math.Pow((1 + rate / 100), yearCounter));
31               output += $"{yearCounter}\t{amount:C}\r\n";
32            }
33
34            displayTextBox.Text = output; // display result
35         }
36      }
37   }
```

Click to increase number of years

NumericUpDown control

Click to decrease number of years

**Fig. 14.36** | Demonstrating the `NumericUpDown` control. (Part 2 of 2.)

For the `NumericUpDown` control named `yearUpDown`, we set the `Minimum` property to `1` and the `Maximum` property to `10`. We left the `Increment` property set to `1`, its default value. These settings specify that users can enter a number of years in the range `1` to `10` in increments of `1`. If we had set the `Increment` to `0.5`, we could also input values such as `1.5` or `2.5`. If you don't modify the `DecimalPlaces` property (`0` by default), `1.5` and `2.5` display as `2` and `3`, respectively. We set the `NumericUpDown`'s **`ReadOnly` property** to `true` to indicate that the user cannot type a number into the control to make a selection. Thus, the user must click the up and down arrows to modify the value in the control. By default, the `ReadOnly` property is set to `false`. The output for this app is displayed in a multiline read-only `TextBox` with a vertical scrollbar, so the user can scroll through the entire output. Notice that `\r\n` is required (lines 24 and 31) to move to the next line in the `TextBox`.

## 14.11 Mouse-Event Handling

This section explains how to handle **mouse events**, such as **clicks** and **moves**, which are generated when the user interacts with a control via the mouse. Mouse events can be handled for any control that derives from class `System.Windows.Forms.Control`. For most mouse events, information about the event is passed to the event-handling method through an object of class **`MouseEventArgs`**, and the delegate used to create the mouse-event handlers is **`MouseEventHandler`**. Each mouse-event-handling method for these events requires an `object` and a `MouseEventArgs` object as arguments.

Class `MouseEventArgs` contains information related to the mouse event, such as the mouse pointer's *x*- and *y*-coordinates, the mouse button pressed (`Right`, `Left` or `Middle`) and the number of times the mouse was clicked. The *x*- and *y*-coordinates of the `MouseEventArgs` object are relative to the control that generated the event—i.e., point (0,0) represents the upper-left corner of the control where the mouse event occurred. Several common mouse events and event arguments are described in Fig. 14.37.

| Mouse events and event arguments | |
|---|---|
| ***Mouse Events with Event Argument of Type `EventArgs`*** | |
| `MouseEnter` | Mouse cursor enters the control's boundaries. |
| `MouseHover` | Mouse cursor hovers within the control's boundaries. |
| `MouseLeave` | Mouse cursor leaves the control's boundaries. |
| ***Mouse Events with Event Argument of Type `MouseEventArgs`*** | |
| `MouseDown` | Mouse button is pressed while the mouse cursor is within a control's boundaries. |
| `MouseMove` | Mouse cursor is moved while in the control's boundaries. |
| `MouseUp` | Mouse button is released when the cursor is over the control's boundaries. |
| `MouseWheel` | Mouse wheel is moved while the control has the focus. |
| ***Class `MouseEventArgs` Properties*** | |
| `Button` | Specifies which mouse button was pressed (`Left`, `Right`, `Middle` or `None`). |
| `Clicks` | The number of times that the mouse button was clicked. |
| `X` | The *x*-coordinate within the control where the event occurred. |
| `Y` | The *y*-coordinate within the control where the event occurred. |

**Fig. 14.37** | Mouse events and event arguments.

Figure 14.38 uses mouse events to draw on a `Form`. Whenever the user *drags* the mouse (i.e., moves the mouse while a mouse button is pressed), small circles appear on the `Form` at the position where each mouse event occurs during the drag operation.

```
// Fig. 14.38: PainterForm.cs
// Using the mouse to draw on a Form.
using System;
using System.Drawing;
using System.Windows.Forms;

namespace Painter
{
   // creates a Form that's a drawing surface
   public partial class PainterForm : Form
   {
      bool ShouldPaint { get; set; } = false; // whether to paint

```

**Fig. 14.38** | Using the mouse to draw on a `Form`. (Part 1 of 2.)

```
        // default constructor
        public PainterForm()
        {
            InitializeComponent();
        }

        // should paint when mouse button is pressed down
        private void PainterForm_MouseDown(object sender, MouseEventArgs e)
        {
            // indicate that user is dragging the mouse
            ShouldPaint = true;
        }

        // stop painting when mouse button is released
        private void PainterForm_MouseUp(object sender, MouseEventArgs e)
        {
            // indicate that user released the mouse button
            ShouldPaint = false;
        }

        // draw circle whenever mouse moves with its button held down
        private void PainterForm_MouseMove(object sender, MouseEventArgs e)
        {
            if (ShouldPaint) // check if mouse button is being pressed
            {
                // draw a circle where the mouse pointer is present
                using (Graphics graphics = CreateGraphics())
                {
                    graphics.FillEllipse(
                        new SolidBrush(Color.BlueViolet), e.X, e.Y, 4, 4);
                }
            }
        }
    }
}
```

**Fig. 14.38** | Using the mouse to draw on a `Form`. (Part 2 of 2.)

In line 12, the program declares property `ShouldPaint`, which determines whether to draw on the `Form`. We want the program to draw only while the mouse button is pressed (i.e., held down). Thus, when the user clicks or holds down a mouse button, the system generates a `MouseDown` event, and the event handler (lines 21–25) sets `ShouldPaint` to `true`. When the user releases the mouse button, the system generates a `MouseUp` event, `ShouldPaint` is set to `false` in the `PainterForm_MouseUp` event handler (lines 28–32) and the program stops drawing. Unlike `MouseMove` events, which occur continuously as the user moves the mouse, the system generates a `MouseDown` event only when a mouse button is first *pressed* and generates a `MouseUp` event only when a mouse button is *released*.

Whenever the mouse moves over a control, the `MouseMove` event for that control occurs. Inside the `PainterForm_MouseMove` event handler (lines 35–46), the program draws only if `ShouldPaint` is `true` (i.e., a mouse button is pressed). In the `using` statement, line 40 calls inherited `Form` method `CreateGraphics` to create a **`Graphics`** object that allows the program to draw on the `Form`. Class `Graphics` provides methods that draw various shapes. For example, lines 42–43 use method **`FillEllipse`** to draw a circle. The first parameter to method `FillEllipse` in this case is an object of class **`SolidBrush`**, which specifies the solid color that will fill the shape. The color is provided as an argument to class `SolidBrush`'s constructor. Type **`Color`** contains numerous predefined color constants—we selected `Color.BlueViolet`. `FillEllipse` draws an oval in a bounding rectangle that's specified by the *x*- and *y*-coordinates of its upper-left corner, its width and its height—the final four arguments to the method. The *x*- and *y*-coordinates represent the location of the mouse event and can be taken from the mouse-event arguments (`e.X` and `e.Y`). To draw a circle, we set the width and height of the bounding rectangle so that they're equal—in this example, both are 4 pixels. `Graphics`, `SolidBrush` and `Color` are all part of the namespace `System.Drawing`. Recall from Chapter 13 that the `using` statement automatically calls `Dispose` on the object that was created in the parentheses following keyword `using`. This is important because `Graphics` objects are a limited resource. Calling `Dispose` on a `Graphics` object ensures that its resources are returned to the system for reuse.

## 14.12 Keyboard-Event Handling

**Key events** occur when keyboard keys are pressed and released. Such events can be handled for any control that inherits from `System.Windows.Forms.Control`. There are three key events—`KeyPress`, `KeyUp` and `KeyDown`. The **`KeyPress`** event occurs when the user presses a character key or the space or backspace keys. The specific key can be determined with property **`KeyChar`** of the event handler's **`KeyPressEventArgs`** argument.

The `KeyPress` event does *not* indicate whether **modifier keys** (e.g., *Shift*, *Alt* and *Ctrl*) were pressed when a key event occurred. If this information is important, the **`KeyUp`** or **`KeyDown`** events can be used. The **`KeyEventArgs`** argument for each of these events contains information about modifier keys. Figure 14.39 lists important key event information. Several properties return values from the **`Keys` enumeration**, which provides constants that specify the various keys on a keyboard. Like the `FontStyle` enumeration (Section 14.7), the `Keys` enumeration is represented with a set of bits, so the enumeration's constants can be combined with the bitwise operators to indicate *multiple keys* pressed at the same time.

| Keyboard events and event arguments | |
|---|---|
| ***Key Events with Event Arguments of Type* `KeyEventArgs`** | |
| `KeyDown` | Generated when a key is initially pressed. |
| `KeyUp` | Generated when a key is released. |
| ***Key Event with Event Argument of Type* `KeyPressEventArgs`** | |
| `KeyPress` | Generated when a key is pressed. Raised after `KeyDown` and before `KeyUp`. |
| ***Class* `KeyPressEventArgs` *Property*** | |
| `KeyChar` | Returns the ASCII character for the key pressed. |
| ***Class* `KeyEventArgs` *Properties*** | |
| `Alt` | Indicates whether the *Alt* key was pressed. |
| `Control` | Indicates whether the *Ctrl* key was pressed. |
| `Shift` | Indicates whether the *Shift* key was pressed. |
| `KeyCode` | Returns the key code for the key as a value from the `Keys` enumeration. This does not include modifier-key information. It's used to test for a specific key. |
| `KeyData` | Returns the key code for a key combined with modifier information as a `Keys` value. This property contains all information about the pressed key. |
| `KeyValue` | Returns the key code as an `int`, rather than as a value from the `Keys` enumeration. This property is used to obtain a numeric representation of the pressed key. The `int` value is known as a Windows virtual key code. |
| `Modifiers` | Returns a `Keys` value indicating any pressed modifier keys (*Alt*, *Ctrl* and *Shift*). This property is used to determine modifier-key information only. |

**Fig. 14.39** | Keyboard events and event arguments.

Figure 14.40 demonstrates the use of the key-event handlers to display a key pressed by a user. The program is a `Form` with two `Label`s that displays the pressed key on one `Label` and modifier key information on the other.

```
// Fig. 14.40: KeyDemo.cs
// Displaying information about the key the user pressed.
using System;
using System.Windows.Forms;

namespace KeyDemo
{
   // Form to display key information when key is pressed
   public partial class KeyDemo : Form
   {
      // default constructor
      public KeyDemo()
      {
         InitializeComponent();
      }
```

**Fig. 14.40** | Displaying information about the key the user pressed. (Part 1 of 2.)

```

      // display the character pressed using KeyChar
      private void KeyDemo_KeyPress(object sender, KeyPressEventArgs e)
      {
         charLabel.Text = $"Key pressed: {e.KeyChar}";
      }

      // display modifier keys, key code, key data and key value
      private void KeyDemo_KeyDown(object sender, KeyEventArgs e)
      {
         keyInfoLabel.Text =
            $"Alt: {(e.Alt ? "Yes" : "No")}\n" +
            $"Shift: {(e.Shift ? "Yes" : "No")}\n" +
            $"Ctrl: {(e.Control ? "Yes" : "No")}\n" +
            $"KeyCode: {e.KeyCode}\n" +
            $"KeyData: {e.KeyData}\n" +
            $"KeyValue: {e.KeyValue}";
      }

      // clear Labels when key released
      private void KeyDemo_KeyUp(object sender, KeyEventArgs e)
      {
         charLabel.Text = "";
         keyInfoLabel.Text = "";
      }
   }
}
```

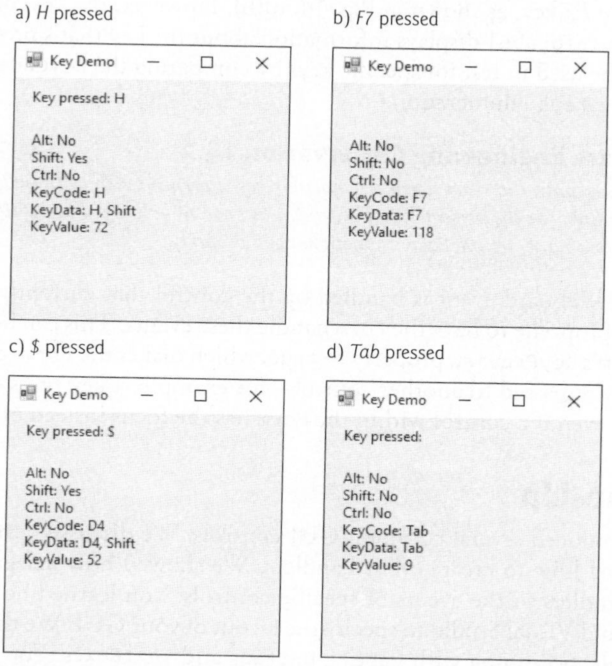

a) *H* pressed

Key Demo

Key pressed: H

Alt: No
Shift: Yes
Ctrl: No
KeyCode: H
KeyData: H, Shift
KeyValue: 72

b) *F7* pressed

Key Demo

Alt: No
Shift: No
Ctrl: No
KeyCode: F7
KeyData: F7
KeyValue: 118

c) *$* pressed

Key Demo

Key pressed: $

Alt: No
Shift: Yes
Ctrl: No
KeyCode: D4
KeyData: D4, Shift
KeyValue: 52

d) *Tab* pressed

Key Demo

Key pressed:

Alt: No
Shift: No
Ctrl: No
KeyCode: Tab
KeyData: Tab
KeyValue: 9

**Fig. 14.40** | Displaying information about the key the user pressed. (Part 2 of 2.)

Control `charLabel` displays the character value of the key pressed, whereas `keyInfoLabel` displays information relating to the pressed key. Because the `KeyDown` and `KeyPress` events convey different information, the `Form` (`KeyDemo`) handles both.

The `KeyPress` event handler (lines 18–21) accesses the `KeyChar` property of the `KeyPressEventArgs` object. This returns the pressed key as a `char`, which we then display in `charLabel` (line 20). If the pressed key is not an ASCII character, then the `KeyPress` event will not occur, and `charLabel` will not display any text. ASCII is a common encoding format for letters, numbers, punctuation marks and other characters. It does not support keys such as the **function keys** (like *F1*) or the modifier keys (*Alt*, *Ctrl* and *Shift*).

The `KeyDown` event handler (lines 24–33) displays information from its `KeyEventArgs` object. The handler tests for the *Alt*, *Shift* and *Ctrl* keys using the `Alt`, `Shift` and `Control` properties that each return a `bool`—`true` if the corresponding key is pressed and `false` otherwise. The handler then displays the `KeyCode`, `KeyData` and `KeyValue` properties.

The `KeyCode` property returns a `Keys` enumeration value (line 30). The `KeyCode` property returns the pressed key, but does not provide any information about modifier keys. Thus, both a capital and a lowercase "a" are represented as the *A* key.

The `KeyData` property (line 31) also returns a `Keys` enumeration value, but also includes modifier-key data. Thus, if "A" is input, the `KeyData` shows that both *A* and *Shift* were pressed. Lastly, `KeyValue` (line 32) returns an `int` representing a pressed key. This `int` is the **key code**. The key code is useful when testing for non-ASCII keys like *F12*.

The `KeyUp` event handler (lines 36–40) clears both `Labels` when the key is released. As we can see from the output, non-ASCII keys are not displayed in `charLabel`, because the `KeyPress` event is not generated. For example, `charLabel` does not display any text when you press the *F7* key, as shown in Fig. 14.40(b). However, the `KeyDown` event still is generated, and `keyInfoLabel` displays information about the key that's pressed. The `Keys` enumeration can be used to test for specific keys by comparing the `KeyCode` of the pressed key to values in the `Keys` enumeration.

**Software Engineering Observation 14.2**

*To cause a control to react when a particular key is pressed (such as* Enter*), handle a key event and test for the pressed key. To cause a `Button` to be clicked when the* Enter *key is pressed on a `Form`, set the `Form`'s `AcceptButton` property.*

By default, a keyboard event is handled by the control that currently has the focus. Sometimes it's appropriate to have the `Form` handle these events. This can be accomplished by setting the `Form`'s `KeyPreview` property to `true`, which makes the `Form` receive keyboard events before they're passed to another control—for example, a key press would raise the `Form`'s `KeyPress`, even if a control within the `Form` has the focus instead of the `Form` itself.

## 14.13 Wrap-Up

This chapter introduced several common GUI controls. We discussed event handling in detail, and showed how to create event handlers. We showed how delegates are used to connect event handlers to the events of specific controls. You learned how to use a control's properties and Visual Studio to specify the layout of your GUI. We then demonstrated several controls, beginning with `Labels`, `Buttons` and `TextBoxes`. You learned how to use `GroupBoxes` and `Panels` to organize other controls. We then demonstrated `CheckBoxes` and RadioButtons, which are state buttons that allow users to select among several options. We displayed images in PictureBox controls, displayed helpful text on a GUI with ToolTip components and specified a range of numeric input values for users with a NumericUpDown control. We then demonstrated how to handle mouse and keyboard events. The next chapter introduces additional GUI controls. You'll learn how to add menus to your GUIs and create Windows Forms apps that display multiple Forms.

# 15

# Graphical User Interfaces with Windows Forms: Part 2

## Objectives

In this chapter you'll:

- Create menus, tabbed windows and multiple document interface (MDI) programs.
- Use the `ListView` and `TreeView` controls for displaying information.
- Create hyperlinks using the `LinkLabel` control.
- Display lists of information in `ListBox`, `CheckedListBox` and `ComboBox` controls.
- Input dates with the `MonthCalendar` control.
- Input date and time data with the `DateTimePicker` control.
- Create custom controls.
- Use visual inheritance to build upon an existing GUI.

**Outline**



## 15.1 Introduction

Here we continue our Windows `Forms` presentation. We start with menus, which present users with logically organized commands (or options). We show how to create menus in the Windows `Forms` designer. We discuss how to input and display dates and times using the `MonthCalendar` and `DateTimePicker` controls. We also introduce `LinkLabel`s that can hyperlink to a file on the current machine or a web page, simply by clicking the mouse.

We demonstrate how to manipulate lists of values via a `ListBox` and `ListView` and how to combine several checkboxes in a `CheckedListBox`. We also create drop-down lists using `ComboBox`es and display data hierarchically with a `TreeView` control. You'll learn two other important GUI elements—tab controls and multiple document interface (MDI) windows. These components enable you to create real-world programs with sophisticated GUIs. You'll use visual inheritance to build upon an existing GUI.

Visual Studio provides many GUI components, several of which are discussed in this (and the previous) chapter. You also can design custom controls and add them to the **ToolBox**, as we demonstrate in this chapter's last example. The techniques presented here form the groundwork for creating more substantial GUIs and custom controls.

## 15.2 Menus

**Menus** provide groups of related commands for Windows `Forms` apps. Although these commands depend on the program, some—such as **Open** and **Save**—are common to many apps. Menus are an integral part of GUIs, because they organize commands without "cluttering" the GUI.

In Fig. 15.1, an expanded menu from Visual Studio lists various commands (called **menu items**), plus **submenus** (menus within a menu). The top-level menus appear in the left portion of the figure, whereas any submenus or menu items are displayed to the right. The menu that contains a menu item is called that menu item's **parent menu**. A menu item that contains a submenu is considered to be the parent of that submenu.

Menus can have *Alt* key shortcuts (also called **access shortcuts**, **keyboard shortcuts** or **hotkeys**), which are accessed by pressing *Alt* and the underlined letter—for example, *Alt* + *F* typically expands the **File** menu. Menu items can have shortcut keys as well (combinations of *Ctrl*, *Shift*, *Alt*, *F1*, *F2*, letter keys, and so on). Some menu items display checkmarks, usually indicating that multiple options on the menu can be selected at once.

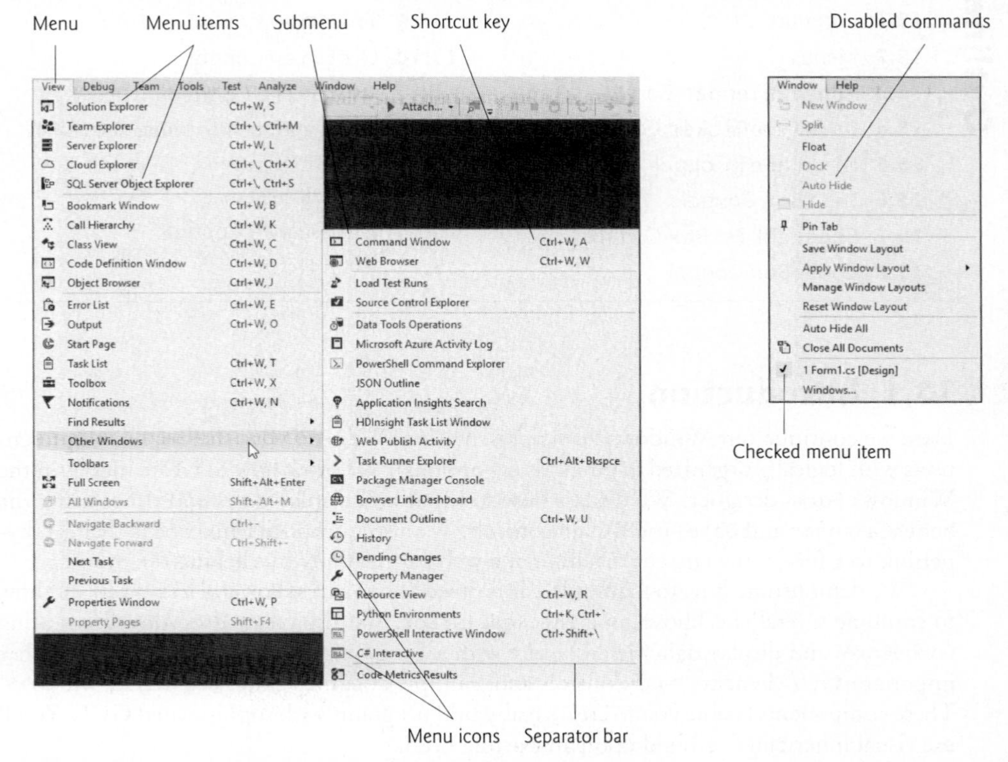


**Fig. 15.1** | Menus, submenus and menu items.

To create a menu, open the **Toolbox** and drag a **MenuStrip** control onto the Form. This creates a menu bar across the top of the Form (below the title bar) and places a MenuStrip icon in the component tray. To select the MenuStrip, click this icon. You can now use **Design** mode to create and edit menus for your app. Menus, like other controls, have properties and events, which can be accessed through the **Properties** window.

To add menu items to the menu, click the **Type Here** TextBox (Fig. 15.2) and type the menu item's name. This action adds an entry to the menu of type **ToolStripMenuItem**. After you press the *Enter* key, the menu item name is added to the menu. Then more **Type Here** TextBoxes appear, allowing you to add items underneath or to the side of the original menu item (Fig. 15.3).

To create an access shortcut, type an ampersand (&) before the character to be underlined. For example, to create the **File** menu item with the letter **F** underlined, type &File. To display an ampersand, type &&. To add other shortcut keys (e.g., *Ctrl* + *F9*) for menu items, set the **ShortcutKeys** property of the appropriate ToolStripMenuItems. To do this, select the down arrow to the right of this property in the **Properties** window. In the window that appears (Fig. 15.4), use the CheckBoxes and drop-down list to select the shortcut keys. When you're finished, click elsewhere on the screen. You can hide the shortcut keys by setting property **ShowShortcutKeys** to false, and you can modify how the shortcut keys are displayed in the menu item by modifying property **ShortcutKeyDisplayString**.

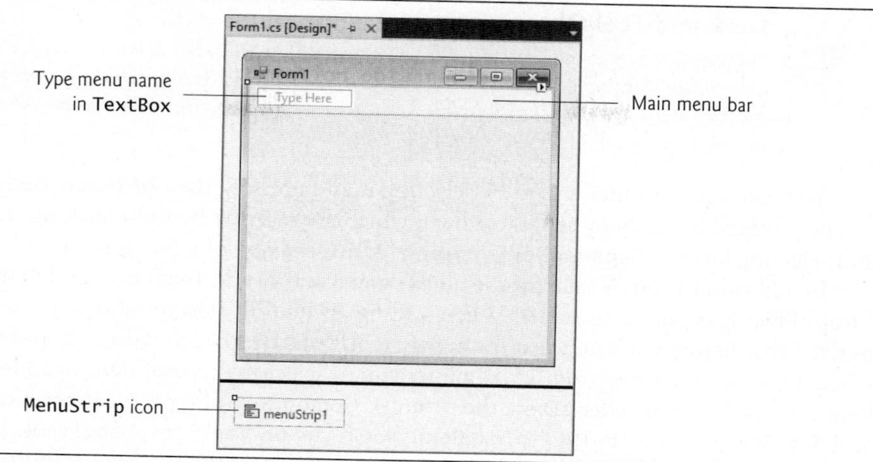


**Fig. 15.2** | Editing menus in Visual Studio.

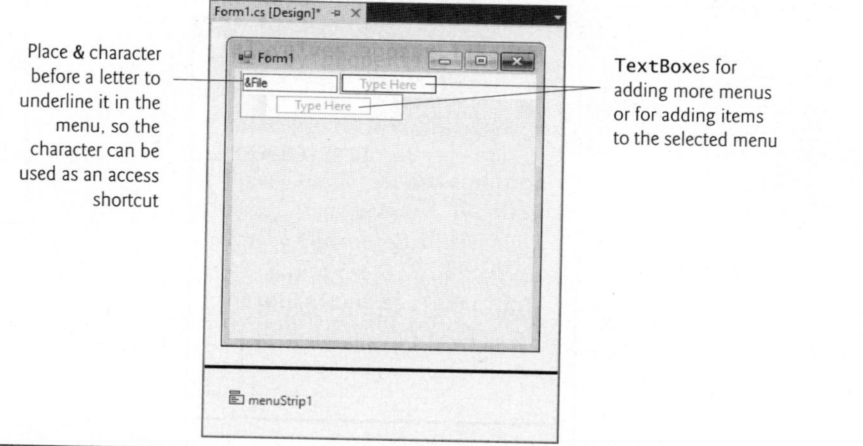


**Fig. 15.3** | Adding `ToolStripMenuItems` to a `MenuStrip`.

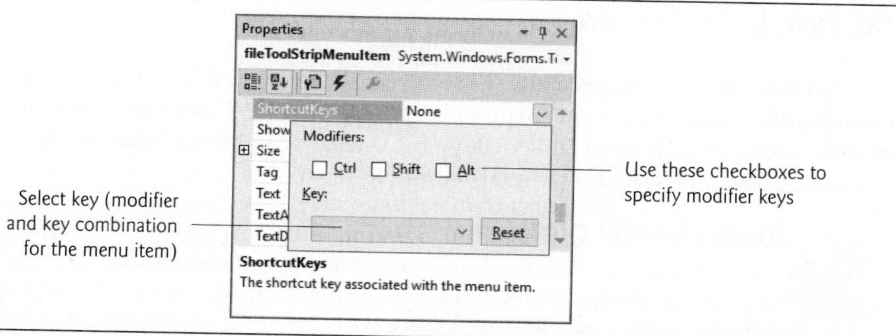


**Fig. 15.4** | Setting a menu item's shortcut keys.

**Look-and-Feel Observation 15.1**

*Buttons can have access shortcuts. Place the & symbol immediately before the desired character in the Button's text. To press the button by using its access key in the running app, the user presses* Alt *and the underlined character. If the underline is not visible when the app runs, press the* Alt *key to display the underlines.*

You can remove a menu item by selecting it and pressing the *Delete* key. Menu items can be grouped logically by **separator bars**, which are inserted by right clicking the menu and selecting **Insert > Separator** or by typing "-" for the text of a menu item.

In addition to text, Visual Studio allows you to easily add `TextBox`es and `ComboBox`es (drop-down lists) as menu items. When adding an item in **Design** mode, you may have noticed that before you enter text for a new item, you're provided with a drop-down list. Clicking the down arrow (Fig. 15.5) allows you to select the type of item to add—**MenuItem** (of type `ToolStripMenuItem`, the default), **ComboBox** (of type `ToolStripComboBox`) and **TextBox** (of type `ToolStripTextBox`). We focus on `ToolStripMenuItem`s. [*Note:* If you view this drop-down list for menu items that are not on the top level, a fourth option appears, allowing you to insert a separator bar.]

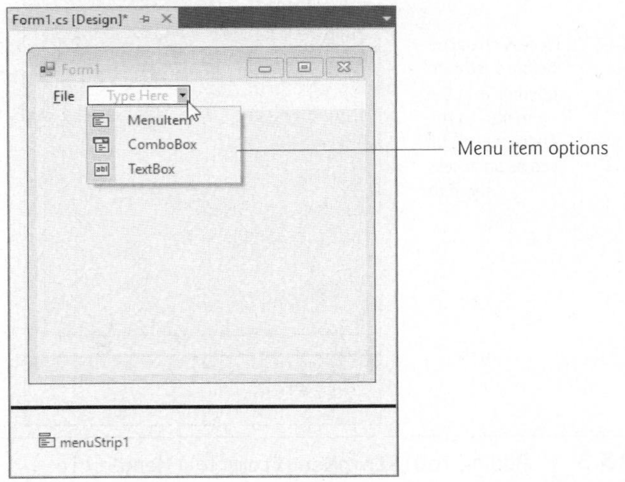


**Fig. 15.5** | Menu-item options.

`ToolStripMenuItem`s generate a **`Click`** event when selected. To create an empty `Click` event handler, double click the menu item in **Design** mode. Common actions in response to these events include displaying dialogs and setting properties. Common menu properties and a common event are summarized in Fig. 15.6.

**Look-and-Feel Observation 15.2**

*It's a convention to place an ellipsis (...) after the name of a menu item (e.g.,* **Save As...***) that requires the user to provide more information—typically through a dialog. A menu item that produces an immediate action without prompting the user for more information (e.g.,* **Save***) should not have an ellipsis following its name.*

| MenuStrip and ToolStripMenuItem properties and an event | Description |
|---|---|
| ***MenuStrip Properties*** | |
| RightToLeft | Causes text to display from right to left. This is useful for languages that are read from right to left. |
| ***ToolStripMenuItem Properties*** | |
| Checked | Indicates whether a menu item is checked. The default value is false, meaning that the menu item is unchecked. |
| CheckOnClick | Indicates that a menu item should appear checked or unchecked as it is clicked. |
| ShortcutKey-DisplayString | Specifies text that should appear beside a menu item for a shortcut key. If left blank, the key names are displayed. Otherwise, the text in this property is displayed for the shortcut key. |
| ShortcutKeys | Specifies the shortcut key for the menu item (e.g., <*Ctrl*>-*F9* is equivalent to clicking a specific item). |
| ShowShortcutKeys | Indicates whether a shortcut key is shown beside menu item text. The default is true, which displays the shortcut key. |
| Text | Specifies the menu item's text. To create an *Alt* access shortcut, precede a character with & (e.g., &File to specify a menu named **File** with the letter **F** underlined). |
| ***Common ToolStripMenuItem Event*** | |
| Click | Generated when an item is clicked or a shortcut key is used. This is the default event when the menu is double clicked in the designer. |

**Fig. 15.6** | MenuStrip and ToolStripMenuItem properties and an event.

Class MenuTestForm (Fig. 15.7) creates a simple menu on a Form. The Form has a top-level **File** menu with menu items **About** (which displays a MessageBox) and **Exit** (which terminates the program). The program also includes a **Format** menu, which contains menu items that change the format of the text on a Label. The **Format** menu has submenus **Color** and **Font**, which change the color and font of the text on a Label.

```
// Fig. 15.7: MenuTestForm.cs
// Using Menus to change font colors and styles.
using System;
using System.Drawing;
using System.Windows.Forms;

namespace MenuTest
{
   // our Form contains a Menu that changes the font color
   // and style of the text displayed in Label
```

**Fig. 15.7** | Using menus to change text font and color. (Part 1 of 5.)

```
    public partial class MenuTestForm : Form
    {
       // constructor
       public MenuTestForm()
       {
          InitializeComponent();
       }

       // display MessageBox when About ToolStripMenuItem is selected
       private void aboutToolStripMenuItem_Click(
          object sender, EventArgs e)
       {
          MessageBox.Show("This is an example\nof using menus.", "About",
             MessageBoxButtons.OK, MessageBoxIcon.Information);
       }

       // exit program when Exit ToolStripMenuItem is selected
       private void exitToolStripMenuItem_Click(object sender, EventArgs e)
       {
          Application.Exit();
       }

       // reset checkmarks for Color ToolStripMenuItems
       private void ClearColor()
       {
          // clear all checkmarks
          blackToolStripMenuItem.Checked = false;
          blueToolStripMenuItem.Checked = false;
          redToolStripMenuItem.Checked = false;
          greenToolStripMenuItem.Checked = false;
       }

       // update Menu state and color display black
       private void blackToolStripMenuItem_Click(
          object sender, EventArgs e)
       {
          // reset checkmarks for Color ToolStripMenuItems
          ClearColor();

          // set color to Black
          displayLabel.ForeColor = Color.Black;
          blackToolStripMenuItem.Checked = true;
       }

       // update Menu state and color display blue
       private void blueToolStripMenuItem_Click(object sender, EventArgs e)
       {
          // reset checkmarks for Color ToolStripMenuItems
          ClearColor();

          // set color to Blue
          displayLabel.ForeColor = Color.Blue;
```

**Fig. 15.7** | Using menus to change text font and color. (Part 2 of 5.)

```
            blueToolStripMenuItem.Checked = true;
        }

        // update Menu state and color display red
        private void redToolStripMenuItem_Click(
            object sender, EventArgs e)
        {
            // reset checkmarks for Color ToolStripMenuItems
            ClearColor();

            // set color to Red
            displayLabel.ForeColor = Color.Red;
            redToolStripMenuItem.Checked = true;
        }

        // update Menu state and color display green
        private void greenToolStripMenuItem_Click(
            object sender, EventArgs e)
        {
            // reset checkmarks for Color ToolStripMenuItems
            ClearColor();

            // set color to Green
            displayLabel.ForeColor = Color.Green;
            greenToolStripMenuItem.Checked = true;
        }

        // reset checkmarks for Font ToolStripMenuItems
        private void ClearFont()
        {
            // clear all checkmarks
            timesToolStripMenuItem.Checked = false;
            courierToolStripMenuItem.Checked = false;
            comicToolStripMenuItem.Checked = false;
        }

        // update Menu state and set Font to Times New Roman
        private void timesToolStripMenuItem_Click(
            object sender, EventArgs e)
        {
            // reset checkmarks for Font ToolStripMenuItems
            ClearFont();

            // set Times New Roman font
            timesToolStripMenuItem.Checked = true;
            displayLabel.Font = new Font("Times New Roman", 14,
                displayLabel.Font.Style);
        }

```

**Fig. 15.7** | Using menus to change text font and color. (Part 3 of 5.)

```
      // update Menu state and set Font to Courier
      private void courierToolStripMenuItem_Click(
         object sender, EventArgs e)
      {
         // reset checkmarks for Font ToolStripMenuItems
         ClearFont();

         // set Courier font
         courierToolStripMenuItem.Checked = true;
         displayLabel.Font = new Font("Courier", 14,
            displayLabel.Font.Style);
      }

      // update Menu state and set Font to Comic Sans MS
      private void comicToolStripMenuItem_Click(
         object sender, EventArgs e)
      {
         // reset checkmarks for Font ToolStripMenuItems
         ClearFont();

         // set Comic Sans font
         comicToolStripMenuItem.Checked = true;
         displayLabel.Font = new Font("Comic Sans MS", 14,
            displayLabel.Font.Style);
      }

      // toggle checkmark and toggle bold style
      private void boldToolStripMenuItem_Click(object sender, EventArgs e)
      {
         // toggle checkmark
         boldToolStripMenuItem.Checked = !boldToolStripMenuItem.Checked;

         // use Xor to toggle bold, keep all other styles
         displayLabel.Font = new Font(displayLabel.Font,
            displayLabel.Font.Style ^ FontStyle.Bold);
      }

      // toggle checkmark and toggle italic style
      private void italicToolStripMenuItem_Click(
         object sender, EventArgs e)
      {
         // toggle checkmark
         italicToolStripMenuItem.Checked =
            !italicToolStripMenuItem.Checked;

         // use Xor to toggle italic, keep all other styles
         displayLabel.Font = new Font(displayLabel.Font,
            displayLabel.Font.Style ^ FontStyle.Italic);
      }
   }
}
```

**Fig. 15.7** | Using menus to change text font and color. (Part 4 of 5.)

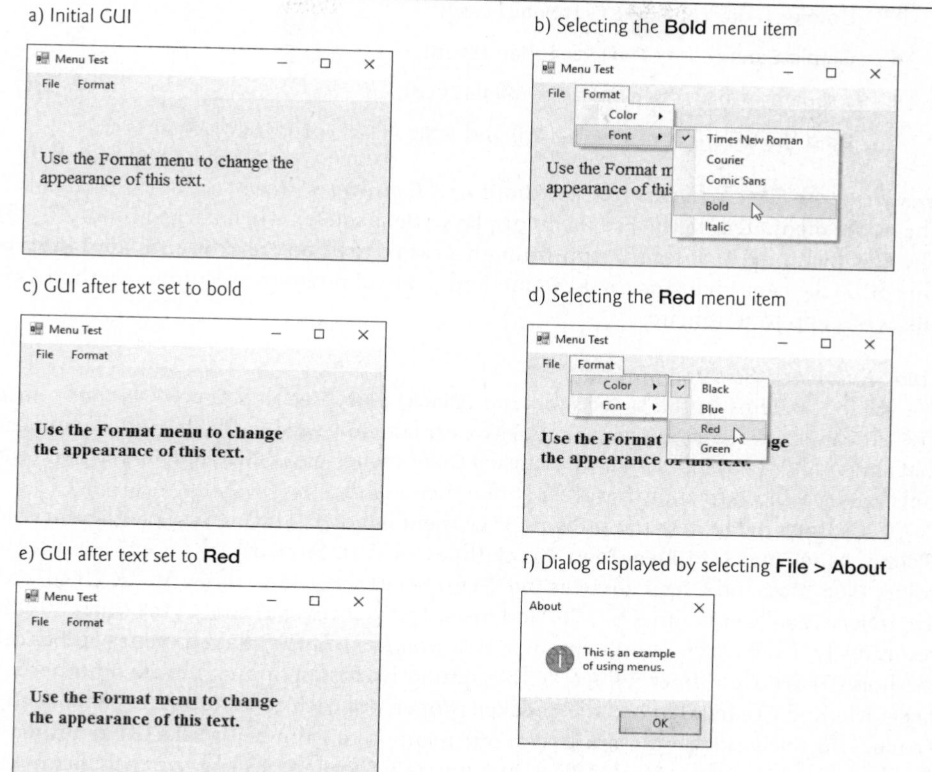


**Fig. 15.7** | Using menus to change text font and color. (Part 5 of 5.)

### *Create the GUI*

To create this GUI, begin by dragging the `MenuStrip` from the **ToolBox** onto the `Form`. Then use **Design** mode to create the menu structure shown in the sample outputs. The **File** menu (`fileToolStripMenuItem`) has menu items

- **About** (`aboutToolStripMenuItem`) and
- **Exit** (`exitToolStripMenuItem`).

The **Format** menu (`formatToolStripMenuItem`) has two submenus. The first submenu, **Color** (`colorToolStripMenuItem`), contains menu items

- **Black** (`blackToolStripMenuItem`),
- **Blue** (`blueToolStripMenuItem`),
- **Red** (`redToolStripMenuItem`) and
- **Green** (`greenToolStripMenuItem`).

The second submenu, **Font** (`fontToolStripMenuItem`), contains menu items

- **Times New Roman** (`timesToolStripMenuItem`),

- **Courier** (`courierToolStripMenuItem`),
- **Comic Sans** (`comicToolStripMenuItem`),
- a separator bar (`dashToolStripMenuItem`),
- **Bold** (`boldToolStripMenuItem`) and **Italic** (`italicToolStripMenuItem`).

### *Handling the* `Click` *Events for the* About *and* Exit *Menu Items*

The **About** menu item in the **File** menu displays a `MessageBox` when clicked (lines 20–25). The **Exit** menu item closes the app through `static` method **`Exit`** of class **`Application`** (line 30). Class `Application`'s `static` methods control program execution. Method `Exit` causes our app to terminate.

### Color *Submenu Events*

We made the items in the **Color** submenu (**Black**, **Blue**, **Red** and **Green**) *mutually exclusive*—the user can select *only one* at a time (we explain how we did this shortly). To indicate that a menu item is selected, we will set each **Color** menu item's **`Checked`** property to `true`. This causes a check to appear to the left of a menu item.

Each **Color** menu item has its own `Click` event handler. The method handler for color **Black** is `blackToolStripMenuItem_Click` (lines 44–53). Similarly, the event handlers for colors **Blue**, **Red** and **Green** are `blueToolStripMenuItem_Click` (lines 56–64), `redToolStripMenuItem_Click` (lines 67–76) and `greenToolStripMenuItem_Click` (lines 79–88), respectively. Each **Color** menu item must be *mutually exclusive*, so each event handler calls method `ClearColor` (lines 34–41) before setting its corresponding `Checked` property to `true`. Method `ClearColor` sets the `Checked` property of each color `ToolStripMenuItem` to `false`, effectively preventing more than one menu item from being selected at a time. In the designer, we initially set the **Black** menu item's `Checked` property to `true`, because at the start of the program, the text on the `Form` is black.

**Software Engineering Observation 15.1**

*The mutual exclusion of menu items is not enforced by the* `MenuStrip`*, even when the* `Checked` *property is* `true`*. You must program this behavior.*

### Font *Submenu Events*

The **Font** menu contains three menu items for fonts (**Courier**, **Times New Roman** and **Comic Sans**) and two menu items for font styles (**Bold** and **Italic**). We added a separator bar between the font and font-style menu items to indicate that these are separate options. A `Font` object can specify only one font at a time but can *set multiple styles at once* (e.g., a font can be both *bold* and italic). We set the font menu items to display checks. As with the **Color** menu, we must enforce mutual exclusion of these items in our event handlers.

Event handlers for font menu items **Times New Roman**, **Courier** and **Comic Sans** are `timesToolStripMenuItem_Click` (lines 100–110), `courierToolStripMenuItem_Click` (lines 113–123) and `comicToolStripMenuItem_Click` (lines 126–136), respectively. These event handlers are similar to those of the **Color** menu items. Each clears the `Checked` properties for all font menu items by calling method `ClearFont` (lines 91–97), then sets the `Checked` property of the menu item that raised the event to `true`. This enforces the mutual exclusion of the font menu items. In the designer, we initially set the **Times New Roman** menu item's `Checked` property to `true`, because this is the original font for the text on the

Form. The event handlers for the **Bold** and **Italic** menu items (lines 139–160) use the bitwise logical exclusive OR (^) operator to combine font styles, as we discussed in Chapter 14.

## 15.3 MonthCalendar Control

Many apps must perform date and time calculations. The .NET Framework provides two controls that allow an app to retrieve date and time information—MonthCalendar and DateTimePicker (Section 15.4).

The **MonthCalendar** (Fig. 15.8) control displays a monthly calendar on the Form. The user can select a date from the currently displayed month or can use the provided arrows to navigate to another month. When a date is selected, it is highlighted. Multiple dates can be selected by clicking dates on the calendar while holding down the *Shift* key. The default event for this control is the **DateChanged** event, which is generated when a new date is selected. Properties are provided that allow you to modify the appearance of the calendar, how many dates can be selected at once, and the minimum date and maximum date that may be selected. MonthCalendar properties and a common MonthCalendar event are summarized in Fig. 15.9.

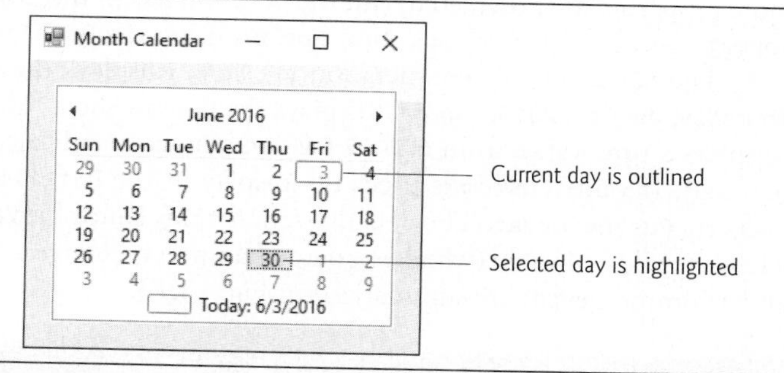


**Fig. 15.8** | MonthCalendar control.

| MonthCalendar properties and an event | Description |
|---|---|
| ***MonthCalendar Properties*** | |
| FirstDayOfWeek | Sets which day of the week is the first displayed for each week in the calendar. |
| MaxDate | The last date that can be selected. |
| MaxSelectionCount | The maximum number of dates that can be selected at once. |
| MinDate | The first date that can be selected. |
| MonthlyBoldedDates | An array of dates that will be displayed in bold in the calendar. |
| SelectionEnd | The last of the dates selected by the user. |
| SelectionRange | The dates selected by the user. |
| SelectionStart | The first of the dates selected by the user. |

**Fig. 15.9** | MonthCalendar properties and an event. (Part 1 of 2.)

| MonthCalendar properties and an event | Description |
|---|---|
| ***Common* MonthCalendar *Event*** | |
| DateChanged | Generated when a date is selected in the calendar. |

**Fig. 15.9** | MonthCalendar properties and an event. (Part 2 of 2.)

## 15.4 DateTimePicker Control

The **DateTimePicker** control (see output of Fig. 15.11) is similar to the MonthCalendar control but displays the calendar when a *down arrow* is selected. The DateTimePicker can be used to retrieve date and time information from the user. A DateTimePicker's **Value** property stores a DateTime object, which always contains both date and time information. You can retrieve the date information from the DateTime object by using property **Date**, and you can retrieve only the time information by using the **TimeOfDay** property.

The DateTimePicker is also more customizable than a MonthCalendar control—more properties are provided to edit the look and feel of the drop-down calendar. Property **Format** specifies the user's selection options using the **DateTimePickerFormat** enumeration. The values in this enumeration are Long (displays the date in long format, as in Thursday, July 10, 2013), Short (displays the date in short format, as in 7/10/2013), Time (displays a time value, as in 5:31:02 PM) and Custom (indicates that a custom format will be used). If value Custom is used, the display in the DateTimePicker is specified using property **CustomFormat**. The default event for this control is **ValueChanged**, which occurs when the selected value (whether a date or a time) is changed. DateTimePicker properties and a common event are summarized in Fig. 15.10.

| DateTimePicker properties and an event | Description |
|---|---|
| ***DateTimePicker Properties*** | |
| CalendarForeColor | Sets the text color for the calendar. |
| CalendarMonthBackground | Sets the calendar's background color. |
| CustomFormat | Sets the custom format string for the date and/or time displayed in the control. |
| Format | Sets the format of the date and/or time used for the date and/or time displayed in the control. |
| MaxDate | The maximum date and time that can be selected. |
| MinDate | The minimum date and time that can be selected. |
| ShowCheckBox | Indicates if a CheckBox should be displayed to the left of the selected date and time. |

**Fig. 15.10** | DateTimePicker properties and an event. (Part 1 of 2.)

| DateTimePicker properties and an event | Description |
|---|---|
| ShowUpDown | Indicates whether the control displays up and down Buttons. Helpful when the DateTimePicker is used to select a time—the Buttons can be used to increase or decrease hour, minute and second. |
| Value | The data selected by the user. |
| ***Common DateTimePicker Event*** | |
| ValueChanged | Generated when the Value property changes, including when the user selects a new date or time. |

**Fig. 15.10** | DateTimePicker properties and an event. (Part 2 of 2.)

Figure 15.11 demonstrates using a DateTimePicker to select an item's drop-off time. Many companies use such functionality—online retailers typically specify the day a package is sent out and the estimated time that it will arrive at your home. The user selects a drop-off day, then an estimated arrival date is displayed. The date is always two days after drop-off, three days if a Sunday is reached (mail is not delivered on Sunday).

```
// Fig. 15.11: DateTimePickerForm.cs
// Using a DateTimePicker to select a drop-off time.
using System;
using System.Windows.Forms;

namespace DateTimePickerTest
{
   // Form lets user select a drop-off date using a DateTimePicker
   // and displays an estimated delivery date
   public partial class DateTimePickerForm : Form
   {
      // constructor
      public DateTimePickerForm()
      {
         InitializeComponent();
      }

      private void dropOffDateTimePicker_ValueChanged(
         object sender, EventArgs e)
      {
         DateTime dropOffDate = dropOffDateTimePicker.Value;

         // add extra time when items are dropped off Sunday
         if (dropOffDate.DayOfWeek == DayOfWeek.Friday ||
            dropOffDate.DayOfWeek == DayOfWeek.Saturday ||
            dropOffDate.DayOfWeek == DayOfWeek.Sunday)
         {
```

**Fig. 15.11** | Using a DateTimePicker to select a drop-off time. (Part 1 of 2.)

```
28             //estimate three days for delivery
29             outputLabel.Text = dropOffDate.AddDays(3).ToLongDateString();
30          }
31          else
32          {
33             // otherwise estimate only two days for delivery
34             outputLabel.Text = dropOffDate.AddDays(2).ToLongDateString();
35          }
36       }
37
38       private void DateTimePickerForm_Load(object sender, EventArgs e)
39       {
40          // user cannot select days before today
41          dropOffDateTimePicker.MinDate = DateTime.Today;
42
43          // user can only select days up to one year in the future
44          dropOffDateTimePicker.MaxDate = DateTime.Today.AddYears(1);
45       }
46    }
47 }
```

a) GUI when app first executes shows current date

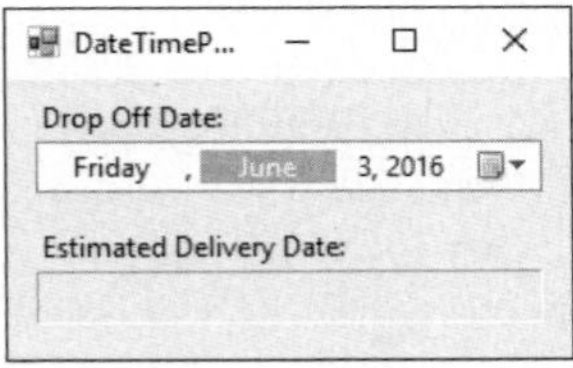


b) Selecting a drop-off date

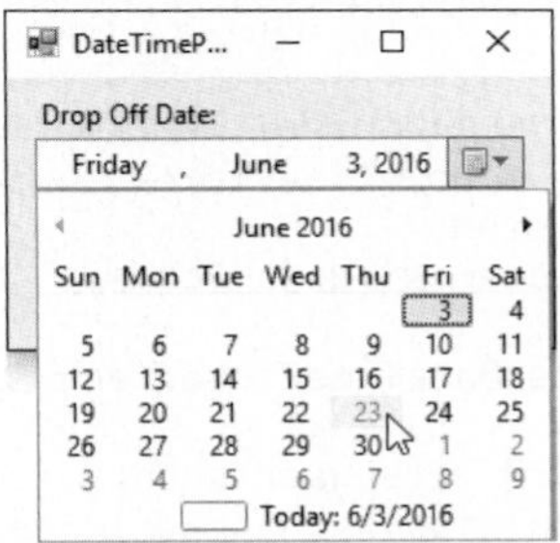


c) GUI after selecting drop-off date

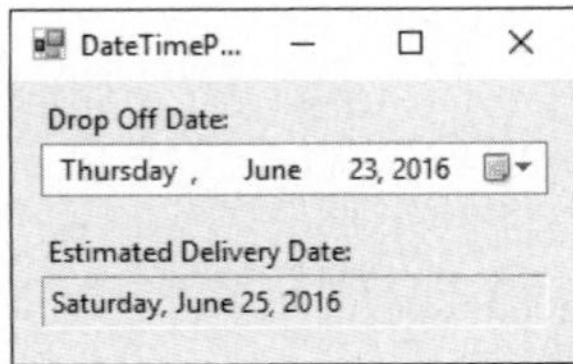


d) GUI showing current and selected dates

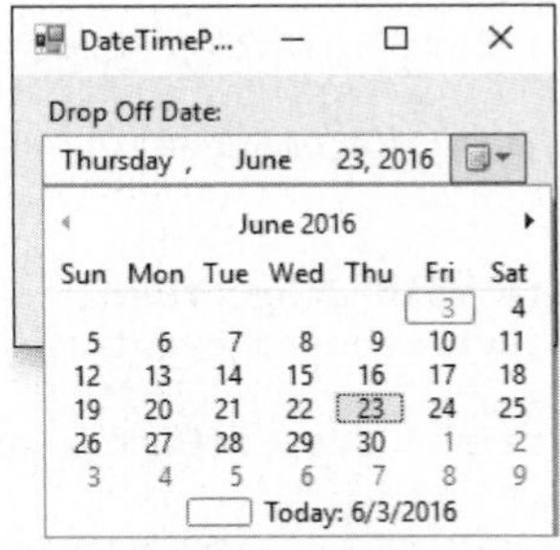


**Fig. 15.11** | Using a `DateTimePicker` to select a drop-off time. (Part 2 of 2.)

The `DateTimePicker` (`dropOffDateTimePicker`) has its `Format` property set to `Long`, so the user can select just a date in this app. When the user selects a date, the `ValueChanged` event occurs. The event handler for this event (lines 18–36) first retrieves the selected date from the `DateTimePicker`'s `Value` property (line 21). Lines 24–26 use the `DateTime` structure's **DayOfWeek** property to determine the day of the week on which the selected date falls. The day values are represented using the **DayOfWeek** enumeration. Lines 29 and 34 use DateTime's **AddDays** method to increase the date by three days or two days, respectively. The resulting date is then displayed in Long format using method **ToLongDateString**.

In this app, we do not want the user to be able to select a drop-off day before the current day, or one that's more than a year into the future. To enforce this, we set the DateTimePicker's **MinDate** and **MaxDate** properties when the Form is loaded (lines 41 and 44). Property Today returns the current day, and method **AddYears** (with an argument of 1) is used to specify a date one year in the future.

Let's take a closer look at the output. This app begins by displaying the current date (Fig. 15.11(a)). In Fig. 15.11(b), we selected the 23rd of June. In Fig. 15.11(c), the estimated arrival date is displayed as the 25th of June. Figure 15.11(d) shows that the 23rd, after it is selected, is highlighted in the calendar.

## 15.5 LinkLabel Control

The **LinkLabel** control displays *links* to other resources, such as files or web pages (Fig. 15.12). A LinkLabel appears as underlined text (colored blue by default). When the mouse moves over the link, the pointer changes to a hand; this is similar to the behavior of a hyperlink in a web page. The link can change color to indicate whether it is not yet visited, previously visited or active (the mouse is over the link and a button is pressed). When clicked, the LinkLabel generates a **LinkClicked** event (see Fig. 15.13). Class LinkLabel is derived from class Label and therefore inherits all of class Label's functionality.

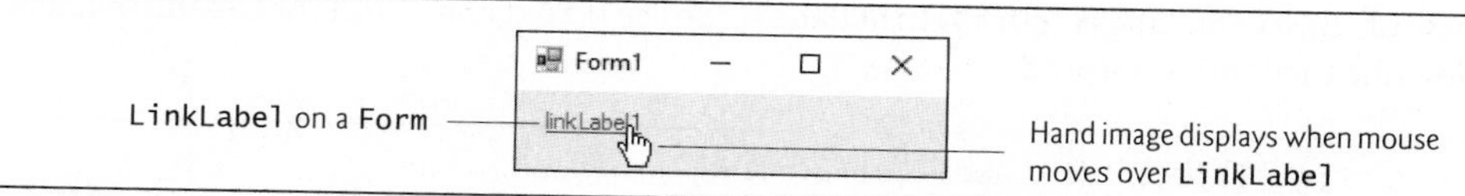


**Fig. 15.12** | LinkLabel control in running program.

**Look-and-Feel Observation 15.3**

*A LinkLabel is the preferred control for indicating that the user can click a link to jump to a resource such as a web page, though other controls can perform similar tasks.*

| LinkLabel properties and an event | Description |
|---|---|
| *Common Properties* | |
| ActiveLinkColor | Specifies the color of the active link when the user is in the process of clicking the link. The default color (typically red) is set by the system. |
| LinkArea | Specifies which portion of text in the LinkLabel is part of the link. |

**Fig. 15.13** | LinkLabel properties and an event. (Part 1 of 2.)

| `LinkLabel` properties and an event | Description |
|---|---|
| `LinkBehavior` | Specifies the link's behavior, such as how the link appears when the mouse is placed over it. |
| `LinkColor` | Specifies the original color of the link before it's been visited. The default color (typically blue) is set by the system. |
| `LinkVisited` | If `true`, the link appears as though it has been visited (its color is changed to that specified by property `VisitedLinkColor`). The default value is `false`. |
| `Text` | Specifies the control's text. |
| `UseMnemonic` | If `true`, the `&` character in the `Text` property acts as a shortcut (similar to the *Alt* shortcut in menus). |
| `VisitedLinkColor` | Specifies the color of a visited link. The default color (typically purple) is set by the system. |
| ***Common Event (Event arguments `LinkLabelLinkClickedEventArgs`)*** | |
| `LinkClicked` | Generated when the link is clicked. This is the default event when the control is double clicked in **Design** mode. |

**Fig. 15.13** | `LinkLabel` properties and an event. (Part 2 of 2.)

Class `LinkLabelTestForm` (Fig. 15.14) uses three `LinkLabel`s to link to the `C:` drive, the Deitel website (`www.deitel.com`) and the Notepad app, respectively. The `Text` properties of the `LinkLabel`s `cDriveLinkLabel`, `deitelLinkLabel` and `notepadLinkLabel` describe each link's purpose.

```
// Fig. 15.14: LinkLabelTestForm.cs
// Using LinkLabels to create hyperlinks.
using System;
using System.Windows.Forms;

namespace LinkLabelTest
{
   // Form using LinkLabels to browse the C:\ drive,
   // load a web page and run Notepad
   public partial class LinkLabelTestForm : Form
   {
      // constructor
      public LinkLabelTestForm()
      {
         InitializeComponent();
      }

      // browse C:\ drive
      private void cDriveLinkLabel_LinkClicked(object sender,
         LinkLabelLinkClickedEventArgs e)
      {
```

**Fig. 15.14** | Using `LinkLabel`s to create hyperlinks. (Part 1 of 3.)

```
            // change LinkColor after it has been clicked
            cDriveLinkLabel.LinkVisited = true;

            System.Diagnostics.Process.Start(@"C:\");
        }

        // load www.deitel.com in web browser
        private void deitelLinkLabel_LinkClicked(object sender,
            LinkLabelLinkClickedEventArgs e)
        {
            // change LinkColor after it has been clicked
            deitelLinkLabel.LinkVisited = true;

            System.Diagnostics.Process.Start("http://www.deitel.com");
        }

        // run app Notepad
        private void notepadLinkLabel_LinkClicked(object sender,
            LinkLabelLinkClickedEventArgs e)
        {
            // change LinkColor after it has been clicked
            notepadLinkLabel.LinkVisited = true;

            // program called as if in run
            // menu and full path not needed
            System.Diagnostics.Process.Start("notepad");
        }
    }
}
```

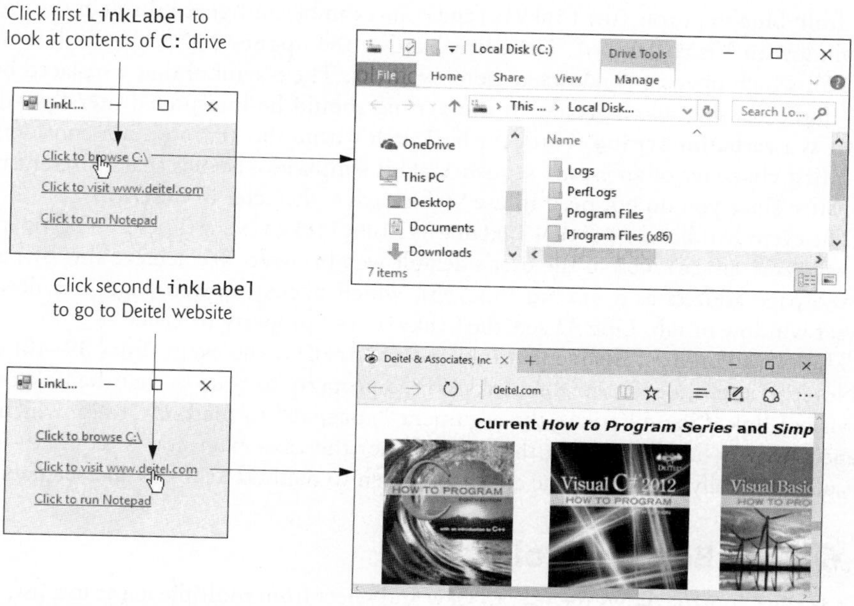

Click first `LinkLabel` to look at contents of `C:` drive

Click second `LinkLabel` to go to Deitel website

**Fig. 15.14** | Using `LinkLabel`s to create hyperlinks. (Part 2 of 3.)

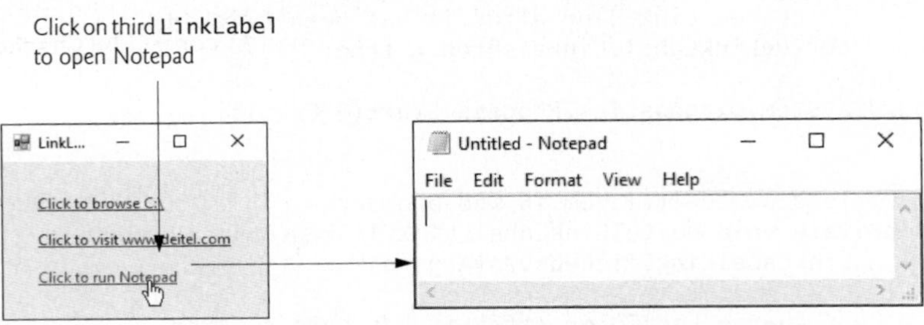


**Fig. 15.14** | Using `LinkLabel`s to create hyperlinks. (Part 3 of 3.)

The event handlers for the `LinkLabel`s call method **`Start`** of class **`Process`** (namespace **`System.Diagnostics`**), which allows you to execute other programs, or load documents or web sites from an app. Method `Start` can take one argument, the file to open, or two arguments, the app to run and its command-line arguments. Method `Start`'s arguments can be in the same form as if they were provided for input to the Windows **Run** command (**Start > Run...**). For apps that are known to Windows, full path names are not needed, and the file extension often can be omitted. To open a file of a type that Windows recognizes (and knows how to handle), simply use the file's full path name. For example, if you a pass the method a `.docx` file, Windows will open it in Microsoft Word (or whatever program is registered to open `.docx` files, if any). The Windows operating system must be able to use the app associated with the given file's extension to open the file.

The event handler for `cDriveLinkLabel`'s `LinkClicked` event browses the `C:` drive (lines 19–26). Line 23 sets the `LinkVisited` property to `true`, which changes the link's color from blue to purple (the `LinkVisited` colors can be configured through the **Properties** window in Visual Studio). The event handler then passes `@"C:\"` to method `Start` (line 25), which opens a **Windows Explorer** window. The `@` symbol that we placed before `"C:\"` indicates that all characters in the `string` should be interpreted literally—this is known as a **verbatim `string`**. Thus, the backslash within the `string` is not considered to be the first character of an escape sequence. This simplifies `string`s that represent directory paths, since you do not need to use \\ for each \ character in the path.

The event handler for `deitelLinkLabel`'s `LinkClicked` event (lines 29–36) opens the web page `www.deitel.com` in the user's default web browser. We achieve this by passing the web-page address as a `string` (line 35), which opens the web page in a new web browser window or tab. Line 33 sets the `LinkVisited` property to `true`.

The event handler for `notepadLinkLabel`'s `LinkClicked` event (lines 39–48) opens the Notepad app. Line 43 sets the `LinkVisited` property to `true` so that the link appears as a visited link. Line 47 passes the argument `"notepad"` to method `Start`, which runs `notepad.exe`. In line 47, neither the full path nor the `.exe` extension is required—Windows automatically recognizes the argument given to method `Start` as an executable file.

## 15.6 ListBox Control

The **`ListBox`** control allows the user to view and select from multiple items in a list. `ListBox`es are static GUI entities, which means that users cannot directly edit the list of items.

The user can be provided with `TextBoxes` and `Buttons` with which to specify items to be added to the list, but the actual additions must be performed in code. The **`CheckedListBox`** control (Section 15.7) extends a `ListBox` by including `CheckBoxes` next to each item in the list. This allows users to place checks on multiple items at once, as is possible with `CheckBox` controls. (Users also can select multiple items from a `ListBox` by setting the `ListBox`'s **`SelectionMode`** property, which is discussed shortly.) Figure 15.15 displays a `ListBox` and a `CheckedListBox`. In both controls, scrollbars appear if the number of items exceeds the `ListBox`'s viewable area.

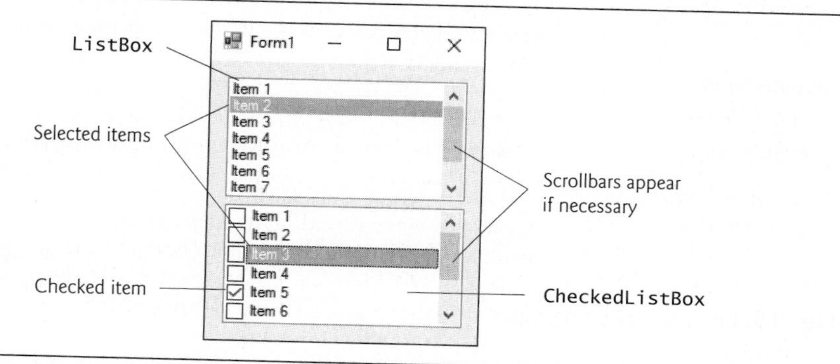


**Fig. 15.15** | `ListBox` and `CheckedListBox` on a `Form`.

Figure 15.16 lists common `ListBox` properties and methods and a common event. The `SelectionMode` property determines the number of items that can be selected. This property has the possible values `None`, `One`, `MultiSimple` and `MultiExtended` (from the **`SelectionMode`** enumeration)—the differences among these settings are explained in Fig. 15.16. The **`SelectedIndexChanged`** event occurs when the user selects a new item.

| `ListBox` properties, methods and an event | Description |
|---|---|
| ***Common Properties*** | |
| `Items` | The collection of items in the `ListBox`. |
| `MultiColumn` | Indicates whether the `ListBox` can display multiple columns. Multiple columns eliminate vertical scrollbars from the display. |
| `SelectedIndex` | Returns the index of the selected item. If no items have been selected, the property returns `-1`. If the user selects multiple items, this property returns only one of the selected indices. If multiple items are selected, use property `SelectedIndices`. |
| `SelectedIndices` | Returns a collection containing the indices for all selected items. |
| `SelectedItem` | Returns a reference to the selected item. If multiple items are selected, it can return any of the selected items. |
| `SelectedItems` | Returns a collection of the selected item(s). |

**Fig. 15.16** | `ListBox` properties, methods and an event. (Part 1 of 2.)

| ListBox properties, methods and an event | Description |
|---|---|
| SelectionMode | Determines the number of items that can be selected and the means through which multiple items can be selected. Values are None, One (the default), MultiSimple (multiple selection allowed) or MultiExtended (multiple selection allowed using a combination of arrow keys or mouse clicks and *Shift* and *Ctrl* keys). |
| Sorted | Indicates whether items are sorted *alphabetically*. Setting this property's value to true sorts the items. The default value is false. |
| ***Common Methods*** | |
| ClearSelected | Deselects every item. |
| GetSelected | Returns true if the item at the specified index is selected. |
| ***Common Event*** | |
| SelectedIndexChanged | Generated when the selected index changes. This is the default event when the control is double clicked in the designer. |

**Fig. 15.16** | ListBox properties, methods and an event. (Part 2 of 2.)

Both the ListBox and CheckedListBox have properties Items, SelectedItem and SelectedIndex. Property **Items** returns a collection of the list items. *Collections* are a common way to manage lists of objects in the .NET framework. Many .NET GUI components (e.g., ListBoxes) use collections to expose lists of internal objects (e.g., items in a ListBox). We discuss collections further in Chapter 19. The collection returned by property Items is represented as an object of type ListBox.ObjectCollection. Property **SelectedItem** returns the ListBox's currently selected item. If the user can select multiple items, use collection **SelectedItems** to return all the selected items as a ListBox.SelectedObjectColection. Property **SelectedIndex** returns the index of the selected item—if there could be more than one, use property **SelectedIndices**, which returns a ListBox.SelectedIndexCollection. If no items are selected, property SelectedIndex returns -1. Method **GetSelected** takes an index and returns true if the corresponding item is selected.

### *Adding Items to **ListBoxes** and **CheckedListBoxes***

To add items to a ListBox or to a CheckedListBox, we must add objects to its Items collection. This can be accomplished by calling method Add to add a string to the ListBox's or CheckedListBox's Items collection. For example, we could write

```
myListBox.Items.Add(myListItem);
```

to add string *myListItem* to ListBox *myListBox*. To add multiple objects, you can either call method Add multiple times or call method AddRange to add an array of objects. Classes ListBox and CheckedListBox each call the submitted object's ToString method to determine the Label for the corresponding object's entry in the list. This allows you to add different objects to a ListBox or a CheckedListBox that later can be returned through properties SelectedItem and SelectedItems.

Alternatively, you can add items to `ListBoxes` and `CheckedListBoxes` visually by examining the `Items` property in the **Properties** window. Clicking the ellipsis button opens the **String Collection Editor**, which contains a text area for adding items; each item appears on a separate line (Fig. 15.17). Visual Studio then writes code to add these `strings` to the `Items` collection inside method `InitializeComponent`.

String Collection Editor

Enter the strings in the collection (one per line):

Item 1
Item 2
Item 3
Item 4
Item 5
Item 6

OK Cancel

**Fig. 15.17** | **String Collection Editor**.

Figure 15.18 uses class `ListBoxTestForm` to add, remove and clear items from `ListBox displayListBox`. Class `ListBoxTestForm` uses `TextBox inputTextBox` to allow the user to type in a new item. When the user clicks the **Add** `Button`, the new item appears in `displayListBox`. Similarly, if the user selects an item and clicks **Remove**, the item is deleted. When clicked, **Clear** deletes all entries in `displayListBox`. The user terminates the app by clicking **Exit**.

The `addButton_Click` event handler (lines 20–24) calls method `Add` of the `Items` collection in the `ListBox`. This method takes a `string` as the item to add to `displayListBox`. In this case, the `string` used is the user input from the `inputTextBox` (line 22). After the item is added, `inputTextBox.Text` is cleared (line 23).

The `removeButton_Click` event handler (lines 27–34) uses method `RemoveAt` to remove an item from the `ListBox`. Event handler `removeButton_Click` first uses property `SelectedIndex` to determine which index is selected. If `SelectedIndex` is not `-1` (i.e., an item is selected), line 32 removes the item that corresponds to the selected index.

```
 1  // Fig. 15.18: ListBoxTestForm.cs
 2  // Program to add, remove and clear ListBox items
 3  using System;
 4  using System.Windows.Forms;
 5
 6  namespace ListBoxTest
 7  {
 8     // Form uses a TextBox and Buttons to add,
 9     // remove, and clear ListBox items
10     public partial class ListBoxTestForm : Form
11     {
12        // constructor
13        public ListBoxTestForm()
14        {
```

**Fig. 15.18** | Program to add, remove and clear `ListBox` items. (Part 1 of 3.)

```
         InitializeComponent();
      }

      // add new item to ListBox (text from input TextBox)
      // and clear input TextBox
      private void addButton_Click(object sender, EventArgs e)
      {
         displayListBox.Items.Add(inputTextBox.Text);
         inputTextBox.Clear();
      }

      // remove item if one is selected
      private void removeButton_Click(object sender, EventArgs e)
      {
         // check whether item is selected; if so, remove
         if (displayListBox.SelectedIndex != -1)
         {
            displayListBox.Items.RemoveAt(displayListBox.SelectedIndex);
         }
      }

      // clear all items in ListBox
      private void clearButton_Click(object sender, EventArgs e)
      {
         displayListBox.Items.Clear();
      }

      // exit app
      private void exitButton_Click(object sender, EventArgs e)
      {
         Application.Exit();
      }
   }
}
```

a) GUI after adding **Dog**, **Cat** and **Chicken** and before adding **Cow**

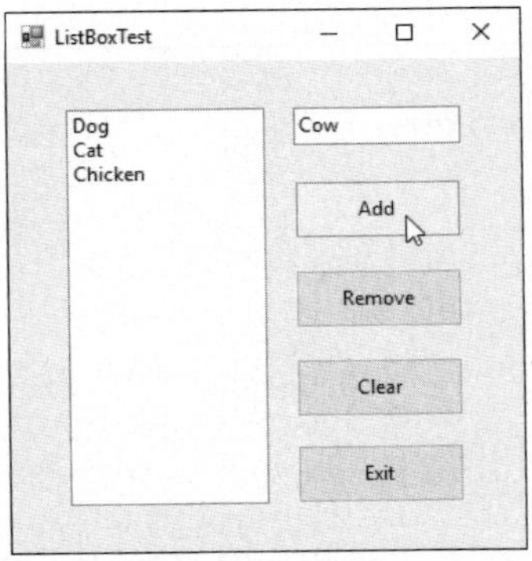

b) GUI after adding **Cow** and before deleting **Chicken**

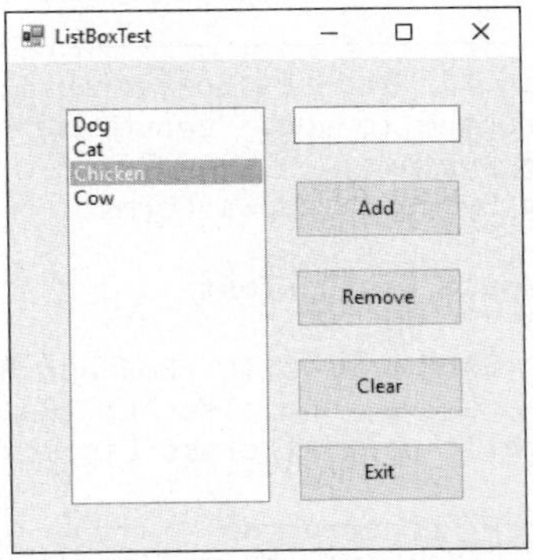

**Fig. 15.18** | Program to add, remove and clear `ListBox` items. (Part 2 of 3.)

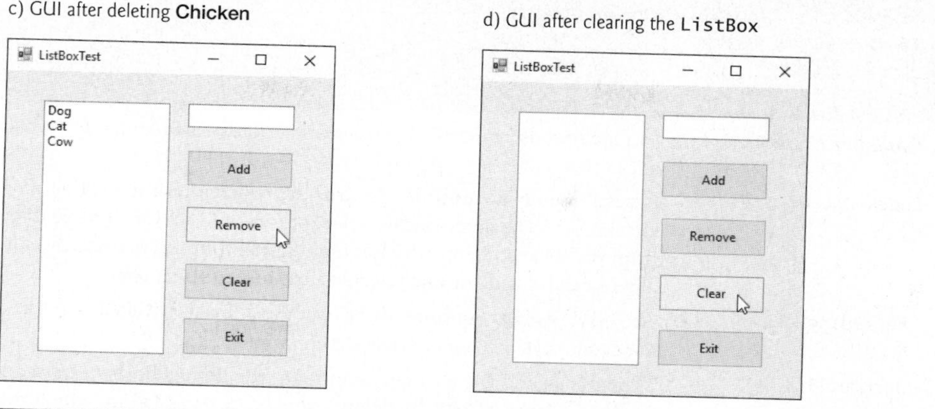


**Fig. 15.18** | Program to add, remove and clear `ListBox` items. (Part 3 of 3.)

The `clearButton_Click` event handler (lines 37–40) calls method `Clear` of the `Items` collection (line 39). This removes all the entries in `displayListBox`. Finally, event handler `exitButton_Click` (lines 43–46) terminates the app by calling method `Application.Exit` (line 45).

## 15.7 CheckedListBox Control

The `CheckedListBox` control derives from `ListBox` and displays a `CheckBox` with each item. Items can be added via methods `Add` and `AddRange` or through the **String Collection Editor**. `CheckedListBoxes` allow multiple items to be checked, but item selection is more restrictive. The only values for the `SelectionMode` property are `None` and `One`. `One` allows a single selection, whereas `None` allows no selections. Because an item must be selected to be checked, you must set the `SelectionMode` to be `One` if you wish to allow users to check items. Thus, toggling property `SelectionMode` between `One` and `None` effectively switches between enabling and disabling the user's ability to check list items. Common properties, a method and an event of `CheckedListBoxes` appear in Fig. 15.19.

**Common Programming Error 15.1**

*The IDE displays an error message if you attempt to set the `SelectionMode` property to `MultiSimple` or `MultiExtended` in the **Properties** window of a `CheckedListBox`. If this value is set programmatically, a runtime error occurs.*

Event **`ItemCheck`** occurs whenever a user checks or unchecks a `CheckedListBox` item. Event-argument properties `CurrentValue` and `NewValue` return `CheckState` values for the current and new state of the item, respectively. A comparison of these values allows you to determine whether the `CheckedListBox` item was checked or unchecked. The `CheckedListBox` control retains the `SelectedItems` and `SelectedIndices` properties (it inherits them from class `ListBox`). However, it also includes properties `CheckedItems` and `CheckedIndices`, which return information about the checked items and indices.

| CheckedListBox properties, a method and an event | Description |
|---|---|
| ***Common Properties*** | *(All the* `ListBox` *properties, methods and events are inherited by* `CheckedListBox`*.)* |
| `CheckedItems` | Accessible only at runtime. Returns the collection of items that are checked as a `CheckedListBox.CheckedItemCollection`. This is distinct from the selected item, which is highlighted (but not necessarily checked). There can be at most one selected item at any given time. |
| `CheckedIndices` | Accessible only at runtime. Returns indices for all checked items as a `CheckedListBox.CheckedIndexCollection`. |
| `CheckOnClick` | When `true` and the user clicks an item, the item is both selected and checked or unchecked. By default, this property is `false`, which means that the user must select an item, then click it again to check or uncheck it. |
| `SelectionMode` | Determines whether items can be selected and checked. The possible values are `One` (the default; allows multiple checks to be placed) or `None` (does not allow any checks to be placed). |
| ***Common Method*** | |
| `GetItemChecked` | Takes an index and returns `true` if the corresponding item is checked. |
| ***Common Event (Event arguments*** **`ItemCheckEventArgs`*****)*** | |
| `ItemCheck` | Generated when an item is checked or unchecked. |
| **`ItemCheckEventArgs`** ***Properties*** | |
| `CurrentValue` | Indicates whether the current item is checked or unchecked. Possible values are `Checked`, `Unchecked` and `Indeterminate`. |
| `Index` | Returns the zero-based index of the item that changed. |
| `NewValue` | Specifies the new state of the item. |

**Fig. 15.19** | `CheckedListBox` properties, a method and an event.

In Fig. 15.20, class `CheckedListBoxTestForm` uses a `CheckedListBox` and a `ListBox` to display a user's selection of books. The `CheckedListBox` allows the user to select multiple titles. In the **String Collection Editor**, items were added for some Deitel books: C, C++, Java, Internet & WWW, Visual Basic, Visual C++ and Visual C# (the abbreviation HTP stands for "How to Program"). The `ListBox` (named `displayListBox`) displays the user's selection. In the screenshots accompanying this example, the `CheckedListBox` appears to the left, the `ListBox` on the right.

```
// Fig. 15.20: CheckedListBoxTestForm.cs
// Using a CheckedListBox to add items to a display ListBox

using System.Windows.Forms;
```

**Fig. 15.20** | Using a `CheckedListBox` to add items to a display `ListBox`. (Part 1 of 2.)

```
5
6   namespace CheckedListBoxTest
7   {
8      // Form uses a checked ListBox to add items to a display ListBox
9      public partial class CheckedListBoxTestForm : Form
10     {
11        // constructor
12        public CheckedListBoxTestForm()
13        {
14           InitializeComponent();
15        }
16
17        // item checked or unchecked
18        // add or remove from display ListBox
19        private void itemCheckedListBox_ItemCheck(
20           object sender, ItemCheckEventArgs e)
21        {
22           // obtain reference of selected item
23           string item = itemCheckedListBox.SelectedItem.ToString();
24
25           // if item checked, add to ListBox
26           // otherwise remove from ListBox
27           if (e.NewValue == CheckState.Checked)
28           {
29              displayListBox.Items.Add(item);
30           }
31           else
32           {
33              displayListBox.Items.Remove(item);
34           }
35        }
36     }
37  }
```

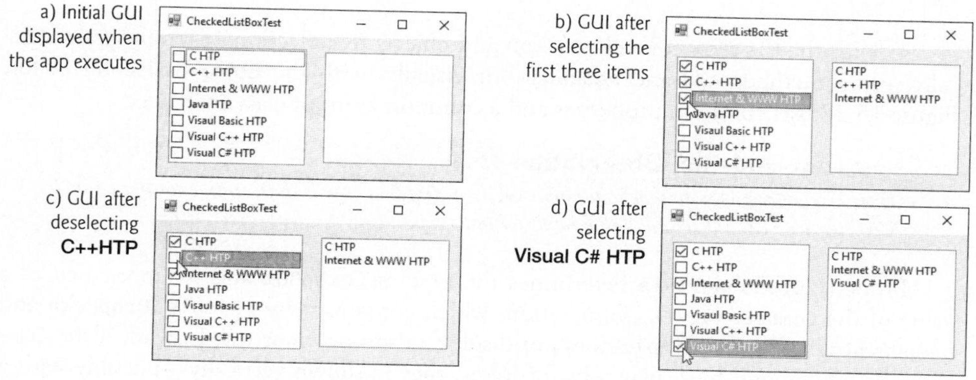

a) Initial GUI displayed when the app executes

b) GUI after selecting the first three items

c) GUI after deselecting **C++HTP**

d) GUI after selecting **Visual C# HTP**

**Fig. 15.20** | Using a `CheckedListBox` to add items to a display `ListBox`. (Part 2 of 2.)

When the user checks or unchecks an item in `itemCheckedListBox`, an `ItemCheck` event occurs and event handler `itemCheckedListBox_ItemCheck` (lines 19–35) executes. An `if...else` statement (lines 27–34) determines whether the user checked or unchecked an item in the CheckedListBox. Line 27 uses the NewValue property to determine whether the item is being checked (CheckState.Checked). If the user checks an item, line 29 adds the checked entry to the ListBox displayListBox. If the user unchecks an item, line 33 removes the corresponding item from displayListBox. This event handler was created by selecting the CheckedListBox in **Design** mode, viewing the control's events in the **Properties** window and double clicking the ItemCheck event. The default event for a CheckedListBox is a SelectedIndexChanged event.

## 15.8 ComboBox Control

The **ComboBox** control combines TextBox features with a **drop-down list**—a GUI component that contains a list from which a value can be selected. A ComboBox usually appears as a TextBox with a down arrow to its right. By default, the user can enter text into the TextBox or click the down arrow to display a list of predefined items. If a user chooses an element from this list, that element is displayed in the TextBox. If the list contains more elements than can be displayed in the drop-down list, a *scrollbar* appears. The maximum number of items that a drop-down list can display at one time is set by property **MaxDropDownItems**. Figure 15.21 shows a sample ComboBox in three different states.

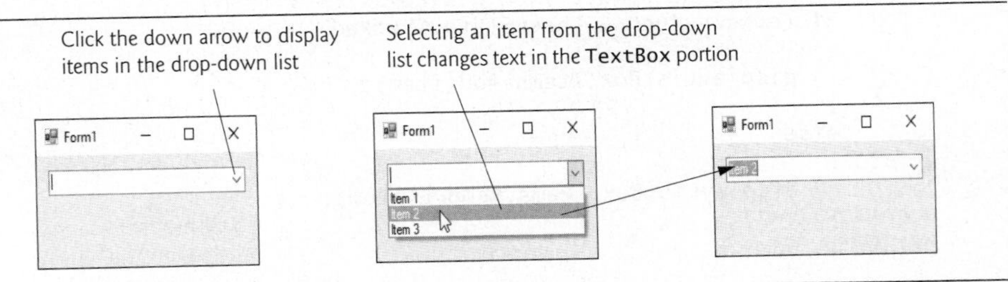


**Fig. 15.21** | ComboBox demonstration.

As with the ListBox control, you can add objects to collection Items programmatically, using methods Add and AddRange, or visually, with the **String Collection Editor**. Figure 15.22 lists common properties and a common event of class ComboBox.

**Look-and-Feel Observation 15.4**

*Use a* ComboBox *to save space on a GUI. A disadvantage is that, unlike with a* ListBox, *the user cannot see available items without expanding the drop-down list.*

Property **DropDownStyle** determines the type of ComboBox and is represented as a value of the **ComboBoxStyle** enumeration, which contains values Simple, DropDown and DropDownList. Option Simple does not display a drop-down arrow. Instead, if the ComboBox is tall enough to display a list of items, they're shown vertically—possibly with a scrollbar to allow the user to view items that cannot fit in the display area. The user also can type in a selection. Style DropDown (the default) displays a drop-down list when the down arrow is clicked (or the down arrow key is pressed). The user can type a new item in the ComboBox. The last style is DropDownList, which displays a drop-down list but does not allow the user to type in the TextBox.

| ComboBox properties and an event | Description |
|---|---|
| ***Common Properties*** | |
| `DropDownStyle` | Determines the type of `ComboBox`. Value `Simple` means that the text portion is editable and the list portion is always visible. Value `DropDown` (the default) means that the text portion is editable but the user must click an arrow button to see the list portion. Value `DropDownList` means that the text portion is not editable and the user must click the arrow button to see the list portion. |
| `Items` | The collection of items in the `ComboBox` control. |
| `MaxDropDownItems` | Specifies the maximum number of items (between `1` and `100`) that the drop-down list can display. If the number of items exceeds the maximum number of items to display, a scrollbar appears. |
| `SelectedIndex` | Returns the index of the selected item, or `-1` if none are selected. |
| `SelectedItem` | Returns a reference to the selected item. |
| `Sorted` | Indicates whether items are sorted alphabetically. Setting this property's value to `true` sorts the items. The default is `false`. |
| ***Common Event*** | |
| `SelectedIndexChanged` | Generated when the selected index changes (such as when a different item is selected). This is the default event when control is double clicked in the designer. |

**Fig. 15.22** | ComboBox properties and an event.

The `ComboBox` control has properties **`Items`** (a collection), **`SelectedItem`** and **`SelectedIndex`**, which are similar to the corresponding properties in `ListBox`. There can be at most one selected item in a `ComboBox`. If no items are selected, then `SelectedIndex` is `-1`. When the selected item changes, a **`SelectedIndexChanged`** event occurs.

Class `ComboBoxTestForm` (Fig. 15.23) allows users to select a shape to draw—circle, ellipse, square or pie (in both filled and unfilled versions)—by using a `ComboBox`. The `ComboBox` in this example is uneditable, so the user cannot type in the `TextBox`.

**Look-and-Feel Observation 15.5**

*Make lists (such as `ComboBoxes`) editable only if the app is designed to accept user-submitted elements. Otherwise, the user might try to enter a custom item that's improper for the purposes of your app.*

```
// Fig. 15.23: ComboBoxTestForm.cs
// Using ComboBox to select a shape to draw.
using System;
using System.Drawing;
using System.Windows.Forms;
```

**Fig. 15.23** | Using `ComboBox` to select a shape to draw. (Part 1 of 3.)

```

namespace ComboBoxTest
{
   // Form uses a ComboBox to select different shapes to draw
   public partial class ComboBoxTestForm : Form
   {
      // constructor
      public ComboBoxTestForm()
      {
         InitializeComponent();
      }

      // get index of selected shape, draw shape
      private void imageComboBox_SelectedIndexChanged(
         object sender, EventArgs e)
      {
         // create graphics object, Pen and SolidBrush
         using (Graphics myGraphics = base.CreateGraphics())

         // create Pen using color DarkRed
         using (Pen myPen = new Pen(Color.DarkRed))

         // create SolidBrush using color DarkRed
         using (SolidBrush mySolidBrush = new SolidBrush(Color.DarkRed))
         {
            // clear drawing area, setting it to color white
            myGraphics.Clear(Color.White);

            // find index, draw proper shape
            switch (imageComboBox.SelectedIndex)
            {
               case 0: // case Circle is selected
                  myGraphics.DrawEllipse(myPen, 50, 50, 150, 150);
                  break;
               case 1: // case Rectangle is selected
                  myGraphics.DrawRectangle(myPen, 50, 50, 150, 150);
                  break;
               case 2: // case Ellipse is selected
                  myGraphics.DrawEllipse(myPen, 50, 85, 150, 115);
                  break;
               case 3: // case Pie is selected
                  myGraphics.DrawPie(myPen, 50, 50, 150, 150, 0, 45);
                  break;
               case 4: // case Filled Circle is selected
                  myGraphics.FillEllipse(mySolidBrush, 50, 50, 150, 150);
                  break;
               case 5: // case Filled Rectangle is selected
                  myGraphics.FillRectangle(
                     mySolidBrush, 50, 50, 150, 150);
                  break;
               case 6: // case Filled Ellipse is selected
                  myGraphics.FillEllipse(mySolidBrush, 50, 85, 150, 115);
                  break;
```

**Fig. 15.23** | Using ComboBox to select a shape to draw. (Part 2 of 3.)

```
59                  case 7: // case Filled Pie is selected
60                     myGraphics.FillPie(
61                        mySolidBrush, 50, 50, 150, 150, 0, 45);
62                     break;
63               }
64            }
65         }
66      }
67   }
```

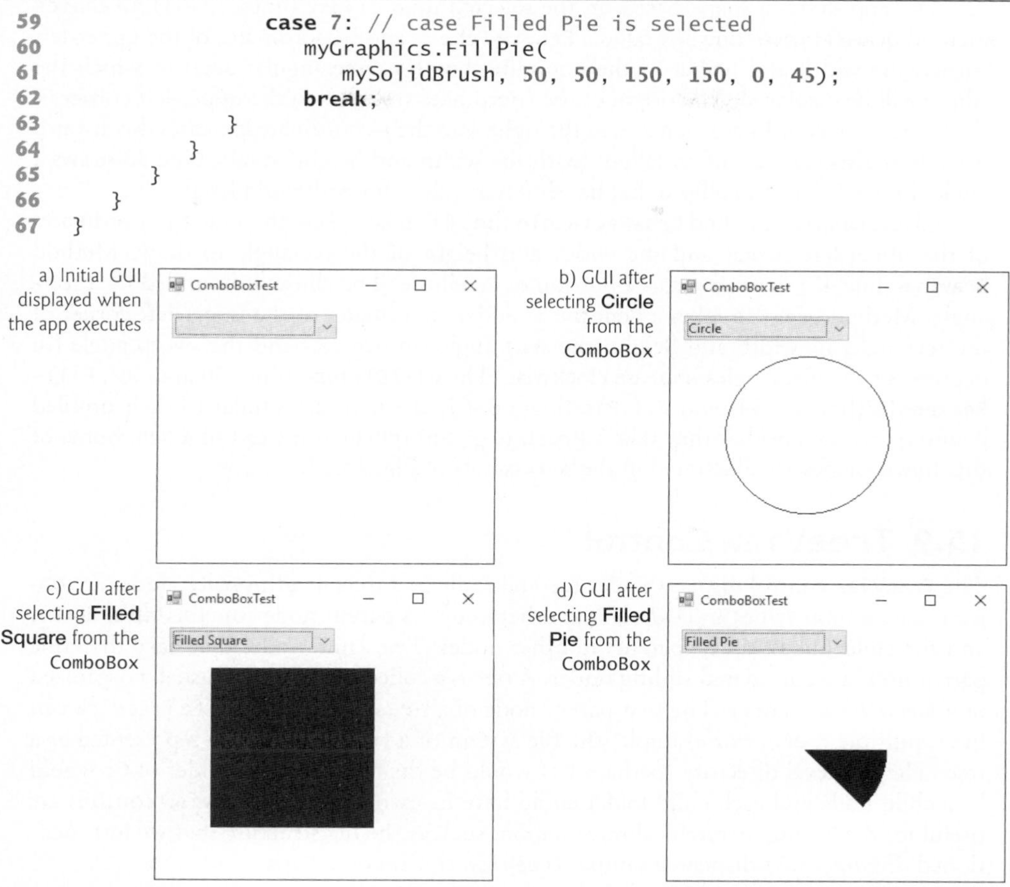

a) Initial GUI displayed when the app executes
ComboBoxTest
b) GUI after selecting **Circle** from the ComboBox
ComboBoxTest
Circle
c) GUI after selecting **Filled Square** from the ComboBox
ComboBoxTest
Filled Square
d) GUI after selecting **Filled Pie** from the ComboBox
ComboBoxTest
Filled Pie


**Fig. 15.23** | Using ComboBox to select a shape to draw. (Part 3 of 3.)

After creating ComboBox imageComboBox, make it uneditable by setting its DropDownStyle to DropDownList in the **Properties** window. Next, add items Circle, Square, Ellipse, Pie, Filled Circle, Filled Square, Filled Ellipse and Filled Pie to the Items collection using the **String Collection Editor**. Whenever the user selects an item from imageComboBox, a SelectedIndexChanged event occurs and event handler imageComboBox_SelectedIndexChanged (lines 19–65) executes. Lines 23–29 create a Graphics object, a Pen and a SolidBrush, which are used to draw on the Form—each is an IDisposable object, so a chained using statement (multiple using clauses before the opening brace at line 30) ensures their Dispose methods are called at the end of the event handler. The Graphics object (line 23) allows a pen or brush to draw on a component, using one of several Graphics methods. The Pen object (line 26) is used by methods DrawEllipse, DrawRectangle and DrawPie (lines 38, 41, 44 and 47) to draw the outlines of their corresponding shapes. The SolidBrush object (line 29) is used by methods FillEllipse, FillRectangle and FillPie (lines 50, 53–54, 57 and 60–61) to fill their corresponding solid shapes. Line 32 colors the entire Form White, using Graphics method **Clear**.

The app draws a shape based on the selected item's index (lines 35–61). `Graphics` method **`DrawEllipse`** (line 38) takes a `Pen`, and the *x*- and *y*-coordinates of the upper-left corner, the width and height of the bounding box (i.e., rectangular area) in which the ellipse will be displayed. The origin of the coordinate system is in the upper-left corner of the `Form`; the *x*-coordinate increases to the right, and the *y*-coordinate increases downward. A circle is a special case of an ellipse (with the width and height equal). Line 38 draws a circle. Line 44 draws an ellipse that has different values for width and height.

Class `Graphics` method **`DrawRectangle`** (line 41) takes a `Pen`, the *x*- and *y*-coordinates of the upper-left corner and the width and height of the rectangle to draw. Method **`DrawPie`** (line 47) draws a pie as a portion of an ellipse. The ellipse is bounded by a rectangle. Method `DrawPie` takes a `Pen`, the *x*- and *y*-coordinates of the upper-left corner of the rectangle, its width and height, the start angle (in degrees) and the sweep angle (in degrees) of the pie. Angles increase clockwise. The **`FillEllipse`** (lines 50 and 56), **`FillRectangle`** (line 53–54) and **`FillPie`** (line 60–61) methods are similar to their unfilled counterparts, except that they take a `Brush` (e.g., `SolidBrush`) instead of a `Pen`. Some of the drawn shapes are illustrated in the screenshots of Fig. 15.23.

## 15.9 TreeView Control

The **`TreeView`** control displays **nodes** hierarchically in a **tree**. Traditionally, nodes are objects that contain values and can refer to other nodes. A **parent node** contains **child nodes**, and the child nodes can be parents to other nodes. Two child nodes that have the same parent node are considered **sibling nodes**. A tree is a collection of nodes, usually organized in a *hierarchical* manner. The first parent node of a tree is the **root** node (a `TreeView` can have multiple roots). For example, the file system of a computer can be represented as a tree. The top-level directory (perhaps `C:`) would be the root, each subfolder of `C:` would be a child node and each child folder could have its own children. `TreeView` controls are useful for displaying hierarchical information, such as the file structure that we just mentioned. Figure 15.24 displays a sample `TreeView` control on a `Form`.

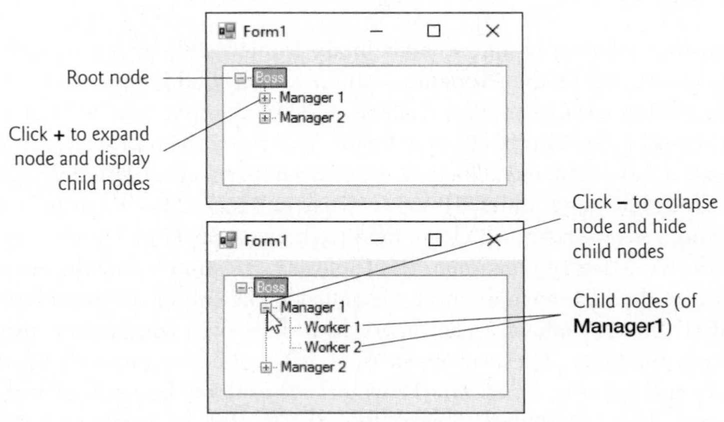


**Fig. 15.24** | `TreeView` displaying a sample tree.

A parent node can be expanded or collapsed by clicking the plus box or minus box to its left. Nodes without children do not have these boxes.

The nodes in a TreeView are instances of class **TreeNode**. Each TreeNode has a **Nodes collection** (type **TreeNodeCollection**), which contains a list of other TreeNodes—known as its children. The Parent property returns a reference to the parent node (or null if the node is a root node). Figures 15.25 and 15.26 list the common properties of TreeViews and TreeNodes, common TreeNode methods and a common TreeView event.

| TreeView properties and an event | Description |
|---|---|
| *Common Properties* | |
| CheckBoxes | Indicates whether CheckBoxes appear next to nodes. A value of true displays CheckBoxes. The default value is false. |
| ImageList | Specifies an ImageList object containing the node icons. An **ImageList** object is a collection that contains Image objects. |
| Nodes | Returns the collection of TreeNodes in the control as a TreeNodeCollection. It contains methods Add (adds a TreeNode object), Clear (deletes the entire collection) and Remove (deletes a specific node). Removing a parent node deletes all of its children. |
| SelectedNode | The selected node. |
| *Common Event (Event arguments* ***TreeViewEventArgs****)* | |
| AfterSelect | Generated after selected node changes. This is the default event when the control is double clicked in the designer. |

**Fig. 15.25** | TreeView properties and an event.

| TreeNode properties and methods | Description |
|---|---|
| *Common Properties* | |
| Checked | Indicates whether the TreeNode is checked (CheckBoxes property must be set to true in the parent TreeView). |
| FirstNode | Specifies the first node in the Nodes collection (i.e., the first child in the tree). |
| FullPath | Indicates the path of the node, starting at the root of the tree. |
| ImageIndex | Specifies the index in the TreeView's ImageList of the image shown when the node is deselected. |
| LastNode | Specifies the last node in the Nodes collection (i.e., the last child in the tree). |
| NextNode | Next sibling node. |
| Nodes | Collection of TreeNodes contained in the current node (i.e., all the children of the current node). It contains methods Add (adds a TreeNode object), Clear (deletes the entire collection) and Remove (deletes a specific node). Removing a parent node deletes all of its children. |

**Fig. 15.26** | TreeNode properties and methods. (Part 1 of 2.)

| TreeNode properties and methods | Description |
|---|---|
| `PrevNode` | Previous sibling node. |
| `SelectedImageIndex` | Specifies the index in the `TreeView`'s `ImageList` of the image to use when the node is selected. |
| `Text` | Specifies the `TreeNode`'s text. |
| *Common Methods* | |
| `Collapse` | Collapses a node. |
| `Expand` | Expands a node. |
| `ExpandAll` | Expands all the children of a node. |
| `GetNodeCount` | Returns the number of child nodes. |

**Fig. 15.26** | `TreeNode` properties and methods. (Part 2 of 2.)

To add nodes to the `TreeView` visually, click the ellipsis next to the `Nodes` property in the **Properties** window. This opens the **TreeNode Editor** (Fig. 15.27), which displays an empty tree representing the `TreeView`. There are `Buttons` to create a root and to add or delete a node. To the right are the properties of the current node. Here you can rename the node.

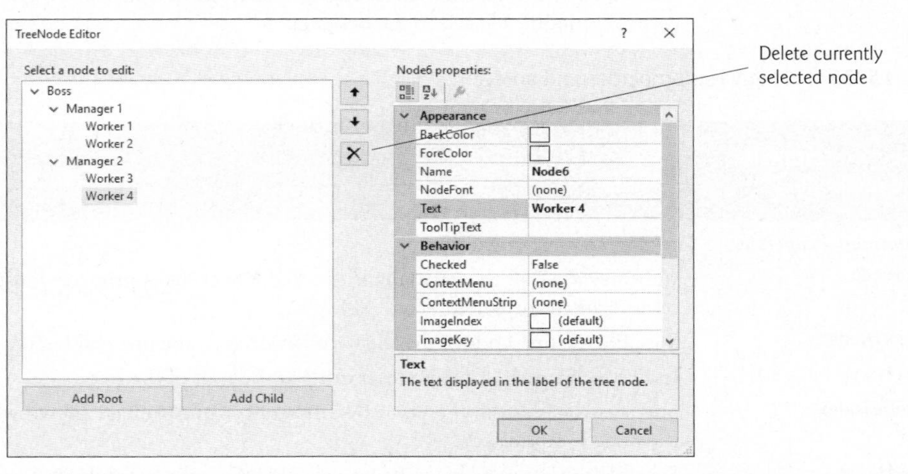


**Fig. 15.27** | TreeNode Editor.

To add nodes programmatically, first create a root node. Create a new `TreeNode` object and pass it a `string` to display. Then call method `Add` to add this new `TreeNode` to the `TreeView`'s `Nodes` collection. Thus, to add a root node to `TreeView` *myTreeView*, write

```
myTreeView.Nodes.Add(new TreeNode(rootLabel));
```

where *myTreeView* is the TreeView to which we are adding nodes, and *rootLabel* is the text to display in *myTreeView*. To add children to a root node, add new TreeNodes to its Nodes collection. We select the appropriate root node from the TreeView by writing

```
myTreeView.Nodes[myIndex]
```

where *myIndex* is the root node's index in *myTreeView*'s Nodes collection. We add nodes to child nodes through the same process by which we added root nodes to *myTreeView*. To add a child to the root node at index *myIndex*, write

```
myTreeView.Nodes[myIndex].Nodes.Add(new TreeNode(ChildLabel));
```

Class TreeViewDirectoryStructureForm (Fig. 15.28) uses a TreeView to display the contents of a directory chosen by the user. A TextBox and a Button are used to specify the directory. First, enter the full path of the directory you want to display. Then click the Button to set the specified directory as the root node in the TreeView. Each subdirectory of this directory becomes a child node. This layout is similar to that used in **Windows Explorer**. Folders can be expanded or collapsed by clicking the plus or minus boxes that appear to their left.

```
// Fig. 15.28: TreeViewDirectoryStructureForm.cs
// Using TreeView to display directory structure.
using System;
using System.Windows.Forms;
using System.IO;

namespace TreeViewDirectoryStructure
{
   // Form uses TreeView to display directory structure
   public partial class TreeViewDirectoryStructureForm : Form
   {
      string substringDirectory; // store last part of full path name

      // constructor
      public TreeViewDirectoryStructureForm()
      {
         InitializeComponent();
      }

      // populate current node with subdirectories
      public void PopulateTreeView(
         string directoryValue, TreeNode parentNode)
      {
         // array stores all subdirectories in the directory
         string[] directoryArray =
            Directory.GetDirectories(directoryValue);

         // populate current node with subdirectories
         try
         {
```

**Fig. 15.28** | Using TreeView to display directory structure. (Part 1 of 3.)

```
            // check to see if any subdirectories are present
            if (directoryArray.Length != 0)
            {
               // for every subdirectory, create new TreeNode,
               // add as a child of current node and recursively
               // populate child nodes with subdirectories
               foreach (string directory in directoryArray)
               {
                  // obtain last part of path name from the full path
                  // name by calling the GetFileNameWithoutExtension
                  // method of class Path
                  substringDirectory =
                     Path.GetFileNameWithoutExtension(directory);

                  // create TreeNode for current directory
                  TreeNode myNode = new TreeNode(substringDirectory);

                  // add current directory node to parent node
                  parentNode.Nodes.Add(myNode);

                  // recursively populate every subdirectory
                  PopulateTreeView(directory, myNode);
               }
            }
         }
         catch (UnauthorizedAccessException)
         {
            parentNode.Nodes.Add("Access denied");
         }
      }

      // handles enterButton click event
      private void enterButton_Click(object sender, EventArgs e)
      {
         // clear all nodes
         directoryTreeView.Nodes.Clear();

         // check if the directory entered by user exists
         // if it does, then fill in the TreeView,
         // if not, display error MessageBox
         if (Directory.Exists(inputTextBox.Text))
         {
            // add full path name to directoryTreeView
            directoryTreeView.Nodes.Add(inputTextBox.Text);

            // insert subfolders
            PopulateTreeView(
               inputTextBox.Text, directoryTreeView.Nodes[ 0 ]);
         }
         // display error MessageBox if directory not found
         else
         {
```

**Fig. 15.28** | Using `TreeView` to display directory structure. (Part 2 of 3.)

```
83                 MessageBox.Show(inputTextBox.Text + " could not be found.",
84                    "Directory Not Found", MessageBoxButtons.OK,
85                    MessageBoxIcon.Error);
86             }
87          }
88       }
89    }
```

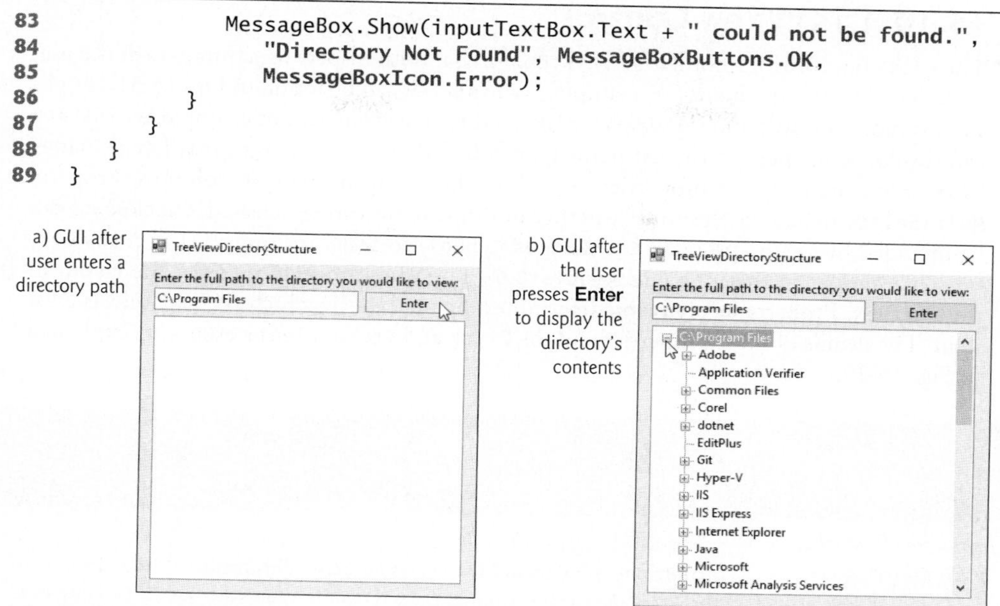


**Fig. 15.28** | Using `TreeView` to display directory structure. (Part 3 of 3.)

When the user clicks the `enterButton`, all the nodes in `directoryTreeView` are cleared (line 66). Then, if the directory exists (line 71), the path entered in `inputTextBox` is used to create the root node. Line 74 adds the directory to `directoryTreeView` as the root node, and lines 77–78 call method `PopulateTreeView` (lines 21–60), which takes a directory (a `string`) and a parent node. Method `PopulateTreeView` then creates child nodes corresponding to the subdirectories of the directory it receives as an argument.

Method `PopulateTreeView` (lines 21–60) obtains a list of subdirectories, using method **`GetDirectories`** of class `Directory` (namespace `System.IO`) in lines 25–26. Method `GetDirectories` takes a `string` (the current directory) and returns an array of `strings` (the subdirectories). If a directory is not accessible for security reasons, an `UnauthorizedAccessException` is thrown. Lines 56–59 catch this exception and add a node containing "`Access denied`" instead of displaying the subdirectories.

If there are accessible subdirectories, lines 42–43 use method `GetFileNameWithoutExtension` of class `Path` to increase readability by shortening the full path name to just the directory name. The **`Path`** class provides functionality for working with `strings` that are file or directory paths. Next, each `string` in the `directoryArray` is used to create a new child node (line 46). We use method `Add` (line 49) to add each child node to the parent. Then method `PopulateTreeView` is called recursively on every subdirectory (line 52), which eventually populates the `TreeView` with the entire directory structure. Our recursive algorithm may cause a delay when the program loads large directories. However, once the folder names are added to the appropriate `Nodes` collection, they can be expanded and collapsed without delay. In the next section, we present an alternate algorithm to solve this problem.

## 15.10 ListView Control

The **ListView** control is similar to a ListBox in that both display lists from which the user can select one or more items (an example of a ListView can be found in Fig. 15.31). ListView is more versatile and can display items in different formats. For example, a ListView can display icons next to the list items (controlled by its SmallImageList, LargeImageList or StateImageList properties) and show the details of items in columns. Property **MultiSelect** (a bool) determines whether multiple items can be selected. CheckBoxes can be included by setting property **CheckBoxes** (a bool) to true, making the ListView's appearance similar to that of a CheckedListBox. The **View** property specifies the layout of the ListBox. Property **Activation** determines the method by which the user selects a list item. The details of these properties and the Click and ItemActivate events are explained in Fig. 15.29.

| ListView properties and events | Description |
|---|---|
| *Common Properties* | |
| Activation | Determines how the user activates an item. This property takes a value in the ItemActivation enumeration. Possible values are OneClick (single-click activation), TwoClick (double-click activation, item changes color when the mouse moves over the item) and Standard (the default; double-click activation, item does not change color). |
| CheckBoxes | Indicates whether items appear with CheckBoxes. true displays CheckBoxes. The default is false. |
| LargeImageList | Specifies the ImageList containing large icons for display. |
| Items | Returns the collection of ListViewItems in the control. |
| MultiSelect | Determines whether multiple selection is allowed. The default is true, which enables multiple selection. |
| SelectedItems | Returns the collection of selected items as a ListView.SelectedListViewItemCollection. |
| SmallImageList | Specifies the ImageList containing small icons for display. |
| View | Determines appearance of ListViewItems. Possible values are LargeIcon (the default; large icon displayed, items can be in multiple columns), SmallIcon (small icon displayed, items can be in multiple columns), List (small icons displayed, items appear in a single column), Details (like List, but multiple columns of information can be displayed per item) and Tile (large icons displayed, information provided to right of icon). |
| *Common Events* | |
| Click | Generated when an item is clicked. This is the default event. |
| ItemActivate | Generated when an item in the ListView is activated (clicked or double clicked). Does not contain the specifics of which item is activated—you can use SelectedItems or SelectedIndices to determine this. |

**Fig. 15.29** | ListView properties and events.

ListView allows you to define the images used as icons for ListView items. To display images, an ImageList component is required. Create one by dragging it to a Form from the **ToolBox**. Then, select the **Images** property in the **Properties** window to display the **Images Collection Editor** (Fig. 15.30). Here you can browse for images that you wish to add to the ImageList, which contains an array of Images. Adding images this way embeds them into the app (like resources), so they do not need to be included separately with the published app. They're not, however, part of the project. In this example, we added images to the ImageList programmatically rather than using the **Images Collection Editor** so that we could use image resources. After creating an empty ImageList, add the file and folder icon images (provided with this chapter's examples) to the project as resources. Next, set property SmallImageList of the ListView to the new ImageList object. Property **SmallImageList** specifies the image list for the small icons. Property **LargeImageList** sets the ImageList for large icons. The items in a ListView are each of type **ListViewItem**. Icons for the ListView items are selected by setting the item's **ImageIndex** property to the appropriate index.

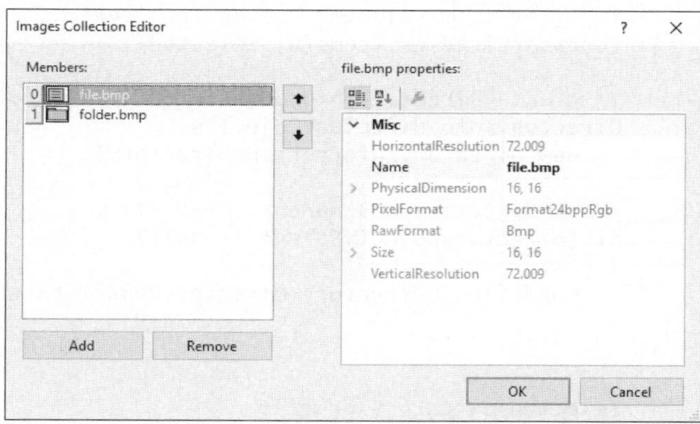


**Fig. 15.30** | **Images Collection Editor** window for an ImageList component.

Class ListViewTestForm (Fig. 15.31) displays files and folders in a ListView, along with small icons representing each file or folder. If a file or folder is inaccessible because of permission settings, a MessageBox appears. The program scans the contents of the directory as it browses, rather than indexing the entire drive at once.

```
// Fig. 15.31: ListViewTestForm.cs
// Displaying directories and their contents in ListView.
using System;
using System.Windows.Forms;
using System.IO;

namespace ListViewTest
{
```

**Fig. 15.31** | Displaying directories and their contents in ListView. (Part 1 of 4.)

```
   // Form contains a ListView which displays
   // folders and files in a directory
   public partial class ListViewTestForm : Form
   {
      // store current directory
      string currentDirectory = Directory.GetCurrentDirectory();

      // constructor
      public ListViewTestForm()
      {
         InitializeComponent();
      }

      // browse directory user clicked or go up one level
      private void browserListView_Click(object sender, EventArgs e)
      {
         // ensure an item is selected
         if (browserListView.SelectedItems.Count != 0)
         {
            // if first item selected, go up one level
            if (browserListView.Items[0].Selected)
            {
               // create DirectoryInfo object for directory
               DirectoryInfo directoryObject =
                  new DirectoryInfo(currentDirectory);

               // if directory has parent, load it
               if (directoryObject.Parent != null)
               {
                  LoadFilesInDirectory(directoryObject.Parent.FullName);
               }
            }

            // selected directory or file
            else
            {
               // directory or file chosen
               string chosen = browserListView.SelectedItems[0].Text;

               // if item selected is directory, load selected directory
               if (Directory.Exists(
                  Path.Combine(currentDirectory, chosen)))
               {
                  LoadFilesInDirectory(
                     Path.Combine(currentDirectory, chosen));
               }
            }

            // update displayLabel
            displayLabel.Text = currentDirectory;
         }
      }

```

**Fig. 15.31** | Displaying directories and their contents in `ListView`. (Part 2 of 4.)

```
      // display files/subdirectories of current directory
      public void LoadFilesInDirectory(string currentDirectoryValue)
      {
         // load directory information and display
         try
         {
            // clear ListView and set first item
            browserListView.Items.Clear();
            browserListView.Items.Add("Go Up One Level");

            // update current directory
            currentDirectory = currentDirectoryValue;
            DirectoryInfo newCurrentDirectory =
               new DirectoryInfo(currentDirectory);

            // put files and directories into arrays
            DirectoryInfo[] directoryArray =
               newCurrentDirectory.GetDirectories();
            FileInfo[] fileArray = newCurrentDirectory.GetFiles();

            // add directory names to ListView
            foreach (DirectoryInfo dir in directoryArray)
            {
               // add directory to ListView
               ListViewItem newDirectoryItem =
                  browserListView.Items.Add(dir.Name);

               newDirectoryItem.ImageIndex = 0;  // set directory image
            }

            // add file names to ListView
            foreach (FileInfo file in fileArray)
            {
               // add file to ListView
               ListViewItem newFileItem =
                  browserListView.Items.Add(file.Name);

               newFileItem.ImageIndex = 1;  // set file image
            }
         }

         // access denied
         catch (UnauthorizedAccessException)
         {
            MessageBox.Show("Warning: Some files may not be " +
               "visible due to permission settings",
               "Attention", 0, MessageBoxIcon.Warning);
         }
      }

      // handle load event when Form displayed for first time
      private void ListViewTestForm_Load(object sender, EventArgs e)
      {
```

**Fig. 15.31** | Displaying directories and their contents in ListView. (Part 3 of 4.)

```
115             // add icon images to ImageList
116             fileFolderImageList.Images.Add(Properties.Resources.folder);
117             fileFolderImageList.Images.Add(Properties.Resources.file);
118 
119             // load current directory into browserListView
120             LoadFilesInDirectory(currentDirectory);
121             displayLabel.Text = currentDirectory;
122         }
123     }
124 }
```

a) GUI showing app's default folder

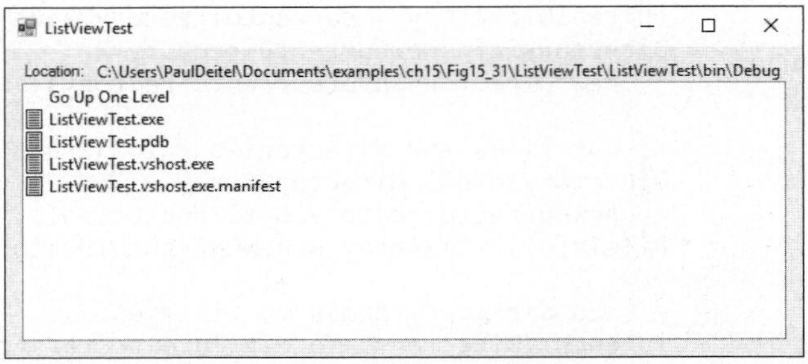

ListViewTest
Location: C:\Users\PaulDeitel\Documents\examples\ch15\Fig15_31\ListViewTest\ListViewTest\bin\Debug
Go Up One Level
ListViewTest.exe
ListViewTest.pdb
ListViewTest.vshost.exe
ListViewTest.vshost.exe.manifest

b) GUI showing the contents of the `c:\Users` directoy

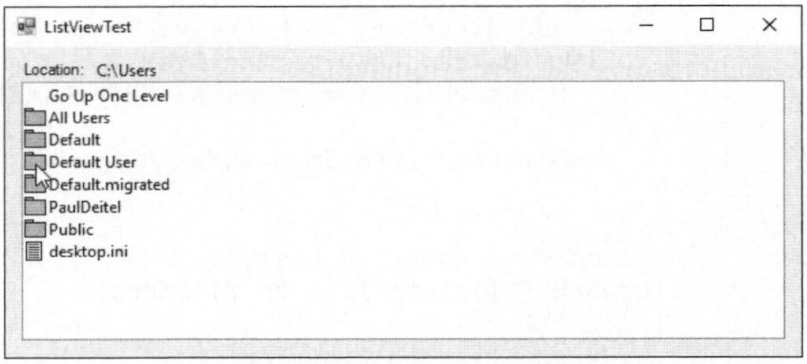

ListViewTest
Location: C:\Users
Go Up One Level
All Users
Default
Default User
Default.migrated
PaulDeitel
Public
desktop.ini

c) Dialog that appears if you try to access a directory for which you do not have permission

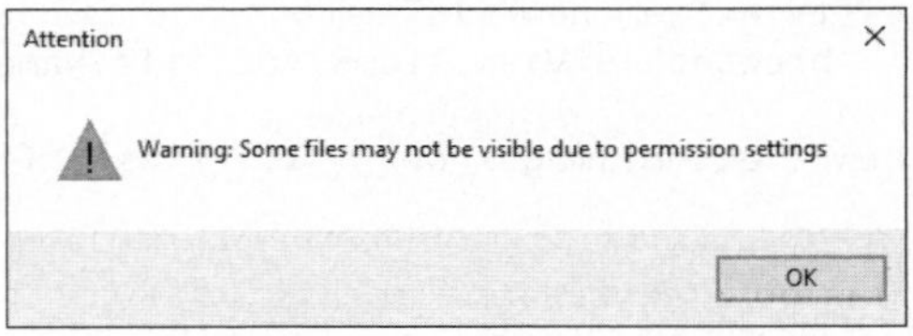

Attention
Warning: Some files may not be visible due to permission settings
OK

**Fig. 15.31** | Displaying directories and their contents in `ListView`. (Part 4 of 4.)

### *Method* `ListViewTestForm_Load`

Method `ListViewTestForm_Load` (lines 113–122) handles the `Form`'s `Load` event. When the app loads, the folder and file icon images are added to the `Images` collection of `fileFolderImageList` (lines 116–117). Since the `ListView`'s `SmallImageList` property is set to this `ImageList`, the `ListView` can display these images as icons for each item. Because the folder icon was added first, it has array index `0`, and the file icon has array index `1`. The app also loads its home directory (obtained at line 14) into the `ListView` when it first loads (line 120) and displays the directory path (line 121).

### *Method* **LoadFilesInDirectory**

The LoadFilesInDirectory method (lines 63–110) populates browserListView with the directory passed to it (currentDirectoryValue). It clears browserListView and adds the element "Go Up One Level". When the user clicks this element, the program attempts to move up one level (we see how shortly). The method then creates a DirectoryInfo object initialized with the string currentDirectory (lines 74–75). If permission is not given to browse the directory, an exception is thrown (and caught in line 104). Method LoadFilesInDirectory works differently from method PopulateTreeView in the previous program (Fig. 15.28). Instead of loading all the folders on the hard drive, method LoadFilesInDirectory loads only the folders and files in the current directory.

Class **DirectoryInfo** (namespace System.IO) enables us to browse or manipulate the directory structure easily. Method **GetDirectories** (line 79) returns an array of DirectoryInfo objects containing the subdirectories of the current directory. Similarly, method **GetFiles** (line 80) returns an array of class **FileInfo** objects containing the files in the current directory. Property **Name** (of both class DirectoryInfo and class FileInfo) contains only the directory or file name, such as temp instead of C:\myfolder\temp. To access the full name, use property **FullName**.

Lines 83–90 and lines 93–100 iterate through the subdirectories and files of the current directory and add them to browserListView. Lines 89 and 99 set the ImageIndex properties of the newly created items. If an item is a directory, we set its icon to a directory icon (index 0); if an item is a file, we set its icon to a file icon (index 1).

### *Method* **browserListView_Click**

Method browserListView_Click (lines 23–60) responds when the user clicks control browserListView. Line 26 checks whether anything is selected. If a selection has been made, line 29 determines whether the user chose the first item in browserListView. The first item in browserListView is always **Go Up One Level**; if it's selected, the program attempts to go up a level. Lines 32–33 create a DirectoryInfo object for the current directory. Line 36 tests property Parent to ensure that the user is not at the root of the directory tree. Property **Parent** indicates the parent directory as a DirectoryInfo object; if no parent directory exists, Parent returns the value null. If a parent directory does exist, line 38 pass the parent directory's full name to LoadFilesInDirectory.

If the user did not select the first item in browserListView, lines 43–55 allow the user to continue navigating through the directory structure. Line 46 creates string chosen and assigns it the text of the selected item (the first item in collection SelectedItems). Lines 49–50 determine whether the user selected a valid directory (rather than a file). Using the Combine method of class Path, the program combines strings currentDirectory and chosen to form the new directory path. The Combine method automatically adds a backslash (\), if necessary, between the two pieces. This value is passed to the **Exists** method of class Directory. Method Exists returns true if its string parameter is a valid directory. If so, the program passes the string to method LoadFilesInDirectory (lines 52–53). Finally, displayLabel is updated with the new directory (line 58).

This program loads quickly, because it indexes only the files in the current directory. A small delay may occur when a new directory is loaded. In addition, changes in the directory structure can be shown by reloading a directory. The previous program (Fig. 15.28) may have a large initial delay, as it loads an entire directory structure.

**Software Engineering Observation 15.2**

*When designing apps that run for long periods of time, you might choose a large initial delay to improve performance throughout the rest of the program. However, in apps that run for only short periods, fast initial loading times and small delays after each action are preferable.*

## 15.11 TabControl Control

The **TabControl** creates tabbed windows, such as those in Visual Studio (Fig. 15.32). This enables you to specify more information in the same space on a Form and group displayed data logically. TabControls contain **TabPage** objects, which are similar to Panels and GroupBoxes in that TabPages also can contain controls. You first add controls to the TabPage objects, then add the TabPages to the TabControl. Only one TabPage is displayed at a time. To add objects to the TabPage and the TabControl, write

```
myTabPage.Controls.Add(myControl);
myTabControl.TabPages.Add(myTabPage);
```

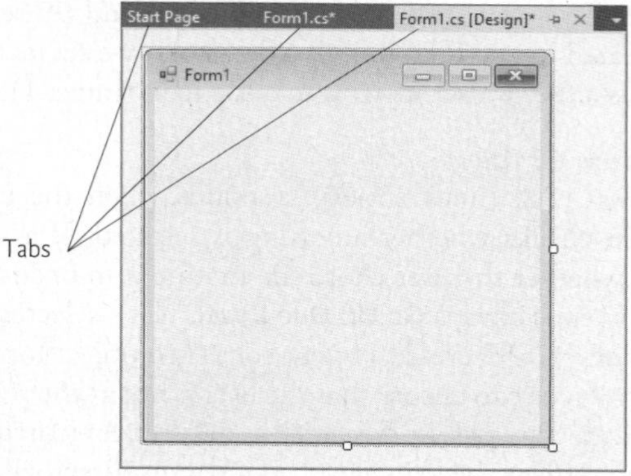


**Fig. 15.32** | Tabbed windows in Visual Studio.

The preceding statements call method Add of the Controls collection and method Add of the TabPages collection. The example adds TabControl *myControl* to TabPage *myTabPage*, then adds *myTabPage* to *myTabControl*. Alternatively, we can use method AddRange to add an array of TabPages or controls to a TabControl or TabPage, respectively. Figure 15.33 depicts a sample TabControl.

You can add TabControls visually by dragging and dropping them onto a Form in **Design** mode. To add TabPages in **Design** mode, click the top of the TabControl, open its *smart tasks menu* and select **Add Tab** (Fig. 15.34). Alternatively, click the **TabPages** property in the **Properties** window and add tabs in the dialog that appears. To change a tab label, set the **Text** property of the TabPage. Clicking the tabs selects the TabControl—to select the TabPage, click the control area underneath the tabs. You can add controls to the TabPage by dragging and dropping items from the **ToolBox**. To view different TabPages, click the appropriate tab (in either design or run mode).

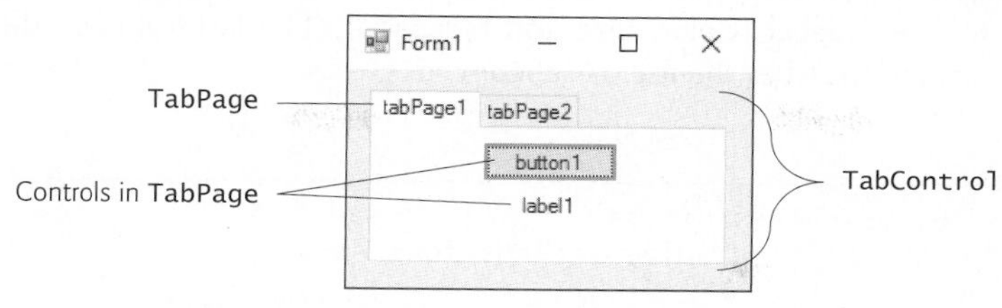


**Fig. 15.33** | `TabControl` with `TabPages` example.

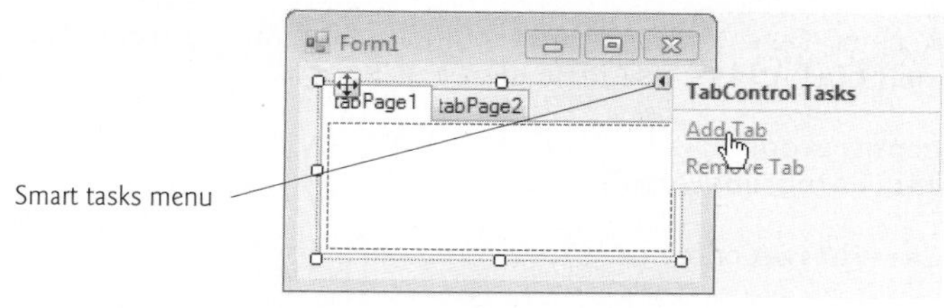


**Fig. 15.34** | `TabPages` added to a `TabControl`.

Common properties and a common event of `TabControls` are described in Fig. 15.35. Each `TabPage` generates a `Click` event when its tab is clicked. Event handlers for this event can be created by double clicking the body of the `TabPage`.

| `TabControl` properties and an event | Description |
|---|---|
| ***Common Properties*** | |
| `ImageList` | Specifies images to be displayed on tabs. |
| `ItemSize` | Specifies the tab size. |
| `Multiline` | Indicates whether multiple rows of tabs can be displayed. |
| `SelectedIndex` | Index of the selected `TabPage`. |
| `SelectedTab` | The selected `TabPage`. |
| `TabCount` | Returns the number of tab pages. |
| `TabPages` | Returns the collection of `TabPages` within the `TabControl` as a `TabControl.TabPageCollection`. |
| ***Common Event*** | |
| `SelectedIndexChanged` | Generated when `SelectedIndex` changes (i.e., another `TabPage` is selected). |

**Fig. 15.35** | `TabControl` properties and an event.

Class UsingTabsForm (Fig. 15.36) uses a TabControl to display various options relating to the text on a label (**Color**, **Size** and **Message**). The last TabPage displays an **About** message, which describes the use of TabControls.

```
// Fig. 15.36: UsingTabsForm.cs
// Using TabControl to display various font settings.
using System;
using System.Drawing;
using System.Windows.Forms;

namespace UsingTabs
{
   // Form uses Tabs and RadioButtons to display various font settings
   public partial class UsingTabsForm : Form
   {
      // constructor
      public UsingTabsForm()
      {
         InitializeComponent();
      }

      // event handler for Black RadioButton
      private void blackRadioButton_CheckedChanged(
         object sender, EventArgs e)
      {
         displayLabel.ForeColor = Color.Black; // change color to black
      }

      // event handler for Red RadioButton
      private void redRadioButton_CheckedChanged(
         object sender, EventArgs e)
      {
         displayLabel.ForeColor = Color.Red; // change color to red
      }

      // event handler for Green RadioButton
      private void greenRadioButton_CheckedChanged(
         object sender, EventArgs e)
      {
         displayLabel.ForeColor = Color.Green; // change color to green
      }

      // event handler for 12 point RadioButton
      private void size12RadioButton_CheckedChanged(
         object sender, EventArgs e)
      {
         // change font size to 12
         displayLabel.Font = new Font(displayLabel.Font.Name, 12);
   }

```

**Fig. 15.36** | Using TabControl to display various font settings. (Part 1 of 2.)

```
        // event handler for 16 point RadioButton
        private void size16RadioButton_CheckedChanged(
           object sender, EventArgs e)
        {
           // change font size to 16
           displayLabel.Font = new Font(displayLabel.Font.Name, 16);
        }

        // event handler for 20 point RadioButton
        private void size20RadioButton_CheckedChanged(
           object sender, EventArgs e)
        {
           // change font size to 20
           displayLabel.Font = new Font(displayLabel.Font.Name, 20);
        }

        // event handler for Hello! RadioButton
        private void helloRadioButton_CheckedChanged(
           object sender, EventArgs e)
        {
           displayLabel.Text = "Hello!"; // change text to Hello!
        }

        // event handler for Goodbye! RadioButton
        private void goodbyeRadioButton_CheckedChanged(
           object sender, EventArgs e)
        {
           displayLabel.Text = "Goodbye!"; // change text to Goodbye!
        }
     }
  }
```

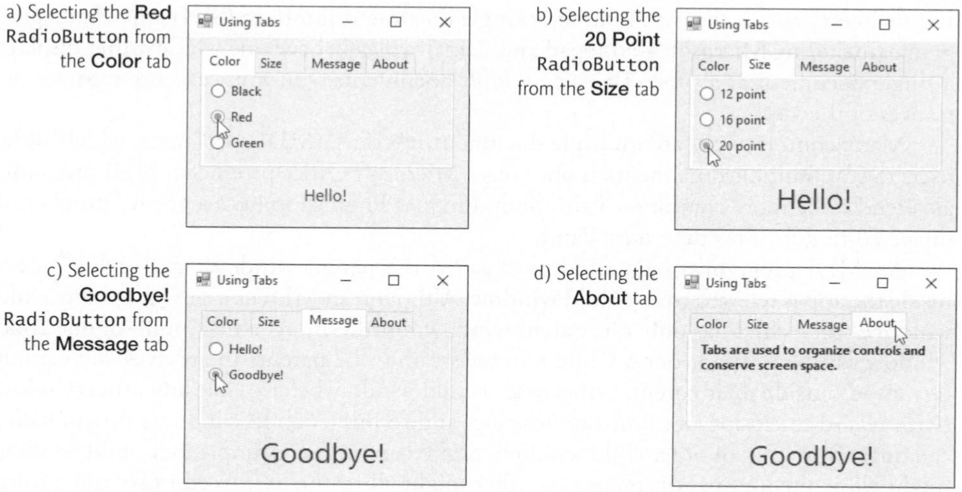
a) Selecting the Red RadioButton from the Color tab
Using Tabs
Color
Size
Message
About
Black
Red
Green
Hello!
b) Selecting the 20 Point RadioButton from the Size tab
Using Tabs
Color
Size
Message
About
12 point
16 point
20 point
Hello!
c) Selecting the Goodbye! RadioButton from the Message tab
Using Tabs
Color
Size
Message
About
Hello!
Goodbye!
Goodbye!
d) Selecting the About tab
Using Tabs
Color
Size
Message
About
Tabs are used to organize controls and conserve screen space.
Goodbye!

**Fig. 15.36** | Using `TabControl` to display various font settings. (Part 2 of 2.)

The textOptionsTabControl and the colorTabPage, sizeTabPage, messageTabPage and aboutTabPage are created in the designer (as described previously):

- The colorTabPage contains three RadioButtons for the colors black (blackRadioButton), red (redRadioButton) and green (greenRadioButton). This TabPage is displayed in Fig. 15.36(a). The CheckedChanged event handler for each RadioButton updates the color of the text in displayLabel (lines 22, 29 and 36).
- The sizeTabPage (Fig. 15.36(b)) has three RadioButtons, corresponding to font sizes 12 (size12RadioButton), 16 (size16RadioButton) and 20 (size20RadioButton), which change the font size of displayLabel—lines 44, 52 and 60, respectively.
- The messageTabPage (Fig. 15.36(c)) contains two RadioButtons for the messages **Hello!** (helloRadioButton) and **Goodbye!** (goodbyeRadioButton). The two RadioButtons determine the text on displayLabel (lines 67 and 74, respectively).
- The aboutTabPage (Fig. 15.36(d)) contains a Label (messageLabel) describing the purpose of TabControls.

**Software Engineering Observation 15.3**

*A* TabPage *can act as a container for a single logical group of* RadioButtons*, enforcing their mutual exclusivity. To place multiple* RadioButton *groups inside a single* TabPage*, you should group* RadioButtons *within* Panels *or* GroupBoxes *contained within the* TabPage*.*

## 15.12 Multiple Document Interface (MDI) Windows

In previous chapters, we have built only **single document interface** (**SDI**) apps. Such programs (including Microsoft's Notepad and Paint) typically have one window that displays a single document at a time. To edit *multiple* documents, you must execute separate instances of the app.

Many complex apps are **multiple document interface** (**MDI**) programs, which allow users to edit multiple documents at once (e.g., Microsoft Office products). MDI programs also tend to be more complex—Paint Shop Pro and Photoshop have a greater number of image-editing features than does Paint.

An MDI program's main window is called the **parent window**, and each window inside the app is referred to as a **child window**. Although an MDI app can have many child windows, each child has only one parent window. Furthermore, a maximum of one child window can be active at once. Child windows cannot be parents themselves and cannot be moved outside their parent. Otherwise, a child window behaves like any other window (with regard to closing, minimizing, resizing, and so on). A child window's functionality can differ from that of other child windows of the parent. For example, one child window might allow the user to edit images, another might allow the user to edit text and a third might display network traffic graphically, but all could belong to the same MDI parent. Figure 15.37 depicts a sample MDI app with two child windows.

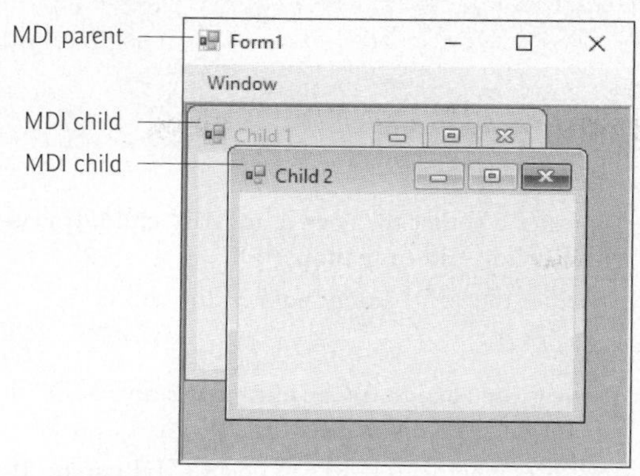


**Fig. 15.37** | MDI parent window and MDI child windows.

To create an MDI `Form`, set a `Form`'s **`IsMdiContainer`** property to `true`. The `Form` changes appearance, as in Fig. 15.38. Next, create a child `Form` class to be added to the `Form`. To do this, right click the project in the **Solution Explorer**, select **Project > Add Windows Form...** and name the file. Edit the `Form` as you like. To add the child `Form` to the parent, we must create a new child `Form` object, set its **`MdiParent`** property to the parent `Form` and call the child `Form`'s `Show` method. In general, to add a child `Form` to a parent, write

```
ChildFormClass childForm = New ChildFormClass();
childForm.MdiParent = parentForm;
childForm.Show();
```

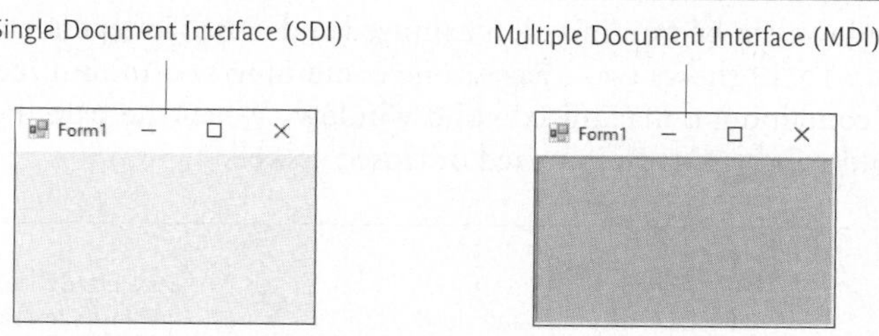


**Fig. 15.38** | SDI and MDI forms.

In most cases, the parent `Form` creates the child, so the *parentForm* reference is `this`. The code to create a child usually lies inside an event handler, which creates a new window in response to a user action. Menu selections (such as **File**, followed by a submenu option of **New**, followed by a submenu option of **Window**) are common techniques for creating new child windows.

Class `Form` property **`MdiChildren`** returns an array of child `Form` references. This is useful if the parent window wants to check the status of all its children (for example, ensuring that all are saved before the parent closes). Property **`ActiveMdiChild`** returns a reference to the active child window; it returns `null` if there are no active child windows. Other features of MDI windows are described in Fig. 15.39.

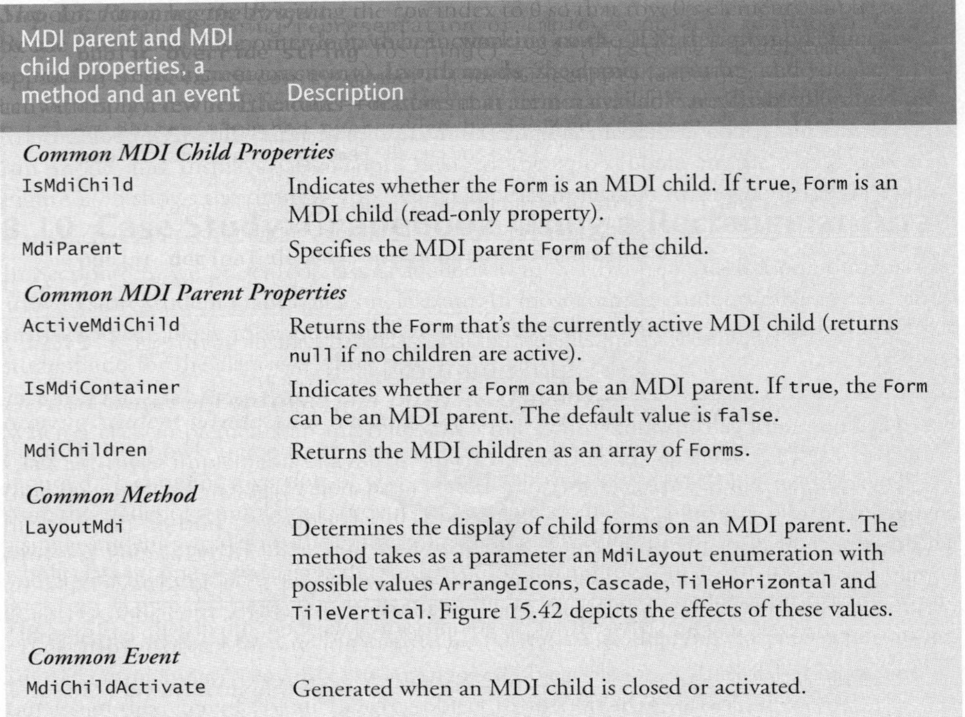

| MDI parent and MDI child properties, a method and an event | Description |
|---|---|
| ***Common MDI Child Properties*** | |
| `IsMdiChild` | Indicates whether the `Form` is an MDI child. If `true`, `Form` is an MDI child (read-only property). |
| `MdiParent` | Specifies the MDI parent `Form` of the child. |
| ***Common MDI Parent Properties*** | |
| `ActiveMdiChild` | Returns the `Form` that's the currently active MDI child (returns `null` if no children are active). |
| `IsMdiContainer` | Indicates whether a `Form` can be an MDI parent. If `true`, the `Form` can be an MDI parent. The default value is `false`. |
| `MdiChildren` | Returns the MDI children as an array of `Forms`. |
| ***Common Method*** | |
| `LayoutMdi` | Determines the display of child forms on an MDI parent. The method takes as a parameter an `MdiLayout` enumeration with possible values `ArrangeIcons`, `Cascade`, `TileHorizontal` and `TileVertical`. Figure 15.42 depicts the effects of these values. |
| ***Common Event*** | |
| `MdiChildActivate` | Generated when an MDI child is closed or activated. |

**Fig. 15.39** | MDI parent and MDI child properties, a method and an event.

Child windows can be minimized, maximized and closed independently of the parent window. Figure 15.40 shows two images: one containing two minimized child windows and a second containing a maximized child window. When the parent is minimized or closed, the child windows are minimized or closed as well.

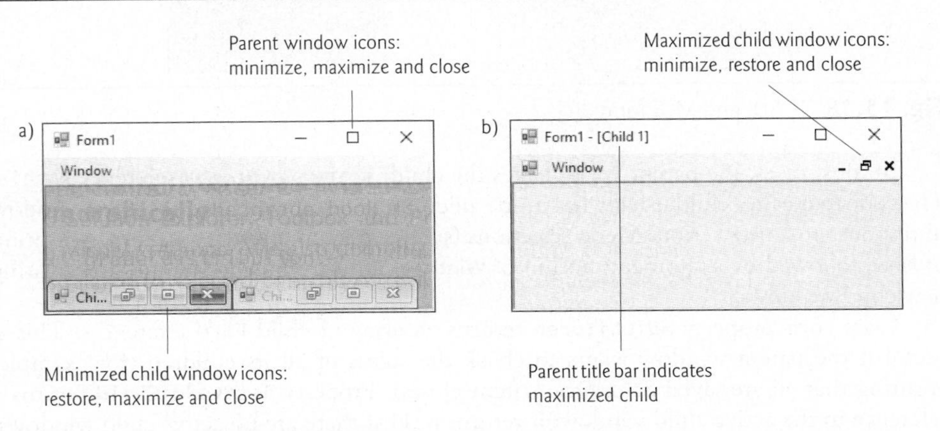


**Fig. 15.40** | Minimized and maximized child windows.

Note the title bar in Fig. 15.40(b) is **Form1 - [Child1]**. When a child window is maximized, its title-bar text is inserted into the parent window's title bar. When a child window is minimized or maximized, its title bar displays a restore icon, which can be used to return the child window to its previous size (its size before it was minimized or maximized).

C# provides a property that helps track which child windows are open in an MDI container. Property **`MdiWindowListItem`** of class `MenuStrip` specifies which menu, if any, displays a list of open child windows that the user can select to bring the corresponding window to the foreground. When a new child window is opened, an entry is added to the end of the list (Fig. 15.41). If ten or more child windows are open, the list includes the option **More Windows...**, which allows the user to select a window from a list in a dialog.

**Good Programming Practice 15.1**

*In an MDI app, include a menu that displays a list of the open child windows. This helps the user select a child window quickly.*

MDI containers allow you to organize the placement of its child windows. The child windows in an MDI app can be arranged by calling method **`LayoutMdi`** of the parent `Form`. Method `LayoutMdi` takes an **`MdiLayout`** enumeration, which can have values `ArrangeIcons`, `Cascade`, `TileHorizontal` and `TileVertical`. **Tiled windows** completely fill the parent and do *not* overlap; such windows can be arranged horizontally (value `TileHorizontal`) or vertically (value `TileVertical`). **Cascaded windows** (value `Cascade`) overlap—each is the same size and displays a visible title bar, if possible. Value `ArrangeIcons` arranges the icons for any minimized child windows. If minimized windows are scattered around the parent window, value `ArrangeIcons` orders them neatly at the bottom-left corner of the parent window. Figure 15.42 illustrates the values of the `MdiLayout` enumeration.

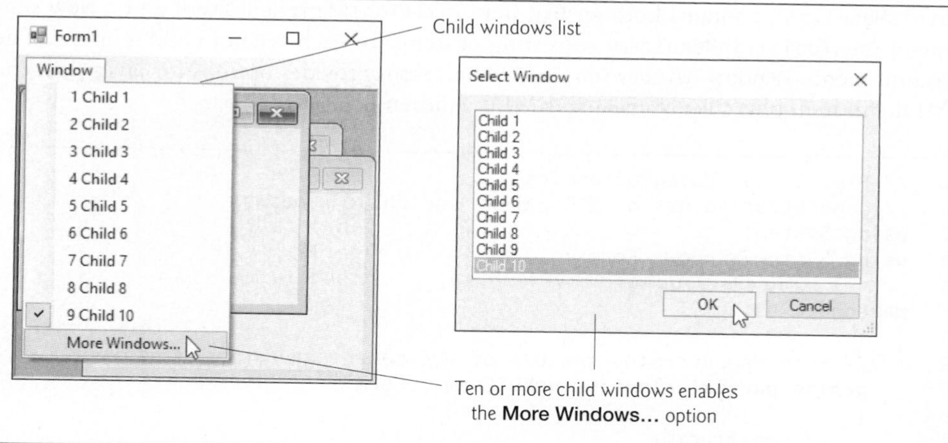


**Fig. 15.41** | `MenuStrip` property `MdiWindowListItem` example.

Class `UsingMDIForm` (Fig. 15.43) demonstrates MDI windows. Class `UsingMDIForm` uses three instances of child `Form` `ChildForm` (Fig. 15.44), each containing a `PictureBox` that displays an image. The parent MDI `Form` contains a menu enabling users to create and arrange child `Forms`.

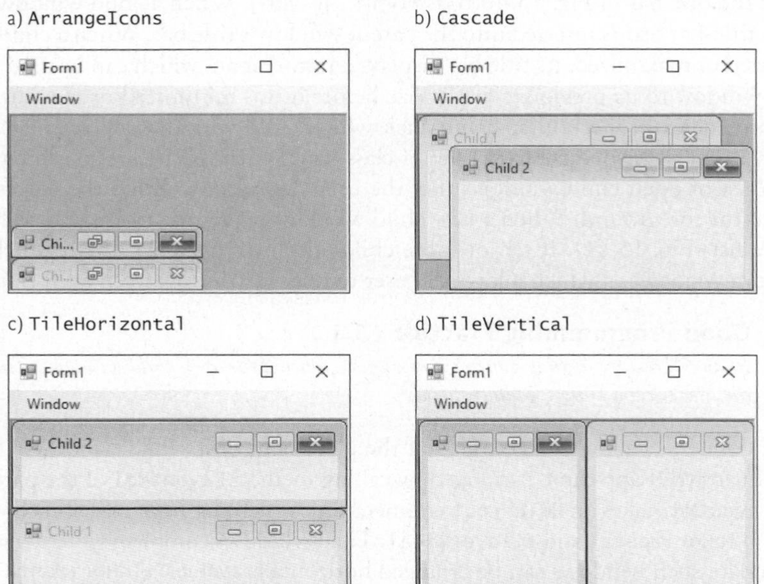


**Fig. 15.42** | `MdiLayout` enumeration values.

### *MDI Parent Form*

Figure 15.43 presents class `UsingMDIForm`—the app's MDI parent `Form`. This `Form`, which is created first, contains two top-level menus. The first of these menus, **File** (`fileToolStripMenuItem`), contains both an **Exit** item (`exitToolStripMenuItem`) and a **New** submenu (`newToolStripMenuItem`) consisting of items for each type of child window. The second menu, **Window** (`windowToolStripMenuItem`), provides options for laying out the MDI children, plus a list of the active MDI children.

```
// Fig. 15.43: UsingMDIForm.cs
// Demonstrating use of MDI parent and child windows.
using System;
using System.Windows.Forms;

namespace UsingMDI
{
   // Form demonstrates the use of MDI parent and child windows
   public partial class UsingMDIForm : Form
   {
      // constructor
      public UsingMDIForm()
      {
         InitializeComponent();
      }

```

**Fig. 15.43** | Demonstrating use of MDI parent and child windows. (Part 1 of 3.)

```
      // create Lavender Flowers image window
      private void lavenderToolStripMenuItem_Click(
         object sender, EventArgs e)
      {
         // create new child
         var child = new ChildForm(
             "Lavender Flowers", "lavenderflowers");
         child.MdiParent = this; // set parent
         child.Show(); // display child
      }

      // create Purple Flowers image window
      private void purpleToolStripMenuItem_Click(
         object sender, EventArgs e)
      {
         // create new child
         var child = new ChildForm(
             "Purple Flowers", "purpleflowers");
         child.MdiParent = this; // set parent
         child.Show(); // display child
      }

      // create Yellow Flowers image window
      private void yellowToolStripMenuItem_Click(
         object sender, EventArgs e)
      {
         // create new child
         var child = new ChildForm(
             "Yellow Flowers", "yellowflowers");
         child.MdiParent = this; // set parent
         child.Show(); // display child
      }

      // exit app
      private void exitToolStripMenuItem_Click(
         object sender, EventArgs e)
      {
         Application.Exit();
      }

      // set Cascade layout
      private void cascadeToolStripMenuItem_Click(
         object sender, EventArgs e)
      {
         this.LayoutMdi(MdiLayout.Cascade);
      }

      // set TileHorizontal layout
      private void tileHorizontalToolStripMenuItem_Click(
         object sender, EventArgs e)
      {
         this.LayoutMdi(MdiLayout.TileHorizontal);
      }
```

**Fig. 15.43** | Demonstrating use of MDI parent and child windows. (Part 2 of 3.)

```
70
71        // set TileVertical layout
72        private void tileVerticalToolStripMenuItem_Click(
73           object sender, EventArgs e)
74        {
75           this.LayoutMdi(MdiLayout.TileVertical);
76        }
77     }
78  }
```

a) Selecting the **Lavender Flowers** menu item

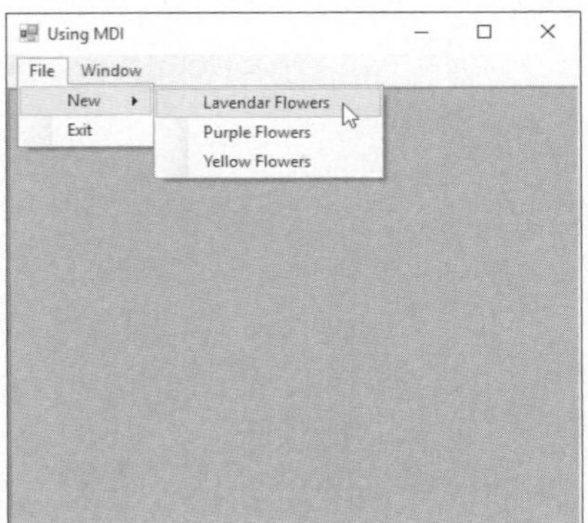


b) **Lavender Flowers** `ChildForm` window displayed

c) Selecting the **Cascade** menu item

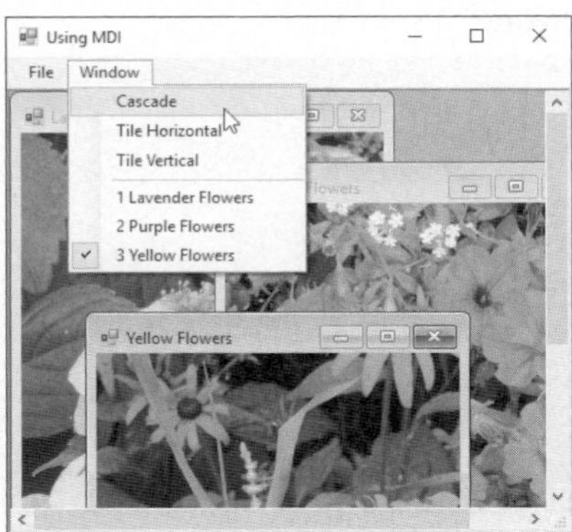


d) Cascaded child windows in an MDI window

**Fig. 15.43** | Demonstrating use of MDI parent and child windows. (Part 3 of 3.)

In the **Properties** window, we set the `Form`'s `IsMdiContainer` property to `true`, making the `Form` an MDI parent. In addition, we set the `MenuStrip`'s `MdiWindowListItem` property to `windowToolStripMenuItem`. This enables the **Window** menu to contain the list of child MDI windows.

The **Cascade** menu item (`cascadeToolStripMenuItem`) has an event handler (`cascadeToolStripMenuItem_Click`, lines 58–62) that arranges the child windows in a cascading manner. The event handler calls method `LayoutMdi` with the argument `Cascade` from the `MdiLayout` enumeration (line 61).

The **Tile Horizontal** menu item (`tileHorizontalToolStripMenuItem`) has an event handler (`tileHorizontalToolStripMenuItem_Click`, lines 65–69) that arranges the child windows in a horizontal manner. The event handler calls method `LayoutMdi` with the argument `TileHorizontal` from the `MdiLayout` enumeration (line 68).

Finally, the **Tile Vertical** menu item (`tileVerticalToolStripMenuItem`) has an event handler (`tileVerticalToolStripMenuItem_Click`, lines 72–76) that arranges the child windows in a vertical manner. The event handler calls method `LayoutMdi` with the argument `TileVertical` from the `MdiLayout` enumeration (line 75).

### *MDI Child* Form

At this point, the app is still incomplete—we must define the MDI child class. To do this, right click the project in the **Solution Explorer** and select **Add > Windows Form....** Then name the new class in the dialog as `ChildForm` (Fig. 15.44). Next, we add a `PictureBox` (`displayPictureBox`) to `ChildForm`. In `ChildForm`'s constructor, line 16 sets the title-bar text. Lines 19–21 retrieve the appropriate image resource, cast it to an `Image` and set `displayPictureBox`'s `Image` property. The images that are used can be found in the `Images` subfolder of this chapter's examples directory.

```
1  // Fig. 15.44: ChildForm.cs
2  // Child window of MDI parent.
3
4  using System.Drawing;
5  using System.Windows.Forms;
6
7  namespace UsingMDI
8  {
9     public partial class ChildForm : Form
10    {
11       public ChildForm(string title, string resourceName)
12       {
13          // Required for Windows Form Designer support
14          InitializeComponent();
15
16          Text = title; // set title text
17
18          // set image to display in PictureBox
19          displayPictureBox.Image =
20             (Image) (Properties.Resources.ResourceManager.GetObject(
21                resourceName));
22       }
23    }
24 }
```

**Fig. 15.44** | Child window of MDI parent.

After the MDI child class is defined, the parent MDI `Form` (Fig. 15.43) can create new child windows. The event handlers in lines 18–48 create a new child `Form` corresponding to the menu item clicked. Lines 22–23, 33–34 and 44–45 create new instances of `ChildForm`. Lines 24, 35 and 46 set each `Child`'s `MdiParent` property to the parent `Form`. Lines 25, 36 and 47 call method `Show` to display each child `Form`.

## 15.13 Visual Inheritance

Chapter 11 discussed how to create classes via inheritance. We've also used inheritance to create `Form`s that display a GUI, by deriving our new `Form` classes from class `System.Windows.Forms.Form`. This is an example of **visual inheritance**. The derived `Form` class contains the functionality of its `Form` base class, including any base-class properties, methods, variables and controls. The derived class also inherits all visual aspects—such as sizing, component layout, spacing between GUI components, colors and fonts.

Visual inheritance enables you to achieve visual consistency. For example, you could define a base `Form` that contains a product's logo, a specific background color, a predefined menu bar and other elements. You then could use the base `Form` throughout an app for uniformity and branding. You also can create controls that inherit from other controls. For example, you might create a custom `UserControl` (discussed in Section 15.14) that's derived from an existing control.

### *Creating a Base* `Form`

Class `VisualInheritanceBaseForm` (Fig. 15.45) derives from `Form`. The output depicts how the `Form` works. The GUI contains two `Label`s with text **Bugs, Bugs, Bugs** and **Copyright 2017, by Deitel & Associates, Inc.**, as well as one `Button` displaying the text **Learn More**. When a user presses the **Learn More** `Button`, method `learnMoreButton_Click` (lines 18–24) is invoked. This method displays a `MessageBox` that provides some informative text.

```
1  // Fig. 15.45: VisualInheritanceBaseForm.cs
2  // Base Form for use with visual inheritance.
3  using System;
4  using System.Windows.Forms;
5
6  namespace VisualInheritanceBase
7  {
8     // base Form used to demonstrate visual inheritance
9     public partial class VisualInheritanceBaseForm : Form
10    {
11       // constructor
12       public VisualInheritanceBaseForm()
13       {
14          InitializeComponent();
15       }
16
17       // display MessageBox when Button is clicked
18       private void learnMoreButton_Click(object sender, EventArgs e)
19       {
20          MessageBox.Show(
21             "Bugs, Bugs, Bugs is a product of deitel.com",
22             "Learn More", MessageBoxButtons.OK,
23             MessageBoxIcon.Information);
24       }
25    }
26 }
```

**Fig. 15.45** | Base `Form` for use with visual inheritance. (Part 1 of 2.)

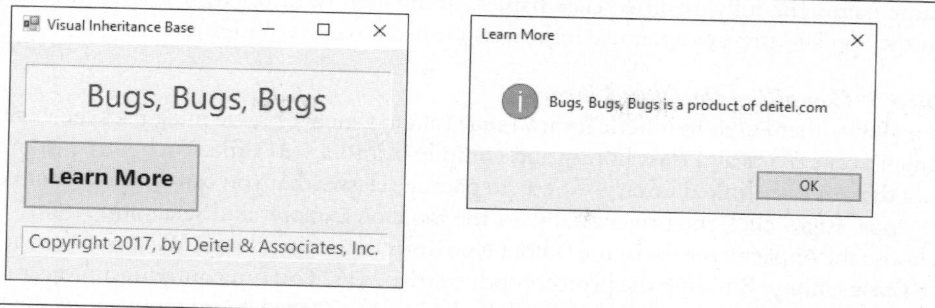


**Fig. 15.45** | Base `Form` for use with visual inheritance. (Part 2 of 2.)

### *Steps for Declaring and Using a Reusable Class*

Before a `Form` (or any class) can be used in multiple apps, it must be placed in a class library to make it reusable. The steps for creating a reusable class are:

1. Declare a `public` class. If the class is not `public`, it can be used only by other classes in the same assembly—that is, compiled into the same DLL or EXE file.
2. Choose a namespace name and add a `namespace` declaration to the source-code file for the reusable class declaration.
3. Compile the class into a class library.
4. Add a reference to the class library in an app.
5. Use the class.

Let's take a look at these steps in the context of this example:

### *Step 1: Creating a* `public` *Class*

For *Step 1* in this discussion, we use the `public` class `VisualInheritanceBaseForm` declared in Fig. 15.45. By default, every new `Form` class you create is declared as a public class.

### *Step 2: Adding the* `namespace` *Declaration*

For *Step 2*, we use the `namespace` declaration that was created for us by the IDE. By default, every new class you define is placed in a namespace with the same name as the project. In almost every example in the text, we've seen that classes from preexisting libraries, such as the .NET Framework Class Library, can be imported into a C# app. Each class belongs to a namespace that contains a group of related classes. As apps become more complex, namespaces help you manage the complexity of app components. Class libraries and namespaces also facilitate software reuse by enabling apps to add classes from other namespaces (as we've done in many examples). We removed the namespace declarations in earlier chapters because they were not necessary.

Placing a class inside a `namespace` declaration indicates that the class is part of the specified namespace. The `namespace` name is part of the fully qualified class name, so the name of class `VisualInheritanceTestForm` is actually `VisualInheritanceBase.VisualInheritanceBaseForm`. You can use this fully qualified name in your apps, or you can write a `using` directive and use the class's simple name (the unqualified class name—`VisualInheritanceBaseForm`) in the app. If another namespace also contains a class with the same name, the fully qualified class names can be used to distinguish between the classes in the app and prevent a name conflict (also called a name collision).

### *Step 3: Compiling the Class Library*

To allow other Forms to inherit from `VisualInheritanceForm`, we must package `VisualInheritanceForm` as a class library and compile it into a **`.dll` file**. Such as file is known as a **dynamically linked library**—a way to package classes that you can reference from other apps. Right click the project name in the **Solution Explorer** and select **Properties**, then choose the **Application** tab. In the **Output type** drop-down list, change **Windows Application** to **Class Library**. Building the project produces the `.dll`. You can configure a project to be a class library when you first create it by selecting the **Class Library** template in the **New Project** dialog. [*Note:* A class library cannot execute as a stand-alone app. The screen captures in Fig. 15.45 were taken before changing the project to a class library.]

### *Step 4: Adding a Reference to the Class Library*

Once the class is compiled and stored in the class library file, the library can be referenced from any app by indicating to Visual Studio where to find the class library file. To visually inherit from `VisualInheritanceBaseForm`, first create a new Windows app. Right click the **References** node in the **Solution Explorer** window and select **Add Reference...** from the pop-up menu that appears. The dialog box that appears will contain a list of class libraries from the .NET Framework. Some class libraries, like the one containing the `System` namespace, are so common that they're added to your app by the IDE. The ones in this list are not.

In the **Reference Manager** dialog box, click **Browse** then click the **Browse...** button. When you build a class library, Visual C# places the `.dll` file in the project's `bin\Debug` or `bin\Release` folder, depending on whether the **Solution Configurations** drop-down list in the IDE's toolbar is set to **Debug** or **Release**. In the **Browse** tab, you can navigate to the directory containing the class library file you created in *Step 3*, as shown in Fig. 15.46. Select the `.dll` file and click **Add**.

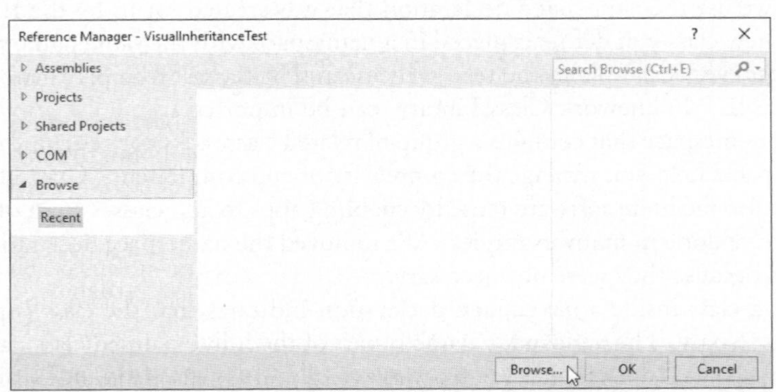


**Fig. 15.46** | Using the **Reference Manager** dialog to browse for a DLL. (Part 1 of 2.)

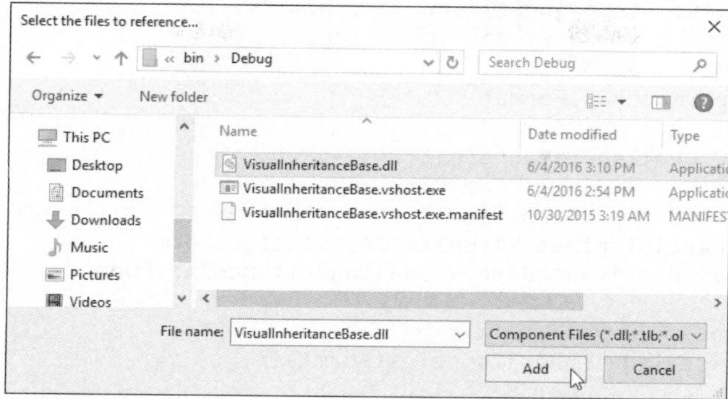


**Fig. 15.46** | Using the **Reference Manager** dialog to browse for a DLL. (Part 2 of 2.)

### *Step 5: Using the Class—Deriving from a Base* `Form`

Open the file that defines the new app's GUI and modify the line that defines the class to indicate that the app's `Form` should inherit from class `VisualInheritanceBaseForm`. The class-declaration line should now appear as follows:

```
public partial class VisualInheritanceTestForm :
   VisualInheritanceBase.VisualInheritanceBaseForm
```

Unless you specify namespace `VisualInheritanceBase` in a `using` directive, you must use the fully qualified name `VisualInheritanceBase.VisualInheritanceBaseForm`. In **Design** view, the new app's `Form` should now display the controls inherited from the base `Form` (Fig. 15.47). We can now add more components to the `Form`.

**Fig. 15.47** | `Form` demonstrating visual inheritance.

### *Class* `VisualInheritanceTestForm`

Class `VisualInheritanceTestForm` (Fig. 15.48) is a derived class of `VisualInheritance-BaseForm`. The output illustrates the functionality of the program. The components, their layouts and the functionality of base class `VisualInheritanceBaseForm` (Fig. 15.45) are inherited by `VisualInheritanceTestForm`. We added an additional `Button` with text **About this Program**. When a user presses this `Button`, method `aboutButton_Click` (Fig. 15.48, lines 19–25) is invoked. This method displays another `MessageBox` providing different informative text (lines 21–24).

```
// Fig. 15.48: VisualInheritanceTestForm.cs
// Derived Form using visual inheritance.
using System;
using System.Windows.Forms;

namespace VisualInheritanceTest
{
   // derived form using visual inheritance
   public partial class VisualInheritanceTestForm :
      VisualInheritanceBase.VisualInheritanceBaseForm
   {
      // constructor
      public VisualInheritanceTestForm()
      {
         InitializeComponent();
      }

      // display MessageBox when Button is clicked
      private void aboutButton_Click(object sender, EventArgs e)
      {
         MessageBox.Show(
            "This program was created by Deitel & Associates.",
            "About This Program", MessageBoxButtons.OK,
            MessageBoxIcon.Information);
      }
   }
}
```

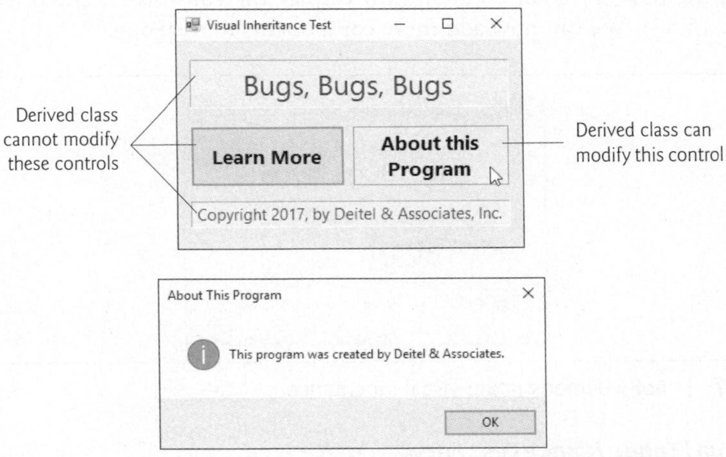


**Fig. 15.48** | Derived Form using visual inheritance.

If a user clicks the **Learn More** button, the event is handled by the base-class event handler `learnMoreButton_Click`. Because `VisualInheritanceBaseForm` uses a `private` access modifier to declare its controls, `VisualInheritanceTestForm` cannot modify the controls inherited from class `VisualInheritanceBaseForm` visually or programmatically. The IDE displays a small icon at the top left of the visually inherited controls to indicate that they're inherited and cannot be altered.

## 15.14 User-Defined Controls

The .NET Framework allows you to create **custom controls**. These custom controls appear in the user's **Toolbox** and can be added to `Forms`, `Panels` or `GroupBoxes` in the same way that we add `Buttons`, `Labels` and other predefined controls. The simplest way to create a custom control is to derive a class from an existing control, such as a `Label`. This is useful if you want to add functionality to an existing control, rather than replacing it with one that provides the desired functionality. For example, you can create a new type of `Label` that behaves like a normal `Label` but has a different appearance. You accomplish this by inheriting from class `Label` and overriding method `OnPaint`.

### *Method **OnPaint***

All controls have an **`OnPaint`** method, which the system calls when a component must be redrawn (such as when the component is resized). The method receives a **`PaintEventArgs`** object, which contains graphics information—property **`Graphics`** is the graphics object used to draw, and property **`ClipRectangle`** defines the rectangular boundary of the control. Whenever the system raises a `Paint` event to draw the control on the screen, the control catches the event and calls its `OnPaint` method. The base class's `OnPaint` should be called explicitly from an overridden `OnPaint` implementation before executing custom-paint code. In most cases, you want to do this to ensure that the original painting code executes in addition to the code you define in the custom control's class.

### *Creating New Controls*

To create a new control composed of existing controls, use class **`UserControl`**. Controls added to a custom control are called **constituent controls**. For example, a programmer could create a `UserControl` composed of a `Button`, a `Label` and a `TextBox`, each associated with some functionality (for example, the `Button` setting the `Label`'s text to that contained in the `TextBox`). The `UserControl` acts as a container for the controls added to it. The `UserControl` contains constituent controls, but it does not determine how these constituent controls are displayed. To control the appearance of each constituent control, you can handle each control's `Paint` event or override `OnPaint`. Both the `Paint` event handler and `OnPaint` are passed a `PaintEventArgs` object, which can be used to draw graphics (lines, rectangles, and so on) on the constituent controls.

Using another technique, a programmer can create a brand-new control by inheriting from class `Control`. This class does not define any specific behavior; that's left to you. Instead, class `Control` handles the items associated with all controls, such as events and sizing handles. Method `OnPaint` should contain a call to the base class's `OnPaint` method, which calls the `Paint` event handlers. You add code that draws custom graphics inside the overridden `OnPaint` method. This technique allows for the greatest flexibility but also requires the most planning. All three approaches are summarized in Fig. 15.49.

| Custom-control techniques and PaintEventArgs properties | Description |
|---|---|
| ***Custom-Control Techniques*** | |
| Inherit from a Windows Forms control | You can do this to add functionality to a preexisting control. If you override method OnPaint, call the base class's OnPaint method. You only can add to the original control's appearance, not redesign it. |
| Create a UserControl | You can create a UserControl composed of multiple preexisting controls (e.g., to combine their functionality). You place drawing code in a Paint event handler or overridden OnPaint method. |
| Inherit from class Control | Define a brand new control. Override method OnPaint, then call base-class method OnPaint and add the code to draw the control. With this method you can customize both control appearance and functionality. |
| ***PaintEventArgs Properties*** | |
| Graphics | The control's graphics object, which is used to draw on the control. |
| ClipRectangle | Specifies the rectangle indicating the boundary of the control. |

**Fig. 15.49** | Custom-control creation.

### *Clock Control*

We create a "clock" control in Fig. 15.50. This is a UserControl composed of a Label and a Timer—whenever the Timer raises an event (once per second in this example), the Label is updated to reflect the current time.

```
// Fig. 15.50: ClockUserControl.cs
// User-defined control with a Timer and a Label.
using System;
using System.Windows.Forms;

namespace ClockExample
{
   // UserControl that displays the time on a Label
   public partial class ClockUserControl : UserControl
   {
      // constructor
      public ClockUserControl()
      {
         InitializeComponent();
      }
```

**Fig. 15.50** | User-defined control with a Timer and a Label. (Part 1 of 2.)

```
16
17          // update Label at every tick
18          private void clockTimer_Tick(object sender, EventArgs e)
19          {
20             // get current time (Now), convert to string
21             displayLabel.Text = DateTime.Now.ToLongTimeString();
22          }
23       }
24    }
```

**Fig. 15.50** | User-defined control with a `Timer` and a `Label`. (Part 2 of 2.)

### *Timers*

**`Timers`** (`System.Windows.Forms` namespace) are non-visual components that generate **`Tick`** events at a set interval. This interval is set by the `Timer`'s **`Interval`** property, which defines the number of milliseconds (thousandths of a second) between events. By default, timers are disabled and do not generate events.

### *Adding a User Control*

This app contains a user control (`ClockUserControl`) and a `Form` that displays the user control. Create a Windows app, then create a `UserControl` class by selecting **Project > Add User Control....** This displays a dialog from which we can select the type of item to add—user controls are already selected. We then name the file (and the class) `ClockUserControl`. Our empty `ClockUserControl` is displayed as a grey rectangle.

### *Designing the User Control*

You can treat this control like a Windows `Form`, meaning that you can add controls using the **ToolBox** and set properties using the **Properties** window. However, instead of creating an app, you're simply creating a new control composed of other controls. Add a `Label` (`displayLabel`) and a `Timer` (`clockTimer`) to the `UserControl`. Set the `Timer` interval to 1000 milliseconds and set `displayLabel`'s text with each `Tick` event (lines 18–22; the default event). To generate events, `clockTimer` must be enabled by setting property `Enabled` to `true` in the **Properties** window.

Structure **`DateTime`** (namespace `System`) contains property **`Now`**, which returns the current time. Method **`ToLongTimeString`** converts `Now` to a `string` containing the current hour, minute and second (along with AM or PM, depending on your locale). We use this to set the time in `displayLabel` in line 21.

Once created, our clock control appears as an item in the **ToolBox** in the section titled *ProjectName* **Components**, where *ProjectName* is your project's name. *You may need to switch to the app's `Form` before the item appears in the* **ToolBox**. To use the control, simply drag it to the `Form` and run the Windows app. We gave the `ClockUserControl` object a white background to make it stand out in the `Form`. Figure 15.50 shows the output of `Clock`, which contains our `ClockUserControl`. There are no event handlers in `Clock`, so we show only the code for `ClockUserControl`.

### *Sharing Custom Controls with Other Developers*

Visual Studio allows you to share custom controls with other developers. To create a `UserControl` that can be exported to other solutions, do the following:

1. Create a new **Class Library** project.
2. Delete `Class1.cs`, initially provided with the app.
3. Right click the project in the **Solution Explorer** and select **Add > User Control....** In the dialog that appears, name the user-control file and click **Add**.
4. Inside the project, add controls and functionality to the `UserControl` (Fig. 15.51).

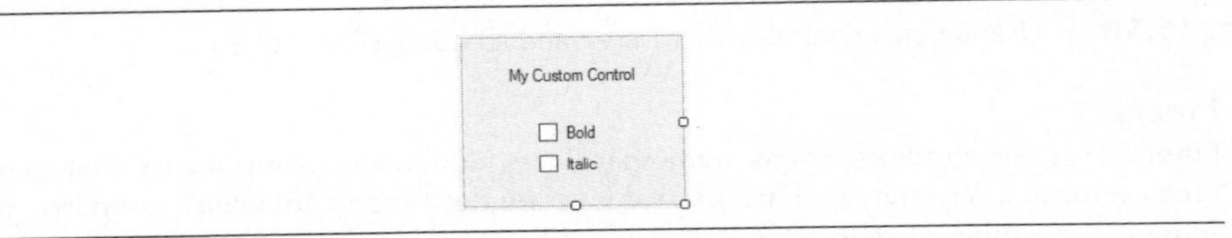


**Fig. 15.51** | Custom-control creation.

5. Build the project. Visual Studio creates a `.dll` file for the `UserControl` in the output directory (`bin/Debug` or `bin/Release`). The file is not executable; class libraries are used to define classes that are reused in other executable apps. You can give the `.dll` file to other developers and they can follow *Steps 6* and *7*.
6. Create a new Windows app.
7. In the new Windows app, right click the **ToolBox** and select **Choose Items....** In the **Choose Toolbox Items** dialog that appears, click **Browse....** Browse for the `.dll` file from the class library created in *Steps 1–5*. The item will then appear in the **.NET Framework Components** tab of the **Choose Toolbox Items** dialog. If it's not already checked, check this item. Click **OK** to add the item to the **Toolbox**. This control can now be added to the `Form` as if it were any other control.

## 15.15 Wrap-Up

Many of today's commercial apps provide GUIs that are easy to use and manipulate. Because of this demand for user-friendly GUIs, the ability to design sophisticated GUIs is an essential programming skill. Visual Studio's IDE makes GUI development quick and easy. In Chapters 14 and 15, we presented basic Windows Forms GUI development techniques. In Chapter 15, we demonstrated how to create menus, which provide users easy access to an app's functionality. You learned the `DateTimePicker` and `MonthCalendar` controls, which allow users to input date and time values. We demonstrated `LinkLabels`, which are used to link the user to an app or a web page. You used several controls that provide lists of data to the user—`ListBoxes`, `CheckedListBoxes` and `ListViews`. We used the `ComboBox` control to create drop-down lists, and the `TreeView` control to display data in hierarchical form. We then introduced complex GUIs that use tabbed windows and multiple document interfaces. The chapter concluded with demonstrations of visual inheritance and creating custom controls. In Chapter 16, we introduce `string` and character processing.

# 16

# Strings and Characters: A Deeper Look

## Objectives

In this chapter you'll:

- Create and manipulate immutable character-string objects of class `string` and mutable character-string objects of class `StringBuilder`.
- Use various methods of classes `string` and `StringBuilder`.
- Manipulate character objects of `struct Char`.
- Use regular-expression classes `Regex` and `Match`.

**Outline**



## 16.1 Introduction

This chapter introduces the .NET Framework Class Library's string- and character-processing capabilities and demonstrates how to use regular expressions to search for patterns in text. The techniques it presents can be employed in most kinds of applications, and particularly in text editors, word processors, page-layout software, computerized typesetting systems and other kinds of text-processing software. Previous chapters presented some basic string-processing capabilities. Now we discuss in detail the text-processing capabilities of class `string` and type `char` from the `System` namespace and class `StringBuilder` from the `System.Text` namespace.

We begin with an overview of the fundamentals of characters and strings in which we discuss *character constants* and *string literals*. We then provide examples of class `string`'s many constructors and methods. The examples demonstrate how to determine the *length* of strings, *copy* strings, *access individual characters* in strings, *search* strings, obtain *substrings* from larger strings, *compare* strings, *concatenate* strings, *replace characters* in strings and convert strings to uppercase or lowercase letters.

Next, we introduce class `StringBuilder`, which is used to assemble strings dynamically. We demonstrate `StringBuilder` capabilities for determining and specifying the *size* of a `StringBuilder`, as well as *appending, inserting, removing* and *replacing* characters in a `StringBuilder` object. We then introduce the character-testing methods of `struct Char` that enable a program to determine whether a character is a digit, a letter, a lowercase letter, an uppercase letter, a punctuation mark or a symbol other than a punctuation mark. Such methods are useful for validating individual characters in user input. In addition, type `Char` provides methods for *converting* a character to *uppercase or lowercase*.

We provide an online section at `http://www.deitel.com/books/CSharp6FP` that discusses *regular expressions*. We present classes `Regex` and `Match` from the `System.Text.RegularExpressions` namespace as well as the symbols that are used to form regular expressions. We then demonstrate how to *find patterns* in a string, *match entire strings to patterns, replace characters* in a string that match a pattern and *split strings* at delimiters specified as a pattern in a regular expression.

## 16.2 Fundamentals of Characters and Strings

Characters are the fundamental building blocks of C# source code. Every program is composed of characters that, when grouped together meaningfully, create a sequence that the compiler interprets as instructions describing how to accomplish a task. A program also can contain **character constants.** A character constant is a character that's represented as an integer value, called a *character code.* For example, the integer value `122` corresponds to the character constant `'z'`. The integer value `10` corresponds to the newline character `'\n'`. Character constants are established according to the **Unicode character set,** an international character set that contains many more symbols and letters than does the ASCII character set (listed in Appendix C). To learn more about Unicode, see `unicode.org`.

A string is a series of characters treated as a unit. These characters can be uppercase letters, lowercase letters, digits and various **special characters:** +, -, *, /, $ and others. A string is an object of type `string`. Just as the C# keyword `object` is an alias for class `Object`, `string` is an alias for class `String` (namespace `System`). We write **string literals,** also called **string constants,** as sequences of characters in double quotation marks, as follows:

```
"John Q. Doe"
"9999 Main Street"
"Waltham, Massachusetts"
"(201) 555-1212"
```

A declaration can assign a `string` literal to a `string` reference. The declaration

```
string color = "blue";
```

initializes the `string` `color` to refer to the `string` literal object `"blue"`.

**Performance Tip 16.1**

*If there are multiple occurrences of the same* `string` *literal object in an app, a single copy of it will be referenced from each location in the program that uses that* `string` *literal. It's possible to share the object in this manner, because* `string` *literal objects are implicitly constant. Such sharing conserves memory.*

### *Verbatim* `strings`

Recall that *backslash characters* in `strings` introduce escape sequences and that placing a literal backslash in a `string` requires \\. On occasion, a `string` will contain multiple literal backslash characters (this often occurs in the name of a file). To avoid excessive backslashes, it's possible to exclude escape sequences and interpret all the characters in a `string` literally, using the `@` character to create what's known as a **verbatim string.** Backslashes within the double quotation marks following the `@` character are not considered to be part of escape sequences. Often this simplifies programming and makes the code easier to read.

For example, consider the `string` in the following assignment:

```
string file = "C:\\MyFolder\\MySubFolder\\MyFile.txt";
```

Using the *verbatim* `string` *syntax,* the assignment can be altered to

```
string file = @"C:\MyFolder\MySubFolder\MyFile.txt";
```

Verbatim `strings` may also span multiple lines, in which case they preserve all newlines, spaces and tabs between the opening `@"` and closing `"` delimiters.

## 16.3 string Constructors

Figure 16.1 demonstrates three of class string's constructors.

```
1  // Fig. 16.1: StringConstructor.cs
2  // Demonstrating string class constructors.
3  using System;
4
5  class StringConstructor
6  {
7     static void Main()
8     {
9        // string initialization
10       char[] characterArray =
11          {'b', 'i', 'r', 't', 'h', ' ', 'd', 'a', 'y'};
12       var originalString = "Welcome to C# programming!";
13       var string1 = originalString;
14       var string2 = new string(characterArray);
15       var string3 = new string(characterArray, 6, 3);
16       var string4 = new string('C', 5);
17
18       Console.WriteLine($"string1 = \"{string1}\"\n" +
19          $"string2 = \"{string2}\"\n" +
20          $"string3 = \"{string3}\"\n" +
21          $"string4 = \"{string4}\"\n");
22    }
23 }
```

```
string1 = "Welcome to C# programming!"
string2 = "birth day"
string3 = "day"
string4 = "CCCCC"
```

**Fig. 16.1** | Demonstrating string class constructors.

Lines 10–11 create the char array characterArray, which contains nine characters. Lines 12–16 declare the strings originalString, string1, string2, string3 and string4. Line 12 assigns string literal "Welcome to C# programming!" to string reference originalString. Line 13 sets string1 to reference the same string literal.

Line 14 assigns to string2 a new string, using the string constructor with a character array argument. The new string contains a copy of the array's characters.

Line 15 assigns to string3 a new string, using the string constructor that takes a char array and two int arguments. The second argument specifies the starting index position (the *offset*) from which characters in the array are to be copied. The third argument specifies the number of characters (the *count*) to be copied from the specified starting position in the array. The new string contains a copy of the specified characters in the array. If the specified offset or count indicates that the program should access an element outside the bounds of the character array, an ArgumentOutOfRangeException is thrown.

Line 16 assigns to string4 a new string, using the string constructor that takes as arguments a character and an int specifying the number of times to repeat that character in the string.

**Software Engineering Observation 16.1**

*In most cases, it's not necessary to make a copy of an existing* `string`*. All* `string`*s are* immutable*—their character contents cannot be changed after they're created. Also, if there are one or more references to a* `string` *(or any reference-type object for that matter), the object cannot be reclaimed by the garbage collector.*

## 16.4 `string` Indexer, Length Property and CopyTo Method

Figure 16.2 presents

- the `string` *indexer* (`[]`) for retrieving any character in a `string`,
- the `string` property `Length`, which returns a `string`'s length and
- the `string` method `CopyTo`, which copies a specified number of characters from a `string` into a `char` array.

```
// Fig. 16.2: StringMethods.cs
// Using the indexer, property Length and method CopyTo
// of class string.
using System;

class StringMethods
{
   static void Main()
   {
      var string1 = "hello there";
      var characterArray = new char[5];

      Console.WriteLine($"string1: \"{string1}\""); // output string1

      // test Length property
      Console.WriteLine($"Length of string1: {string1.Length}");

      // loop through characters in string1 and display reversed
      Console.Write("The string reversed is: ");

      for (int i = string1.Length - 1; i >= 0; --i)
      {
         Console.Write(string1[i]);
      }

      // copy characters from string1 into characterArray
      string1.CopyTo(0, characterArray, 0, characterArray.Length);
      Console.Write("\nThe character array is: ");

      foreach (var element in characterArray)
      {
         Console.Write(element);
      }
```

**Fig. 16.2** | `string` indexer, `Length` property and `CopyTo` method. (Part 1 of 2.)

```
34
35          Console.WriteLine("\n");
36       }
37    }
```

```
string1: "hello there"
Length of string1: 11
The string reversed is: ereht olleh
The character array is: hello
```

**Fig. 16.2** | `string` indexer, `Length` property and `CopyTo` method. (Part 2 of 2.)

Line 16 uses `string` property `Length` to determine the number of characters in `string1`. Like arrays, `string`s always know their own size.

Lines 21–24 display the characters of `string1` in reverse order using the `string` indexer (`[]`), which treats a `string` as an array of `char`s and returns the character at a specific index in the `string`. As with arrays, the first element of a `string` has index 0.

**Common Programming Error 16.1**

*Attempting to access a character that's outside a* `string`*'s bounds results in an* `IndexOutOfRangeException`.

Line 27 uses `string` method `CopyTo` to copy the characters of `string1` into a character array (`characterArray`). The first argument given to method `CopyTo` is the index from which the method begins copying characters in the `string`. The second argument is the character array into which the characters are copied. The third argument is the index specifying the starting location at which the method begins placing the copied characters into the character array. The last argument is the number of characters that the method will copy from the `string`. Lines 30–33 output the `char` array contents one character at a time.

We used a `for` statement in lines 21–24 to demonstrate a `string`'s `Length` property and the `string` indexer, using them to display the `string` in reverse. That loop could have been implemented with `foreach` and the **Reverse extension method** as in

```
foreach (var element in string1.Reverse())
{
   Console.Write(element);
}
```

Method `Reverse` is one of many LINQ extension methods and requires a `using` directive for the namespace `System.Linq`.

## 16.5 Comparing strings

The next two examples demonstrate various methods for *comparing* `string`s. To understand how one `string` can be "greater than" or "less than" another, consider the process of alphabetizing a series of last names. The reader would, no doubt, place `"Jones"` before `"Smith"`, because the first letter of `"Jones"` comes before the first letter of `"Smith"` in the alphabet. The alphabet is more than just a set of 26 letters—it's an ordered list of characters in which each letter occurs in a specific position. For example, Z is more than just a letter of the alphabet; it's specifically the twenty-sixth letter of the alphabet. Computers can order characters alphabetically because they're represented internally as numeric codes and those codes are ordered according to the alphabet so, for example, `'a'` is less than `'b'`—see Appendix C.

### *Comparing* `string`*s with* `Equals`*,* `CompareTo` *and the Equality Operator (==)*

Class `string` provides several ways to compare `string`s. Figure 16.3 demonstrates methods `Equals` and `CompareTo` and the equality operator (==).

```
// Fig. 16.3: StringCompare.cs
// Comparing strings
using System;

class StringCompare
{
   static void Main()
   {
      var string1 = "hello";
      var string2 = "good bye";
      var string3 = "Happy Birthday";
      var string4 = "happy birthday";

      // output values of four strings
      Console.WriteLine($"string1 = \"{string1}\"" +
         $"\nstring2 = \"{string2}\"" +
         $"\nstring3 = \"{string3}\"" +
         $"\nstring4 = \"{string4}\"\n");

      // test for equality using Equals method
      if (string1.Equals("hello"))
      {
         Console.WriteLine("string1 equals \"hello\"");
      }
      else
      {
         Console.WriteLine("string1 does not equal \"hello\"");
      }

      // test for equality with ==
      if (string1 == "hello")
      {
         Console.WriteLine("string1 equals \"hello\"");
      }
      else
      {
         Console.WriteLine("string1 does not equal \"hello\"");
      }

      // test for equality comparing case
      if (string.Equals(string3, string4)) // static method
      {
```

**Fig. 16.3** | Comparing `string`s. (Part 1 of 2.)

```
43            Console.WriteLine("string3 equals string4");
44         }
45         else
46         {
47            Console.WriteLine("string3 does not equal string4");
48         }
49
50         // test CompareTo
51         Console.WriteLine(
52            $"\nstring1.CompareTo(string2) is {string1.CompareTo(string2)}");
53         Console.WriteLine(
54            $"string2.CompareTo(string1) is {string2.CompareTo(string1)}");
55         Console.WriteLine(
56            $"string1.CompareTo(string1) is {string1.CompareTo(string1)}");
57         Console.WriteLine(
58            $"string3.CompareTo(string4) is {string3.CompareTo(string4)}");
59         Console.WriteLine(
60            $"string4.CompareTo(string3) is {string4.CompareTo(string3)}");
61      }
62   }
```

```
string1 = "hello"
string2 = "good bye"
string3 = "Happy Birthday"
string4 = "happy birthday"

string1 equals "hello"
string1 equals "hello"
string3 does not equal string4

string1.CompareTo(string2) is 1
string2.CompareTo(string1) is -1
string1.CompareTo(string1) is 0
string3.CompareTo(string4) is 1
string4.CompareTo(string3) is -1
```

**Fig. 16.3** | Comparing strings. (Part 2 of 2.)

The condition in line 21 uses `string` method `Equals` to compare `string1` and literal `string` `"hello"` (the argument) to determine whether they're equal. Method `Equals` (inherited from `object` and overridden in `string`) tests two `string`s for equality (i.e., checks whether the `string`s have *identical contents*). The method returns `true` if the objects are equal and `false` otherwise. In this case, the condition returns `true`, because `string1` references `string` literal object `"hello"`. Method `Equals` uses word sorting rules that do not depend on your system's currently selected culture. Comparing `"hello"` with `"HELLO"` would return `false`, because the lowercase letters are different from the corresponding uppercase letters.

The condition in line 31 uses class `string`'s *overloaded equality operator (==)* to compare `string` `string1` with the literal `string` `"hello"` for equality. In C#, the equality operator also compares the contents of two `string`s. Thus, the condition in the `if` statement evaluates to `true`, because the values of `string1` and `"hello"` are equal.

Line 41 tests whether string3 and string4 are equal to illustrate that comparisons are indeed case sensitive. Here, static method Equals is used to compare the values of two strings. "Happy Birthday" does not equal "happy birthday", so the condition fails, and the message "string3 does not equal string4" is output (line 47).

Lines 51–60 use string method CompareTo to compare strings. The method returns 0 if the strings are equal, a negative value if the string that invokes CompareTo is less than the string that's passed as an argument and a positive value if the string that invokes CompareTo is greater than the string that's passed as an argument.

Notice that CompareTo considers string3 to be greater than string4. The only difference between these two strings is that string3 contains two uppercase letters in positions where string4 contains lowercase letters. The method uses sorting rules that are case and culture sensitive.

### *Determining Whether a String Begins or Ends with a Specified String*

Figure 16.4 tests whether a string begins or ends with a given string. Method StartsWith determines whether a string starts with the string passed to the method as an argument. Method EndsWith determines whether a string ends with the string passed to the method as an argument.

```
// Fig. 16.4: StringStartEnd.cs
// Demonstrating StartsWith and EndsWith methods.
using System;

class StringStartEnd
{
   static void Main()
   {
      string[] strings = {"started", "starting", "ended", "ending"};

      // test every string to see if it starts with "st"
      foreach (var element in strings)
      {
         if (element.StartsWith("st"))
         {
            Console.WriteLine($"\"{element}\" starts with \"st\"");
         }
      }

      Console.WriteLine();

      // test every string to see if it ends with "ed"
      foreach (var element in strings)
      {
         if (element.EndsWith("ed"))
         {
            Console.WriteLine($"\"{element}\" ends with \"ed\"");
         }
      }

```

**Fig. 16.4** | Demonstrating StartsWith and EndsWith methods. (Part 1 of 2.)

```
31         Console.WriteLine();
32      }
33   }
```

```
"started" starts with "st"
"starting" starts with "st"

"started" ends with "ed"
"ended" ends with "ed"
```

**Fig. 16.4** | Demonstrating `StartsWith` and `EndsWith` methods. (Part 2 of 2.)

Line 9 defines an array of `string`s, which contains `"started"`, `"starting"`, `"ended"` and `"ending"`. Line 14 uses method `StartsWith`, which takes a `string` argument. The condition in the `if` statement determines whether the current `element` starts with the characters `"st"`. If so, the method returns `true`, and the `element` is displayed along with a message.

Line 25 uses method `EndsWith` to determine whether the current `element` ends with the characters `"ed"`. If so, the method returns `true`, and the `element` is displayed along with a message.

## 16.6 Locating Characters and Substrings in `string`s

In many apps, it's necessary to search for a character or set of characters in a `string`. For example, a programmer creating a word processor would want to provide capabilities for searching through documents. Figure 16.5 demonstrates some versions of `string` methods `IndexOf`, `IndexOfAny`, `LastIndexOf` and `LastIndexOfAny`, which search for a specified character or substring in a `string`. We perform all searches in this example on the `string` `letters` (line 9).

```
1   // Fig. 16.5: StringIndexMethods.cs
2   // Using string-searching methods.
3   using System;
4
5   class StringIndexMethods
6   {
7      static void Main()
8      {
9         var letters = "abcdefghijklmabcdefghijklm";
10        char[] searchLetters = {'c', 'a', '$'};
11
12        // test IndexOf to locate a character in a string
13        Console.WriteLine($"First 'c' is located at index " +
14           letters.IndexOf('c'));
15        Console.WriteLine("First 'a' starting at 1 is located at index " +
16           letters.IndexOf('a', 1));
17        Console.WriteLine("First '$' in the 5 positions starting at 3 " +
18           $"is located at index " + letters.IndexOf('$', 3, 5));
19
```

**Fig. 16.5** | Using `string`-searching methods. (Part 1 of 3.)

```
         // test LastIndexOf to find a character in a string
         Console.WriteLine($"\nLast 'c' is located at index " +
            letters.LastIndexOf('c'));
         Console.WriteLine("Last 'a' up to position 25 is located at " +
            "index " + letters.LastIndexOf('a', 25));
         Console.WriteLine("Last '$' in the 5 positions ending at 15 " +
            "is located at index " + letters.LastIndexOf('$', 15, 5));

         // test IndexOf to locate a substring in a string
         Console.WriteLine("\nFirst \"def\" is located at index " +
            letters.IndexOf("def"));
         Console.WriteLine("First \"def\" starting at 7 is located at " +
            "index " + letters.IndexOf("def", 7));
         Console.WriteLine("First \"hello\" in the 15 positions " +
            "starting at 5 is located at index " +
            letters.IndexOf("hello", 5, 15));

         // test LastIndexOf to find a substring in a string
         Console.WriteLine("\nLast \"def\" is located at index " +
            letters.LastIndexOf("def"));
         Console.WriteLine("Last \"def\" up to position 25 is located " +
            "at index " + letters.LastIndexOf("def", 25));
         Console.WriteLine("Last \"hello\" in the 15 positions " +
            "ending at 20 is located at index " +
            letters.LastIndexOf("hello", 20, 15));

         // test IndexOfAny to find first occurrence of character in array
         Console.WriteLine("\nFirst 'c', 'a' or '$' is " +
            "located at index " + letters.IndexOfAny(searchLetters));
         Console.WriteLine("First 'c', 'a' or '$' starting at 7 is " +
            "located at index " + letters.IndexOfAny(searchLetters, 7));
         Console.WriteLine("First 'c', 'a' or '$' in the 5 positions " +
            "starting at 7 is located at index " +
            letters.IndexOfAny(searchLetters, 7, 5));

         // test LastIndexOfAny to find last occurrence of character
         // in array
         Console.WriteLine("\nLast 'c', 'a' or '$' is " +
            "located at index " + letters.LastIndexOfAny(searchLetters));
         Console.WriteLine("Last 'c', 'a' or '$' up to position 1 is " +
            "located at index " +
            letters.LastIndexOfAny(searchLetters, 1));
         Console.WriteLine("Last 'c', 'a' or '$' in the 5 positions " +
            "ending at 25 is located at index " +
            letters.LastIndexOfAny(searchLetters, 25, 5));
      }
   }
```

```
First 'c' is located at index 2
First 'a' starting at 1 is located at index 13
First '$' in the 5 positions starting at 3 is located at index -1
```

**Fig. 16.5** | Using `string`-searching methods. (Part 2 of 3.)

```
Last 'c' is located at index 15
Last 'a' up to position 25 is located at index 13
Last '$' in the 5 positions ending at 15 is located at index -1

First "def" is located at index 3
First "def" starting at 7 is located at index 16
First "hello" in the 15 positions starting at 5 is located at index -1

Last "def" is located at index 16
Last "def" up to position 25 is located at index 16
Last "hello" in the 15 positions ending at 20 is located at index -1

First 'c', 'a' or '$' is located at index 0
First 'c', 'a' or '$' starting at 7 is located at index 13
First 'c', 'a' or '$' in the 5 positions starting at 7 is located at index -1

Last 'c', 'a' or '$' is located at index 15
Last 'c', 'a' or '$' up to position 1 is located at index 0
Last 'c', 'a' or '$' in the 5 positions ending at 25 is located at index -1
```

**Fig. 16.5** | Using string-searching methods. (Part 3 of 3.)

Lines 14, 16 and 18 use method IndexOf to locate the first occurrence of a character or substring in a string. If it finds a character, IndexOf returns the index of the specified character in the string; otherwise, IndexOf returns -1. The expression in line 16 uses a method IndexOf with two arguments—the character to search for and the starting index at which the search should begin. The method does not examine any characters that occur prior to the starting index (in this case, 1). The expression in line 18 uses method IndexOf with three arguments—the character to search for, the index at which to start searching and the number of characters to search.

Lines 22, 24 and 26 use method LastIndexOf to locate the last occurrence of a character in a string. Method LastIndexOf performs the search from the end to the beginning of the string. If it finds the character, LastIndexOf returns the index of the specified character in the string; otherwise, LastIndexOf returns -1. There are three versions of method LastIndexOf. The expression in line 22 uses the version that takes as an argument the character for which to search. The expression in line 24 uses the version that takes two arguments—the character for which to search and the highest index from which to begin searching backward for the character. The expression in line 26 uses a third version of method LastIndexOf that takes three arguments—the character for which to search, the starting index from which to start searching backward and the number of characters (the portion of the string) to search.

Lines 29–44 use versions of IndexOf and LastIndexOf that take a string instead of a character as the first argument. These versions of the methods perform identically to those described above except that they search for sequences of characters (or substrings) that are specified by their string arguments.

Lines 47–64 use methods IndexOfAny and LastIndexOfAny, which take an array of characters as the first argument. These versions of the methods also perform identically to those described above, except that they return the index of the first or last occurrence of any of the characters in the character-array argument, respectively.

**Common Programming Error 16.2**

*In the overloaded methods `LastIndexOf` and `LastIndexOfAny` that take three parameters, the second argument must be greater than or equal to the third. This might seem counterintuitive, but remember that the search moves from the end of the string toward the start of the string.*

## 16.7 Extracting Substrings from strings

Class `string` provides two `Substring` methods, which create a new `string` by copying part of an existing `string`. Each method returns a new `string`. Figure 16.6 demonstrates both methods.

```
1  // Fig. 16.6: SubString.cs
2  // Demonstrating the string Substring method.
3  using System;
4
5  class SubString
6  {
7     static void Main()
8     {
9        var letters = "abcdefghijklmabcdefghijklm";
10
11       // invoke Substring method and pass it one parameter
12       Console.WriteLine("Substring from index 20 to end is " +
13          $"\"{letters.Substring(20)}\"");
14
15       // invoke Substring method and pass it two parameters
16       Console.WriteLine("Substring from index 0 of length 6 is " +
17          $"\"{letters.Substring(0, 6)}\"");
18    }
19 }
```

```
Substring from index 20 to end is "hijklm"
Substring from index 0 of length 6 is "abcdef"
```

**Fig. 16.6** | Demonstrating the `string` `Substring` method.

The statement in line 13 uses the `Substring` method that takes one `int` argument. The argument specifies the starting index from which the method copies characters in the original `string`. The substring returned contains a copy of the characters from the starting index to the end of the `string`. If the index specified in the argument is outside the bounds of the `string`, the program throws an `ArgumentOutOfRangeException`.

The second version of method `Substring` (line 17) takes two `int` arguments. The first argument specifies the starting index from which the method copies characters from the original `string`. The second argument specifies the length of the substring to copy. The substring returned contains a copy of the specified characters from the original `string`. If the supplied length of the substring is too large (i.e., the substring tries to retrieve characters past the end of the original `string`), an `ArgumentOutOfRangeException` is thrown.

## 16.8 Concatenating strings

The + operator is not the only way to perform string concatenation. The static method Concat of class string (Fig. 16.7) concatenates two strings and returns a new string containing the combined characters from both original strings. Line 15 appends the characters from string2 to the end of a copy of string1, using method Concat. The method call in line 15 does not modify the original strings.

```
1  // Fig. 16.7: SubConcatenation.cs
2  // Demonstrating string class Concat method.
3  using System;
4
5  class StringConcatenation
6  {
7     static void Main()
8     {
9        var string1 = "Happy ";
10       var string2 = "Birthday";
11
12       Console.WriteLine($"string1 = \"{string1}\"");
13       Console.WriteLine($"string2 = \"{string2}\"");
14       Console.WriteLine("\nResult of string.Concat(string1, string2) = " +
15          string.Concat(string1, string2));
16       Console.WriteLine($"string1 after concatenation = {string1}");
17    }
18 }
```

```
string1 = "Happy "
string2 = "Birthday"

Result of string.Concat(string1, string2) = Happy Birthday
string1 after concatenation = Happy
```

**Fig. 16.7** | Demonstrating string class Concat method.

## 16.9 Miscellaneous string Methods

Class string provides several methods that return modified copies of strings. Figure 16.8 demonstrates string methods Replace, ToLower, ToUpper and Trim.

```
// Fig. 16.8: StringMethods2.cs
// Demonstrating string methods Replace, ToLower, ToUpper and Trim

using System;

class StringMethods2
{
   static void Main()
   {
```

**Fig. 16.8** | Demonstrating string methods Replace, ToLower, ToUpper and Trim. (Part 1 of 2.)

```
10         var string1 = "cheers!";
11         var string2 = "GOOD BYE ";
12         var string3 = "   spaces   ";
13
14         Console.WriteLine($"string1 = \"{string1}\"\n" +
15            $"string2 = \"{string2}\"\n" +
16            $"string3 = \"{string3}\"");
17
18         // call method Replace
19         Console.WriteLine("\nReplacing \"e\" with \"E\" in string1: " +
20            $"\"{string1.Replace('e', 'E')}\"");
21
22         // call ToLower and ToUpper
23         Console.WriteLine(
24            $"\nstring1.ToUpper() = \"{string1.ToUpper()}\"" +
25            $"\nstring2.ToLower() = \"{string2.ToLower()}\"");
26
27         // call Trim method
28         Console.WriteLine(
29            $"\nstring3 after trim = \"{string3.Trim()}\"");
30
31         Console.WriteLine($"\nstring1 = \"{string1}\"");
32      }
33   }
```

```
string1 = "cheers!"
string2 = "GOOD BYE "
string3 = "   spaces   "

Replacing "e" with "E" in string1: "chEErs!"

string1.ToUpper() = "CHEERS!"
string2.ToLower() = "good bye "

string3 after trim = "spaces"

string1 = "cheers!"
```

**Fig. 16.8** | Demonstrating `string` methods `Replace`, `ToLower`, `ToUpper` and `Trim`. (Part 2 of 2.)

Line 20 uses `string` method `Replace` to return a new `string`, replacing every occurrence in `string1` of character `'e'` with `'E'`. Method `Replace` takes two arguments—a `char` for which to search and another `char` with which to replace all matching occurrences of the first argument. The original `string` remains unchanged. If there are no occurrences of the first argument in the `string`, the method returns the original `string`. An overloaded version of this method allows you to provide two `string`s as arguments.

The `string` method `ToUpper` generates a new `string` (line 24) that replaces any *lowercase* letters in `string1` with their *uppercase* equivalents (using the current culture's rules). The method returns a new `string` containing the converted `string`; the original `string` remains *unchanged*. If there are no characters to convert, the original `string` is returned. Line 25 uses `string` method `ToLower` to return a new `string` in which any *uppercase* letters in `string2` are replaced by their *lowercase* equivalents (using the current culture's rules). The original `string` is *unchanged*. As with `ToUpper`, if there are *no* characters to convert to lowercase, method `ToLower` returns the *original* `string`.

Line 29 uses string method Trim to remove all *whitespace characters* that appear at the beginning and end of a string. Without otherwise altering the original string, the method returns a new string that contains the string, but *omits* leading and trailing *whitespace* characters. This method is particularly useful for retrieving user input (i.e., via a TextBox). Another version of method Trim takes a character array and returns a copy of the string that does not begin or end with any of the characters in the array argument.

## 16.10 Class StringBuilder

The string class provides many capabilities for processing strings. However a string's contents can *never* change. Operations that seem to concatenate strings are in fact creating new strings—the += operator creates a new string and assigns its reference to the variable on the left of the += operator.

The next several sections discuss the features of class StringBuilder (namespace System.Text), used to create and manipulate dynamic string information—i.e., *mutable* strings. Every StringBuilder can store a certain number of characters that's specified by its capacity. Exceeding the capacity of a StringBuilder causes the capacity to expand to accommodate the additional characters. As we'll see, members of class StringBuilder, such as methods Append and AppendFormat, can be used for *concatenation* like the operators + and += for class string—without creating any new string objects. StringBuilder is particularly useful for manipulating in place a large number of strings, as it's much more efficient than creating individual immutable strings.

**Performance Tip 16.2**

*Objects of class string are immutable (i.e., constant strings), whereas objects of class StringBuilder are mutable. C# can perform certain optimizations involving strings (such as the sharing of one string among multiple references), because it knows these objects will not change.*

### *StringBuilder Constructors*

Class StringBuilder provides six overloaded constructors. Class StringBuilderConstructor (Fig. 16.9) demonstrates three of these overloaded constructors. Line 10 employs the no-parameter StringBuilder constructor to create a StringBuilder that contains no characters and has an implementation-specific *default initial capacity*. Line 11 uses the StringBuilder constructor that takes an int argument to create a StringBuilder that contains no characters and has the *initial capacity* specified in the int argument (i.e., 10). Line 12 uses the StringBuilder constructor that takes a string argument to create a StringBuilder containing the characters of the string argument—the initial capacity might differ from the string's size. Lines 14–16 implicitly use StringBuilder method ToString to obtain string representations of the StringBuilders' contents.

```
1  // Fig. 16.9: StringBuilderConstructor.cs
2  // Demonstrating StringBuilder class constructors.
3  using System;
4  using System.Text;
```

**Fig. 16.9** | Demonstrating StringBuilder class constructors. (Part 1 of 2.)

```

class StringBuilderConstructor
{
   static void Main()
   {
      var buffer1 = new StringBuilder();
      var buffer2 = new StringBuilder(10);
      var buffer3 = new StringBuilder("hello");

      Console.WriteLine($"buffer1 = \"{buffer1}\"");
      Console.WriteLine($"buffer2 = \"{buffer2}\"");
      Console.WriteLine($"buffer3 = \"{buffer3}\"");
   }
}
```

```
buffer1 = ""
buffer2 = ""
buffer3 = "hello"
```

**Fig. 16.9** | Demonstrating `StringBuilder` class constructors. (Part 2 of 2.)

## 16.11 Length and Capacity Properties, EnsureCapacity Method and Indexer of Class StringBuilder

Class `StringBuilder` provides the `Length` and `Capacity` properties to return the number of characters currently in a `StringBuilder` and the number of characters that a `StringBuilder` can store without allocating more memory, respectively. These properties also can be used to increase or decrease the length or the capacity of the `StringBuilder`. Method `EnsureCapacity` allows you to reduce the number of times that a `StringBuilder`'s capacity must be increased. The method ensures that the `StringBuilder`'s capacity is at least the specified value. Figure 16.10 demonstrates these methods and properties.

```
// Fig. 16.10: StringBuilderFeatures.cs
// StringBuilder size manipulation.
using System;
using System.Text;

class StringBuilderFeatures
{
   static void Main()
   {
      var buffer = new StringBuilder("Hello, how are you?");

      // use Length and Capacity properties
      Console.WriteLine($"buffer = {buffer}" +
         $"\nLength = {buffer.Length}" +
         $"\nCapacity = {buffer.Capacity}");
```

**Fig. 16.10** | `StringBuilder` size manipulation. (Part 1 of 2.)

```
16
17         buffer.EnsureCapacity(75); // ensure a capacity of at least 75
18         Console.WriteLine($"\nNew capacity = {buffer.Capacity}");
19
20         // truncate StringBuilder by setting Length property
21         buffer.Length = 10;
22         Console.Write($"New length = {buffer.Length}\n\nbuffer = ");
23
24         // use StringBuilder indexer
25         for (int i = 0; i < buffer.Length; ++i)
26         {
27            Console.Write(buffer[i]);
28         }
29
30         Console.WriteLine();
31      }
32   }
```

```
buffer = Hello, how are you?
Length = 19
Capacity = 19

New capacity = 75
New length = 10

buffer = Hello, how
```

**Fig. 16.10** | StringBuilder size manipulation. (Part 2 of 2.)

The program contains one StringBuilder, called buffer. Line 10 uses the StringBuilder constructor that takes a string argument to create a StringBuilder and initialize it to "Hello, how are you?". Lines 13–15 output the StringBuilder's content, length and capacity.

Line 17 expands the StringBuilder's capacity to a minimum of 75 characters. If new characters are added to a StringBuilder so that its length exceeds its capacity, the capacity *grows* to accommodate the additional characters in the same manner as if method EnsureCapacity had been called.

Line 21 uses property Length to set the StringBuilder's length to 10—this does *not* change the Capacity. If the specified length is less than the StringBuilder's current number of characters, the contents are *truncated* to the specified length. If the specified length is greater than the current number of characters, null characters (that is, '\0' characters) are appended to the StringBuilder until the total number of characters is equal to the specified length. Lines 25–28 use StringBuilder's indexer to display each character. This for statement could be replaced with the following foreach:

```
foreach (var element in buffer)
{
   Console.Write(element);
}
```

## 16.12 Append and AppendFormat Methods of Class StringBuilder

Class StringBuilder provides overloaded Append methods that allow various types of values to be added to the end of a StringBuilder. The Framework Class Library provides versions for each simple type and for character arrays, strings and objects. (Remember that method ToString produces a string representation of any object.) Each method takes an argument, converts it to a string and appends it to the StringBuilder. Figure 16.11 uses several Append methods (lines 22–40) to attach the variables' string representations in lines 10–18 to the end of the StringBuilder.

```
1  // Fig. 16.11: StringBuilderAppend.cs
2  // Demonstrating StringBuilder Append methods.
3  using System;
4  using System.Text;
5
6  class StringBuilderAppend
7  {
8     static void Main()
9     {
10       object objectValue = "hello";
11       var stringValue = "good bye";
12       char[] characterArray = {'a', 'b', 'c', 'd', 'e', 'f'};
13       var booleanValue = true;
14       var characterValue = 'Z';
15       var integerValue = 7;
16       var longValue = 1000000L; // L suffix indicates a long literal
17       var floatValue = 2.5F; // F suffix indicates a float literal
18       var doubleValue = 33.333;
19       var buffer = new StringBuilder();
20
21       // use method Append to append values to buffer
22       buffer.Append(objectValue);
23       buffer.Append("  ");
24       buffer.Append(stringValue);
25       buffer.Append("  ");
26       buffer.Append(characterArray);
27       buffer.Append("  ");
28       buffer.Append(characterArray, 0, 3);
29       buffer.Append("  ");
30       buffer.Append(booleanValue);
31       buffer.Append("  ");
32       buffer.Append(characterValue);
33       buffer.Append("  ");
34       buffer.Append(integerValue);
35       buffer.Append("  ");
36       buffer.Append(longValue);
37       buffer.Append("  ");
38       buffer.Append(floatValue);
39       buffer.Append("  ");
40       buffer.Append(doubleValue);
```

**Fig. 16.11** | Demonstrating StringBuilder Append methods. (Part 1 of 2.)

```

            Console.WriteLine($"buffer = {buffer.ToString()}");
        }
    }
```

```
buffer = hello  good bye  abcdef  abc  True  Z  7  1000000  2.5  33.333
```

**Fig. 16.11** | Demonstrating StringBuilder Append methods. (Part 2 of 2.)

Class `StringBuilder` also provides method `AppendFormat`, which converts a `string` to a specified format, then appends it to the `StringBuilder`. The example in Fig. 16.12 demonstrates `AppendFormat`.

```
// Fig. 16.12: StringBuilderAppendFormat.cs
// Demonstrating method AppendFormat.
using System;
using System.Text;

class StringBuilderAppendFormat
{
   static void Main()
   {
      var buffer = new StringBuilder();

      // formatted string
      var string1 = "This {0} costs: {1:C}.\n\n";

      // string1 argument array
      var objectArray = new object[2] {"car", 1234.56};

      // append to buffer formatted string with argument
      buffer.AppendFormat(string1, objectArray);

      // formatted string
      string string2 = "Number:\n{0:d3}.\n\n" +
         "Number right aligned with spaces:\n{0,4}.\n\n" +
         "Number left aligned with spaces:\n{0,-4}.";

      // append to buffer formatted string with argument
      buffer.AppendFormat(string2, 5);

      // display formatted strings
      Console.WriteLine(buffer.ToString());
   }
}
```

```
This car costs: $1,234.56.

Number:
005.
```

**Fig. 16.12** | Demonstrating method AppendFormat. (Part 1 of 2.)

```
Number right aligned with spaces:
   5.

Number left aligned with spaces:
5   .
```

**Fig. 16.12** | Demonstrating method `AppendFormat`. (Part 2 of 2.)

Line 13 declares a **format `string`** that consists of text and **format items**. Each format item in braces (`{}`) is a placeholder for a value. Format items also may include the same optional formatting you've seen throughout this book in interpolated `string`s. Line 16 declares and initializes an array of `object`s that will be formatted. Line 19 shows a version of `AppendFormat` that takes two parameters—a format `string` and an array of `object`s to serve as the arguments to the format `string`. The `object` at index `0` of the array is formatted by the format item `"{0}"`, which simply produces the `object`'s `string` representation. The `object` at index `1` of the array is formatted by the format item `"{1:C}"`, which formats the `object` as currency.

Lines 22–24 declare another format `string` with three format specifiers:

- The first—`{0:d3}`—formats a three-digit integer value. Any number having fewer than three digits will have leading zeros.
- The second—`{0,4}`—formats a `string` in a right-aligned field of four characters.
- The third—`{0,-4}`—formats a `string` in a left-aligned field of four characters.

Line 27 uses a version of `AppendFormat` that takes two parameters—a format `string` and an object to format. In this case, the object is the number `5`, which is formatted by all three format specifiers. The output displays the result of applying these two versions of `AppendFormat` with their respective arguments.

## 16.13 `Insert`, `Remove` and `Replace` Methods of Class `StringBuilder`

Class `StringBuilder` provides overloaded `Insert` methods to allow various types of data to be inserted at any position in a `StringBuilder`. The class provides versions for each simple type and for character arrays, `string`s and `object`s. Each method takes its second argument, converts it to a `string` and inserts the `string` into the `StringBuilder` in front of the character in the position specified by the first argument. The index specified by the first argument must be greater than or equal to `0` and less than the `StringBuilder`'s length; otherwise, the program throws an `ArgumentOutOfRangeException`.

Class `StringBuilder` also provides method `Remove` for deleting any portion of a `StringBuilder`. Method `Remove` takes two arguments—the index at which to begin deletion and the number of characters to delete. The sum of the starting index and the number of characters to be deleted must always be less than the `StringBuilder`'s length; otherwise, the program throws an `ArgumentOutOfRangeException`. The `Insert` and `Remove` methods are demonstrated in Fig. 16.13.

```
// Fig. 16.13: StringBuilderInsertRemove.cs
// Demonstrating methods Insert and Remove of the
// StringBuilder class.
using System;
using System.Text;

class StringBuilderInsertRemove
{
   static void Main()
   {
      object objectValue = "hello";
      var stringValue = "good bye";
      char[] characterArray = {'a', 'b', 'c', 'd', 'e', 'f'};
      var booleanValue = true;
      var characterValue = 'K';
      var integerValue = 7;
      var longValue = 1000000L; // L suffix indicates a long literal
      var floatValue = 2.5F; // F suffix indicates a float literal
      var doubleValue = 33.333;
      var buffer = new StringBuilder();

      // insert values into buffer
      buffer.Insert(0, objectValue);
      buffer.Insert(0, "  ");
      buffer.Insert(0, stringValue);
      buffer.Insert(0, "  ");
      buffer.Insert(0, characterArray);
      buffer.Insert(0, "  ");
      buffer.Insert(0, booleanValue);
      buffer.Insert(0, "  ");
      buffer.Insert(0, characterValue);
      buffer.Insert(0, "  ");
      buffer.Insert(0, integerValue);
      buffer.Insert(0, "  ");
      buffer.Insert(0, longValue);
      buffer.Insert(0, "  ");
      buffer.Insert(0, floatValue);
      buffer.Insert(0, "  ");
      buffer.Insert(0, doubleValue);
      buffer.Insert(0, "  ");

      Console.WriteLine($"buffer after Inserts: \n{buffer}\n");

      buffer.Remove(10, 1); // delete 2 in 2.5
      buffer.Remove(4, 4);  // delete .333 in 33.333

      Console.WriteLine($"buffer after Removes:\n{buffer}");
   }
}
```

```
buffer after Inserts:
  33.333  2.5  10000000  7  K  True  abcdef  good bye  hello
```

**Fig. 16.13** | Demonstrating methods `Insert` and `Remove` of the `StringBuilder` class. (Part 1 of 2.)

```
buffer after Removes:
 33  .5  10000000  7  K  True  abcdef  good bye  hello
```

**Fig. 16.13** | Demonstrating methods `Insert` and `Remove` of the `StringBuilder` class. (Part 2 of 2.)

Another useful method included with `StringBuilder` is `Replace`, which searches for a specified `string` or character and *substitutes* another `string` or character all occurrences. Figure 16.14 demonstrates this method.

```
1  // Fig. 16.14: StringBuilderReplace.cs
2  // Demonstrating method Replace.
3  using System;
4  using System.Text;
5
6  class StringBuilderReplace
7  {
8     static void Main()
9     {
10       var builder1 = new StringBuilder("Happy Birthday Jane");
11       var builder2 = new StringBuilder("goodbye greg");
12
13       Console.WriteLine($"Before replacements:\n{builder1}\n{builder2}");
14
15       builder1.Replace("Jane", "Greg");
16       builder2.Replace('g', 'G', 0, 5);
17
18       Console.WriteLine($"\nAfter replacements:\n{builder1}\n{builder2}");
19    }
20 }
```

```
Before Replacements:
Happy Birthday Jane
good bye greg

After replacements:
Happy Birthday Greg
Goodbye greg
```

**Fig. 16.14** | Demonstrating method `Replace`.

Line 15 uses method `Replace` to replace all instances of `"Jane"` with the `"Greg"` in `builder1`. Another overload of this method takes two characters as parameters and *replaces* each occurrence of the first character with the second. Line 16 uses an overload of `Replace` that takes four parameters, of which the first two are both characters or both `string`s and the second two are `int`s. The method replaces all instances of the first character with the second character (or the first `string` with the second), beginning at the index specified by the first `int` and continuing for a count specified by the second `int`. Thus, in this case, `Replace` looks through only five characters, starting with the character at index `0`. As the output illustrates, this version of `Replace` replaces `g` with `G` in the word `"goodbye"`, but not in `"greg"`. This is because the `g`s in `"greg"` are not in the range indicated by the `int` arguments (i.e., between indexes `0` and `4`).

## 16.14 Char Methods

Section 10.13 introduced structs for representing value types. The simple types are actually aliases for struct types. For instance, an int is defined by struct System.Int32, a long by System.Int64 and so on. All struct types derive from class **ValueType**, which derives from object. Also, all struct types are implicitly sealed.

In the struct **System.Char**—which is the struct for characters and represented by C# keyword char—most methods are static, take at least one character argument and perform either a test or a manipulation on the character. We present several of these in the next example. Figure 16.15 demonstrates static methods that test characters to determine whether they're of a specific character type and static methods that perform case conversions on characters.

```
// Fig. 16.15: StaticCharMethods.cs
// Demonstrates static character-testing and case-conversion methods
// from Char struct
using System;

class StaticCharMethods
{
   static void Main(string[] args)
   {
      Console.Write("Enter a character: ");
      var character = char.Parse(Console.ReadLine());

      Console.WriteLine($"is digit: {char.IsDigit(character)}");
      Console.WriteLine($"is letter: {char.IsLetter(character)}");
      Console.WriteLine(
         $"is letter or digit: {char.IsLetterOrDigit(character)}");
      Console.WriteLine($"is lower case: {char.IsLower(character)}");
      Console.WriteLine($"is upper case: {char.IsUpper(character)}");
      Console.WriteLine($"to upper case: {char.ToUpper(character)}");
      Console.WriteLine($"to lower case: {char.ToLower(character)}");
      Console.WriteLine(
         $"is punctuation: {char.IsPunctuation(character)}");
      Console.WriteLine($"is symbol: {char.IsSymbol(character)}");
   }
}
```

```
Enter a character: A
is digit: False
is letter: True
is letter or digit: True
is lower case: False
is upper case: True
to upper case: A
to lower case: a
is punctuation: False
is symbol: False
```

**Fig. 16.15** | Demonstrates static character-testing and case-conversion methods from Char struct. (Part 1 of 2.)

```
Enter a character: 8
is digit: True
is letter: False
is letter or digit: True
is lower case: False
is upper case: False
to upper case: 8
to lower case: 8
is punctuation: False
is symbol: False
```

```
Enter a character: @
is digit: False
is letter: False
is letter or digit: False
is lower case: False
is upper case: False
to upper case: @
to lower case: @
is punctuation: True
is symbol: False
```

```
Enter a character: m
is digit: False
is letter: True
is letter or digit: True
is lower case: True
is upper case: False
to upper case: M
to lower case: m
is punctuation: False
is symbol: False
```

```
Enter a character: +
is digit: False
is letter: False
is letter or digit: False
is lower case: False
is upper case: False
to upper case: +
to lower case: +
is punctuation: False
is symbol: True
```

**Fig. 16.15** | Demonstrates `static` character-testing and case-conversion methods from `Char` `struct`. (Part 2 of 2.)

After the user enters a character, lines 13–23 analyze it. Line 13 uses `Char` method `IsDigit` to determine whether `character` is defined as a digit. If so, the method returns `true`; otherwise, it returns `false` (note that `bool` values are capitalized for output). Line

14 uses `Char` method `IsLetter` to determine whether `character` is a letter. Line 16 uses `Char` method `IsLetterOrDigit` to determine whether character `character` is a letter or a digit.

The methods in lines 17–20 are culture sensitive. Line 17 uses `Char` method `IsLower` to determine whether `character` is a *lowercase* letter. Line 18 uses `Char` method `IsUpper` to determine whether `character` is an *uppercase* letter.

Line 19 uses `Char` method `ToUpper` to convert `character` to its *uppercase* equivalent. The method returns the converted character if the it has an uppercase equivalent; otherwise, the method returns its *original* argument.

Line 20 uses `Char` method `ToLower` to convert `character` to its *lowercase* equivalent. The method returns the converted character if the character has a lowercase equivalent; otherwise, the method returns its *original* argument.

Line 22 uses `Char` method `IsPunctuation` to determine whether `character` is a punctuation mark, such as `"!"`, `":"` or `")"`. Line 23 uses `Char` method `IsSymbol` to determine whether character `character` is a symbol, such as `"+"`, `"="` or `"^"`.

Structure type `Char` also contains other methods not shown in this example. Many of the `static` methods are similar—for instance, `IsWhiteSpace` is used to determine whether a certain character is a whitespace character (e.g., newline, tab or space). The `struct` also contains several `public` instance methods; many of these, such as methods `ToString` and `Equals`, are methods that we have seen before in other classes. This group includes method `CompareTo`, which is used to compare one character value with another.

## 16.15 Introduction to Regular Expressions (Online)

This online section is available via the book's webpage at

```
http://www.deitel.com/books/CSharp6FP
```

In this section, we introduce **regular expressions**—specially formatted strings used to find patterns in text. They can be used to ensure that data is in a particular format. For example, a U.S. zip code must consist of five digits, or five digits followed by a dash followed by four more digits. Compilers use regular expressions to *validate* program syntax. If the program code does *not* match the regular expression, the compiler indicates that there's a syntax error. We discuss classes `Regex` and `Match` from the `System.Text.RegularExpressions` namespace as well as the symbols used to form regular expressions. We then demonstrate how to find patterns in a string, match entire strings to patterns, replace characters in a string that match a pattern and split strings at delimiters specified as a pattern in a regular expression.

## 16.16 Wrap-Up

This chapter presented the Framework Class Library's `string`- and character-processing capabilities. We overviewed the fundamentals of characters and strings. You saw how to determine the length of strings, copy strings, access the individual characters in strings, search strings, obtain substrings from larger strings, compare strings, concatenate strings, replace characters in strings and convert strings to uppercase or lowercase letters.

We showed how to use class `StringBuilder` to build strings dynamically. You learned how to determine and specify the size of a `StringBuilder` object, and how to append, insert, remove and replace characters in a `StringBuilder` object. We then introduced the character-testing methods of type `Char` that enable a program to determine whether a character is a digit, a letter, a lowercase letter, an uppercase letter, a punctuation mark or a symbol other than a punctuation mark, and the methods for converting a character to uppercase or lowercase.

In the next chapter, you'll learn how to read data from and write data to text files. We'll also demonstrate C#'s object-serialization mechanism that can convert objects into bytes so you can output and input objects.

# 17

# Files and Streams

## Objectives

In this chapter you'll:

- Create, read, write and update files.
- Use classes `File` and `Directory` to obtain information about files and directories on your computer.
- Use LINQ to search through directories.
- Become familiar with sequential-access file processing.
- Use classes `FileStream`, `StreamReader` and `StreamWriter` to read text from and write text to files.
- Use classes `FileStream` and `BinaryFormatter` to read objects from and write objects to files.

Outline



## 17.1 Introduction

Variables and arrays offer only *temporary* storage of data—the data is lost when a local variable "goes out of scope" or when the program terminates. By contrast, **files** (and databases, which we cover in Chapter 20) are used for long-term retention of large amounts of data, even after the program that created the data terminates. Data maintained in files often is called **persistent data**. Computers store files on **secondary storage devices**, such as hard drives, solid-state drives, flash drives, DVDs and tapes. In this chapter, we explain how to create, update and process data files in C# programs.

We overview some of the Framework Class Library's file-processing classes. We then create Windows `Forms` apps that write to and read from *text files* that are *human readable* and binary files that store entire objects in binary format. Finally, we present examples that show how you can determine information about the files and directories on your computer.

## 17.2 Files and Streams

C# views each file as a sequential **stream** of bytes (Fig. 17.1). Each file ends either with an **end-of-file marker** or at a specific byte number that's recorded in a system-maintained administrative data structure, because file organization is operating-system dependent. A C# program processing a stream of bytes simply receives an indication from the operating system when it reaches the end of the stream—the program does *not* need to know how the underlying platform represents files or streams.

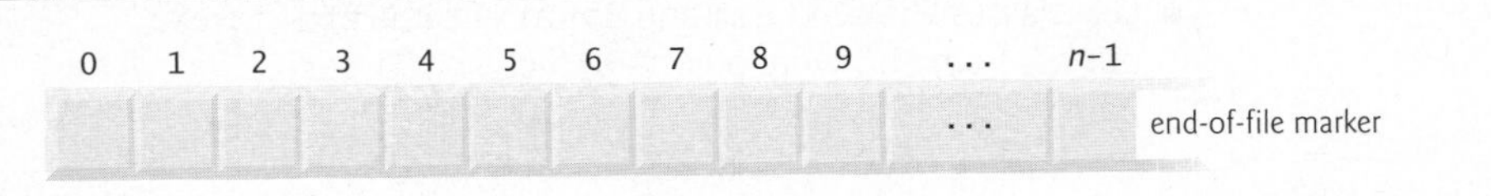


**Fig. 17.1** | C#'s view of an $n$-byte file.

### *Standard Streams in Console Apps*

When a file is opened, an object is created and a stream is associated with the object. When a console app executes, the runtime environment creates three stream objects that are accessible via properties **`Console.Out`**, **`Console.In`** and **`Console.Error`**, respectively. These objects use streams to facilitate communication between a program and a particular file or device. `Console.In` refers to the **standard input stream object**, which enables a program to input data from the keyboard. `Console.Out` refers to the **standard output stream object**, which enables a program to output data to the screen. `Console.Error` refers to the **standard error stream object**, which enables a program to output error messages to the screen. These can be redirected to other files or devices. We've been using `Console.Out` and `Console.In` in our console apps:

- `Console` methods `Write` and `WriteLine` use `Console.Out` to perform output, and
- `Console` methods `Read` and `ReadLine` use `Console.In` to perform input.

### *File-Processing Classes*

There are many file-processing classes in the Framework Class Library. The **`System.IO` namespace** includes stream classes such as **`StreamReader`** (for text input from a stream), **`StreamWriter`** (for text output to a stream) and **`FileStream`** (for both input from and output to a stream). These stream classes inherit from `abstract` classes **`TextReader`**, **`TextWriter`** and `Stream`, respectively. `Console.In` and `Console.Error` are of type `TextWriter`. `Console.In` is of type `TextReader`. The system creates objects of `TextReader` and `TextWriter` derived classes to initialize `Console` properties `Console.In` and `Console.Out`.

Abstract class **`Stream`** provides functionality for representing streams as bytes. Classes `FileStream`, **`MemoryStream`** and **`BufferedStream`** (all from namespace `System.IO`) inherit from class `Stream`. Class `FileStream` can be used to write data to and read data from files. Class `MemoryStream` enables the transfer of data directly to and from memory—this is much faster than reading from and writing to external devices.

Class `BufferedStream` uses **buffering** to transfer data to or from a stream. Buffering is an I/O performance-enhancement technique, in which each output operation is directed to a region in memory, called a **buffer**, that's large enough to hold the data from *many* output operations. Then actual transfer to the output device is performed in one large **physical output operation** each time the buffer fills. The output operations directed to the output buffer in memory often are called **logical output operations**. Buffering also can be used to speed input operations by initially reading more data than is required into a buffer, so subsequent reads get data from high-speed memory rather than a slower external device.

In this chapter, we use key stream classes to implement file-processing programs that create and manipulate sequential-access files.

## 17.3 Creating a Sequential-Access Text File

C# imposes *no* structure on files. Thus, the concept of a "record" does *not* exist in C# files. This means that you must structure files to meet the requirements of your apps. The next few examples use text and special characters to organize our own concept of a "record."

### *Class* `BankUIForm`

The following examples demonstrate file processing in a bank-account maintenance app. These programs have similar user interfaces, so we created reusable class `BankUIForm` (Fig. 17.2) to encapsulate the common GUI (see the screen capture in Fig. 17.2). Class

BankUIForm (part of the BankLibrary project with this chapter's examples) contains four Labels and four TextBoxes. Methods ClearTextBoxes (lines 22–30), SetTextBoxValues (lines 33–51) and GetTextBoxValues (lines 54–59) clear, set the text in and get the text from the TextBoxes, respectively. Using *visual inheritance*—presented in Section 15.13—you can extend this class to create the GUIs for several examples in this chapter. Recall that to reuse class BankUIForm, you must compile the GUI into a class library, then add a reference to the new class library's DLL in each project that will reuse it (see Section 15.13).

```
1  // Fig. 17.2: BankUIForm.cs
2  // A reusable Windows Form for the examples in this chapter.
3  using System;
4  using System.Windows.Forms;
5
6  namespace BankLibrary
7  {
8     public partial class BankUIForm : Form
9     {
10       protected int TextBoxCount { get; set; } = 4; // number of TextBoxes
11
12       // enumeration constants specify TextBox indices
13       public enum TextBoxIndices {Account, First, Last, Balance}
14
15       // parameterless constructor
16       public BankUIForm()
17       {
18          InitializeComponent();
19       }
20
21       // clear all TextBoxes
22       public void ClearTextBoxes()
23       {
24          // iterate through every Control on form
25          foreach (Control guiControl in Controls)
26          {
27             // if Control is TextBox, clear it
28             (guiControl as TextBox)?.Clear();
29          }
30       }
31
32       // set text box values to string-array values
33       public void SetTextBoxValues(string[] values)
34       {
35          // determine whether string array has correct length
36          if (values.Length != TextBoxCount)
37          {
38             // throw exception if not correct length
39             throw (new ArgumentException(
40                $"There must be {TextBoxCount} strings in the array",
41                nameof(values)));
42          }
```

**Fig. 17.2** | A reusable Windows Form for the examples in this chapter's apps. (Part 1 of 2.)

```
         else // set array values if array has correct length
         {
            // set array values to TextBox values
            accountTextBox.Text = values[(int) TextBoxIndices.Account];
            firstNameTextBox.Text = values[(int) TextBoxIndices.First];
            lastNameTextBox.Text = values[(int) TextBoxIndices.Last];
            balanceTextBox.Text = values[(int) TextBoxIndices.Balance];
         }
      }

      // return TextBox values as string array
      public string[] GetTextBoxValues()
      {
         return new string[] {
            accountTextBox.Text, firstNameTextBox.Text,
            lastNameTextBox.Text, balanceTextBox.Text};
      }
   }
}
```

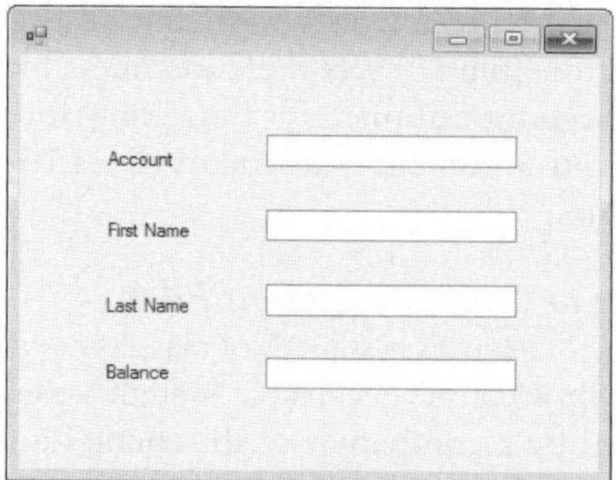


**Fig. 17.2** | A reusable Windows `Form` for the examples in this chapter's apps. (Part 2 of 2.)

### *Class* **Record**

Figure 17.3 contains class `Record` that Figs. 17.4, 17.6 and 17.7 use for maintaining the information in each record that's written to or read from a file. This class also belongs to the `BankLibrary`, so it's located in the same project as class `BankUIForm`.

```
// Fig. 17.3: Record.cs
// Class that represents a data record.
namespace BankLibrary
{
   public class Record
   {
      public int Account { get; set; }
      public string FirstName { get; set; }
      public string LastName { get; set; }
      public decimal Balance { get; set; }
```

**Fig. 17.3** | Class that represents a data record. (Part 1 of 2.)

```
11
12         // parameterless constructor sets members to default values
13         public Record() : this(0, string.Empty, string.Empty, 0M) { }
14
15         // overloaded constructor sets members to parameter values
16         public Record(int account, string firstName,
17            string lastName, decimal balance)
18         {
19            Account = account;
20            FirstName = firstName;
21            LastName = lastName;
22            Balance = balance;
23         }
24      }
25   }
```

**Fig. 17.3** | Class that represents a data record. (Part 2 of 2.)

Class `Record` contains *auto-implemented properties* `Account`, `FirstName`, `LastName` and `Balance` (lines 7–10), which collectively represent all the information for a record. The parameterless constructor (line 13) sets these members by calling the four-argument constructor with `0` for the account number, `string.Empty` for the first and last name and `0.0M` for the balance. The four-argument constructor (lines 16–23) sets these members to the specified parameter values.

### *Using a Character Stream to Create an Output File*

Class `CreateFileForm` (Fig. 17.4) uses instances of class `Record` to create a *sequential-access file* that might be used in an accounts-receivable system—i.e., a program that organizes data regarding money owed by a company's credit clients. For each client, the program obtains an account number and the client's first name, last name and balance (i.e., the amount of money that the client owes to the company for previously received goods and services). The data obtained for each client constitutes a record for that client. In this app, the account number is used as the *record key*—files are created and maintained in account-number order. This program assumes that the user enters records in account-number order. However, a comprehensive accounts-receivable system would provide a *sorting* capability, so the user could enter the records in any order. When you create a **Windows Forms Application** project for this app, be sure to add a reference to `BankLibrary.dll` and to change the base class from `Form` to `BankUIForm`. See Section 15.13 for information on adding a reference to a class library.

```
// Fig. 17.4: CreateFileForm.cs
// Creating a sequential-access file.
using System;
using System.Windows.Forms;
using System.IO;
using BankLibrary;

```

**Fig. 17.4** | Creating a sequential-access file. (Part 1 of 5.)

```
namespace CreateFile
{
   public partial class CreateFileForm : BankUIForm
   {
      private StreamWriter fileWriter; // writes data to text file

      // parameterless constructor
      public CreateFileForm()
      {
         InitializeComponent();
      }

      // event handler for Save Button
      private void saveButton_Click(object sender, EventArgs e)
      {
         // create and show dialog box enabling user to save file
         DialogResult result; // result of SaveFileDialog
         string fileName; // name of file containing data

         using (var fileChooser = new SaveFileDialog())
         {
            fileChooser.CheckFileExists = false; // let user create file
            result = fileChooser.ShowDialog();
            fileName = fileChooser.FileName; // name of file to save data
         }

         // ensure that user clicked "OK"
         if (result == DialogResult.OK)
         {
            // show error if user specified invalid file
            if (string.IsNullOrEmpty(fileName))
            {
               MessageBox.Show("Invalid File Name", "Error",
                  MessageBoxButtons.OK, MessageBoxIcon.Error);
            }
            else
            {
               // save file via FileStream
               try
               {
                  // open file with write access
                  var output = new FileStream(fileName,
                     FileMode.OpenOrCreate, FileAccess.Write);

                  // sets file to where data is written
                  fileWriter = new StreamWriter(output);

                  // disable Save button and enable Enter button
                  saveButton.Enabled = false;
                  enterButton.Enabled = true;
               }
               catch (IOException)
               {
```

**Fig. 17.4** | Creating a sequential-access file. (Part 2 of 5.)

```
                  // notify user if file does not exist
                  MessageBox.Show("Error opening file", "Error",
                     MessageBoxButtons.OK, MessageBoxIcon.Error);
               }
            }
         }
      }

      // handler for enterButton Click
      private void enterButton_Click(object sender, EventArgs e)
      {
         // store TextBox values string array
         string[] values = GetTextBoxValues();

         // determine whether TextBox account field is empty
         if (!string.IsNullOrEmpty(values[(int) TextBoxIndices.Account]))
         {
            // store TextBox values in Record and output it
            try
            {
               // get account-number value from TextBox
               int accountNumber =
                  int.Parse(values[(int) TextBoxIndices.Account]);

               // determine whether accountNumber is valid
               if (accountNumber > 0)
               {
                  // Record containing TextBox values to output
                  var record = new Record(accountNumber,
                     values[(int) TextBoxIndices.First],
                     values[(int) TextBoxIndices.Last],
                     decimal.Parse(values[(int) TextBoxIndices.Balance]);

                  // write Record to file, fields separated by commas
                  fileWriter.WriteLine(
                     $"{record.Account},{record.FirstName}," +
                     $"{record.LastName},{record.Balance}");
               }
               else
               {
                  // notify user if invalid account number
                  MessageBox.Show("Invalid Account Number", "Error",
                     MessageBoxButtons.OK, MessageBoxIcon.Error);
               }
            }
            catch (IOException)
            {
               MessageBox.Show("Error Writing to File", "Error",
                  MessageBoxButtons.OK, MessageBoxIcon.Error);
            }
            catch (FormatException)
            {
```

**Fig. 17.4** | Creating a sequential-access file. (Part 3 of 5.)

```
               MessageBox.Show("Invalid Format", "Error",
                  MessageBoxButtons.OK, MessageBoxIcon.Error);
            }
         }

         ClearTextBoxes(); // clear TextBox values
      }

      // handler for exitButton Click
      private void exitButton_Click(object sender, EventArgs e)
      {
         try
         {
            fileWriter?.Close(); // close StreamWriter and underlying file
         }
         catch (IOException)
         {
            MessageBox.Show("Cannot close file", "Error",
               MessageBoxButtons.OK, MessageBoxIcon.Error);
         }

         Application.Exit();
      }
   }
}
```

a) BankUI graphical user interface with three additional controls

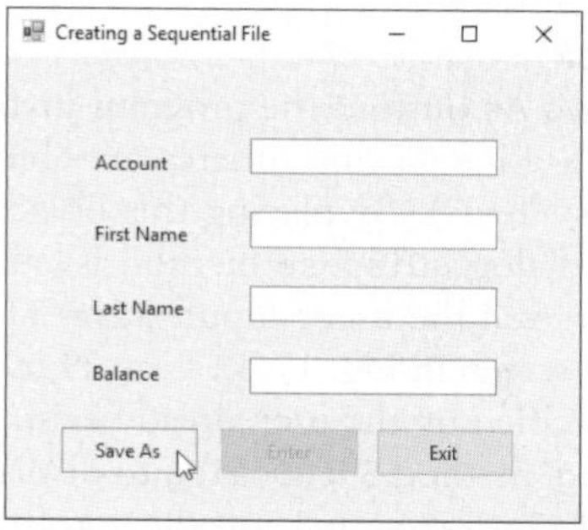

b) Save File dialog

Files and directories

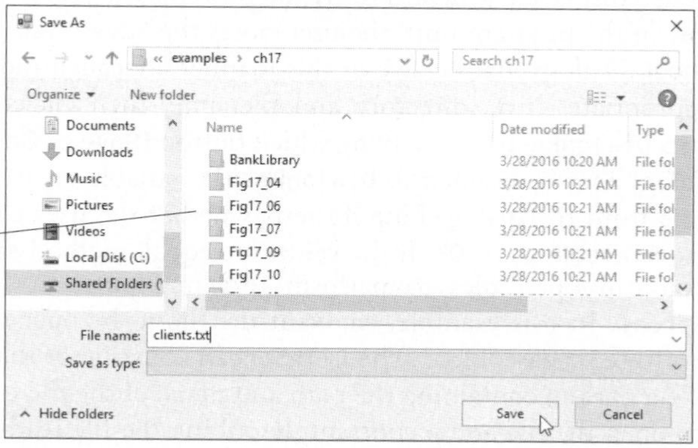

**Fig. 17.4** | Creating a sequential-access file. (Part 4 of 5.)

c) Account 100, "Nancy Brown", saved with a balance of -25.54

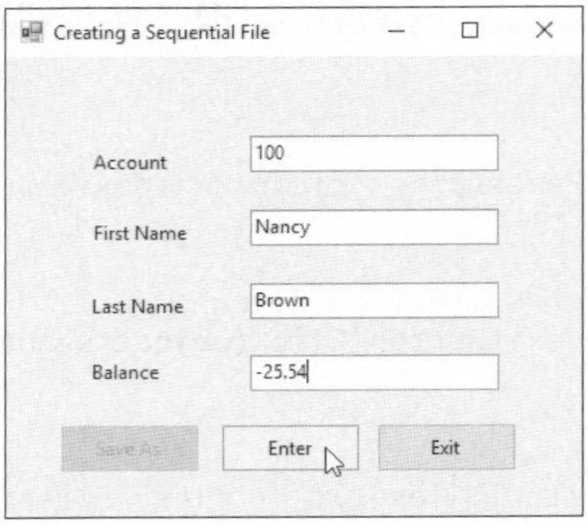

Creating a Sequential File

Account 100

First Name Nancy

Last Name Brown

Balance -25.54

Save As Enter Exit

**Fig. 17.4** | Creating a sequential-access file. (Part 5 of 5.)

Class `CreateFileForm` either creates or opens a file (depending on whether one exists), then allows the user to write records to it. The `using` directive in line 6 enables us to use the classes of the `BankLibrary` namespace; this namespace contains class `BankUIForm`, from which class `CreateFileForm` inherits (line 10). Class `CreateFileForm`'s GUI enhances that of class `BankUIForm` with buttons **Save As**, **Enter** and **Exit**.

### *Method* `saveButton_Click`

When the user clicks the **Save As** button, the program invokes the event handler `saveButton_Click` (lines 21–67). Line 27 instantiates an object of class **`SaveFileDialog`** (namespace `System.Windows.Forms`). By placing this object in a `using` statement (lines 27–32), we ensure that the dialog's `Dispose` method is called to release its resources as soon as the program has retrieved the user's input. `SaveFileDialog` objects are used for selecting files (see the second screen in Fig. 17.4). Line 29 indicates that the dialog should not check if the filename specified by the user already exists (this is actually the default). Line 30 calls `SaveFileDialog` method `ShowDialog` to display the dialog.

When displayed, a `SaveFileDialog` prevents the user from interacting with any other window in the program until the user closes the `SaveFileDialog` by clicking either **Save** or **Cancel**. Dialogs that behave in this manner are called **modal dialogs**. The user selects the appropriate drive, directory and filename, then clicks **Save**. Method **`ShowDialog`** returns a `DialogResult` specifying which button (**Save** or **Cancel**) the user clicked to close the dialog. This is assigned to `DialogResult` variable `result` (line 30). Line 31 gets the filename from the dialog. Line 35 tests whether the user clicked **OK** by comparing this value to `DialogResult.OK`. If the values are equal, method `saveButton_Click` continues.

You can open files to perform text manipulation by creating objects of class `FileStream`. In this example, we want the file to be opened for *output*, so lines 49–50 create a `FileStream` object. The `FileStream` constructor that we use receives three arguments—a `string` containing the path and name of the file to open, a constant describing how to open the file and a constant describing the file read-write permissions. The constant `FileMode.OpenOrCreate` (line 50) indicates that the `FileStream` object should open the file if it *exists* or create the file if it *does not exist.*

Note that the contents of an existing file are *overwritten* by the FileStream. To *preserve* the original contents of a file, use FileMode.Append. There are other FileMode constants describing how to open files; we introduce these constants as we use them in examples. The constant FileAccess.Write indicates that the program can perform only *write* operations with the FileStream object. There are two other constants for the third constructor parameter—FileAccess.Read for read-only access and FileAccess.ReadWrite for both read and write access.

Line 59 catches an **IOException** if there's a problem opening the file or creating the StreamWriter. If so, the program displays an error message (lines 62–63). If no exception occurs, the file is open for writing.

**Common Programming Error 17.1**

*Failure to open a file before attempting to use it in a program is a logic error.*

### *Method* enterButton_Click

After typing information into each TextBox, the user clicks **Enter**, which calls enterButton_Click (lines 70–119) to save the data from the TextBoxes into the user-specified file. If the user entered a *valid* account number (i.e., an integer greater than zero), lines 89–92 create a Record containing the TextBox values. If the user entered *invalid* data in one of the TextBoxes (such as nonnumeric characters in the **Balance** field), the program throws a FormatException. The catch block in lines 111–115 handles such exceptions by notifying the user (via a MessageBox) of the improper format.[1]

If the user entered *valid* data, lines 95–97 write the record to the file by invoking method WriteLine of the StreamWriter object that was created at line 53. Method WriteLine writes a sequence of characters to a file. The StreamWriter object is constructed with a FileStream argument that specifies the file to which the StreamWriter will output text. Class StreamWriter (like most of the classes we discuss in this chapter) belongs to the System.IO namespace. Finally, the TextBoxes are cleared so the user can begin typing the next record's data.

### *Method* exitButton_Click

When the user clicks **Exit**, exitButton_Click (lines 122–135) executes. Line 126 closes the StreamWriter (if it is not null), which automatically closes the underlying FileStream. Then, line 134 terminates the program. Note that method Close is called in a try block. Method Close throws an IOException if the file or stream cannot be closed properly. In this case, it's important to notify the user that the information in the file or stream might be *corrupted*.

**Performance Tip 17.1**

*Releasing resources explicitly when they're no longer needed makes them immediately available for reuse by other programs, thus improving resource utilization.*

---

1. We could prevent these exceptions by using int.TryParse in line 83 and decimal.TryParse—we chose not to in this chapter's apps, because doing so adds many lines of logic to the apps (which are already long). However, it's considered better practice to prevent such exceptions.

*Sample Data*

To test the program, we entered information for the accounts shown in Fig. 17.5. The program does not depict how the data records are stored in the file. To verify that the file has been created successfully, we create a program in the next section to read and display the file. Since this is a *text file*, you can actually open it in any *text editor* to see its contents.

| Account number | First name | Last name | Balance |
|---|---|---|---|
| 100 | Nancy | Brown | -25.54 |
| 200 | Stacey | Dunn | 314.33 |
| 300 | Doug | Barker | 0.00 |
| 400 | Dave | Smith | 258.34 |
| 500 | Sam | Stone | 34.98 |

**Fig. 17.5** | Sample data for the program of Fig. 17.4.

## 17.4 Reading Data from a Sequential-Access Text File

The previous section demonstrated how to create a file for use in sequential-access apps. In this section, we discuss how to read (or retrieve) data sequentially from a file. Class `ReadSequentialAccessFileForm` (Fig. 17.6) reads records from the file created by the program in Fig. 17.4, then displays the contents of each record. Much of the code in this example is similar to that of Fig. 17.4, so we discuss only the unique aspects of the app.

```
// Fig. 17.6: ReadSequentialAccessFileForm.cs
// Reading a sequential-access file.
using System;
using System.Windows.Forms;
using System.IO;
using BankLibrary;

namespace ReadSequentialAccessFile
{
   public partial class ReadSequentialAccessFileForm : BankUIForm
   {
      private StreamReader fileReader; // reads data from a text file

      // parameterless constructor
      public ReadSequentialAccessFileForm()
      {
         InitializeComponent();
      }

```

**Fig. 17.6** | Reading a sequential-access file. (Part 1 of 4.)

```
      // invoked when user clicks the Open button
      private void openButton_Click(object sender, EventArgs e)
      {
         // create and show dialog box enabling user to open file
         DialogResult result; // result of OpenFileDialog
         string fileName; // name of file containing data

         using (OpenFileDialog fileChooser = new OpenFileDialog())
         {
            result = fileChooser.ShowDialog();
            fileName = fileChooser.FileName; // get specified name
         }

         // ensure that user clicked "OK"
         if (result == DialogResult.OK)
         {
            ClearTextBoxes();

            // show error if user specified invalid file
            if (string.IsNullOrEmpty(fileName))
            {
               MessageBox.Show("Invalid File Name", "Error",
                  MessageBoxButtons.OK, MessageBoxIcon.Error);
            }
            else
            {
               try
               {
                  // create FileStream to obtain read access to file
                  FileStream input = new FileStream(
                     fileName, FileMode.Open, FileAccess.Read);

                  // set file from where data is read
                  fileReader = new StreamReader(input);

                  openButton.Enabled = false; // disable Open File button
                  nextButton.Enabled = true; // enable Next Record button
               }
               catch (IOException)
               {
                  MessageBox.Show("Error reading from file",
                     "File Error", MessageBoxButtons.OK,
                     MessageBoxIcon.Error);
               }
            }
         }
      }

      // invoked when user clicks Next button
      private void nextButton_Click(object sender, EventArgs e)
      {
         try
         {
```

**Fig. 17.6** | Reading a sequential-access file. (Part 2 of 4.)

```
            // get next record available in file
            var inputRecord = fileReader.ReadLine();

            if (inputRecord != null)
            {
               string[] inputFields = inputRecord.Split(',');

               // copy string-array values to TextBox values
               SetTextBoxValues(inputFields);
            }
            else
            {
               // close StreamReader and underlying file
               fileReader.Close();
               openButton.Enabled = true; // enable Open File button
               nextButton.Enabled = false; // disable Next Record button
               ClearTextBoxes();

               // notify user if no records in file
               MessageBox.Show("No more records in file", string.Empty,
                  MessageBoxButtons.OK, MessageBoxIcon.Information);
            }
         }
         catch (IOException)
         {
            MessageBox.Show("Error Reading from File", "Error",
               MessageBoxButtons.OK, MessageBoxIcon.Error);
         }
      }
   }
}
```

a) BankUI graphical user interface with an Open File button

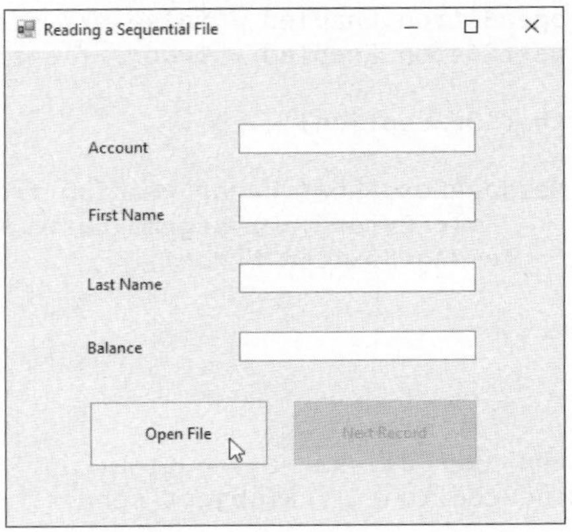


**Fig. 17.6** | Reading a sequential-access file. (Part 3 of 4.)

b) `OpenFileDialog` window

c) Reading account 100

d) User is shown a messagebox when all records have been read

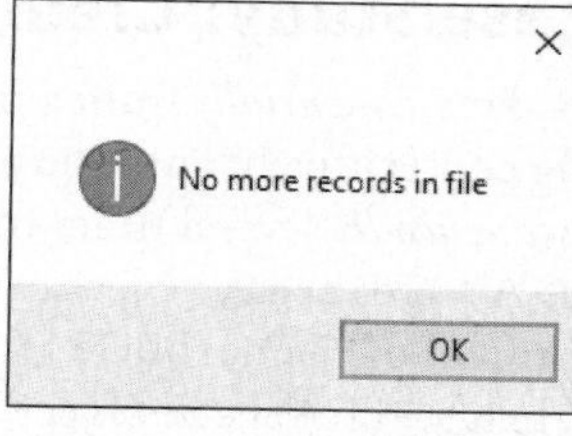


**Fig. 17.6** | Reading a sequential-access file. (Part 4 of 4.)

### *Method* `openButton_Click`

When the user clicks **Open File**, the program calls event handler `openButton_Click` (lines 21–66). Line 27 creates an **`OpenFileDialog`**, and line 29 calls its `ShowDialog` method to display the **Open** dialog (see the second screenshot in Fig. 17.6). The behavior and GUI for the **Save** and **Open** dialog types are identical, except that **Save** is replaced by **Open**. If the user selects a *valid* filename, lines 49–50 create a `FileStream` object and assign it to reference `input`. We pass constant `FileMode.Open` as the second argument to the `FileStream` constructor to indicate that the `FileStream` should open the file if it exists or throw a **`FileNotFoundException`** if it does not. (In this example, the `FileStream` constructor will *not* throw a `FileNotFoundException`, because the `OpenFileDialog` is configured to check that the file exists.) In the last example (Fig. 17.4), we wrote text to the file using a `FileStream` object with *write-only access*. In this example (Fig. 17.6), we specify *read-only access* to the file by passing constant `FileAccess.Read` as the third argument to the `FileStream` constructor. This `FileStream` object is used to create a `StreamReader` object in line 53. The `FileStream` object specifies the file from which the `StreamReader` object will read text.

**Error-Prevention Tip 17.1**

*Open a file with the `FileAccess.Read` file-open mode if its contents should not be modified. This prevents unintentional modification of the contents.*

### *Method* `nextButton_Click`

When the user clicks the **Next Record** button, the program calls event handler `nextButton_Click` (lines 69–101), which reads the next record from the user-specified file. (The user must click **Next Record** after opening the file to view the first record.) Line 74 calls `StreamReader` method `ReadLine` to read the next record. If an error occurs while reading the file, an `IOException` is thrown (caught at line 96), and the user is notified (lines 98–99). Otherwise, line 76 determines whether `StreamReader` method `ReadLine` returned `null` (i.e., there's no more text in the file). If not, line 78 uses `string` method **`Split`** to separate the stream of characters that was read from the file into tokens (`string`s) that represent the `Record`'s properties—the second argument indicates that the tokens are delimited by commas in this file. Line 81 displays the `Record` values in the `TextBox`es. If `ReadLine` returns `null`, the program closes the `StreamReader` object (line 86), automatically closing the `FileStream` object, then notifies the user that there are no more records (lines 92–93).

## 17.5 Case Study: Credit-Inquiry Program

To retrieve data *sequentially* from a file, programs normally start from the *beginning* of the file, reading consecutively until the desired data is found. It sometimes is necessary to process a file *sequentially* several times (from the *beginning* of the file) during the execution of a program. A `FileStream` object can *reposition* its **file-position pointer** (which contains the byte number of the next byte to be read from or written to the file) to *any* position in the file. When a `FileStream` object is opened, its *file-position pointer* is set to *byte position 0* (i.e., the *beginning* of the file).

We now present a program that builds on the concepts employed in Fig. 17.6. Class `CreditInquiryForm` (Fig. 17.7) is a credit-inquiry program that enables a credit manager to search for and display account information for those customers with credit balances (i.e., customers to whom the company owes money), zero balances (i.e., customers who do not owe the company money) and debit balances (i.e., customers who owe the company money for previously received goods and services). We use a `RichTextBox` in the program to display the account information. `RichTextBox`es provide more functionality than regular `TextBox`es—for example, `RichTextBox`es offer method `Find` for searching individual strings and method `LoadFile` for displaying file contents. Classes `RichTextBox` and `TextBox` both inherit from `abstract` class `System.Windows.Forms.TextBoxBase`. In this example, we chose a `RichTextBox`, because it displays multiple lines of text by default, whereas a regular `TextBox` displays only one. Alternatively, we could have specified that a `TextBox` object display *multiple* lines of text by setting its `Multiline` property to `true`.

The program displays buttons that enable a credit manager to obtain credit information. The **Open File** button opens a file for gathering data. The **Credit Balances** button displays a list of accounts that have credit balances, the **Debit Balances** button displays a list of accounts that have debit balances and the **Zero Balances** button displays a list of accounts that have zero balances. The **Done** button exits the app.

```
// Fig. 17.7: CreditInquiryForm.cs
// Read a file sequentially and display contents based on
// account type specified by user (credit, debit or zero balances).
using System;
using System.Windows.Forms;
using System.IO;
using BankLibrary;

namespace CreditInquiry
{
   public partial class CreditInquiryForm : Form
   {
      private FileStream input; // maintains the connection to the file
      private StreamReader fileReader; // reads data from text file

      // parameterless constructor
      public CreditInquiryForm()
      {
         InitializeComponent();
      }

      // invoked when user clicks Open File button
      private void openButton_Click(object sender, EventArgs e)
      {
         // create dialog box enabling user to open file
         DialogResult result;
         string fileName;

         using (OpenFileDialog fileChooser = new OpenFileDialog())
         {
            result = fileChooser.ShowDialog();
            fileName = fileChooser.FileName;
         }

         // exit event handler if user clicked Cancel
         if (result == DialogResult.OK)
         {
            // show error if user specified invalid file
            if (string.IsNullOrEmpty(fileName))
            {
               MessageBox.Show("Invalid File Name", "Error",
                  MessageBoxButtons.OK, MessageBoxIcon.Error);
            }
            else
            {
               // create FileStream to obtain read access to file
               input = new FileStream(fileName,
                  FileMode.Open, FileAccess.Read);

               // set file from where data is read
               fileReader = new StreamReader(input);

```

**Fig. 17.7** | Credit-inquiry program. (Part 1 of 5.)

```
            // enable all GUI buttons, except for Open File button
            openButton.Enabled = false;
            creditButton.Enabled = true;
            debitButton.Enabled = true;
            zeroButton.Enabled = true;
         }
      }
   }

   // invoked when user clicks credit balances,
   // debit balances or zero balances button
   private void getBalances_Click(object sender, System.EventArgs e)
   {
      // convert sender explicitly to object of type button
      Button senderButton = (Button) sender;

      // get text from clicked Button, which stores account type
      string accountType = senderButton.Text;

      // read and display file information
      try
      {
         // go back to the beginning of the file
         input.Seek(0, SeekOrigin.Begin);

         displayTextBox.Text =
            $"Accounts with {accountType}{Environment.NewLine}";

         // traverse file until end of file
         while (true)
         {
            // get next Record available in file
            string inputRecord = fileReader.ReadLine();

            // when at the end of file, exit method
            if (inputRecord == null)
            {
               return;
            }

            // parse input
            string[] inputFields = inputRecord.Split(',');

            // create Record from input
            var record =
               new Record(int.Parse(inputFields[0]), inputFields[1],
                  inputFields[2], decimal.Parse(inputFields[3]));

            // determine whether to display balance
            if (ShouldDisplay(record.Balance, accountType))
            {
```

**Fig. 17.7** | Credit-inquiry program. (Part 2 of 5.)

```
                  // display record
                  displayTextBox.AppendText($"{record.Account}\t" +
                     $"{record.FirstName}\t{record.LastName}\t" +
                     $"{record.Balance:C}{Environment.NewLine}");
               }
            }
         }
         catch (IOException)
         {
            MessageBox.Show("Cannot Read File", "Error",
               MessageBoxButtons.OK, MessageBoxIcon.Error);
         }
      }

      // determine whether to display given record
      private bool ShouldDisplay(decimal balance, string accountType)
      {
         if (balance > 0M && accountType == "Credit Balances")
         {
            return true; // should display credit balances
         }
         else if (balance < 0M && accountType == "Debit Balances")
         {
            return true; // should display debit balances
         }
         else if (balance == 0 && accountType == "Zero Balances")
         {
            return true; // should display zero balances
         }

         return false;
      }

      // invoked when user clicks Done button
      private void doneButton_Click(object sender, EventArgs e)
      {
         // close file and StreamReader
         try
         {
            fileReader?.Close(); // close StreamReader and underlying file
         }
         catch (IOException)
         {
            // notify user of error closing file
            MessageBox.Show("Cannot close file", "Error",
               MessageBoxButtons.OK, MessageBoxIcon.Error);
         }

         Application.Exit();
      }
   }
}
```

**Fig. 17.7** | Credit-inquiry program. (Part 3 of 5.)

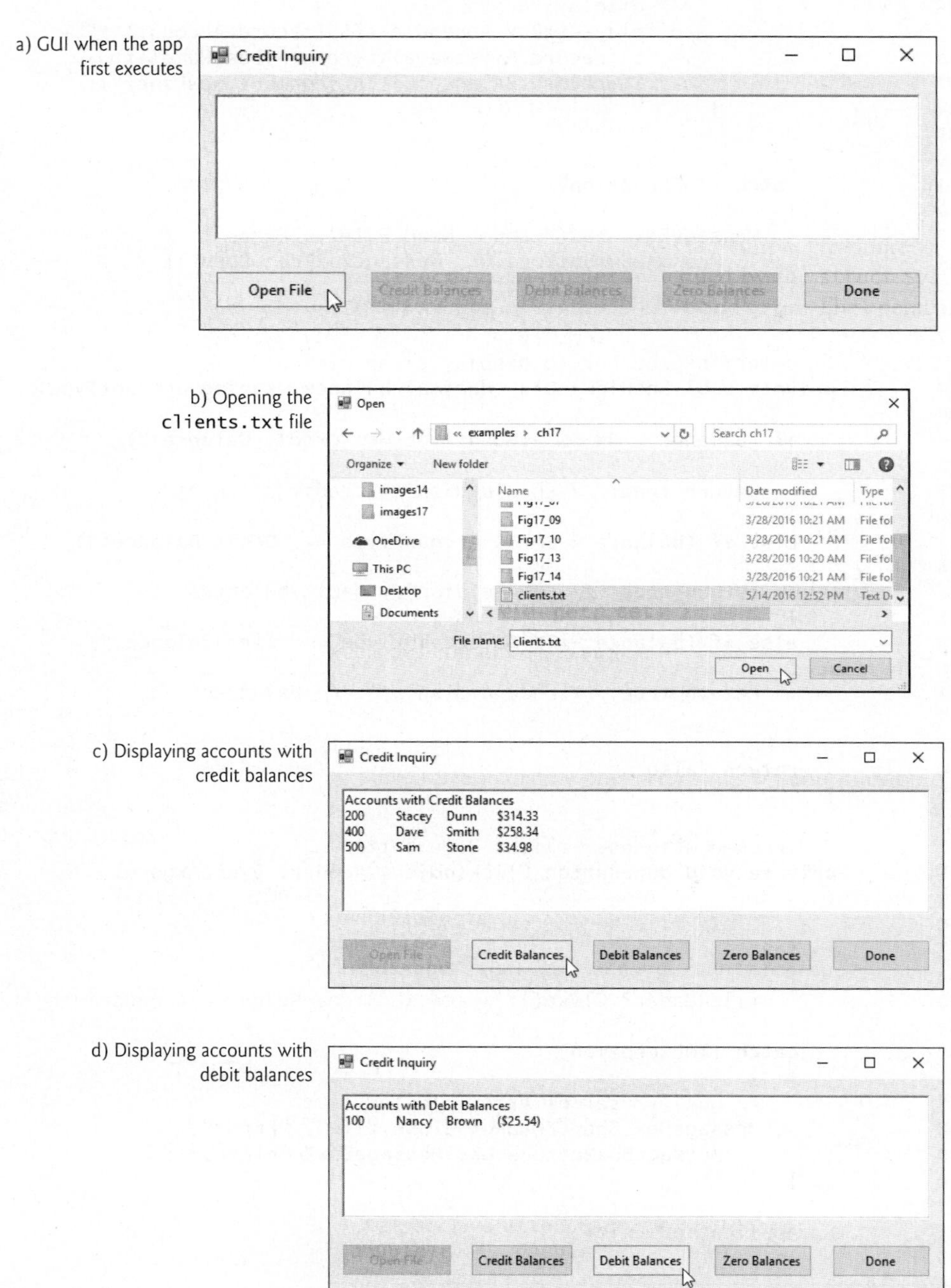


**Fig. 17.7** | Credit-inquiry program. (Part 4 of 5.)

e) Displaying accounts with zero balances

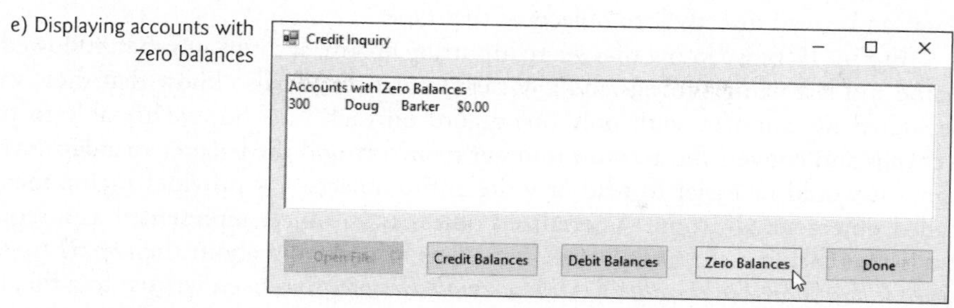


**Fig. 17.7** | Credit-inquiry program. (Part 5 of 5.)

When the user clicks the **Open File** button, the program calls the event handler `openButton_Click` (lines 23–60). Line 29 creates an `OpenFileDialog`, and line 31 calls its `ShowDialog` method to display the **Open** dialog, in which the user selects the file to open. Lines 47–48 create a `FileStream` object with *read-only file access* and assign it to reference `input`. Line 51 creates a `StreamReader` object that we use to read text from the `FileStream`.

When the user clicks **Credit Balances**, **Debit Balances** or **Zero Balances**, the program invokes method `getBalances_Click` (lines 64–116). Line 67 casts the `sender` parameter, which is an `object` reference to the control that generated the event, to a `Button` object. Line 70 extracts the `Button` object's text, which the program uses to determine which type of accounts to display. Line 76 uses `FileStream` method **`Seek`** to reset the *file-position pointer* back to the *beginning* of the file. `FileStream` method `Seek` allows you to reset the *file-position pointer* by specifying the number of bytes it should be *offset* from the file's *beginning*, *end* or *current* position. The part of the file you want to be *offset* from is chosen using constants from the **`SeekOrigin`** enumeration. In this case, our stream is offset by `0` bytes from the file's *beginning* (`SeekOrigin.Begin`). Line 102 use `private` method `ShouldDisplay` (lines 119–135) to determine whether to display each record in the file. The `while` loop obtains each record by repeatedly calling `StreamReader` method `ReadLine` (line 85) and splitting the text into *tokens* (line 94) that are used to initialize object `record` (lines 97–99). Line 88 determines whether the *file-position pointer* has reached the end of the file, in which case `ReadLine` returns `null`. If so, the program returns from method `getBalances_Click` (line 90).

## 17.6 Serialization

Section 17.3 demonstrated how to write the individual fields of a `Record` object to a text file, and Section 17.4 demonstrated how to read those fields from a file and place their values in a `Record` object in memory. In the examples, `Record` was used to *aggregate* the information for one record. When the instance variables for a `Record` were output to a disk file as text, certain information was lost, such as the type of each value. For instance, if the value `"3"` is read from a text file, there's no way to tell if the value came from an `int`, a `string` or a `decimal`. We have only data, not type information, on disk. If the program that's going to read this data "knows" what object type the data corresponds to, then the data can be read directly into objects of that type.

In Fig. 17.6, we know that we're inputting an `int` account number, followed by first name and last name `string`s and a `decimal` balance. We also know that these values are separated by commas, with only one record on each line. So, we are able to parse the `string`s and convert the account number to an `int` and the balance to a `decimal`. Sometimes it would be easier to read or write entire objects. C# provides such a mechanism, called **object serialization**. A **serialized object** is an object represented as a sequence of bytes that includes the *object's data*, as well as information about the *object's type* and the *types of data stored in the object*. After a *serialized object* has been written to a file, it can be read from the file and **deserialized**—that is, the type information and bytes that represent the object and its data can be used to *recreate* the object in memory.

Class **`BinaryFormatter`** (namespace **`System.Runtime.Serialization.Formatters.Binary`**) enables entire objects to be written to or read from a stream in binary format. `BinaryFormatter` method **`Serialize`** writes an object's representation to a file. `BinaryFormatter` method **`Deserialize`** reads this representation from a file and *reconstructs* the original object. Both methods throw a **`SerializationException`** if an error occurs during *serialization* or *deserialization*. Both methods require a `Stream` object (e.g., the `FileStream`) as a parameter so that the `BinaryFormatter` can access the correct stream.

In Sections 17.7–17.8, we create and manipulate *sequential-access files* using *object serialization*. Object serialization is performed with *byte-based streams*, so the sequential files created and manipulated will be *binary files*. Binary files are not human-readable. For this reason, we write a separate app that reads and displays *serialized objects*. Other serialization formats are available that are both human- and machine-readable. For example,

- the `XmlSerializer` class (namespace `System.Xml.Serialization`) can read and write objects in XML (Extensible Markup Language) format and
- the `DataContractJsonSerializer` class (namespace `System.Runtime.Serialization.Json`) can read and write objects in JSON (JavaScript Object Notation) format.

XML and JSON are popular formats for transferring data over the Internet.

## 17.7 Creating a Sequential-Access File Using Object Serialization

We begin by creating and writing *serialized objects* to a *sequential-access file*. In this section, we reuse much of the code from Section 17.3, so we focus only on the new features.

### *Defining the* `RecordSerializable` *Class*

Let's modify class `Record` (Fig. 17.3) so that objects of this class can be *serialized*. Class `RecordSerializable` (Fig. 17.8; part of the `BankLibrary` project) is marked with what is-known as an attribute—**`[Serializable]`** (line 7)—this attribute indicates to the CLR that `RecordSerializable` objects can be *serialized*. Classes that represent serializable types must include this attribute in their declarations or must implement *interface* **`ISerializable`**.

```
// Fig. 17.8: RecordSerializable.cs
// Serializable class that represents a data record.
using System;

namespace BankLibrary
{
   [Serializable]
   public class RecordSerializable
   {
      public int Account { get; set; }
      public string FirstName { get; set; }
      public string LastName { get; set; }
      public decimal Balance { get; set; }

      // default constructor sets members to default values
      public RecordSerializable()
         : this(0, string.Empty, string.Empty, 0M) {}

      // overloaded constructor sets members to parameter values
      public RecordSerializable(int account, string firstName,
         string lastName, decimal balance)
      {
         Account = account;
         FirstName = firstName;
         LastName = lastName;
         Balance = balance;
      }
   }
}
```

**Fig. 17.8** | `Serializable` class that represents a data record.

In a class that's marked with the `[Serializable]` attribute or that implements interface `ISerializable`, you must ensure that every instance variable of the class is also *serializable*. All simple-type variables and `string`s are *serializable*. For variables of *reference types*, you must check the class declaration (and possibly its base classes) to ensure that the type is *serializable*. By default, array objects are serializable. However, if the array contains references to other objects, those objects may or may not be serializable.

### *Using a Serialization Stream to Create an Output File*

Next, we'll create a sequential-access file with *serialization* (Fig. 17.9). To test this program, we used the sample data from Fig. 17.5 to create a file named `clients.ser`—we chose the extension `.ser` to indicate that the file stores serialized objects. Since the sample screen captures are the same as Fig. 17.4, they are not shown here. Line 15 creates a `BinaryFormatter` for writing *serialized objects*. Lines 55–56 open the `FileStream` to which this program writes the *serialized objects*. The `string` argument that's passed to the `FileStream`'s constructor represents the name and path of the file to be opened. This specifies the file to which the *serialized objects* will be written.

```
// Fig. 17.9: CreateFileForm.cs
// Creating a sequential-access file using serialization.
using System;
using System.Windows.Forms;
using System.IO;
using System.Runtime.Serialization.Formatters.Binary;
using System.Runtime.Serialization;
using BankLibrary;

namespace CreateFile
{
   public partial class CreateFileForm : BankUIForm
   {
      // object for serializing RecordSerializables in binary format
      private BinaryFormatter formatter = new BinaryFormatter();
      private FileStream output; // stream for writing to a file

      // parameterless constructor
      public CreateFileForm()
      {
         InitializeComponent();
      }

      // handler for saveButton_Click
      private void saveButton_Click(object sender, EventArgs e)
      {
         // create and show dialog box enabling user to save file
         DialogResult result;
         string fileName; // name of file to save data

         using (SaveFileDialog fileChooser = new SaveFileDialog())
         {
            fileChooser.CheckFileExists = false; // let user create file

            // retrieve the result of the dialog box
            result = fileChooser.ShowDialog();
            fileName = fileChooser.FileName; // get specified file name
         }

         // ensure that user clicked "OK"
         if (result == DialogResult.OK)
         {
            // show error if user specified invalid file
            if (string.IsNullOrEmpty(fileName))
            {
               MessageBox.Show("Invalid File Name", "Error",
                  MessageBoxButtons.OK, MessageBoxIcon.Error);
            }
            else
            {
               // save file via FileStream if user specified valid file
               try
               {
```

**Fig. 17.9** | Creating a sequential-access file using serialization. (Part 1 of 3.)

```
                  // open file with write access
                  output = new FileStream(fileName,
                     FileMode.OpenOrCreate, FileAccess.Write);

                  // disable Save button and enable Enter button
                  saveButton.Enabled = false;
                  enterButton.Enabled = true;
               }
               catch (IOException)
               {
                  // notify user if file could not be opened
                  MessageBox.Show("Error opening file", "Error",
                     MessageBoxButtons.OK, MessageBoxIcon.Error);
               }
            }
         }
      }

      // handler for enterButton Click
      private void enterButton_Click(object sender, EventArgs e)
      {
         // store TextBox values string array
         string[] values = GetTextBoxValues();

         // determine whether TextBox account field is empty
         if (!string.IsNullOrEmpty(values[(int) TextBoxIndices.Account]))
         {
            // store TextBox values in RecordSerializable and serialize it
            try
            {
               // get account-number value from TextBox
               int accountNumber = int.Parse(
                  values[(int) TextBoxIndices.Account]);

               // determine whether accountNumber is valid
               if (accountNumber > 0)
               {
                  // RecordSerializable to serialize
                  var record = new RecordSerializable(accountNumber,
                     values[(int) TextBoxIndices.First],
                     values[(int) TextBoxIndices.Last],
                     decimal.Parse(values[(int) TextBoxIndices.Balance]));

                  // write Record to FileStream (serialize object)
                  formatter.Serialize(output, record);
               }
               else
               {
                  // notify user if invalid account number
                  MessageBox.Show("Invalid Account Number", "Error",
                     MessageBoxButtons.OK, MessageBoxIcon.Error);
               }
            }
```

**Fig. 17.9** | Creating a sequential-access file using serialization. (Part 2 of 3.)

```
107             catch (SerializationException)
108             {
109                MessageBox.Show("Error Writing to File", "Error",
110                   MessageBoxButtons.OK, MessageBoxIcon.Error);
111             }
112             catch (FormatException)
113             {
114                MessageBox.Show("Invalid Format", "Error",
115                   MessageBoxButtons.OK, MessageBoxIcon.Error);
116             }
117          }
118
119          ClearTextBoxes(); // clear TextBox values
120       }
121
122       // handler for exitButton Click
123       private void exitButton_Click(object sender, EventArgs e)
124       {
125          // close file
126          try
127          {
128             output?.Close(); // close FileStream
129          }
130          catch (IOException)
131          {
132             MessageBox.Show("Cannot close file", "Error",
133                MessageBoxButtons.OK, MessageBoxIcon.Error);
134          }
135
136          Application.Exit();
137       }
138    }
139 }
```

**Fig. 17.9** | Creating a sequential-access file using serialization. (Part 3 of 3.)

This program assumes that data is input correctly and in record-number order. Method `enterButton_Click` (lines 73–120) performs the write operation. Lines 92–95 create and initialize a `RecordSerializable` object. Line 98 calls `Serialize` to write the `RecordSerializable` object to the output file. Method `Serialize` takes the `FileStream` object as the first argument so that the `BinaryFormatter` can write its second argument to the correct file. The app does not specify how to format the objectfor output—`Serialize` handles these details. If a problem occurs during *serialization*, a `SerializationException` occurs.

In the sample execution (Fig. 17.9), we entered five accounts—the same as in Fig. 17.5. The program does not show how the data records actually appear in the file. Remember that we are now using *binary files*, which are *not* human readable. To verify that the file was created successfully, the next section presents a program to read the file's contents.

## 17.8 Reading and Deserializing Data from a Binary File

The preceding section showed how to create a *sequential-access file* using *object serialization*. In this section, we discuss how to read serialized objects sequentially from a file.

Figure 17.10 reads and displays the contents of the `clients.ser` file created by the program in Fig. 17.9. The sample screen captures are identical to those of Fig. 17.6, so they are not shown here. Line 15 creates the `BinaryFormatter` that will be used to read objects. The program opens the file for input by creating a `FileStream` object (lines 51–52). The name of the file to open is specified as the first argument to the `FileStream` constructor.

The program reads objects from a file in event handler `nextButton_Click` (lines 61–93). We use method `Deserialize` (of the `BinaryFormatter` created in line 15) to read the data (lines 67–68). Note that we cast the result of `Deserialize` to type `RecordSerializable` (line 67)—`Deserialize` returns a reference of type `object`, so we must perform this cast to access properties that belong to class `RecordSerializable`. If an error occurs during *deserialization* or the end of the file is reached, a `SerializationException` is thrown, and the `FileStream` object is closed (line 83).

```
1  // Fig. 17.10: ReadSequentialAccessFileForm.cs
2  // Reading a sequential-access file using deserialization.
3  using System;
4  using System.Windows.Forms;
5  using System.IO;
6  using System.Runtime.Serialization.Formatters.Binary;
7  using System.Runtime.Serialization;
8  using BankLibrary;
9
10 namespace ReadSequentialAccessFile
11 {
12    public partial class ReadSequentialAccessFileForm : BankUIForm
13    {
14       // object for deserializing RecordSerializable in binary format
15       private BinaryFormatter reader = new BinaryFormatter();
16       private FileStream input; // stream for reading from a file
17
18       // parameterless constructor
19       public ReadSequentialAccessFileForm()
20       {
21          InitializeComponent();
22       }
23
24       // invoked when user clicks the Open button
25       private void openButton_Click(object sender, EventArgs e)
26       {
27          // create and show dialog box enabling user to open file
28          DialogResult result; // result of OpenFileDialog
29          string fileName; // name of file containing data
30
31          using (OpenFileDialog fileChooser = new OpenFileDialog())
32          {
33             result = fileChooser.ShowDialog();
34             fileName = fileChooser.FileName; // get specified name
35          }
36
```

**Fig. 17.10** | Reading a sequential-access file using deserialization. (Part 1 of 3.)

```
         // ensure that user clicked "OK"
         if (result == DialogResult.OK)
         {
            ClearTextBoxes();

            // show error if user specified invalid file
            if (string.IsNullOrEmpty(fileName))
            {
               MessageBox.Show("Invalid File Name", "Error",
                  MessageBoxButtons.OK, MessageBoxIcon.Error);
            }
            else
            {
               // create FileStream to obtain read access to file
               input = new FileStream(
                  fileName, FileMode.Open, FileAccess.Read);

               openButton.Enabled = false; // disable Open File button
               nextButton.Enabled = true;  // enable Next Record button
            }
         }
      }

      // invoked when user clicks Next button
      private void nextButton_Click(object sender, EventArgs e)
      {
         // deserialize RecordSerializable and store data in TextBoxes
         try
         {
            // get next RecordSerializable available in file
            RecordSerializable record =
               (RecordSerializable) reader.Deserialize(input);

            // store RecordSerializable values in temporary string array
            var values = new string[] {
               record.Account.ToString(),
               record.FirstName.ToString(),
               record.LastName.ToString(),
               record.Balance.ToString()
            };

            // copy string-array values to TextBox values
            SetTextBoxValues(values);
         }
         catch (SerializationException)
         {
            input?.Close(); // close FileStream
            openButton.Enabled = true; // enable Open File button
            nextButton.Enabled = false; // disable Next Record button

            ClearTextBoxes();

```

**Fig. 17.10** | Reading a sequential-access file using deserialization. (Part 2 of 3.)

```
            // notify user if no RecordSerializables in file
            MessageBox.Show("No more records in file", string.Empty,
               MessageBoxButtons.OK, MessageBoxIcon.Information);
         }
      }
   }
}
```

**Fig. 17.10** | Reading a sequential-access file using deserialization. (Part 3 of 3.)

## 17.9 Classes File and Directory

Files are organized in directories (also called folders). Classes File and Directory enable programs to manipulate files and directories on disk. Class **File** can determine information about files and can be used to open files for reading or writing. We discussed techniques for writing to and reading from files in previous sections.

Figure 17.11 lists several of class File's static methods for manipulating and determining information about files. We demonstrate several of these methods in Fig. 17.13.

| static Method | Description |
|---|---|
| AppendText | Returns a StreamWriter that appends text to an existing file or creates a file if one does not exist. |
| Copy | Copies a file to a new file. |
| Create | Creates a file and returns its associated FileStream. |
| CreateText | Creates a text file and returns its associated StreamWriter. |
| Delete | Deletes the specified file. |
| Exists | Returns true if the specified file exists and false otherwise. |
| GetCreationTime | Returns a DateTime object representing when the file/directory was created. |
| GetLastAccessTime | Returns a DateTime object representing when the file/directory was last accessed. |
| GetLastWriteTime | Returns a DateTime object representing when the file/directory was last modified. |
| Move | Moves the specified file to a specified location. |
| Open | Returns a FileStream associated with the specified file and equipped with the specified read/write permissions. |
| OpenRead | Returns a read-only FileStream associated with the specified file. |
| OpenText | Returns a StreamReader associated with the specified file. |
| OpenWrite | Returns a write FileStream associated with the specified file. |

**Fig. 17.11** | File class static methods (partial list).

Class **Directory** provides capabilities for manipulating directories. Figure 17.12 lists some of class Directory's static methods for directory manipulation. Figure 17.13 demonstrates several of these methods, as well. The **DirectoryInfo** object returned by method **CreateDirectory** contains information about a directory. Much of the information contained in class `DirectoryInfo` also can be accessed via the methods of class `Directory`.

| `static` Method | Description |
|---|---|
| `CreateDirectory` | Creates a directory and returns its associated `DirectoryInfo` object. |
| `Delete` | Deletes the specified directory. |
| `Exists` | Returns `true` if the specified directory exists and `false` otherwise. |
| `GetDirectories` | Returns a `string` array containing the names of the subdirectories in the specified directory. |
| `GetFiles` | Returns a `string` array containing the names of the files in the specified directory. |
| `GetCreationTime` | Returns a `DateTime` object representing when the directory was created. |
| `GetLastAccessTime` | Returns a `DateTime` object representing when the directory was last accessed. |
| `GetLastWriteTime` | Returns a `DateTime` object representing when items were last written to the directory. |
| `Move` | Moves the specified directory to a specified location. |

**Fig. 17.12** | `Directory` class `static` methods.

### 17.9.1 Demonstrating Classes `File` and `Directory`

Class `FileTestForm` (Fig. 17.13) uses `File` and `Directory` methods to access file and directory information. The `Form` contains the `inputTextBox`, in which the user enters a file or directory name. For each key that the user presses while typing in the `TextBox`, the program calls `inputTextBox_KeyDown` (lines 19–76). If the user presses the *Enter* key (line 22), this method displays either the file's or directory's contents, depending on the text the user input. (If the user does not press the *Enter* key, this method returns without displaying any content.)

```
1  // Fig. 17.13: FileTestForm.cs
2  // Using classes File and Directory.
3  using System;
4  using System.Windows.Forms;
5  using System.IO;
6
7  namespace FileTest
8  {
9     // displays contents of files and directories
10    public partial class FileTestForm : Form
11    {
12       // parameterless constructor
13       public FileTestForm()
14       {
```

**Fig. 17.13** | Using classes `File` and `Directory`. (Part 1 of 4.)

```
            InitializeComponent();
        }

        // invoked when user presses key
        private void inputTextBox_KeyDown(object sender, KeyEventArgs e)
        {
           // determine whether user pressed Enter key
           if (e.KeyCode == Keys.Enter)
           {
              // get user-specified file or directory
              string fileName = inputTextBox.Text;

              // determine whether fileName is a file
              if (File.Exists(fileName))
              {
                 // get file's creation date, modification date, etc.
                 GetInformation(fileName);

                 // display file contents through StreamReader
                 try
                 {
                    // obtain reader and file contents
                    using (var stream = new StreamReader(fileName))
                    {
                       outputTextBox.AppendText(stream.ReadToEnd());
                    }
                 }
                 catch (IOException)
                 {
                    MessageBox.Show("Error reading from file",
                       "File Error", MessageBoxButtons.OK,
                       MessageBoxIcon.Error);
                 }
              }
              // determine whether fileName is a directory
              else if (Directory.Exists(fileName))
              {
                 // get directory's creation date,
                 // modification date, etc.
                 GetInformation(fileName);

                 // obtain directory list of specified directory
                 string[] directoryList =
                    Directory.GetDirectories(fileName);

                 outputTextBox.AppendText("Directory contents:\n");

                 // output directoryList contents
                 foreach (var directory in directoryList)
                 {
                    outputTextBox.AppendText($"{directory}\n");
                 }
              }
```

**Fig. 17.13** | Using classes File and Directory. (Part 2 of 4.)

```
            else
            {
               // notify user that neither file nor directory exists
               MessageBox.Show(
                  $"{inputTextBox.Text} does not exist", "File Error",
                  MessageBoxButtons.OK, MessageBoxIcon.Error);
            }
         }
      }

      // get information on file or directory,
      // and output it to outputTextBox
      private void GetInformation(string fileName)
      {
         outputTextBox.Clear();

         // output that file or directory exists
         outputTextBox.AppendText($"{fileName} exists\n");

         // output when file or directory was created
         outputTextBox.AppendText(
            $"Created: {File.GetCreationTime(fileName)}\n" +
            Environment.NewLine);

         // output when file or directory was last modified
         outputTextBox.AppendText(
            $"Last modified: {File.GetLastWriteTime(fileName)}\n" +
            Environment.NewLine);

         // output when file or directory was last accessed
         outputTextBox.AppendText(
            $"Last accessed: {File.GetLastAccessTime(fileName)}\n" +
            Environment.NewLine);
      }
   }
}
```

a) Viewing the contents of file "quotes.txt"

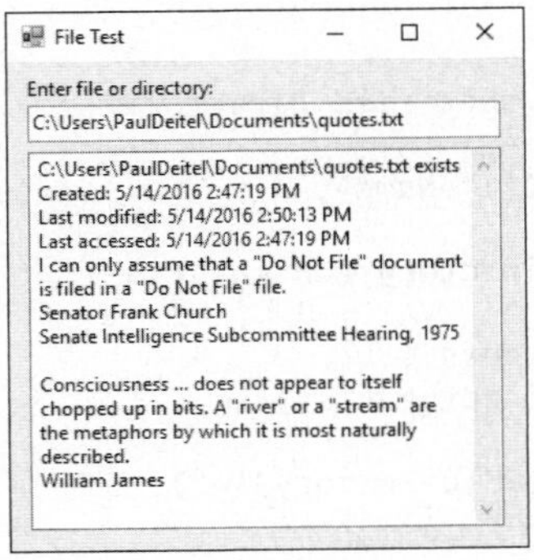

File Test

Enter file or directory:

C:\Users\PaulDeitel\Documents\quotes.txt

C:\Users\PaulDeitel\Documents\quotes.txt exists
Created: 5/14/2016 2:47:19 PM
Last modified: 5/14/2016 2:50:13 PM
Last accessed: 5/14/2016 2:47:19 PM
I can only assume that a "Do Not File" document is filed in a "Do Not File" file.
Senator Frank Church
Senate Intelligence Subcommittee Hearing, 1975

Consciousness ... does not appear to itself chopped up in bits. A "river" or a "stream" are the metaphors by which it is most naturally described.
William James

b) Viewing all directories in C:\Program Files\

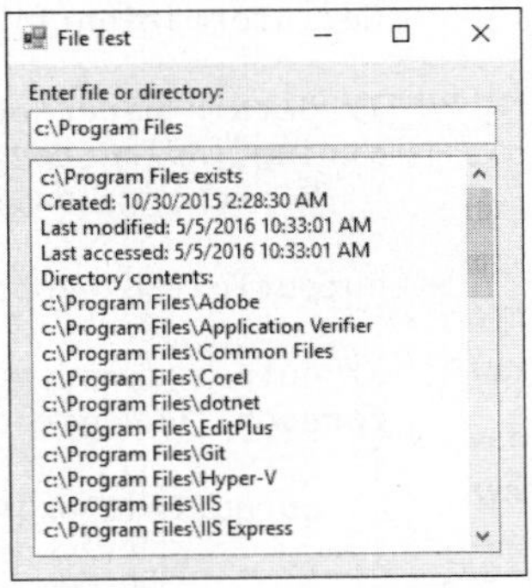

File Test

Enter file or directory:

c:\Program Files

c:\Program Files exists
Created: 10/30/2015 2:28:30 AM
Last modified: 5/5/2016 10:33:01 AM
Last accessed: 5/5/2016 10:33:01 AM
Directory contents:
c:\Program Files\Adobe
c:\Program Files\Application Verifier
c:\Program Files\Common Files
c:\Program Files\Corel
c:\Program Files\dotnet
c:\Program Files\EditPlus
c:\Program Files\Git
c:\Program Files\Hyper-V
c:\Program Files\IIS
c:\Program Files\IIS Express

**Fig. 17.13** | Using classes File and Directory. (Part 3 of 4.)

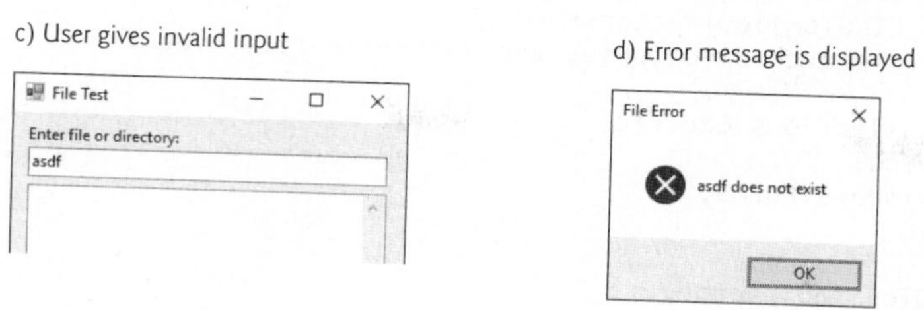


**Fig. 17.13** | Using classes `File` and `Directory`. (Part 4 of 4.)

Line 28 uses `File` method `Exists` to determine whether the user-specified text is the name of an existing file. If so, line 31 invokes `private` method `GetInformation` (lines 80–101), which calls `File` methods `GetCreationTime` (line 89), `GetLastWriteTime` (line 94) and `GetLastAccessTime` (line 99) to access file information. When method `GetInformation` returns, line 37 instantiates a `StreamReader` for reading text from the file. The `StreamReader` constructor takes as an argument a `string` containing the name and path of the file to open. Line 39 calls `StreamReader` method **`ReadToEnd`** to read the entire contents of the file as a `string`, then appends the `string` to `outputTextBox`. Once the file has been read, the `using` block disposes of the corresponding object, which closes the file.

If line 28 determines that the user-specified text is not a file, line 50 determines whether it's a directory using `Directory` method **`Exists`**. If the user specified an *existing* directory, line 54 invokes method `GetInformation` to access the directory information. Lines 57–58 call `Directory` method **`GetDirectories`** to obtain a `string` array containing the names of the subdirectories in the specified directory. Lines 63–66 display each element in the `string` array. Note that, if line 50 determines that the user-specified text is *not* a directory name, lines 71–73 notify the user that the name the user entered does not exist as a file or directory.

### 17.9.2 Searching Directories with LINQ

We now consider another example that uses file- and directory-manipulation capabilities. Class `LINQToFileDirectoryForm` (Fig. 17.14) uses LINQ with classes `File`, `Path` and `Directory` to report the number of files of each file type that exist in the specified directory path. The program also serves as a "clean-up" utility—when it finds a file that has the `.bak` filename extension (i.e., a *backup* file), the program displays a `MessageBox` asking the user whether that file should be removed, then responds appropriately to the user's input. This example also uses *LINQ to Objects* to help delete the backup files.

When the user clicks **Search Directory**, the program invokes `searchButton_Click` (lines 23–62), which searches recursively through the directory path specified by the user. If the user inputs text in the `TextBox`, line 27 calls `Directory` method `Exists` to determine whether that text is a valid directory. If it's not, lines 30–31 notify the user of the error.

```
// Fig. 17.14: LINQToFileDirectoryForm.cs
// Using LINQ to search directories and determine file types.
using System;
using System.Collections.Generic;
using System.Linq;
using System.Windows.Forms;
using System.IO;

namespace LINQToFileDirectory
{
   public partial class LINQToFileDirectoryForm : Form
   {
      // store extensions found, and number of each extension found
      Dictionary<string, int> found = new Dictionary<string, int>();

      // parameterless constructor
      public LINQToFileDirectoryForm()
      {
         InitializeComponent();
      }

      // handles the Search Directory Button's Click event
      private void searchButton_Click(object sender, EventArgs e)
      {
         // check whether user specified path exists
         if (!string.IsNullOrEmpty(pathTextBox.Text) &&
            !Directory.Exists(pathTextBox.Text))
         {
            // show error if user does not specify valid directory
            MessageBox.Show("Invalid Directory", "Error",
               MessageBoxButtons.OK, MessageBoxIcon.Error);
         }
         else
         {
            // directory to search; if not specified use current directory
            string currentDirectory =
               (!string.IsNullOrEmpty(pathTextBox.Text)) ?
                  pathTextBox.Text : Directory.GetCurrentDirectory();

            directoryTextBox.Text = currentDirectory; // show directory

            // clear TextBoxes
            pathTextBox.Clear();
            resultsTextBox.Clear();

            SearchDirectory(currentDirectory); // search the directory

            // allow user to delete .bak files
            CleanDirectory(currentDirectory);

            // summarize and display the results
            foreach (var current in found.Keys)
            {
```

**Fig. 17.14** | Using LINQ to search directories and determine file types. (Part 1 of 3.)

```
               // display the number of files with current extension
               resultsTextBox.AppendText(
                  $"* Found {found[current]} {current} files." +
                  Environment.NewLine);
            }

            found.Clear(); // clear results for new search
         }
      }

      // search directory using LINQ
      private void SearchDirectory(string folder)
      {
         // files contained in the directory
         string[] files = Directory.GetFiles(folder);

         // subdirectories in the directory
         string[] directories = Directory.GetDirectories(folder);

         // find all file extensions in this directory
         var extensions =
            from file in files
            group file by Path.GetExtension(file);

         foreach (var extension in extensions)
         {
            if (found.ContainsKey(extension.Key))
            {
               found[extension.Key] += extension.Count(); // update count
            }
            else
            {
               found[extension.Key] = extension.Count(); // add count
            }
         }

         // recursive call to search subdirectories
         foreach (var subdirectory in directories)
         {
            SearchDirectory(subdirectory);
         }
      }

      // allow user to delete backup files (.bak)
      private void CleanDirectory(string folder)
      {
         // files contained in the directory
         string[] files = Directory.GetFiles(folder);

         // subdirectories in the directory
         string[] directories = Directory.GetDirectories(folder);
```

**Fig. 17.14** | Using LINQ to search directories and determine file types. (Part 2 of 3.)

```
            // select all the backup files in this directory
            var backupFiles =
               from file in files
               where Path.GetExtension(file) == ".bak"
               select file;

            // iterate over all backup files (.bak)
            foreach (var backup in backupFiles)
            {
               DialogResult result = MessageBox.Show(
                  $"Found backup file {Path.GetFileName(backup)}. Delete?",
                  "Delete Backup", MessageBoxButtons.YesNo,
                  MessageBoxIcon.Question);

               // delete file if user clicked 'yes'
               if (result == DialogResult.Yes)
               {
                  File.Delete(backup); // delete backup file
                  --found[".bak"]; // decrement count in Dictionary

                  // if there are no .bak files, delete key from Dictionary
                  if (found[".bak"] == 0)
                  {
                     found.Remove(".bak");
                  }
               }
            }

            // recursive call to clean subdirectories
            foreach (var subdirectory in directories)
            {
               CleanDirectory(subdirectory);
            }
         }
      }
   }
```

a) GUI after entering a directory to search and pressing **Search Directory**

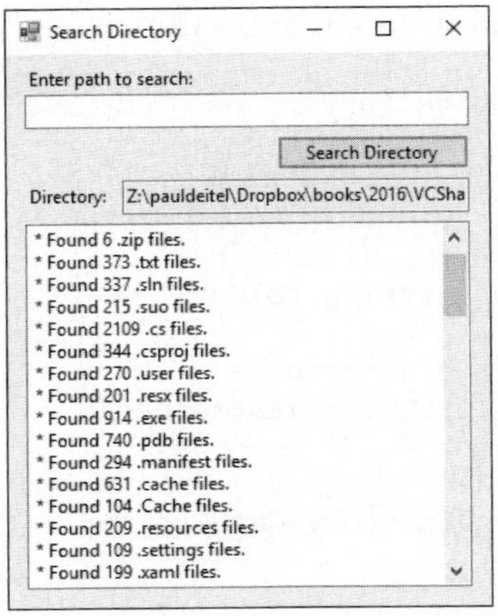

Search Directory

Enter path to search:

Search Directory

Directory: Z:\pauldeitel\Dropbox\books\2016\VCSha

* Found 6 .zip files.
* Found 373 .txt files.
* Found 337 .sln files.
* Found 215 .suo files.
* Found 2109 .cs files.
* Found 344 .csproj files.
* Found 270 .user files.
* Found 201 .resx files.
* Found 914 .exe files.
* Found 740 .pdb files.
* Found 294 .manifest files.
* Found 631 .cache files.
* Found 104 .Cache files.
* Found 209 .resources files.
* Found 109 .settings files.
* Found 199 .xaml files.

b) Dialog that appears to confirm deletion of a `.bak` file

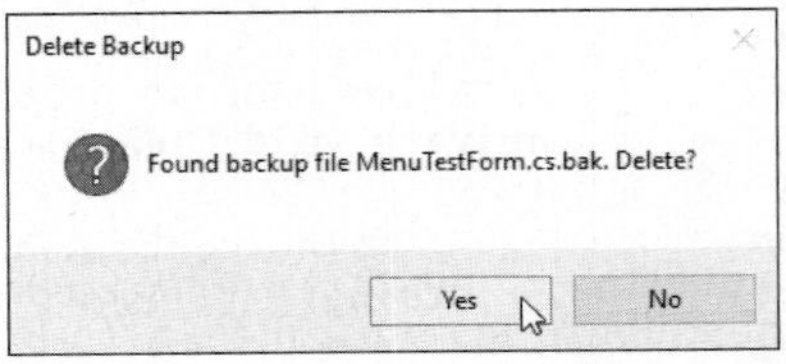

Delete Backup

Found backup file MenuTestForm.cs.bak. Delete?

Yes No

**Fig. 17.14** | Using LINQ to search directories and determine file types. (Part 3 of 3.)

### *Method* `SearchDirectory`

Lines 36–38 get the current directory (if the user did not specify a path) or the specified directory. Line 46 passes the directory name to *recursive* method `SearchDirectory` (lines 65–95). Line 68 calls `Directory` method **`GetFiles`** to get a `string` array containing filenames in the specified directory. Line 71 calls `Directory` method `GetDirectories` to get a `string` array containing the subdirectory names in the specified directory.

Lines 74–76 use LINQ to get the filename extensions in the `files` array. **`Path`** method **`GetExtension`** obtains the extension for the specified filename. We use the LINQ **`group by`** clause to group the results by filename extension. For each filename-extension group returned by the LINQ query, lines 78–88 use LINQ method `Count` to determine the number of occurrences of that extension in the `files` array.

Class `LINQToFileDirectoryForm` uses a `Dictionary` (declared in line 14) to store each filename extension and the corresponding number of filenames with that extension. A **`Dictionary`** (namespace `System.Collections.Generic`) is a collection of *key–value pairs*, in which each *key* has a corresponding *value*. Class `Dictionary` is a *generic class* like class `List` (presented in Section 9.4). Line 14 indicates that the `Dictionary found` contains pairs of `string`s and `int`s, which represent the filename extensions and the number of files with those extensions, respectively. Line 80 uses `Dictionary` method **`ContainsKey`** to determine whether the specified filename extension has been placed in the `Dictionary` previously. If this method returns `true`, line 82 adds the count of the number of files with a given extention to the current total for that extension that's stored in the `Dictionary`. Otherwise, line 86 inserts a new *key–value pair* into the `Dictionary` for the new filename extension and its extension count. Lines 91–94 recursively call `SearchDirectory` for each subdirectory in the current directory—depending on the number of files and folders, this operation could take substantial time to complete.

### *Method* `CleanDirectory`

When method `SearchDirectory` returns, line 49 calls `CleanDirectory` (lines 98–139) to search for all files with extension `.bak`. Lines 101 and 104 obtain the list of filenames and list of directory names in the current directory, respectively. The LINQ query in lines 107–110 locates all filenames in the current directory that have the `.bak` extension. Lines 113–132 iterate through the results and ask the user whether each file should be deleted. If the user clicks **Yes** in the dialog, line 123 uses `File` method **`Delete`** to remove the file from disk, and line 124 subtracts 1 from the total number of `.bak` files. If the number of `.bak` files remaining is `0`, line 129 uses `Dictionary` method **`Remove`** to delete the key–value pair for `.bak` files from the `Dictionary`. Lines 135–138 recursively call `CleanDirectory` for each subdirectory in the current directory. After each subdirectory has been checked for `.bak` files, method `CleanDirectory` returns, and lines 52–58 display the summary of filename extensions and the number of files with each extension. Line 52 uses `Dictionary` property **`Keys`** to get all the keys. Line 56 uses the `Dictionary`'s indexer to get the value for the current key. Finally, line 60 uses `Dictionary` method **`Clear`** to delete the contents of the `Dictionary`.

## 17.10 Wrap-Up

In this chapter, you used file processing to manipulate persistent data. We overviewed several file-processing classes from the `System.IO` namespace. We showed how to use sequential-access file processing to manipulate records in text files. We then discussed the differences between text-file processing and object serialization, and used serialization to store entire objects in and retrieve entire objects from files. Finally, you used class `File` to manipulate files, and classes `Directory` and `DirectoryInfo` to manipulate directories.

In the next chapter, we introduce *generics*, which allow you to declare a family of classes and methods that implement the same functionality on *any* type.

18

# Generics

## Objectives

In this chapter you'll:

- Create generic methods that perform identical tasks on arguments of different types.
- Create a generic `Stack` class that can be used to store objects of a specific type.
- Understand how to overload generic methods with nongeneric methods or with other generic methods.
- Understand the kinds of constraints that can be applied to a type parameter.
- Apply multiple constraints to a type parameter.

Outline



## 18.1 Introduction

In this chapter, we introduce C# generics and demonstrate how to create generic methods and a generic class.

### *`object`-Based Data Structure Disadvantages*

You can store any `object` in our data structures. One inconvenient aspect of storing `object` references occurs when retrieving them from a collection. An app normally needs to process specific types of objects. As a result, the `object` references obtained from a collection typically need to be *downcast* to an appropriate type to allow the app to process the objects correctly. In addition, data of value types (e.g., `int` and `double`) must be *boxed* to be manipulated with `object` references, which increases the overhead of processing such data. Most importantly, processing all data as type `object` limits the C# compiler's ability to perform type checking.

### *Compile-Time Type Safety*

Though we can easily create data structures that manipulate any type of data as `object`s, it would be nice if we could detect type mismatches at compile time—this is known as **compile-time type safety**. For example, if a `Stack` should store only `int` values, attempting to push a `string` onto that `Stack` should cause a compile-time error. Similarly, a `Sort` method should be able to compare elements that are all guaranteed to have the same type. If we create type-specific versions of class `Stack` and method `Sort`, the C# compiler would certainly be able to ensure compile-time type safety. However, this would require that we create many copies of the same basic code.

### *Generics*

This chapter discusses generics, which provide the means to create the general models mentioned above. **Generic methods** enable you to specify, with a *single method declaration, a set of related methods.* **Generic classes** enable you to specify, with a *single class declaration, a set of related classes.* Similarly, **generic interfaces** enable you to specify, with a *single interface declaration, a set of related interfaces.* Generics provide *compile-time type safety.* [*Note:* You also can implement generic `struct`s and `delegate`s.] So far in this book, we've used the generic types `List` (Chapter 9) and `Dictionary` (Chapter 17).

We can write a generic method for sorting an array, then invoke the generic method separately with an `int` array, a `double` array, a `string` array and so on, to sort each different type of array. The compiler performs **type checking** to ensure that the array passed to the sorting method contains only elements of the correct type. We can write a single generic `Stack` class, then instantiate `Stack` objects for a stack of `int`s, a stack of `double`s, a stack of `string`s and so on. The compiler performs *type checking* to ensure that the `Stack` stores *only* elements of the correct type.

This chapter presents examples of generic methods and generic classes. Chapter 19, Generic Collections; Functional Programming with LINQ/PLINQ, discusses the .NET Framework's generic collections classes. A *collection* is a data structure that maintains a group of related objects or values. The .NET Framework collection classes use generics to allow you to specify the exact types of object that a particular collection will store.

## 18.2 Motivation for Generic Methods

Overloaded methods are often used to perform similar operations on different types of data. To understand the motivation for generic methods, let's begin with an example (Fig. 18.1) that contains three overloaded `DisplayArray` methods (lines 23–31, lines 34–42 and lines 45–53). These methods display the elements of an `int` array, a `double` array and a `char` array, respectively. Soon, we'll reimplement this program more concisely and elegantly using a *single* generic method.

```
1  // Fig. 18.1: OverloadedMethods.cs
2  // Using overloaded methods to display arrays of different types.
3  using System;
4
5  class OverloadedMethods
6  {
7     static void Main(string[] args)
8     {
9        // create arrays of int, double and char
10       int[] intArray = {1, 2, 3, 4, 5, 6};
11       double[] doubleArray = {1.1, 2.2, 3.3, 4.4, 5.5, 6.6, 7.7};
12       char[] charArray = {'H', 'E', 'L', 'L', 'O'};
13
14       Console.Write("Array intArray contains: ");
15       DisplayArray(intArray); // pass an int array argument
16       Console.Write("Array doubleArray contains: ");
17       DisplayArray(doubleArray); // pass a double array argument
18       Console.Write("Array charArray contains: ");
19       DisplayArray(charArray); // pass a char array argument
20    }
21
22    // output int array
23    private static void DisplayArray(int[] inputArray)
24    {
25       foreach (var element in inputArray)
26       {
27          Console.Write($"{element} ");
28       }
29
30       Console.WriteLine();
31    }
```

**Fig. 18.1** | Using overloaded methods to display arrays of different types. (Part 1 of 2.)

```
32
33     // output double array
34     private static void DisplayArray(double[] inputArray)
35     {
36        foreach (var element in inputArray)
37        {
38           Console.Write($"{element} ");
39        }
40
41        Console.WriteLine();
42     }
43
44     // output char array
45     private static void DisplayArray(char[] inputArray)
46     {
47        foreach (var element in inputArray)
48        {
49           Console.Write($"{element} ");
50        }
51
52        Console.WriteLine();
53     }
54  }
```

```
Array intArray contains: 1 2 3 4 5 6
Array doubleArray contains: 1.1 2.2 3.3 4.4 5.5 6.6 7.7
Array charArray contains: H E L L O
```

**Fig. 18.1** | Using overloaded methods to display arrays of different types. (Part 2 of 2.)

The program begins by declaring and initializing three arrays—six-element `int` array `intArray` (line 10), seven-element `double` array `doubleArray` (line 11) and five-element `char` array `charArray` (line 12). Then, lines 14–19 output the arrays.

When the compiler encounters a method call, it attempts to locate a method declaration that has the *same* method name and parameters that *match* the argument types in the method call. In this example, each `DisplayArray` call exactly matches one of the `DisplayArray` method declarations. For example, line 15 calls `DisplayArray` with `intArray` as its argument. At compile time, the compiler determines argument `intArray`'s type (i.e., `int[]`), attempts to locate a method named `DisplayArray` that specifies a single `int[]` parameter (which it finds at lines 23–31) and sets up a call to that method. Similarly, when the compiler encounters the `DisplayArray` call at line 17, it determines argument `doubleArray`'s type (i.e., `double[]`), then attempts to locate a method named `DisplayArray` that specifies a single `double[]` parameter (which it finds at lines 34–42) and sets up a call to that method. Finally, when the compiler encounters the `DisplayArray` call at line 19, it determines argument `charArray`'s type (i.e., `char[]`), then attempts to locate a method named `DisplayArray` that specifies a single `char[]` parameter (which it finds at lines 45–53) and sets up a call to that method.

Study each `DisplayArray` method. Note that the array element type (`int`, `double` or `char`) appears in *one* location in each method—the method header (lines 23, 34 and 45). Each `foreach` statement header (lines 25, 36 and 47) uses `var` to infer the element type from the method's parameter. If we were to replace the element types in each method's header with a generic name (such as T for "type"), then all three methods would look like the one in Fig. 18.2. It appears that if we can replace the array element type in each of the three methods with a single "generic type parameter," then we should be able to declare one DisplayArray method that can display the elements of *any* array. The method in Fig. 18.2 *will not compile*, because its syntax is not correct. We declare a generic DisplayArray method with the proper syntax in Fig. 18.3.

```
private static void DisplayArray(T[] inputArray)
{
   foreach (var element in inputArray)
   {
      Console.Write($"{element} ");
   }

   Console.WriteLine();
}
```

**Fig. 18.2** | DisplayArray method in which actual type names have been replaced by convention with the generic name T. Again, this code will *not* compile.

## 18.3 Generic-Method Implementation

If the operations performed by several overloaded methods are identical for each argument type, the overloaded methods can be more compactly and conveniently coded using a generic method. You can write a single generic-method declaration that can be called at different times with arguments of different types. Based on the types of the arguments passed to the generic method, the compiler handles each method call appropriately.

Figure 18.3 reimplements the app of Fig. 18.1 using a generic DisplayArray method (lines 24–32). Note that the DisplayArray method calls in lines 15, 17 and 19 are identical to those of Fig. 18.1, the outputs of the two apps are identical and the code in Fig. 18.3 is 22 lines *shorter* than that in Fig. 18.1. As illustrated in Fig. 18.3, generics enable us to create and test our code once, then *reuse* it for many different types of data. This effectively demonstrates the expressive power of generics.

```
1  // Fig. 18.3: GenericMethod.cs
2  // Using a generic method to display arrays of different types.
3  using System;
4
5  class GenericMethod
6  {
7     static void Main()
8     {
9        // create arrays of int, double and char
10       int[] intArray = {1, 2, 3, 4, 5, 6};
11       double[] doubleArray = {1.1, 2.2, 3.3, 4.4, 5.5, 6.6, 7.7};
12       char[] charArray = {'H', 'E', 'L', 'L', 'O'};
```

**Fig. 18.3** | Using a generic method to display arrays of different types. (Part 1 of 2.)

```
13
14          Console.Write("Array intArray contains: ");
15          DisplayArray(intArray); // pass an int array argument
16          Console.Write("Array doubleArray contains: ");
17          DisplayArray(doubleArray); // pass a double array argument
18          Console.Write("Array charArray contains: ");
19          DisplayArray(charArray); // pass a char array argument
20       }
21
22       // output array of all types
23       private static void DisplayArray<T>(T[] inputArray)
24       {
25          foreach (var element in inputArray)
26          {
27             Console.Write($"{element} ");
28          }
29
30          Console.WriteLine();
31       }
32    }
```

```
Array intArray contains: 1 2 3 4 5 6
Array doubleArray contains: 1.1 2.2 3.3 4.4 5.5 6.6 7.7
Array charArray contains: H E L L O
```

**Fig. 18.3** | Using a generic method to display arrays of different types. (Part 2 of 2.)

Line 23 begins method `DisplayArray`'s declaration, which is `static` so that `Main` can call `DisplayArray`. All generic method declarations have a **type-parameter list** delimited by angle brackets (<T> in this example) that follows the method's name. Each type-parameter list contains one or more **type parameters**, separated by commas (e.g., `Dictionary<K, V>`). A type parameter is an identifier that's used in place of actual type names. The type parameters can be used to declare the return type, the parameter types and local variable types in a generic method declaration; the type parameters act as placeholders for **type arguments** that represent the types of data that will be passed to the generic method.

The type-parameter names throughout the method declaration (if any) must match those declared in the type-parameter list. Also, a type parameter can be declared *only once* in the type-parameter list but can appear *more than once* in the method's parameter list. Type-parameter names need *not* be unique among separate generic methods.

**Common Programming Error 18.1**

*If you forget to include the type-parameter list when declaring a generic method, the compiler will not recognize the type-parameter names when they're encountered in the method. This results in compilation errors.*

Method `DisplayArray`'s type-parameter list (line 23) declares type parameter `T` as the placeholder for the array-element type that `DisplayArray` will output. Note that `T` appears in the parameter list as the array-element type (line 23). This is the same location where the overloaded `DisplayArray` methods of Fig. 18.1 specified `int`, `double` or `char` as the element type. The remainder of `DisplayArray` is identical to the version presented in

Fig. 18.1. In this example though, the `foreach` statement infers `element`'s type from the array type passed to the method.

As in Fig. 18.1, the program of Fig. 18.3 begins by declaring and initializing six-element `int` array `intArray` (line 10), seven-element `double` array `doubleArray` (line 11) and five-element `char` array `charArray` (line 12). Then each array is output by calling `DisplayArray` (lines 15, 17 and 19)—once with argument `intArray`, once with argument `doubleArray` and once with argument `charArray`.

When the compiler encounters a method call such as line 15, it analyzes the set of methods (both nongeneric and generic) that might match the method call, looking for a method that best matches the call. If there's no matching method, or if there's more than one best match, the compiler generates an error.

In the case of line 15, the compiler determines that the best match occurs if the type parameter `T` in line 23 of method `DisplayArray`'s declaration is replaced with the type of the elements in the method call's argument `intArray` (i.e., `int`). Then the compiler sets up a call to `DisplayArray` with `int` as the type argument for the type parameter `T`. This is known as the type-inferencing process. The same process is repeated for the calls to method `DisplayArray` in lines 17 and 19.

**Common Programming Error 18.2**

*If the compiler cannot find a single nongeneric or generic method declaration that's a best match for a method call, or if there are multiple best matches, a compilation error occurs.*

For each variable declared with a type parameter, the compiler checks whether the operations performed on the variable are allowed for all types that the type parameter can assume. By default, a type parameter can assume any type, but we'll show in Section 18.4 that you can restrict this to specific types. The only operation performed on each array element in this example is to output its `string` representation. Line 27 performs an *implicit* `ToString` call on the current array element. Since all objects have a `ToString` method, the compiler is satisfied that line 27 performs a valid operation for *any* array element.

By declaring `DisplayArray` as a generic method in Fig. 18.3, we eliminated the need for the overloaded methods of Fig. 18.1, saving 22 lines of code and creating a *reusable* method that can output the string representations of the elements in *any* one-dimensional array, not just arrays of `int`, `double` or `char` elements.

### *Value Types vs. Reference Types in Generics*

The compiler handles value and reference types differently in generic method calls. When a value-type argument is used for a given type parameter, the compiler generates a version of the method that's specific to the value type—if one has been generated previously, the compiler reuses that one. So in Fig. 18.3, the compiler generates three versions of method `DisplayArray`—one each for types `int`, `double` and `char`. If `DisplayArray` were called with a reference type, the compiler would also generate a *single* version of the method that's used by all reference types.

### *Explicit Type Arguments*

You also can use **explicit type arguments** to indicate the exact type that should be used to call a generic function. For example, line 15 could be written as

```
DisplayArray<int>(intArray); // pass an int array argument
```

The preceding method call explicitly provides the type argument (int) that should be used to replace type parameter T in line 23. Though not required here, an explicit type argument would be required if the compiler cannot infer the type from the method's argument(s).

## 18.4 Type Constraints

In this section, we present a generic Maximum method that determines and returns the largest of its three arguments (all of the same type). The generic method in this example uses the type parameter to declare *both* the method's return type *and* its parameters. Normally, when comparing values to determine which one is greater, you would use the > operator. However, this operator is not overloaded for use with every type that's built into the Framework Class Library or that might be defined by extending those types. By default, generic code is restricted to performing operations that are guaranteed to work for every possible type. Thus, an expression like value1 < value2 is not allowed unless the compiler can ensure that the operator < is provided for every type that will ever be used in the generic code. Similarly, you cannot call a method or access a property on a generic-type variable unless the compiler can ensure that all types that will ever be used in the generic code support that method. For this reason, generic code supports only the methods of class object by default.

### 18.4.1 IComparable<T> Interface

It's possible to compare two objects of the *same* type if that type implements the generic interface **IComparable<T>** (of namespace System). A benefit of implementing this interface is that such objects can be used with the *sorting* and *searching* methods of classes in the System.Collections.Generic namespace—we discuss those methods in Chapter 19.

C#'s simple types *all* implement IComparable<T> via their .NET Framework Class Library types. For example, the Double value type (for simple type double) implements IComparable<Double>, and the Int32 value type (for simple type int) implements IComparable<Int32>. Types that implement IComparable<T> *must* declare a CompareTo method for comparing objects. For example, if we have two ints, int1 and int2, they can be compared with the expression:

```
int1.CompareTo(int2)
```

Method CompareTo must return

- 0 if the objects are equal,
- a negative integer if int1 is less than int2 or
- a positive integer if int1 is greater than int2.

### 18.4.2 Specifying Type Constraints

Even though IComparable<T> objects can be compared, by default they cannot be used with generic code, because *not* all types implement interface IComparable<T>. However, we can restrict the types that can be used with a generic method or class to ensure that the types meet the method's or class's requirements. This is accomplished with **type constraints**.

Figure 18.4 declares method `Maximum` (lines 18–35) with a type constraint that requires each of the method's arguments to be of type `IComparable<T>`. This restriction is important, because *not* all objects can be compared via a `CompareTo` method. However, all `IComparable<T>` objects are *guaranteed* to have a `CompareTo` method, which we use in method `Maximum` to determine the largest of its three arguments. In addition, because there's only one type parameter, all three arguments must be of the same type.

```
1  // Fig. 18.4: MaximumTest.cs
2  // Generic method Maximum returns the largest of three objects.
3  using System;
4
5  class MaximumTest
6  {
7     static void Main()
8     {
9        Console.WriteLine($"Maximum of 3, 4 and 5 is {Maximum(3, 4, 5)}\n");
10       Console.WriteLine(
11          $"Maximum of 6.6, 8.8 and 7.7 is {Maximum(6.6, 8.8, 7.7)}\n");
12       Console.WriteLine("Maximum of pear, apple and orange is " +
13          $"{Maximum("pear", "apple", "orange")}\n");
14    }
15
16    // generic function determines the
17    // largest of the IComparable<T> objects
18    private static T Maximum<T>(T x, T y, T z) where T : IComparable<T>
19    {
20       var max = x; // assume x is initially the largest
21
22       // compare y with max
23       if (y.CompareTo(max) > 0)
24       {
25          max = y; // y is the largest so far
26       }
27
28       // compare z with max
29       if (z.CompareTo(max) > 0)
30       {
31          max = z; // z is the largest
32       }
33
34       return max; // return largest object
35    }
36 }
```

```
Maximum of 3, 4 and 5 is 5
Maximum of 6.6, 8.8 and 7.7 is 8.8
Maximum of pear, apple and orange is pear
```

**Fig. 18.4** | Generic method `Maximum` returns the largest of three objects.

### *Specifying the Type Constraint with a* `where` *Clause*

Generic method `Maximum` uses type parameter `T` as the return type of the method (line 18), as the type of method parameters `x`, `y` and `z` (line 18), and as the inferred type of local variable max (line 20). The **where** clause (after the parameter list in line 18) specifies the type constraint for type parameter T. In this case, the type constraint

```
where T : IComparable<T>
```

indicates that this method requires the type argument to implement interface `IComparable<T>`. If no type constraint is specified, the default type constraint is `object`. If you pass to `Maximum` a value of a type that does not match the type constraint, the compiler generates an error. Note once again, that we declared `Maximum` `static` so `Main` can call it—generic methods are not required to be `static` in every case.

### *Kinds of Type Constraints*

C# provides several kinds of type constraints:

- A **class constraint** indicates that the type argument must be an object of a specific base class or one of its subclasses.
- An **interface constraint** indicates that the type argument's class must implement a specific interface. The type constraint in line 18 is an interface constraint, because `IComparable<T>` is an interface.
- You can specify that the type argument must be a reference type or a value type by using the **reference-type constraint** (`class`) or the **value-type constraint** (`struct`), respectively.
- Finally, you can specify a **constructor constraint—new()**—to indicate that the generic code can use operator `new` to create new objects of the type represented by the type parameter. If a type parameter is specified with a constructor constraint, the type argument's class must provide a `public` parameterless or default constructor to ensure that objects of the class can be created without passing constructor arguments; otherwise, a compilation error occurs.

### *Applying Multiple Type Constraints*

It's possible to apply **multiple constraints** to a type parameter. To do so, simply provide a comma-separated list of constraints in the `where` clause. If you have a class constraint, reference-type constraint or value-type constraint, it must be listed first—only one of these types of constraints can be used for each type parameter. Interface constraints (if any) are listed next. The constructor constraint is listed last (if there is one).

### *Analyzing the Code*

Method `Maximum` assumes that its first argument (`x`) is the largest and assigns it to local variable `max` (line 20). Next, the `if` statement at lines 23–26 determines whether `y` is greater than `max`. The condition invokes `y.CompareTo(max)`. If `y` is greater than `max`—that is, `CompareTo` returns a value greater than 0—then `y` is assigned to variable `max` (line 25). Similarly, the statement at lines 29–32 determines whether `z` is greater than `max`. If so, line 31 assigns `z` to `max`. Then, line 34 returns `max` to the caller.

In `Main` (lines 7–14), line 9 calls `Maximum` with the integers `3`, `4` and `5`. Generic method `Maximum` is a match for this call, but its arguments must implement interface `IComparable<T>` to ensure that they can be compared. Type `int` is a synonym for `Int32`, which implements interface `IComparable<int>`. Thus, `int`s (and other simple types) are valid arguments to method `Maximum`.

Line 11 passes three `double` arguments to `Maximum`. Again, this is allowed because `double` is a synonym for `Double`, which implements `IComparable<double>`. Line 13 passes `Maximum` three `strings`, which are also `IComparable<string>` objects. We intentionally placed the largest value in a different position in each method call (lines 9, 11 and 13) to show that the generic method always finds the maximum value, regardless of its position in the argument list and regardless of the inferred type argument.

*Value Types vs. Reference Types in Generics*

In this example, the compiler generates three versions of method `Maximum`, based on the calls in `Main`. Customized `Maximum` methods are generated for types `int` and `double` and, because `string` is a class, a third version of `Maximum` is generated for all reference types—the runtime then determines the reference type argument from the method call. For more details on how the runtime handles generics for value and reference types, see

```
https://msdn.microsoft.com/library/f4a6ta2h
```

## 18.5 Overloading Generic Methods

A generic method may be **overloaded**. Each overloaded method must have a unique signature (as discussed in Chapter 7). A class can provide two or more generic methods with the *same* name but *different* method parameters. For example, we could provide a second version of generic method `DisplayArray` (Fig. 18.3) with the additional parameters `lowIndex` and `highIndex` that specify the portion of the array to output.

A generic method can be overloaded by nongeneric methods with the same method name. When the compiler encounters a method call, it searches for the method declaration that best matches the method name and the argument types specified in the call. For example, generic method `DisplayArray` of Fig. 18.3 could be overloaded with a version specific to `strings` that outputs the `strings` in tabular format—the non-generic version of a method takes precedence over a generic version. If the compiler cannot match a method call to either a nongeneric method or a generic method, or if there's ambiguity due to multiple possible matches, the compiler generates an error.

## 18.6 Generic Classes

The concept of a data structure (e.g., a stack) that contains data elements can be understood independently of the element type it manipulates. A generic class provides a means for describing a class in a *type-independent* manner. We can then instantiate type-specific versions of the generic class. This capability is an opportunity for software reusability.

With a generic class, you can use a simple, concise notation to indicate the actual type(s) that should be used in place of the class's type parameter(s). At compilation time, the compiler ensures your code's type safety, and the runtime system replaces type parameters with type arguments to enable your client code to interact with the generic class.

One generic `Stack` class, for example, could be the basis for creating many `Stack` classes (e.g., "`Stack` of `double`," "`Stack` of `int`," "`Stack` of `char`," "`Stack` of `Employee`"). Figure 18.5 presents a generic `Stack` class declaration. This class should not be confused with the class `Stack` from namespace `System.Collections.Generics`. A generic class declaration is similar to a nongeneric class declaration, except that the class name is followed by a type-parameter list (line 5) and, optionally, one or more constraints on its type parameter. Type parameter `T` represents the element type the `Stack` will manipulate. As with generic methods, the type-parameter list of a generic class can have one or more type parameters separated by commas. Type parameter `T` is used throughout the `Stack` class declaration (Fig. 18.5) to represent the element type. Class `Stack` declares variable `elements` as an array of type `T` (line 8). This array (created at line 25) will store the `Stack`'s elements. [*Note:* This example implements a `Stack` as an array, but they also can be implemented as linked lists.]

```
1  // Fig. 18.5: Stack.cs
2  // Generic class Stack.
3  using System;
4
5  public class Stack<T>
6  {
7     private int top; // location of the top element
8     private T[] elements; // array that stores stack elements
9
10    // parameterless constructor creates a stack of the default size
11    public Stack()
12       : this(10) // default stack size
13    {
14       // empty constructor; calls constructor at line 18 to perform init
15    }
16
17    // constructor creates a stack of the specified number of elements
18    public Stack(int stackSize)
19    {
20       if (stackSize <= 0) // validate stackSize
21       {
22          throw new ArgumentException("Stack size must be positive.");
23       }
24
25       elements = new T[stackSize]; // create stackSize elements
26       top = -1; // stack initially empty
27    }
28
29    // push element onto the stack; if unsuccessful,
30    // throw FullStackException
31    public void Push(T pushValue)
32    {
33       if (top == elements.Length - 1) // stack is full
34       {
35          throw new FullStackException(
36             $"Stack is full, cannot push {pushValue}");
37       }
38
39       ++top; // increment top
40       elements[top] = pushValue; // place pushValue on stack
41    }
```

**Fig. 18.5** | Generic class `Stack`. (Part 1 of 2.)

```
42
43       // return the top element if not empty,
44       // else throw EmptyStackException
45       public T Pop()
46       {
47          if (top == -1) // stack is empty
48          {
49             throw new EmptyStackException("Stack is empty, cannot pop");
50          }
51
52          --top; // decrement top
53          return elements[top + 1]; // return top value
54       }
55    }
```

**Fig. 18.5** | Generic class `Stack`. (Part 2 of 2.)

As with generic methods, when a generic class is compiled, the compiler performs type checking on the class's type parameters to ensure that they can be used with the code in the generic class. For value-types, the compiler generates a custom version of the class for each unique value type used to create a new `Stack` object, and for reference types, the compiler generates a single additional custom `Stack`. The constraints determine the operations that can be performed on the type parameters. For reference types, the runtime system replaces the type parameters with the actual types. For class `Stack`, no type constraint is specified, so the default type constraint, `object`, is used. The scope of a generic class's type parameter is the entire class.

### `Stack` *Constructors*

Class `Stack` has two constructors. The parameterless constructor (lines 11–15) passes the default stack size (`10`) to the one-argument constructor, using the syntax `this` (line 12) to invoke another constructor in the same class. The one-argument constructor (lines 18–27) validates the `stackSize` argument and creates an array of the specified `stackSize` (if it's greater than `0`) or throws an exception, otherwise.

### `Stack` *Method* `Push`

Method `Push` (lines 31–41) first determines whether an attempt is being made to push an element onto a full `Stack`. If so, lines 35–36 throw a `FullStackException` (declared in Fig. 18.6). If the `Stack` is not full, line 39 increments the `top` counter to indicate the new top position, and line 40 places the argument in that location of array `elements`.

### `Stack` *Method* `Pop`

Method `Pop` (lines 45–54) first determines whether an attempt is being made to pop an element from an empty `Stack`. If so, line 49 throws an `EmptyStackException` (declared in Fig. 18.7). Otherwise, line 52 decrements the `top` counter to indicate the new top position, and line 53 returns the original top element of the `Stack`.

### *Classes* `FullStackException` *and* `EmptyStackException`

Classes `FullStackException` (Fig. 18.6) and `EmptyStackException` (Fig. 18.7) each provide a parameterless constructor, a one-argument constructor of exception classes (as discussed in Section 13.8) and a two-argument constructor for creating a new exception using an existing one. The parameterless constructor sets the default error message while the other two constructors set custom error messages.

```
// Fig. 18.6: FullStackException.cs
// FullStackException indicates a stack is full.
using System;

public class FullStackException : Exception
{
   // parameterless constructor
   public FullStackException() : base("Stack is full")
   {
      // empty constructor
   }

   // one-parameter constructor
   public FullStackException(string exception) : base(exception)
   {
      // empty constructor
   }

   // two-parameter constructor
   public FullStackException(string exception, Exception inner)
      : base(exception, inner)
   {
      // empty constructor
   }
}
```

**Fig. 18.6** | `FullStackException` indicates a stack is full.

```
// Fig. 18.7: EmptyStackException.cs
// EmptyStackException indicates a stack is empty.
using System;

public class EmptyStackException : Exception
{
   // parameterless constructor
   public EmptyStackException() : base("Stack is empty")
   {
      // empty constructor
   }

   // one-parameter constructor
   public EmptyStackException(string exception) : base(exception)
   {
      // empty constructor
   }

```

**Fig. 18.7** | `EmptyStackException` indicates a stack is empty. (Part 1 of 2.)

```
    // two-parameter constructor
    public EmptyStackException(string exception, Exception inner)
       : base(exception, inner)
    {
       // empty constructor
    }
}
```

**Fig. 18.7** | `EmptyStackException` indicates a stack is empty. (Part 2 of 2.)

### *Demonstrating Class* `Stack`

Now, let's consider an app (Fig. 18.8) that uses our generic `Stack` class. Lines 13–14 declare variables of type `Stack<double>` (pronounced "`Stack` of `double`") and `Stack<int>` (pronounced "`Stack` of `int`"). The types `double` and `int` are the `Stack`'s type arguments. The compiler replaces the type parameters in the generic class and performs type checking. Method `Main` instantiates objects `doubleStack` of size `5` (line 18) and `intStack` of size `10` (line 19), then calls methods `TestPushDouble` (declared in lines 28–47), `TestPopDouble` (declared in lines 50–71), `TestPushInt` (declared in lines 74–93) and `TestPopInt` (declared in lines 96–117) to manipulate the two `Stack`s in this example.

```
1  // Fig. 18.8: StackTest.cs
2  // Testing generic class Stack.
3  using System;
4
5  class StackTest
6  {
7     // create arrays of doubles and ints
8     private static double[] doubleElements =
9        {1.1, 2.2, 3.3, 4.4, 5.5, 6.6};
10    private static int[] intElements =
11       {1, 2, 3, 4, 5, 6, 7, 8, 9, 10, 11};
12
13    private static Stack<double> doubleStack; // stack stores doubles
14    private static Stack<int> intStack; // stack stores ints
15
16    static void Main()
17    {
18       doubleStack = new Stack<double>(5); // stack of doubles
19       intStack = new Stack<int>(10); // stack of ints
20
21       TestPushDouble(); // push doubles onto doubleStack
22       TestPopDouble(); // pop doubles from doubleStack
23       TestPushInt(); // push ints onto intStack
24       TestPopInt(); // pop ints from intStack
25    }
26
27    // test Push method with doubleStack
28    private static void TestPushDouble()
29    {
```

**Fig. 18.8** | Testing generic class `Stack`. (Part 1 of 4.)

```
      // push elements onto stack
      try
      {
         Console.WriteLine("\nPushing elements onto doubleStack");

         // push elements onto stack
         foreach (var element in doubleElements)
         {
            Console.Write($"{element:F1} ");
            doubleStack.Push(element); // push onto doubleStack
         }
      }
      catch (FullStackException exception)
      {
         Console.Error.WriteLine($"\nMessage: {exception.Message}");
         Console.Error.WriteLine(exception.StackTrace);
      }
   }

   // test Pop method with doubleStack
   private static void TestPopDouble()
   {
      // pop elements from stack
      try
      {
         Console.WriteLine("\nPopping elements from doubleStack");

         double popValue; // store element removed from stack

         // remove all elements from stack
         while (true)
         {
            popValue = doubleStack.Pop(); // pop from doubleStack
            Console.Write($"{popValue:F1} ");
         }
      }
      catch (EmptyStackException exception)
      {
         Console.Error.WriteLine($"\nMessage: {exception.Message}");
         Console.Error.WriteLine(exception.StackTrace);
      }
   }

   // test Push method with intStack
   private static void TestPushInt()
   {
      // push elements onto stack
      try
      {
         Console.WriteLine("\nPushing elements onto intStack");

```

**Fig. 18.8** | Testing generic class Stack. (Part 2 of 4.)

```
         // push elements onto stack
         foreach (var element in intElements)
         {
            Console.Write($"{element} ");
            intStack.Push(element); // push onto intStack
         }
      }
      catch (FullStackException exception)
      {
         Console.Error.WriteLine($"\nMessage: {exception.Message}");
         Console.Error.WriteLine(exception.StackTrace);
      }
   }

   // test Pop method with intStack
   private static void TestPopInt()
   {
      // pop elements from stack
      try
      {
         Console.WriteLine("\nPopping elements from intStack");

         int popValue; // store element removed from stack

         // remove all elements from stack
         while (true)
         {
            popValue = intStack.Pop(); // pop from intStack
            Console.Write($"{popValue:F1} ");
         }
      }
      catch (EmptyStackException exception)
      {
         Console.Error.WriteLine($"\nMessage: {exception.Message}");
         Console.Error.WriteLine(exception.StackTrace);
      }
   }
}
```

```
Pushing elements onto doubleStack
1.1 2.2 3.3 4.4 5.5 6.6
Message: Stack is full, cannot push 6.6
   at Stack`1.Push(T pushValue) in C:\Users\PaulDeitel\Documents\
      examples\ch20\Fig20_05_08\Stack\Stack\Stack.cs:line 35
   at StackTest.TestPushDouble() in C:\Users\PaulDeitel\Documents\
      examples\ch20\Fig20_05_08\Stack\Stack\StackTest.cs:line 39

Popping elements from doubleStack
5.5 4.4 3.3 2.2 1.1
Message: Stack is empty, cannot pop
   at Stack`1.Pop() in C:\Users\PaulDeitel\Documents\
      examples\ch20\Fig20_05_08\Stack\Stack\Stack.cs:line 49
   at StackTest.TestPopDouble() in C:\Users\PaulDeitel\Documents\
      examples\ch20\Fig20_05_08\Stack\Stack\StackTest.cs:line 62
```

**Fig. 18.8** | Testing generic class Stack. (Part 3 of 4.)

```
Pushing elements onto intStack
1 2 3 4 5 6 7 8 9 10 11
Message: Stack is full, cannot push 11
   at Stack`1.Push(T pushValue) in C:\Users\PaulDeitel\Documents\
      examples\ch20\Fig20_05_08\Stack\Stack\Stack.cs:line 35
   at StackTest.TestPushInt() in C:\Users\PaulDeitel\Documents\
      examples\ch20\Fig20_05_08\Stack\Stack\StackTest.cs:line 85

Popping elements from intStack
10 9 8 7 6 5 4 3 2 1
Message: Stack is empty, cannot pop
   at Stack`1.Pop() in C:\Users\PaulDeitel\Documents\
      examples\ch20\Fig20_05_08\Stack\Stack\Stack.cs:line 49
   at StackTest.TestPopInt() in C:\Users\PaulDeitel\Documents\
      examples\ch20\Fig20_05_08\Stack\Stack\StackTest.cs:line 109
```

**Fig. 18.8** | Testing generic class `Stack`. (Part 4 of 4.)

### *Method* `TestPushDouble`

Method `TestPushDouble` (lines 28–47) invokes method `Push` to place the `double` values `1.1`, `2.2`, `3.3`, `4.4` and `5.5` from `doubleElements` onto `doubleStack`. The `foreach` statement terminates when the test program attempts to `Push` a sixth value onto `doubleStack` (which is full, because `doubleStack` can store only five elements), causing the method to throw a `FullStackException` (Fig. 18.6). Lines 42–46 of Fig. 18.8 catch this exception and display the message and stack-trace information. The stack trace indicates the exception that occurred and shows that `Stack` method `Push` generated the exception at line 35 of the file `Stack.cs` (Fig. 18.5). The trace also shows that method `Push` was called by `StackTest` method `TestPushDouble` at line 39 of `StackTest.cs`. This information enables you to determine the methods on the method-call stack at the time that the exception occurred. Because the program catches the exception, the C# runtime environment considers the exception to have been handled, and the program can continue executing.

### *Method* `TestPopDouble`

Method `TestPopDouble` (Fig. 18.8, lines 50–71) invokes `Stack` method `Pop` in an infinite `while` loop to remove all the values from the stack. Note in the output that the values are popped off in *last-in, first-out order*—this, of course, is the defining characteristic of stacks. The `while` loop (lines 60–64) continues until the stack is empty. An `EmptyStackException` occurs when an attempt is made to pop from the empty stack. This causes the program to proceed to the `catch` block (lines 66–70) and handle the exception, so the program can continue executing. When the test program attempts to `Pop` a sixth value, the `doubleStack` is empty, so method `Pop` throws an `EmptyStackException`.

### *Methods* `TestPushInt` *and* `TestPopInt`

Method `TestPushInt` (lines 74–93) invokes `Stack` method `Push` to place values onto `intStack` until it's full. Method `TestPopInt` (lines 96–117) invokes `Stack` method `Pop` to remove values from `intStack` until it's empty. Again, values pop in last-in, first-out order.

### *Creating Generic Methods to Test Class* `Stack<T>`

Note that the code in methods `TestPushDouble` and `TestPushInt` is virtually identical for pushing values onto `Stack`s. Similarly the code in methods `TestPopDouble` and `TestPopInt` is virtually identical for popping values from Stacks. This presents another opportunity to use generic methods. Figure 18.9 declares generic method TestPush (lines 33–53) to perform the same tasks as TestPushDouble and TestPushInt in Fig. 18.8—that is, Push values onto a Stack<T>. Similarly, generic method TestPop (lines 56–77) performs the same tasks as TestPopDouble and TestPopInt in Fig. 18.8—that is, Pop values off a Stack<T>.

```
1  // Fig. 18.9: StackTest.cs
2  // Testing generic class Stack.
3  using System;
4  using System.Collections.Generic;
5
6  class StackTest
7  {
8     // create arrays of doubles and ints
9     private static double[] doubleElements =
10       {1.1, 2.2, 3.3, 4.4, 5.5, 6.6};
11    private static int[] intElements =
12       {1, 2, 3, 4, 5, 6, 7, 8, 9, 10, 11};
13
14    private static Stack<double> doubleStack; // stack stores doubles
15    private static Stack<int> intStack; // stack stores int objects
16
17    static void Main()
18    {
19       doubleStack = new Stack<double>(5); // stack of doubles
20       intStack = new Stack<int>(10); // stack of ints
21
22       // push doubles onto doubleStack
23       TestPush(nameof(doubleStack), doubleStack, doubleElements);
24       // pop doubles from doubleStack
25       TestPop(nameof(doubleStack), doubleStack);
26       // push ints onto intStack
27       TestPush(nameof(doubleStack), intStack, intElements);
28       // pop ints from intStack
29       TestPop(nameof(doubleStack), intStack);
30    }
31
32    // test Push method
33    private static void TestPush<T>(string name, Stack<T> stack,
34       IEnumerable<T> elements)
35    {
36       // push elements onto stack
37       try
38       {
39          Console.WriteLine($"\nPushing elements onto {name}");
40
41          // push elements onto stack
42          foreach (var element in elements)
43          {
```

**Fig. 18.9** | Testing generic class Stack. (Part 1 of 3.)

```
               Console.Write($"{element} ");
               stack.Push(element); // push onto stack
            }
         }
         catch (FullStackException exception)
         {
            Console.Error.WriteLine($"\nMessage: {exception.Message}");
            Console.Error.WriteLine(exception.StackTrace);
         }
      }

      // test Pop method
      private static void TestPop<T>(string name, Stack<T> stack)
      {
         // pop elements from stack
         try
         {
            Console.WriteLine($"\nPopping elements from {name}");

            T popValue; // store element removed from stack

            // remove all elements from stack
            while (true)
            {
               popValue = stack.Pop(); // pop from stack
               Console.Write($"{popValue} ");
            }
         }
         catch (EmptyStackException exception)
         {
            Console.Error.WriteLine($"\nMessage: {exception.Message}");
            Console.Error.WriteLine(exception.StackTrace);
         }
      }
   }
```

```
Pushing elements onto doubleStack
1.1 2.2 3.3 4.4 5.5 6.6
Message: Stack is full, cannot push 6.6
   at Stack`1.Push(T pushValue) in C:\Users\PaulDeitel\Documents\
      examples\ch20\Fig20_09\Stack\Stack\Stack.cs:line 35
   at StackTest.TestPush[T](String name, Stack`1 stack, IEnumerable`1
      elements) in C:\Users\PaulDeitel\Documents\examples\ch20\Fig20_09\
      Stack\Stack\StackTest.cs:line 45

Popping elements from doubleStack
5.5 4.4 3.3 2.2 1.1
Message: Stack is empty, cannot pop
   at Stack`1.Pop() in C:\Users\PaulDeitel\Documents\
      examples\ch20\Fig20_09\Stack\Stack\Stack.cs:line 49
   at StackTest.TestPop[T](String name, Stack`1 stack) in
      C:\Users\PaulDeitel\Documents\examples\ch20\Fig20_09\Stack\
      Stack\StackTest.cs:line 68
```

**Fig. 18.9** | Testing generic class `Stack`. (Part 2 of 3.)

```
Pushing elements onto intStack
1 2 3 4 5 6 7 8 9 10 11
Message: Stack is full, cannot push 11
   at Stack`1.Push(T pushValue) in C:\Users\PaulDeitel\Documents\
      examples\ch20\Fig20_09\Stack\Stack\Stack.cs:line 35
   at StackTest.TestPush[T](String name, Stack`1 stack, IEnumerable`1
      elements) in C:\Users\PaulDeitel\Documents\examples\ch20\Fig20_09\
      Stack\Stack\StackTest.cs:line 45

Popping elements from intStack
10 9 8 7 6 5 4 3 2 1
Message: Stack is empty, cannot pop
   at Stack`1.Pop() in C:\Users\PaulDeitel\Documents\
      examples\ch20\Fig20_09\Stack\Stack\Stack.cs:line 49
   at StackTest.TestPop[T](String name, Stack`1 stack) in
      C:\Users\PaulDeitel\Documents\examples\ch20\Fig20_09\Stack\
      Stack\StackTest.cs:line 68
```

**Fig. 18.9** | Testing generic class `Stack`. (Part 3 of 3.)

Method `Main` (Fig. 18.9, lines 17–30) creates the `Stack<double>` (line 19) and `Stack<int>` (line 20) objects. Lines 23–29 invoke generic methods `TestPush` and `TestPop` to test the `Stack` objects.

Generic method `TestPush` (lines 33–53) uses type parameter `T` (specified at line 33) to represent the data type stored in the `Stack`. The generic method takes three arguments—a `string` that represents the name of the `Stack` object for output purposes, an object of type `Stack<T>` and an `IEnumerable<T>` that contains the elements that will be `Push`ed onto `Stack<T>`. The compiler enforces consistency between the type of the `Stack` and the elements that will be pushed onto the `Stack` when `Push` is invoked, which is the type argument of the generic method call. Generic method `TestPop` (lines 56–77) takes two arguments—a `string` that represents the name of the `Stack` object for output purposes and an object of type `Stack<T>`.

## 18.7 Wrap-Up

This chapter introduced generics. We discussed how generics ensure compile-time type safety by checking for type mismatches at compile time. You learned that the compiler will allow generic code to compile only if all operations performed on the type parameters in the generic code are supported for all types that could be used with the generic code. You also learned how to declare generic methods and classes using type parameters. We demonstrated how to use a type constraint to specify the requirements for a type parameter—a key component of compile-time type safety. We discussed several kinds of type constraints, including reference-type constraints, value-type constraints, class constraints, interface constraints and constructor constraints. We also discussed how to implement multiple type constraints for a type parameter. Finally, we showed how generics improve code reuse. In the next chapter, we demonstrate the .NET Framework Class Library's collection classes, interfaces and algorithms. Collection classes are pre-built data structures that you can reuse in your apps, saving you time.

# 19

# Generic Collections; Functional Programming with LINQ/PLINQ

## Objectives

In this chapter you'll:

- See additional .NET generic collections.
- Manipulate arrays with class `Array`'s `static` methods.
- Provide a `using static` directive to access a class's `static` members without fully qualifying their names.
- Iterate through a collection with enumerators.
- Use generic collections `SortedDictionary` and `LinkedList`.
- Use the C# 6 null-conditional `?[]` operator to access array or collection elements.
- Use C# 6 index initializers to initialize a dictionary.
- Store method references in delegate variables, then use those variables to invoke the corresponding methods.
- Use lambda expressions to create anonymous methods and refer to those methods via delegate variables.
- Use LINQ method-call syntax and lambdas to demonstrate functional programming techniques.
- Parallelize LINQ operations with PLINQ for multicore performance.
- Be introduced to covariance and contravariance for generic types.

Outline



## 19.1 Introduction

For the vast majority of apps, there's no need to build custom data structures. Instead, you can use the *prepackaged* data-structure classes provided by the .NET Framework. These are known as **collection classes**—they store collections of data. Each instance of one of these classes is a **collection** of items. Some examples of collections are the cards you hold in a card game, the songs stored in your computer, the real-estate records in your local registry of deeds (which map book numbers and page numbers to property owners), and the players on your favorite sports team.

### *Use the Existing Collection Classes Rather Than Building Your Own*

Collection classes enable you to store sets of items by using *existing* data structures, without concern for how they're implemented. This is a nice example of code reuse. You can code faster and expect excellent performance, maximizing execution speed and minimizing memory consumption. In this chapter, we discuss

- the collection interfaces that declare each collection type's capabilities
- the implementation classes
- the **enumerators** that iterate through collections (these are like iterators in languages like C++ and Java).

*Collections Namespaces*
The .NET Framework provides several namespaces dedicated to collections:

- **`System.Collections`** contains collections that store `object`s. Such collections can store objects of many different types at the same time, because all C# types derive directly or indirectly from `object`. You might encounter this namespace's classes, such as `ArrayList`, `Stack` and `Hashtable`, in C# legacy code prior to the introduction of generics in C# 2.0 (2005). **Legacy code** uses older programming techniques—possibly including language and library features that a programming language no longer supports or that have been superseded by newer capabilities.
- **`System.Collections.Generic`** contains generic collections, such as the `List<T>` (Section 9.4) and `Dictionary<K, V>` (Section 17.9) classes, that store objects of types you specify when you create the collection. You should use the generic collections—rather than the `object`-based legacy collections—to take advantage of compile-time type checking of your collection-processing code.
- **`System.Collections.Concurrent`** contains so-called thread-safe generic collections for use in multithreaded applications.
- **`System.Collections.Specialized`** contains collections that are optimized for specific scenarios, such as manipulating collections of bits.

*Delegates and Lambda Expressions*
In Section 14.3.3, we introduced the concept of a *delegate*—an object that holds a reference to a method. Delegates enable apps to store methods as data and to pass a method as an argument to another method. In event handling, a delegate stores a reference to the event-handler method that will be called when a user interacts with a GUI control. In this chapter, we'll discuss delegates in more detail and introduce lambda expressions, which allow you to define **anonymous methods** that can be used with delegates. Here we'll focus on using lambdas to pass method references to methods that specify delegate parameters.

*Introduction to Functional Programming*
So far, we've demonstrated three programming paradigms:

- structured programming (also known as procedural programming)
- object-oriented programming
- generic programming (which we'll continue discussing in this chapter).

Sections 19.10–19.11 define and introduce functional programming, showing how to use it with LINQ to Objects to write code more concisely and with fewer bugs than programs written with other techniques. In Section 19.12, with one additional method call, we'll demonstrate how *PLINQ (Parallel LINQ)* can improve LINQ to Objects performance substantially on multicore systems. Many earlier examples can be reimplemented using functional-programming techniques.

## 19.2 Collections Overview

All collection classes in the .NET Framework implement some combination of the collection interfaces that declare the operations to be performed on various types of collections.

Figure 19.1 lists some of the collection interfaces in namespace `System.Collections.Generic`, which also have legacy `object`-based analogs in `System.Collections`. Many collection classes implement these interfaces. You may also provide implementations specific to your own requirements.

| Interface | Description |
|---|---|
| `IEnumerable<T>` | An object that can be enumerated—for example, a `foreach` loop can iterate over such an object's elements. This interface contains one method, `GetEnumerator`, which returns an `IEnumerator<T>` object, which (as you'll see in Section 19.3) can be used manually to iterate through a collection. In fact, `foreach` uses a collection's `IEnumerator<T>` object behind the scenes. `ICollection<T>` extends `IEnumerable<T>` so all collection classes implement `IEnumerable` directly or indirectly. |
| `ICollection<T>` | The interface from which interfaces `IList<T>` and `IDictionary<K,V>` inherit. Contains a `Count` property to determine the size of a collection and a `CopyTo` method for copying a collection's contents to a traditional array, and an `IsReadOnly` property. |
| `IList<T>` | An ordered collection that can be manipulated like an array. Provides a `[]` operator (known as an **indexer**) for accessing elements with an `int` index. Also has methods for searching and modifying a collection, including `Add`, `Remove`, `Contains` and `IndexOf`. |
| `IDictionary<K,V>` | A collection of values, indexed by an arbitrary "key" object of type `K`. Provides an indexer (`[]`) for accessing elements by key and methods for modifying the collection (e.g., `Add`, `Remove`). `IDictionary<K,V>` property `Keys` contains all the keys, and property `Values` contains all the stored values. |

**Fig. 19.1** | Some common generic collection interfaces.

### *Namespace* `System.Collections.Generic`

With the collections of the `System.Collections.Generic` namespace, you can specify the exact type that will be stored in a collection. This provides two key benefits over the `object`-based legacy collections:

- *Compile-time type checking* ensures that you're using appropriate types with your collection and, if not, the compiler issues error messages.
- Any item you retrieve from a generic collection will have the correct type. With `object`-based collections, any item you retrieve is returned as an `object`. Then, you must *explicitly cast* the `object` to the type that your program manipulates. This could lead to `InvalidCastException`s at execution time if the referenced object does not have the appropriate type.

Generic collections are especially useful for storing value types, since they eliminate the overhead of boxing and unboxing required with `object`-based legacy collections.

In this chapter, we continue our discussion of data structures and collections with additional built-in array capabilities, as well as the generic `SortedDictionary` and `LinkedList` classes. Namespace `System.Collections.Generic` provides many other data structures, including **`Stack<T>`**, **`Queue<T>`** and **`SortedList<K,V>`** (a collection of *key–value* pairs that are sorted by key and can be accessed either by key or by index). Figure 19.2 summarizes many of the collection classes—for a complete list, visit

```
https://msdn.microsoft.com/library/system.collections.generic
```

The collection classes have many common capabilities specified by the interfaces the classes implement. Once you know how to use a few collections (like `List`, `Dictionary`, `LinkedList` and `SortedDictionary`), you can figure out how to use the others via their online documentation, which includes sample code.

| Class | Implements interface | Description |
|---|---|---|
| ***`System`* namespace** | | |
| `Array` | `IList` | The base class of all conventional arrays. See Section 19.3. |
| ***`System.Collections.Generic`* namespace** | | |
| `Dictionary<K, V>` | `IDictionary<K, V>` | A generic, unordered collection of key–value pairs that can be accessed rapidly by key. See Section 17.9.2. |
| `LinkedList<T>` | `ICollection<T>` | A generic doubly linked list. See Section 19.5. |
| `List<T>` | `IList<T>` | A generic array-based list. See Section 9.4. |
| `Queue<T>` | `ICollection<T>` | A generic first-in, first-out (FIFO) collection. |
| `SortedDictionary<K,V>` | `IDictionary<K, V>` | A `Dictionary` that sorts the data by the keys in a binary tree. See Section 19.4. |
| `SortedList<K, V>` | `IDictionary<K, V>` | Similar to a `SortedDictionary`, but uses arrays internally. If the data already exists and is sorted before insertion in a collection, then inserting in a `SortedList` is faster than a `SortedDictionary`. If the data is not sorted, insertion in a `SortedDictionary` is faster. |
| `Stack<T>` | `ICollection<T>` | A generic last-in, first-out (LIFO) collection. |
| ***Legacy collections of the `System.Collections` namespace*** | | |
| `ArrayList` | `IList` | Mimics conventional arrays, but will grow or shrink as needed to accommodate the number of elements. |

**Fig. 19.2** | Some .NET Framework collection classes. (Part 1 of 2.)

| Class | Implements interface | Description |
|---|---|---|
| `BitArray` | `ICollection` | A memory-efficient array of bits in which each bit's `0` or `1` value represents the `bool` value `false` or `true`. |
| `Hashtable` | `IDictionary` | An unordered collection of key–value pairs that can be accessed rapidly by key. |
| `Queue` | `ICollection` | A first-in, first-out (FIFO) collection. |
| `SortedList` | `IDictionary` | A collection of key–value pairs that are sorted by key and can be accessed either by key or by index. |
| `Stack` | `ICollection` | A last-in, first-out (LIFO) collection. |

**Fig. 19.2** | Some .NET Framework collection classes. (Part 2 of 2.)

We also discuss the `IEnumerator<T>` interface. Each collection class's enumerator allows you to iterate through the collection. Although these enumerators have different implementations, they all implement the `IEnumerator<T>` interface so that an app can iterate through a collection's elements (e.g., with a `foreach` statement). In the next section, we begin our discussion by examining enumerators and the capabilities for array manipulation. Collection classes directly or indirectly implement `ICollection<T>` and `IEnumerable<T>` (or their `object`-based equivalents `ICollection` and `IEnumerable` for legacy collections).

## 19.3 Class Array and Enumerators

Chapter 8 presented basic array-processing capabilities. All arrays implicitly inherit from `abstract` base class `Array` (namespace `System`); this class defines property `Length`, which specifies the number of elements in the array. In addition, class `Array` provides `static` methods that provide algorithms for processing arrays. Typically, class `Array` overloads these methods—for example, `Array` method `Reverse` can reverse the order of the elements in an entire array or in a specified range of elements. For a complete list of class `Array`'s `static` methods visit

```
https://msdn.microsoft.com/library/system.array
```

Figure 19.3 demonstrates several `static` methods of class `Array`.

```
// Fig. 19.3: UsingArray.cs
// Array class static methods for common array manipulations.
using System;
using static System.Array;
```

**Fig. 19.3** | `Array` class `static` methods for common array manipulations. (Part 1 of 3.)

```
using System.Collections;

// demonstrate algorithms of class Array
class UsingArray
{
   private static int[] intValues = {1, 2, 3, 4, 5, 6};
   private static double[] doubleValues = {8.4, 9.3, 0.2, 7.9, 3.4};
   private static int[] intValuesCopy;

   // method Main demonstrates class Array's methods
   static void Main()
   {
      intValuesCopy = new int[intValues.Length]; // defaults to zeroes

      Console.WriteLine("Initial array values:\n");
      PrintArrays(); // output initial array contents

      // sort doubleValues
      Sort(doubleValues); // unqualified call to Array static method Sort

      // copy intValues into intValuesCopy
      Array.Copy(intValues, intValuesCopy, intValues.Length);

      Console.WriteLine("\nArray values after Sort and Copy:\n");
      PrintArrays(); // output array contents
      Console.WriteLine();

      // search for 5 in intValues
      int result = Array.BinarySearch(intValues, 5);
      Console.WriteLine(result >= 0 ?
         $"5 found at element {result} in intValues" :
         "5 not found in intValues");

      // search for 8763 in intValues
      result = Array.BinarySearch(intValues, 8763);
      Console.WriteLine(result >= 0 ?
         $"8763 found at element {result} in intValues" :
         "8763 not found in intValues");
   }

   // output array content with enumerators
   private static void PrintArrays()
   {
      Console.Write("doubleValues: ");

      // iterate through the double array with an enumerator
      IEnumerator enumerator = doubleValues.GetEnumerator();

      while (enumerator.MoveNext())
      {
         Console.Write($"{enumerator.Current} ");
      }

```

**Fig. 19.3** | Array class static methods for common array manipulations. (Part 2 of 3.)

```
58          Console.Write("\nintValues: ");
59
60          // iterate through the int array with an enumerator
61          enumerator = intValues.GetEnumerator();
62
63          while (enumerator.MoveNext())
64          {
65             Console.Write($"{enumerator.Current} ");
66          }
67
68          Console.Write("\nintValuesCopy: ");
69
70          // iterate through the second int array with a foreach statement
71          foreach (var element in intValuesCopy)
72          {
73             Console.Write($"{element} ");
74          }
75
76          Console.WriteLine();
77       }
78    }
```

```
Initial array values:

doubleValues: 8.4 9.3 0.2 7.9 3.4
intValues: 1 2 3 4 5 6
intValuesCopy: 0 0 0 0 0 0

Array values after Sort and Copy:

doubleValues: 0.2 3.4 7.9 8.4 9.3
intValues: 1 2 3 4 5 6
intValuesCopy: 1 2 3 4 5 6

5 found at element 4 in intValues
8763 not found in intValues
```

**Fig. 19.3** | Array class static methods for common array manipulations. (Part 3 of 3.)

### 19.3.1 C# 6 using static Directive 6

The using directives in lines 3 and 5 include the namespaces System (for classes Array and Console) and System.Collections (for interface IEnumerator, which we discuss shortly). Line 4 introduces C# 6's **using static directive** for accessing a type's static members without fully qualifying their names—in this case, class Array's static members. Line 23

```
Sort(doubleValues); // unqualified call to Array static method Sort
```

shows an *unqualified call* to Array static method Sort, which is equivalent to

```
Array.Sort(doubleValues); // call to Array static method Sort
```

Though we could use unqualified calls for all of class Array's static members in this example (e.g., Copy in line 26 and BinarySearch in lines 33 and 39), the code is easier to read with the fully qualified method calls, which make it absolutely clear which class contains a given static method.

### 19.3.2 Class UsingArray's static Fields

Our test class declares three `static` array variables (lines 10–12). The first two lines initialize `intValues` and `doubleValues` to an `int` and `double` array, respectively. `static` variable `intValuesCopy` is intended to demonstrate the `Array`'s `Copy` method—it's initially `null`, so it does not yet refer to an array.

Line 17 initializes `intValuesCopy` to an `int` array with the same length as array `intValues`. Line 20 calls the `PrintArrays` method (lines 46–77) to output the initial contents of all three arrays. We discuss the `PrintArrays` method shortly. The output of Fig. 19.3 shows that each element of array `intValuesCopy` is initialized to the default value `0`.

### 19.3.3 Array Method Sort

Line 23 uses `static Array` method **`Sort`** to sort array `doubleValues` in ascending order. The elements in the array must implement the `IComparable` interface (as all simple types do), which enables method `Sort` to compare elements to determine their order.

### 19.3.4 Array Method Copy

Line 26 uses `static Array` method **`Copy`** to copy elements from array `intValues` to array `intValuesCopy`. The first argument is the array to copy (`intValues`), the second argument is the destination array (`intValuesCopy`) and the third argument is an `int` representing the number of elements to copy (in this case, `intValues.Length` specifies all elements). Class `Array` also provides overloads for copying portions of arrays.

### 19.3.5 Array Method BinarySearch

Lines 33 and 39 invoke `static Array` method **`BinarySearch`** to perform binary searches on array `intValues`. Method `BinarySearch` receives the *sorted* array in which to search and the key for which to search. The method returns the index in the array at which it finds the key (or a negative number if the key was not found). `BinarySearch` assumes that it receives a sorted array. Its behavior on an *unsorted* array is *undefined*.

### 19.3.6 Array Method GetEnumerator and Interface IEnumerator

Method `PrintArrays` (lines 46–77) uses class `Array`'s methods to iterate over the elements of the arrays. Class `Array` implements the **`IEnumerable`** interface (the non-generic version of `IEnumerable<T>`). All arrays inherit implicitly from `Array`, so both the `int[]` and `double[]` array types implement `IEnumerable` interface method **`GetEnumerator`**, which returns an enumerator that can *iterate* over the collection—this method always returns an enumerator positioned *before the first element*. Interface **`IEnumerator`** (which all enumerators implement) defines methods **`MoveNext`** and **`Reset`** and property **`Current`**:

- `MoveNext` moves the enumerator to the next element in the collection. The first call to `MoveNext` positions the enumerator at the *first* element of the collection—if there is an element, `MoveNext` returns `true`; otherwise, the method returns `false`.
- Method `Reset` positions the enumerator before the first element of the collection.

- Read-only property `Current` returns the object at the current location in the collection (determined by the last call to `MoveNext`).

Enumerators cannot be used to *modify* the contents of collections, only to obtain the contents.

**Common Programming Error 19.1**

*If a collection is modified after an enumerator is created for that collection, the enumerator immediately becomes invalid—for this reason, enumerators are said to be "fail fast." Any calls to the enumerator's* `Reset` *or* `MoveNext` *methods after this point throw* `InvalidOperationException`*s. This is true for collections, but not for arrays.*

When an enumerator is returned by the `GetEnumerator` method in line 51, it's initially positioned *before* the first element in `Array doubleValues`. Then when line 53 calls `MoveNext` in the first iteration of the `while` loop, the enumerator advances to the first element in `doubleValues`. The `while` statement in lines 53–56 iterates over each element until the enumerator passes the end of `doubleValues` and `MoveNext` returns `false`. In each iteration, we use the enumerator's `Current` property to obtain and output the current array element. Lines 63–66 iterate over array `intValues`.

### 19.3.7 Iterating Over a Collection with foreach

Lines 71–74 use a `foreach` statement to iterate over the collection. Both `foreach` and an enumerator loop over the elements of an array one by one in consecutive order. Neither allows you to modify the elements during the iteration. This is not a coincidence. Every `foreach` statement implicitly obtains an enumerator via the `GetEnumerator` method and uses the enumerator's `MoveNext` method and `Current` property to traverse the collection, just as we did explicitly in lines 51–56 and 61–66. For this reason, you should use the `foreach` statement to iterate over *any* collection that implements `IEnumerable` or `IEnumerable<T>`—as you saw for class `List<T>` in Section 9.4. Even class `string` implements `IEnumerable<char>` so you can iterate over a `string`'s characters.

### 19.3.8 Array Methods Clear, IndexOf, LastIndexOf and Reverse

Other `static Array` methods include:

- **`Clear`** which sets a range of elements to `0`, `false` or `null`, as appropriate.
- **`IndexOf`** which locates the first occurrence of an object in an array or portion of an array.
- **`LastIndexOf`** which locates the last occurrence of an object in an array or portion of an array.
- **`Reverse`** which reverses the contents of an array or portion of an array.

## 19.4 Dictionary Collections

A **dictionary** is the general term for a collection of key–value pairs. Section 17.9.2 introduced the generic `Dictionary` collection. In this section, we discuss fundamentals of how a `Dictionary` works, then demonstrate the related `SortedDictionary` collection.

### 19.4.1 Dictionary Fundamentals

When an app creates objects of new or existing types, it needs to manage those objects efficiently. This includes sorting and retrieving objects. Sorting and retrieving information with arrays is efficient if some aspect of your data directly matches the key value and if those keys are *unique* and *tightly packed*. If you have 100 employees with nine-digit social security numbers and you want to store and retrieve employee data by using the social security number as a key, it would nominally require an array with 1,000,000,000 elements, because there are 1,000,000,000 unique nine-digit numbers. If you have an array that large, you could get high performance storing and retrieving employee records by simply using the social security number as the array index, but it would be a huge waste of memory. Many apps have this problem—either the keys are of the wrong type (i.e., not non-negative integers), or they're of the right type but are sparsely spread over a large range.

#### *Hashing*

What's needed is a high-speed scheme for converting keys such as social security numbers and inventory part numbers to unique array indices. Then, when an app needs to store something, the scheme could convert the key rapidly to an index and the record of information could be stored at that location in the array. Retrieval occurs the same way—once the app has a key for which it wants to retrieve the data record, the app simply applies the conversion to the key, which produces the array index where the data resides in the array and retrieves the data.

The scheme we describe here is the basis of a technique called **hashing**. Why the name? Because, when we convert a key into an array index, we literally *scramble* the bits, making a "hash" of the number. The number actually has no real significance beyond its usefulness in storing and retrieving this particular data record. Data structures that use hashing are commonly called **hash tables** (like class `Hashtable` in the `System.Collections` namespace). A hash table is one way to implement a dictionary—class `Dictionary<K,V>` in the `System.Collections.Generic` namespace is implemented as a hash table.

#### *Collisions*

A glitch in the scheme occurs when there are **collisions** (i.e., two different keys "hash into" the same cell, or element, in the array). Since we cannot sort two different data records to the *same* space, we need to find an alternative home for all records beyond the first that hash to a particular array index. One scheme for doing this is to "hash again" (i.e., to reapply the hashing transformation to the key to provide a next candidate cell in the array). The hashing process is designed so that with just a few hashes, an available cell will be found.

Another scheme uses one hash to locate the first candidate cell. If the cell is occupied, successive cells are searched linearly until an available cell is found. Retrieval works the same way—the key is hashed once, the resulting cell is checked to determine whether it contains the desired data. If it does, the search is complete. If it does not, successive cells are searched linearly until the desired data is found.

The most popular solution to hash-table collisions is to have each cell of the table be a hash "bucket"—typically, a linked list of all the key–value pairs that hash to that cell. This is the solution that the .NET Framework's `Dictionary` class implements.

### *Load Factor*

The **load factor** affects the performance of hashing schemes. The load factor is the ratio of the number of objects stored in the hash table to the total number of cells of the hash table. As this ratio gets *higher*, the chance of collisions tends to *increase*.

#### Performance Tip 19.1

*The load factor in a hash table is a classic example of a* ***space/time trade-off****. By increasing the load factor, we get better memory utilization, but the app runs slower due to increased hashing collisions. By decreasing the load factor, we get better speed because of reduced hashing collisions, but we get poorer memory utilization because a larger portion of the hash table remains empty.*

### *Hash Function*

A **hash function** performs a calculation that determines where to place data in the hash table. The hash function is applied to the key in a key–value pair of objects. Any `object` can be used as a key. For this reason, class `object` defines method **`GetHashCode`**, which all objects inherit. Most classes that are candidates to be used as keys in a hash table, such as `string`, override this method to provide one that performs efficient hash-code calculations for a specific type.

## 19.4.2 Using the `SortedDictionary` Collection

The .NET Framework provides several implementations of dictionaries that implement the `IDictionary<K,V>` interface (described in Fig. 19.1). The app in Fig. 19.4 demonstrates the generic class **`SortedDictionary`**. Unlike class `Dictionary`—which is implemented as a hash table—class `SortedDictionary` stores its key–value pairs in a binary search tree. As the class name suggests, the entries in `SortedDictionary` are sorted by key. For key types that implement `IComparable<T>`, the `SortedDictionary` uses the results of `IComparable<T>` method `CompareTo` to sort the keys. Despite these implementation details, we use the same `public` methods, properties and indexers with classes `Dictionary` and `SortedDictionary`. In many scenarios, these classes are interchangeable—this is the beauty of object-oriented programming.

#### Performance Tip 19.2

*Because class `SortedDictionary` keeps its elements sorted in a binary tree, obtaining or inserting a key–value pair takes O(log n) time, which is fast compared to linear searching, then inserting.*

```
// Fig. 19.4: SortedDictionaryTest.cs
// App counts the number of occurrences of each word in a string
// and stores them in a generic sorted dictionary.
using System;
using System.Text.RegularExpressions;
using System.Collections.Generic;
```

**Fig. 19.4** | App counts the number of occurrences of each word in a `string` and stores them in a generic sorted dictionary. (Part 1 of 3.)

```

class SortedDictionaryTest
{
   static void Main()
   {
      // create sorted dictionary based on user input
      SortedDictionary<string, int> dictionary = CollectWords();

      DisplayDictionary(dictionary); // display sorted dictionary content
   }

   // create sorted dictionary from user input
   private static SortedDictionary<string, int> CollectWords()
   {
      // create a new sorted dictionary
      var dictionary = new SortedDictionary<string, int>();

      Console.WriteLine("Enter a string: "); // prompt for user input
      string input = Console.ReadLine(); // get input

      // split input text into tokens
      string[] words = Regex.Split(input, @"\s+");

      // processing input words
      foreach (var word in words)
      {
         var key = word.ToLower(); // get word in lowercase

         // if the dictionary contains the word
         if (dictionary.ContainsKey(key))
         {
            ++dictionary[key];
         }
         else
         {
            // add new word with a count of 1 to the dictionary
            dictionary.Add(key, 1);
         }
      }

      return dictionary;
   }

   // display dictionary content
   private static void DisplayDictionary<K, V>(
      SortedDictionary<K, V> dictionary)
   {
      Console.WriteLine(
         $"\nSorted dictionary contains:\n{"Key",-12}{"Value",-12}");

```

**Fig. 19.4** | App counts the number of occurrences of each word in a `string` and stores them in a generic sorted dictionary. (Part 2 of 3.)

```
57          // generate output for each key in the sorted dictionary
58          // by iterating through the Keys property with a foreach statement
59          foreach (var key in dictionary.Keys)
60          {
61             Console.WriteLine($"{key,-12}{dictionary[key],-12}");
62          }
63
64          Console.WriteLine($"\nsize: {dictionary.Count}");
65       }
66    }
```

```
Enter a string:
We few, we happy few, we band of brothers

Sorted dictionary contains:
Key          Value
band         1
brothers     1
few,         2
happy        1
of           1
we           3

size: 6
```

**Fig. 19.4** | App counts the number of occurrences of each word in a `string` and stores them in a generic sorted dictionary. (Part 3 of 3.)

Lines 4–6 contain `using` directives for namespaces `System` (for class `Console`), `System.Text.RegularExpressions` (for class `Regex`) and `System.Collections.Generic` (for class `SortedDictionary`). Generic class `SortedDictionary` takes two type arguments:

- the first specifies the type of key (i.e., `string`) and
- the second the type of value (i.e., `int`).

Class `SortedDictionaryTest` declares three `static` methods:

- Method `CollectWords` (lines 19–48) inputs a sentence and returns a `SortedDictionary<string, int>` in which the keys are the words in the sentence and the values are the number of times each word appears in the sentence.
- Method `DisplayDictionary` (lines 51–65) displays the `SortedDictionary` passed to it in column format.
- Method `Main` (lines 10–16) simply invokes `CollectWords` (line 13), then passes the `SortedDictionary<string, int>` returned by `CollectWords` to `DisplayDictionary` in line 15.

### *Method* `CollectWords`

Method `CollectWords` (lines 19–48) begins by initializing local variable `dictionary` with a new `SortedDictionary<string, int>` (line 22). Lines 24–25 prompt the user and input a sentence as a `string`. We use `static` method `Split` of class `Regex` (introduced in the online section of Chapter 16 at `http://www.deitel.com/books/CSharp6FP`) in line 28 to divide the string by its whitespace characters. In the regular expression \s+, \s means *whitespace* and + means one or more of the expression to its left—so the words are separated by one or more whitespace characters, which are discarded. This creates an array of "words," which we then store in local variable words.

### SortedDictionary *Methods* ContainsKey *and* Add

Lines 31–45 iterate through the array words. Each word is converted to lowercase with string method ToLower, then stored in variable key (line 33). Next, line 36 calls SortedDictionary method **ContainsKey** to determine whether the word is in the dictionary. If so, that word occurred previously in the sentence. If the SortedDictionary does *not* contain an entry for the word, line 43 uses SortedDictionary method **Add** to create a new entry in the dictionary, with the lowercase word as the key and 1 as the value.

**Common Programming Error 19.2**

*Using the* Add *method to add a key that already exists in the hash table causes an* **ArgumentException***.*

### SortedDictionary *Indexer*

If the word is already a key in the hash table, line 38 uses the SortedDictionary's indexer to obtain and set the key's associated value (the word count) in the dictionary. Using the set accessor with a key that does not exist in the hash table creates a new entry, as if you had used the Add method, so line 43 could have been written as

```
dictionary[key] = 1;
```

**Common Programming Error 19.3**

*Invoking the* get *accessor of a* SortedDictionary *indexer with a key that does not exist in the collection causes a* **KeyNotFoundException***.*

### *Method* DisplayDictionary

Line 47 returns the dictionary to the Main method, which then passes it to method DisplayDictionary (lines 51–65), which displays all the key–value pairs. This method uses read-only property **Keys** (line 59) to get an ICollection<T> that contains all the keys. Because the interface ICollection<T> extends IEnumerable<T>, we can use this collection in the foreach statement in lines 59–62 to iterate over the keys. This loop accesses and outputs each key and its corresponding value using the iteration variable and the SortedDictionary indexer's get accessor. Each key and value is displayed *left aligned* in a field width of 12 positions. Because a SortedDictionary stores its key–value pairs in a binary search tree, the key–value pairs are displayed with the keys in sorted order. Line 64 uses SortedDictionary property **Count** to get the number of key–value pairs in the dictionary.

### *Iterating Over a* SortedDictionary*'s* KeyValuePairs

Lines 59–62 could have also used the foreach statement with the SortedDictionary object itself, instead of using the Keys property. If you use a foreach statement with a SortedDictionary object, the iteration variable will be of type **KeyValuePair<K,V>**. The enumerator of a SortedDictionary uses the KeyValuePair<K,V> struct value type to store key–value pairs. KeyValuePair<K,V> provides properties Key and Value for retrieving the key and value of the current element.

### *SortedDictionary's* **Values** *Property*

If you do not need the keys, class SortedDictionary also provides a read-only **Values** property that gets an ICollection<T> of all the values stored in the SortedDictionary. You could use this property to iterate through the values stored in the SortedDictionary without regard for their corresponding keys.

## 19.5 Generic LinkedList Collection

Section 9.4 introduced the generic List<T> collection, which defines an array-based list implementation. Here, we discuss class **LinkedList<T>**, which defines a doubly linked list that an app can navigate both forwards and backwards. A LinkedList<T> contains nodes of generic class **LinkedListNode<T>**. Each node contains property **Value** and read-only properties **Previous** and **Next**. The Value property's type matches LinkedList<T>'s single type parameter because it contains the data stored in the node. Previous gets a reference to the preceding node in the linked list (or null if the node is the first of the list). Similarly, Next gets a reference to the subsequent reference in the linked list (or null if the node is the last of the list). We demonstrate a few linked-list manipulations in Fig. 19.5.

```
// Fig. 19.5: LinkedListTest.cs
// Using LinkedLists.
using System;
using System.Collections.Generic;

class LinkedListTest
{
   private static readonly string[] colors =
      {"black", "yellow", "green", "blue", "violet", "silver"};
   private static readonly string[] colors2 =
      {"gold", "white", "brown", "blue", "gray"};

   // set up and manipulate LinkedList objects
   static void Main()
   {
      var list1 = new LinkedList<string>();

      // add elements to first linked list
      foreach (var color in colors)
      {
         list1.AddLast(color);
      }

      // add elements to second linked list via constructor
      var list2 = new LinkedList<string>(colors2);

      Concatenate(list1, list2); // concatenate list2 onto list1
      PrintList(list1); // display list1 elements

      Console.WriteLine("\nConverting strings in list1 to uppercase\n");
      ToUppercaseStrings(list1); // convert to uppercase string
```

**Fig. 19.5** | Using LinkedLists. (Part 1 of 3.)

```
         PrintList(list1); // display list1 elements

         Console.WriteLine("\nDeleting strings between BLACK and BROWN\n");
         RemoveItemsBetween(list1, "BLACK", "BROWN");

         PrintList(list1); // display list1 elements
         PrintReversedList(list1); // display list in reverse order
      }

      // display list contents
      private static void PrintList<T>(LinkedList<T> list)
      {
         Console.WriteLine("Linked list: ");

         foreach (var value in list)
         {
            Console.Write($"{value} ");
         }

         Console.WriteLine();
      }

      // concatenate the second list on the end of the first list
      private static void Concatenate<T>(
         LinkedList<T> list1, LinkedList<T> list2)
      {
         // concatenate lists by copying element values
         // in order from the second list to the first list
         foreach (var value in list2)
         {
            list1.AddLast(value); // add new node
         }
      }

      // locate string objects and convert to uppercase
      private static void ToUppercaseStrings(LinkedList<string> list)
      {
         // iterate over the list by using the nodes
         LinkedListNode<string> currentNode = list.First;

         while (currentNode != null)
         {
            string color = currentNode.Value; // get value in node
            currentNode.Value = color.ToUpper(); // convert to uppercase
            currentNode = currentNode.Next; // get next node
         }
      }

      // delete list items between two given items
      private static void RemoveItemsBetween<T>(
         LinkedList<T> list, T startItem, T endItem)
      {
```

**Fig. 19.5** | Using `LinkedLists`. (Part 2 of 3.)

```
84         // get the nodes corresponding to the start and end item
85         LinkedListNode<T> currentNode = list.Find(startItem);
86         LinkedListNode<T> endNode = list.Find(endItem);
87
88         // remove items after the start item
89         // until we find the last item or the end of the linked list
90         while ((currentNode.Next != null) && (currentNode.Next != endNode))
91         {
92            list.Remove(currentNode.Next); // remove next node
93         }
94      }
95
96      // display reversed list
97      private static void PrintReversedList<T>(LinkedList<T> list)
98      {
99         Console.WriteLine("Reversed List:");
100
101        // iterate over the list by using the nodes
102        LinkedListNode<T> currentNode = list.Last;
103
104        while (currentNode != null)
105        {
106           Console.Write($"{currentNode.Value} ");
107           currentNode = currentNode.Previous; // get previous node
108        }
109
110        Console.WriteLine();
111     }
112  }
```

```
Linked list:
black yellow green blue violet silver gold white brown blue gray

Converting strings in list1 to uppercase

Linked list:
BLACK YELLOW GREEN BLUE VIOLET SILVER GOLD WHITE BROWN BLUE GRAY

Deleting strings between BLACK and BROWN

Linked list:
BLACK BROWN BLUE GRAY
Reversed List:
GRAY BLUE BROWN BLACK
```

**Fig. 19.5** | Using `LinkedLists`. (Part 3 of 3.)

Lines 16–25 create `LinkedLists` of `strings` named `list1` and `list2` and fill them with the contents of arrays `colors` and `colors2`, respectively. `LinkedList` is a *generic class* that has one type parameter for which we specify the type argument `string` in this example (lines 16 and 25).

### *`LinkedList` Methods `AddLast` and `AddFirst`*

We demonstrate two ways to fill the lists. Lines 19–22 use the `foreach` statement and method **`AddLast`** to fill `list1`. The `AddLast` method creates a new `LinkedListNode` (with the node's value available via the `Value` property) and appends this node to the end of the list. There's also an **`AddFirst`** method that inserts a node at the beginning of the list.

Line 25 invokes the constructor that takes an `IEnumerable<T>` parameter. All arrays implement the generic interfaces `IList<T>` and `IEnumerable<T>` with the array's element type as the type argument, so a `string` array implements `IEnumerable<string>`. Thus, `colors2` is an `IEnumerable<string>` and can be passed to the `List<string>` constructor to initialize the `List`. This constructor copies array `colors2`'s contents into `list2`.

### *Methods That Test Class* `LinkedList`

Line 27 calls *generic method* `Concatenate` (lines 55–64) to append all elements of `list2` to the end of `list1`. Line 28 calls method `PrintList` (lines 42–52) to output `list1`'s contents. Line 31 calls method `ToUppercaseStrings` (lines 67–78) to convert each `string` element to uppercase, then line 32 calls `PrintList` again to display the modified `strings`. Line 35 calls method `RemoveItemsBetween` (lines 81–94) to remove the elements between `"BLACK"` and `"BROWN"`—not including either. Line 37 outputs the list again, then line 38 invokes method `PrintReversedList` (lines 97–111) to display the list in *reverse* order.

### *Generic Method* `Concatentate`

Generic method `Concatenate` (lines 55–64) iterates over its second parameter (`list2`) with a `foreach` statement and calls method `AddLast` to append each value to the end of its first parameter (`list1`). The `LinkedList` class's enumerator loops over the values of the nodes, not the nodes themselves, so the iteration variable is inferred to be of the `LinkedList`'s element type `T`. Notice that this creates a new node in `list1` for each node in `list2`. One `LinkedListNode` cannot be a member of more than one `LinkedList`. If you want the same data to belong to more than one `LinkedList`, you must make a copy of the node for each list to avoid `InvalidOperationExceptions`.

### *Generic Method* `PrintList` *and Method* `ToUppercaseStrings`

Generic method `PrintList` (lines 42–52) similarly uses a `foreach` statement to iterate over the values in a `LinkedList`, and outputs them. Method `ToUppercaseStrings` (lines 67–78) takes a linked list of `strings` and converts each `string` value to uppercase. This method replaces the `strings` stored in the list, so we cannot use a `foreach` statement as in the previous two methods. Instead, we obtain the first `LinkedListNode` via the `First` property (line 70) and use a sentinel-controlled `while` statement to loop through the list (lines 72–77). Each iteration of the `while` statement obtains and updates the contents of `currentNode` via property `Value` (line 74), using `string` method `ToUpper` to create an uppercase version of the `string` (line 75). Then line 76 moves to the next node in the list by assigning to `currentNode` the value of `currentNode.Next`, which refers to the `LinkedList`'s next node. The `Next` property of the `LinkedList`'s last node is `null`, so when the `while` statement iterates past the end of the list, the loop exits.

### *Method* `ToUppercaseStrings` *is not a Generic Method*

It does not make sense to declare `ToUppercaseStrings` as a generic method, because it uses the `string`-specific methods of the values in the nodes.

**Software Engineering Observation 19.1**

*For maximal code reuse, define methods with generic type parameters whenever possible.*

### *Generic Method* **RemoveItemsBetween**

Generic method RemoveItemsBetween (lines 81–94) removes a range of items between two nodes. Lines 85–86 obtain the two "boundary" nodes of the range by using method **Find**, which performs a linear search on the list and returns the first node that contains a value equal to Find's argument, or null if the value is not found. We store the node preceding the range in local variable currentNode and the node following the range in endNode.

Lines 90–93 remove all the elements between currentNode and endNode. Each iteration of the loop removes the node following currentNode by invoking method **Remove** (line 92), which takes a LinkedListNode, splices it out of the LinkedList, and fixes the references of the surrounding nodes. After the Remove call, currentNode's Next property now refers to the node *following* the node just removed, and that node's Previous property refers to currentNode. The while statement continues to loop until there are no nodes left between currentNode and endNode, or until currentNode is the last node in the list. An overloaded version of method Remove performs a linear search for a specified value and removes the first node in the list that contains it.

### *Method* **PrintReversedList**

Method PrintReversedList (lines 97–111) displays the list backwards by navigating the nodes manually. Line 102 obtains the last element of the list via the **Last** property and stores it in currentNode. The while statement in lines 104–108 iterates through the list backwards by assigning to currentNode the value of currentNode.Previous (the previous node in the list). The loop terminates when currentNode.Previous is null. Note how similar this code is to lines 70–77, which iterated through the list from the beginning to the end.

## 19.6 C# 6 Null Conditional Operator ?[]

6

Section 13.9 introduced nullable types and C# 6's null-conditional operator (?.), which checks whether a reference is null before using it to call a method or access a property. C# 6 provides another **null-conditional operator, ?[]**, for arrays and for collections that support the [] indexing operator.

Assume that a class Employee has a decimal Salary property and that an app defines a List<Employee> named employees. The statement

```
decimal? salary = employees?[0]?.Salary;
```

uses both null-conditional operators and executes as follows:

- First the ?[] operator determines whether employees is null. If so, the expression employees?[0]?.Salary short circuits—that is, it terminates immediately—and the expression evaluates to null. In the preceding statement, this is assigned to the nullable decimal variable salary. If employees is not null, employees?[0] accesses the element at position 0 of the List<Employee>.
- Element 0 could be null or a reference to an Employee object, so we use the ?. operator to check whether employees?[0] is null. If so, once again the entire expression evaluates to null, which is assigned to the nullable decimal variable salary; otherwise, the property Salary's value is assigned to salary.

Note in the preceding statement that salary *must* be declared as a nullable type, because the expression employees?[0]?.Salary can return null or a decimal value.

## 6 19.7 C# 6 Dictionary Initializers and Collection Initializers

C# 6 supports two new features with respect to initializing collections—index initializers and using collection initializers with collections that have an `Add` extension method.

### *C# 6 Index Initializers*

Prior to C# 6, you could use a fully braced collection initializer to initialize a `Dictionary`'s key–value pairs. For example, if you have a `Dictionary<string, int>` named `toolInventory`, you could create and initialize it as follows:

```
var toolInventory = new Dictionary<string, int>{
   {"Hammer", 13},
   {"Saw", 17},
   {"Screwdriver", 7}
};
```

This is shorthand for creating the `Dictionary` then using its `Add` method to add each key–value pairs.

6 C# 6 introduces the **index initializers**, which enable you to clearly indicate the key and the value in each key–value pair as follows:

```
var toolInventory = new Dictionary<string, int>{
   ["Hammer"] = 13,
   ["Saw"] = 17,
   ["Screwdriver"] = 7
};
```

### *C# 6 Collection Initializers Now Support Collections with* `Add` *Extension Methods*

Prior to C# 6, any collection that defined an `Add` instance method could be initialized with a collection initializer. As of C# 6, the compiler also supports collection initializers for any
6 collection that has an `Add` extension method.

## 19.8 Delegates

In Section 14.3.3, we introduced the concept of a *delegate*—an object that holds a reference to a method.[1] You can call a method through a variable of a delegate type—thus *delegating* to the referenced method the responsibilty of performing a task. Delegates also allow you to pass methods to and from other methods. We introduced delegates in the context of GUI event handlers, but they're used in many areas of the .NET Framework. For example, in Chapter 9, we introduced LINQ query syntax. The compiler converts such LINQ queries into calls to extension methods—many of which have delegate parameters. Figure 19.6 declares and uses a delegate type. In Section 19.11, we'll use delegates in the context of LINQ extension methods.

1. This is similar to function pointers and function objects (also called functors) in C++.

```
// Fig. 19.6: Delegates.cs
// Using delegates to pass functions as arguments.
using System;
using System.Collections.Generic;

class Delegates
{
   // delegate for a function that receives an int and returns a bool
   public delegate bool NumberPredicate(int number);

   static void Main()
   {
      int[] numbers = {1, 2, 3, 4, 5, 6, 7, 8, 9, 10};

      // create an instance of the NumberPredicate delegate type
      NumberPredicate evenPredicate = IsEven;

      // call IsEven using a delegate variable
      Console.WriteLine(
         $"Call IsEven using a delegate variable: {evenPredicate(4)}");

      // filter the even numbers using method IsEven
      List<int> evenNumbers = FilterArray(numbers, evenPredicate);

      // display the result
      DisplayList("Use IsEven to filter even numbers: ", evenNumbers);

      // filter the odd numbers using method IsOdd
      List<int> oddNumbers = FilterArray(numbers, IsOdd);

      // display the result
      DisplayList("Use IsOdd to filter odd numbers: ", oddNumbers);

      // filter numbers greater than 5 using method IsOver5
      List<int> numbersOver5 = FilterArray(numbers, IsOver5);

      // display the result
      DisplayList("Use IsOver5 to filter numbers over 5: ", numbersOver5);
   }

   // select an array's elements that satisfy the predicate
   private static List<int> FilterArray(int[] intArray,
      NumberPredicate predicate)
   {
      // hold the selected elements
      var result = new List<int>();

      // iterate over each element in the array
      foreach (var item in intArray)
      {
         // if the element satisfies the predicate
         if (predicate(item)) // invokes method referenced by predicate
         {
```

**Fig. 19.6** | Using delegates to pass functions as arguments. (Part 1 of 2.)

```
54                 result.Add(item); // add the element to the result
55             }
56         }
57
58         return result; // return the result
59     }
60
61     // determine whether an int is even
62     private static bool IsEven(int number) => number % 2 == 0;
63
64     // determine whether an int is odd
65     private static bool IsOdd(int number) => number % 2 == 1;
66
67     // determine whether an int is greater than 5
68     private static bool IsOver5(int number) => number > 5;
69
70     // display the elements of a List
71     private static void DisplayList(string description, List<int> list)
72     {
73         Console.Write(description); // display the output's description
74
75         // iterate over each element in the List
76         foreach (var item in list)
77         {
78             Console.Write($"{item} "); // print item followed by a space
79         }
80
81         Console.WriteLine(); // add a new line
82     }
83 }
```

```
Call IsEven using a delegate variable: True
Use IsEven to filter even numbers: 2 4 6 8 10
Use IsOdd to filter odd numbers: 1 3 5 7 9
Use IsOver5 to filter numbers over 5: 6 7 8 9 10
```

**Fig. 19.6** | Using delegates to pass functions as arguments. (Part 2 of 2.)

### 19.8.1 Declaring a Delegate Type

Line 9 defines a delegate type named `NumberPredicate`. A variable of this type can store a reference to any method that takes one `int` argument and returns a `bool`. A delegate type is declared by preceding a method header with keyword `delegate` (placed after any access specifiers, such as `public` or `private`) and following the method header with a semicolon. A `delegate` type declaration includes the method header only—the header describes a set of methods with specific parameters and a specific return type.

### 19.8.2 Declaring a Delegate Variable

Line 16 declares `evenPredicate` as a `NumberPredicate` variable and initializes it with a reference to the expression-bodied `IsEven` method (line 62). Since method `IsEven`'s signature matches the `NumberPredicate` delegate's signature, `IsEven` can be referenced by a variable of type `NumberPredicate`. Variable `evenPredicate` can now be used as an alias for method `IsEven`. A `NumberPredicate` variable can hold a reference to any method that receives an `int` and returns a `bool`. Lines 19–20 use variable `evenPredicate` to call method `IsEven`, then display the result. The method referenced by the delegate is called using the delegate variable's name in place of the method's name, as in

```
evenPredicate(4)
```

### 19.8.3 Delegate Parameters

The real power of delegates is in passing method references as arguments to methods, as we do in this example with method `FilterArray` (lines 42–59). The method takes as arguments

- an `int` array and
- a `NumberPredicate` that references a method used to filter the array elements.

The method returns a `List<int>` containing only the `int`s that satisfy the condition specified by the `NumberPredicate`. `FilterArray` returns a `List`, because we don't know in advance how many elements will be included in the result.

The `foreach` statement (lines 49–56) calls the method referenced by the `NumberPredicate` delegate (line 52) once for each element of the array. If the method call returns `true`, the element is included in `result`. The `NumberPredicate` is guaranteed to return either `true` or `false`, because any method referenced by a `NumberPredicate` must return a `bool`—as specified by the definition of the `NumberPredicate` delegate type (line 9). Line 23 passes to `FilterArray` the `int` array (`numbers`) and the `NumberPredicate` that references the `IsEven` method (`evenPredicate`). `FilterArray` then calls the `NumberPredicate` delegate on each array element. Line 23 assigns the `List` returned by `FilterArray` to variable `evenNumbers` and line 26 calls method `DisplayList` (lines 71–82) to display the results.

### 19.8.4 Passing a Method Name Directly to a Delegate Parameter

Line 29 calls method `FilterArray` to select the odd numbers in the array. In this case, we pass the method name `IsOdd` (defined in line 65) as `FilterArray`'s second argument, rather than creating a `NumberPredicate` variable. Line 32 displays the results showing only the odd numbers. Line 35 calls method `FilterArray` to select the numbers greater than 5 in the array, using method `IsOver5` (defined in line 68) as `FilterArray`'s second argument. Line 38 displays the elements that are greater than 5.

## 19.9 Lambda Expressions

**Lambda expressions** allow you to define simple, **anonymous methods**—that is, methods that do not have names and that are defined where they are assigned to a delegate or passed to a delegate parameter. In many cases, working with lambda expressions can reduce the size of your code and the complexity of working with delegates. As you'll see in later examples, lambda expressions are particularly powerful when combined with the `where` clause in LINQ queries. Figure 19.7 reimplements the example of Fig. 19.6 using lambda expressions rather than explicitly declared methods `IsEven`, `IsOdd` and `IsOver5`.

```
// Fig. 19.7: Lambdas.cs
// Using lambda expressions.
using System;
using System.Collections.Generic;

class Lambdas
{
   // delegate for a function that receives an int and returns a bool
   public delegate bool NumberPredicate(int number);

   static void Main(string[] args)
   {
      int[] numbers = {1, 2, 3, 4, 5, 6, 7, 8, 9, 10};

      // create an instance of the NumberPredicate delegate type using an
      // implicit lambda expression
      NumberPredicate evenPredicate = number => number % 2 == 0;

      // call a lambda expression through a variable
      Console.WriteLine(
         $"Use a lambda-expression variable: {evenPredicate(4)}");

      // filter the even numbers using a lambda expression
      List<int> evenNumbers = FilterArray(numbers, evenPredicate);

      // display the result
      DisplayList("Use a lambda expression to filter even numbers: ",
         evenNumbers);

      // filter the odd numbers using an explicitly typed lambda
      // expression
      List<int> oddNumbers =
         FilterArray(numbers, (int number) => number % 2 == 1);

      // display the result
      DisplayList("Use a lambda expression to filter odd numbers: ",
         oddNumbers);

      // filter numbers greater than 5 using an implicit lambda statement
      List<int> numbersOver5 =
         FilterArray(numbers, number => {return number > 5;});

      // display the result
      DisplayList("Use a lambda expression to filter numbers over 5: ",
         numbersOver5);
   }

   // select an array's elements that satisfy the predicate
   private static List<int> FilterArray(
      int[] intArray, NumberPredicate predicate)
   {
      // hold the selected elements
      var result = new List<int>();
```

**Fig. 19.7** | Using lambda expressions. (Part 1 of 2.)

```
54
55          // iterate over each element in the array
56          foreach (var item in intArray)
57          {
58             // if the element satisfies the predicate
59             if (predicate(item))
60             {
61                result.Add(item); // add the element to the result
62             }
63          }
64
65          return result; // return the result
66       }
67
68       // display the elements of a List
69       private static void DisplayList(string description, List<int> list)
70       {
71          Console.Write(description); // display the output's description
72
73          // iterate over each element in the List
74          foreach (int item in list)
75          {
76             Console.Write($"{item} "); // print item followed by a space
77          }
78
79          Console.WriteLine(); // add a new line
80       }
81    }
```

```
Use a lambda expression variable: True
Use a lambda expression to filter even numbers: 2 4 6 8 10
Use a lambda expression to filter odd numbers: 1 3 5 7 9
Use a lambda expression to filter numbers over 5: 6 7 8 9 10
```

**Fig. 19.7** | Using lambda expressions. (Part 2 of 2.)

### 19.9.1 Expression Lambdas

A lambda expression (line 17)

```
number => number % 2 == 0
```

begins with a parameter list (`number` in this case). The parameter list is followed by the `=>` **lambda operator** (read as "goes to") and an expression that represents the lambda's body. The lambda expression in line 17 uses the `%` operator to determine whether the parameter's `number` value is an even `int`. The value produced by the expression—`true` if the `int` is even, `false` otherwise—is implicitly returned by the lambda expression. The lambda in line 17 is called an **expression lambda**, because it has a single expression to the right of the lambda operator. Note that we do not specify a return type for the lambda expression—the return type is inferred from the return value or, in some cases, from a delegate's return type. The lambda expression in line 17 is equivalent to the `IsEven` method in Fig. 19.6. Note that C# 6's expression-bodied methods use a similar syntax to expression lambdas, including the lambda operator (`=>`). 6

### 19.9.2 Assigning Lambdas to Delegate Variables

In line 17 of Fig. 19.7, the lambda expression is assigned to a variable of type `NumberPredicate`—the delegate type declared in line 9. A delegate can hold a reference to a lambda expression. As with traditional methods, a method defined by a lambda expression must have a signature that's compatible with the delegate type. The `NumberPredicate` delegate can hold a reference to any method that receives an `int` and returns a `bool`. Based on this, the compiler is able to infer that the lambda expression in line 17 defines a method that implicitly takes an `int` as an argument and returns the `bool` result of the expression in its body.

Lines 20–21 display the result of calling the lambda expression defined in line 17. The lambda expression is called via the variable that references it (`evenPredicate`). Line 24 passes `evenPredicate` to method `FilterArray` (lines 49–66), which is identical to the method used in Fig. 19.6—it uses the `NumberPredicate` delegate to determine whether an array element should be included in the result. Lines 27–28 display the filtered results.

### 19.9.3 Explicitly Typed Lambda Parameters

Lambda expressions often are used as arguments to methods with delegate-type parameters, rather than defining and referencing a separate method or defining a delegate variable that references a lambda. Lines 32–33 select the odd array elements with the lambda

```
(int number) => number % 2 == 1
```

In this case, the lambda is passed directly to method `FilterArray` and is implicitly stored in the `NumberPredicate` delegate parameter.

The lambda expression's input parameter `number` is explicitly typed as an `int` here—sometimes this is necessary to avoid ambiguity that would lead to compilation errors (though that is not the case here). When specifying a lambda parameter's type and/or when a lambda has more than one parameter, you must enclose the parameter list in parentheses as in line 33. The lambda expression in line 33 is equivalent to the `IsOdd` method defined in Fig. 19.6. Lines 36–37 of Fig. 19.7 display the filtered results.

### 19.9.4 Statement Lambdas

Lines 40–41 use the lambda

```
number => {return number > 5;}
```

to find the `int`s greater than `5` in the array and store the results. This lambda is equivalent to the `IsOver5` method in Fig. 19.6.

The preceding lambda is called a **statement lambda**, because it contains a statement block—one or more statements enclosed in braces (`{}`)—to the right of the lambda operator. This lambda's signature is compatible with the `NumberPredicate` delegate, because the parameter `number`'s type is inferred to be `int` and the statement in the lambda returns a `bool`. For additional information on lambdas, visit

```
https://msdn.microsoft.com/library/bb397687
```

## 19.10 Introduction to Functional Programming

So far, you've seen structured, object-oriented and generic programming techniques in C#. Though you often used .NET Framework classes and interfaces to perform various tasks, you typically determined *what* you wanted to accomplish in a task, then specified precisely *how* to accomplish it.

For example, let's assume that *what* you'd like to accomplish is to sum the elements of an `int` array named `values` (the *data source*). You might use the following code:

```
var sum = 0;

for (var counter = 0; counter < values.Length; ++counter)
{
   sum += values[counter];
}
```

This loop specifies precisely *how* to add each array element's value to the `sum`—with a `for` iteration statement that processes each element one at a time, adding its value to the `sum`. This technique is known as **external iteration**—because *you* specify how to iterate, not the library—and requires you to access the elements sequentially from beginning to end in a single thread of execution. To perform the preceding task, you also create two variables (`sum` and `counter`) that are *mutated* repeatedly—their values *change* as the iteration is performed. You performed many similar array and collection tasks, such as displaying the elements of an array, summarizing the faces of a die that was rolled 60,000,000 times, calculating the average of an array's elements and more.

### *External Iteration Is Error Prone*

The problem with external iteration is that even in this simple loop, there are many opportunities for error. You could, for example,

- initialize variable `sum` incorrectly,
- initialize control variable `counter` incorrectly,
- use the wrong loop-continuation condition,
- increment control variable `counter` incorrectly or
- incorrectly add each value in the array to the `sum`.

### *Internal Iteration*

In **functional programming**, you specify *what* you want to accomplish in a task, but *not how* to accomplish it. As you'll see, to sum a numeric data source's elements (such as those in an array or collection), you can use LINQ capabilities that allow you to say, "Here's a data source, give me the sum of its elements." You do *not* need to specify *how* to iterate through the elements or declare and use *any* mutable (that is, modifiable) variables. This is known as **internal iteration**, because the *library* code (behind the scenes) iterates through all the elements to perform the task.[2]

2. Systems developers have been familiar with the "*what* vs. *how*" distinction for decades. They begin a systems development effort by defining a *requirements document* that specifies *what* the system is supposed to do. Then, they use tools, such as the UML, to design the system, which specifies *how* the system should be built to meet the requirements. In the online chapters, we build the software for a very simple ATM. We begin with a requirements document that specifies *what* the software is supposed to do, then we use the UML to specify *how* the software should do it. We specify the final details of *how* by writing the actual C# code.

A key aspect of functional programming is **immutability**—not modifying the data source being processed or any other program state, such as counter-control variables in loops. By using internal iteration, you eliminate from your programs common errors that are caused by modifying data incorrectly. This makes it easier to write correct code.

#### *Filter, Map and Reduce*

Three common functional-programming operations that you'll perform on collections of data are *filter*, *map* and *reduce*:

- A **filter** operation results in a *new* collection containing only the elements that satisfy a condition. For example, you might filter a collection of `int`s to locate only the even integers, or you might filter a collection of `Employee`'s to locate people in a specific department of a large company. Filter operations *do not modify* the original collection.
- A **map** operation results in a *new* collection in which each element of the original collection is mapped to a new value (possibly of a different type)—e.g., mapping numeric values to the squares of the numeric values. The new collection has the same number of elements as the collection that was mapped. Map operations *do not modify* the original collection.
- A **reduce** operation combines the elements of a collection into a single new value typically using a lambda that specifies how to combine the elements. For example, you might reduce a collection of `int` grades from zero to 100 on an exam to the number of students who passed with a grade greater than or equal to 60. Reduce operations *do not modify* the original collection.

In the next section, we'll demonstrate filter, map and reduce operations using class `Enumerable`'s LINQ to Objects extension methods `Where`, `Select` and `Aggregate`, respectively. The extension methods defined by class `Enumerable` operate on collections that implement the interface `IEnumerable<T>`.

#### *C# and Functional Programming*

Though C# was not originally designed as a functional-programming language, C#'s LINQ query syntax and LINQ extension methods support functional-programming techniques, such as internal iteration and immutability. In addition, C# 6's getter-only, auto-implemented properties make it easier to define immutable types. We expect future versions of C# and most other popular programming languages to include more functional-programming capabilities that make implementing programs with a functional style more natural.

## 19.11 Functional Programming with LINQ Method-Call Syntax and Lambdas

In Chapter 9, we introduced LINQ, demonstrated LINQ query syntax and introduced some LINQ extension methods. The same tasks you can perform with LINQ query syntax can also be performed with various LINQ extension methods and lambdas. In fact, the compiler translates LINQ query syntax into calls to LINQ extension methods that receive lambdas as arguments. For example, lines 21–24 of Fig. 9.2

```
var filtered =
   from value in values // data source is values
   where value > 4
   select value;
```

can be written as

```
var filtered = values.Where(value => value > 4);
```

Figure 19.8 demonstrates simple functional programming techniques using a list of integers.

```
// Fig. 19.8: FunctionalProgramming.cs
// Functional programming with LINQ extension methods and lambdas.
using System;
using System.Collections.Generic;
using System.Linq;

namespace FilterMapReduce
{
   class FunctionalProgramming
   {
      static void Main()
      {
         var values = new List<int> {3, 10, 6, 1, 4, 8, 2, 5, 9, 7};

         Console.Write("Original values: ");
         values.Display(); // call Display extension method

         // display the Min, Max, Sum and Average
         Console.WriteLine($"\nMin: {values.Min()}");
         Console.WriteLine($"Max: {values.Max()}");
         Console.WriteLine($"Sum: {values.Sum()}");
         Console.WriteLine($"Average: {values.Average()}");

         // sum of values via Aggregate
         Console.WriteLine("\nSum via Aggregate method: " +
            values.Aggregate(0, (x, y) => x + y));

         // sum of squares of values via Aggregate
         Console.WriteLine("Sum of squares via Aggregate method: " +
            values.Aggregate(0, (x, y) => x + y * y));

         // product of values via Aggregate
         Console.WriteLine("Product via Aggregate method: " +
            values.Aggregate(1, (x, y) => x * y));

         // even values displayed in sorted order
         Console.Write("\nEven values displayed in sorted order: ");
         values.Where(value => value % 2 == 0) // find even integers
               .OrderBy(value => value) // sort remaining values
               .Display(); // show results

```

**Fig. 19.8** | Functional programming with LINQ extension methods and lambdas. (Part 1 of 2.)

```
42            // odd values multiplied by 10 and displayed in sorted order
43            Console.Write(
44               "Odd values multiplied by 10 displayed in sorted order: ");
45            values.Where(value => value % 2 != 0) // find odd integers
46                  .Select(value => value * 10) // multiply each by 10
47                  .OrderBy(value => value) // sort the values
48                  .Display(); // show results
49
50            // display original values again to prove they were not modified
51            Console.Write("\nOriginal values: ");
52            values.Display(); // call Display extension method
53         }
54      }
55
56      // declares an extension method
57      static class Extensions
58      {
59         // extension method that displays all elements separated by spaces
60         public static void Display<T>(this IEnumerable<T> data)
61         {
62            Console.WriteLine(string.Join(" ", data));
63         }
64      }
65   }
```

```
Original values: 3 10 6 1 4 8 2 5 9 7

Min: 1
Max: 10
Sum: 55
Average: 5.5

Sum via Aggregate method: 55
Sum of squares via Aggregate method: 385
Product via Aggregate method: 3628800

Even values displayed in sorted order: 2 4 6 8 10
Odd values multiplied by 10 displayed in sorted order: 10 30 50 70 90

Original values: 3 10 6 1 4 8 2 5 9 7
```

**Fig. 19.8** | Functional programming with LINQ extension methods and lambdas. (Part 2 of 2.)

### *Extension Method* `Display`

Throughout this example, we display the results of various operations by calling our own extension method named `Display`, which is defined in the `static class Extensions` (lines 57–64). The method uses `string` method `Join` to concatenate the `IEnumerable<T>` argument's elements separated by spaces.

Note at the beginning and end of `Main` that when we call `Display` directly on the `values` collection (lines 16 and 52) the same values are displayed in the same order. These outputs confirm that the functional-programming operations performed throughout `Main` (which we discuss in Sections 19.11.1–19.11.4) do not modify the contents of the original `values` collection.

### 19.11.1 LINQ Extension Methods `Min`, `Max`, `Sum` and `Average`

Class `Enumerable` (namespace `System.Linq`) defines various LINQ extension methods for performing common *reduction* operations including:

- **`Min`** (line 19) returns the smallest value in the collection.
- **`Max`** (line 20) returns the largest value in the collection.
- **`Sum`** (line 21) returns the sum of all the values in the collection.
- **`Average`** (line 22) returns the average of all the values in the collection.

#### *Iteration and Mutation Are Hidden from You*

Note in lines 19–22 that for each of these reduction operations:

- We simply say *what* we want to accomplish, not *how* to accomplish it—there are no iteration details in the app.
- *No mutable variables* are used in the app to perform these operations.
- The `values` collection is *not modified* (confirmed by the output of line 52).

In fact, the LINQ operations have no *side effects* that modify the original collection or any other variables in the app—a key aspect of functional programming.

Of course, behind the scenes iteration and mutable variables *are* required:

- All four extension methods iterate through the collection and must keep track of the current element they're processing.
- While iterating through the collection, `Min` and `Max` must store the current smallest and largest items, respectively, and `Sum` and `Average` must keep track of the total of the elements processed so far—all of these require mutating a local variable that's hidden from you.

The other operations in Sections 19.11.2–19.11.4 also require iteration and mutable variables, but the *library*—which has already been thoroughly debugged and tested—handles these details for you. To see how LINQ extension methods like `Min`, `Max`, `Sum` and `Average` implement these concepts, check out class `Enumerable` in the .NET source code at

```
https://github.com/dotnet/corefx/tree/master/src/System.Linq/src/
   System/Linq
```

Class `Enumerable` is divided into many `partial` classes—you can find methods `Min`, `Max`, `Sum` and `Average` in the files `Min.cs`, `Max.cs`, `Sum.cs` and `Average.cs`.

### 19.11.2 `Aggregate` Extension Method for Reduction Operations

You can define your own *reductions* with the **`Aggregate`** LINQ extension method. For example, the call to `Aggregate` in lines 25–26 sums the elements of `values`. The version of `Aggregate` used here receives two arguments:

- The first argument (`0`) is a value that helps you begin the reduction operation. When summing the elements of a collection, we begin with the value `0`. Shortly, we'll use 1 to begin calculating the *product* of the elements.
- The second argument is a delegate of type **`Func`** (namespace `System`) that represents a method which receives two arguments of the same type and returns a value—there are many versions of type `Func` that specify from 0 to 16 arguments of any

type. In this case, we pass the following lambda expression, which returns the sum of its two arguments:

```
(x, y) => x + y
```

Once for each element in the collection, `Aggregate` calls this lambda expression.

- On the first call to the lambda, parameter `x`'s value is `Aggregate`'s first argument (`0`) and parameter `y`'s value is the first `int` in `values` (`3`), producing the value `3` (0 + 3).
- Each subsequent call to the lambda uses the result of the previous call as the lambda's first argument and the next element of the collection as the second. On the second call to the lambda, parameter `x`'s value is the result of the first calculation (`3`) and parameter `y`'s value is the *second* `int` in `values` (`10`), producing the sum `13` (3 + 10).
- On the third call to the lambda, parameter `x`'s value is the result of the previous calculation (`13`) and parameter `y`'s value is the *third* `int` in `values` (`6`), producing the sum `19` (13 + 6).

This process continues producing a running total of the values until they've all been used, at which point the final sum is returned by `Aggregate`. Note again that *no mutable variables* are used to reduce the collection to the sum of its elements and that the original `values` collection is *not* modified.

### *Summing the Squares of the Values with Method* `Aggregate`

Lines 29–30 use `Aggregate` to calculate the sums of the squares of `values`' elements. The lambda in this case,

```
(x, y) => x + y * y
```

adds the *square* of the current value to the running total. Evaluation of the reduction proceeds as follows:

- On the first call to the lambda, parameter `x`'s value is `Aggregate`'s first argument (`0`) and parameter `y`'s value is the first `int` in `values` (`3`), producing the value `9` ($0 + 3^2$).
- On the next call to the lambda, parameter `x`'s value is the result of the first calculation (`9`) and parameter `y`'s value is the *second* `int` in `values` (`10`), producing the sum `109` ($9 + 10^2$).
- On the next call to the lambda, parameter `x`'s value is the result of the previous calculation (`109`) and parameter `y`'s value is the *third* `int` in `values` (`6`), producing the sum `145` ($109 + 6^2$).

This process continues producing a running total of the squares of the elements until they've all been used, at which point the final sum is returned by `Aggregate`. Note again that *no mutable variables* are used to reduce the collection to the sum of its squares and that the original `values` collection is *not* modified.

### *Calculating the Product of the Values with Method* `Aggregate`

Lines 33–34 use `Aggregate` to calculate the product of `values`' elements. The lambda

```
(x, y) => x * y
```

multiplies its two arguments. Because we're producing a product, we begin with the value `1` in this case. Evaluation of the reduction proceeds as follows:

- On the first call to the lambda, parameter `x`'s value is `Aggregate`'s first argument (`1`) and parameter `y`'s value is the *first* `int` in `values` (`3`), producing the value `3` (1 * 3).
- On the next call to the lambda, parameter `x`'s value is the result of the first calculation (`3`) and parameter `y`'s value is the *second* `int` in `values` (`10`), producing the sum `30` (3 * 10).
- On the next call to the lambda, parameter `x`'s value is the result of the previous calculation (`30`) and parameter `y`'s value is the *third* `int` in `values` (`6`), producing the sum `180` (30 * 6).

This process continues producing a running product of the elements until they've all been used, at which point the final product is returned. Note again that *no mutable variables* are used to reduce the collection to the product of its elements and that the original `values` collection is *not* modified.

### 19.11.3 The Where Extension Method for Filtering Operations

Lines 38–40 *filter* the even integers in `values`, *sort* them in ascending order and display the results. You *filter* elements to produce a *new* collection of results that match a condition known as a *predicate*. LINQ extension method **`Where`** (line 38) receives as its argument a `Func` delegate for a method that receives one argument and returns a `bool` indicating whether a given element should be included in the collection returned by `Where`.

The lambda in line 38:

```
value => value % 2 == 0
```

receives a value and returns a `bool` indicating whether the `value` satisfies the predicate—in this case, if the value it receives is divisible by 2.

#### *Sorting the Results*

The **`OrderBy` extension method** receives as its argument a `Func` delegate representing a method that receives one parameter and returns a value that's used to order the results. In this case (line 39), the lambda expression

```
value => value
```

simply returns its argument, which `OrderBy` uses to sort the values in ascending order—for descending order you'd use `OrderByDescending`. Note again that *no mutable variables* are used to filter or sort the collection and that the original `values` collection is *not* modified.

#### *Deferred Execution*

Calls to `Where` and `OrderBy` use the same *deferred execution* we discussed in Section 9.5.2—they aren't evaluated until you iterate over the results. In lines 38–40 (Fig. 19.8), this occurs when our `Display` extension method is called (line 40). This means you can save the operation into a variable for future execution, as in

```
var evenIntegers =
   values.Where(value => value % 2 == 0) // find even integers
      .OrderBy(value => value); // sort remaining values
```

You can execute the operation by iterating over `evenIntegers` later. Each time you execute the operation, the current elements in `values` will be filtered and sorted. So, if you modify `values` by adding more even integers to the collection, these will appear in the results when you iterate over `evenIntegers`.

### 19.11.4 `Select` Extension Method for Mapping Operations

Lines 45–48 *filter* the odd integers in `values`, *multiply* each odd integer by 10, *sort* the values in ascending order and display the results. The new feature here is the *mapping* operation that takes each value and multiplies it by 10. Mapping transforms a collection's elements to new values, which sometimes are of different types from the original elements.

LINQ extension method **`Select`** receives as its argument a `Func` delegate for a method that receives one argument and maps it to a new value (possibly of another type) that's included in the collection returned by `Select`. The lambda in line 46:

```
value => value * 10
```

multiplies its `value` argument by `10`, thus mapping it to a new value. Line 47 sorts the results. Calls to `Select` are *deferred* until you iterate over the results—in this case, when our `Display` extension method is called (line 48). Note again that *no mutable variables* are used to map the collection's elements and that the original `values` collection is *not* modified.

## 19.12 PLINQ: Improving LINQ to Objects Performance with Multicore

Today's computers are likely to have multicore processors with four or eight cores. One vendor already offers a 61-core processor[3] and future processors are likely to have many more cores. Your computer's operating system shares the cores among operating system tasks and the apps running at a given time.

#### *Threads*

A concept called *threads* enables the operating system to run parts of an app concurrently—for example, while the *user-interface thread* (commonly called the *GUI thread*) waits for the user to interact with a GUI control, separate threads in the same app could be performing other tasks like complex calculations, downloading a video, playing music, sending an e-mail, etc. Though all of these tasks can make progress concurrently, they may do so by sharing one processor core.

#### *Sharing Processors*

With multicore processors, apps can operate truly in parallel (that is, simultaneously) on separate cores. In addition, the operating system can allow one app's threads to operate truly in parallel on separate cores, possibly increasing the app's performance substantially. Parallelizing apps and algorithms to take advantage of multiple cores is difficult and highly error prone, especially if those tasks share data that can be modified by one or more of the tasks.

#### *PLINQ (Parallel LINQ)*

In Section 19.10, we mentioned that a benefit of functional programming and internal iteration is that the library code (behind the scenes) iterates through all the elements of a

3. The website `http://processors.specout.com` shows a range of processors with 1 to 61 cores.

collection to perform a task. Another benefit is that you can easily ask the library to perform a task with *parallel processing* to take advantage of a processor's multiple cores. This is the purpose of **PLINQ (Parallel LINQ)**—an implementation of the LINQ to Objects extension methods that parallelizes the operations for increased performance. PLINQ handles for you the error-prone aspects of breaking tasks into smaller pieces that can execute in *parallel* and coordinating the results of those pieces, making it easier for you to write high-performance apps that take advantage of multicore processors.

### *Demonstrating PLINQ*

Figure 19.9 demonstrates the LINQ to Objects and PLINQ extension methods `Min`, `Max` and `Average` operating on a 10,000,000-element array of random `int` values (created in lines 13–15). As with LINQ to Objects, the PLINQ versions of these operations *do not modify* the original collection. We time the operations to show the substantial performance improvements of PLINQ (using multiple cores) over LINQ to Objects (using a single core). For the remainder of this discussion we refer to LINQ to Objects simply as LINQ.

```
1  // Fig. 19.9: ParallelizingWithPLINQ.cs
2  // Comparing performance of LINQ and PLINQ Min, Max and Average methods.
3  using System;
4  using System.Linq;
5
6  class ParallelizingWithPLINQ
7  {
8     static void Main()
9     {
10       var random = new Random();
11
12       // create array of random ints in the range 1-999
13       int[] values = Enumerable.Range(1, 10000000)
14                         .Select(x => random.Next(1, 1000))
15                         .ToArray();
16
17       // time the Min, Max and Average LINQ extension methods
18       Console.WriteLine(
19          "Min, Max and Average with LINQ to Objects using a single core");
20       var linqStart = DateTime.Now; // get time before method calls
21       var linqMin = values.Min();
22       var linqMax = values.Max();
23       var linqAverage = values.Average();
24       var linqEnd = DateTime.Now; // get time after method calls
25
26       // display results and total time in milliseconds
27       var linqTime = linqEnd.Subtract(linqStart).TotalMilliseconds;
28       DisplayResults(linqMin, linqMax, linqAverage, linqTime);
29
30       // time the Min, Max and Average PLINQ extension methods
31       Console.WriteLine(
32          "\nMin, Max and Average with PLINQ using multiple cores");
```

**Fig. 19.9** | Comparing performance of LINQ and PLINQ `Min`, `Max` and `Average` methods. (Part 1 of 2.)

```
        var plinqStart = DateTime.Now; // get time before method calls
        var plinqMin = values.AsParallel().Min();
        var plinqMax = values.AsParallel().Max();
        var plinqAverage = values.AsParallel().Average();
        var plinqEnd = DateTime.Now; // get time after method calls

        // display results and total time in milliseconds
        var plinqTime = plinqEnd.Subtract(plinqStart).TotalMilliseconds;
        DisplayResults(plinqMin, plinqMax, plinqAverage, plinqTime);

        // display time difference as a percentage
        Console.WriteLine("\nPLINQ took " +
           $"{((linqTime - plinqTime) / linqTime):P0}" +
           " less time than LINQ");
     }

     // displays results and total time in milliseconds
     static void DisplayResults(
        int min, int max, double average, double time)
     {
        Console.WriteLine($"Min: {min}\nMax: {max}\n" +
           $"Average: {average:F}\nTotal time in milliseconds: {time:F}");
     }
  }
```

```
Min, Max and Average with LINQ to Objects using a single core
Min: 1
Max: 999
Average: 499.96
Total time in milliseconds: 179.03

Min, Max and Average with PLINQ using multiple cores
Min: 1
Max: 999
Average: 499.96
Total time in milliseconds: 80.99

PLINQ took 55 % less time than LINQ
```

```
Min, Max and Average with LINQ to Objects using a single core
Min: 1
Max: 999
Average: 500.07
Total time in milliseconds: 152.13

Min, Max and Average with PLINQ using multiple cores
Min: 1
Max: 999
Average: 500.07
Total time in milliseconds: 89.05

PLINQ took 41 % less time than LINQ
```

**Fig. 19.9** | Comparing performance of LINQ and PLINQ `Min`, `Max` and `Average` methods. (Part 2 of 2.)

### *Generating a Range of* **ints** *with Enumerable Method* **Range**

Using functional techniques, lines 13–15 create an array of 10,000,000 random ints. Class Enumerable provides static method **Range** to produce an IEnumerable<int> containing integer values. The expression

```
Enumerable.Range(1, 10000000)
```

produces an IEnumerable<int> containing the values 1 through 10,000,000—the first argument specifies the starting value in the range and the second specifies the number of values to produce. Next, line 14 uses LINQ extension method Select to *map* every element to a random integer in the range 1–999. The lambda

```
x => random.Next(1, 1000)
```

ignores its parameter (x) and simply returns a random value that becomes part of the IEnumerable<int> returned by Select. Finally, line 15 calls extension method **ToArray**, which returns an array of ints containing the elements produced by the Select operation. Note that class Enumerable also provides extension method **ToList** to obtain a List<T> rather than an array.

### **Min**, **Max** *and* **Average** *with LINQ*

To calculate the total time required for the LINQ Min, Max and Average extension-method calls, we use type DateTime's **Now** property to get the current time before (line 20) and after (line 24) the LINQ operations. Lines 21–23 perform Min, Max and Average on the array values. Line 27 uses DateTime method **Subtract** to compute the difference between the end and start times, which is returned as a **TimeSpan**. We then store the TimeSpan's **TotalMilliseconds** value for use in a later calculation showing PLINQ's percentage improvement over LINQ.

### **Min**, **Max** *and* **Average** *with PLINQ*

Lines 33–41 perform the same tasks as lines 20–28, but use PLINQ Min, Max and Average extension-method calls to demonstrate the performance improvement over LINQ. To initiate parallel processing, lines 34–36 invoke IEnumerable<T> extension method **AsParallel** (from class **ParallelEnumerable**), which returns a **ParallelQuery<T>** (in this example, T is int). An object that implements ParallelQuery<T> can be used with PLINQ's parallelized versions of the LINQ extension methods. Class ParallelEnumerable defines the ParallelQuery<T> (PLINQ) parallelized versions as well as several PLINQ-specific extension methods. For more information on the extension methods defined in class ParallelEnumerable, visit

```
https://msdn.microsoft.com/library/system.linq.parallelenumerable
```

### *Performance Difference*

Lines 44–46 calculate and display the percentage improvement in processing time of PLINQ over LINQ. As you can see from the sample outputs, the simple choice of PLINQ (via AsParallel) decreased the total processing time substantially—55% and 41% less time in the two sample outputs. We ran the app many more times (using up to three cores) and processing-time savings were generally within the 41–55% range—though we did have a 61% savings on one sample execution. The overall savings will be affected by your processor's number of cores and by what else is running on your computer.

## 19.13 (Optional) Covariance and Contravariance for Generic Types

C# supports *covariance* and *contravariance* of generic interface and delegate types. We'll consider these concepts in the context of arrays, which have always been covariant and contravariant in C#.

### *Covariance in Arrays*

Recall our `Employee` class hierarchy from Section 12.5, which consisted of the base class `Employee` and the derived classes `SalariedEmployee`, `HourlyEmployee`, `CommissionEmployee` and `BasePlusCommissionEmployee`. Assuming the declarations

```
SalariedEmployee[] salariedEmployees = {
   new SalariedEmployee("Bob", "Blue", "111-11-1111", 800M),
   new SalariedEmployee("Rachel", "Red", "222-22-2222", 1234M) };
Employee[] employees;
```

we can write the following statement:

```
employees = salariedEmployees;
```

Even though the array type `SalariedEmployee[]` does *not* derive from the array type `Employee[]`, the preceding assignment *is* allowed because class `SalariedEmployee` is a derived class of `Employee`.

Similarly, suppose we have the following method, which displays the `string` representation of each `Employee` in its `employees` array parameter:

```
void PrintEmployees(Employee[] employees)
```

We can call this method with the array of `SalariedEmployees`, as in

```
PrintEmployees(salariedEmployees);
```

and the method will correctly display the `string` representation of each `SalariedEmployee` object in the argument array. Assigning an array of a derived-class type to an array variable of a base-class type is an example of **covariance**.

### *Covariance in Generic Types*

Covariance works with several *generic interface and delegate types*, including `IEnumerable<T>`. Arrays and generic collections implement the `IEnumerable<T>` interface. Using the `salariedEmployees` array declared previously, consider the following statement:

```
IEnumerable<Employee> employees = salariedEmployees;
```

In earlier versions of C#, this generated a compilation error. Interface `IEnumerable<T>` is now covariant, so the preceding statement *is* allowed. If we modify method `PrintEmployees`, as in

```
void PrintEmployees(IEnumerable<Employee> employees)
```

we can call `PrintEmployees` with the array of `SalariedEmployee` objects, because that array implements the interface `IEnumerable<SalariedEmployee>` and because a `SalariedEmployee` *is an* `Employee` and because `IEnumerable<T>` is covariant. Covariance like this works *only* with *reference* types that are related by a class hierarchy.

### *Contravariance in Arrays*

Previously, we showed that an array of a derived-class type (salariedEmployees) can be assigned to an array variable of a base-class type (employees). Now, consider the following statement, which has *always* compiled in C#:

```
SalariedEmployee[] salariedEmployees2 =
   (SalariedEmployee[]) employees;
```

Based on the previous statements, we know that the Employee array variable employees currently refers to an array of SalariedEmployees. Using a cast operator to assign employees—an array of base-class-type elements—to salariedEmployees2—an array of derived-class-type elements—is an example of **contravariance**. The preceding cast will fail at runtime if employees is *not* an array of SalariedEmployees.

### *Contravariance in Generic Types*

To understand contravariance in generic types, consider a SortedSet of SalariedEmployees. Class **SortedSet<T>** maintains a set of objects in sorted order—no duplicates are allowed. The objects placed in a SortedSet must implement the **IComparable<T> interface**. For classes that do not implement this interface, you can still compare their objects using an object that implements the **IComparer<T> interface**. This interface's Compare method compares its two arguments and returns 0 if they're equal, a negative integer if the first object is less than the second, or a positive integer if the first object is greater than the second.

Our Employee hierarchy classes do not implement IComparable<T>. Let's assume we wish to sort Employees by social security number. We can implement the following class to compare any two Employees:

```
class EmployeeComparer : IComparer<Employee>
{
   int IComparer<Employee>.Compare(Employee a, Employee b)
   {
      return a.SocialSecurityNumber.CompareTo(
         b.SocialSecurityNumber);
   }
}
```

Method Compare returns the result of comparing the two Employees' social security numbers using string method CompareTo.

Now consider the following statement, which creates a SortedSet:

```
SortedSet<SalariedEmployee> set =
   new SortedSet<SalariedEmployee>(new EmployeeComparer());
```

When the type argument does *not* implement IComparable<T>, you must supply an appropriate IComparer<T> object to compare the objects that will be placed in the SortedSet. Since, we're creating a SortedSet of SalariedEmployees, the compiler expects the IComparer<T> object to implement the IComparer<SalariedEmployee>. Instead, we provided an object that implements IComparer<Employee>. The compiler allows us to provide an IComparer for a base-class type where an IComparer for a derived-class type is expected because interface IComparer<T> supports contravariance.

*Web Resources*
For a list of covariant and contravariant interface types, visit

```
https://msdn.microsoft.com/library/dd799517#VariantList
```

It's also possible to create your own types that support covariance and contravariance. For information, visit

```
https://msdn.microsoft.com/library/mt654058
```

## 19.14 Wrap-Up

This chapter introduced the prepackaged collection classes provided by the .NET Framework. We presented the hierarchy of interfaces that many of the collection classes implement, overviewed many of the implementation classes and introduced enumerators that enable programs to iterate through collections.

We discussed the .NET Framework namespaces dedicated to collections, including `System.Collections` for `object`-based collections and `System.Collections.Generic` for generic collections—such as the `List<T>`, `LinkedList<T>`, `Dictionary<K,V>` and `SortedDictionary<K,V>` classes—that store objects of types you specify when you create the collection. We also mentioned the namespace `System.Collections.Concurrent` containing so-called thread-safe generic collections for use in multithreaded applications, and `System.Collections.Specialized` containing collections that are optimized for specific scenarios, such as manipulating collections of bits.

You saw how to use class `Array` to perform array manipulations. We continued our discussion of delegates that hold references to methods and introduced lambda expressions, which allow you to define anonymous methods that can be used with delegates. We focused on using lambdas to pass method references to methods that specify delegate parameters.

We provided a brief introduction to functional programming, showing how to use it to write code more concisely and with fewer bugs than programs written with previous techniques. In particular, we used LINQ extension methods and lambdas to implement functional operations that manipulated lists of values.

In Chapter 20, we begin our discussion of databases, which organize data in such a way that the data can be selected and updated quickly. We introduce the ADO.NET Entity Framework and LINQ to Entities, which allow you to write LINQ queries that are used to query databases.

# 20

# Databases and LINQ

## Objectives

In this chapter you'll:

- Be introduced to the relational database model.
- Use an ADO.NET Entity Data Model to create classes for interacting with a database via LINQ to Entities.
- Use LINQ to retrieve and manipulate data from a database.
- Add data sources to projects.
- Use the IDE's drag-and-drop capabilities to display database tables in apps.
- Use data binding to move data seamlessly between GUI controls and databases.
- Create Master/Detail views that enable you to select a record and display its details.

Outline



## 20.1 Introduction

A **database** is an organized collection of data. A **database management system (DBMS)** provides mechanisms for storing, organizing, retrieving and modifying data. Many of today's most popular DBMSs manage *relational databases*, which organize data simply as tables with *rows* and *columns*.

Some popular proprietary DBMSs are Microsoft SQL Server, Oracle, Sybase and IBM DB2. PostgreSQL, MariaDB and MySQL are popular *open-source* DBMSs that can be downloaded and used *freely* by anyone. In this chapter, we use a version of Microsoft's SQL Server that's installed with Visual Studio. It also can be downloaded separately from

```
https://www.microsoft.com/en-us/server-cloud/products/sql-server-
editions/sql-server-express.aspx
```

### *SQL Server Express*

SQL Server Express provides many features of Microsoft's full (fee-based) SQL Server product, but has some limitations, such as a maximum database size of 10GB. A SQL Server Express database file can be easily migrated to a full version of SQL Server. You can learn more about the SQL Server versions at

```
https://www.microsoft.com/en-us/server-cloud/products/sql-server-
editions/overview.aspx
```

The version of SQL Server bundled with Visual Studio Community is called **SQL Server Express LocalDB**. It's meant for development and testing of apps on your computer.

### *Structured Query Language (SQL)*

A language called **Structured Query Language** (SQL)—pronounced "sequel"—is an international standard used with relational databases to perform **queries** (that is, to request information that satisfies given criteria) and to manipulate data. For years, programs that accessed a relational database passed SQL queries as `strings` to the database management system, then processed the results.

### *LINQ to Entities and the ADO.NET Entity Framework*

A logical extension of querying and manipulating data in databases is to perform similar operations on *any* sources of data, such as arrays, collections (like the `Items` collection of a `ListBox`) and files. Chapter 9 introduced *LINQ to Objects* and used it to manipulate data stored in arrays. **LINQ to Entities** allows you to manipulate data stored in a relational database—in our case, a SQL Server Express database. As with LINQ to Objects, the IDE provides *IntelliSense* for your LINQ to Entities queries.

The **ADO.NET Entity Framework** (**EF**) enables apps to interact with data in various forms, including data stored in relational databases. You'll use the ADO.NET Entity Framework and Visual Studio to create a so-called *entity data model* that represents the database, then use LINQ to Entities to manipulate objects in the entity data model. Though you'll manipulate data in a *SQL Server Express* database in this chapter, the ADO.NET Entity Framework works with *most* popular database management systems. Behind the scenes, the ADO.NET Entity Framework generates SQL statements that interact with a database.

This chapter introduces general concepts of relational databases, then implements several database apps using the ADO.NET Entity Framework, LINQ to Entities and the IDE's tools for working with databases. Databases are at the heart of most "industrial strength" apps.

## 20.2 Relational Databases

A **relational database** organizes data in **tables**. Figure 20.1 illustrates a sample `Employees` table that might be used in a personnel system. The table stores the attributes of employees. Tables are composed of **rows** (also called records) and **columns** (also called **fields**) in which values are stored. This table consists of six rows (one per employee) and five columns (one per attribute). The attributes are the employee's

- ID,
- name,
- department,
- salary and
- location.

The `ID` column of each row is the table's **primary key**—a column (or group of columns) requiring a *unique* value that cannot be duplicated in other rows. This guarantees that each primary-key value can be used to identify *one* row. A primary key composed of two or more columns is known as a **composite key**—in this case, every combination of column values in the composite key must be unique. Good examples of primary-key columns in other apps are a book's ISBN number in a book information system or a part number in an inventory system—values in each of these columns must be unique. We show an example of a composite primary key in Section 20.3. LINQ to Entities *requires every table to have a primary key* to support updating the data in tables. The rows in

| Number | Name | Department | Salary | Location |
|---|---|---|---|---|
| 23603 | Jones | 413 | 1100 | New Jersey |
| 24568 | Kerwin | 413 | 2000 | New Jersey |
| 34589 | Larson | 642 | 1800 | Los Angeles |
| 35761 | Myers | 611 | 1400 | Orlando |
| 47132 | Neumann | 413 | 9000 | New Jersey |
| 78321 | Stephens | 611 | 8500 | Orlando |

Row; Primary key; Column

**Fig. 20.1** | `Employees` table sample data.

Fig. 20.1 are displayed in *ascending order* by primary key. But they could be listed in *descending order* or in no particular order at all.

Each *column* represents a different data *attribute*. Some column values may be duplicated between rows. For example, three different rows in the `Employees` table's `Department` column contain the number 413, indicating that these employees work in the same department.

*Selecting Data Subsets*

You can use LINQ to Entities to define queries that *select subsets* of the data from a table. For example, a program might select data from the `Employees` table to create a query result that shows where each department is located, in ascending order by `Department` number (Fig. 20.2).

| Department | Location |
|---|---|
| 413 | New Jersey |
| 611 | Orlando |
| 642 | Los Angeles |

**Fig. 20.2** | Distinct `Department` and `Location` data from the `Employees` table.

## 20.3 A Books Database

We now consider a simple `Books` database that stores information about some Deitel books. First, we overview the database's tables. A database's tables, their fields and the relationships among them are collectively known as a **database schema**. The ADO.NET Entity Framework uses a database's schema to define classes that enable you to interact with the database. Sections 20.5–20.8 show how to manipulate the `Books` database. The database file—`Books.mdf`—is provided with this chapter's examples. SQL Server database files have the `.mdf` ("master data file") filename extension.

***`Authors`* *Table***

The database consists of three tables: `Authors`, `Titles` and `AuthorISBN`. The `Authors` table (described in Fig. 20.3) consists of three columns that maintain each author's unique

ID number, first name and last name, respectively. Figure 20.4 contains the sample data from the `Authors` table.

| Column | Description |
|---|---|
| `AuthorID` | Author's ID number in the database. In the `Books` database, this integer column is defined as an **identity** column, also known as an **autoincremented** column—for each row inserted in the table, the `AuthorID` value is increased by 1 automatically to ensure that each row has a unique `AuthorID`. This is the *primary key*. |
| `FirstName` | Author's first name (a string). |
| `LastName` | Author's last name (a string). |

**Fig. 20.3** | `Authors` table of the `Books` database.

| AuthorID | FirstName | LastName |
|---|---|---|
| 1 | Paul | Deitel |
| 2 | Harvey | Deitel |
| 3 | Abbey | Deitel |
| 4 | Sue | Green |
| 4 | John | Purple |

**Fig. 20.4** | Data from the `Authors` table.

### `Titles` *Table*

The `Titles` table (described in Fig. 20.5) consists of four columns that maintain information about each book in the database, including its ISBN, title, edition number and copyright year. Figure 20.6 contains the data from the `Titles` table.

| Column | Description |
|---|---|
| `ISBN` | ISBN of the book (a string). The table's primary key. ISBN is an abbreviation for "International Standard Book Number"—a numbering scheme that publishers worldwide use to give every book a *unique* identification number. |
| `Title` | Title of the book (a string). |
| `EditionNumber` | Edition number of the book (an integer). |
| `Copyright` | Copyright year of the book (a string). |

**Fig. 20.5** | `Titles` table of the `Books` database.

| ISBN | Title | EditionNumber | Copyright |
|---|---|---|---|
| 0132151006 | Internet & World Wide Web How to Program | 5 | 2012 |
| 0133807800 | Java How to Program | 10 | 2015 |
| 0132575655 | Java How to Program, Late Objects Version | 10 | 2015 |
| 0133976890 | C How to Program | 8 | 2016 |
| 0133406954 | Visual Basic 2012 How to Program | 6 | 2014 |
| 0134601548 | Visual C# How to Program | 6 | 2017 |
| 0134448235 | C++ How to Program | 10 | 2016 |
| 0134444302 | Android How to Program | 3 | 2016 |
| 0134289366 | Android 6 for Programmers: An App-Driven Approach | 3 | 2016 |
| 0133965260 | iOS 8 for Programmers: An App-Driven Approach with Swift | 3 | 2015 |
| 0134021363 | Swift for Programmers | 1 | 2015 |

**Fig. 20.6** | Data from the `Titles` table of the `Books` database.

### *`AuthorISBN` Table of the `Books` Database*

The `AuthorISBN` table (described in Fig. 20.7) consists of two columns that maintain ISBNs for each book and their corresponding authors' ID numbers. This table associates authors with their books. The `AuthorID` column is a **foreign key**—a column in this table that matches the primary-key column in another table (that is, `AuthorID` in the `Authors` table). The `ISBN` column is also a *foreign key*—it matches the primary-key column (that is, `ISBN`) in the `Titles` table. A database might consist of many tables. A goal of a database's designer is to minimize the amount of duplicated data among the database's tables. Foreign keys, which are specified when a database table is created in the database, link the data in multiple tables. Together the `AuthorID` and `ISBN` columns in this table form a *composite primary key*. Every row in this table *uniquely* matches *one* author to *one* book's ISBN. Figure 20.8 contains the data from the `AuthorISBN` table of the `Books` database.

| Column | Description |
|---|---|
| `AuthorID` | The author's ID number, a foreign key to the `Authors` table. |
| `ISBN` | The ISBN for a book, a foreign key to the `Titles` table. |

**Fig. 20.7** | `AuthorISBN` table of the `Books` database.

| AuthorID | ISBN | AuthorID | ISBN |
|---|---|---|---|
| 1 | 0132151006 | 1 | 0132575655 |
| 1 | 0133807800 | 1 | 0133976890 |

**Fig. 20.8** | Data from the `AuthorISBN` table of the `Books` database. (Part 1 of 2.)

| AuthorID | ISBN | AuthorID | ISBN |
|---|---|---|---|
| 1 | 0133406954 | 2 | 0133406954 |
| 1 | 0134601548 | 2 | 0134601548 |
| 1 | 0134448235 | 2 | 0134448235 |
| 1 | 0134444302 | 2 | 0134444302 |
| 1 | 0134289366 | 2 | 0134289366 |
| 1 | 0133965260 | 2 | 0133965260 |
| 1 | 0134021363 | 2 | 0134021363 |
| 2 | 0132151006 | 3 | 0132151006 |
| 2 | 0133807800 | 3 | 0133406954 |
| 2 | 0132575655 | 4 | 0134289366 |
| 2 | 0133976890 | 5 | 0134289366 |

**Fig. 20.8** | Data from the `AuthorISBN` table of the `Books` database. (Part 2 of 2.)

Every foreign-key value must appear as another table's primary-key value so the DBMS can ensure that the foreign key value is valid. For example, the DBMS ensures that the `AuthorID` value for any particular row of the `AuthorISBN` table (Fig. 20.8) is valid by checking that there is a row in the `Authors` table with that `AuthorID` as the primary key.

Foreign keys also allow related data in multiple tables to be selected from those tables—this is known as **joining** the data. There's a **one-to-many relationship** between a primary key and a corresponding foreign key—e.g., an author can write many books and a book can be written by many authors. So a foreign key can appear many times in its own table but only *once* (as the primary key) in another table. For example, the `ISBN 0132151006` can appear in several rows of `AuthorISBN` but only once in `Titles`, where `ISBN` is the primary key.

### *Entity-Relationship Diagram for the* **Books** *Database*

Figure 20.9 is an **entity-relationship (ER) diagram** for the `Books` database. This diagram shows the tables in the database and the relationships among them.

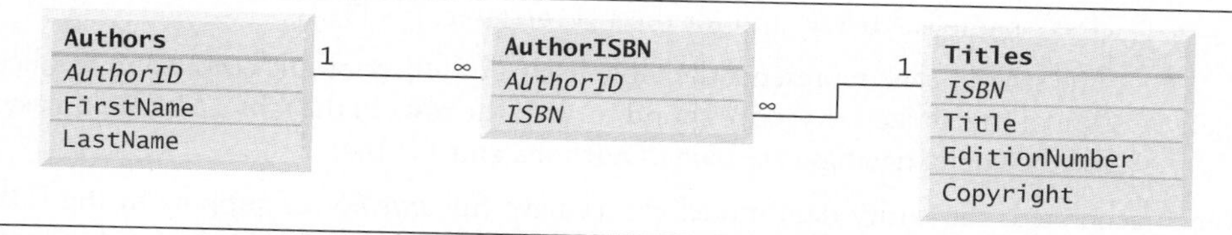


**Fig. 20.9** | Entity-relationship diagram for the `Books` database.

### *Primary Keys*

The first compartment in each box contains the table's name. The names in italic font are *primary keys*—*`AuthorID`* in the `Authors` table, `AuthorID` and `ISBN` in the `AuthorISBN` table, and `ISBN` in the `Titles` table. Every row *must* have a value in the primary-key column (or group of columns), and the value of the key must be *unique* in the table; otherwise, the DBMS will report an error. The names `AuthorID` and `ISBN` in the `AuthorISBN` table are both italic—together these form a *composite primary key* for the `AuthorISBN` table.

*Relationships Between Tables*
The lines connecting the tables in Fig. 20.9 represent the *relationships* among the tables. Consider the line between the `Authors` and `AuthorISBN` tables. On the `Authors` end of the line, there's a `1`, and on the `AuthorISBN` end, an infinity symbol (∞). This indicates a *one-to-many relationship*—for each author in the `Authors` table, there can be an arbitrary number of ISBNs for books written by that author in the `AuthorISBN` table (that is, an author can write any number of books). Note that the relationship line links the `AuthorID` column in the `Authors` table (where `AuthorID` is the primary key) to the `AuthorID` column in the `AuthorISBN` table (where `AuthorID` is a foreign key)—the line between the tables links the primary key to the matching foreign key.

The line between the `Titles` and `AuthorISBN` tables illustrates a *one-to-many relationship*—one book can be written by many authors. Note that the line between the tables links the *primary key* `ISBN` in the `Titles` table to the corresponding *foreign key* in the `AuthorISBN` table. Figure 20.9 illustrates that the sole purpose of the `AuthorISBN` table is to provide a **many-to-many relationship** between the `Authors` and `Titles` tables—an author can write many books, and a book can have many authors.

## 20.4 LINQ to Entities and the ADO.NET Entity Framework

When using the ADO.NET Entity Framework, you interact with the database via classes that the IDE generates from the database schema. You'll initiate this process by adding a new **ADO.NET Entity Data Model** to your project (as you'll see in Section 20.5.1).

*Classes Generated in the Entity Data Model*
For the `Authors` and `Titles` tables in the `Books` database, the IDE creates two classes each in the data model:

- The first class represents a row of the table and contains properties for each column in the table. Objects of this class—called **row objects**—store the data from individual rows of the table. The IDE uses the singular version of a table's plural name as the row class's name. For the `Books` database's `Authors` table, the row class's name is `Author`, and for the `Titles` table, it's `Title`.
- The second class represents the table itself. An object of this class stores a collection of row objects that correspond to all of the rows in the table. The table classes for the `Books` database are named `Authors` and `Titles`.

Once generated, the entity data model classes have full *IntelliSense* support in the IDE. Section 20.7 demonstrates queries that use the relationships among the `Books` database's tables to join data.

*Relationships Between Tables in the Entity Data Model*
You'll notice that we did not mention the `Books` database's `AuthorISBN` table. Recall that this table links

- each author in the `Authors` table to that author's books in the `Titles` table, and
- each book in the `Titles` table to the book's authors in the `Authors` table.

The entity data model's generated classes include the relationships between tables. For example, the `Author` row class contains a **navigation property** named `Titles` which provides access to the `Title` objects representing all the books written by that author. The IDE automatically adds the "`s`" to "`Title`" to indicate that this property represents a collection of `Title` objects. Similarly, the `Title` row class contains a navigation property named `Authors`, which provides access to the `Author` objects representing a given book's authors.

### *`DbContext` Class*

A **`DbContext`** (namespace **`System.Data.Entity`**) manages the data flow between the program and the database. When the IDE generates the *entity data model's* row and table classes, it also creates a derived class of `DbContext` that's specific to the database being manipulated. For the `Books` database, this derived class has properties for the `Authors` and `Titles` tables. As you'll see, these can be used as data sources for manipulating data in LINQ queries and in GUIs. Any changes made to the data managed by the `DbContext` can be saved back to the database using the `DbContext`'s **`SaveChanges` method**.

### *`IQueryable<T>` Interface*

LINQ to Entities works through interface **`IQueryable<T>`**, which inherits from interface `IEnumerable<T>` introduced in Chapter 9. When a LINQ to Entities query on an `IQueryable<T>` object executes against the database, the results are loaded into objects of the corresponding entity data model classes for convenient access in your code.

### *Using Extension Methods to Manipulate `IQueryable<T>` Objects*

Recall that extension methods add functionality to an existing class without modifying the class's source code. In Chapter 9, we introduced several LINQ extension methods, including `First`, `Any`, `Count`, `Distinct`, `ToArray` and `ToList`. These methods, which are defined as `static` methods of class `Enumerable` (namespace `System.Linq`), can be applied to any object that implements the `IEnumerable<T>` interface, such as arrays, collections and the results of LINQ to Objects queries.

In this chapter, we use a combination of the LINQ query syntax and LINQ extension methods to manipulate database contents. The extension methods we use are defined as `static` methods of class **`Queryable`** (namespace `System.Linq`) and can be applied to any object that implements the `IQueryable<T>` interface—these include various entity data model objects and the results of LINQ to Entities queries.

## 20.5 Querying a Database with LINQ

In this section, we demonstrate how to

- *connect* to a database,
- *query* it and
- *display* the results of the query.

There is little code in this section—the IDE provides *visual programming* tools and *wizards* that simplify accessing data in apps. These tools establish database connections and create the objects necessary to view and manipulate the data through Windows `Forms` GUI controls—a technique known as **data binding**.

For the examples in Sections 20.5–20.8, we'll create one solution that contains *several* projects. One will be a reusable class library containing the ADO.NET Entity Data Model for interacting with the `Books` database. The other projects will be Windows `Forms` apps that use the ADO.NET Entity Data Model in the class library to manipulate the database.

Our first example performs a simple query on the `Books` database from Section 20.3. We retrieve the entire `Authors` table, ordered by the authors' last name, then first name. We then use data binding to display the data in a **`DataGridView`**—a control from namespace `System.Windows.Forms` that can display data from a data source in tabular format. The basic steps we'll perform are:

- Create the ADO.NET entity data model classes for manipulating the database.
- Add the entity data model object that represents the `Authors` table as a data source.
- Drag the `Authors` table data source onto the **Design** view to create a GUI for displaying the table's data.
- Add code that allows the app to interact with the database.

The GUI for the program is shown in Fig. 20.10. All of the controls in this GUI are automatically generated when we drag a *data source* that represents the `Authors` table onto the `Form` in **Design** view. The **`BindingNavigator`** toolbar at the top of the window is a collection of controls that allow you to navigate through the records in the `DataGridView` that fills the rest of the window.

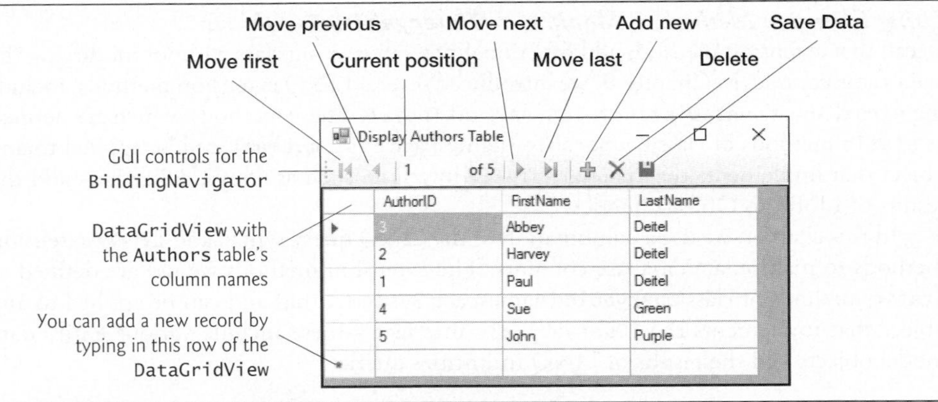


**Fig. 20.10** | GUI for the **Display Authors Table** app.

The `BindingNavigator`'s controls help you add records, delete records, modify existing records and save your changes to the database. You can add a new record by pressing the **Add new** button

then entering the new author's first and last name in the `DataGridView`. You can delete an existing record by selecting an author (either in the `DataGridView` or via the controls on the `BindingNavigator`) and pressing the **Delete** button

You can edit an existing record by clicking the first-name or last-name field for that record and typing the new value. To save your changes to the database, click the **Save Data** button 

Empty values are not allowed in the `Authors` table of the `Books` database, so if you attempt to save a record that does not contain a value for both the first name and last name, an exception occurs.

## 20.5.1 Creating the ADO.NET Entity Data Model Class Library

This section presents the steps required to create the entity data model from an existing database. A *model* describes the data that you'll be manipulating—in our case, the data represented by the tables in the `Books` database.

### *Step 1: Creating a Class Library Project for the ADO.NET Entity Data Model*

Select **File > New > Project…** to display the **New Project** dialog, then select **Class Library** from the **Visual C#** templates and name the project `BooksExamples`. Click **OK** to create the project, then delete the `Class1.cs` file from the **Solution Explorer**.

### *Step 2: Adding the ADO.NET Entity Data Model to the Class Library*

To interact with the database, you'll add an ADO.NET entity data model to the class library project. This will also configure the connection to the database.

1. *Adding the ADO.NET Entity Data Model.* Right click the `BooksExamples` project in the **Solution Explorer**, then select **Add > New Item…** to display the **Add New Item** dialog (Fig. 20.11). From the **Data** category select **ADO.NET Entity Data Model** and name the model `BooksModel`—this will be the name of a file (with the filename extension `.edmx`) that configures the entity data model. Click **Add** to add the entity data model to the class library and display the **Entity Data Model Wizard** dialog.

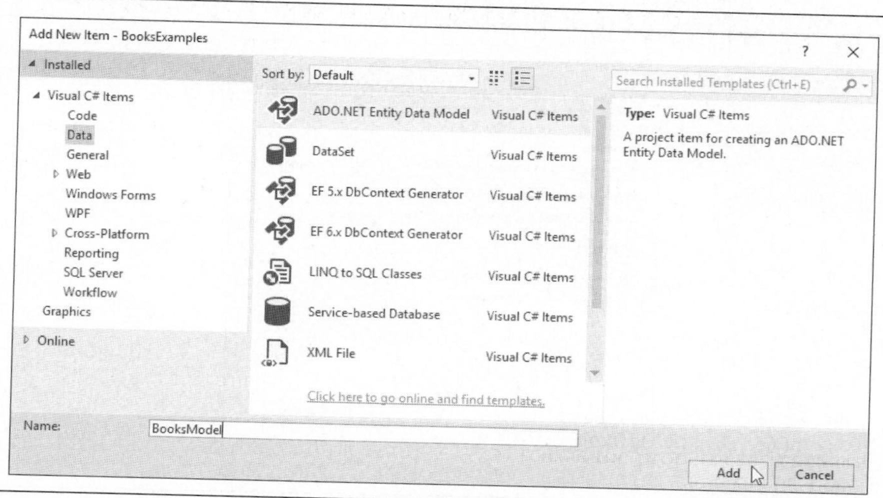


**Fig. 20.11** | Selecting **ADO.NET Entity Data Model** in the **Add New Item** Dialog.

2. *Choosing the Model Contents.* The **Choose Model Contents** step in the **Entity Data Model Wizard** dialog (Fig. 20.12) enables you to specify the entity data model's contents. The model in these examples will consist of data from the `Books` database, so select **EF Designer from database** and click **Next >** to display the **Choose Your Data Connection** step.

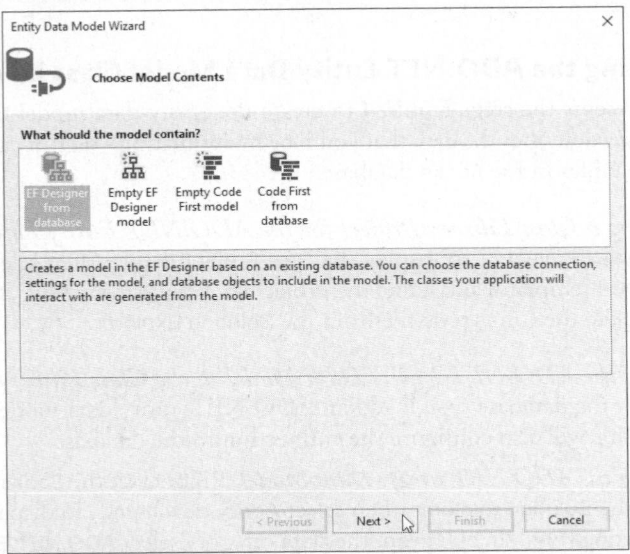


**Fig. 20.12** | **Entity Data Model Wizard** dialog's **Choose Model Contents** step.

3. *Choosing the Data Connection.* In the **Choose Your Data Connection** step, click **New Connection...** to display the **Connection Properties** dialog (Fig. 20.13). (If

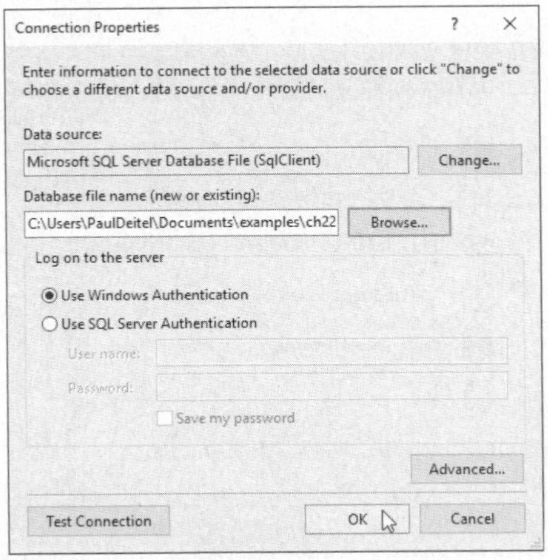

**Fig. 20.13** | **Connection Properties** dialog.

the IDE displays a **Choose Data Source** dialog, select **Microsoft SQL Server Database File** and click **Continue**.) For the **Data source** field, if **Microsoft SQL Server Database File (SqlClient)** is not displayed, click **Change...**, select **Microsoft SQL Server Database File (SqlClient)** and click **OK**. Next, click **Browse...** to the right of the **Database file name** field to locate and select the `Books.mdf` file in the `Databases` directory included with this chapter's examples. You can click **Test Connection** to verify that the IDE can connect to the database through SQL Server Express. Click **OK** to create the connection. Figure 20.14 shows the **Connection string** for the `Books.mdf` database. This contains the information that the ADO.NET Entity Framework requires to connect to the database at runtime. Click **Next >**. A dialog will appear asking if you'd like to add the database file to your project. Click **Yes** to move to the next step.

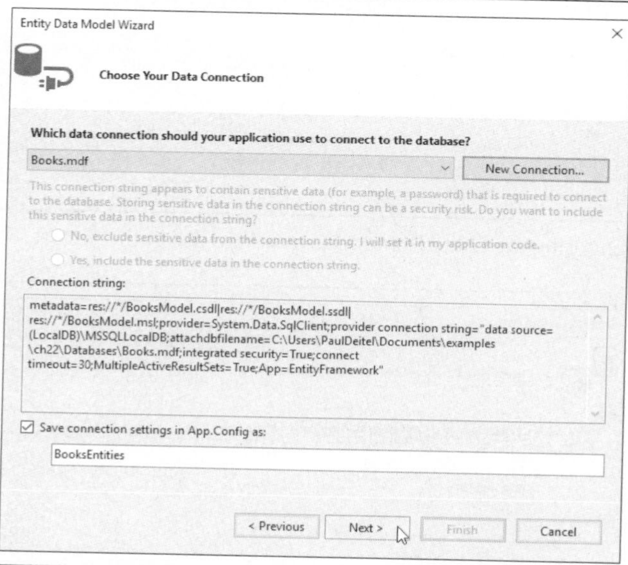


**Fig. 20.14** | **Choose Your Data Connection** step after selecting `Books.mdf`.

4. *Choosing the Entity Framework Version.* In the **Choose Your Version** step, select the **Entity Framework 6.x** (Fig. 20.15), then click **Next >**. This adds the latest version of the Entity Framework to your project.
5. *Choosing the Database Objects to Include in the Model.* In the **Choose Your Database Objects and Settings** step, you'll specify the parts of the database that should be used in the ADO.NET Entity Data Model. Select the **Tables** node as shown in Fig. 20.16, then click **Finish**. At this point, the IDE will download the Entity Framework 6.x templates you need and add them to your project. You may see one or more **Security Warning** dialogs—Visual Studio displays these when you attempt to use downloaded content in your projects. Click **OK** to dismiss each dialog. These warnings are intended primarily for cases in which a Visual Studio template is downloaded from an untrusted website.

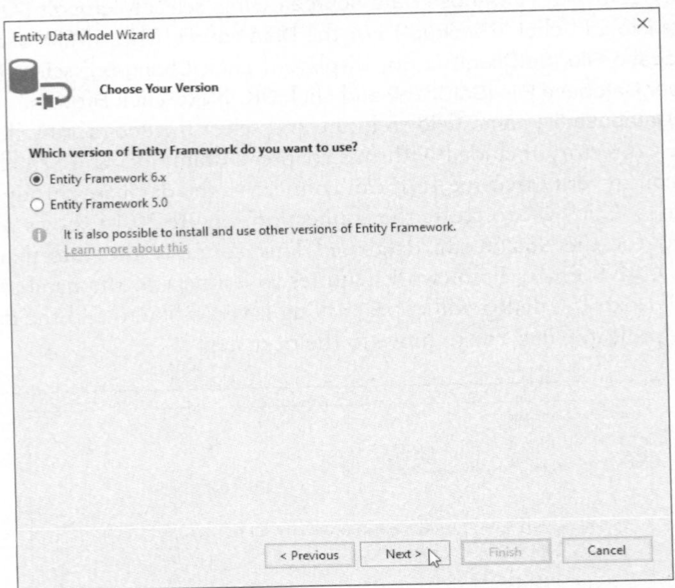


**Fig. 20.15** | Choosing the Entity Framework version to use in the project.

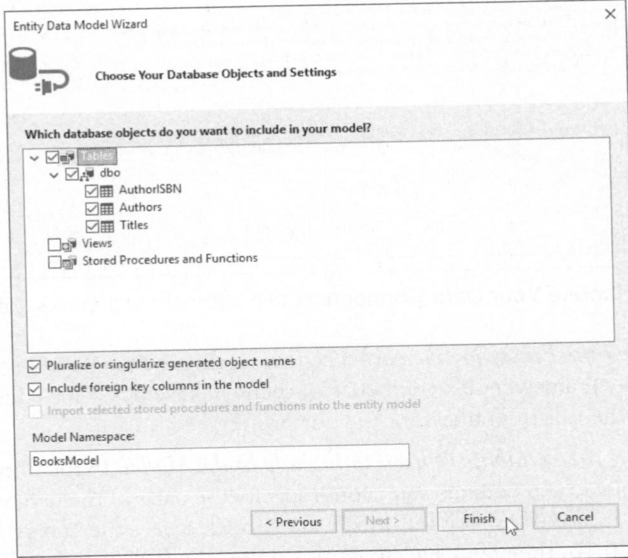


**Fig. 20.16** | Selecting the database's tables to include in the ADO.NET Entity Data Model.

6. ***Viewing the Entity Data Model Diagram in the Model Designer.*** At this point, the IDE creates the entity data model and displays a diagram (Fig. 20.17) in the *model designer*. The diagram contains **Author** and **Title** *entities*—these represent

authors and titles in the database and the properties of each. Notice that the IDE renamed the `Title` column of the `Titles` table as `Title1` to avoid a naming conflict with the class `Title` that represents a row in the table. The line between the entities indicates a relationship between authors and titles—this relationship is implemented in the `Books` database as the `AuthorISBN` table. The asterisk (*) at each end of the line indicates a *many-to-many relationship*—each author can author many titles and each title can have many authors. The **Navigation Properties** section in the **Author** entity contains the **Titles** property, which connects an author to all titles written by that author. Similarly, the **Navigation Properties** section in the **Title** entity contains the **Authors** property, which connects a title to all of its authors.

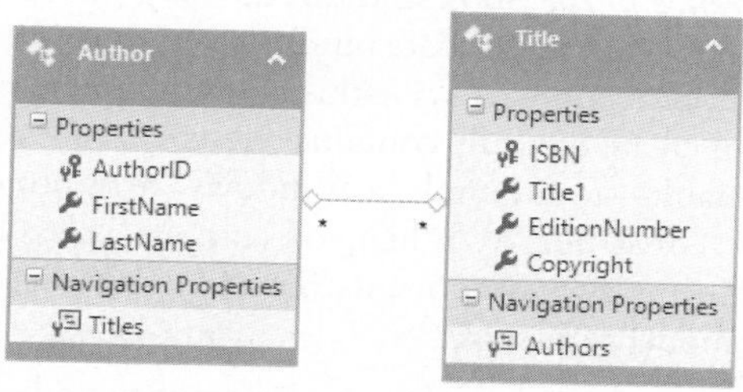


**Fig. 20.17** | Entity data model diagram for the **Author** and **Title** entities.

7. ***Building the Class Library.*** Select **Build > Build Solution** to build the class library that you'll reuse in the next several examples—this will compile the entity data model classes that were generated by the IDE.[1] When you build the class library, the IDE generates the classes that you can use to interact with the database. These include a class for each table you selected from the database and a derived class of `DbContext` named `BooksEntities` that enables you to programmatically interact with the database—the IDE created the name `BooksEntities` (Fig. 20.14) by adding `Entities` to the database file's base name (`Books` in `Books.mdf`). Building the project causes the IDE to execute a script that creates and compiles the entity data model classes.

## 20.5.2 Creating a Windows Forms Project and Configuring It to Use the Entity Data Model

Recall that the next several examples will all be part of *one* solution containing several projects—the class library project with our reusable model and individual Windows `Forms` apps for each example. In this section, you'll create a new Windows `Forms` app and configure it to be able to use the entity data model that you created in the preceding section.

### *Step 1: Creating the Project*

To add a new Windows Forms project to the existing solution:

1. If you get an error message indicating that the IDE can't copy the `.mdf` file to the `bin\Debug` folder because it's in use, close Visual Studio, then reopen the project and try to build the solution again.

1. Right click **Solution 'BooksExamples'** (the solution name) in **Solution Explorer** and select **Add > New Project...** to display the **Add New Project** dialog.
2. Select **Windows Forms Application** from the **Visual C# > Windows > Classic Desktop** category, name the project `DisplayTable` and click **OK**.
3. Change the name of the `Form1.cs` source file to `DisplayAuthorsTable.cs`. The IDE updates the `Form`'s class name to match the source file. Set the `Form`'s **Text** property to `Display Authors Table`.
4. Right click the `DisplayTable` project's name in the **Solution Explorer**, then select **Set as Startup Project** to configure the solution so that project `DisplayTable` will execute when you select **Debug > Start Debugging** (or press *F5*).

### *Step 2: Adding a Reference to the* `BooksExamples` *Class Library*

To use the entity data model classes for data binding, you must first add a reference to the class library you created in Section 20.5.1—this allows the new project to use that class library. Each project you create typically contains references to several .NET class libraries (called *assemblies*) by default—for example, a Windows `Forms` project contains a reference to the `System.Windows.Forms` library. When you compile a class library, the IDE creates a `.dll` file containing the library's components. To add a reference to the class library containing the entity data model's classes:

1. Right click the `DisplayTable` project's **References** node in the **Solution Explorer** and select **Add Reference....**
2. In the left column of the **Reference Manager** dialog that appears, select **Projects** to display the other projects in this solution, then in center of the dialog ensure that the checkbox next to `BooksExamples` is checked and click **OK**. `BooksExamples` should now appear in the projects **References** node.

### *Step 3: Adding a Reference to* `EntityFramework`

You'll also need a reference to the `EntityFramework` library to use the ADO.NET Entity Framework. This library was added by the IDE to the `BooksExamples` class library project when we created the entity data model, but you also must add the `EntityFramework` library to each app that will use the entity data model. To add an `EntityFramework` library reference to a project:

1. Right click the project's name in the **Solution Explorer** and select **Manage NuGet Packages...** to display the **NuGet** tab in Visual Studio's editors area. **NuGet** is a tool (known as a *package manager*) that that helps you download and manage libraries (known as *packages*) used by your projects.
2. In the dialog that appears, click **Browse**, then select the **EntityFramework by Microsoft** and click **Install** (Fig. 20.18).
3. The IDE will ask you to review the changes. Click **OK**.
4. The IDE will ask you to accept the `EntityFramework` license. Click **I Accept** to complete the installation.

`EntityFramework` should now appear in the projects **References** node. You can now close the **NuGet** tab.

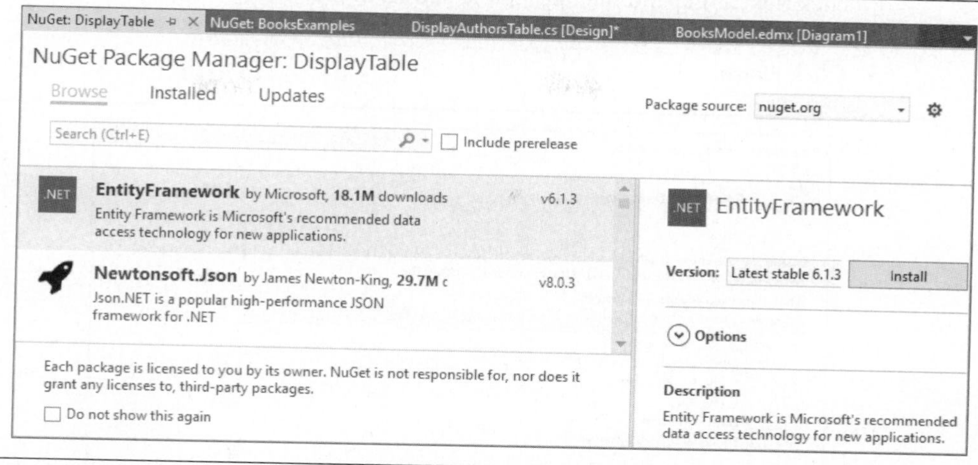


**Fig. 20.18** | Selecting and installing the **EntityFramework** in the **NuGet** tab.

*Step 4: Adding the Connection String to the Windows Forms App*

Each app that will use the entity data model also requires the *connection string* that tells the Entity Framework how to connect to the database. The connection string is stored in the `BooksExamples` class library's `App.Config` file. In the **Solution Explorer**, open the `BooksExamples` class library's `App.Config` file, then copy the `connectionStrings` element (lines 7–9 in our file), which has the format:

```
<connectionStrings>
    Connection string information appears here
</connectionStrings>
```

Next, open the `App.Config` file in the `DisplayTable` project and paste the connection string information *after* the line containing `</entityFramework>` and *before* the line containing `</configuration>`. Save, then close the `App.Config` file.

### 20.5.3 Data Bindings Between Controls and the Entity Data Model

You'll now use the IDE's drag-and-drop GUI design capabilities to create the GUI for interacting with the `Books` database. You must write a small amount of code to enable the autogenerated GUI to interact with the entity data model. You'll now perform the steps to display the contents of the `Authors` table in a GUI.

*Step 1: Adding a Data Source for the* `Authors` *Table*

To use the entity data model classes for data binding, you must first add them as a *data source*. To do so:

1. Select **View > Other Windows > Data Sources** to display the **Data Sources window** at the left side of the IDE, then in that window click the **Add New Data Source...** link to display the **Data Source Configuration Wizard**.
2. The Entity Data Model classes are used to create *objects* representing the tables in the database, so we'll use an **Object data source**. In the dialog, select **Object** and

click **Next >**. Expand the tree view as shown in Fig. 20.19 and ensure that **Author** is checked. An object of this class will be this app's *data source*.

3. Click **Finish**.

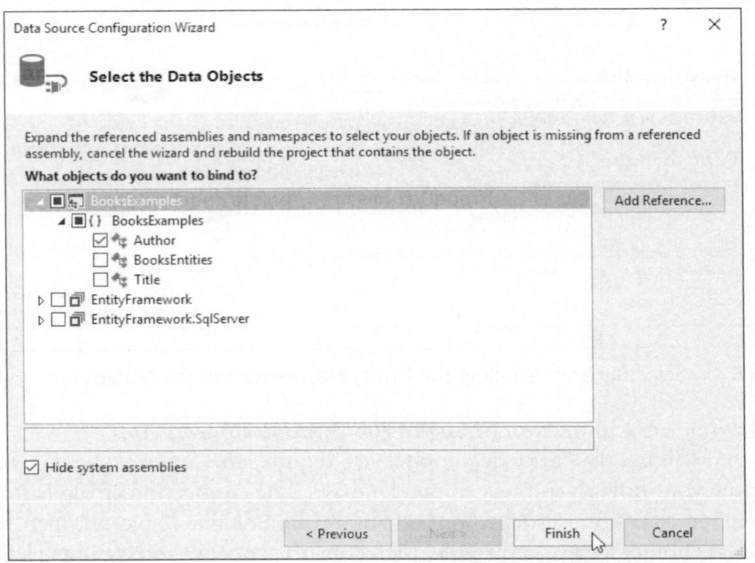


**Fig. 20.19** | Selecting the Entity Data Model class `Author` as the data source.

The `Authors` table in the database is now a data source that can be bound to a GUI control that obtains author data automatically. In the **Data Sources** window (Fig. 20.20), you can see the `Author` class that you added in the previous step. We expanded the node to show `Author`'s properties, representing columns of the database's `Authors` table, as well as the `Titles` navigation property, representing the relationship between the database's `Authors` and `Titles` tables.

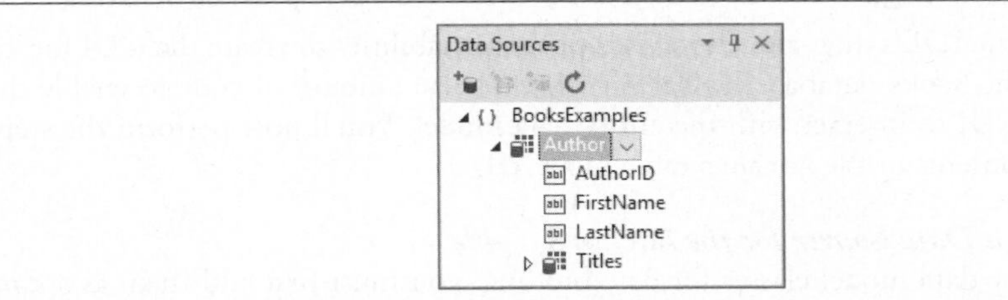


**Fig. 20.20** | **Data Sources** window showing the expanded `Author` class as a data source.

### *Step 2: Creating GUI Elements*

Next, you'll use the **Design** view to create a `DataGridView` control that can display the `Authors` table's data. To do so:

1. Switch to **Design** view for the `DisplayAuthorsTable` class.

2. Click the **Author** node in the **Data Sources** window—it should change to a drop-down list. Open the drop-down by clicking the down arrow and ensure that the `DataGridView` option is selected—this is the GUI control that will be used to display and interact with the data.
3. Drag the **Author** node from the **Data Sources** window onto the `Form` in **Design** view. You'll need to resize the `Form` to fit the `DataGridView`.

The IDE creates a `DataGridView` (Fig. 20.21) with column names representing all the properties for an `Author`, including the `Titles` navigation property.

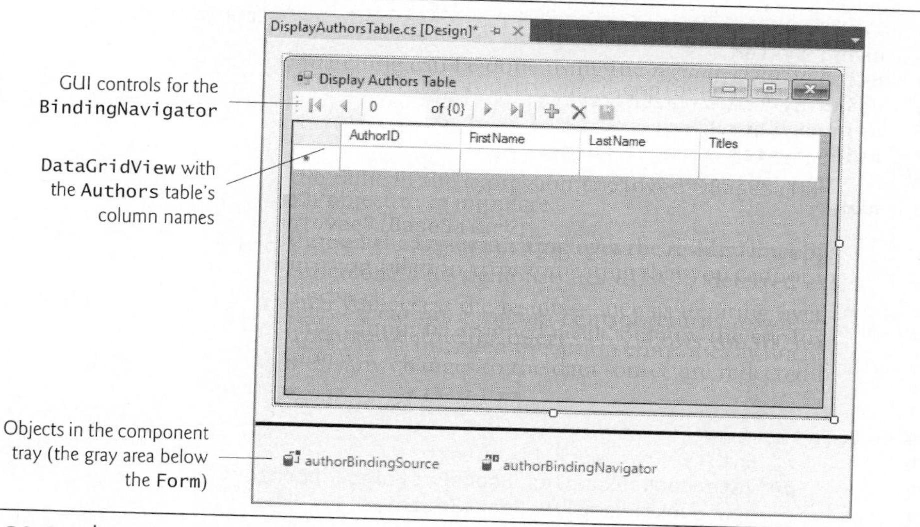


**Fig. 20.21** | Component tray holds nonvisual components in **Design** view.

The IDE also creates a **`BindingNavigator`** that contains `Buttons` for

- moving between entries,
- adding entries,
- deleting entries and
- saving changes to the database.

In addition, the IDE generates a **`BindingSource`** (`authorBindingSource`), which handles the transfer of data between the *data source* and the *data-bound controls* on the `Form`. Nonvisual components such as the `BindingSource` and the nonvisual aspects of the `BindingNavigator` appear in the *component tray*—the gray region below the `Form` in **Design** view. The IDE names the `BindingNavigator` and `BindingSource` (`authorBindingNavigator` and `authorBindingSource`, respectively) based on the data source's name (`Author`). We use the default names for automatically generated components throughout this chapter to show exactly what the IDE creates.

To make the `DataGridView` occupy the *entire* window below the `BindingNavigator`, select the `DataGridView`, then use the **Properties** window to set the `Dock` property to `Fill`. You can stretch the window horizontally to see all the `DataGridView` columns. We do not use the Titles column in this example, so right click the DataGridView and select **Edit Columns...** to display the **Edit Columns** dialog. Select **Titles** in the **Selected Columns** list, click **Remove** to remove that column, then click **OK**.

### *Step 3: Connecting the Data Source to the* authorBindingSource

The final step is to connect the data source to the authorBindingSource, so that the app can interact with the database. Figure 20.22 shows the code needed to obtain data from the database and to save any changes that the user makes to the data back into the database.

```
// Fig. 20.22: DisplayAuthorsTable.cs
// Displaying data from a database table in a DataGridView.
using System;
using System.Data.Entity;
using System.Data.Entity.Validation;
using System.Linq;
using System.Windows.Forms;

namespace DisplayTable
{
   public partial class DisplayAuthorsTable : Form
   {
      // constructor
      public DisplayAuthorsTable()
      {
         InitializeComponent();
      }

      // Entity Framework DbContext
      private BooksExamples.BooksEntities dbcontext =
         new BooksExamples.BooksEntities();

      // load data from database into DataGridView
      private void DisplayAuthorsTable_Load(object sender, EventArgs e)
      {
         // load Authors table ordered by LastName then FirstName
         dbcontext.Authors
            .OrderBy(author => author.LastName)
            .ThenBy(author => author.FirstName)
            .Load();

         // specify DataSource for authorBindingSource
         authorBindingSource.DataSource = dbcontext.Authors.Local;
      }

      // click event handler for the Save Button in the
      // BindingNavigator saves the changes made to the data
      private void authorBindingNavigatorSaveItem_Click(
         object sender, EventArgs e)
      {
         Validate(); // validate the input fields
         authorBindingSource.EndEdit(); // complete current edit, if any
```

**Fig. 20.22** | Displaying data from a database table in a DataGridView. (Part 1 of 2.)

```
43
44             // try to save changes
45             try
46             {
47                dbcontext.SaveChanges(); // write changes to database file
48             }
49             catch(DbEntityValidationException)
50             {
51                MessageBox.Show("FirstName and LastName must contain values",
52                   "Entity Validation Exception");
53             }
54          }
55       }
56    }
```

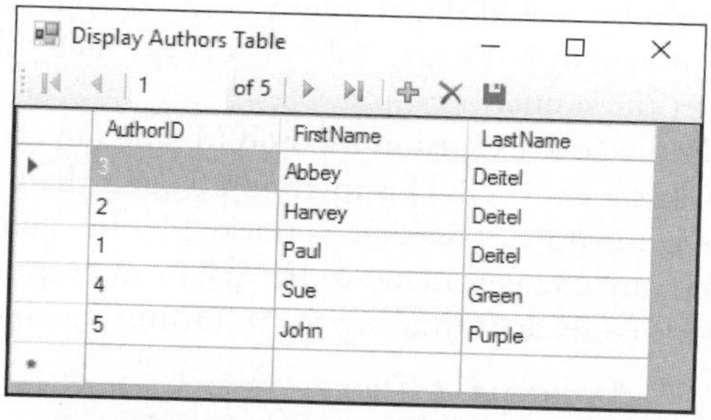

Display Authors Table

1 of 5

| | AuthorID | FirstName | LastName |
|---|---|---|---|
| ▶ | 3 | Abbey | Deitel |
| | 2 | Harvey | Deitel |
| | 1 | Paul | Deitel |
| | 4 | Sue | Green |
| | 5 | John | Purple |
| * | | | |

**Fig. 20.22** | Displaying data from a database table in a `DataGridView`. (Part 2 of 2.)

### *Creating the* `DbContext` *Object*

As mentioned in Section 20.4, a `DbContext` object interacts with the database on the app's behalf. The `BooksEntities` class (a derived class of `DbContext`) was automatically generated by the IDE when you created the entity data model classes to access the `Books` database (Section 20.5.1). Lines 20–21 create an object of this class named `dbcontext`.

### `DisplayAuthorsTable_Load` *Event Handler*

You can create the `Form`'s `Load` event handler (lines 24–34) by double clicking the `Form`'s title bar in **Design** view. In this app, we allow data to move between the `DbContext` and the database by using LINQ to Entities extension methods to extract data from the `BooksEntities`'s `Authors` property (lines 27–30), which corresponds to the `Authors` table in the database. The expression

```
dbcontext.Authors
```

indicates that we wish to get data from the `Authors` table.

The **`OrderBy` extension method** call

```
   .OrderBy(author => author.LastName)
```

indicates that the rows of the table should be retrieved in ascending order by the authors' last names. Extension method `OrderBy` receives as its argument a `Func` delegate (namespace `System`) representing a method that receives one parameter and returns a value that's used to order the results. In this case, we pass a lambda expression that defines an anonymous method in which

- the parameter `author` (an object of the `Author` entity data model class) is passed to the method, and
- the expression to the right of the lambda operator (=>)—the `author`'s `LastName` in this case—is implicitly returned by the method.

The lambda expression infers `author`'s type from `dbcontext.Authors`—which contains `Author` objects—and infers the lambda's return type (`string`) from `author.LastName`.

When there are multiple authors with the same last name, we'd like them to be listed in ascending order by first name as well. The **`ThenBy` extension method** call

```
.ThenBy(author => author.FirstName)
```

enables you to order results by an additional column. This is applied to the `Author` objects that have already been ordered by last name. Like `OrderBy`, `ThenBy` also receives a `Func` delegate that's used to order the results.

Finally, line 30 calls the **`Load` extension method** (defined in class **`DbExtensions`** from the namespace `System.Data.Entity`). This method executes the LINQ to Entities query and loads the results into memory. This data is tracked by the `BookEntities` `DbContext` in local memory so that any changes made to the data can eventually be saved into the database. Lines 27–30 are equivalent to using the following statement:

```
(from author in dbcontext.Authors
 orderby author.LastName, author.FirstName
 select author).Load();
```

Line 33 sets the `authorBindingSource`'s **`DataSource` property** to the `Local` property of the `dbcontext.Authors` object. In this case, the `Local` property is an `ObservableCollection<Author>` that represents the query results that were loaded into memory by lines 27–30. When a `BindingSource`'s `DataSource` property is assigned an **`ObservableCollection<T>`** (namespace `System.Collections.ObjectModel`), the GUI that's bound to the `BindingSource` is notified of any changes to the data so the GUI can be updated accordingly. In addition, changes made by the user to the data in the GUI will be tracked so the `DbContext` can eventually save those changes to the database.

### *`authorBindingNavigatorSaveItem_Click` Event Handler: Saving Modifications to the Database*

If the user modifies the data in the `DataGridView`, we'd also like to save the modifications in the database. By default, the `BindingNavigator`'s **Save Data** `Button`

is disabled. To enable it, right click this `Button`'s icon in the `BindingNavigator` and select **Enabled**. Then, double click the icon to create its `Click` event handler and add the code in the method's body (lines 41–53).

Saving the data entered in the `DataGridView` back to the database is a three-step process. First, the `Form`'s controls are validated (line 41) by calling the inherited `Validate` method—if any control has an event handler for the `Validating` event, it executes. You typically handle this event to determine whether a control's contents are valid. Next, line

42 calls **EndEdit** on the `authorBindingSource`, which forces it to save any pending changes into the `BooksEntities` model in memory. Finally, line 47 calls `SaveChanges` on the `BooksEntities` object (`dbcontext`) to store any changes into the database. We placed this call in a `try` statement, because the `Authors` table does not allow empty values for the first name and last name—these rules were configured when we originally created the database. When `SaveChanges` is called, any changes stored into the `Authors` table must satisfy the table's rules. If any do not, a `DBEntityValidationException` occurs.

## 20.6 Dynamically Binding Query Results

Next we show how to perform several different queries and display the results in a `DataGridView`. This app only reads data from the entity data model, so we disabled the buttons in the `BindingNavigator` that enable the user to add and delete records—simply select each button and set its **Enabled** property to `False` in the **Properties** window. You also could delete these buttons from the `BindingNavigator`. Later, we'll explain why we do not support modifying the database in this example.

The **Display Query Results** app (Figs. 20.23–20.25) allows the user to select a query from the `ComboBox` at the bottom of the window, then displays the results of the query.

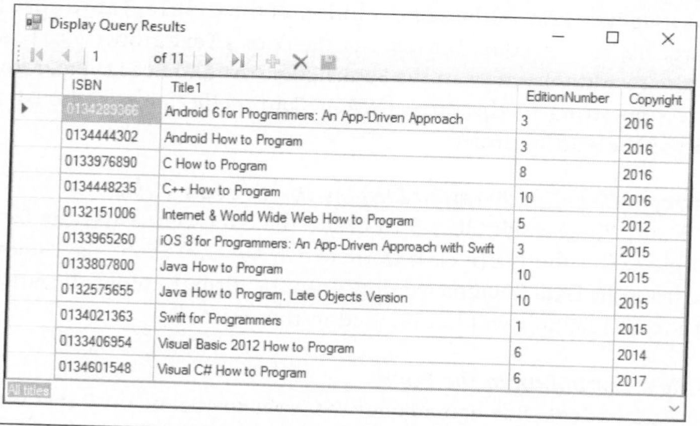

Display Query Results

1 of 11

| ISBN | Title1 | EditionNumber | Copyright |
|---|---|---|---|
| 0134289366 | Android 6 for Programmers: An App-Driven Approach | 3 | 2016 |
| 0134444302 | Android How to Program | 3 | 2016 |
| 0133976890 | C How to Program | 8 | 2016 |
| 0134448235 | C++ How to Program | 10 | 2016 |
| 0132151006 | Internet & World Wide Web How to Program | 5 | 2012 |
| 0133965260 | iOS 8 for Programmers: An App-Driven Approach with Swift | 3 | 2015 |
| 0133807800 | Java How to Program | 10 | 2015 |
| 0132575655 | Java How to Program, Late Objects Version | 10 | 2015 |
| 0134021363 | Swift for Programmers | 1 | 2015 |
| 0133406954 | Visual Basic 2012 How to Program | 6 | 2014 |
| 0134601548 | Visual C# How to Program | 6 | 2017 |

All titles

**Fig. 20.23** | Results of the **Display Query Results** app's **All titles** query, which shows the contents of the `Titles` table ordered by the book titles.

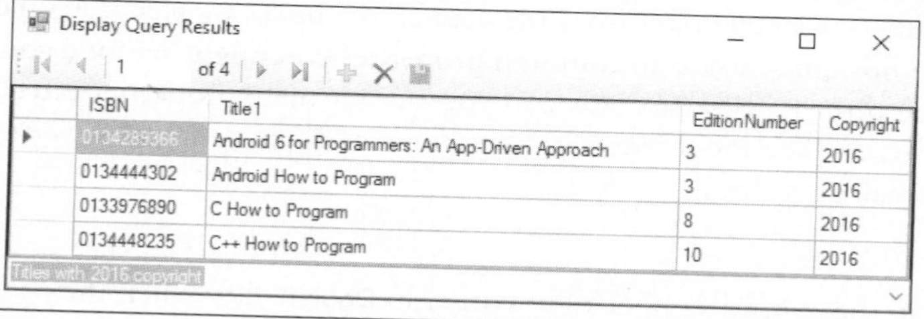

Display Query Results

1 of 4

| ISBN | Title1 | EditionNumber | Copyright |
|---|---|---|---|
| 0134289366 | Android 6 for Programmers: An App-Driven Approach | 3 | 2016 |
| 0134444302 | Android How to Program | 3 | 2016 |
| 0133976890 | C How to Program | 8 | 2016 |
| 0134448235 | C++ How to Program | 10 | 2016 |

Titles with 2016 copyright

**Fig. 20.24** | Results of the **Display Query Results** app's **Titles with 2016 copyright** query.

Display Query Results

1 of 7

| ISBN | Title1 | EditionNumber | Copyright |
|---|---|---|---|
| 0134444302 | Android How to Program | 3 | 2016 |
| 0133976890 | C How to Program | 8 | 2016 |
| 0134448235 | C++ How to Program | 10 | 2016 |
| 0132151006 | Internet & World Wide Web How to Program | 5 | 2012 |
| 0133807800 | Java How to Program | 10 | 2015 |
| 0133406954 | Visual Basic 2012 How to Program | 6 | 2014 |
| 0134601548 | Visual C# How to Program | 6 | 2017 |

Titles ending with "How to Program"

**Fig. 20.25** | Results of the **Display Query Results** app's **Titles ending with "How to Program"** query.

## 20.6.1 Creating the Display Query Results GUI

Perform the following steps to build the **Display Query Results** app's GUI.

*Step 1: Creating the Project*
Perform the steps in Section 20.5.2 to create a new **Windows Forms Application** project named `DisplayQueryResult` in the same solution as the `DisplayTable` app. Rename the `Form1.cs` source file to `TitleQueries.cs`. Set the `Form`'s **Text** property to `Display Query Results`. Be sure to add references to the `BooksExamples` and `EntityFramework` libraries, add the connection string to the project's `App.Config` file and set the `DisplayQuery-Result` project as the startup project.

*Step 2: Creating a* `DataGridView` *to Display the* `Titles` *Table*
Follow *Steps 1* and *2* in Section 20.5.3 to create the data source and the `DataGridView`. For this example, select the `Title` class (rather than `Author`) as the data source, and drag the **Title** node from the **Data Sources** window onto the form. Remove the `Authors` column from the `DataGridView`, as it will not be used in this example.

*Step 3: Adding a* `ComboBox` *to the* `Form`
In **Design** view, add a `ComboBox` named `queriesComboBox` below the `DataGridView` on the `Form`. Users will select which query to execute from this control. Set the `ComboBox`'s `Dock` property to `Bottom` and the `DataGridView`'s `Dock` property to `Fill`.

Next, you'll add the names of the queries to the `ComboBox`. Open the `ComboBox`'s **String Collection Editor** by right clicking the `ComboBox` and selecting **Edit Items...**. You also can access the **String Collection Editor** from the `ComboBox`'s *smart tag menu*. A **smart tag menu** provides you with quick access to common properties you might set for a control (such as the `Multiline` property of a `TextBox`), so you can set these properties directly in **Design** view, rather than in the **Properties** window. You can open a control's *smart tag menu* by clicking the small arrowhead

that appears in the control's upper-right corner in **Design** view when the control is selected. In the **String Collection Editor**, add the following three items to `queriesComboBox`—one for each of the queries we'll create:

1. All titles
2. Titles with 2016 copyright
3. Titles ending with "How to Program"

### 20.6.2 Coding the Display Query Results App

Next you'll create the code for this app (Fig. 20.26).

```
// Fig. 20.26: TitleQueries.cs
// Displaying the result of a user-selected query in a DataGridView.
using System;
using System.Data.Entity;
using System.Linq;
using System.Windows.Forms;

namespace DisplayQueryResult
{
   public partial class TitleQueries : Form
   {
      public TitleQueries()
      {
         InitializeComponent();
      }

      // Entity Framework DbContext
      private BooksExamples.BooksEntities dbcontext =
         new BooksExamples.BooksEntities();

      // load data from database into DataGridView
      private void TitleQueries_Load(object sender, EventArgs e)
      {
         dbcontext.Titles.Load(); // load Titles table into memory

         // set the ComboBox to show the default query that
         // selects all books from the Titles table
         queriesComboBox.SelectedIndex = 0;
      }

      // loads data into titleBindingSource based on user-selected query
      private void queriesComboBox_SelectedIndexChanged(
         object sender, EventArgs e)
      {
         // set the data displayed according to what is selected
         switch (queriesComboBox.SelectedIndex)
         {
            case 0: // all titles
               // use LINQ to order the books by title
               titleBindingSource.DataSource =
                  dbcontext.Titles.Local.OrderBy(book => book.Title1);
               break;
```

**Fig. 20.26** | Displaying the result of a user-selected query in a DataGridView. (Part 1 of 2.)

```
43                case 1: // titles with 2016 copyright
44                   // use LINQ to get titles with 2016
45                   // copyright and sort them by title
46                   titleBindingSource.DataSource =
47                      dbcontext.Titles.Local
48                         .Where(book => book.Copyright == "2016")
49                         .OrderBy(book => book.Title1);
50                   break;
51                case 2: // titles ending with "How to Program"
52                   // use LINQ to get titles ending with
53                   // "How to Program" and sort them by title
54                   titleBindingSource.DataSource =
55                      dbcontext.Titles.Local
56                         .Where(
57                            book => book.Title1.EndsWith("How to Program"))
58                         .OrderBy(book => book.Title1);
59                   break;
60             }
61
62             titleBindingSource.MoveFirst(); // move to first entry
63          }
64       }
65    }
```

**Fig. 20.26** | Displaying the result of a user-selected query in a `DataGridView`. (Part 2 of 2.)

### *Customizing the* `Form`*'s* `Load` *Event Handler*

Create the `TitleQueries_Load` event handler (lines 22–29) by double clicking the title bar in **Design** view. When the `Form` loads, it should display the complete list of books from the `Titles` table, sorted by title. Line 24 calls the `Load` extension method on the `BookEntities` `DbContext`'s `Titles` property to load the `Titles` table's contents into memory. Rather than defining the same LINQ query as in lines 40–41, we can programmatically cause the `queriesComboBox_SelectedIndexChanged` event handler to execute simply by setting the `queriesComboBox`'s `SelectedIndex` to `0` (line 28).

### *`queriesComboBox_SelectedIndexChanged` Event Handler*

Next you must write code that executes the appropriate query each time the user chooses a different item from `queriesComboBox`. Double click `queriesComboBox` in **Design** view to generate a `queriesComboBox_SelectedIndexChanged` event handler (lines 32–63) in the `TitleQueries.cs` file. In the event handler, add a `switch` statement (lines 36–60). Each `case` in the `switch` will change the `titleBindingSource`'s `DataSource` property to the results of a query that returns the correct set of data. The data bindings created by the IDE *automatically* update the `titleDataGridView` *each time* we change its `DataSource`. The `BindingSource` maintains a **`Position`** property that represents the current item in the data source. The **`MoveFirst` method** of the `BindingSource` (line 62) sets the `Position` property to `0` to move to the first row of the result each time a query executes. The results of the queries in lines 40–41, 46–49 and 54–58 are shown in Figs. 20.23–20.25, respectively. Because we do not modify the data in this app, each of the queries is performed on the in-memory representation of the `Titles` table, which is accessible through `dbcontext.Titles.Local`.

### *Ordering the Books By Title*

Lines 40–41 invoke the `OrderBy` extension method on `dbcontext.Titles.Local` to order the `Title` objects by their `Title1` property values. As we mentioned previously, the IDE renamed the `Title` column of the database's `Titles` table as `Title1` in the generated `Title` entity data model class to avoid a naming conflict with the class's name. Recall that `Local` returns an `ObservableCollection<T>` containing the row objects of the specified table—in this case, `Local` returns an `ObservableCollection<Title>`. When you invoke `OrderBy` on an `ObservableCollection<T>`, the method returns an `IOrderedEnumerable<T>`. We assign that object to the `titleBindingSource`'s `DataSource` property. When the `DataSource` property changes, the `DataGridView` iterates through the contents of the `IEnumerable<T>` and displays the data.

### *Selecting Books with 2016 Copyright*

Lines 46–49 filter the titles displayed by using the **`Where` extension method** with the lambda expression

```
book => book.Copyright == "2016"
```

as an argument. The `Where` extension method expects as its parameter a `Func` delegate representing a method that receives one parameter and returns a `bool` indicating whether the method's argument matches the specified criteria. The lambda expression used here takes one `Title` object (named `book`) as its parameter and uses it to check whether the given `Title`'s `Copyright` property (a `string` in the database) is equal to `2014`. A lambda expression that's used with the `Where` extension method must return a `bool` value. Only `Title` objects for which this lambda expression returns `true` will be selected. We use `OrderBy` to order the results by the `Title1` property so the books are displayed in ascending order by title. The type of the lambda's `book` parameter is *inferred* from `dbcontext.Titles.Local`, which contains `Title` objects. As soon as the `titleBindingSource`'s `DataSource` property changes, the `DataGridView` is updated with the query results.

### *Selecting Books with Titles That End in "How to Program"*

Lines 54–58 filter the titles displayed by using the `Where` extension method with the lambda expression

```
book => book.Title1.EndsWith("How to Program")
```

as an argument. This lambda expression takes one `Title` object (named `book`) as its parameter and uses it to check whether the given `Title`'s `Title1` property value ends with `"How to Program"`. The expression `books.Title1` returns the `string` stored in that property, then we use the string class's `EndsWith` method to perform the test. We order the results by the `Title1` property so the books are displayed in ascending order by title.

## 20.7 Retrieving Data from Multiple Tables with LINQ

In this section, you'll perform LINQ to Entities queries using the LINQ query syntax that was introduced in Chapter 9. In particular, you'll learn how to obtain query results that combine data from multiple tables (Figs. 20.27–20.29). The **Joining Tables with LINQ** app uses LINQ to Entities to combine and organize data from multiple tables, and shows the results of queries that perform the following tasks:

- Get a list of all the authors and the ISBNs of the books they've authored, sorted by last name, then first name (Fig. 20.27).
- Get a list of all the authors and the titles of the books they've authored, sorted by last name, then first name; for each author sort the titles alphabetically (Fig. 20.28).
- Get a list of all the book titles grouped by author, sorted by last name, then first name; for a given author sort the titles alphabetically (Fig. 20.29).

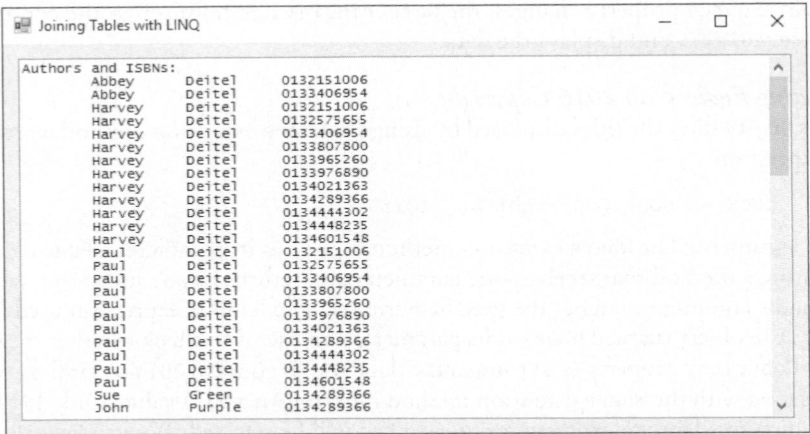


**Fig. 20.27** | **Joining Tables with LINQ** app showing the list of authors and the ISBNs of the books they've authored. The authors are sorted by last name, then first name.

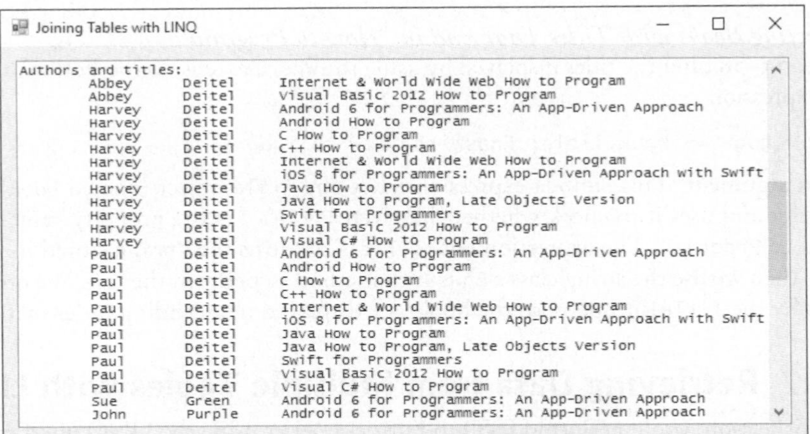


**Fig. 20.28** | **Joining Tables with LINQ** app showing the list of authors and the titles of the book's they've authored. The authors are sorted by last name, then first name, and the titles for a given author are sorted alphabetically.

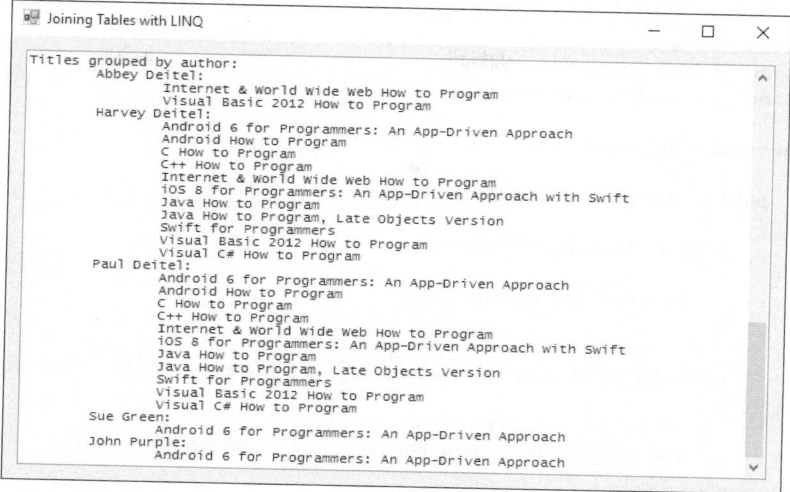


**Fig. 20.29** | **Joining Tables with LINQ** app showing the list of titles grouped by author. The authors are sorted by last name, then first name, and the titles for a given author are sorted alphabetically.

### *GUI for the* Joining Tables with LINQ *App*

For this example (Fig. 20.30–Fig. 20.33), perform the steps in Section 20.5.2 to create a new **Windows Forms Application** project named `JoinQueries` in the same solution as the previous examples. Rename the `Form1.cs` source file to `JoiningTableData.cs`. Set the `Form`'s **Text** property to `Joining Tables with LINQ`. Be sure to add references to the `Books-Examples` and `EntityFramework` libraries, add the connection string to the project's `App.Config` file and set the `JoinQueries` project as the startup project. We set the following properties for the `outputTextBox`:

- `Font` property: Set to `Lucida Console` to display the output in a fixed-width font.
- `Multiline` property: Set to `True` so that multiple lines of text can be displayed.
- `Anchor` property: Set to `Top, Bottom, Left, Right` so that you can resize the window and the `outputTextBox` will resize accordingly.
- `Scrollbars` property: Set to `Vertical`, so that you can scroll through the output.

### *Creating the* `DbContext`

The code uses the entity data model classes to combine data from the tables in the `Books` database and display the relationships between the authors and books in three different ways. We split the code for class `JoiningTableData` into several figures (Figs. 20.30–20.33) for presentation purposes. As in previous examples, the `DbContext` object (Fig. 20.30, line 19) allows the program to interact with the database.

```
1  // Fig. 20.30: JoiningTableData.cs
2  // Using LINQ to perform a join and aggregate data across tables.
3  using System;
4  using System.Linq;
5  using System.Windows.Forms;
6
7  namespace JoinQueries
8  {
9     public partial class JoiningTableData : Form
10    {
11       public JoiningTableData()
12       {
13          InitializeComponent();
14       }
15
16       private void JoiningTableData_Load(object sender, EventArgs e)
17       {
18          // Entity Framework DbContext
19          var dbcontext = new BooksExamples.BooksEntities();
20
```

**Fig. 20.30** | Creating the `BooksEntities` for querying the `Books` database.

### *Combining Author Names with the ISBNs of the Books They've Written*

The first query (Fig. 20.31, lines 22–26) *joins* data from two tables and returns a list of author names and the ISBNs representing the books they've written, sorted by `LastName`, then `FirstName`. The query takes advantage of the properties in the entity data model classes that were created based on foreign-key relationships between the database's tables. These properties enable you to easily combine data from related rows in multiple tables.

```
21          // get authors and ISBNs of each book they co-authored
22          var authorsAndISBNs =
23             from author in dbcontext.Authors
24             from book in author.Titles
25             orderby author.LastName, author.FirstName
26             select new {author.FirstName, author.LastName, book.ISBN};
27
28          outputTextBox.AppendText("Authors and ISBNs:");
29
30          // display authors and ISBNs in tabular format
31          foreach (var element in authorsAndISBNs)
32          {
33             outputTextBox.AppendText($"\r\n\t{element.FirstName,-10} " +
34                $"{element.LastName,-10} {element.ISBN,-10}");
35          }
36
```

**Fig. 20.31** | Getting a list of authors and the ISBNs of the books they've authored.

The first `from` clause (line 23) gets each `author` from the `Authors` table. The second `from` clause (line 24) uses the `Author` class's `Titles` property to get the ISBNs for the current `author`. The entity data model uses the foreign-key information stored in the database's `AuthorISBN` table to get the appropriate ISBNs. The combined result of the two `from` clauses is a collection of all the authors and the ISBNs of the books they've authored. The two `from` clauses introduce *two* range variables into the scope of this query—other clauses can access both range variables to combine data from multiple tables. Line 25 orders the results by the `author`'s `LastName`, then `FirstName`. Line 26 creates a new anonymous type containing an `author`'s `FirstName` and `LastName` from the `Authors` table and the `ISBN` for one of that author's `books` from the `Titles` table.

### *Anonymous Types*

Recall from Section 9.3.5 that a LINQ query's `select` clause can create an anonymous type with the properties specified in the initializer list—in this case, `FirstName`, `LastName` and `ISBN` (line 26). Note that all properties of an anonymous type are `public` and *read-only*. Because the type has no name, you must use *implicitly typed local variables* to store references to objects of anonymous types (e.g., line 31). Also, in addition to the `ToString` method in an anonymous type, the compiler provides an `Equals` method, which compares the properties of the anonymous object that calls the method and the anonymous object that it receives as an argument.

### *Combining Author Names with the Titles of the Books They've Written*

The second query (Fig. 20.32, lines 38–42) gives similar output, but uses the foreign-key relationships to get the title of each book that an author wrote.

```
37          // get authors and titles of each book they co-authored
38          var authorsAndTitles =
39             from book in dbcontext.Titles
40             from author in book.Authors
41             orderby author.LastName, author.FirstName, book.Title1
42             select new {author.FirstName, author.LastName, book.Title1};
43
44          outputTextBox.AppendText("\r\n\r\nAuthors and titles:");
45
46          // display authors and titles in tabular format
47          foreach (var element in authorsAndTitles)
48          {
49             outputTextBox.AppendText($"\r\n\t{element.FirstName,-10} " +
50                $"{element.LastName,-10} {element.Title1}");
51          }
52
```

**Fig. 20.32** | Getting a list of authors and the titles of the books they've authored.

The first `from` clause (line 39) gets each `book` from the `Titles` table. The second `from` clause (line 40) uses the generated `Authors` property of the `Title` class to get only the authors for the current `book`. The entity data model uses the foreign-key information stored in the database's `AuthorISBN` table to get the appropriate authors. The `author` objects give us access to the names of the current book's authors. The `select` clause (line 42) uses the `author` and `book` range variables to get the `FirstName` and `LastName` of each author from the `Authors` table and the title of one of the author's books from the `Titles` table.

### *Organizing Book Titles by Author*

Most queries return results with data arranged in a relational-style table of rows and columns. The last query (Fig. 20.33, lines 55–62) returns hierarchical results. Each element in the results contains the name of an `Author` and a list of `Titles` that the author wrote. The LINQ query does this by using a *nested query* in the `select` clause. The outer query iterates over the authors in the database. The inner query takes a specific author and retrieves all titles that the author wrote. The `select` clause (lines 58–62) creates an anonymous type with two properties:

- The property `Name` (line 58) is initialized with a `string` that separates the author's first and last names by a space.
- The property `Titles` (lines 59–62) is initialized with the result of the nested query, which returns the title of each book written by the current `author`.

In this case, we're providing names for each property in the new anonymous type. When you create an anonymous type, you can specify the name for each property by using the format *name* = *value*.

```
53             // get authors and titles of each book
54             // they co-authored; group by author
55             var titlesByAuthor =
56                from author in dbcontext.Authors
57                orderby author.LastName, author.FirstName
58                select new {Name = author.FirstName + " " + author.LastName,
59                   Titles =
60                      from book in author.Titles
61                      orderby book.Title1
62                      select book.Title1};
63
64             outputTextBox.AppendText("\r\n\r\nTitles grouped by author:");
65
66             // display titles written by each author, grouped by author
67             foreach (var author in titlesByAuthor)
68             {
69                // display author's name
70                outputTextBox.AppendText($"\r\n\t{author.Name}:");
71
72                // display titles written by that author
73                foreach (var title in author.Titles)
74                {
75                   outputTextBox.AppendText($"\r\n\t\t{title}");
76                }
77             }
78          }
79       }
80    }
```

**Fig. 20.33** | Getting a list of titles grouped by authors.

The range variable `book` in the nested query iterates over the current author's books using the `Titles` property. The `Title1` property of a given `book` returns the `Title` column from that row of the `Titles` table in the database.

The nested `foreach` statements (lines 67–77) use the anonymous type's properties to output the hierarchical results. The outer loop displays the author's name and the inner loop displays the titles of all the books written by that author.

## 20.8 Creating a Master/Detail View App

Figure 20.34 shows a so-called **master/detail view**—one part of the GUI (the master) allows you to select an entry, and another part (the details) displays detailed information about that entry. When the app first loads, it displays the name of the first author in the data source and shows that author's books in the `DataGridView`. When you use the buttons on the `BindingNavigator` to change authors, the app displays the details of the books written by the corresponding author—Fig. 20.34 shows the second author's books. This app only reads data from the entity data model, so we disabled the buttons in the `BindingNavigator` that enable the user to add and delete records. When you run the app, experiment with the `BindingNavigator`'s controls. The DVD-player-like buttons of the `BindingNavigator` allow you to change the currently displayed row.

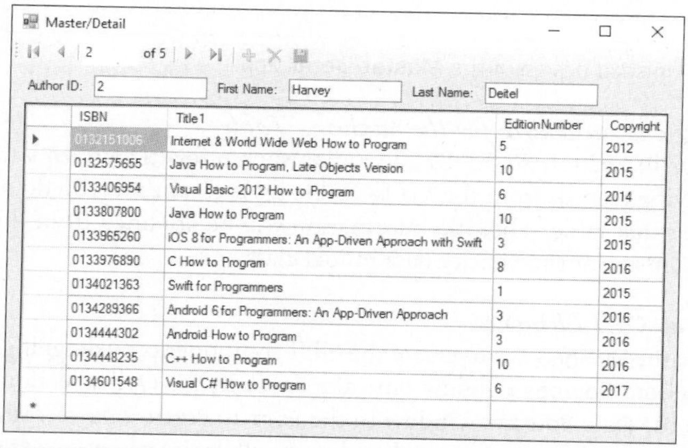

Master/Detail

2 of 5

Author ID: 2 First Name: Harvey Last Name: Deitel

| ISBN | Title1 | EditionNumber | Copyright |
|---|---|---|---|
| 0132151006 | Internet & World Wide Web How to Program | 5 | 2012 |
| 0132575655 | Java How to Program, Late Objects Version | 10 | 2015 |
| 0133406954 | Visual Basic 2012 How to Program | 6 | 2014 |
| 0133807800 | Java How to Program | 10 | 2015 |
| 0133965260 | iOS 8 for Programmers: An App-Driven Approach with Swift | 3 | 2015 |
| 0133976890 | C How to Program | 8 | 2016 |
| 0134021363 | Swift for Programmers | 1 | 2015 |
| 0134289366 | Android 6 for Programmers: An App-Driven Approach | 3 | 2016 |
| 0134444302 | Android How to Program | 3 | 2016 |
| 0134448235 | C++ How to Program | 10 | 2016 |
| 0134601548 | Visual C# How to Program | 6 | 2017 |

**Fig. 20.34** | **Master/Detail** app displaying books for an author in the data source.

### 20.8.1 Creating the Master/Detail GUI

You've seen that the IDE can automatically generate the `BindingSource`, `BindingNavigator` and GUI elements when you drag a data source onto the `Form`. You'll now use two `BindingSources`—one for the master list of authors and one for the titles associated with a given author. Both will be generated by the IDE. The completed GUI that you'll now build is shown in Fig. 20.35.

*Step 1: Creating the Project*

Follow the instructions in Section 20.5.2 to create and configure a new **Windows Forms Application** project called `MasterDetail`. Name the source file `Details.cs` and set the `Form`'s `Text` property to **Master/Detail**. Be sure to add references to the `BooksExamples` and `EntityFramework` libraries, add the connection string to the project's `App.Config` file and set the `MasterDetail` project as the startup project.

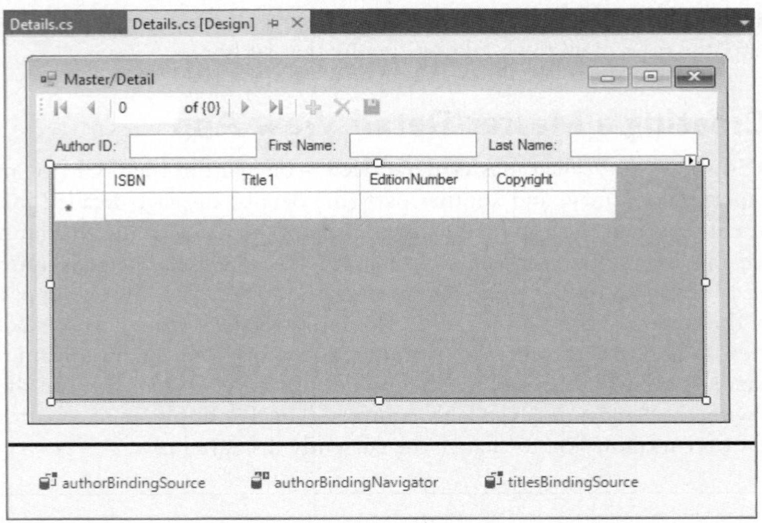


**Fig. 20.35** | Finished design of the **Master/Detail** app.

### *Step 2: Adding a Data Source for the* `Authors` *Table*

Follow the steps in Section 20.5.3 to add a data source for the `Authors` table. Although you'll be displaying records from the `Titles` table for each author, you do not need to add a data source for that table. The title information will be obtained from the `Titles` navigation property in the `Author` entity data model class.

### *Step 3: Creating GUI Elements*

Next, you'll use the **Design** view to create the GUI components by dragging-and-dropping items from the **Data Sources** window onto the `Form`. In the earlier sections, you dragged an object from the **Data Sources** window to the `Form` to create a `DataGridView`. The IDE allows you to specify the type of control(s) that it will create when you drag-and-drop an object from the **Data Sources** window onto a `Form`. To do so:

1. Switch to **Design** view for the `Details` class.
2. Click the **Author** node in the **Data Sources** window—it should change to a drop-down list. Open the drop-down by clicking the down arrow and select the **Details** option—this indicates that we'd like to generate `Label`–`TextBox` pairs that represent each column of the `Authors` table.
3. Drag the **Author** node from the **Data Sources** window onto the `Form` in **Design** view. This creates the `authorBindingSource`, the `authorBindingNavigator` and the `Label`–`TextBox` pairs that represent each column in the table. Initially, the controls appear as shown in Fig. 20.36. We rearranged the controls as shown in Fig. 20.35.
4. By default, the `Titles` navigation property is implemented in the entity data model classes as a `HashSet<Title>`. To bind the data to GUI controls properly, you must change this to an `ObservableCollection<Title>`. To do this, expand

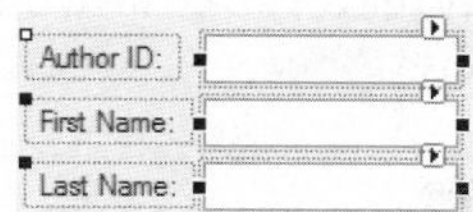


**Fig. 20.36** | Details representation of an Author.

the class library project's BooksModel.edmx node in the **Solution Explorer**, then expand the BooksModel.tt node and open Author.cs in the editor. Add a using statement for the namespace System.Collections.ObjectModel. Then, in the Author constructor change HashSet to ObservableCollection, and in the Titles property's declaration, change ICollection to ObservableCollection. Right click the class library project in the **Solution Explorer** and select **Build** to recompile the class.

5. Select the MasterDetail project in the **Solution Explorer**. Next, click the **Titles** node that's nested in the **Author** node in the **Data Sources** window—it should change to a drop-down list. Open the drop-down by clicking the down arrow and ensure that the DataGridView option is selected—this is the GUI control that will be used to display the data from the Titles table that corresponds to a given author.
6. Drag the **Titles** node onto the Form in **Design** view. This creates the titlesBindingSource and the DataGridView. This control is only for *viewing* data, so set its ReadOnly property to True using the **Properties** window. Because we dragged the **Titles** node from the **Author** node in the **Data Sources** window, the DataGridView will automatically display the books for the currently selected author once we bind the author data to the authorBindingSource.

We used the DataGridView's Anchor property to anchor it to all four sides of the Form. We also set the Form's Size and MinimumSize properties to 550, 300 to set the Form's initial size and minimum size, respectively.

### 20.8.2 Coding the Master/Detail App

The code to display an author and the corresponding books (Fig. 20.37) is straightforward. Lines 18–19 create the DbContext. The Form's Load event handler (lines 22–32) orders the Author objects by LastName (line 26) and FirstName (line 27), then loads them into memory (line 28). Next, line 31 assigns dbcontext.Authors.Local to the authorBindingSource's DataSource property. At this point:

- the BindingNavigator displays the number of Author objects and indicates that the first one in the results is selected,
- the TextBoxes display the currently selected Author's AuthorID, FirstName and LastName property values, and
- the currently selected Author's titles are automatically assigned to the titlesBindingSource's DataSource, which causes the DataGridView to display those titles.

Now, when you use the `BindingNavigator` to change the selected `Author`, the corresponding titles are displayed in the `DataGridView`.

```
// Fig. 20.37: Details.cs
// Using a DataGridView to display details based on a selection.
using System;
using System.Data.Entity;
using System.Linq;
using System.Windows.Forms;

namespace MasterDetail
{
   public partial class Details : Form
   {
      public Details()
      {
         InitializeComponent();
      }

      // Entity Framework DbContext
      BooksExamples.BooksEntities dbcontext =
         new BooksExamples.BooksEntities();

      // initialize data sources when the Form is loaded
      private void Details_Load(object sender, EventArgs e)
      {
         // load Authors table ordered by LastName then FirstName
         dbcontext.Authors
            .OrderBy(author => author.LastName)
            .ThenBy(author => author.FirstName)
            .Load();

         // specify DataSource for authorBindingSource
         authorBindingSource.DataSource = dbcontext.Authors.Local;
      }
   }
}
```

**Fig. 20.37** | Using a `DataGridView` to display details based on a selection.

## 20.9 Address Book Case Study

Our final example implements a simple `AddressBook` app (with sample outputs in (Figs. 20.38–20.40) that enables users to perform the following tasks on the database `AddressBook.mdf` (which is included in the directory with this chapter's examples):

- Insert new contacts.
- Find contacts whose last names begin with the specified letters.
- Update existing contacts.
- Delete contacts.

We populated the database with six fictional contacts.

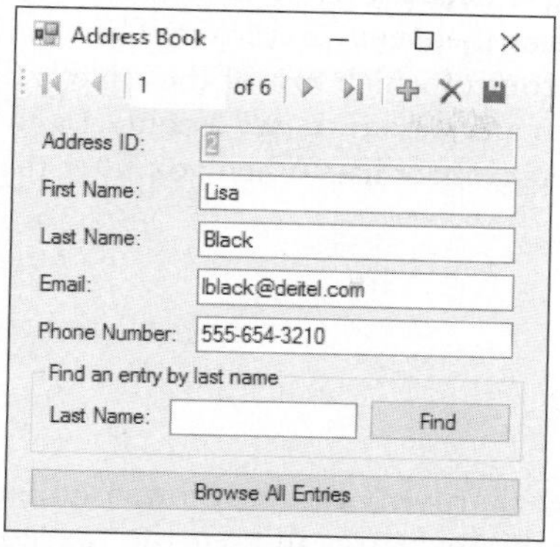

**Fig. 20.38** | Use the `BindingNavigator`'s controls to navigate through the contacts.

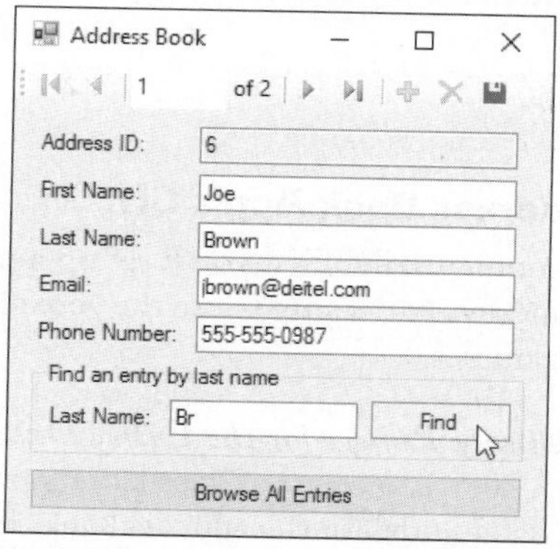

**Fig. 20.39** | Type a search string in the **Last Name** `TextBox`, then press **Find** to locate contacts whose last names begin with that string. Only two names start with **Br**, so the `BindingNavigator` shows the first of two matching records.

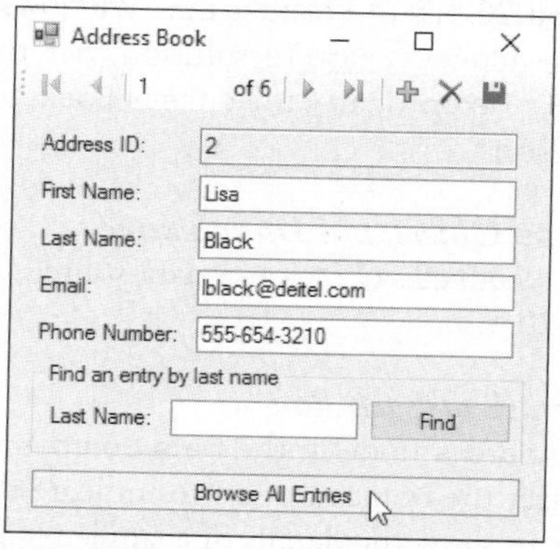

**Fig. 20.40** | Click **Browse All Entries** to clear a search and return to browsing all contacts.

Rather than displaying a database table in a `DataGridView`, this app presents the details of one contact at a time in several `TextBox`es. The `BindingNavigator` at the top of the window allows you to control which *row* of the table is displayed at any given time. The `BindingNavigator` also allows you to *add* a contact and *delete* a contact—but only when browsing the complete contact list. When you filter the contacts by last name, the app disables the **Add new**

and **Delete**

buttons (we'll explain why shortly). Clicking **Browse All Entries** enables these buttons again. Adding a row clears the `TextBox`es and sets the `TextBox` to the right of **Address ID** to zero to indicate that the `TextBox`es now represent a new record. When you save a new entry, the **Address ID** field is automatically changed from zero to a unique ID number by the database. No changes are made to the underlying database unless you click the **Save Data** button:

### 20.9.1 Creating the Address Book App's GUI

We discuss the app's code momentarily. First you'll set up a new solution containing the entity data model and a Windows `Forms` app. Close the `BooksExamples` solution you used in this chapter's previous examples.

#### *Step 1: Creating a* Class Library *Project for the Entity Data Model*

Perform the steps in Section 20.5.1 to create a **Class Library** project named `AddressExample` that contains an entity data model for the `AddressBook.mdf` database, which contains only an `Addresses` table with `AddressID`, `FirstName`, `LastName`, `Email` and `PhoneNumber` columns. Name the entity data model `AddressModel`. The `AddressBook.mdf` database is located in the `Databases` folder with this chapter's examples.

#### *Step 2: Creating a* Windows Forms Application *Project for the* AddressBook *App*

Perform the steps in Section 20.5.2 to create a new **Windows Forms Application** project named `AddressBook` in the `AddressExample` solution. Set the `Form`'s filename to `Contacts.cs`, then set the `Form`'s **Text** property to `Address Book`. Set the `AddressBook` project as the solution's startup project.

#### *Step 3: Adding the* Address *Object as a Data Source*

Add the entity data model's `Address` object as a data source, as you did with the `Author` object in *Step 1* of Section 20.5.3.

#### *Step 4: Displaying the Details of Each Row*

In **Design** view, select the **Address** node in the **Data Sources** window. Click the **Address** node's down arrow and select the **Details** option to indicate that the IDE should create a set of `Label`–`TextBox` pairs to show the details of a single record at a time.

### *Step 5: Dragging the* **`Address`** *Data-Source Node to the* **`Form`**

Drag the `Address` node from the **Data Sources** window to the `Form`. This automatically creates a `BindingNavigator` and the `Labels` and `TextBoxes` corresponding to the columns of the database table. The fields are placed in alphabetical order. Reorder the components, using **Design** view, so they're in the order shown in Fig. 20.38. You'll also want to change the tab order of the controls. To do so, select **View > Tab Order**, then click the `TextBoxes` from top to bottom in the order they appear in Fig. 20.38.

### *Step 5: Making the* **`AddressID TextBox ReadOnly`**

The `AddressID` column of the `Addresses` table is an *autoincremented identity column*, so users should *not* be allowed to edit the values in this column. Select the `TextBox` for the `AddressID` and set its `ReadOnly` property to `True` using the **Properties** window.

### *Step 6: Adding Controls to Allow Users to Specify a Last Name to Locate*

While the `BindingNavigator` allows you to browse the address book, it would be more convenient to be able to find a specific entry by last name. To add this functionality to the app, we must create controls to allow the user to enter a last name and provide event handlers to perform the search.

Add a `Label` named `findLabel`, a `TextBox` named `findTextBox`, and a `Button` named `findButton`. Place these controls in a `GroupBox` named `findGroupBox`, then set its `Text` property to **Find an entry by last name.** Set the `Text` property of the `Label` to `Last Name:` and set the `Text` property of the `Button` to `Find`.

### *Step 7: Allowing the User to Return to Browsing All Rows of the Database*

To allow users to return to browsing all the contacts after searching for contacts with a specific last name, add a `Button` named `browseAllButton` below the `findGroupBox`. Set the `Text` property of `browseAllButton` to **Browse All Entries**.

## 20.9.2 Coding the Address Book App

The `Contacts.cs` code-behind file is split into several figures (Figs. 20.41–20.45) for presentation purposes.

### *Method* **`RefreshContacts`**

As we showed in previous examples, we must connect the `addressBindingSource` that controls the GUI with the `DbContext` that interacts with the database. In this example, we declare the `AddressEntities DbContext` object at line 20 of Fig. 20.41, but create it and initiate the data binding in the `RefreshContacts` method (lines 23–45), which is called from several other methods in the app. When this method is called, if `dbcontext` is not `null`, we call its `Dispose` method, then create a `new AddressEntities DbContext` at line 32. We do this so we can re-sort the data in the entity data model. If we maintained one `dbcontext.Addresses` object in memory for the duration of the program and the user changed a person's last name or first name, the records would still remain in their original order in the `dbcontext.Addresses` object, even if that order is incorrect. Lines 36–39 order the `Address` objects by `LastName`, then `FirstName` and load the objects into memory. Then line 42 sets the `addressBindingSource`'s `DataSource` property to `dbcontext.Addresses.Local` to bind the data in memory to the GUI.

```
// Fig. 20.41: Contact.cs
// Manipulating an address book.
using System;
using System.Data;
using System.Data.Entity;
using System.Data.Entity.Validation;
using System.Linq;
using System.Windows.Forms;

namespace AddressBook
{
   public partial class Contacts : Form
   {
      public Contacts()
      {
         InitializeComponent();
      }

      // Entity Framework DbContext
      private AddressExample.AddressBookEntities dbcontext = null;

      // fill our addressBindingSource with all rows, ordered by name
      private void RefreshContacts()
      {
         // Dispose old DbContext, if any
         if (dbcontext != null)
         {
            dbcontext.Dispose();
         }

         // create new DbContext so we can reorder records based on edits
         dbcontext = new AddressExample.AddressBookEntities();

         // use LINQ to order the Addresses table contents
         // by last name, then first name
         dbcontext.Addresses
            .OrderBy(entry => entry.LastName)
            .ThenBy(entry => entry.FirstName)
            .Load();

         // specify DataSource for addressBindingSource
         addressBindingSource.DataSource = dbcontext.Addresses.Local;
         addressBindingSource.MoveFirst(); // go to first result
         findTextBox.Clear(); // clear the Find TextBox
      }

```

**Fig. 20.41** | Creating the `BooksEntities` and defining method `RefreshContacts` for use in other methods.

### *Method* `Contacts_Load`

Method `Contacts_Load` (Fig. 20.42) calls `RefreshContacts` (line 50) so that the first record is displayed when the app starts. As before, you create the `Load` event handler by double clicking the `Form`'s title bar.

```
47         // when the form loads, fill it with data from the database
48         private void Contacts_Load(object sender, EventArgs e)
49         {
50            RefreshContacts(); // fill binding with data from database
51         }
52
```

**Fig. 20.42** | Calling `RefreshContacts` to fill the `TextBoxes` when the app loads.

### *Method* `addressBindingNavigatorSaveItem_Click`

Method `addressBindingNavigatorSaveItem_Click` (Fig. 20.43) saves the changes to the database when the `BindingNavigator`'s **Save Data** `Button` is clicked. (Remember to enable this button.) The `AddressBook` database requires values for the first name, last name, phone number and e-mail. If a field is empty when you attempt to save, a `DbEntityValidationException` exception occurs. We call `RefreshContacts` (line 72) after saving to re-sort the data and move back to the first element.

```
53         // Click event handler for the Save Button in the
54         // BindingNavigator saves the changes made to the data
55         private void addressBindingNavigatorSaveItem_Click(
56            object sender, EventArgs e)
57         {
58            Validate(); // validate input fields
59            addressBindingSource.EndEdit(); // complete current edit, if any
60
61            // try to save changes
62            try
63            {
64               dbcontext.SaveChanges(); // write changes to database file
65            }
66            catch (DbEntityValidationException)
67            {
68               MessageBox.Show("Columns cannot be empty",
69                  "Entity Validation Exception");
70            }
71
72            RefreshContacts(); // change back to updated unfiltered data
73         }
74
```

**Fig. 20.43** | Saving changes to the database when the user clicks **Save Data**.

### *Method* `findButton_Click`

Method `findButton_Click` (Fig. 20.44) uses LINQ query syntax (lines 81–85) to select only people whose last names start with the characters in the `findTextBox`. The query sorts the results by last name, then first name. In LINQ to Entities, you *cannot* bind a LINQ query's results directly to a `BindingSource`'s `DataSource`. So, line 88 calls the query object's `ToList` method to get a `List` representation of the filtered data and assigns the `List` to the `BindingSource`'s `DataSource`. When you convert the query result to a `List`, only changes to *existing* records in the `DbContext` are tracked by the `DbContext`—any records that you add or remove while viewing the filtered data would be lost. For this reason we disabled the **Add new** and **Delete** buttons when the data is filtered. When you enter a last name and click **Find**, the `BindingNavigator` allows the user to browse only the rows containing the matching last names. This is because the data source bound to the `Form`'s controls (the result of the LINQ query) has changed and now contains only a limited number of rows.

```
      // use LINQ to create a data source that contains only people
      // with last names that start with the specified text
      private void findButton_Click(object sender, EventArgs e)
      {
         // use LINQ to filter contacts with last names that
         // start with findTextBox contents
         var lastNameQuery =
            from address in dbcontext.Addresses
            where address.LastName.StartsWith(findTextBox.Text)
            orderby address.LastName, address.FirstName
            select address;

         // display matching contacts
         addressBindingSource.DataSource = lastNameQuery.ToList();
         addressBindingSource.MoveFirst(); // go to first result

         // don't allow add/delete when contacts are filtered
         bindingNavigatorAddNewItem.Enabled = false;
         bindingNavigatorDeleteItem.Enabled = false;
      }

```

**Fig. 20.44** | Finding the contacts whose last names begin with a specified `String`.

### *Method* `browseAllButton_Click`

Method `browseAllButton_Click` (Fig. 20.45) allows users to return to browsing all the rows after searching for specific rows. Double click `browseAllButton` to create a `Click` event handler. The event handler enables the **Add new** and **Delete** buttons, then calls `RefreshContacts` to restore the data source to the full list of people (in sorted order) and clear the `findTextBox`.

```
      // reload addressBindingSource with all rows
      private void browseAllButton_Click(object sender, EventArgs e)
      {
         // allow add/delete when contacts are not filtered
         bindingNavigatorAddNewItem.Enabled = true;
         bindingNavigatorDeleteItem.Enabled = true;
         RefreshContacts(); // change back to initial unfiltered data
      }
   }
}
```

**Fig. 20.45** | Allowing the user to browse all contacts.

## 20.10 Tools and Web Resources

Our LINQ Resource Center at `www.deitel.com/LINQ` contains many links to additional information, including blogs by Microsoft LINQ team members, sample chapters, tutorials, videos, downloads, FAQs, forums, webcasts and other resource sites.

A useful tool for learning LINQ is LINQPad

```
http://www.linqpad.net
```

which allows you to execute and view the results of any C# or Visual Basic expression, including LINQ queries. It also supports the ADO.NET Entity Framework and LINQ to Entities.

This chapter is meant as an introduction to databases, the ADO.NET Entity Framework and LINQ to Entities. Microsoft's Entity Framework site

```
https://msdn.microsoft.com/en-us/data/aa937723
```

provides lots of additional information on working with the ADO.NET Entity Framework and LINQ to Entities, including tutorials, videos and more.

## 20.11 Wrap-Up

This chapter introduced the relational database model, the ADO.NET Entity Framework, LINQ to Entities and Visual Studio's visual programming tools for working with databases. You examined the contents of a simple `Books` database and learned about the relationships among the tables in the database. You used LINQ to Entities and the entity data model classes generated by the IDE to retrieve data from, add new data to, delete data from and update data in a SQL Server Express database.

We discussed the entity data model classes automatically generated by the IDE, such as the `DbContext` class that manages an app's interactions with a database. You learned how to use the IDE's tools to connect to databases and to generate entity data model classes based on an existing database's schema. You then used the IDE's drag-and-drop capabilities to automatically generate GUIs for displaying and manipulating database data. In the next chapter, we'll show how to use asynchronous programming with C#'s `async` modifier and `await` operator to take advantage of multicore architectures.

# Asynchronous Programming with `async` and `await`

## Objectives

In this chapter you'll:

- Understand what asynchronous programming is and how it can improve the performance of your apps.
- Use the `async` modifier to indicate that a method is asynchronous.
- Use an `await` expression to wait for an asynchronous task to complete execution so that an `async` method can continue its execution.
- Take advantage of multicore processors by executing tasks asynchronously via Task Parallel Library (TPL) features.
- Use `Task` method `WhenAll` to wait for multiple tasks to complete before an `async` method continues.
- Time multiple tasks running on a single-core system and a dual-core system (all with the same processor speeds) to determine the performance improvement when these tasks are run on the dual-core system.
- Use an `HttpClient` to invoke a web service asynchronously.
- Show an asynchronous task's progress and intermediate results.

Outline



## 21.1 Introduction

It would be nice if we could focus our attention on performing only one task at a time and doing it well. That's usually difficult to do in a complex world in which there's so much going on at once. This chapter presents C#'s capabilities for developing programs that create and manage multiple tasks. As we'll demonstrate, this can greatly improve program performance, especially on multicore systems.

### *Concurrency*

When we say that two tasks are operating **concurrently**, we mean that they're both *making progress* at once. Until recently, most computers had only a single processor. Operating systems on such computers execute tasks concurrently by rapidly switching between them, doing a small portion of each before moving on to the next, so that all tasks keep progressing. For example, it's common for personal computers to compile a program, send a file to a printer, receive electronic mail messages over a network and more, concurrently. Tasks like these that proceed independently of one another are said to execute asynchronously and are referred to as **asynchronous tasks**.

### *Parallelism*

When we say that two tasks are operating **in parallel**, we mean that they're executing *simultaneously*. In this sense, parallelism is a subset of concurrency. The human body performs a great variety of operations in parallel. Respiration, blood circulation, digestion, thinking and walking, for example, can occur in parallel, as can all the senses—sight, hearing, touch, smell and taste. It's believed that this parallelism is possible because the human brain is thought to contain billions of "processors." Today's multicore computers have multiple processors that can perform tasks in parallel.

### *Multithreading*

C# makes concurrency available to you through the language and APIs. C# programs can have multiple **threads of execution**, where each thread has its own method-call stack, allowing it to execute concurrently with other threads while sharing with them application-wide resources such as memory and files. This capability is called **multithreading**.

**Performance Tip 21.1**

*A problem with single-threaded applications that can lead to poor responsiveness is that lengthy activities must complete* before *others can begin. In a multithreaded application, threads can be distributed across multiple cores (if available) so that multiple tasks execute in parallel and the application can operate more efficiently. Multithreading can also increase performance on single-processor systems—when one thread cannot proceed (because, for example, it's waiting for the result of an I/O operation), another can use the processor.*

### *Multithreading Is Difficult*

People find it difficult to jump between concurrent trains of thought. To see why multithreaded programs can be difficult to write and understand, try the following experiment: Open three books to page 1, and try reading the books concurrently. Read a few words from the first book, then a few from the second, then a few from the third, then loop back and read the next few words from the first book, the second and so on. After this experiment, you'll appreciate many of the challenges of multithreading—switching between the books, reading briefly, remembering your place in each book, moving the book you're reading closer so that you can see it and pushing the books you're not reading aside—and, amid all this chaos, trying to comprehend the content of the books!

### *Asynchronous Programming,* `async` *and* `await`

To take full advantage of multicore architectures you need to write applications that can process tasks *asynchronously*. **Asynchronous programming** is a technique for writing apps containing tasks that can execute asynchronously, which can improve app performance and GUI responsiveness in apps with long-running or compute-intensive tasks. Before languages like C#, such apps were implemented with operating-system primitives available only to experienced systems programmers. Then C# and other programming languages began enabling app developers to specify concurrent operations. Initially, these capabilities were complex to use, which led to frequent and subtle bugs.

The `async` modifier and `await` operator greatly simplify asynchronous programming, reduce errors and enable your apps to take advantage of the processing power in today's multicore computers, smartphones and tablets. Many .NET classes for web access, file processing, networking, image processing and more have methods that return `Task` objects for use with `async` and `await`, so you can take advantage of asynchronous programming model. This chapter presents a simple introduction to asynchronous programming with `async` and `await`.

## 21.2 Basics of async and await

Before async and await, it was common for a method that was called *synchronously* (i.e., performing tasks one after another in order) in the calling thread to launch a long-running task *asynchronously* and to provide that task with a *callback method* (or, in some cases, register an event handler) that would be invoked once the asynchronous task completed. This style of coding is simplified with async and await.

### 21.2.1 async Modifier

The **async modifier** indicates that a method or lambda expression contains at least one await expression. An async method executes its body in the same thread as the calling method. (Throughout the remainder of this discussion, we'll use the term "method" to mean "method or lambda expression.")

### 21.2.2 await Expression

An **await expression**, which can appear *only* in an async method, consists of the **await operator** followed by an expression that returns an *awaitable entity*—typically a Task object (as you'll see in Section 21.3), though it is possible to create your own awaitable entities. Creating awaitable entities is beyond the scope of our discussion. For more information, see

```
http://blogs.msdn.com/b/pfxteam/archive/2011/01/13/10115642.aspx
```

When an async method encounters an **await** expression:

- If the asynchronous task has already completed, the async method simply continues executing.
- Otherwise, program control returns to the async method's caller until the asynchronous task completes execution. This allows the caller to perform other work that does not depend on the results of the asynchronous task.

When the asynchronous task completes, control returns to the async method and continues with the next statement after the await expression.

**Software Engineering Observation 21.1**

*The mechanisms for determining whether to return control to an async method's caller or continue executing an async method, and for continuing an async method's execution when the asynchronous task completes, are handled entirely by code that's written for you by the compiler.*

### 21.2.3 async, await and Threads

The async and await mechanism does *not* create new threads. If any threads are required, the method that you call to start an asynchronous task on which you await the results is responsible for creating the threads that are used to perform the asynchronous task. For example, we'll show how to use class Task's Run method in several examples to start new threads of execution for executing tasks asynchronously. Task method Run returns a Task on which a method can await the result.

## 21.3 Executing an Asynchronous Task from a GUI App

This section demonstrates the benefits of executing compute-intensive tasks asynchronously in a GUI app.

### 21.3.1 Performing a Task Asynchronously

Figure 21.1 demonstrates executing an asynchronous task from a GUI app. Consider the GUI at the end of Fig. 21.1. In the GUI's top half, you can enter an integer, then click **Calculate** to calculate that integer's Fibonacci value (discussed momentarily) using a compute-intensive recursive implementation (Section 21.3.2). Starting with integers in the 40s (on our test computer), the recursive calculation can take seconds or even minutes to calculate. If this calculation were to be performed *synchronously*, the GUI would *freeze* for that amount of time and the user would not be able to interact with the app (as we'll demonstrate in Fig. 21.2). We launch the calculation *asynchronously* and have it execute on a *separate* thread so the GUI remains *responsive*. To demonstrate this, in the GUI's bottom half, you can click **Next Number** repeatedly to calculate the next Fibonacci number by simply adding the two previous numbers in the sequence. For the screen captures in Fig. 21.1, we used the top half of the GUI to calculate `Fibonacci(45)`, which took over a minute on our test computer. While that calculation proceeded in a separate thread, we clicked **Next Number** repeatedly to demonstrate that we could still interact with the GUI and that the iterative Fibonacci calculation is much more efficient.

#### *A Compute-Intensive Algorithm: Calculating Fibonacci Numbers Recursively*

The examples in this section and in Sections 21.4–21.5 each perform a compute-intensive *recursive* Fibonacci calculation (defined in the `Fibonacci` method at lines 53–63). The Fibonacci series

0, 1, 1, 2, 3, 5, 8, 13, 21, …

begins with 0 and 1, and each subsequent Fibonacci number is the sum of the previous two Fibonacci numbers. The Fibonacci series can be defined *recursively* as follows:

$$\begin{aligned} &\text{Fibonacci}(0) = 0 \\ &\text{Fibonacci}(1) = 1 \\ &\text{Fibonacci}(n) = \text{Fibonacci}(n-1) + \text{Fibonacci}(n-2) \end{aligned}$$

```
1  // Fig. 21.1: FibonacciForm.cs
2  // Performing a compute-intensive calculation from a GUI app
3  using System;
4  using System.Threading.Tasks;
5  using System.Windows.Forms;
6
7  namespace FibonacciTest
8  {
9     public partial class FibonacciForm : Form
10    {
11       private long n1 = 0; // initialize with first Fibonacci number
12       private long n2 = 1; // initialize with second Fibonacci number
```

**Fig. 21.1** | Performing a compute-intensive calculation from a GUI app. (Part 1 of 3.)

```
      private int count = 1; // current Fibonacci number to display

      public FibonacciForm()
      {
         InitializeComponent();
      }

      // start an async Task to calculate specified Fibonacci number
      private async void calculateButton_Click(object sender, EventArgs e)
      {
         // retrieve user's input as an integer
         int number = int.Parse(inputTextBox.Text);

         asyncResultLabel.Text = "Calculating...";

         // Task to perform Fibonacci calculation in separate thread
         Task<long> fibonacciTask = Task.Run(() => Fibonacci(number));

         // wait for Task in separate thread to complete
         await fibonacciTask;

         // display result after Task in separate thread completes
         asyncResultLabel.Text = fibonacciTask.Result.ToString();
      }

      // calculate next Fibonacci number iteratively
      private void nextNumberButton_Click(object sender, EventArgs e)
      {
         // calculate the next Fibonacci number
         long temp = n1 + n2; // calculate next Fibonacci number
         n1 = n2; // store prior Fibonacci number in n1
         n2 = temp; // store new Fibonacci
         ++count;

         // display the next Fibonacci number
         displayLabel.Text = $"Fibonacci of {count}:";
         syncResultLabel.Text = n2.ToString();
      }

      // recursive method Fibonacci; calculates nth Fibonacci number
      public long Fibonacci(long n)
      {
         if (n == 0 || n == 1)
         {
            return n;
         }
         else
         {
            return Fibonacci(n - 1) + Fibonacci(n - 2);
         }
      }
   }
}
```

**Fig. 21.1** | Performing a compute-intensive calculation from a GUI app. (Part 2 of 3.)

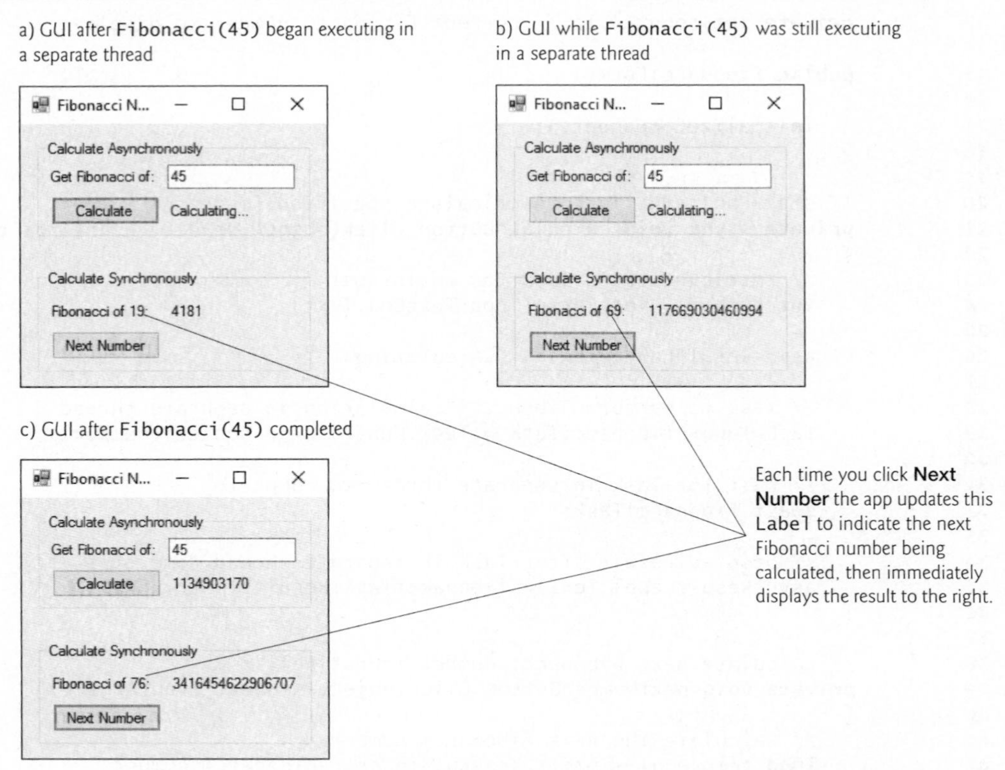

a) GUI after Fibonacci(45) began executing in a separate thread
b) GUI while Fibonacci(45) was still executing in a separate thread
c) GUI after Fibonacci(45) completed
Fibonacci N...
Calculate Asynchronously
Get Fibonacci of: 45
Calculate
Calculating...
1134903170
Calculate Synchronously
Fibonacci of 19: 4181
Fibonacci of 69: 117669030460994
Fibonacci of 76: 3416454622906707
Next Number
Each time you click Next Number the app updates this Label to indicate the next Fibonacci number being calculated, then immediately displays the result to the right.


**Fig. 21.1** | Performing a compute-intensive calculation from a GUI app. (Part 3 of 3.)

### *Exponential Complexity*

A word of caution is in order about recursive methods like the one we use here to generate Fibonacci numbers. The number of recursive calls that are required to calculate the *n*th Fibonacci number is on the order of $2^n$. This rapidly gets out of hand as *n* gets larger. Calculating only the 20th Fibonacci number would require on the order of $2^{20}$ or about a million calls, calculating the 30th Fibonacci number would require on the order of $2^{30}$ or about a billion calls, and so on. This **exponential complexity** can humble even the world's most powerful computers! Calculating just Fibonacci(47) recursively—even on today's most recent desktop and notebook computers—can take minutes.

## 21.3.2 Method `calculateButton_Click`

The **Calculate** button's event handler (lines 21–36) initiates the call to method `Fibonacci` in a separate thread and displays the results when the call completes. The method is declared `async` (line 21) to indicate to the compiler that the method will initiate an asynchronous task and `await` the results. In an `async` method, you write code that looks as if it executes sequentially, and the compiler handles the complicated issues of managing asynchronous execution. This makes your code easier to write, debug, modify and maintain, and reduces errors.

### 21.3.3 Task Method Run: Executing Asynchronously in a Separate Thread

Line 29 creates and starts a **`Task<TResult>`** (namespace **`System.Threading.Tasks`**), which *promises* to return a result of generic type `TResult` *at some point* in the future. Class `Task` is part of .NET's *Task Parallel Library (TPL)* for parallel and asynchronous programming. The version of class `Task`'s `static` method **`Run`** used in line 29 receives a **`Func<TResult>` delegate** (delegates were introduced in Section 14.3.3) as an argument and executes a method in a *separate thread*. The delegate `Func<TResult>` represents any method that takes *no arguments* and returns a *result* of the type specified by the `TResult` type parameter. The return type of the method you pass to `Run` is used by the compiler as the type argument for `Run`'s `Func` delegate and for the `Task` that `Run` returns.

Method `Fibonacci` requires an argument, so line 29 passes the *lambda expression*

```
() => Fibonacci(number)
```

which takes *no arguments*—this lambda encapsulates the call to `Fibonacci` with the argument `number` (the value entered by the user). The lambda expression *implicitly* returns the `Fibonacci` call's result (a `long`), so it meets the `Func<TResult>` delegate's requirements. In this example, `Task`'s `static` method `Run` creates and returns a `Task<long>`. The compiler *infers* the type `long` from the return type of method `Fibonacci`. We could declare local variable `fibonacciTask` (line 29) with `var`—we explicitly used the type `Task<long>` for clarity, because `Task` method `Run`'s return type is not obvious from the call.

### 21.3.4 awaiting the Result

Next, line 32 `await`s the result of the `fibonacciTask` that's executing asynchronously. If the `fibonacciTask` is *already complete*, execution continues with line 35. Otherwise, control returns to `calculateButton_Click`'s caller (the GUI event-handling thread) until the result of the `fibonacciTask` is available. This allows the GUI to remain *responsive* while the `Task` executes. Once the `Task` completes, `calculateButton_Click` continues execution at line 35, which uses `Task` property **`Result`** to get the value returned by `Fibonacci` and display it on `asyncResultLabel`.

An `async` method can perform statements between those that launch an asynchronous `Task` and `await` the results. In such a case, the method continues executing those statements after launching the asynchronous `Task` until it reaches the `await` expression.

Lines 29 and 32 can be written more concisely as

```
long result = await Task.Run(() => Fibonacci(number));
```

In this case, the `await` operator unwraps and returns the `Task`'s result—the `long` returned by method `Fibonacci`. You can then use the `long` value directly without accessing the `Task`'s `Result` property.

### 21.3.5 Calculating the Next Fibonacci Value Synchronously

When you click **Next Number**, the event handler `nextNumberButton_Click` (lines 39–50) executes. Lines 42–45 add the previous two Fibonacci numbers stored in instance variables `n1` and `n2` to determine the next number in the sequence, update instance variables `n1` and n2 to their new values and increment instance variable count. Then lines 48–49 update the GUI to display the Fibonacci number that was just calculated.

The code in the **Next Number** event handler is performed in the GUI thread of execution that processes user interactions with controls. Handling such short computations in this thread does *not* cause the GUI to become unresponsive. Because the longer Fibonacci computation is performed in a *separate thread*, it's possible to get the next Fibonacci number *while the recursive computation is still in progress*.

## 21.4 Sequential Execution of Two Compute-Intensive Tasks

Figure 21.2 uses the recursive Fibonacci method that we introduced in Section 21.3. The example sequentially performs the calculations Fibonacci(46) (line 22) and Fibonacci(45) (line 35) when the user clicks the **Start Sequential Fibonacci Calls** Button. Note that once you click the Button, the app becomes nonresponsive. This occurs because the Fibonacci calculations are performed in the GUI thread—once the calculations complete, you'll be able to interact with the app again. Before and after each Fibonacci call, we capture the time (as a DateTime; Section 15.4) so that we can calculate the total time required for *that* calculation and the total time required for *both* calculations. In this app, we used DateTime's overloaded minus (-) operator to calculate the differences between DateTimes (lines 27, 40 and 45)—like method Subtract introduced previously, the minus (-) operator returns a TimeSpan.

The first two outputs show the results of executing the app on a *dual-core* Windows 10 computer. The last two outputs show the results of executing the app on a single-core Windows 10 computer. In all cases, the cores operated at the same speed. The app *always* took longer to execute (in our testing) on the single-core computer, because the processor was being *shared* between this app and all the others that happened to be executing on the computer at the same time. On the dual-core system, one of the cores could have been handling the "other stuff" executing on the computer, reducing the demand on the core performing the synchronous calculation. Results may vary across systems based on processor speeds, the number of cores, apps currently executing and the chores the operating system is performing.

```
1  // Fig. 21.2: SynchronousTestForm.cs
2  // Fibonacci calculations performed sequentially
3  using System;
4  using System.Windows.Forms;
5
6  namespace FibonacciSynchronous
7  {
8     public partial class SynchronousTestForm : Form
9     {
10       public SynchronousTestForm()
11       {
12          InitializeComponent();
13       }
```

**Fig. 21.2** | Fibonacci calculations performed sequentially. (Part 1 of 3.)

```
      // start sequential calls to Fibonacci
      private void startButton_Click(object sender, EventArgs e)
      {
         // calculate Fibonacci (46)
         outputTextBox.Text = "Calculating Fibonacci(46)\r\n";
         outputTextBox.Refresh(); // force outputTextBox to repaint
         DateTime startTime1 = DateTime.Now; // time before calculation
         long result1 = Fibonacci(46); // synchronous call
         DateTime endTime1 = DateTime.Now; // time after calculation

         // display results for Fibonacci(46)
         outputTextBox.AppendText($"Fibonacci(46) = {result1}\r\n");
         double minutes = (endTime1 - startTime1).TotalMinutes;
         outputTextBox.AppendText(
            $"Calculation time = {minutes:F6} minutes\r\n\r\n");

         // calculate Fibonacci (45)
         outputTextBox.AppendText("Calculating Fibonacci(45)\r\n");
         outputTextBox.Refresh(); // force outputTextBox to repaint
         DateTime startTime2 = DateTime.Now;
         long result2 = Fibonacci(45); // synchronous call
         DateTime endTime2 = DateTime.Now;

         // display results for Fibonacci(45)
         outputTextBox.AppendText($"Fibonacci(45) = {result2}\r\n");
         minutes = (endTime2 - startTime2).TotalMinutes;
         outputTextBox.AppendText(
            $"Calculation time = {minutes:F6} minutes\r\n\r\n");

         // show total calculation time
         double totalMinutes = (endTime2 - startTime1).TotalMinutes;
         outputTextBox.AppendText(
            $"Total calculation time = {totalMinutes:F6} minutes\r\n");
      }

      // Recursively calculates Fibonacci numbers
      public long Fibonacci(long n)
      {
         if (n == 0 || n == 1)
         {
            return n;
         }
         else
         {
            return Fibonacci(n - 1) + Fibonacci(n - 2);
         }
      }
   }
}
```

**Fig. 21.2** | Fibonacci calculations performed sequentially. (Part 2 of 3.)

*a) Outputs on a Dual-Core Windows 10 Computer*

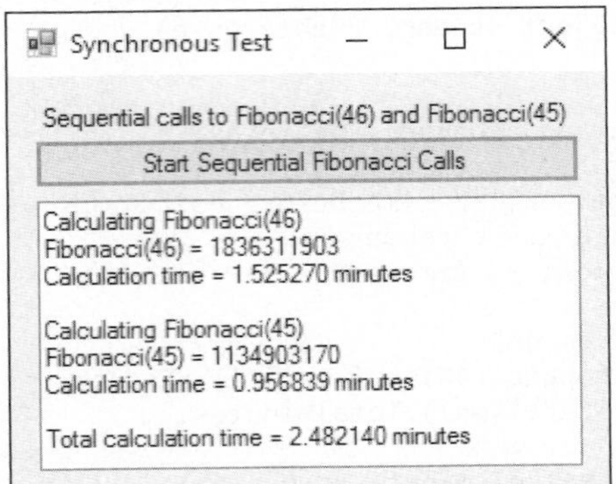


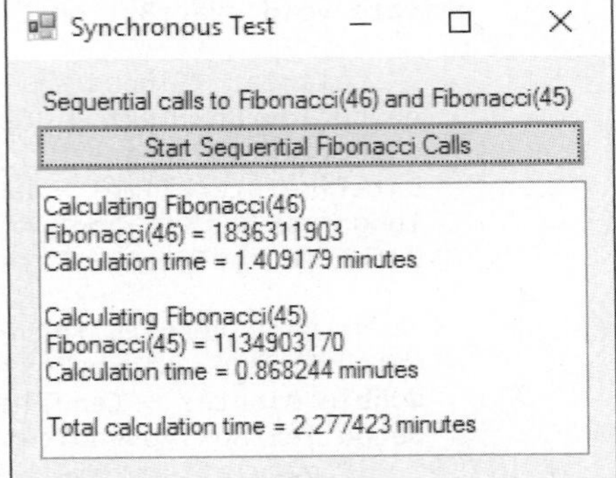


*b) Outputs on a Single-Core Windows 10 Computer*

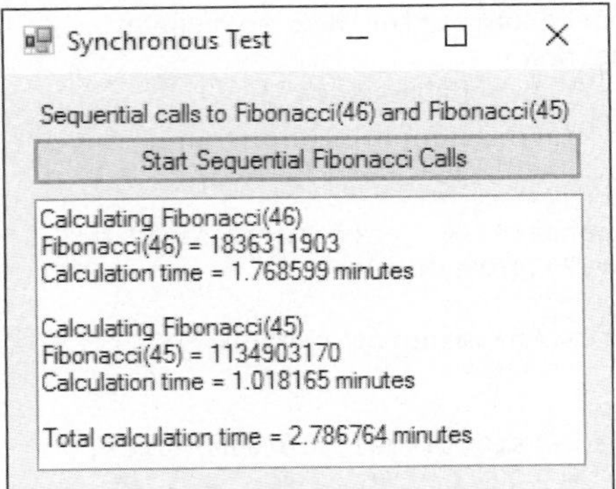


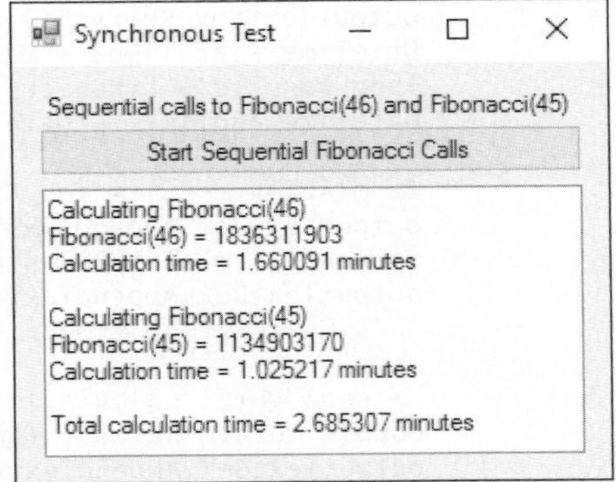


**Fig. 21.2** | Fibonacci calculations performed sequentially. (Part 3 of 3.)

## 21.5 Asynchronous Execution of Two Compute-Intensive Tasks

When you run any program, its tasks compete for processor time with the operating system, other programs and other activities that the operating system is running on your behalf. When you execute the next example, the time to perform the Fibonacci calculations can vary based on your computer's processor speed, number of cores and what else is running on your computer. It's like a drive to the supermarket—the time it takes can vary based on traffic conditions, weather, timing of traffic lights and other factors.

Figure 21.3 also uses the recursive `Fibonacci` method, but the two initial calls to `Fibonacci` execute in *separate threads*. The first two outputs show the results on a *dual-core* computer. Though execution times varied, the total time to perform both `Fibonacci` calculations (in our tests) was typically *significantly less* than the total sequential-execution time in Fig. 21.2. Dividing the compute-intensive calculations into threads and running them on a dual-core system does *not* perform the calculations *twice as fast*, but they'll typically run *faster* than when performed *in sequence* on one core. Though the total time was the compute time for the longer calculation, this is not always the case, as there's overhead inherent in using threads to perform separate Tasks.

The last two outputs show that executing calculations in multiple threads on a single-core processor can actually take *longer* than simply performing them synchronously, due to the overhead of sharing *one* processor among the app's threads, all the other apps executing on the computer and the chores the operating system was performing.

```
// Fig. 21.3: AsynchronousTestForm.cs
// Fibonacci calculations performed in separate threads
using System;
using System.Threading.Tasks;
using System.Windows.Forms;

namespace FibonacciAsynchronous
{
   public partial class AsynchronousTestForm : Form
   {
      public AsynchronousTestForm()
      {
         InitializeComponent();
      }

      // start asynchronous calls to Fibonacci
      private async void startButton_Click(object sender, EventArgs e)
      {
         outputTextBox.Text =
            "Starting Task to calculate Fibonacci(46)\r\n";

         // create Task to perform Fibonacci(46) calculation in a thread
         Task<TimeData> task1 = Task.Run(() => StartFibonacci(46));

         outputTextBox.AppendText(
            "Starting Task to calculate Fibonacci(45)\r\n");

         // create Task to perform Fibonacci(45) calculation in a thread
         Task<TimeData> task2 =  Task.Run(() => StartFibonacci(45));

         await Task.WhenAll(task1, task2); // wait for both to complete

         // determine time that first thread started
         DateTime startTime =
            (task1.Result.StartTime < task2.Result.StartTime) ?
            task1.Result.StartTime : task2.Result.StartTime;

         // determine time that last thread ended
         DateTime endTime =
            (task1.Result.EndTime > task2.Result.EndTime) ?
            task1.Result.EndTime : task2.Result.EndTime;

```

**Fig. 21.3** | Fibonacci calculations performed in separate threads. (Part 1 of 3.)

```
         // display total time for calculations
         double totalMinutes = (endTime - startTime).TotalMinutes;
         outputTextBox.AppendText(
            $"Total calculation time = {totalMinutes:F6} minutes\r\n");
      }

      // starts a call to Fibonacci and captures start/end times
      TimeData StartFibonacci(int n)
      {
         // create a TimeData object to store start/end times
         var result = new TimeData();

         AppendText($"Calculating Fibonacci({n})");
         result.StartTime = DateTime.Now;
         long fibonacciValue = Fibonacci(n);
         result.EndTime = DateTime.Now;

         AppendText($"Fibonacci({n}) = {fibonacciValue}");
         double minutes =
            (result.EndTime - result.StartTime).TotalMinutes;
         AppendText($"Calculation time = {minutes:F6} minutes\r\n");

         return result;
      }

      // Recursively calculates Fibonacci numbers
      public long Fibonacci(long n)
      {
         if (n == 0 || n == 1)
         {
            return n;
         }
         else
         {
            return Fibonacci(n - 1) + Fibonacci(n - 2);
         }
      }

      // append text to outputTextBox in UI thread
      public void AppendText(String text)
      {
         if (InvokeRequired) // not GUI thread, so add to GUI thread
         {
            Invoke(new MethodInvoker(() => AppendText(text)));
         }
         else // GUI thread so append text
         {
            outputTextBox.AppendText(text + "\r\n");
         }
      }
   }
}
```

**Fig. 21.3** | Fibonacci calculations performed in separate threads. (Part 2 of 3.)

*a) Outputs on a Dual-Core Windows 10 Computer*

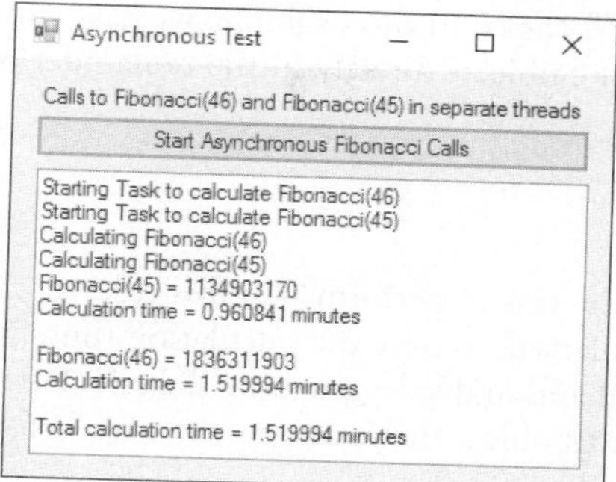


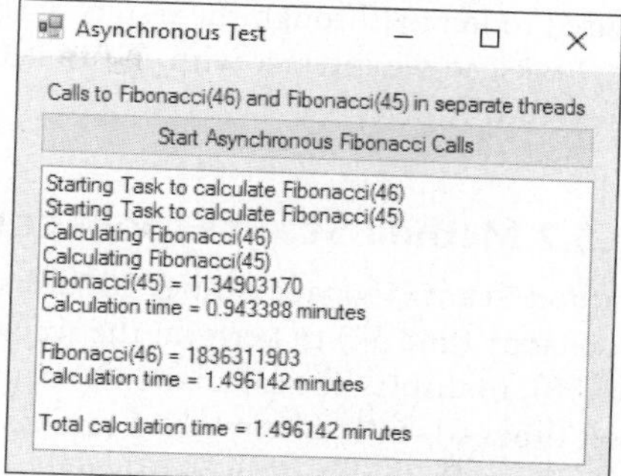


*b) Outputs on a Single-Core Windows 10 Computer*

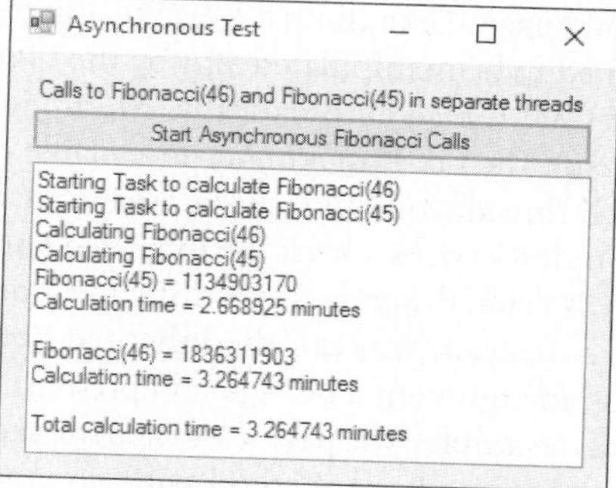


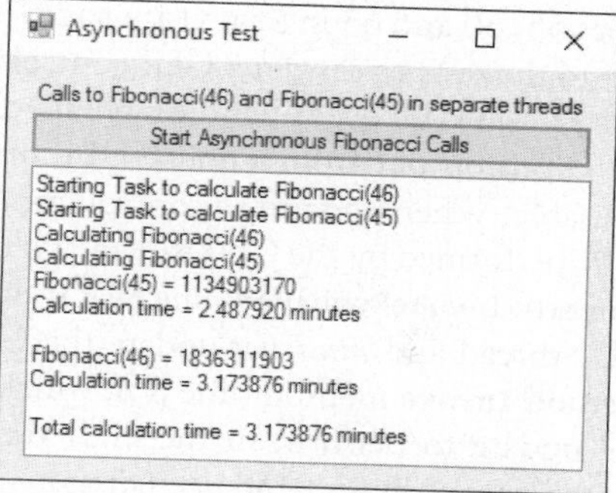


**Fig. 21.3** | Fibonacci calculations performed in separate threads. (Part 3 of 3.)

### 21.5.1 `await`ing Multiple Tasks with Task Method `WhenAll`

In method `startButton_Click`, lines 23 and 29 use `Task` method `Run` to create and start `Task`s that execute method `StartFibonacci` (lines 50–66)—one to calculate `Fibonacci(46)` and one to calculate `Fibonacci(45)`. To show the total calculation time, the app must wait for *both* `Task`s to complete *before* executing lines 34–46. You can wait for *multiple* `Task`s to complete by `await`ing the result of `Task static` method **`WhenAll`** (line 31), which returns a `Task` that waits for *all* of `WhenAll`'s argument `Task`s to complete and places *all* the results in an array. In this app, the `Task`'s `Result` is a `TimeData[]`, because both of `WhenAll`'s argument `Task`s execute methods that return `TimeData` objects. Class `TimeData` is defined as follows in this project's `TimeData.cs` file:

```
class TimeData
{
   public DateTime StartTime { get; set; }
   public DateTime EndTime { get; set; }
}
```

We use objects of this class to store the time just before and immediately after the call to Fibonacci—we use these properties to perform time calculations. The TimeData array can be used to iterate through the results of the awaited Tasks. In this example, we have only two Tasks, so we interact with the task1 and task2 objects directly in the remainder of the event handler.

### 21.5.2 Method StartFibonacci

Method StartFibonacci (lines 50–66) specifies the task to perform—in this case, to call Fibonacci (line 57) to perform the recursive calculation, to time the calculation (lines 56 and 58), to display the calculation's result (line 60) and to display the time the calculation took (lines 61–63). The method returns a TimeData object that contains the time before and after each thread's call to Fibonacci.

### 21.5.3 Modifying a GUI from a Separate Thread

Lines 55, 60 and 63 in StartFibonacci call method AppendText (lines 82–92) to append text to the outputTextBox. GUI controls are designed to be manipulated *only* by the GUI thread—all GUI event handlers are invoked in the GUI thread automatically. Modifying GUI controls one from a non-GUI thread can corrupt the GUI, making it unreadable or unusable. When updating a control from a non-GUI thread, you *must schedule* that update to be performed by the GUI thread. To do so in Windows Forms, check the inherited Form property **InvokeRequired** (line 84). If this property is true, the code is executing in a non-GUI thread and *must not* update the GUI directly. Instead, you call the inherited Form method **Invoke** method (line 86), which receives as an argument a Delegate representing the update to perform in the GUI thread. In this example, we pass a MethodInvoker (namespace System.Windows.Forms)—a Delegate that invokes a method with no arguments and a void return type. We initialize the MethodInvoker with a *lambda expression* that calls AppendText. Line 86 *schedules* this MethodInvoker to execute in the GUI thread. When the method is called from the GUI thread, line 90 updates the outputTextBox. Similar concepts also apply to WPF and Universal Windows Platform GUIs.

### 21.5.4 awaiting One of Several Tasks with Task Method WhenAny

Similar to WhenAll, class Task also provides static method **WhenAny**, which enables you to wait for any one of several Tasks specified as arguments to complete. WhenAny returns the Task that completes first. One use of WhenAny might be to initiate several Tasks that perform the same complex calculation on computers around the Internet, then wait for any one of those computers to send results back. This would allow you to take advantage of computing power that's available to you to get the result as fast as possible. In this case, it's up to you to decide whether to cancel the remaining Tasks or allow them to continue executing. For details on how to do this, see

```
https://msdn.microsoft.com/library/jj155758
```

Another use of WhenAny might be to download several large files—one per Task. In this case, you might want all the results eventually, but you'd like to start processing immediately the results from the first Task that returns. You could then call WhenAny again for the remaining Tasks that are still executing.

## 21.6 Invoking a Flickr Web Service Asynchronously with HttpClient

In this section, we present a **Flickr Viewer** app that allows you to search for photos on Flickr (flickr.com)—one of the first photo-sharing websites—then browse through the results. The app uses an asynchronous method to invoke a Flickr **web service**—that is, a software component that can receive method calls over the Internet using standard web technologies.

### *XML and LINQ to XML*

Many web services return data in XML (Extensible Markup Language) format. XML is a widely supported standard for describing data that is commonly used to exchange that data between applications over the Internet. XML describes data in a way that both human beings and computers can understand.

The Flickr web-service method we use in this example returns XML by default. We'll use LINQ to XML, which is built into the .NET platform, to process the data returned by Flickr. We'll explain in Section 21.6.3 the small amount of XML and LINQ to XML needed.

### *REST Web Service*

Flickr provides a so-called REST (Representational State Transfer) web service that can receive method calls via standard web technologies. As you'll see, the app invokes a Flickr web-service method via a URL, just as you'd use to access a web page from a web browser.

### *Asynchronously Invoking a Web Service*

Because there can be unpredictably long delays while awaiting a web-service response, asynchronous Tasks are frequently used in GUI apps that invoke web services (or perform network communication in general) to ensure that the apps remain responsive to their users.

### *A Flickr API Key Is Required*

To run this example on your computer, ***you must obtain your own Flickr API key*** at

```
https://www.flickr.com/services/apps/create/apply
```

and use it to replace the words YOUR API KEY HERE inside the quotes in line 18 of Fig. 21.4. This key is a unique string of characters and numbers that enables Flickr to track your usage of its APIs. Be sure to read the Flickr API's Terms of Use carefully.

### *Flicker Viewer App*

Our **Flickr Viewer** app (Fig. 21.4) allows you to search by tag for photos that users worldwide have uploaded to Flickr. Tagging—or labeling content—is part of the collaborative nature of social media. A tag is any user-supplied word or phrase that helps organize web content. Tagging items with meaningful words or phrases creates a strong identification of the content. Flickr uses the tags to improve its photo-search service, giving users better results.

```
// Fig. 21.4: FickrViewerForm.cs
// Invoking a web service asynchronously with class HttpClient
using System;
using System.Drawing;
using System.IO;
using System.Linq;
using System.Net.Http;
using System.Threading.Tasks;
using System.Windows.Forms;
using System.Xml.Linq;

namespace FlickrViewer
{
   public partial class FickrViewerForm : Form
   {
      // Use your Flickr API key here--you can get one at:
      // https://www.flickr.com/services/apps/create/apply
      private const string KEY = "YOUR API KEY HERE";

      // object used to invoke Flickr web service
      private static HttpClient flickrClient = new HttpClient();

      Task<string> flickrTask = null; // Task<string> that queries Flickr

      public FickrViewerForm()
      {
         InitializeComponent();
      }

      // initiate asynchronous Flickr search query;
      // display results when query completes
      private async void searchButton_Click(object sender, EventArgs e)
      {
         // if flickrTask already running, prompt user
         if (flickrTask?.Status != TaskStatus.RanToCompletion)
         {
            var result = MessageBox.Show(
               "Cancel the current Flickr search?",
               "Are you sure?", MessageBoxButtons.YesNo,
               MessageBoxIcon.Question);

            // determine whether user wants to cancel prior search
            if (result == DialogResult.No)
            {
               return;
            }
            else
            {
               flickrClient.CancelPendingRequests(); // cancel search
            }
         }
```

**Fig. 21.4** | Invoking a web service asynchronously with class `HttpClient`. (Part 1 of 3.) [Photos used in this example ©Paul Deitel. All rights reserved.]

```

         // Flickr's web service URL for searches
         var flickrURL = "https://api.flickr.com/services/rest/?method=" +
            $"flickr.photos.search&api_key={KEY}&" +
            $"tags={inputTextBox.Text.Replace(" ", ",")}" +
            "&tag_mode=all&per_page=500&privacy_filter=1";

         imagesListBox.DataSource = null; // remove prior data source
         imagesListBox.Items.Clear(); // clear imagesListBox
         pictureBox.Image = null; // clear pictureBox
         imagesListBox.Items.Add("Loading..."); // display Loading...

         // invoke Flickr web service to search Flickr with user's tags
         flickrTask = flickrClient.GetStringAsync(flickrURL);

         // await flickrTask then parse results with XDocument and LINQ
         XDocument flickrXML = XDocument.Parse(await flickrTask);

         // gather information on all photos
         var flickrPhotos =
            from photo in flickrXML.Descendants("photo")
            let id = photo.Attribute("id").Value
            let title = photo.Attribute("title").Value
            let secret = photo.Attribute("secret").Value
            let server = photo.Attribute("server").Value
            let farm = photo.Attribute("farm").Value
            select new FlickrResult
            {
               Title = title,
               URL = $"https://farm{farm}.staticflickr.com/" +
                  $"{server}/{id}_{secret}.jpg"
            };
         imagesListBox.Items.Clear(); // clear imagesListBox

         // set ListBox properties only if results were found
         if (flickrPhotos.Any())
         {
            imagesListBox.DataSource = flickrPhotos.ToList();
            imagesListBox.DisplayMember = "Title";
         }
         else // no matches were found
         {
            imagesListBox.Items.Add("No matches");
         }
      }

      // display selected image
      private async void imagesListBox_SelectedIndexChanged(
         object sender, EventArgs e)
      {
```

**Fig. 21.4** | Invoking a web service asynchronously with class `HttpClient`. (Part 2 of 3.) [Photos used in this example ©Paul Deitel. All rights reserved.]

```
            if (imagesListBox.SelectedItem != null)
            {
               string selectedURL =
                  ((FlickrResult) imagesListBox.SelectedItem).URL;

               // use HttpClient to get selected image's bytes asynchronously
               byte[] imageBytes =
                  await flickrClient.GetByteArrayAsync(selectedURL);

               // display downloaded image in pictureBox
               MemoryStream memoryStream = new MemoryStream(imageBytes);
               pictureBox.Image = Image.FromStream(memoryStream);
            }
         }
      }
   }
```

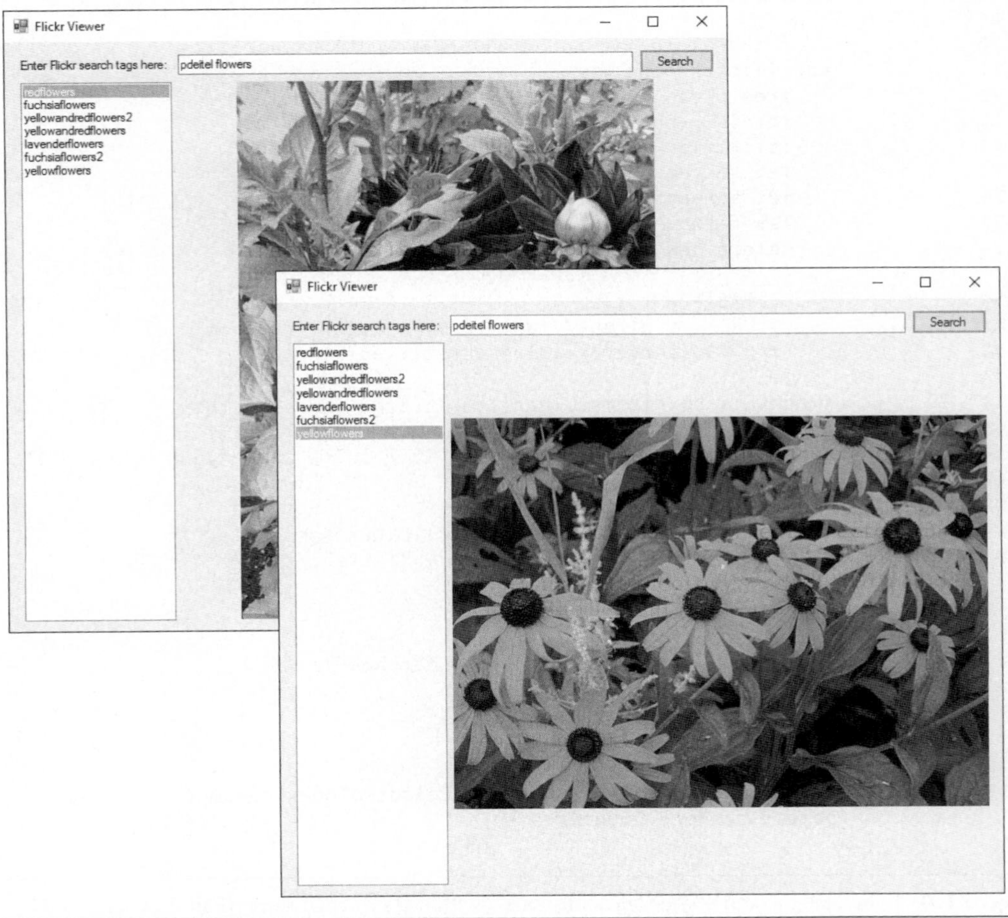


**Fig. 21.4** | Invoking a web service asynchronously with class `HttpClient`. (Part 3 of 3.) [Photos used in this example ©Paul Deitel. All rights reserved.]

As shown in Fig. 21.4, you can type one or more tags (e.g., "pdeitel flowers") into the `TextBox`. When you click the **Search** `Button`, the application invokes the Flickr web service that searches for photos, which returns an XML document containing links to the first 500 (or fewer if there are not 500) results that match the tags you specify. We use LINQ to XML to parse the results and display a list of photo titles in a `ListBox`. When you select an image's title in the `ListBox`, the app uses another asynchronous `Task` to download the full-size image from Flickr and display it in a `PictureBox`.

### 21.6.1 Using Class `HttpClient` to Invoke a Web Service

This app uses class **`HttpClient`** (namespace `System.Net.Http`) to interact with Flickr's web service and retrieve photos that match the search tags. Line 21 creates the `static` `HttpClient` object `flickrClient` that's used in this app to download data from Flickr. Class `HttpClient` is one of many .NET classes that support asynchronous programming with `async` and `await`. In `searchButton_Click` (lines 32–96), we use class `HttpClient`'s **`GetStringAsync`** method to start a new `Task` (line 65). When we create that `Task`, we assign it to instance variable `flickrTask` (declared in line 23) so that we can test whether the `Task` is still executing when the user initiates a new search.

**Software Engineering Observation 21.2**

*An `HttpClient` object is typically declared `static` so it can be used by all of an app's threads. According to the `HttpClient` documentation, a `static` `HttpClient` object can be used from multiple threads of execution.*

### 21.6.2 Invoking the Flickr Web Service's `flickr.photos.search` Method

Method `searchButton_Click` (lines 32–96) initiates the *asynchronous* Flickr search, so it's declared as an `async` method. First, lines 35–51 check whether you started a search previously and, if so, whether that search has already completed (lines 34–35). If an existing search is still being performed, we display a dialog asking if you wish to cancel the search (lines 37–40). If you click **No**, the event handler simply returns. Otherwise, we call the `HttpClient`'s **`CancelPendingRequests`** method to terminate the search (line 49).

Lines 54–57 create the URL that invokes Flickr's `flickr.photos.search` web-service method, which searches for photos, based on the provided parameters. You can learn more about this method's parameters and the format of the URL for invoking the method at

```
https://www.flickr.com/services/api/flickr.photos.search.html
```

In this example, we specify values for the following `flickr.photos.search` parameters:

- `api_key`—Your Flickr API key. Remember that you must obtain your own key from `https://www.flickr.com/services/apps/create/apply`.
- `tags`—A comma-separated list of the tags for which to search. In our sample executions it was `"pdeitel,flowers"`. If the user separates the tags with spaces, the app replaces the spaces with commas.
- `tag_mode`—We use the `all` mode to get results that match *all* the tags specified in the search. You also can use `any` to get results that match *one or more* of the tags.

- per_page—The maximum number of results to return (up to 500). If this parameter is omitted, the default is 100.
- privacy_filter—1 indicates only *publicly accessible* photos should be returned.

Line 65 calls class HttpClient's GetStringAsync method, which uses the URL specified as the string argument to request information from a web server. Because this URL represents a call to a web-service method, calling GetStringAsync will invoke the Flickr web service to perform the search. GetStringAsync returns a Task<string> representing a *promise* to eventually return a string containing the search results. Line 68 then awaits the Task's result. At this point, if the Task is complete, method searchButton_Click's execution continues at line 71; otherwise, program control returns to method searchButton_Click's caller until the results are received. This allows the GUI thread of execution to handle other events, so the GUI remains *responsive* while the search is ongoing. Thus, you could decide to start a *different* search at any time (which cancels the original search in this app).

### 21.6.3 Processing the XML Response

When the Task completes, program control continues in method searchButton_Click at line 68 where the app begins processing the XML returned by the web service. A sample of the XML is shown in Fig. 21.5.

```
1  <rsp stat="ok">
2     <photos page="1" pages="1" perpage="500" total="5">
3        <photo id="8708146820" owner="8832668@N04" secret="40fabab966"
4           server="8130" farm="9" title="fuchsiaflowers" ispublic="1"
5           isfriend="0" isfamily="0"/>
6        <photo id="8707026559" owner="8832668@N04" secret="97be93bb05"
7           server="8115" farm="9" title="redflowers" ispublic="1"
8           isfriend="0" isfamily="0"/>
9        <photo id="8707023603" owner="8832668@N04" secret="54db053efd"
10          server="8263" farm="9" title="yellowflowers" ispublic="1"
11          isfriend="0" isfamily="0"/>
12    </photos>
13 </rsp>
```

**Fig. 21.5** | Sample XML response from the Flickr APIs.

#### *XML Elements and Attributes*

XML represents data as **elements, attributes** and text. XML delimits elements with **start tags** and **end tags**. A start tag consists of the element name, possibly followed by *attributeName=value* pairs, all enclosed in **angle brackets**. For example, line 1 in the sample XML

```
<rsp stat="ok">
```

is the start tag for an rsp element containing the entire web-service *response*. This tag also contains the attribute stat (for "status")—the value "ok" indicates that the Flickr web-service request was successful. An end tag consists of the element name preceded by a **forward slash** (/) in angle brackets (for example, </rsp> in line 13, which denotes "end of response").

An element's start and end tags enclose

- text that represents a piece of data or
- other nested elements—for example, the rsp element contains one photos element (lines 2–12) and the photos element contains five photo elements (lines 3–11) representing the photos that were found by the web service.

An element is *empty* if it does not contain text or nested elements between its start and end tags. Such an element can be represented by a start tag that ends with />. For example, lines 3–5 define an empty photo element with several *attribute=value* pairs in the start tag.

### *Class* **XDocument** *and LINQ to XML*

Namespace **System.Xml.Linq** contains the classes used to manipulate XML using LINQ to XML—we use several of these classes to process the Flickr response. Once the app receives the XML search results, line 68 (Fig. 21.4) uses **XDocument** method **Parse** to convert into an XDocument object the string of XML returned by the await expression. LINQ to XML can query an XDocument to extract data from the XML.

Lines 71–83 use LINQ to XML to gather from each photo element in the XDocument the attributes required to locate the corresponding photo on Flickr:

- XDocument method **Descendants** (line 72) returns a list of **XElement** objects representing the elements with the name specified as an argument—in this case, the photo elements.
- Lines 73–77 use XElement method **Attribute** to extract **XAttributes** representing the element's id, title, secret, server and farm attributes from the current photo XElement.
- XAttribute property **Value** (lines 73–77) returns the value of a given attribute.

For each photo, we create an object of class FlickrResult (located in this project's FlickrResult.cs file) containing:

- A Title property—initialized with the photo element's title attribute and used cnnto display the photo's title in the app's ListBox.
- A URL property—assembled from the photo element's id, secret, server and farm (a *farm* is a collection of servers on the Internet) attributes. The format of the URL for each image is specified at

```
http://www.flickr.com/services/api/misc.urls.html
```

We use a FlickrResult's URL in imagesListBox_SelectedIndexChanged (Section 21.6.5) to download the corresponding photo when the user selects it in the ListBox.

## 21.6.4 Binding the Photo Titles to the ListBox

If there are any results (line 87), lines 89–90 *bind* the results' titles to the ListBox. You cannot bind a LINQ query's result directly to a ListBox, so line 89 invokes LINQ method ToList on the flickrPhotos LINQ query to convert it to a List first, then assigns the result to the ListBox's DataSource property. This indicates that the List's data should be used to populate the ListBox's Items collection. The List contains FlickrResult objects, so line 90 sets the ListBox's DisplayMember property to indicate that each FlickrResult's Title property should be displayed in the ListBox.

### 21.6.5 Asynchronously Downloading an Image's Bytes

Method imagesListBox_SelectedIndexChanged (lines 99–115) is declared async because it awaits an *asynchronous* download of a photo. Lines 104–105 get the URL property of the selected ListBox item. Then lines 108–109 invoke HttpClient's **GetByteArrayAsync** method, which gets a byte array containing the photo. The method uses the URL specified as the method's string argument to request the photo from Flickr and returns a Task<byte[]>—a *promise* to return a byte[] once the task completes execution. The event handler then awaits the result. When the Task completes, the await expression returns the byte[]. Line 112 creates a MemoryStream from the byte[] (which allows reading bytes as a stream from an array in memory), then line 113 uses the Image class's static FromStream method to create an Image from the byte array and assign it to the PictureBox's Image property to display the selected photo.

## 21.7 Displaying an Asynchronous Task's Progress

Our last example shows how to display an asynchronous task's progress and intermediate results. Figure 21.6 presents class FindPrimes, which asynchronously determines whether each value from 2 up to a user-entered value is a prime number. During the asynchronous testing of each value, we update a TextBox with each prime that's found and update a **ProgressBar** and Label to show the percentage of the testing that has been completed so far.

```
// Fig. 21.6: FindPrimes.cs
// Displaying an asynchronous task's progress and intermediate results
using System;
using System.Linq;
using System.Threading.Tasks;
using System.Windows.Forms;

namespace FindPrimes
{
   public partial class FindPrimesForm : Form
   {
      // used to enable cancelation of the async task
      private bool Canceled { get; set; } = false;
      private bool[] primes; // array used to determine primes

      public FindPrimesForm()
      {
         InitializeComponent();
         progressBar.Minimum = 2; // 2 is the smallest prime number
         percentageLabel.Text = $"{0:P0}"; // display 0 %
      }

      // handles getPrimesButton's click event
      private async void getPrimesButton_Click(object sender, EventArgs e)
      {
         // get user input
         var maximum = int.Parse(maxValueTextBox.Text);
```

**Fig. 21.6** | Displaying an asynchronous task's progress and intermediate results. (Part 1 of 3.)

```

         // create array for determining primes
         primes = Enumerable.Repeat(true, maximum).ToArray();

         // reset Canceled and GUI
         Canceled = false;
         getPrimesButton.Enabled = false; // disable getPrimesButton
         cancelButton.Enabled = true; // enable cancelButton
         primesTextBox.Text = string.Empty; // clear primesTextBox
         statusLabel.Text = string.Empty; // clear statusLabel
         percentageLabel.Text = $"{0:P0}"; // display 0 %
         progressBar.Value = progressBar.Minimum; // reset progressBar min
         progressBar.Maximum = maximum; // set progressBar max

         // show primes up to maximum
         int count = await FindPrimes(maximum);
         statusLabel.Text = $"Found {count} prime(s)";
      }

      // displays prime numbers in primesTextBox
      private async Task<int> FindPrimes(int maximum)
      {
         var primeCount = 0;

         // find primes less than maximum
         for (var i = 2; i < maximum && !Canceled; ++i)
         {
            // if i is prime, display it
            if (await Task.Run(() => IsPrime(i)))
            {
               ++primeCount; // increment number of primes found
               primesTextBox.AppendText($"{i}{Environment.NewLine}");
            }

            var percentage = (double)progressBar.Value /
               (progressBar.Maximum - progressBar.Minimum + 1);
            percentageLabel.Text = $"{percentage:P0}";
            progressBar.Value = i + 1; // update progress
         }

         // display message if operation was canceled
         if (Canceled)
         {
            primesTextBox.AppendText($"Canceled{Environment.NewLine}");
         }

         getPrimesButton.Enabled = true; // enable getPrimesButton
         cancelButton.Enabled = false; // disable cancelButton
         return primeCount;
      }

```

**Fig. 21.6** | Displaying an asynchronous task's progress and intermediate results. (Part 2 of 3.)

```
79         // check whether value is a prime number
80         // and mark all multiples as not prime
81         public bool IsPrime(int value)
82         {
83            // if value is prime, mark all of multiples
84            // as not prime and return true
85            if (primes[value])
86            {
87               // mark all multiples of value as not prime
88               for (var i = value + value; i < primes.Length; i += value)
89               {
90                  primes[i] = false; // i is not prime
91               }
92
93               return true;
94            }
95            else
96            {
97               return false;
98            }
99         }
100
101        // if user clicks Cancel Button, stop displaying primes
102        private void cancelButton_Click(object sender, EventArgs e)
103        {
104           Canceled = true;
105           getPrimesButton.Enabled = true; // enable getPrimesButton
106           cancelButton.Enabled = false; // disable cancelButton
107        }
108     }
109  }
```

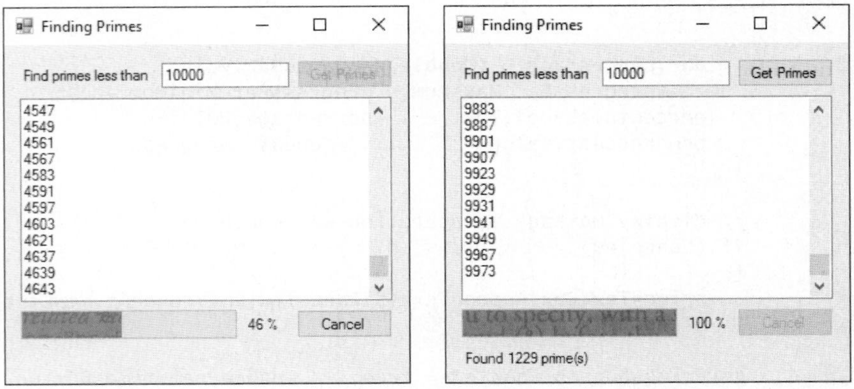

**Fig. 21.6** | Displaying an asynchronous task's progress and intermediate results. (Part 3 of 3.)

### *Sieve of Eratosthenes*

Line 14 declares the bool array primes, which we use with the **Sieve of Eratosthenes** algorithm (https://wikipedia.org/wiki/Sieve_of_Eratosthenes) to find all prime numbers less than a maximum value. The Sieve of Eratosthenes takes a list of integers and, beginning with the first prime, filters out all multiples of that prime. It then moves to the next number not yet filtered out, which is the next prime, then eliminates all of its multiples. It continues until all nonprimes have been filtered out. Algorithmically, we begin with element 2 of the `bool` array (ignoring elements 0 and 1) and set the elements at all indices that are multiples of 2 to `false` to indicate that they're divisible by 2 and thus not prime. We then move to the next array element, check whether it's `true`, and if so set all of its multiples to `false` to indicate that they're divisible by the current index. When the algorithm completes, all indices that contain `true` are prime, as they have no divisors. The Sieve of Eratosthenes in this example is implemented by methods `FindPrimes` (lines 48–77) and `IsPrime` (lines 81–99). Each time `IsPrime` determines that a specific number is prime, it immediately eliminates all multiples of that number.[1]

### *Constructor*

Class `FindPrimesForm`'s constructor (lines 16–21) sets `progressBar`'s `Minimum` property to 2—the first prime number—and sets the `percentageLabel`'s `Text` to 0 formatted as a whole-number percentage. In the format specifier `P0`, `P` indicates that the value should be formatted as a percentage and `0` indicates zero decimal places.

### `async` *Method* `getPrimesButton_Click`

When the user enters a number in the `maxValueTextBox` and presses the **Get Primes** `Button`, method `getPrimesButton_Click` (lines 24–45) is called. This method is declared `async` because it will `await` the results of the `FindPrimes` method. Line 27 gets the `maximum` value entered by the user, then line 30 creates a `bool` array with that number of elements and fills it with `true` values. The elements with indices that are not prime numbers will eventually be set to `false`. `Enumerable` `static` method **`Repeat`** creates a list of elements containing its first argument's value. The second argument specifies the length of the list. We then call `ToArray` on the result to get an array representation of the elements. `Repeat` is a *generic* method—the type of the list it returns is determined by the first argument's type.

Lines 33–40 reset the `Canceled` property to `false` and reset the GUI to prepare to determine the prime numbers. Lines 39–40 reset the `progressBar`'s `Value` to the `Minimum` value and set `Maximum` to the new value entered by the user. As we test each number from 2 to the maximum to determine whether its prime, we'll set the `progressBar`'s `Value` property to the current number being tested. As this number increases, the `progressBar` will fill proportionally with color to show the asynchronous task's progress.

Line 43 calls `async` method `FindPrimes` to begin the process of finding prime numbers. Upon completion, `FindPrimes` returns the number of primes less than the maximum value entered by the user, which the app then displays at line 44.

---

1. Visit `https://en.wikipedia.org/wiki/Sieve_of_Eratosthenes` to learn more about the Sieve of Eratosthenes. The algorithm as implemented in Fig. 21.6 is inefficient—it keeps eliminating multiples of primes even after the array already represents all primes up to the maximum entered by the user. The algorithm is complete once it eliminates the multiples of all primes that are less than or equal to the *square root* of the maximum value. As an exercise, you could update the algorithm, then modify the code that updates the `ProgressBar` and percentage `Label` so that they indicate the progress of the algorithm, rather than the progress of checking whether each number in the range is prime.

### *async Method FindPrimes*

The async method FindPrimes implements the Sieve of Eratosthenes algorithm, displays the primes that are found and updates the progressBar and percentage completion. Line 50 initially sets primeCount to 0 to indicate that no primes have been found yet. Lines 53–66 iterate through the values from 2 up to, but not including, the maximum entered by the user. For each value, line 56 launches an async Task to determine whether that value is prime and awaits the Task's result. When that result is returned, if it's true, line 58 increments primeCount to indicate that a prime number was found and line 59 appends that number's string representation to the primesTextBox's text—thus displaying one of the intermediate results. Regardless of whether a value is prime, lines 62–64 calculate the percentage of the loop that has completed so far and display that percentage, and line 65 updates the progressBar's Value.

At any point during the execution of FindPrimes, the user could click the app's **Cancel** Button, in which case property Canceled will be set to true and the loop will terminate early. If this occurs, lines 69–72 display "Canceled" in the primesTextBox.

### *Method IsPrime*

Method IsPrime (lines 81–99) is called by async method FindPrimes to perform part of the Sieve of Eratosthenes. IsPrime tests whether its value argument is prime by checking the corresponding element in array primes (line 85). If value is prime, lines 88–91 set to false the primes elements at all indices that are multiples of value, then line 93 returns true to indicate that value is prime; otherwise, the method returns false.

### *Method cancelButton_Click*

When the user clicks the **Cancel** Button, method cancelButton_Click (lines 102–107) sets property Canceled to true, then enables the **Get Primes** Button and disables the **Cancel** Button. When the condition at line 53 is evaluated next, the loop in method FindPrimes terminates.

## 21.8 Wrap-Up

In this chapter, you learned how to use the async modifier, await operator and Tasks to perform long-running or compute-intensive tasks asynchronously. You learned that tasks that proceed independently of one another are said to execute asynchronously and are referred to as asynchronous tasks.

We showed that multithreading enables threads to execute concurrently with other threads while sharing application-wide resources such as memory and processors. To take full advantage of multicore architecture, we wrote applications that processed tasks asynchronously. You learned that asynchronous programming is a technique for writing apps containing tasks that can execute asynchronously, which can improve app performance and GUI responsiveness in apps with long-running or compute-intensive tasks.

To provide a convincing demonstration of asynchronous programming, we presented several apps:

- The first showed how to execute a compute-intensive calculation asynchronously in a GUI app so that the GUI remained responsive while the calculation executed.

- The second app performed two compute-intensive calculations synchronously (sequentially). When that app executed, the GUI froze because the calculations were performed in the GUI thread. The third app executed the same compute-intensive calculations asynchronously. We executed these two apps on single-core and dual-core computers to demonstrate the performance of each program in each scenario.
- The fourth app used class `HttpClient` to interact with the Flickr website to search for photos. You learned that class `HttpClient` is one of many built-in .NET Framework classes that can initiate asynchronous tasks for use with `async` and `await`.
- The last app demonstrated how to show an asynchronous task's progress in a `ProgressBar`.

We hope you've enjoyed the book and we wish you great success!

# Operator Precedence Chart

Operators are shown in decreasing order of precedence from top to bottom with each level of precedence separated by a horizontal line. The associativity of the operators is shown in the right column.

| Operator | Type | Associativity |
|---|---|---|
| `.` | member access | left-to-right |
| `?.` | null-conditional member access | |
| `()` | method call | |
| `[]` | element access | |
| `?[]` | null-conditional element access | |
| `++` | postfix increment | |
| `--` | postfix decrement | |
| `nameof` | string representation of an identifier | |
| `new` | object creation | |
| `typeof` | get `System.Type` object for a type | |
| `sizeof` | get size in bytes of a type | |
| `checked` | checked evaluation | |
| `unchecked` | unchecked evaluation | |
| `+` | unary plus | right-to-left |
| `-` | unary minus | |
| `!` | logical negation | |
| `~` | bitwise complement | |
| `++` | prefix increment | |
| `--` | prefix decrement | |
| (*type*) | cast | |
| `*` | multiplication | left-to-right |
| `/` | division | |
| `%` | remainder | |

**Fig. A.1** | Operator precedence chart (Part 1 of 2.).

| Operator | Type | Associativity |
|---|---|---|
| + | addition | left-to-right |
| - | subtraction | |
| >> | right shift | left-to-right |
| << | left shift | |
| < | less than | left-to-right |
| > | greater than | |
| <= | less than or equal to | |
| >= | greater than or equal to | |
| is | type comparison | |
| as | type conversion | |
| != | is not equal to | left-to-right |
| == | is equal to | |
| & | logical AND | left-to-right |
| ^ | logical XOR | left-to-right |
| \| | logical OR | left-to-right |
| && | conditional AND | left-to-right |
| \|\| | conditional OR | left-to-right |
| ?? | null coalescing | right-to-left |
| ?: | conditional | right-to-left |
| = | assignment | right-to-left |
| *= | multiplication assignment | |
| /= | division assignment | |
| %= | remainder assignment | |
| += | addition assignment | |
| -= | subtraction assignment | |
| <<= | left shift assignment | |
| >>= | right shift assignment | |
| &= | logical AND assignment | |
| ^= | logical XOR assignment | |
| \|= | logical OR assignment | |

**Fig. A.1** | Operator precedence chart (Part 2 of 2.).

# B

# Simple Types

| Type | Size in bits | Value range | Standard |
|---|---|---|---|
| bool | 8 | true or false | |
| byte | 8 | 0 to 255, inclusive | |
| sbyte | 8 | –128 to 127, inclusive | |
| char | 16 | '\u0000' to '\uFFFF' (0 to 65535), inclusive | Unicode |
| short | 16 | –32768 to 32767, inclusive | |
| ushort | 16 | 0 to 65535, inclusive | |
| int | 32 | –2,147,483,648 to 2,147,483,647, inclusive | |
| uint | 32 | 0 to 4,294,967,295, inclusive | |
| float | 32 | *Approximate negative range:*<br>–3.4028234663852886E+38 to<br>–1.40129846432481707E–45<br>*Approximate positive range:*<br>1.40129846432481707E–45 to<br>3.4028234663852886E+38<br>*Other supported values:*<br>positive and negative zero<br>positive and negative infinity<br>not-a-number (NaN) | IEEE 754<br>IEC 60559 |
| long | 64 | –9,223,372,036,854,775,808 to<br>9,223,372,036,854,775,807, inclusive | |
| ulong | 64 | 0 to 18,446,744,073,709,551,615, inclusive | |

**Fig. B.1** | Simple types. (Part 1 of 2.)

| Type | Size in bits | Value range | Standard |
| --- | --- | --- | --- |
| `double` | 64 | *Approximate negative range:*<br>–1.7976931348623157E+308 to<br>–4.94065645841246544E–324<br>*Approximate positive range:*<br>4.94065645841246544E–324 to<br>1.7976931348623157E+308<br>*Other supported values:*<br>positive and negative zero<br>positive and negative infinity<br>not-a-number (NaN) | IEEE 754<br>IEC 60559 |
| `decimal` | 128 | *Negative range:*<br>–79,228,162,514,264,337,593,543,950,335<br>(–7.9E+28) to –1.0E–28<br>*Positive range:*<br>1.0E–28 to<br>79,228,162,514,264,337,593,543,950,335<br>(7.9E+28) | |

**Fig. B.1** | Simple types. (Part 2 of 2.)

### *Additional Simple Type Information*

- This appendix is based on information from the **Types** section of Microsoft's C# 6 specification. A draft of this document can be found at:

```
http://msdn.microsoft.com/vcsharp/aa336809
```

- Values of type `float` have seven digits of precision.
- Values of type `double` have 15–16 digits of precision.
- Values of type `decimal` are represented as integer values that are scaled by a power of 10. Values between –1.0 and 1.0 are represented exactly to 28 digits.
- For more information on IEEE 754 visit `http://grouper.ieee.org/groups/754/`.
- For more information on Unicode, visit `http://unicode.org`.

# C

# ASCII Character Set

| | 0 | 1 | 2 | 3 | 4 | 5 | 6 | 7 | 8 | 9 |
|---|---|---|---|---|---|---|---|---|---|---|
| **0** | nul | soh | stx | etx | eot | enq | ack | bel | bs | ht |
| **1** | nl | vt | ff | cr | so | si | dle | dc1 | dc2 | dc3 |
| **2** | dc4 | nak | syn | etb | can | em | sub | esc | fs | gs |
| **3** | rs | us | sp | ! | " | # | $ | % | & | ' |
| **4** | ( | ) | * | + | , | - | . | / | 0 | 1 |
| **5** | 2 | 3 | 4 | 5 | 6 | 7 | 8 | 9 | : | ; |
| **6** | < | = | > | ? | @ | A | B | C | D | E |
| **7** | F | G | H | I | J | K | L | M | N | O |
| **8** | P | Q | R | S | T | U | V | W | X | Y |
| **9** | Z | [ | \ | ] | ^ | _ | ' | a | b | c |
| **10** | d | e | f | g | h | i | j | k | l | m |
| **11** | n | o | p | q | r | s | t | u | v | w |
| **12** | x | y | z | { | \| | } | ~ | del | | |

**Fig. C.1** | ASCII Character Set.

The digits at the left of the table are the left digits of the decimal equivalent (0–127) of the character code, and the digits at the top of the table are the right digits opf the character code. For example, the character code for "F" is 70, and the character code for "&" is 38.

Most users of this book are interested in the ASCII character set used to represent English characters on many computers. The ASCII character set is a subset of the Unicode character set used by C# to represent characters from most of the world's languages. For more information on the Unicode character set, see `http://unicode.org`.

# Index

## Symbols



## A

## D

## E

## F

## H



## I

## J



## K



## L

## N

## O

## U



## V



## W